THE HOUSE STYLE BOOK

THE HOUSE STYLE BOOK

Chief Contributing Editor Deyan Sudjic

Mitchell Beazley

The House Style Book

Chief Contributing Editor
Deyan Sudjic

Contributors
Jill Blake
Annie Clark
Alex Dingwall-Main
Susanna Goodden
José Manser
Sarah Miller
David Pearce
Hugh Pearman
Barty Phillips
Ted Stevens
Alan Wakeford
Julia Watson

Edited and designed by Mitchell Beazley International Ltd
14-15 Manette Street, London W1V 5LB

Project Manager/Art Editor	Kelly Flynn
Editor	Fiona Duncan
Associate Editor	Leonie Hamilton
Deputy Editor	Amanda Evans
Designers	Paul Drayson, Ruth Levy
Editorial Assistant	Lynne Lynch
Picture research	Diana Korchien
Production	Peter Phillips
Indexers	Richard and Hilary Bird
Editorial Director	Jack Tresidder
Art Director	Tony Cobb

ISBN 0 85533 538 6

Filmset by The Montage Filmsetting Company, London, England
Reproduction by Chelmer Litho Reproductions, Maldon, Essex
Printed in Spain by
Printer Industria Grafica S.A.
Sant Vincenc dels Horts Barcelona
D.L.B. 25172-1984

HOW THE BOOK WORKS

Style is very much a matter of individual confidence. The purpose of this book is first to pick out, from the confusion of designs that fill the pages of interior decorating magazines, six underlying approaches and analyse how they work; second to build on this foundation with hundreds of illustrations that show good style in practice, room by room throughout the house, as well as in fixtures and fittings.

PART ONE: STYLE provides the overview, not only to today's dominant trends in style, but to such general aspects as architecture and furniture, colour and space. The styles analysed in this section are shown in their purest forms, not because most of us wish — or can afford — to apply any one of them consistently but in order to provide a basis for understanding and modifying style.

PART TWO: LIVING AREAS breaks the house into its separate components, each with its own complex challenges. Here, in the longest section of the book, styles are inevitably mixed and fragmented, compared and contrasted. References back to the opening section are overlaid by all the considerations of cost, personal whim or individual possession, comfort or function, that influence the way we choose to design or decorate rooms in practice. The illustrations are chosen to suggest ideas, solutions, opportunities, as well as to illustrate stylish treatments of individual areas.

PART THREE: DETAILS returns to the overall view of the house, but this time to such practical aspects as surfaces, paint finishes, hardware, lighting, heating and storage systems, with advice too on how to use other people's help — or do it yourself.

CONTENTS

STYLE 8

THE MEANING OF STYLE 11
COUNTRY HOUSE 12
HARD EDGE 19
CITY TRADITIONAL 26
POST MODERN 33
DECORATOR 40
ECLECTIC 47

INDIVIDUAL STYLE 53
The minimum 54
A converted prison 56
Deco tech 58
The home office 60
The pool house 62

WORKING WITH COLOUR 64
CONTEMPORARY FURNITURE 70

ARCHITECTURE 74
The evolution of the house 75
Taking on the terraced house 81
Taking on the historic house 82
Taking on the unorthodox house 84

WORKING WITH SPACE 86
Constraints 88
Potential 90
Combining and dividing 92
Gaining space 94

Using furniture 96

LIVING AREAS 98

HALLS 100
Making an entrance 102
The practicalities 104

LIVING ROOMS 106
Planning 108
Focal points 110
Installing a fireplace 112
Displaying art 113
Details 114
Formal living 116
Urban living 118
Rural living 120
Merging with the garden 122
Loose-fit living 124
Furniture 126
Relaxing 130
Taming the hardware 132

DINING ROOMS 134
Finding your style 135
The practicalities 138
Formal dining 140
Flexible dining 142
Furniture 144
Table settings 148

Finishing touches 150

KITCHENS 152
Planning 154
The practicalities 156
Family kitchens 158
Cooks' kitchens 162
Functional kitchens 164
Designer kitchens 166
Tiny kitchens 167
Eating in the kitchen 168
Ideas 170
Equipment 172
Appliances 174
Batterie de cuisine 176

WORK AREAS 179
The traditional study 180
The office 182
The workshop 184
The laundry and utility room 186

BEDROOMS 188
Finding your style 190
Details 192
Storage 195
Beds 196
The software 198
The flexible bedroom 202
Bed and bathroom 204

CONTENTS

BATHROOMS 206
Planning 208
The practicalities 210
The bathroom as a room 212
Finding your style 214
Baths and showers 216
Basins, bidets and lavatories 218
Details 220

CHILDREN'S ROOMS 222
The nursery 223
Room to grow 224
A room of their own 226
Playrooms 228
Furniture 230
Safety 232

ONE ROOM LIVING 234
Planning and practicalities 236
The high life 238
Studios 240
Sharers 242
Space saving ideas 244
Kitchens and bathrooms 245

CONVERSIONS AND EXTENSIONS 248
Converting the attic 250
Raising the roof 252
A brighter outlook 254
Building at the back 256

Conservatories 260
Blending old with new 262

GARDENS 264
The budget 266
The plan 268
The components 270
Decorative effects 272
Garden furniture 273
Roof gardens 274
Indoor plants 276

DETAILS 278

FLOORS 280
Hard floors 281
Semi-hard floors 283
Soft floors 284
Semi-soft floors 286
Rugs 286

WALLS 288
Practicalities 289
Wallcoverings 290
Paint 292
Paint effects 295
Details 297

WINDOWS 298
The view from the inside 300

Curtains, blinds and shutters 302
Window dressing 304

LIGHTING 305
The basics 306
Lighting systems 308

STORAGE 314
Showing off 316
Hiding away 318

FIXTURES AND FITTINGS 320
Security 324

HEATING AND ENERGY 326
THE PAPERWORK 330
DEALING WITH THE EXPERTS 331
BE YOUR OWN INTERIOR DESIGNER 334

DO-IT-YOURSELF 338
Painting 339
Wallpapers 343
Tiles 346
Floors 348
Mouldings 350
Basic shelving 351
Curtains and blinds 352

INDEX 354
ACKNOWLEDGEMENTS 360
CREDITS 360

THE MEANING OF STYLE

Interiors are like clothes. Of course they have to keep us warm and comfortable, but that isn't the whole point. We also use them to say things about ourselves, and to try and give our homes their identity. They should be practical, but there has to be room for the question of style as well; for this is what makes the difference between an impersonal hotel room, and a warm and welcoming home.

When we choose our clothes, we tend to use bits and pieces from several different fashion looks to suit our moods and express our individual preferences, and we do the same with furniture, wallpaper and colour. They do not change with quite the frenetic pace of the fashion world's annual collections perhaps, but the colours do date, and the shapes and materials do go in and out of style. It isn't simply a matter of good taste, whatever that elusive concept may mean. Flying china ducks on the wall, and Art Deco table lamps fashioned like galleons in full sail would once have sent sensitive aesthetes into paroxysms of scorn. Now we've become subtler about the way that we see things. To have china ducks on the wall today is an elaborate double bluff. Of course you know that they are meant to be bad taste, but by putting them in invisible quotation marks, you can still enjoy them.

Because homes last so much longer, and offer so many more ways of putting across a message than clothes, they are far more complex in style terms. But the process by which styles come and go is very much the same. In both fashion and interior design there are the star designers who are responsible for putting together the looks that the glossies love to illustrate. Interior design has its equivalents of Zandra Rhodes and Ralph Lauren. They can afford to be wilful, extreme and flamboyant, even to go totally over the top. But then they are in business to make their mark, not to live with the consequences.

Style is not just a question of the overall look; it also depends on what could be called the hardware: the tables, chairs, accessories and so on, which is where the manufacturers and retailers have a part to play. There are the top flight firms in furniture and lighting, the equivalents perhaps of the Diors and Chanels, most of whom seem to be Italian. Despite the aura of culture with which they like to surround their activities, they are in the business of selling. It is in their interests to keep changing the look of their products, and to ensure that the fashion constantly changes. Then there are the second and third tier manufacturers and the high street retailers who take their lead from the stars with affordable copies a year or so behind.

Designing a home successfully means finding the right balance between style and function, between fashion and comfort. It is certainly not about slapping on a look regardless of what kind of home you live in, or the practicalities of what you need. And that is as true when you are working with a professional designer's help, when cost may not be such a major issue, as it is when, as for most of us, style is a case of carefully balancing budgets, and making the most of as little as possible.

We live in style conscious times. There has never been such a wide range of options to choose from. There are no unchallenged arbiters of taste anymore, and almost anything is possible. In a city street you can find a miniature recreation of a country house, complete with stripped pine Adam fireplace to take the stiff white invitation cards right next door to a house which is open plan and aggressively high tech. So long as they suit the needs of their owners, and achieve what they set out to do, both are equally appropriate.

To help give an idea of the style ground rules, it is possible to pick out different themes. We have identified six particular individual styles: they are not universal prescriptions, and the boundaries between them are fluid. But they do offer a way of getting to grips with what can otherwise appear to be an alarmingly nebulous and very personal subject.

Of course the styles are not mutually exclusive: it's possible to use them side by side in different rooms, or even to mix some of them together in the same room. Most of us do just that, as we acquire and retire bits of furniture or redecorate piecemeal. In no particular order, the six styles which have been identified, and which are described in detail on the following pages are: country house, hard edge, city traditional, post modern, decorator and eclectic.

But style is not just a question of categorizing things. It is a personal expression too, so we also look at five homes created for, or by, five different owners. They demonstrate how style works in creating a complete house.

Equally, style depends on being able to use colour to good advantage, and we go into detail on how colour works. Finally, style has to do with the furniture and accessories that you choose, so we complete this chapter with a look at contemporary and influential furniture.

COUNTRY HOUSE

Despite the aura of timeless unchanging tradition that surrounds the country house look, the way in which people see their ideal country home has undergone sharp changes. In the egalitarian 1970s, the rural cottage was the model for the dreams of countless town dwellers; both as a weekend retreat, and as the inspiration for the decoration of their everyday urban home. We tended to see the past through a haze of romantic nostalgia, and thoroughly sanitized of rural squalor.

Helped by the advertising industry, key images such as pine matchboard panelling, Welsh dressers and brightly coloured enamel teapots became inextricably associated with naturalness, a wholesome refuge in a world increasingly swamped by the artificial and the machine made. Of course the naturalness was often more apparent than real, and so popular did the cottage look become that it was severely over-exposed. Pine eventually became a short-hand way of summing up the whole style.

Yet the rural house is still as potent an image as ever, albeit in a softer, gentler sort of way. Perhaps appropriately, given the very different social climate of the present, the new inspiration is not the cottage, but the more generously scaled country house. The look is more sophisticated, less innocent in flavour, but still calculatingly pretty, and puts a premium on materials and finishes that mellow as they grow older, that look more and more comfortable as they wear.

The idea is not to ape the impossibly glossy formality of the grand stately homes, but instead to achieve the comfortable, lived-in naturalness of the smaller country houses, where rich rugs are allowed to sit directly on stone flagged floors, where simple fresh paint finishes highlight worn old woodwork, above all where fading upholstery and slightly threadbare furniture won't look out of place, and where the family Labrador doesn't have to be banned from the living room for fear of making a mess.

Providing it originally had the quality to take a few knocks, a dining table with one rickety leg, unmatching chairs, and laid with odd cutlery, can look just as good as a squeaky clean, immaculate spread. The essence of the style is in the different appeals of the warm charm of a second-hand reconditioned wood-burning range in the kitchen, set against the intimidating technological glitter of a chrome and glass space-age split-level oven that needs a second glance to make quite certain it's not the television.

But a self-conscious 'rustic' effect won't look right either. Gingham tablecloths, and an over abundance of copper kettles and horse brasses just looks fake.

The desired effect may be natural

3 The faded charm of the country house style can be equally effective in a city setting. An atmosphere redolent of a Victorian country conservatory is evoked with a cane chaise longue, wrought iron and cane furniture, a black and white marble floor, and groups of flowers and plants. Modern lighting plays a part: a chrome uplighter emits a subtle light, and looks elegant in its setting.

1 Plain painted brick walls can look appropriate, set off by gold-framed engravings, a tapestry screen and an antique urn filled with dried grasses.

2 Soft focus lighting is an important part of the look – the aged finishes and rich colours can't take the exposure of harsh natural or artificial light. Candlelight is not only subtle, but also reminiscent of bygone times.

4 A battered antique cabinet on a pastel wall – just one of the many elements that combine to create the finished picture.

5 Even in quite small country houses it is possible to play up the grandeur of a stately home with a well-placed classical bust and opulent drapes.

1 Provided everything has weathered down to the same elegantly faded colours, and the textures match, it is impossible to put too much into a room like this. Even the chandelier, which would look intimidating in other surroundings, seems a natural part of this room.

2 Consider having wood finishes for floors and furniture that look better the more they are used. With pictures, flowers and fresh pink walls, the simple chest and bare floorboards suggest the prettiness of a cottage.

3 The country house style depends not so much on showing off beautiful individual pieces, as creating, with many different elements, an overall ordered and lived-in effect.

looking and easy to live with, but that does not mean it can be achieved without careful planning and a clear idea of the end result. Furniture, decoration and architecture all need to be knitted together to achieve the effect. Ideas from different styles can be blended to help reinforce the feeling that this is a home which has been created gradually over the years, rather than conjured into being overnight by the wave of a decorator's magic wand.

The approach has to be a pragmatic one. The starting point is the house itself, its inherent character and the peculiarities of its individual architectural style. As knowledge of the way in which historic houses were originally decorated and lived in has grown, so has a concern for making sure that later alterations do not mask that original character. When making changes the important details should be left intact. Thus structural changes will tend to be minimal, aimed primarily at stripping the house back to what it was, rather than imposing a new and unsympathetic style.

There is a lot to be said for leaving well alone — a collection of irregular little rooms can often be more useful, and much easier to keep warm, than one large open space. Of course there is still room for sympathetic changes too.

If practicality is a major considera-tion, then this is an appropriate style to choose. Around the entrance, for example, floor finishes should be tough, a sensible precaution in town or country against mud being tramped in. Buffer areas around the doors, halls or lobbies full of Wellingtons and coat racks serve the same purpose. Stone flags or quarry tiles are the traditional materials. But if you are setting out to achieve a country flavour that doesn't rely entirely on traditional styles, Italian ceramic floor tiles in beige or white may raise eyebrows, but will look just as good.

The furniture should be a mixture; a sprinkling of 'good' pieces, traditional antiques — a mahogany dining table perhaps, with one or two claw-footed chairs, a grandfather clock, handsome gilt framed mirrors — as well as the newer kind of antique refectory tables

and dressers. But the country look also stretches to take in contemporary furniture that has the right qualities, a large generously proportioned sofa perhaps, in a natural finish loose cover. And there is room for cheaper, simpler old furniture too, from junk rather than antique shops. The country house style is very straight-faced: kitsch and jokes don't fit in at all, and neither do plastics or chrome.

Stripped, sanded and polished finishes can still look good — whether it's a sanded chair or floorboards showing around the edge of a carpet. But sanding should be carried out sparingly. Don't go overboard: it can fit in well with a washed-out pastel colour scheme, but over-stripping is definitely too much of a good thing. And it certainly isn't an authentic treatment for period panelling, doors or architraves which would originally have been painted or stained.

Country colours are fresh and subtle, delicate pastels that fade well, pale blues, greys, sand and oatmeal, with doors and cornices picked out in white. Small scale print fabrics and wallpapers are right too. Decorating in this style provides a chance to indulge magpie instincts. Rooms lend themselves to groups of pictures, busy with incident; tables and mantlepieces covered in a clutter of objects, anything from sets of toy soldiers to old scientific instruments. Very untraditional spotlights can play an important part in lighting such collections effectively.

In the bedrooms the ideal is the four poster, but much less elaborate furnish-ings can provide an equally attractive rural feeling – a simple washstand with a Victorian ceramic jug, for example. In the bathroom if you have old fittings – like big old tubs with lion's feet, or huge old taps – keep them. Modern alternatives never look as good, and in any case are hardly ever scaled to match the same proportions.

In the living room, the visual focus will almost inevitably be the fireplace. An open log fire is still inseparable in most people's minds with country house comfort. Again, if you are trying to produce a non-traditional country look, you could use a studio stove to fulfil the same function. If you already

1 A big old country barn, complete with exposed timber rafters and antlers on the walls, has been civilized with well-stuffed club armchairs and an architectural folly – the bookcase.

2 If you have roughcast stone walls and a whitewashed fireplace, make the most of their textures by choosing mellow furnishings and siting your local lighting carefully.

have a handsome classical mantlepiece complete with matching fire surround, you are very lucky. It's a detail for which no satisfactory modern replacement has ever been found. If your house has lost its fireplace, and you want to install one, it should not be too difficult, provided that the flue is still in the wall. As far as the mantlepiece and the grate are concerned, second-hand specimens from an architectural salvage firm will generally look a lot better than the repro duction Adam kind, which always look anaemic by comparison with the real thing.

The dining room, if there is one, is the place for candlelit formality and ancestral portraits. Here, light fittings may present a problem as they tend to do generally with this style. Electricity of course came too late for the golden age of the country house. Some purists have been known to stick to gas and oil lamps; certainly the so-called

'traditional' designs for electric lights, those central rose glass chandeliers that hide light bulbs uncomfortably, simply look awkward, and don't provide a particularly attractive quality of light. Wall brackets disguised as half melted plastic candles look even worse. Much better then to go for a simple modern design. Floor standing uplighters are particularly good: not only do they give an attractive diffuse light source, bouncing off walls and ceiling, but they don't require cables running through fragile plaster or panelling either.

The country house look is inspired by a particular approach to rural houses, but it can work just as well in a town house or apartment. It's not a question of recreating a rustic fantasy in a wildly inappropriate setting, but simply of picking out the essential elements of colour, material, finishes and furniture, and deploying them in town.

3   The good life – a feast in a country kitchen. The succulent spread makes a startling contrast to this rural room, with its old stone fireplace and walls, quarry tiled floor, rows of dried flowers and jars filled with beans.

4   At the heart of country living is the open fire. This basic hole in the wall grate is perfect for toasting teatime crumpets. A loose patchwork cover rescues an armchair past retiring age, and complements the room.

5   There is always a place for flowers; here imaginatively arranged in a mis-matching pair of china vases.

1 Traditional trompe l'oeil techniques can do much to embellish an interior in an appropriate style. Even a comparatively humble hall can be transformed with neoclassical paintwork, marbling and murals augmented by a sophisticated fabric wallcovering and voluptuously swagged drapes to create a metropolitan air.

2 Country house comes to town: a pretty patchwork quilt is

3 Elaborately fringed and gathered curtains emphasize the elegant proportions of the windows in this gracious Georgian drawing room.

In the late 1970s high tech rose to fame amid a welter of curly cables, perforated steel shelves and coloured pipes. As a brand new interior design style it quickly found favour with many people who were tired of traditional approaches. High tech, however, has proved itself no passing fad; it is here to stay and furthermore it has formed the basis of an even newer look which we call hard edge. Not as naively fashion conscious as high tech in its early days, hard edge deploys industrial chic in a tamer, cooler, more sophisticated way. Here we take a look at high tech and its more recent offspring.

The name high tech was coined by Joan Kron and Suzanne Slesin in the late 1970s for the title of their book on what they called the industrial style. But as an idea it has been around much longer — it has been appropriated by architects and designers in their own homes for years, and at first they became alarmed at seeing it develop into a popular trend.

High tech depends on a tough minded, no-nonsense look. It is spare and plain and undecorated rather than soft and squashy. Angles are sharp rather than curved, colours are solid rather than patterned. Metal, glass, rubber and plastic are the favoured materials, while wood is looked down on by the real enthusiasts as too messy and inexact for serious consideration.

Part of the fun of high tech is in recycling objects originally designed for heavy duty industrial use in a domestic setting: beds made out of scaffolding and Kee Klamps, or, in the living room, studded rubber Freudenberg flooring first developed for use in airport terminals. It is a style calculated to appeal to anybody who has ever enjoyed playing with a Meccano set.

High tech looks particularly at home in big, open plan loft style spaces — inspired by the old New York warehouses that were turned into studios and living spaces by SoHo artists in the 1970s, and which have since become a way of life in other cities such as London and Paris. Given the acres of space in a loft, big photographers' floods can make fine lampshades, and gym lockers work well as ready made

Hard edge is for perfectionists. The idea is to use simple geometric shapes, minimal colours, a variety of textures, and to abolish clutter. It's not easy to live with, but is stunning when it works.

high tech wardrobes. But in the space conscious surroundings that most of us live in, it is more sensible to concentrate on the smaller details. The style is so strong and positive that a little can go a very long way. In the kitchen, show off your batterie de cuisine by keeping it attached to a wall-mounted metal grid rack. Use Dexion racking and plastic industrial storage bins for the vegetables. Yacht hawser makes an elegant high tech balustrade for metal handrails.

In these design conscious days, high tech is the enthusiasts' style, for whom it can become an all-consuming passion. They search high and low for exactly the right kind of matt black toaster to go with the look of the kitchen, or to find the Braun wall-mounted clock with the *right* flexible hose-pipe connector. For those who live highly organized tidy lives, it's the perfect way of taming clutter. Everything has its place.

High tech is, however, short on warmth and cosiness. If those are the qualities that you are looking for, you will probably concentrate on other styles. Yet, in the right hands, high tech has inspired some ravishing modern houses. One of the first belonged to Charles Eames — the American architect and designer, who was an early prophet of the joys of industrial products. He set out to prove the point by designing himself a house in California that consisted entirely of off-the-shelf components from the catalogues of manufacturers supplying pre-fabricated factories. From this unlikely source he succeeded in producing a beautiful sunlit house of great elegance. He proved that simple and unadorned interiors do not have to look stark or antiseptic. Ever since, other architects have tried to follow his example, one of the most recent being Michael Hopkins with his glass, steel and aluminium house in London.

High tech mixes the very practical — cheap, clever ideas for using unusual things — with objects that might look functional, but which in reality are not. Watch out, for example, for all those dust-gathering surfaces that come from using open wire mesh shelves.

Though it might seem most appropriate for new modern buildings, this style can look very appropriate in some types of historic buildings too. With mellow quarry tiled floors and massive old timber beams, the spindly metal of high tech furniture, with its temporary, about-to-be-moved look, can be just the right way of minimizing the visual imposition of the present on the character of the old.

The rather more serious hard edge look is the grown-up version of high tech, and is inspired by the pioneering modernists of the Bauhaus — people like Le Corbusier who once described the house as a machine for living, and the furniture designer Marcel Breuer.

Like high tech, it is self-consciously modern – part of the revival of interest in design that took place at the start of the 1980s when the stripped pine nostalgia of the urban country cottage of the 1970s began, to some people at least, to look both tired and inappropriate. Its owners want to show that they are forward-looking and unstuffy. The look comes originally from the design community, who see it as rational, flexible and understated, and who enjoy the disciplines of achieving such contrived simplicity.

Hard edge relies on the classic furniture of the early modern designers

1 Perforated steel has become almost a cliché of the high tech look, but there is sound reason for using it. Cutting holes in the steel lightens its weight without losing its strength.

3

2   The high tech house, with its glass walls and open plan structure, where partitions have been reduced to Venetian blinds. The classic Eames' chair in the foreground is a natural part of the style.

3   Gerrit Rietveld zigzag timber chairs provide a natural finish in this sleek dining room.

4   Stunning in their highly polished monochrome setting, these specially made table and stools owe much to engineering design.

4

1 The industrial aesthetic, suitably tidied up, creates a stylish and polished environment. However, the only genuine industrial component in this sophisticated interior designed by Eva Jiricna is the sliding door gear. Even the doors themselves had to be specially made.

— who predominantly worked in black leather and chrome. Many of the original pieces are now being manufactured in much larger quantities than they ever were in the 1930s. Like all classics they have acquired a timelessness that keeps them from dating. And their very simplicity, pure geometric shapes and lack of applied decoration, means that they have avoided taking on a period flavour.

Room colours are restrained, running from neutral whites to greys. They form a background which allows objects in them to stand out like spotlit works of art. Simplicity on this scale doesn't come cheap. The smooth white walls scraped clean of any ornaments have to be in perfect shape: there's no scope to hide any imperfections with clutter. Nonetheless there is room for a slightly wider range of accessories and finishes than with high tech. Parquet floors and bentwood chairs can mix well with the simplicity of steel furniture. So too can Persian rugs.

Hard edge is for perfectionists. The aim is to provide a calm, neutral and undramatic background for everyday life, with as much as possible of the clutter and mess hidden out of sight in built-in furniture that is itself almost invisibly unobtrusive. It's a very architectural style; the emphasis is on integrating all the disparate elements in a room or in a house, into a single, cohesive, almost sculptural whole. Walls, floors, and furniture all run into each other. The effect is achieved by using as few different materials, finishes and colours as possible — so a kitchen for example may have the same white tiles on the floor, the walls, and on the work surfaces. Or a living room may have plain grey carpet, a similar tone for the curtains, and all the furniture in white covers. The technique ties the whole design together, giving the impression that everything belongs, thereby increasing the sense of spaciousness.

The style calls for consistency and discipline, with relief coming from just one or two carefully chosen objects left to make their presence felt. Perhaps a single, highly sculptural Italian quartz halogen bulb uplighter, with its blue ground glass shade throwing the walls

2 Once floor and wall finishes have been pared down to a minimum – just bare white walls and a marble floor – the furniture will stand out like works of art. This Eileen Gray sofa can happily bear the attention.

3 Not a switch or a light socket out of place, this hard edge interior is almost monastic in its starkness.

4 For the purist, the style must be carried through to every minute detail of the interior. Here, even the book-shelves have been specially engineered, hung by steel yacht hawser from special brackets.

into relief. Or else a carefully framed and painstakingly positioned print or painting. Design gestures need to be large scale and generous — a pair of simple sofas facing each other, grouped low tables — so that furniture layouts form a pattern, carefully calculated to produce the exact effect, rather than a confused, random clutter which achieves nothing.

This is a demanding style, more of a way of life really, and it is not possible to do things by halves. The style must be applied throughout a home if it is to look comfortable, from a kitchen as meticulously planned as a hospital operating theatre, to a sculptural bedroom and bathroom. Unless every detail, large and small, is just right, the whole thing will look wrong. That means everything from door knobs to washing machines, by way of the sofas and the book shelves. If you can manage it, the effect is stunning — a soothing atmosphere that can make you feel happy to be at home on even the dullest of days.

The secret is to use as few elements as possible, to their maximum effect. The starting point is to empty a room of all but the essentials, then to put back as little as possible. When funds

are limited, it is possible to plan a programme of purchases step by step, rather like building up a top quality hi-fi system component by component. Simplicity takes some adapting to, but it doesn't mean simple minded, or easy. With the extras reduced to a minimum, the feel and look of the materials that you do use become of major importance. Light is a special priority — from the way in which daylight is allowed to filter in through silver Venetian blinds, to the modelling and shadows cast by artificial light. So too is the surface texture of the walls — there is a world of difference between a matt and a gloss white paint for example.

The few accessories that you use have to work extra hard: it could be an Alvar Aalto glass vase with cut flowers in it, classic modern crockery or simple table lamps, all of which add up to an air of quiet sophistication.

2

1 Cool, understated white walls, grey woodwork and black leather Le Corbusier chairs set the mood for this sophisticated urban living room. A painting introduces a splash of bright yellow for relief.

2 Metal and glass are not without their decorative possibilities. The sun filtering through these Venetian blinds creates a rich texture and pattern on floor and wall.

1

3 In designing this striking, imaginative staircase made out of scaffolding poles and building site clamps, architect Pierre Botschi has adhered to the original concept of high tech – the recycling of industrial components in a domestic setting.

CITY TRADITIONAL

The model for this sophisticated style is the grand town house, but today it is used to great effect in far humbler dwellings. As escalating property prices have forced many young people to abandon hope of a chic town house and seek potential in hitherto run-down inner city suburbs, so the city traditional look has gained in popularity. It is based partly on a country flavour, so warm, natural materials and fresh pretty colours are important. But also, in equal measure, it has to do with creating a nostalgic sense of period.

One of the effects of the style is to give gentrified houses a feeling of how they would once have been, before they fell on hard times. But the city traditional look is also a matter of taste. It is a style that is used to suggest a confident, settled lifestyle, where novelty for novelty's sake is frowned on, and where new technology is kept firmly in its proper place. (Although that does not mean that the video machine is hidden inside a mock Chippendale cabinet.)

Sometimes, for example when gutting and rebuilding a terraced Georgian house that has been split up into a rabbit warren of tiny flats and awkward bed-sitting rooms, there is scope for genuinely putting back what would once have existed. But more often than not, the kind of house which nowadays receives the attentions of the gentrifiers would never have been particularly elevated on the social scale. Such are the vagaries of fluctuating property values that what were once humble artisans' cottages in grimy areas are now sought after pieces of real estate.

In such circumstances, the city traditional look is particularly popular. It helps to reinforce the new-found status of the house. But it needs to be applied with care if it is not to look pretentious or overblown in much smaller scaled rooms than those for which it was originally intended.

The inspiration is the manor house, or at least the Victorian idea of what an 18th century manor house would have looked like. And that has long been the approved style for a certain type of urban upper middle class home, in which over elaborate design is looked

The fireplace is a natural point of focus in a room like this. It has been given even greater emphasis by the symmetrical arrangement of pictures, wall candelabra and a traditionally framed mirror. Great care has been taken to give the mantlepiece a distressed gold paint finish.

Avoid any sense of self-consciousness with this style. The furniture is arranged in one informal group around the fireplace and another around a low table. The chairs do not have to match, but must all work together to create an atmosphere that lives up to the dignified setting.

Architectural bookcases are the superior forerunners of built-in cupboards. If you have them, keep them, and fill them with old leather, gold-blocked books – the perfect accessories for this look. Even if your drawing room is not on such a grand scale, it is worth keeping in mind the mellow effect of old leather as a decorative element.

No matter how ornate the chandelier, don't attempt to match the light switch. Simple plastic is much less of an intrusion than pretentious brass scrolls. Here the switches are camouflaged even further by being the same colour as the wall.

A room of sumptuous tones of gold, warm leather armchairs and mellow woodwork needs some sort of visual contrast, however small. In this case, a simple white vase, ashtray and cigarette holder grouped together on one small table provide the drama that this room needs.

Natural materials are an essential ingredient of this look. If you discover floorboards in good condition, don't hide them under fitted carpet, but clean, polish and seal them to bring out the warm glow of the wood. If you like a little warmth underfoot, then one oriental rug placed in the middle of the room is appropriate.

upon with suspicion, and in which tradition is important. Now that those original patrons have scattered far beyond their traditional habitat to what would once have been considered novel or even unsuitable locations, the look has been tidied up and turned into a style in its own right, in just the way that the fashion designers have taken the classic gentleman's wardrobe and used it as a starting point for an elegant fashion look.

Hunting prints and stags' heads are clearly going too far, but there is scope for formality and symmetry in internal layouts and arrangements. Rooms will tend to have traditional names in such homes, the drawing room, study and dining room, which will instantly help to conjure up the desired effect.

Walls are embellished, often using the newly rediscovered techniques of

the past. They are dragged and stippled, stencilled and *trompe l'oeil* painted. Combing and dragging both have a Victorian heritage when they were highly developed skills. Now they have more potential for do-it-yourself, and have become the starting point for a variety of different looks. In a tightly controlled form, delicate small scale stippled or cracked finishes look traditional and offer a more personal, intimate touch than similar mechanical wallpaper effects. In a coarser, freer form stippling can also be used in much less conventional, traditional ways.

Curtains are gathered and tucked, hemmed and swagged. Pelmets or elaborate curtain rods are equally acceptable. Festoon blinds, and even fabric tent ceilings have a place too. The effect is to create a rich, opulent looking romantic background, which is

1 Furniture should be arranged sympathetically to complement the room's architecture. Here, an alcove makes the perfect setting for a sofa framed by a pair of palm trees.

2 Details are all important: an interesting arrangement of bric-a-brac and flowers makes an appealing focus to this window bay.

3

5

4

3 The furniture and fittings in this early Georgian house hark back to the interests of that era. Egyptian-style bookcases flank the fireplace, and modern lights have been completely transformed with an Egyptian motif.

4 If your collection fits in with the mood of your house, don't hesitate to show it off.

also, in a kind of soft focus, exactly the opposite to the assertive 'architectural' look, in which walls are seen as pure, sculptural elements. And indeed the city traditional look is in many other ways its exact opposite, and likely to appeal to a very different person.

The ideal city house or apartment will have some sort of hall, even if it's only a vestigial one. It provides space to establish the tone you want to set throughout the house. A few well chosen objects and pictures will go a long way to getting the message across.

This is not the kind of look that calls for an open approach, although some walls may have to be knocked through, especially in the gentrified terraced

house. The idea is to emulate the traditional Georgian house plan which features a double living room, sometimes divided by folding partition doors, so reordering a plan to give more dignity and space to the principal rooms may be necessary.

It is possible to opt for strong colours in some places; provided that they are used in the right setting. Solid dark green with the woodwork picked out in white will throw a room into sharp relief, highlighting the objects in it, and can suggest a suitably lordly background, redolent of libraries full of ancient leather-bound volumes and faded gilt-framed pictures.

If you are trying to apply this kind

of look to a relatively modest house or apartment with small rooms, it is important not to overdo it. Put in too much furniture, and you will find yourself tripping over it, not admiring it. And a huge oil painting on the wall will simply look intimidating and over-scaled. Yet it is possible to sketch in the look deftly with just one or two carefully chosen elements in a way that is far more convincing. A sombre oil painting in a gilt frame does not have to be large to be effective. A few pieces of richly polished mahogany furniture that are not too large, a glass-fronted cabinet with a collection of antique porcelain cups or plates can all help to establish the right kind of atmosphere and texture.

Furniture is traditional, and arranged with formal symmetry. In the living room a pair of sofas, probably covered in big floral print covers with contrasting piping, and soft cushions covered in fabric that co-ordinates, but not so obviously that it shouts at you, will flank the fireplace. The sofas will be accompanied by low tables, covered with carefully placed magazines and large books, and vases of arranged flowers. There will be other circular tables, swathed in floor length fabric and carrying photographs, objets d'art and lamps with huge fabric shades. These do not have to be old; there is no objection to new things so long as they are not aggressively modern. The secret is to look as non-designery as possible, to suggest unselfconscious comfort and solid, self-assured traditional good taste.

There is scope too for a few pieces of exotica within the look. A chinoiserie folding screen perhaps, Indian miniatures on the wall, a set of Piranesi engravings, or a pair of ceramic obelisks. Architectural features such as skirting boards, dados and cornices should certainly be retained. If they have gone missing already, they will need to be replaced. If you are trying to create a traditional atmosphere, nothing looks so immediately wrong as a missing cornice, making the room seem mean and ungenerous. Where a room has been divided, there is often a cornice on three walls but not the partition. There are many craftsmen

who can reproduce a matching piece of cornice for the fourth wall.

The model setting for this style is by its very nature a hierarchical one: well-proportioned formal living rooms, with a much more modestly scaled kitchen — after all it would have been used by servants almost exclusively — a master bedroom, with several smaller subsidiary bedrooms. All of which adds up to not such a bad model for today. It offers a choice between dressing up to live up to the main rooms and relaxing in the less prominent ones. Out of public sight in the bedrooms there is scope for more individual touches than in the public rooms. Bedrooms can be planned around a four-poster, or a brass bedstead — still a favourite, and one which works very well with this look. In the bedroom, painted and stencilled floorboards and American rag quilts also complement this style.

If you want to be consistent with the rest of the house, the kitchen should have a servants' hall flavour to it: plain deal table, dresser, open shelves and schoolroom clock. Built-in kitchen units

will probably be there, but they will be unobtrusive, made of wood rather than plastic laminate faced.

City gardens will necessarily be modestly scaled in most cases, but it is still possible to carry on the flavour of the house even if there isn't a lawn big enough to play croquet on. Hard surfaced gardens using flagstones, paviours and pergolas with small planting beds and moss can look very good. And Edwardian conservatories, their glazing bars painted white, will form a handsome adjunct to any house.

With a light touch, the city traditional look manages to mix sophistication with traditional comfort, but its faintly establishment aura will not be to everyone's taste. It is calculated to appeal to instinctive collectors rather than purists or the compulsively tidy. It respects architectural character, and provides an easy, relaxed background. To work best however, it needs a suitable setting, restraint, and a careful eye for the right pieces of furniture, and the colours and finishes to go with them.

1

2

1 Robert and Sandi Lacey use the classical proportions of their town house as a setting for a rich and elaborate collection of exotica. Big soft cushions on deep opulent sofas add to the feeling of luxurious comfort.

2 A pale colour scheme for the walls allows the richly textured ceiling to stand out in this attractive period interior.

3 Flashy gadgets and space-age ovens are not permitted to dominate the city traditional kitchen. Glass-fronted cupboards and shelves displaying china, a huge bowl of flowers and a range are much more in keeping with this style.

1 Rather than matching furniture of a similar style, why not match shapes? Here, the shape of an antique chair back is reflected in the Deco lampshade, and the trim of the shade echoed in the lacey curtain

2 Furniture from a number of different periods all looks at home in this quietly relaxed living room.

3 Even though the fireplace no longer works, it still forms a natural focal point – an effect that is reinforced by the carefully arranged prints, all in matching frames, on the chimney breast.

POST MODERN

Contemporary design has been through a crisis, which still isn't over. From the 1930s until about the middle of the 1970s there was just one mainstream approach to the design of modern architecture, interiors and furniture. Underpinning it was the notion that any design problem could be solved simply by looking at the functional needs. If you analysed the problem carefully enough, you would not only end up with the best possible design but one which would look good too, ran the theory.

Along with this came a set of preconceptions that started out as ideals, but simply ended up as dogmatic prejudices — ornament and decoration for example were considered to be irrational, even, in some undefined way, dishonest. Consistency and minimalism were considered to be virtues in their own right, and the aesthetic aspired to was the simplicity of machinery.

In theory all this might have sounded fine, but in the long run it resulted in a lot of tidy and over-simplified boxes. In the hands of the best designers, modernism produced work of the highest quality. But their followers, who mechanically tried to apply the same formulas, simply churned out dreary office blocks that looked like shoe boxes, and living rooms with all the warmth and charm of an airport lounge. Simplicity was just too difficult for them. But the dogma also maintained that simple uncluttered surfaces were more efficient, cheaper and more practical, even in a subtle way, more moral, than any other approach.

So modernism became an extremely repressive creed, shutting out any kind of alternative. Yet in fact many of its precepts turned out to be the exact opposite of the truth. Simple unadorned shapes and surfaces are often more difficult and more expensive to make than complicated ornate ones. Decoration for example can be a highly efficient way of hiding an awkward joint. Even more importantly, the simple-minded functionalism of some of the modernists missed out completely on many of the less quantifiable but still essential purposes of design. Modernism

1 It is the combination of gentle classical details with sharp purist lines that is the hallmark of post modernism.

2 Shape and form play an important part in this style. The curve of a halogen desk lamp flirts with the strict proportions of a single column, and is subtly echoed in the shape of the arum lilies.

3 All the elements of post modernism are here: conspicuously redundant columns, laminate surfaces, ceiling and walls painted like clouds.

is an abstract style, it doesn't make any concessions to the symbolic or personal aspects of design.

When in the 1970s the public outcry at the sterility of the excesses of modernism had become so loud that it triggered off a collective crisis of confidence among the architectural profession, the repercussions were quickly felt in interiors too, so close are the theoretical underpinnings of both disciplines. Post modernism is the profession's response to that crisis. In many ways it sets out to be the exact opposite of the modernism which it seeks to replace.

Post modernism aims to be complicated and ambiguous, to be representational rather than abstract, to use colours that would once have been regarded as frivolous, even to incorporate wit and humour, and references to many different architectural periods.

In interior planning, the post modern approach seeks to get away from the simplicity and clarity of the

1　Post modernism has had a far-reaching influence – even extending into areas of product design. This vacuum cleaner, designed by Michele de Lucchi, is a familiar object, given a new lease of life with toy-like colours and shapes.

2　An apartment in which the Memphis-inspired new wave has run riot. The marble-clad 1930s hall makes a striking setting for a Sottsass table and painted clouds.

3

modern interior where you can see at a glance all there is to see. A post modern plan by contrast avoids big simple open spaces, preferring to create a series of small-scale spaces that reveal themselves gradually as you move through them, and a complicated interlocking set of levels. In interiors, post modernism began as a revolt against what was beginning to be seen as the stifling constraints of conventional good taste and all the sterility that implied. The glossy perfection of the Italians of the 1970s in particular was simply looking something of a bore.

The new movement started in America and in Milan, and initially looked deliberately outrageous and extreme in contrast to the sobriety of so much orthodox modernism whose conventions and sensibilities it deliberately set out to flout. But now with growing acceptance, the post modernists are settling into a calmer, and totally serious approach to design.

In Milan in particular, the Memphis

group of designers — whose members come from Japan, America and Britain as well as from Italy itself — have developed a highly influential collection of furniture and fabrics, ceramics and glass in an entirely original post modern style. Rather than retreat into nostalgia the Memphis group set out to create a new approach. They use challenging juxtapositions of materials, colours that would once have been dismissed as naive, and mockingly non-functional details: bookcases that parody the sleek built-in units of the major manufacturers, sideboards that look apparently broken, coffee tables with splayed and spindly legs. Memphis triggered off one of those cross-over moments in the history of taste, when everything that had up until then seemed good became bad, and what had been written off as bad became a virtue.

Memphis' impact has been astonishing. In Italy all the mainstream manufacturers of furniture rushed to produce Memphis-inspired designs.

4

5

3 Practicality is not the priority of this unorthodox table; but its strong primary colours and combination of playful shapes make it a dramatic focus for this Californian interior.

4 Outlandish post modern furniture sits happily next to perforated metal high tech benches. An appropriately bland background is provided by the white walls, curtains and floor – the only detail allowed to stand out is the gleaming timber ceiling.

5 The post modern approach out of doors. Contrasting pinks, glass brick windows, square paving stones, even the tall straight palms are the elements that create the look.

1 A traditionally proportioned living room, transformed by new finishes and materials. The gloss ceiling complements the brushed steel fireplace, and reflects the overstuffed scarlet satin armchairs.

2 This cool, tranquil room is decorated in different shades of related colours. The chairs are Bauhaus modern classics; the cornice and column hark back to earlier times.

3 The mood here is definitely 1950s thanks to the strong colours and simple geometric shapes. The furniture has been arranged with graph paper precision.

New colour combinations emerged at the same time, and so did new ways of using materials. Printed pattern laminates came into their own, used by Memphis not as pale imitations of natural finishes, or in quietly neutral tones but in bright jagged patterns that revelled in their artificiality.

In America the post modern look has already made rapid strides toward becoming part of the mainstream of design, and other countries are following. It is not to be confused with simple revivalism, a style which uses period details in a straightforward way, one period at a time, with the idea of creating a particular image. Post modernists will cheerfully deploy classical columns and plasterwork cornices alongside Charles Rennie Mackintosh chairs and elaborate Art Deco fireplaces.

Such devices are not meant to be taken seriously, nor as period pieces. They are put together in completely untraditional ways, one style on top of another. Columns are deliberately distorted, or stop short of the ceilings that they might be expected to be supporting. They are painted in subversive pinks and blues.

According to Charles Jencks, the architectural critic who has been one of post modernism's leading proponents, the point of the style is to put back into design all those expressive and symbolic qualities that modernism took away in the name of standardization and mass production. Just as in the field of product design, the mood has turned against packaging everything in anonymous black boxes which make video machines look indistinguishable from electric fan heaters, and toward designs that express symbolically what a product does, so the post modernist interior design attempts to celebrate the rituals of everyday life. Post modernists are trying to invent a system of ornament and decoration that is appropriate for modern materials and production methods.

Post modernism is still growing. It represents an attitude of mind among designers that can take in a wide variety of different approaches. In France it includes the work of Ricardo Boffill, who is building housing estates

4 The features of this room – the moulding, French windows, parquet floor – remain intact; there are even one or two antiques dotted around. But the vivid colours, strong patterns and abundance of visual jokes make it clear that this is a highly unconventional interior.

5 Traditional plasterwork and elaborate architectural detailing provide a particularly striking context for the nonconformist shapes and unusual colours of this room.

around Paris that are modelled closely on giant classical monuments, with bedrooms contained in huge columns, or in the form of Roman aqueducts. In Britain it is represented, among many others, by Terry Farrell, architect of the celebrated TV-AM studios, who attempts to create designs which tell stories as you move around them. In London, Charles Jencks' own house is built around a 52 step staircase which serves as a calendar for important family events, and boasts a kitchen in which classical columns are decorated with a frieze made up of wooden spoons in the place of a rather more orthodox classical motif.

The post modern approach is permissive and relaxed. Sometimes it is even playful and funny. The overall effect is more important than making a fetish out of being consistent in every detail and each finish, which makes it highly suitable as a style for applying to existing interiors. Accidents of proportion and scale can sometimes be the starting point of a design, as can features that already exist in a room that you have decided to decorate.

In the kitchen, marbling cheap standard chipboard units, or equipping them with stick-on, pre-formed cornices that can be bought inexpensively by the metre will give an instant touch of post modern splendour. Similarly, in the living room, an existing storage system can be given a face-lift and a post modern flavour by applying flat cut-out columns and a pediment, or grouping the units to form a pattern.

Don't be afraid to use colour in unorthodox ways. Post modernism uses a much broader palette than conventional good taste would allow.
Trompe l'oeil murals can help to change the character of a room too — and its function can provide useful clues for the choice of subject matter. Illusions created by the use of paint and mirrors can increase the interest of an interior, or improve on its proportions.

For a post modern interior, this kind of ambiguity between what is real and what is not, is a valued quality. It is possible to play surrealist tricks with apparently solid materials and elements. A fireplace for example can be made to look as if it is floating in mid-air by setting it into a mirror-faced wall. Even such apparently honest-to-goodness high tech materials as Dexion shelving can have their character transformed by painting them a frivolous pastel shade and using them with Lloyd loom basket weave chairs and plastic flowers. One London designer has even put studded rubber to similar uses, creating an indoor beach out of strips of yellow and blue rubber, with cardboard waves, dangling sea gulls, beach umbrella and life belts to complete the illusion.

1

1 **This striking architectural setting needs little embellishment; but what few pieces of furniture there are have to make bold statements. The rich dark wood of the grand piano is a dramatic contrast to the white walls and pale pink tinge seen through the doors.**

2 **Pigeon holes with an architectural emphasis. By making clever use of cornices and pediments these storage units dominate the room.**

2

3 The face of the new-look, Italian interior. Instant tongue-in-cheek character is given to the neutral background with specially made textured laminate furniture, wedge-shaped units and playful stools.

4 Transformed by a careful selection of furniture this small room assumes larger proportions. The sofa is by Charles Eames, the floorlight is Italian; together they give this basic, functional interior a fresh look.

5 There are times when the hi-fi need not be camouflaged. As a free-standing system, sitting purposefully on the floor, it can look like a natural part of the furniture.

DECORATOR

The decorator look is instantly recognizable, not so much as a particular style, but as an approach. It can be equally appropriate with a traditional or with a modern flavour, or a combination of both. It works in town apartments and in country houses. It is international, although different countries use it with a different emphasis. In Britain it is the gentlemanly aesthete decorators who have made the running, first David Hicks, now David Mlinaric. In America the look is altogether glossier and more flamboyant.

What distinguishes the style everywhere though, is the calculating eye for the picturesque and the dramatic flair with which it is applied. It is expensive, and looks it. Every piece of furniture, and every object is placed with elaborate care for the effect of its colour and texture on the overall design. It's done with the same painstaking attention to detail as the propping and art direction of a film set. The locating of chairs and bowls of flowers is carried out with a theatrical elaboration. Lighting plays a particularly important part, as well it might, for this is a species of stage setting.

The look has grown up gradually as the decorator, or the interior designer, as some of them prefer to be called, has emerged as a professional in his own right. In contrast to the architect, who in general is happier manipulating space, cutting holes here, deploying new walls there, inserting new floors and so on, the decorator is much more skilled at dealing with surfaces, textures and details.

Carried to extremes, this approach can come uncomfortably close to self-parody. An indigestibly rich mixture of items of furniture from every period, arranged with fetishistic care without thought for how people will actually live with them, will simply end up looking pretentious. In the 1970s one could come across decorated homes in which clear perspex rocking chairs co-existed uneasily with brass mounted ivory tusks, 18th century black boys and French Empire mirrors, all contained in blood red rooms and lit by enough dazzling spotlights to equip an entire Italian restaurant.

The excesses were a perhaps inevitable by-product of the way in which decorators worked. Each needed to build up a strong, instantly recognizable style of their own so that their message could be picked up and broadcast by the glossy shelter magazines. And some of their clients may have been to blame as well — demanding more decorating than was always appropriate. As one designer put it, "it took courage to realize that the best advice to give some clients was simply to paint their living room in two shades of white".

All this is not to decry the talents of the serious decorators. It is a highly skilled task. And the influence of talented tastemakers on the rest of us is considerable. It is not something that just anybody can do well, but there are techniques and skills to be learnt from looking at the way in which the decorators work.

The best decorators have a good grasp of architectural skills too, allowing them to ensure that their designs are not simply a skin deep layer applied to existing walls like wrapping paper. Their aim is to provide a domestic setting which reinforces, or even flatters the way in which their clients want to live and to present themselves to the world. It means providing a kitchen which is not only convenient, but in which practicalities do not submerge style either. It should be the kind of place which will make you feel better on a rainy Sunday morning over your orange juice and croissant. The dining room should have enough glamour and glitter to add a little sparkle to a dinner party. If the living room is where you do your entertaining, a successful decorator's design should encourage people to feel relaxed, and able to sit and talk to each other at ease. That can mean providing several different seating focuses — perhaps a series of small tables as well as the more conventional sofa groups.

The decorator works without preconceptions or allegiances to any one particular style, but has a catholic willingness to borrow an idea or a motif that seems appropriate from a variety of different sources. It is not, generally speaking, the decorators who are the

innovators, but they are best at putting other people's innovations to use.

Thus decorators were quickly able to incorporate developments in modern lighting techniques such as recessed downlighters and spotlamps. And equally they moved to exploit the picturesque qualities of the slick Italian furniture designs of the 1970s, clean, sculptural and often using flamboyant new materials. These they blended with the ornate antiques that had always been part of their repertoire, along with such classics of the 1930s as the Mies van der Rohe flat steel cantilevered dining chairs.

These and many other items are all standard parts of the decorator's palette, to be deployed in patterns and groups as part of overall interior design schemes. One small square table, for example, sitting all by itself can look lost and insignificant. Four identical tables grouped together and softened with a bowl full of spotlit daffodils will make a much more positive statement. The successful decorator's interior will look calm and effortless. Every last picture and light switch may have been positioned with graph paper precision, but it certainly shouldn't look thus.

Artfully treated as a stage set, this dining room embraces the decorator style with exuberance. A large mirror reflects candlelight onto the highly polished mahogany furniture. The cloth draped around the walls and loosely over the chairs is just casual enough to avoid self-consciousness. Although the room bristles with antiques, it doesn't attempt to be a historical replica. They have been selected to achieve an overall effect rather than for their individual qualities.

The decorator's preferred order of work is to start from the front door and work his way through the whole house, creating a total look by linking rooms, halls and stairs, in a way that is beyond the means of most of us. But it is still possible to adapt some of their ideas to a more modest approach.

Consistency — and at the same time knowing when to break the rules — is one of the keys to a successful decorator look. You can achieve much more by limiting yourself to a range of colours and finishes and using them to help you select everything in a room, rather than simply acquiring a haphazard collection of unco-ordinated bits and pieces. Work out a spectrum of colours that you plan to use first. If you opt for celadon green in the living room for example, echo a celadon carpet with toning walls, and matching loose covers for the sofa. Accessories and fittings should also echo the main colour, but just occasionally there is scope to throw in an obviously clashing shade that will bring out the best in the sober greens.

Bear in mind the tactile qualities of the materials you use. The decorator look makes the most of the use of contrasting gloss and matt finishes, and uses lighting schemes to bring out the highlights in them — rich looking glossy lacquers, gloss paint walls, and so on (finishes incidentally which can equally well be applied to furniture and fittings). Gleaming metal highlights, which can look especially good after dark, are part of the style too. More traditionally inspired decorators like to work with fabrics, to create a rich mixture of pattern with pattern, co-ordinating curtains with lampshade and upholstery and combining materials of different texture and weight.

But perhaps the most critical element that the decorator has to work with is space. To look right, an interior must be able to use large amounts of space, or else (and it's just as good if it can be done well), give the impression that it has created an abundance of space. Nothing else gives such an instant impression of opulence as the sense of being able to swim in an apparently endless indoor area.

Low screened lights, creating a soft glow around the velvety sofa, offer an inviting background for intimate after-dinner conversation.

Textures are very important in this room; soft cushions contrast with the rougher, coarser textures of the rush matting on the floor, the basket weave lampshade, and the cane chair and low table – all of which cleverly present different variations on the same theme.

Pattern making, by juxtaposing a collection of exotic objects, helps to give the interior the appearance of a carefully considered painting.

Even the base of the table lamp carries on the same basket weave theme, as does the flower basket. A rough wood frame makes an interesting variation on the traditional coffee table.

The richly embroidered cloth draped over the circular table adds a touch of luxury – and offers relief from the rough natural textures that predominate.

An artful use of mirror on the chimney breast; it plays tricks with the gilt-framed prints hung over it, making them look as if they are floating in space.

The decorator look is calculated to come into its own after dark. Candlelight and sparkling spotlamps are reflected in mirrors, and gleam in the glossy sheen of an ancient laquered screen.

Chairs don't have to match, but the plain loose covers give a sense of continuity and don't detract from the splendours of the table setting.

Don't overdo the finishing touches; half a dozen simple, but well-chosen objects that complement each other can achieve much more than a flashy, flamboyant display.

A folding screen helps to create a more intimate sense of enclosure around the dining table.

A dark wood table is particularly effective in this kind of setting for dinner with a sense of occasion.

Strategically positioned mirrors can help of course. So can a collection of low, horizontal surfaces, rather than large vertical pieces of furniture. And using light to divert attention away from the wall surfaces helps too, as does working with just one or two pale colours throughout a scheme; it allows walls, floor and furniture to merge into one. But the simplest of techniques in increasing the apparent size of a room is to banish all superfluous furniture and clutter. Nothing makes a room seem bigger than keeping its contents down to a minimum, perhaps just a small table, lit by a low slung pendant light, and a couple of chairs. The decorator look is particularly geared to keeping the evidence of daily life's mundane necessities out of sight. Cynics might explain the success of this in terms of carefully posed magazine photographs, or an abundance of domestic help.

The look is particularly prone to the swings of fashion and taste, not to say to fads. It has a tendency to move toward the extremes, giving it a sensational appeal. Its practitioners have dabbled in Art Nouveau and are currently caught up in a bout of interest in Art Deco, which after all began as decorator style.

Its extremes are not calculated to appeal to the puritanical British who are naturally suspicious of indulgence and sensuousness. Yet there are signs that a new, softer and less stylized decorators' look is enjoying increasing popularity in Britain, and is even influencing the more hedonistically inclined Americans. Gradually the look is moving toward a more natural approach, one which is helping to revive the almost forgotten craft skills such as furniture making and painting techniques and elevating them to the realms of high fashion.

1 These life size statues are the kind of flamboyant antiques that are at their best when lit and positioned with an eye for drama.

2 and 3   A carefully
co-ordinated colour
scheme, based on shades
of white and pale beige,
makes the most of this
light, airy room. Several
low, horizontal surfaces
are used as platforms for
architectural ornaments,
and carefully placed
books and flowers. The
geometrically patterned
floor provides a strong
visual basis which is
continued in the panelled
walls and heavy
moulding.

1 Flashes of red, like strokes of a paintbrush, rescue this carefully limited scheme of greys and white from flatness. The mink coloured walls throw the pictures into sharp relief – the contrast makes the pattern of the frames almost as important as the pictures themselves.

2 The lifesize stag provides a flamboyant touch to this ordered room. The medieval style fireplace contrasts with the surroundings but echoes the presence of a hunted animal.

3 Bold, geometric and carefully placed matching tables have their impact on the room softened by pale unobtrusive colours. Two symmetrically placed downlighters draw the eye to the focus of the room – the fireplace.

This is the style for people who don't like following the rules. They want to mix and match ideas that catch their fancy, and use them to express their individuality by the personal touches they apply. The look is very close to the advertising and music businesses in its inspiration, and like them, it is restless and twitchy, always on the look out for something new. There are three basic ingredients: a non-specific nostalgia for the past — it can be for any period from Victoriana to the 1960s, but the past is getting closer all the time; an instinct for collecting weird and wonderful memorabilia, and wanting to show it off; and finally, a certain calculated reluctance to take things too seriously.

The joy of an eclectic approach to decoration is that it allows you to have your cake and eat it, to indulge in a taste for the wilful and the not quite respectable, but at the same time to be able to step back a few paces and say that you didn't really mean it, that you were only joking. It is a style which is always highly sensitive to changes in the design climate, but though the details fluctuate, the readiness to accept new ideas is always there.

In the 1970s the Biba department store elevated the style to a way of life, sparking off a whole crop of Art Deco living rooms with gold dancing girl table lamps, fake leopard skin rugs and glamorous gloss black walls. It was followed rapidly by a merry-go-round of other styles — from ethnic Afghan tents to 1950s revivals revelling in what had been until recently embarrassingly bad (or was it good?) taste.

What distinguishes the eclectic look, though, is its ability to keep its tongue firmly in its cheek. To succeed as an interior style, it needs to juggle the three basic elements of nostalgia, obsessive collecting and flippancy. Veer too far in any one direction and it will come unstuck and appear mawkishly unfunny, the room cluttered with table lamps disguised as ducks, or turned into a dry and dusty museum.

Some highly successful eclectic interiors do, of course, border on the positively dotty. One London art school lecturer for example, has his entire kitchen painted to look like a giant

Refusing to take any one style entirely seriously, the eclectic approach is all about breaking the rules. Jon Weallans uses sleek 1960s chrome and glass for his dining table, but then wittily undermines its purpose by adding an Arts and Crafts sideboard, and a frankly bad taste flower vase.

1 Eclectic interiors depend on an element of mix and match. But in order for this rather more sophisticated version of the eclectic style to work, there must be a disciplined control of colours and finishes. Architect Tom Brent has successfully done this in his London warehouse.

2 and 3 The artificial silk sofa cover tones perfectly with the gold painted screen and the natural, untreated plaster walls. The 1920s cinema fascia crowns this area of soft colours and textures and distinguishes it from the rest of the room.

4 and 5 Unusual wood graining paint techniques are used throughout Tom Brent's warehouse – on the wooden building structure, walls, chairs and even the dining table. The effect is that of a space which is tobacco-mellow and warm.

6 Reminiscent of a pre-war cinema, the gold paint and maroon carpets in the mezzanine bedroom capture the nostalgia of this richly decorative period.

piece of De Stijl abstract art, with red, blue and yellow as the only colours. And his living room is an essay in recycled militaria, camouflage netting draped over the sofa, olive drab walls, with a couple of jerry cans doing duty as a coffee table. If you feel you can live with it, that's fine. For the rest of us, it's certainly fun to see.

For the less committed, who don't plan to take things to extremes, eclecticism still offers a chance of making a strong personal statement, and doing it with a minimum of expenditure. You can make do at one end of the eclectic scale simply with a strong colour sense, an eye for the

antiques of the future, and a bit of nerve. At the other, eclecticism can blossom into all kinds of lush exotica: lofts filled with jukeboxes and pinball tables, small semi-detached houses dominated by obsessive collections of coronation mugs and giant-sized poster blow-ups on the wall.

The look is built up painstakingly, layer upon layer, like a collage. One Art Deco teapot by itself will simply look like a curiosity. A whole wall of them on specially built mirrored shelves will provide the focus for a complete room, giving it instant character and identity. Bric-a-brac of all kinds can be transformed from the mundane simply

by the way in which it is grouped, arranged and displayed. Carefully chosen junk shop delights may not look very much in isolation, but used as part of an overall design scheme that puts a premium on rich swirling patterns and textures, they add up to something much more positive than the sum total of the parts individually.

Eclectic enthusiasts play an important part in identifying new looks, and turning them into a part of mainstream interior design taste. They were the first to see the joys of Victoriana and Art Deco, and even of those once dreadful Scandinavian modern three piece suites from the

1950s, helping them along the way to becoming sought-after collector's items.

The inspiration may be a film, or an exhibition which suddenly sparks off an interest in a new kind of style, or else it can simply be a matter of individual enthusiasms. Either way it is a comfortable, accommodating look that is not intimidating, but which can instead offer great latitude. Things don't have to be perfect, or match each other. Pieces of furniture or accessories can come and go according to changes in enthusiasm, and the room will still look good. The effect can be built up gradually, adding a piece of furniture here, or a fabric there, rather than

1

1 The most unlikely bits and pieces can be pressed into service to achieve this look. One clown's mask in its plastic wrapping would simply look untidy; five make a point.

2 Eclecticism should be fun. It is a style built up with a wide range of objects that together say something about the owner. The trademarks are familiar – the goose light, old teapots and tin toys – it is the way they are assembled that makes the individual statement.

2

deliberately setting out to make a dramatic new statement from scratch, and then rigidly sticking to it.

The style is equally at home on a small, modest scale in a suburban house, or on a much grander scale as an exotic collector's piece. But because it is always slightly at odds with respectable notions of good taste, it invariably has a hint of the non-conformist about it.

Colour and pattern both play an important part. The colours in an eclectic scheme will tend to be frivolous, or theatrical, or even deliberately designed to set the purist's teeth just slightly on edge by breaking the rules a little. Nursery colours, pinks and washed out baby blues used in the living room can be one way of achieving this. Or else an apparently tasteful use of cream, subverted by a thin stripe of lime green or flame orange around the skirting. Or strong, glossy reds or blacks which can provide a useful background to a collection of objects on the wall, and help to make one aware of

the calculatedly theatrical effect on your surroundings.

Cheap and quick transformations can be achieved by repainting junk shop furniture. A set of old kitchen chairs could be gloss painted in different primary colours. A collection of different chairs could be linked visually by painting them the same colour, or even stencilling or marbling them. Lloyd loom basket weave chairs — once so reminiscent of dreary seaside nursing homes — freshly painted in soft pink or lavender, became an almost essential ingredient in the eclectic repertoire.

Finishes and materials that are obviously pretending to be something else are especially favoured: bamboo style chests of drawers, lino that looks like marble, wallpaper that looks like leopard skin and so on. Patterns can be mixed in profusion: carpets, fabrics and paint can all be used in this way.

Specific themes are important to this style. A theme may be pain-stakingly consistent, as for example in

the detailed recreation of a 1940s period flavour, right down to using massive old refrigerators with lightning flash door handles, lino on the floor, and huge old sofas that look like dodgem cars. Or it can be a collection of plastic memorabilia from a range of periods.

The starting point for a theme might be a piece of recycled architectural salvage. A ritzy 1930s Art Deco mirror, for example, could provide the theme for a complete Grand Hotel style bathroom, with big old fashioned taps and sunburst stencil motif on the side of the bath panels. A kitchen design might spring from an Edwardian glass fronted shop counter, put to use instead of modern fitted units.

With flair and a good eye, the eclectic approach conjures an air of sophisticated knowing in which nothing is quite what it seems, and in which a great diversity of objects work together to provide a highly personal picture about the kind of person who lives with them.

3 Not the most practical of tables but, in true eclectic manner, a witty and attractive way of displaying a collection of china. The glass top is held up by three variously coloured chairs, and all those rules about colour co-ordination are blatantly ignored.

3

1   Eclecticism is not for perfectionists. Particularly if it means making virtue of a room's defects – in this case the damp patches. Here a plan chest is used to prop up the side table.

2   Dougie Fields' slightly sinister living room gets its edge from the '50s nostalgia and collection of artist's palette inspired furniture.

3   Not for the faint-hearted, this bathroom is out and out bad taste to some people, but that is exactly the point Dougie Fields is making.

THE MINIMUM

John Pawson designs interiors that demand a certain amount of commitment from those who live in them. They are not for those who enjoy clutter, or who can tolerate untidiness. Rather, they are exercises in reducing possessions to their barest minimum, no decorative frills, no assertive pieces of furniture, no pictures on the walls. Almost nothing at all in fact. He creates self-contained environments, from which the outside world is carefully excluded. Only sunlight is allowed to penetrate, and even that only through carefully controlled Venetian blinds that turn it into an abstract pattern on the floor.

Such a minimalist approach makes apparently even the smallest of decisions, the exact distance of a chair from a wall or the position of a light switch, take on unusual importance.

This apartment, on the ground floor of a large Victorian house, was originally a warren of small rooms, built around a well. Pawson has moved all the walls, to create a large double-volume space at the front, in which a vestigial kitchen is provided. The marble worktop has a sink and a hob set into it; the oven is concealed in the storage wall opposite. At the rear of the apartment are two bedrooms, and a wide corridor with more storage space concealed within a run of cupboards.

The bedrooms are not bedrooms in the conventional sense in that they have no beds or permanent furniture. Futon mattresses are brought out at night for sleeping purposes. During the day they go back into the cupboards. Pictures too are only temporary, hung on the walls at whim, then returned to their storage cupboards.

4

2

3

1 Even in the kitchen visual distractions are kept to a minimum. An elegantly detailed sink and hob are let into the marble worktop. Only Richard Sapper's chrome kettle is allowed to remain on show.

2 The corridor, lit by ankle level recessed lights, is treated with as much meticulous care as the rooms themselves.

3 The bedroom by night. Totally empty during the day, in the evening a bed, in the form of a surprisingly comfortable Japanese futon, is allowed out of storage.

4 Pawson has deliberately kept the number of textures and finishes throughout the apartment to a minimum. All the walls are white; all the floors and skirtings are of wood, Venetian blinds adorn all the windows. Only the craftsmanlike chairs provide a lighter touch, a necessary relief in such disciplined surroundings.

5 In an almost bare room, the patterns cast by the sun filtering through Venetian blinds become a major element in the design.

6 At the back of the apartment the corridor has been widened to provide storage for household belongings and appliances – even the washing machine and dryer are hidden inside the cupboards.

7 Two rooms and a corridor have been opened out to create a large living area. In an interior as sparse as this the quality of the details becomes vital. Only the perfectly preserved Victorian cornice remains of the old interior.

A CONVERTED PRISON

Architect Nigel Crump and his painter wife Midori have created a home and a studio out of a mainly Victorian building, used at various times as a school and a factory, but best known as a women's prison. They have managed with skill one of the most difficult tasks facing those who attempt to recycle industrial buildings – retaining the essential character, but also creating an interior that is practical for family life.

When the Crumps bought the building, they had a plain, almost windowless barn of a place, with brick walls supporting a pitched roof. They wanted to keep the open feeling, but also to arrange the space to provide a studio where Midori could work undisturbed, and a couple of rooms for children and occasional guests. The conversion had to be achieved within a tight budget, and needed to be realized over a long period to spread the cost.

The main two storey space has been left intact; bare brick walls, domesticated by pictures and bookshelves, visibly betray the industrial origins of the building. The windows have not been altered, leaving the character of the place intact from the outside. But to bring more sunshine in, large glass rooflights have been inserted.

A mezzanine level has been installed in one corner, to provide a sleeping platform. Underneath it is the bathroom, contained in a simple timber cabin whose proportions betray Midori's Japanese origins. The kitchen is built in a little outhouse that comes spilling out of the main structure, and which also houses a conventional children's bedroom. Midori's studio is divided from the main living space by a full height timber-framed screen, made using traditional Japanese techniques, without nails.

1

3

2

4

6

7

1 A welter of different architectural styles sit happily on the outside of the old prison housing the Crumps' studio.

2 Sand-blasted brick walls make a gritty contrast to a collection of antiques and pictures.

3 The master bedroom is a mezzanine high in the rafters – an arrangement that preserves the open studio flavour.

4 Translucent paper screens bring light into the internal bathroom without loss of privacy.

5 The kitchen/dining room is not open plan, keeping cooking smells and clutter in exile.

6 A Japanese screen divides Midori's studio from the main room. Unpretentious furniture sets a relaxed mood.

7 New rooflights inserted into the original structure keep luxuriant houseplants healthy.

DECO TECH

Top fashion retailer Joseph Ettedgui, better known simply as Joseph, was born in Morocco, has shops in New York and London, and spends much of his time in Paris and Tokyo. His home, however, is in London, where he says he prefers to live because of the relaxed way of life it offers. Outside, the Knightsbridge block of apartments where he lives is nondescript. Inside Joseph and his architect Eva Jiricna have collaborated to create a world apart, an interior that has none of the dowdy feel that usually accompanies such impersonal places.

The apartment originally had a layout akin to a racetrack, small rooms opening off both sides of a dark corridor. All that has been swept away to create a single 'L'-shaped living area, with the kitchen at one end, screened by a partition wall that stops at eye level. Bedroom and bathroom are fitted into the short side of the 'L', linked by intercommunicating doors.

Demolishing the walls means that light comes into the living area from two different directions, always a good way of creating a space that is pleasant to be in. The geometry of the layout ensures that, although the apartment is open, there is plenty of scope for different areas within it to develop their own character. The style blends Joseph's enthusiasm for collecting Art Deco, and the monochrome look of the 1920s, with Eva Jiricna's commitment to modern materials like steel, and high tech tricks such as the commercial glass-fronted, walk-in refrigerator.

Together, the two forces have combined to produce a svelte, sophisticated interior, in which the stained ash floor creates an attractive foil to the brushed steel that Jiricna has used for many of the apartment's specially designed fittings.

The partnership between Joseph and Jiricna, who designed his previous apartment and his latest shops, is a good example of how an expert and a client can work together, pooling ideas and requirements, to produce a successful and exciting result.

1

2

3

1 The original layout has been opened up, eliminating corridors and small cell-like rooms to create one calm, well-proportioned space. The dining chairs are 1920s classics designed by Mallet-Stevens, and the rug is by Eileen Gray. Eva Jiricna designed the special steel picture mount.

2 The black and white bedroom is calmer and softer than the rest of the apartment – there is no steel here, just glass shelves and dark, stained wood.

3 Travertine and stainless steel make a surreal mixture in the bathroom, accentuated by the drinking fountain and authentic ship's porthole that is used as a window and can be seen reflected in the mirror.

4 High tech is dominant in the kitchen; stainless steel units create a professional restaurant flavour.

5 Joseph has chosen a few select pieces of Art Deco glass from his collection to soften the austere lines of Jiricna's design.

6 The living area combines Jiricna's severe modern approach with Joseph's fondness for the 1920s. The chairs are by Eileen Gray, and it all adds up to a quiet evocation of monochrome modernism.

7 Floodlit by a huge Fortuny umbrella light, Joseph poses in an empty corner of his apartment.

THE HOME OFFICE

Jo van Heyningen and Birkin Haward designed their house to function both as a family home, and as a place to work. It is built on land at the end of the garden of an existing house, and faces onto a side road. The chosen site meant not only a restriction on the height of the house, but also demanded a plan which took into account the need to provide for privacy. This has been achieved by building the house around an enclosed courtyard. All the rooms can then look out over this space with large glass windows, secure that they are not overlooked by outsiders, and work can go on uninterrupted. Work area and living room are clearly defined, but integrated by the use of similar furniture.

The courtyard is itself designed to function as an outdoor room in the summer. On one side is the main two storey house, at the other side is a single storey wing, which offers the possibility of becoming a self-contained apartment when children grow into teenagers, and want independence.

In the main part of the house, the family living room, kitchen and dining room are all in one, built on the ground floor along with the remaining bedrooms. The more formal living area for adults in need of a rest from the hurly burly of family life is upstairs, combined with a studio workspace. This gives the house a feeling of calm and serenity, enforced by the cool and unfussy interior design. The floor at the upper level is cut short at one end to allow the family room below to have a double height volume above it, emphasizing its importance – and making it one of the pleasantest parts of the house to be in. The height restriction imposed by planning constraints means that the upper level is lit by windows fitted into the slope of the roof.

1 Squeezed into a small city site the house presents a blank exterior, softened by ivy, to preserve the privacy of its occupants.

2 The private side: sliding glass doors open out onto a sun-filled courtyard.

3 The kitchen, elegantly simple with plain white units and quarry tile floor. The stainless steel stove acts as a focus for the house.

4 In the studio area, stools and work surface are designed to match and to echo the wood-framed windows and creamy walls.

5 Children's rooms and kitchen being downstairs, the upper level can remain a calm, peaceful adult preserve.

6 Above the two storey entrance hall, sloping glass roof panels and cotton blinds give a marvellously airy effect with splashes of colour from prints on the wall and dangling kites.

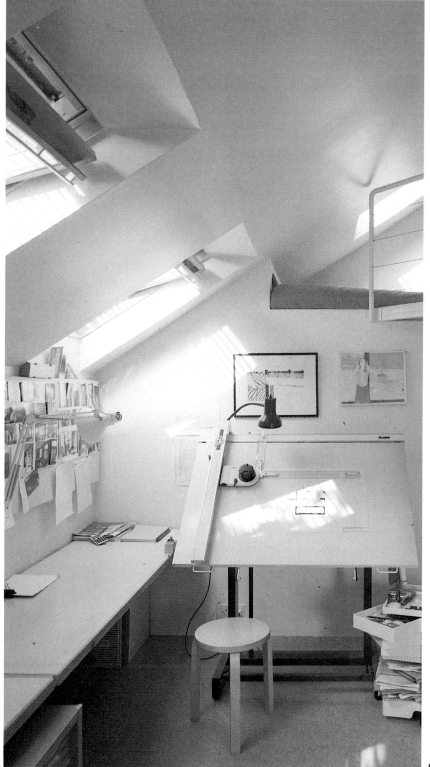

4

5

6

THE POOL HOUSE

Francisco Gilardi lives in a house that could easily have become a museum piece. He persuaded Luis Barragan, Mexico's greatest architect, to come out of semi-retirement and build him a home in Mexico City. But though it has all the perfection of detail and proportion that are the trademarks of Barragan's calm style of architecture, it is still a modestly scaled and attractive place to live.

Mexico City is one of the world's less endearing capitals: polluted, overcrowded and sprawling, Gilardi's house provides a retreat from all this. Although centrally located, and in a busy street packed in close with its neighbours, it is an oasis of tranquillity.

At the centre of the house is a swimming pool, integrated with the dining room. Across an open courtyard lies the rest of the house which contains the living room and bedrooms. The pool is used as a part of the composition – sunlight bounces off the rippling water to create a pattern of reflections on the far wall and a stunning background for leisurely meals.

Barragan's technique is to reinterpret the traditions of Mexican vernacular architecture, and to use its materials to create abstract patterns and textures that have many of the spare, simple qualities of the original. Walls are roughcast plaster both inside and out, finished in a selection of pastel and more vivid shades of coloured wash. The floors, where they are not carpeted, are of hefty clay tiles, and the staircases are made of pine.

Against this stark background, furniture is an important softening influence. Gilardi has chosen large sofas, simple in their shape but using soft welcoming textured covers. And here and there stands a colonial Spanish antique or two, taking the edge off the house's modernity.

1

2

3

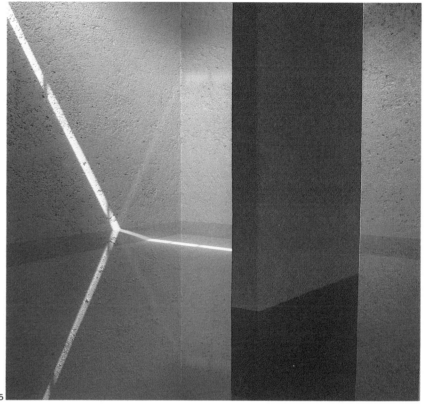

1 The house is built around a courtyard – with a cloister linking the main building to the pool room at the back.

2 The Spanish colonial wardrobe was a gift from the architect to help soften the feeling of newness in the house.

3 In Mexico's harsh sunlight minimal window openings make sense.

4 Furniture in natural materials co-exist well with the roughcast walls.

5 A structural pillar rises out of the pool like a dramatic sculpture, pierced by a single shaft of sunlight reflected from the water.

6 More like a vast abstract painting than a simple rectangle of water, the pool forms a stunning centrepiece for the dining room.

WORKING WITH COLOUR

Colour is a crucial factor in any interior. It can clearly have a dominating effect on the feel of a room — in both the physical and the emotional senses.

Yet so much of the discussion on this subject is wrapped up in impenetrable layers of pseudo-scientific mumbo-jumbo and questionable pop-psychology. All sorts of half-proved theories exist. There are suggestions that yellow for example is associated with mental disturbance, apparently because of the colours that Van Gogh used, to say nothing of the bold assertions that some colours suit certain people's astrological signs. And of course there are numerous prescriptions for using colours and patterns to affect the apparent proportions of a room.

It is not altogether surprising that colour is the subject of so many sweeping claims. Colour has always been associated with myth and ritual — imperial purple, black for mourning, white for purity. Even today, for example, it is impossible to use certain colours to paint modern skyscrapers in Hong Kong for fear of bad luck.

Like all subjects which combine a scientific basis with aesthetic applications, there is a continual temptation to try and work out cut and dried mathematical rules setting out colour combinations, the meaning of particular shades and so on. The rules might be much more convincing if the way in which we see colours did not depend on so many uncontrollable variables, such as the kind of artificial light that they are seen in, the time of day, or the frame of an individual's mind at the time. And of course colours themselves are not constant — they fade and change with age.

The colour spectrum

First, it is important to bear in mind how we experience colour. White daylight is made up of all the colours of the spectrum. The colour of an object or a surface depends on the physical composition of that surface, which determines what part of the spectrum of white light falling on it is reflected, and what part is absorbed. What we call a red object is one which absorbs the whole of the spectrum except for the red component which is reflected back. But if we use certain types of neon light, or tungsten bulbs which do not emit quite the same balance of the spectrum as daylight, we will get a slightly different effect, with a blue or yellow tinge to all the colours in a room.

Primary and secondary colours

The paint and dye spectrum is made up of the three primary colours: red, blue and yellow. All the other colours are a result of mixing the three primaries in varying proportions.

Orange, green and violet are the secondary colours — each made up by mixing two of the primaries in equal proportions.

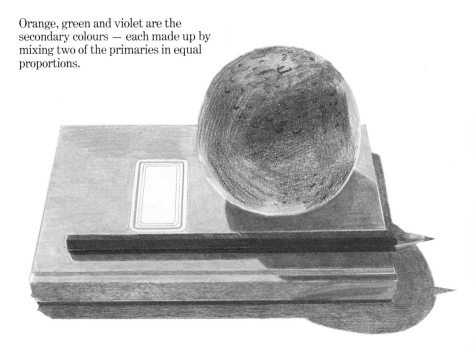

harmonious schemes. The use of dramatic contrasting colours creates restless tensions, but can be highly effective in some applications. Contrasting colours used in similar tones can also look good together.

To be visually comfortable, most people need to be able to see different kinds of colour. Too much of one shade is visually tiring — you need a relief to rest the eyes. Theatrically dramatic colour schemes using only one shade can be effective at first, but if you spend too much time with them, even an apparently neutral all grey look will be too demanding for comfort unless there is some visual relief.

The complementary colours are pairs of colours which have a strong effect on each other apparently vibrating when positioned next to one another.

Complementary pairs are composed of one primary colour, and the secondary colour which is made up by mixing the *other* two primaries: red and green, blue and orange, yellow and violet.

Colours close to each other in the spectrum will work well together, and can be used to help create subtle and

The effect of colour

We can describe the spectrum as falling into two distinct groups, the warm and the cool. The warm colours, from yellow through orange to red appear to have very different properties from the cool ones — ranging from green through blue to violet. Painters have long relied on the way that colours appear to behave when used with each other to create a sense of space and depth on a flat canvas. It is generally recognized that the warm colours appear to advance forward out of the picture plane towards us, while the cool blues retreat away. One American researcher went so far as to claim that you could demonstrate this as a fact by looking at the relative amount of damage suffered by blue and red cars. His studies showed that because most drivers find the apparent gap between two parked blue cars larger than it really is, blue cars get dented more often than red ones.

The claims made for the emotional effects of colour are equally far-reaching. Laboratory experiments have shown that red stimulates the whole nervous system. But in an all blue room, blood pressure, heart beat and breathing rate all fall slightly. One Scandinavian study even suggests that in blue rooms people have a tendency to turn up the heating to compensate for the apparent visual coldness.

It is important then to be aware of the potential effects that colour can have on us. But in practice we have an instinctive response to colour anyway, choosing a range with which we feel comfortable. The reasons for the choices we make are usually highly personal. But though taste is an individual question there is also an underlying cycle which seems to determine the way in which we use colour, and how we respond to it.

Fashion is partly the cause. Suddenly, and apparently quite unpredictably, it can dictate that grey is *the* colour of the season, and decree with equal authority that it will be red for the autumn. Next year, grey and red will be passé, and other colours will have taken their place.

More fundamentally, we change our ideas every few years about the ways in which colour can be used. In the 1960s and early '70s the tendency was to put bright splashes of primary accent colours — it could be orange, or pink, or lime green — into neutral white, beige or cream backgrounds. The result was to make individual objects stand out in space. Adjoining walls might each display a different and contrasting colour, possibly with stripes across them, or even different colours used to delineate different functions. Within this kind of scheme, fabrics would be equally simple — stripes and checks of pure colours.

New colour treatments are moving in a very different direction. In general the saturated pure colours are disappearing, to be replaced by a far wider range of subtler, much less assertive colours. Stone and grey, umber and beige are used in a whole variety of colours that blend in with each other. With so many different yet related colours being used in a room, the effect is to integrate everything in it, and create a much richer and more sophisticated sensation than the old approach which relied on the instant attraction of primaries.

Choosing a colour scheme
An effective colour scheme needs to take into account all the elements that make up an interior, balancing them against each other. Choose the carpet with the walls and furniture in mind too. Select the curtain fabric to co-ordinate with the wallpaper. And

make sure that the colour scheme extends to the pictures and accessories. It is often the smallest finishing touches that bring the colour in a room alive, and they need to be used with just as much thought as the major components.

Colour can be introduced into an interior in many different ways, from the spines of a row of paperbacks on a bookshelf or the fresh and delicate tones of a bowl of cut flowers, to the more obvious techniques of papering and painting the walls.

The floor finish is a particularly crucial element, whether it is a carpet in a single solid colour, patterned rugs or geometric tiles. A uniform pale colour can very effectively be used to tie a series of spaces together, increasing the apparent size of a room, and forming a good visual platform for the rest of the design.

In the kitchen, colour can come from pots and pans, spice jars, fruit on open shelves, even from packaging and bottles. Household appliances are gradually becoming available in a much wider range of colours than the once universal white. Manufacturers are bringing out cookers and freezers, dishwashers and washing machines in beiges and pastels, even occasionally in stronger browns, greens, dark greys and blues.

In the bathroom the coloured suite had become something of a cliché. White is a much more timeless classic shade, though bright primaries can look good too, and black can be a very sophisticated choice. Colour in this case can come from a stack of vivid towels, or even an elegantly enamelled tap.

Taking advantage of colour

If you want to make the pictures on your walls stand out, do so dramatically by giving them an all white background, which will act like a spotlight. Equally, a dark background can have a similar effect, making the pattern of the spaces between the pictures visually important too. Think about the time of day you will be using a room most. Those schemes that depend on dark colours, strong shades and glossy and rich finishes can make a place look its best after dark.

Try not to forget about natural colours. Morning sunlight filtering through a Venetian blind onto plain white walls can provide all the colour a room needs. The green of a lawn outside, or a plant indoors can do the same.

Colour has an architectural role too. Certain shades, such as Adam green for example can be used to evoke a period atmosphere. And if you are lucky enough to have an architecturally distinguished interior, colour can be used to emphasize it. Conversely, colour schemes can camouflage shortcomings, such as dents in the wall and unsightly pipes.

CONTEMPORARY FURNITURE

According to one design critic, this is the century in which the "ultimate test of architectural genius has become whether or not one can design a new kind of chair". Certainly there is an unprecedented amount of effort and energy going into the design of furniture now. It has moved from being a functional background to, in some cases, the focus of an interior, with chairs, tables and sofas acquiring almost the flavour of works of art, to be displayed rather than sat on. In many cases this is taking things much too far, but nevertheless furniture does have an important part to play in building up the look of an interior.

Comfort in all this is not usually a dominating factor. Many new chairs, if not actually miniature buildings designed by frustrated architects, certainly owe more to architectural slogans than they do to the principles of ergonomics. Comfort is not after all an exact science; often the chair that looks comfortable *is* comfortable. But don't let yourself be seduced entirely by looks; practicality is important too. Sofas are an expensive item these days, so make sure that yours won't be irreparably ruined the very first time that somebody spills a glass of wine over it.

The evolution of modern furniture

Modern furniture really began with Michael Thonet, sometime cabinet-maker to the imperial Austro-Hungarian court. In 1840 he patented a bentwood process, opening the way to mass-producing furniture on an unprecedented scale. Thonet's bentwood and cane classic dining chairs have been sold in their millions. Though they were designed in the 1860s they are still in production today, and look as timeless as ever.

The bentwood process, a complicated matter of steaming, clamping and gluing slivers of wood on a production line, allows for sinuous, seamless shapes. Perhaps the most perfect of the Thonet designs are the classic dining café chair, now copied by countless other firms, and the curvaceous armchair, first produced in 1870. Both chairs will work with almost any kind of interior since they have become such

familiar objects that they can melt away into the background. Yet examine them closely and you will find how handsome they still look.

It was after World War I that the *avant-garde* really began to produce the modern classics of furniture that in many cases are only now beginning to go into full mass production. The Dutch De Stijl group was among the first with Gerrit Rietveld's Red-Blue chair, designed in 1918. It looked astonishing then, as it still does today, a series of sculptural floating planes and voids. Reitveld claimed that he had designed it in an attempt to produce a chair which anyone could afford, and which could be made from simple, machine-cut shapes fitted together with glued dowels. Comfortable, however, it is not. Rietveld himself is reported to have badly bruised his ankles at least once in an incautious attempt to rise from his creation too quickly.

From 1930s to today

Of all the pioneering modern designers of the 1930s, Marcel Breuer has probably had the most impact on the ordinary living room. He designed the first successful tubular steel cantilevered chair, now known as the Cesca, which in various copies is an international best-seller. Breuer was still in his early twenties when he designed it, inspired by the economy and strength of the tubular steel of his bicycle frame.

Breuer was so taken by the potential of the material that he immediately saw its applications to furniture. The first result was the Wassily armchair, originally designed for the house of a fellow professor at the Bauhaus, made up of nine pieces of steel tube with a canvas or leather seat, back and arm rests. First publicized in 1925, it served as the inspiration for other classic designs by Mies van der Rohe and Le Corbusier, and is still in production today, including several inexpensive versions.

In France Le Corbusier used extravagant materials to turn tubular steel furniture into a luxury item. In 1928 he designed the Basculant, inspired partly by the traditional officer's camp chair, but transformed by the use of skins and leather for the

1

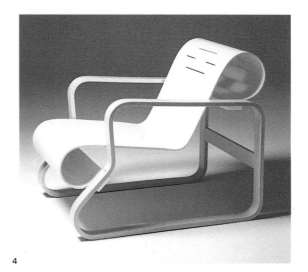

2

3

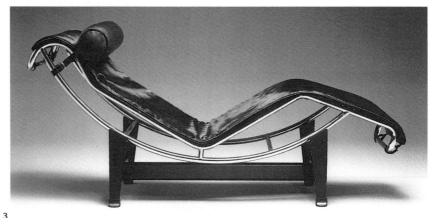

4

1 The classic bentwood café chair, sold in millions since its first appearance in the 1860s, and still as fresh as ever.

2 Hans Coray's Landi chair – a breakthrough in the use of aluminium. Designed in the 1930s, it is now a modern classic.

3 This chaise longue, designed by Le Corbuier, transformed tubular steel into a luxury material.

4 Finnish architect Alvar Aalto's experiments with plywood produced his elegant chairs.

5

8

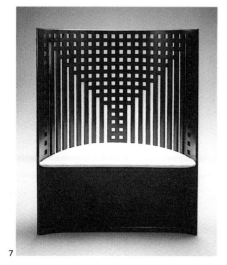

7

6

9

5 Furniture as sculpture: Gerrit Rietveld's red and blue chair; not quite as uncomfortable as it looks.

6 Inspired by a bicycle – Marcel Breuer's Wassily chair.

7 Charles Rennie Mackintosh's Art Nouveau masterpiece.

8 Mies van der Rohe's Barcelona and Cantilever side chairs. Both were designed for particular buildings and are the last word in refined simplicity.

9 Le Corbusier's Grand Confort, a modern version of the traditional club armchair.

seat. Then came his chaise longue, memorably described by Tom Wolfe as being capable of delivering a karate chop to the back of the neck of unwary occupants. Le Corbusier himself claimed he had been inspired by watching westerns in which the villain lazes on the porch of the saloon, his feet propped on the rail, while he smokes a cheroot. Le Corbusier's chaise longue can be adjusted on its chromed steel runners to suit a variety of positions, from sitting to reclining. The Grand Confort, based on a reworking of the traditional club armchair went even further in the pursuit of overstuffed opulence, grasping five fat leather cushions within a steel cradle.

Alvar Aalto's furniture, which reverted to wood just at the time when the world was being flooded with coils of tubular steel, could be explained in terms of his humanism. Or else simply because of the fact that two thirds of his native Finland is covered by forest. Aalto himself said that achieving "a springy seat merely with a few bent tubes and some tightly stretched bits of leather is in itself a clever technical achievement." But Aalto believed that cleverness was not enough on its own. "Such objects," he wrote, "can often suffer from a considerable lack of human qualities."

While Aalto valued tradition, it did not stop him experimenting with new techniques. He developed ingenious new methods of working with plywood,

bending and gluing it to create a series of memorable designs, including the elaborate Paimio armchair with hoop-shaped arms, and the classic stool he designed for a library in Finland for which he was also the architect.

Hans Coray designed only one important chair, the Landi. Ironically enough, it was originally intended to be a humble park chair for the Swiss National Exhibition in Zurich. It was the first chair to make use of the newly discovered aluminium alloy, at that time still an untested material. Coray's design uses profiled channel legs that are entirely rigid, but employs the innate flexibility of aluminium to produce a comfortable seat. With its distinctive perforated shape the Landi

71

still looks innovative and adventurous, and was a true piece of high tech decades before the term was coined.

Quite apart from the power and quality of any of his individual designs, Charles Eames was most impressive for the range of his achievements. The other major furniture designers of the 20th century have all tended to limit their output either to a short period, or a particular material. Marcel Breuer, for example, produced his outstanding work in a brief three years — and all of it in tubular steel. Le Corbusier designed three chairs in just one year, and thereafter virtually gave up. But Eames was involved with furniture throughout the greater part of his career as a designer, and was equally at home with plywood, aluminium, steel and fibreglass.

Not only are his designs technically excellent, they are aesthetically outstanding too. His plywood and leather lounge chair, with swivelling

base and ottoman stool was *the* modern chair of the 1960s, mercilessly plagiarized. And unlike so many of the designs of that period, it still looks as good as ever today.

For a time it seemed as if plastic would be to the 1960s what tubular steel had been to the 1930s. Verner Panton's flowing stackable chair of 1960 is the most striking of the genre, though not particularly successful commercially, Robin Day's polypropylene chair is aesthetically much more modest, but was an instant success, selling by the hundred thousand. Designed in 1969, Gian Carlo Piretti's folding Plia chair, with its clear plastic back and seat, and elegant one piece aluminium joint, marked the end of the plastics era, as the oil price rises of the early 1970s put an end to the cheapness of plastic.

Furniture in the 1970s saw a decade of Italian dominance — and of two designers in particular, Vico Magistretti

1 **A post modern approach to table design, the Tangram can be used as one single table or in separate units.**

2 **Fred Scott's Supporto chair was designed for the office, but is still an elegant option for the dining room.**

3 **Vico Magistretti's inspiration for his Sinbad chair was the traditional horseblanket thrown casually over a curvaceous metal frame.**

4 **Luxury in contemporary style: Charles Eames' lounge chair.**

5 **Also designed by Charles Eames, this aluminium pair is equally appropriate in an office or domestic setting.**

and Mario Bellini, who both produced a steady stream of elegant, highly polished furniture designs.

Magistretti is particularly influenced by craft traditions. He is responsible for the sophisticated version of the rush-seated peasant chair that can be seen in countless bistros. And he also used the traditional English horse-blanket as the starting point for his Sinbad chair.

In England Rodney Kinsman's OMK Designs were the outstanding success of the 1970s. Working mainly in sheet metal, perforated and folded into shape, Kinsman designed a series of well-priced and attractive light-weight sofas, chairs, tables and storage units.

By the start of the 1980s, Ettore Sottsass and his fellow designers in the Memphis group had set out to undermine the carefully sophisticated Italian look, with their deliberately outrageous designs — and they have had considerable success.

Living with furniture

Furniture is not simply a matter of showing off individual pieces, although of course that does have its place, and can be a highly effective way of establishing the character of an interior. It also needs to be acquired with an eye both on the kind of interior that you want to create and on your practical needs.

If space is at a premium, it is important not to try to cram too much into a room. There are all kinds of space-saving designs available, and these are now much more stylish than their predecessors, which had a distinct air of Heath Robinson about them.

Folding chairs that stack flat, or which can even be hung on a wall are especially useful in the kitchen, or as overflow dining chairs. Folding tables are a possibility too, particularly the kind which can be fixed to the wall, and flap down out of the way when not in use. In rooms that have to double up as

a spare bedroom the divan bed can be a good answer, or the futon mattress which converts into a makeshift sofa.

Built-in furniture is not always such a good idea. The more people move, the less popular it becomes. It can be seriously inflexible too — it is very difficult to change your mind about how you want built-in furniture arranged once it has all been installed. However the main advantage is that you can build this type of furniture with a specific purpose in mind.

Having a definite plan on how you want to arrange your furniture, and knowing in advance what you will be buying piece by piece as the money becomes available, helps to make the most of limited space, and ensures that everything you purchase will work visually and functionally with every-thing else. In more spacious interiors furniture can take on an architectural role, helping to subdivide spaces to define their character.

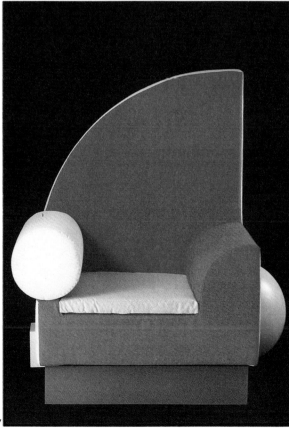

6 Sophisticated version of the Italian peasant chair – rush seat and stained beach wood – designed by Magistretti.

7 Peter Shire's Bel Air chair for the Memphis collection, a complete break with conventional good taste.

8 The wink chair, designed by Toshiyuki Kita, has a hinged structure and folding Mickey Mouse ears. The cover comes off to give a change of mood.

ARCHITECTURE

Few of us live in a brand new house; indeed many of us prefer not to do so. The character, solidity and wealth of detail of the older house and the chance to preserve something of the past all have appeal. Yet unlike even the smallest household appliance, the house itself — the biggest purchase most of us ever make — comes without a manual for maintenance or repair, and even when new it is sold without instructions. When it comes to alterations to your home, whether it was built a decade or a century ago, you have to rely on your eyes.

A little basic knowledge about your house is necessary before you start work on it. Its age, origin, construction and location, the quality of the original work, and an idea of how the various materials can be treated, repaired or replaced are all important. House plans have developed gradually over many centuries, and existing ones must be altered sympathetically to meet modern requirements. Also remember your surroundings; major external changes may have an effect on the whole area, as well as on your neighbour's temper. This is where official planning and building controls play a part — as well as for health and safety factors (see The Paperwork).

Although most of us live in houses built over the last century, some people are lucky enough to live in historic houses, parts of which might date back to medieval times. Their conservation is widely supported these days, and living in such a house entails making the most of its inheritance. It may mean maintaining a property in a manner sympathetic to its original character, or bringing a derelict building back into use, or finding a new purpose for a redundant structure.

The following pages look both at the general evolution of houses and at specific problems that some houses present; in particular ordinary terraced houses, historic houses and unorthodox buildings — such as barns, warehouses and chapels — currently being converted into homes. Although this section deals mainly with developments in Britain, the resurgence of interest in the style and charm of older houses is a worldwide trend.

THE EVOLUTION OF THE HOUSE

Very old houses are very rare. In England, few survive from before the reign of Elizabeth I, during which time the population was only about five million — most of whom lived in rural hovels which have long since disappeared. Only in the 19th century did towns and cities greatly expand; indeed the Victorian period experienced more building than in all previous ages put together.

Houses that date from before 1700 are most often to be found in the country. Medieval, 16th and 17th century buildings exist in the centres of country towns in many countries, especially in more remote areas, but even then they are often disguised behind 18th or 19th century facades.

In most places people have moved from the centre of town into ever-spreading 19th, then 20th century suburbs. Now that even major companies have moved out to suburban offices, there is often a chance to re-colonize town centres as places in which to live. Great discoveries are there to be made. It is possible to find features from many centuries jumbled together in just one house; even in 19th century terraced houses there are layers to be unravelled, though it may only be a boarded-up bannister, or a blocked-up fireplace.

Not all old buildings are equally interesting. The wealthier the original builder, the better the materials, construction and details. However, often quite humble buildings were of high quality because they were built by a rich landowner on his estate, or by the church or a charitable institution. Many redundant 19th century buildings, such as chapels and railway stations are equally well built.

Since prehistoric times the house has been, and still is, constantly evolving. By looking at common plan types, regional forms of construction and decorations — that is, by studying vernacular or local architecture, we can trace the history of the house, and place any type of building in its historical context.

Chimneys first appeared in the 12th century, but only in very grand buildings such as castles and monasteries. Elsewhere central fire-places remained in use as more people could share their heat. A wooden screen was used to separate the kitchen (which soon acquired a primitive hooded wall fireplace) from the hall, and sometimes there was a

1 Regency Nash terrace.

2 Splendidly ornate brass knocker.

3 A stone-built farmhouse with original small windows and new slate roof.

4 Early 18th century town houses in two tones of brick.

5 Modern architecture of character: Michael Hopkins' minimal steel and glass house.

6 Once derelict Victorian warehouse, now resurrected as studio apartments.

7 Rubbed brickwork window opening in original condition.

8 Architect Tom Brent's delightfully quirky and eccentric house.

gallery above. This arrangement created a passageway from the front to the back of the building, where the staircase was often installed, and which was the origin of the entrance hall in all later houses. In Britain, the hall was later subdivided horizontally by the insertion of one or two floors. The attic floor with sloping ceilings was occupied by servants.

While no two old houses will be exactly the same, clear similarities can be recognized in those built at similar stages in the evolution of the house, and in those situated in close geographical proximity, where climate and the availability of materials were the principal considerations. A farmhouse in the northwest of England, for example, will probably be stone-built because of the local availability of stone; it will be a long house, with a low roof, tucked into the hillside against the wind; the walls will be thick and windows small as protection against weather.

In America, the early settlers brought their architecture with them, building in Virginia and New England similar kinds of houses to those they had left behind. Further south, the plantation houses adapted European classical design to a totally different climate.

Window size is another key factor in dating houses: early examples were unglazed, providing ventilation as well as light, except in the coldest weather when the shutters would be closed. Glass was very scarce and costly until the 16th century, and not generally available until the 19th century.

If you buy one of these early houses, you will be faced with a whole series of conflicts between the essential character of the building and the accepted modern standards for window size and ceiling heights. Give character the edge as much as you can, particularly on the main elevation and in the relationship between windows and walls. The older the building, the smaller the area of window; so resist the temptation to put large modern windows into an old house, and by doing so destroy one of the most important features of a historic building.

Up until the early part of

1

2

3

4

the 20th century, most houses were built using traditional techniques and materials in local styles that evolved very gradually over the years. Architecture in the fullest sense was left to the grander buildings — palaces, mansions and churches — and from these, stylistic tricks were borrowed to embellish humbler houses, such as a window with a Gothic arch or classic columns around a doorway for a touch of importance.

With the 20th century however, things changed dramatically. First of all building became an industry more than a craft to cope with the vastly increased population. This industrialization meant that all the traditional styles, which are based on the technical demands of constructing a house by hand with local materials, became redundant. It meant that you could apply any style you pleased to the outside of your basic mass-produced

1 Late 16th century Kentish hall house, with timber-framed structure.

2 A wide-fronted 18th century house with Gothic battlements.

3 Built with few variations in many hundreds of thousands, the Victorian terraced house.

4 Large-scale Edwardian semi-detached houses.

5 Turn of the century house in San Francisco with elaborate decoration.

6 Colonial India's gift to the English suburb — a 1930s bow-fronted bungalow.

7 Michael Graves brought decoration back to the modern house when the charms of the flat-topped box style began to pall.

8 Luxury liner: architects like Richard Meir have given the ideas of the early moderns a new lease of life.

box of a house, and that is exactly what happened. The Victorian builders leafed through their pattern books and turned out suburban castles, or rustic cottages to order.

After World War I, modernism in architecture was conceived as a reaction against all this. Houses were made by machines, went the thinking of people like Le Corbusier and Walter Gropius, so they should look like them too. Pitched roofs were swept away, brickwork was covered up with white plaster, windows became increasingly larger, and were set in metal frames. The idea was revolutionary at first, and in the 1930s and 1940s, a string of beautiful modern houses that were like highly polished pieces of sculpture were built, into which the traditional constraints of small cellular rooms were dropped.

The trouble of course was that houses aren't the same as refrigerators — you can't build them on a production line; and when they are finished they have to stand up to the weather. In a rainy climate a pitched roof is far more practical than a flat roof.

Although there are still a number of architects who are taking the idea of the modern glass-walled box to ever further and more striking extremes, the move back towards houses that relate to history and tradition has gathered pace in the last decade.

The importance of local materials

Until the 19th century most buildings were constructed entirely from materials available within a few miles. In country areas houses were often built from materials that could be dug out of the actual site; such as rough stone for the walls or clay to make bricks, help stick the stones together, or contribute to the make-up of the wattle and daub for infill panels in a timber-framed building.

Half timbering The brickwork and roofing materials used in British houses, for example, give important clues to the age of the building, as illustrated in the following pages. Buildings constructed in and before the 17th or even the early 18th century are usually oak framed. During the last hundred years of this

period, brick panels or 'nogging' gradually replaced wattle and daub as infill. Although houses were frequently constructed with an entirely brick facade, there would be a wooden frame behind.

In general oak framing should be left untreated — apart from the thin coat of lime wash which gives a silvery finish — both inside and out.

Brickwork Bricks came in a multitude of different shapes and sizes, before the introduction of the now standard 225 x 75mm (9 x 3in.) design. The Romans used long, thin bricks, almost like tiles; Elizabethan bricks were not much thicker; and Georgian brickwork was the most beautiful. Colour and texture varied according to the clay, and also the method of firing in the kiln. Colours range from pale cream to dark reds and browns. They were all handmade until the mid-19th century. Modern machine made bricks applied with sand or other fake colourings should in no circumstance be used to repair a fine old building.

The variations in the bricks themselves are matched by the many

different kinds of patterns or 'bonds' of laying. Cavity brickwork became the norm in the early part of this century, when 'stretcher' (simply a brick lengthways) became the only practical bond.

The use of decoratively moulded bricks or ones of different colours was popular in Elizabethan times and again in the 19th century. Patterns were also attempted in the 1960s, but were usually crude because of a lack of craftsmanship and decent bricks. On Georgian houses, the doors and windows were often framed with darker coloured bricks than had been used on the walls, and arched with soft red bricks which were carefully rubbed to taper and so hold up an almost flat arch. These kinds of bricks are known as 'red rubbers'.

The mortar joints or 'pointing' between the bricks presented builders with another opportunity for detailed work. The mortar was usually made of sand or fine grit and lime and was only slightly recessed. 18th and 19th century builders tried to make narrow and very regular joints (in the finest stone masonry they are almost

1 Timber beams in their original state; thick coats of black tar were an unsightly later addition.

2 Builders would enrich walls with different coloured bands of brickwork.

3 Simple, bold patterns made by concentric arches around the door.

4 and 5 Harsh modern bricks compare unfavourably with mellow 18th century ones. Bear in mind the difference when contemplating alterations or additions.

6 A decorative flourish on the cross-shaped end of a tie rod, inserted for a very practical reason: to stop the wall falling outwards.

7 Deep pantiles, an early alternative to slates.

invisible), which in brickwork required very evenly sized bricks — quite the opposite of the rustic handmade bricks we now admire. These bricks were expensive at the time, so builders often made the wide, irregular pointing look precise by cutting a thin groove and inserting a strip of lime putty, which is known as 'tuck pointing'. Like all other traditional crafts, this can be reproduced with care, but should never be faked by painting on white lines, for example. New or repaired pointing should not be coloured up to match the old; it will weather in time. Avoid taking short cuts in the restoration and maintenance of your old house.

Roofing Thatch was the universal roofing material in medieval times, except for the very important buildings which were stone slated. Clay tiles became common in the 17th century in southeast England, although they never reached the universal and picturesque applications that they did in the Mediterranean coastal towns, where deeply modelled curved pantiles give the local architecture its characteristic quality. In Northern

Europe stone slates were still prevalent in the 17th century; thick ones came from the English Cotswolds, for example, while a thinner slate was found in Northamptonshire, where the limestone was laid down geologically in thin beds.

Regional variations can also be seen in the different types of tiles. 'Peg tiles', for example, are small and flat with holes for wooden pegs, by which they were fixed, and are found particularly in Kent and Sussex. Similar types of plain tiles were used in the same areas for cladding walls as well, in which case they overlapped. When fixed flat, that is edge to edge so that they looked like brickwork, they were called 'mathematical tiles'. Common in East Anglia and the East Midlands, 'pantiles' are larger and have an 'S' shaped curve, which shows as a clear ridge down the roof. With all clay tiles there are variations in colour, even on the same roof — something which is very difficult to reproduce with modern alternatives. Handmade tiles can still be bought; second-hand ones, although difficult to find, will probably be

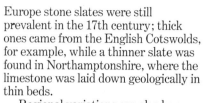

8 Hanging clay tiles, used instead of bricks or weatherboard on outer walls.

9 The original slate roofs are gradually disappearing from these Victorian houses, to be replaced by modern concrete tiles.

10 Carved detail, 19th century.

11 On really ornate Victorian buildings, even blank windows came in for the full decorative treatment.

12 Now almost unobtainable except at huge cost — sturdy slates from North Wales.

13 Carved terracotta, now almost a lost art.

14 Thatch is still keeping out the rain.

slightly cheaper and well worth looking out for.

In the more westerly regions of Britain, blue slate has been the predominant roofing material for at least two centuries. It is still produced in Cornwall, Cumberland and principally in North Wales.

Our 20th century towns and cities exhibit almost every kind of style and material from tile-hanging to mock Tudor beams, although there has recently been a move to reinforce local traditions, using both regional materials and forms of construction.

Doors and windows

In looking for features which will help you to date your house, to recognize its historic 'type' and its particular regional qualities, the design of windows and doors can be very misleading. The walls and even the roof may well last the whole life of a building, while the doors and windows will probably have been changed several times.

Very early windows had no glass, and were usually divided by square sectioned oak vertical bars set at an angle in the frame. The diamond shaped recesses for the bars and grooves for sliding shutters are often visible. The tiny panes of early glass were divided by lead 'cames', in a

diamond pattern in Tudor times and with slightly larger rectangular or square divisions in the 17th century. All these windows, if they opened at all, were 'side hung' casements, but the 18th century saw the first sash, or vertically sliding windows.

During this century the metal window has become popular. Types range from the steel windows of the 1920s and 1930s to the plastic coated steel or aluminium windows of today which slide in any direction, pivot or are simply side-hung. These modern windows look fine in new houses, but are hardly ever suitable in old ones; not only is the material inappropriate, but both the windows and the sheets of glass are too large, and the frames are too thin.

Many of the observations made about windows apply equally to doors. Pre-Georgian doors were small and low, though often quite wide. They were vertically boarded and usually made of oak until 1800, when it was replaced by softwood. Such doors were used in cottages up until the last century. Panelled doors were universally used in 18th and 19th century terraces. The idea of inserting glass into the top half of the door only became popular about a century ago, perhaps to light the narrower and smaller halls typical of the houses built at that time.

1 Large sheets of glass characterize the Victorian sliding sash.

2 Familiar features of the 19th century — a glass panel in the door and decorative cast iron railings.

3 A 1980s steel-framed tilting window.

4 Wrap-around windows with metal frames and a strong 1930s period flavour.

5 The Venetian window — a recurring theme in classical architecture.

6 Tudor leaded casements.

7 A Georgian portico with fanlight and original columns.

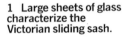

TAKING ON THE TERRACED HOUSE

If you live in a terraced house, it is important to realize that your house is part of one large structure, both in construction and appearance. It cannot therefore be considered in isolation from its neighbours. You can't simply enlarge or deepen your basement or build a roof extension without endangering the walls of the neighbouring houses. In fact to make either of these structural alterations, you need the agreement of your neighbours as well as the local authority. The degree of work that can be undertaken depends on the thickness of the walls and the depth and soundness of the foundations; both are likely to be superior in houses built after about 1840. Throughout history there have been ups and downs in the quality of workmanship and materials. In Britain, most periods of mass expansion in housing, such as mid-Georgian, to a lesser extent late Victorian, and the post-war 1930s and 1960s housing booms were times of poor work. Later Georgian, mid-Victorian, Edwardian and current housing are of a better standard.

The question of the overall appearance of the terrace — especially if it is 'listed' or in a conservation area, must also be considered. One roof extension on an otherwise uniform block can spoil the whole look of a street. There are certain — not unreasonable — regulations, requiring, for example, that the front of an extension be set back so that it cannot be seen from the street; or, if a whole terrace is in natural brick, or cream-painted stucco, that no-one paints their house a vivid colour which would be inconsistent with the rest. On the other hand it would be going too far to control the colour of your window paint, front door or even, as has happened in the past, curtains. If it is a terraced house, your home is not your castle, to the extent that it can be if it is detached and in its own grounds.

You will have more freedom to expand at the back of a terrace, although this opportunity may have been taken already. Few houses built before 1890 had internal bathrooms and lavatories, or even adequate kitchens, so rear extensions of that period are

1 A late 19th century terrace, already modernized — note the roof lights on the right — and with ridge-backed roofs to help drainage.

2 and 3 Narrow-fronted Georgian terraced houses are often so small that you will need to build out. This terrace has valley roof gutters, which can mean damp problems.

common. But, whereas 19th century houses usually have deep and wide foundations (or footings), extensions and even bay windows were often added without good footings adequately tied in to the main structure. Sometimes there is evidence of a parting of company — a problem that can be rectified, but usually at considerable cost.

Another problem which you are likely to encounter with nearly all pre-1900 houses is rising damp, unless a damp-proof course (DPC) has been laid (nowadays it is usually silicon injected into the solid walls). Don't be too concerned, however, about the occasional damp wall or room — improved heating and ventilation, simply unblocking the fireplaces for example, will do a great deal to help.

Perhaps the major practical upsets

with the terraced house are caused by the roof — its structure and method of drainage. The roof of a terraced house is usually concealed behind a brick parapet, and slopes down from a high point at the party walls to a more or less flat 'valley' running from front to back and supported by a main beam from the middle of the front elevation to the middle of the rear. Here you will see an opening below the parapet coping and a square hopper head, which discharges water into a downpipe, made of lead if it is very old, otherwise cast iron, unless it has recently been replaced in plastic — a perfectly practical material, although it doesn't enhance the property's character.

Difficulties are likely to arise through the lack of gutters on the roof. Water, the chief enemy of all buildings, tends to lie on flat areas, which can be

asphalted, bituminous-felted or, best of all, lead-covered, and eventually seeps through these areas of flat roofing and rots the wooden beams below. For this very reason later Victorian houses returned to the pre-Georgian roof pattern of a steeply sloping roof with the ridge across the centre of the house, parallel to the front and back walls. The roof was constructed of tiles or slates, and overhanging eaves carried the rain over the top of the walls into gutters, clear of the building. This sensible arrangement has many advantages and remains in use today. Its wooden structure and flexible covering allows the movement that takes place in most buildings to occur without trouble, a degree of ventilation keeps the materials in good order, and there is, of course, useful storage space under the eaves.

TAKING ON THE HISTORIC HOUSE

In moving into a historic house, the basic rule is to retain as much 'period' character as possible, whilst incorporating the modern comforts and services you require. You have to compromise with an old house; and the older, more rare and beautiful it is, the more sacrifices in convenience you will have to make. If you want vast open spaces and picture windows, then convert a 19th century warehouse or chapel, not a 16th century cottage. If you have splendid panelling then you will have to do without central heating which will crack it. If you have hand-painted 18th century Chinese wallpaper, tapestries or fine water colour paintings, you should avoid bright lighting — especially natural light — in those rooms.

Structural changes can of course be made, bearing in mind that almost any wall can be knocked down with the use of cunningly concealed reinforced steel joists (RSJs). In fact many internal walls are not load-bearing, which is something that you can discover for yourself by examining the floorboards in the room above, or the ceiling joists if it is on the top floor. The joists will run in the opposite direction to the boards and will be supported at either end on a wall or beam. Do not swing the sledge hammer, however, without getting an expert — an architect, a surveyor or a builder — to check that the wall is not load-bearing first.

The drawback of making dramatic structural alterations to an old house, whose structure has inevitably moved over the years and will continue to do so as the water table in the earth beneath it changes, is that they could cause distortions to the house. These stresses will cause cracks, which may not be serious, but will, at the very least, damage your decoration. This is not to say that no structural changes are advisable; one of the joys of owning and refurbishing an old house is the opportunity for sweeping away later changes and subdivisions, and rediscovering its original character.

In making changes to a historic house your eye is your best guide. You will see, for example, where the plaster ceiling cornice has been interrupted; where a narrow modern door with a thin architrave has been inserted; where one floor has been divided from another by a door on a landing; where a finely proportioned room has been partitioned (perhaps in a house which has been split up into small flats); or where the turned bannisters on the stairs have been boarded up.

Aim to make the best of your house, rather than transform it into something else; to do this, you have to train your eye to recognize original features, even if they are heavily disguised. Proportions and heights of rooms, and plaster and wood details provide some clues. Are there, for example, shutters which have been nailed up and painted, crying out to be released and stripped? A whole range of fixtures, such as fireplaces, cupboards, and even bathroom fittings, can provide historic evidence, and, unless there is a good reason for removing them, don't. A glimpse at a few houses of different periods will give several more pointers.

Stone-built cottages

An air of cosiness will be created by the characteristic small windows and thick walls of the stone cottage, which is only likely to be marred by the odd patch of damp. This can be dealt with by an injected damp course. Internal walls will probably be thickly and unevenly lime-plastered, and the ground floor may well be brick or stone paved; it is important to keep these features, which are integral to this type of house. If there is rising damp, lift up the paviours and re-lay them on a new concrete slab with a bituminous or polythene damp-proof membrane laid between.

Doors, both inside and out, are usually vertically boarded, and wider and lower than modern doors; they may have hand made wrought iron hinges and 'Norfolk latches'. Only the front door is likely to be panelled. You may need to accustom yourself to low beams and ceilings as well as doors, and resist your instinct to raise them or lower floors. There is a minimum ceiling height required by law, but the local authorities are prepared to negotiate in the case of historic buildings. The upstairs floors will probably have wide oak floorboards, which may be uneven and worm-eaten. They can be cleaned, treated with worm killer and polished so they gleam in a way no modern boards can. Remember that all old timbers, especially beams, are oversized in terms of structural requirements (unless they are badly rotted where they enter the wall or the ground), and there will certainly be plenty of strength left in them.

A small 19th century or modern fireplace may well be blocking up a large inglenook, and you could even find a bread oven here too. But resist the temptation to strip everything in sight. Brick and stone were plastered and wood was painted for the good reasons of protection, preservation and to deter dust.

Timber-framed houses

Many of the problems and opportunities for renovation which exist in stone-built cottages are also found in timber-framed houses. The outside walls

present more of a problem, however, being less thick, and not so warm or waterproof. The inner lining of plaster is even more essential both for insulation and for covering the cracks between the wooden frame members and the wattle and daub or brick 'nogging' infill panels. Oak is a hardy and good-looking material, but it's worth bearing in mind that it was originally used for structural purposes, and was not intended to be exposed as has become the fashion.

Early town houses

Being of the same date and constructed of similar materials as stone cottages and timber-framed houses, early town houses should be treated in much the same way. They may be more difficult to decipher however, especially if they are on a busy main street, where facades will have been rebuilt, side passages blocked up and shop fronts either inserted or removed. The parts at the back are likely to be older than the front, but in any case there may be fine details, such as plaster ceilings and oak panelling, in rooms recently used for shop storage. If you find oak panelling, it should be stripped, cleaned and polished with turps and beeswax.

Georgian and later houses

Many of the characteristics of terraced houses are shared by detached 18th and 19th century houses. There may be good quality ornamental plaster-work, softwood panelling and fireplaces with cast iron grates and wood or marble surrounds. The woodwork of the doors and staircases will also be of high quality, as will such details as window shutters. If you want to paint your woodwork, choose light colours, but not dead white. Plaster walls will have been painted in slightly darker colours; the shades deepened dramatically as the 19th century progressed, and even softwood was often 'grained' to look like oak. The extent to which you wish to reproduce original colour schemes is a matter of personal choice.

1 A stone-built cottage, with small windows and thick walls to keep the cold out and the warm in.

2 Characteristic diamond panes in 14th century leaded casement windows.

3 Once a West Coast bank — its splendid columns signifying financial probity — now lofty apartments.

4 Weatherboard hangings — widely used in certain areas.

5 Four variations on the Georgian theme, all different, but all in harmony.

6 Elaborate cast iron work for the grander Georgian town house.

7 and 8 Once derelict early 19th century houses restored to their original condition.

9 A palatial facade to a late 19th century terrace.

TAKING ON THE UNORTHODOX HOUSE

It is not only terraced and historic houses which attract the attention of modernizers and restorers. There has recently been an unprecedented burst of recycling into new homes of the kind of buildings that were never originally intended for domestic purposes. Sometimes it is the location that is the attraction; or else it can simply be a commitment to preserving old buildings; or an enthusiasm for living in distinctive and unusual spaces. Converting such buildings can sometimes even make sound economic sense, creating — if all goes well — valuable property at a bargain price. Although these buildings are of many different types, which are listed below, they fall into three distinct categories.

Unusual historic buildings

Perhaps the most difficult for a restorer to handle are those structures with a wealth of intact historic detail, such as churches, chapels and castles. Conventional domestic plans are often impossible here, and big, open plan layouts that respect the original character are essential. If you can't live without large picture windows for example, don't try converting a 19th century church with narrow Gothic windows. Keeping the damp at bay, and installing heating are often problems too. Putting in modern wiring and plumbing can play havoc with ancient structures, and can be very expensive, especially if, there has never been any provision for main drainage.

There are two principal strategies for dealing with this sort of building. One is to make any necessary new additions, both on the outside and the inside, such as bathrooms or partition walls, in a style that is consciously different from the original fabric, showing quite clearly what is new and what is not. The other is to minimize the difference using matching materials and finishes. Either way you will need an expert's advice. An architect, preferably one with experience of working on this type of structure, can help you to see the potential of a building, and warn you about the problems that may lurk beneath the surface. Some plan forms will never

make satisfactory homes, others are much more pliable. Call in an expert to help you decide which you are looking at before you commit yourself.

Large industrial buildings

Disused industrial spaces — warehouses in particular — have become chic and fashionable places in which to live. The problem here is making sufficient structural changes to meet the stringent building regulations — window areas are often too small in relation to the floor area, exposed timber beams need to be protected against fire, escape staircases have to be installed, and of course you need planning permission to convert from industrial to residential occupation.

Taking on a complete warehouse building is a daunting and intimidating task; working with others to tackle a floor each is more manageable.

This type of deep plan, open structure has sparked off a totally new loft lifestyle, where furniture rather than walls is used to define areas, within one huge space. It is certainly not for agrophobics. Yet while initially living in one giant space can be very attractive, in many cases, the space has gradually been subdivided by partitions. Recently an effort has been made to tame the essentially industrial flavour of this type of building.

Flexibility and adaptability depends on the windows. If you can only get daylight from one wall, the potential for

subdivision is severely limited, and big open plans are essential. If there are windows on all the main walls your freedom to manipulate the space is much greater.

Smaller buildings

Old railway buildings, redundant police stations and schools are often more likely to approximate to a domestic scale. There may be difficulties in deciding what to do about the lavatories or the cells, for example, but otherwise these can be the basis for the simplest type of conversion, although they don't always provide the most exciting results. The following are the main types of disused buildings which are gaining a new life as beautiful and unusual houses.

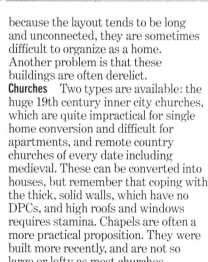

1 A redundant tea warehouse has been reclaimed to provide low-cost studio apartments.

2 A converted railway station makes an attractive chalet-style home. Where the track once ran, a patio has now been built.

3 With all the charms of a waterside setting, a white-painted clapboard mill has been converted into two modern apartments.

4 Sturdily-built chapels offer great potential for domestic conversion. Although these windows are new, their Gothic shape enhances the original flavour of the building.

5 Careful restoration of this Cotswold stone barn, now a weekend house, has preserved its original character and mellow stonework.

6 and 7 An old watermill with all its original features intact, is now a spacious home in a picturesque location.

Country mansions Bargains can still be found in remote parts of the country: Some of the larger country houses have been very successfully divided up into several holiday and retirement homes. Obviously you need a considerable amount of money to deal with the building problems, unless you can obtain a restoration grant. A management structure and some continuing expenditure will be required to maintain the estate.

Old railway stations Unused stations and other buildings, such as signal boxes and railway cottages come up for sale from time to time. On some lines the trains still rush by, on others rabbits and hares have taken over the old embankments. The buildings are sturdy structures in brick or stone. But

because the layout tends to be long and unconnected, they are sometimes difficult to organize as a home. Another problem is that these buildings are often derelict.

Churches Two types are available: the huge 19th century inner city churches, which are quite impractical for single home conversion and difficult for apartments, and remote country churches of every date including medieval. These can be converted into houses, but remember that coping with the thick, solid walls, which have no DPCs, and high roofs and windows requires stamina. Chapels are often a more practical proposition. They were built more recently, and are not so large or lofty as most churches.

Barns Though posing problems of

scale similar to churches, above all barns exemplify the dilemma of how to create a comfortable home while still preserving the essential quality of the building. There is no point in buying a fine barn with a beautiful oak roof and ending up with something which looks like a suburban villa. Preserve the atmosphere of the barn by using existing openings wherever you can for new windows and doors, and by avoiding the addition of brick chimneys, porches, garages, sun lounges, and even dormer windows as far as possible. This may well mean that you don't use every foot of space; a first floor may only occupy part of the building, allowing your main living room to reach right up to the magnificent timber roof. Stairs have to be carefully planned too; they

should not entail cutting through one of the main beams. And in these circumstances the best chimneys are unobtrusive cylindrical metal flues.

Wind and water mills Many of the points which apply to the conversion of barns also apply to mills, but here there is the added interest — and problem — of the machinery if it survives. Much of the beauty of a mill lies not in the outside shell, but in the water wheel or the sails, together with the simple and robust mechanism which transfers their power to the grinding stones. If it is possible to incorporate it into your home, keep the mill machinery and make a feature of it. Windmills shorn of their sails and with gaping windows inserted can look like large and unhappy pepperpots.

WORKING WITH SPACE

Few of us ever get the chance to design a home from scratch. We live in houses or apartments that were built many years ago for people who lived very differently. Such buildings have often been subject to radical alterations as their status, or that of their occupants changed. Or else we buy new homes that will almost certainly have been built to a standard builder's plan, exactly like that of many thousands of identical homes and aimed at a non-existent average occupant.

Either way, the result is a gap between what we need and want of a home, and what it can provide. It may be that we are faced with interiors that are stubbornly awkward, with bathrooms opening off kitchens, corridors that are profligate in their use of space, meandering through a warren of cell-like little rooms, and kitchens housed in cramped, dank basements. Or we may simply find that as family circumstances change, so do our requirements of a home. Teenage children will probably want their own room; a home office may become necessary; even more fundamentally, our tastes may change. Whereas we once enjoyed living in wide open plan spaces, we may eventually decide that we feel happier in traditional rooms, with greater wall space to hang pictures, and with enough privacy to let several activities take place in the home at the same time without interfering with each other.

The most successful way to deal with all these problems is not to treat the existing layout of your home as a burdensome handicap that cannot be altered, but instead to regard it as a resource, from which a layout of character and individuality that meets your requirements can be created. The secret is to develop the skill of being able to work with space; to see the potential of an interior with a key wall removed, a new door punched off a corridor, or a relocated kitchen.

Space is the basic ingredient of an interior. The quality of individual spaces, and the way in which they run into each other, establishes not just the functional performance of an interior, but also its character. Given enough money, you can carry out virtually any

kind of internal surgery on a house. It is possible to install new staircases, new window openings, new mezzanine floor levels and so on. With enough steel to hold up the roof, you could go as far as taking out all the walls and floors in the house to create one gigantic new space. But before you start calling in the demolition men, you should pause to work out exactly what you want to achieve, and how best to accomplish it.

If you want a more spacious living room for example, it may simply be a question of rethinking your furniture – most homes have more than is strictly necessary. Think carefully about the purpose of every piece you have, and if

you find that a sofa is only there for show, or that a particular table is never used, consider moving them elsewhere. With fewer pieces, grouped in the most compact way, you may find the extra sense of space that you are after without pulling down any walls.

Equally, you should think through the implications of demolishing walls. Two rooms may be more useful than one, and you may find that a large open space is much harder and more expensive to keep warm than a series of more intimate rooms.

Try to think of all the rooms in your home in relation to each other. If you swap functions around, it may be possible to get the result that you want

without resorting to building work.

If you already have a large, spacious interior and you want to create individual areas within it, it may again be a case of redistributing the furniture rather than erecting new walls. Bookcases can make effective room dividers, and grouping sofas together can form an unusual focus to a room.

The quality of a space is affected by several exterior factors which should be taken into account. For example, when you are thinking about which rooms to use for what purposes, bear in mind the effect of the sun. Early morning sunshine is delightful at breakfast, so think about which windows face east

when you are planning your kitchen. Equally a bleak view or a noisy road can blight a living room, and remedial action in this case might simply be to put up curtains or even a screen.

Lofty ceilings can be an asset to large rooms. In small ones, they can be merely oppressive, so think about the possibility of lowering the ceiling, either cosmetically by stretching fabric across it, or using strongly focused lighting, or physically by inserting a mezzanine floor. Consider also the possibility of changing floor levels. If you have the headroom, raising the level of the floor can improve your views out, and change the proportions of a room for the better.

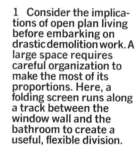

1 Consider the implications of open plan living before embarking on drastic demolition work. A large space requires careful organization to make the most of its proportions. Here, a folding screen runs along a track between the window wall and the bathroom to create a useful, flexible division.

2 A grandly scaled room of Edwardian proportions. This splendid galleried area with its richly panelled walls is a perfect setting for boldly patterned fabrics — the kilims, for instance. For more intimate moments there is a sheltered alcove around the fireplace.

CONSTRAINTS

Making the best use of the space within your home depends on working with its fabric, not against it. Most houses have a fundamental character, a feel, almost like a grain in wood. And unless you are intent on the sort of design which makes a point of deliberately flouting its setting, by playing up the contrast between an old building and a completely new interior, you should not cut across that grain. Tiny cottages with thick walls do not take comfortably to being transformed into open plan spaces. Big open barns with handsome timber beams are best left as undivided as possible if their essential character is not to be obliterated. And handsome, well-proportioned Georgian rooms should not be interfered with. On the other hand it can be very satsifying to strip out later additions and alterations and recreate the original qualities of a house. The kind of constraints you will come across can be divided into structural, legal and practical.

Structural

A variety of constructional methods are used for the walls and floors of houses. Before you start making elaborate plans to alter your interiors, you should work out what kind of construction you are dealing with. This can be a complicated business. And since you will need to get the approval of your local authority for all but the most elementary changes, it may be necessary to call in a professional.

Broadly there are two kinds of internal partition, the load-bearing and the non-load-bearing varieties. Removing the latter is a relatively straightforward business. You may have to relocate any water or gas pipes or electric cables that are channelled through it, but you will not have to make any alternative structural arrangements. Load-bearing walls on the other hand are a more problematic affair. They may carry the weight of the walls or the floors above them, and if they are to be removed, a supporting beam will need to be inserted across the gap to take the weight, and transfer it to the foundations.

In more recently constructed houses, partitions can be made of

blockwork or brickwork, but more often they are of timber posts and faced with plasterboard. Ascertaining which walls are load-bearing and which are not is a complicated business, and sometimes even the experts can be surprised by unexpected supporting beams within walls that are apparently unstructural.

However, if there is another wall running in exactly the same position on the floor above, then you can be fairly certain that you are dealing with a load-bearing wall. And if the floor-boards on the floor above don't run parallel to the wall you are investigating, that is a sign that you are looking at a non-load-bearing wall.

As well as knocking down internal walls, it is possible to open up your floor – either by inserting a new staircase, or in some cases – creating a double height room over part, or all of the floor area of the room below. To do so you will need to cut through some of the floor joists – the deep timber beams which span between the load-bearing walls of a house – and it will be necessary to provide an alternative means of transferring the load that the joists were carrying to the walls. A new deep timber joist trimming around the opening to neighbouring joists, or even a steel joist, will be needed. This is a job for an expert, and you will have to show structural calculations to your local authority to prove that what you are doing is safe.

Legal

The legal considerations when altering the spaces within your home must be taken into account at an early stage. There is a legal minimum height, 2.3m (7ft 6in.) for a habitable room as defined by British planning law. When you are dealing with sloping ceilings, as for example in an attic, there are formulae which define a minimum proportion of the floor area which has that headroom. Similarly a habitable room must have a window or windows which provide an opening that is at least one tenth of the floor area. In practice these rules are unlikely to trouble you when you are dealing with an existing home, except when you are building an extension, creating new rooms in the basement or attic, or

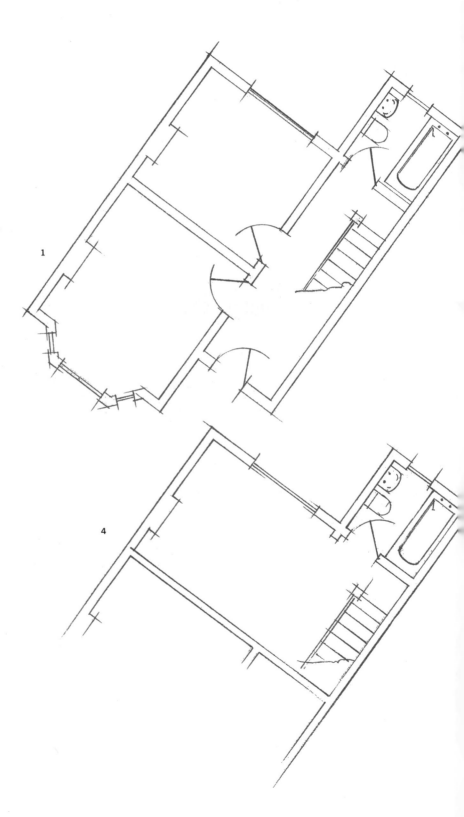

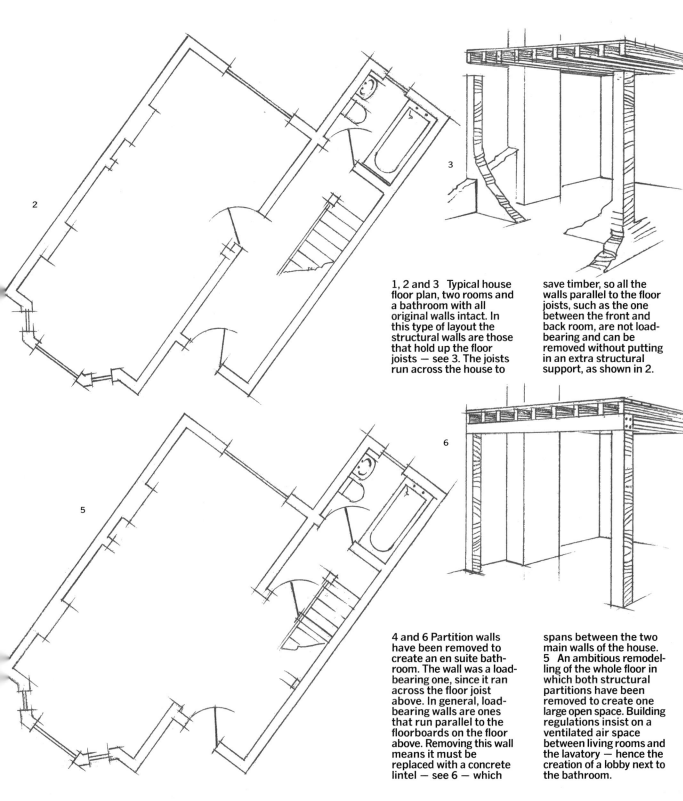

1, 2 and 3 Typical house floor plan, two rooms and a bathroom with all original walls intact. In this type of layout the structural walls are those that hold up the floor joists — see 3. The joists run across the house to save timber, so all the walls parallel to the floor joists, such as the one between the front and back room, are not load-bearing and can be removed without putting in an extra structural support, as shown in 2.

4 and 6 Partition walls have been removed to create an en suite bathroom. The wall was a load-bearing one, since it ran across the floor joist above. In general, load-bearing walls are ones that run parallel to the floorboards on the floor above. Removing this wall means it must be replaced with a concrete lintel — see 6 — which spans between the two main walls of the house. **5** An ambitious remodelling of the whole floor in which both structural partitions have been removed to create one large open space. Building regulations insist on a ventilated air space between living rooms and the lavatory — hence the creation of a lobby next to the bathroom.

trying to make two rooms out of one. You may find that you have to insert one or more new windows when carrying out these alterations.

The regulations also specify that you must not position your bathroom or lavatory in such a way that it opens directly off a habitable room. Obviously a corridor, or a store room does not count as a habitable room. An exception is made for bedrooms, provided that there is a second bathroom elsewhere in the home. The minimum requirement when locating a lavatory off a kitchen or a living room, is that there is a hall, or lobby between, with a door off each room. This can shrink into what is called a 'ventilated airspace'–a windowless lobby fitted with two doors and an extractor fan.

Practical

The practical constraints on planning space within your home are more straightforward. It is important to strike a balance between the conflicting needs of a household, so that quiet studying for example can take place at the same time as television watching. This combination will require you to keep individual rooms for each function – preferably separated from each other by a sound barrier, such as another room or a hall.

Should you wish to merge your dining room, living room and kitchen into one large space, then it is important to make sure that your kitchen area is well ventilated, otherwise cooking smells will infiltrate all the other areas. If you are planning this kind of radical restructuring throughout the house, you should also try to ensure that you can reach the bedrooms without having to pass through the main space. With large-scale open plan interiors, it is a good idea, for the sake of privacy, to position the bedrooms as far away as possible from the front door.

Remember when considering knocking down walls that large rooms are more difficult, and more expensive, to keep warm than small ones. In the latter you can turn off radiators when they are not in use; in large single spaces it has to be a full scale heating system or nothing at all.

POTENTIAL

What can be achieved from restructuring the spaces within your home depends very much on the raw material with which you are starting. It might be that you simply enlarge an existing kitchen by knocking through into the redundant scullery next door to create a single space. It can mean relocating a door to create a longer length of uninterrupted wall space to fit in a range of units, or more simply, changing the direction of its swing.

On the other hand, it might be the complete transformation of a house. In the traditional terraced house for example, which is typically one room thick, with a staircase rising from front to back alongside a living and dining room, it is possible to open out the staircase wall, and to remove the partition walls to create an open space.

Victorian basements, often a warren of little rooms and nooks, can make big kitchens, thus freeing the existing kitchen for another purpose. Or, with separate access, they can make good self-contained apartments.

If your problem is a poor relationship of rooms – awkward corridors for example, or cramped staircases – explore the possibility of adding an extension onto the house in such a way that you link the rooms you want to connect. Doors knocked out of the original outside wall create a smooth transition between the two.

If space is at a premium, then you might consider removing redundant chimney breasts, mantlepieces and built-in cupboards. Think carefully however before removing a fireplace and blocking off the flue; once gone they can be quite hard to replace. And even if they are not in use, fireplaces often provide an attractive visual element in a room. On the other hand, taking out the fireplaces can offer you much more flexibility in arranging your interiors, especially in kitchens, where their removal would create valuable space for long straight runs of equipment and work surfaces.

Extending up into the attic, or even adding an extra storey can offer wide scope for creating a dramatic interior. High ceilings are always attractive, especially when combined with mezzanines and different levels.

5

7

6

8

1 and 2 From the outside, this old school building remains unchanged. Inside a transformation has taken place. The vast, high-ceilinged rooms have been divided with new partitions which stop just short of both the ceiling and original walls, to differentiate clearly between old and new. Angular 'windows' in the new walls are the antithesis of the original rounded window shapes, thus creating a strong architectural feel.

3 The distinctly unpanoramic view is shut out from this room with a translucent screen running right across the window. Extra space is created by knocking the old corridor wall back to the stairs.

4 Timber-framed houses are perfect candidates for opening up, since the newly exposed beams remain to create subtle divisions between the different areas without the barrier made by a solid wall.

5 Rearranging the levels internally will instantly remove the 'box-like' impression many houses give. This device also allows daylight to flood into the house from complicated angles.

6 Low screen walls, looking more like upstanding floorboards, separate the kitchen from the main room in this warehouse conversion.

7 A large single space occasionally needs breaking up. A Venetian blind is a simple and smart way of providing an instant visual barrier whenever it is required.

8 Folding screens have a dual purpose in any large space – as decorative and functional pieces. This one, providing a splash of bright pink on the polished wood, hides a cloakroom area.

COMBINING AND DIVIDING

The two simplest ways of altering your space are knocking down a wall and putting one up. Both have pros and cons, depending on the layout of your house and your requirements.

Making one room from two
Perhaps the most commonly undertaken piece of spatial juggling is the creation of one large room out of two or more smaller ones. Before doing anything rash, you should weigh up the benefits and disadvantages of what you are planning. For example if you plan to sell up in the short term, you may reduce the value of your property by cutting the number of rooms.

Find out the implications of what you plan to do. Removing a non-load-bearing wall, for instance (see page 88), is a relatively simple task, and it is possible to make good the damage so that no traces of the vanished wall remain. On the other hand taking out a structural wall means putting back a supporting beam to carry the weight. It can either be concrete or a steel lintel. But in each case, unless you can contrive to hide the beam within the depth of the floor space above, there

1

2

3

will be a downstand beam left showing, to mark the original room divisions. You will probably also need to leave nibs of the old wall at each end, to provide a firm support for the new structural beam.

Decide how big an opening you will really need. It can sometimes have just as much impact on the overall performance of a house to put in a new door as it can to take out a complete wall. And often when faced with the many constraints of removing a load-bearing wall, it may be better to admit frankly that you are dealing with two rooms, and deliberately make the opening between them no more than a door. Or you might want to think about creating an archway in the centre of the dividing wall. Alternatively, if there is a major structural element in the middle of the wall, such as a chimney stack, then the only practical approach may be just to remove the pieces of wall at either side, leaving a central column.

When you are removing a partition that has been inserted after a house was completed, you will automatically find yourself improving the proportions. If you are taking out an original wall, try visualizing the proportions of the new space before you do it.

To complete the transformation and to make the most of the new sense of spaciousness you have created, it is a good idea to treat the wall and floor surfaces as part of a single unified design. Using the same floor covering throughout a large room, especially if it has a strong geometric pattern such as white tiles, can be a good way of making the two halves read as one. Colour can also be used to play the same role.

If you have a decorative cornice or frieze, and have been left with spaces where a new opening has been made, you can buy small pieces of ready-made plasterwork to bridge the gaps.

Making two rooms from one

There are many circumstances in which it may be necessary or desirable to partition off space to create a new room: for example, when you want to build a bathroom that leads off an existing bedroom, or want to divide a bedroom to create another smaller bedroom or perhaps a new study.

You must make sure that both the resulting rooms will meet the local standards governing the dimensions and characteristics of habitable rooms (see page 88). Aim to locate your new partition wall so that any existing windows are positioned in a sensible place; windows hard against a corner, for example, will look like awkward afterthoughts. Nor should you be tempted to split a room into two simply by running a new partition up to the middle of an existing window bay. It is not only crude and extremely unsightly, but, with an airgap around the end of the partition will result in a lack of acoustic privacy.

The raw materials for creating a new room are basic, and very straight-forward. A timber stud frame, made up of vertical and horizontal pieces of timber, with diagonal bracing for rigidity, is nailed together, and in turn the assembly is nailed to the floor. Plasterboard sheets are attached to the framework, then coated in a skimcoat of plaster, ready for a decorative treatment. Stability is provided in this type of wall by the shape of the floor plan, while turns and right-angled corners provide the rigidity.

A more sophisticated means of creating two rooms out of one is to use sliding partition walls, mounted in floor and ceiling tracks which can be pushed back out of the way when not needed. If there is no room for a door opening into the new room you are creating, employ a sliding door.

1 A chimney breast left intact to take the weight of the original load-bearing wall.

2 A circular window through one wall and an arch linking the room with a corridor create a series of spaces that transforms the layout.

3 A non-load-bearing wall demolished to create a single room the length of the house.

4 A square opening knocked through a load-bearing wall, leaving enough of the structure to support a boxed-in beam.

5 Three separate rooms linked by removing the dividing walls and continuing the same colour scheme.

GAINING SPACE

Look around your home – notice how much space is wasted in areas such as stairwells, or long, thin corridors, or even by ceilings too tall for the size of the room. With some thought it is quite possible to make profitable use of this extra space.

Mezzanines

The grandly scaled proportions of Victorian and Edwardian buildings, where ceilings are far more generous than today's skimpy minimum heights, offer plenty of scope for inserting mezzanine floor levels. These can be both a practical means of getting the most out of a space, and an attractive new element in an interior.

Obviously rooms of particularly dignified proportions should not be marred by a heavy timber platform fitted unsympathetically across one wall. An elegant free-standing steel structure, specially fabricated from scaffolding tubing, may sometimes be a more graceful alternative, and makes better structural sense.

In such houses, the corridors and stairs will often have equally generous ceiling heights, and these areas can make excellent settings for timber mezzanines, providing storage space, or even a spare guest bed.

A timber mezzanine is made up from joists which span two load-bearing walls, with the platform's upper surface formed from chipboard or plywood. The depth of the joists will need to be increased in direct proportion to the distance they have to span. So the relatively narrow spaces in corridors and at the top of staircases make sound economic sense for mezzanines, provided of course that they are wide enough to be usable.

Line up the bottom of the platform with the top of the nearest door. If you aim to use the platform simply for

1 Burrowing up into the roof here provides extra space in two ways. It makes the whole room feel more spacious, and allows a work area to be created in the eaves.

2 A lofty entrance hall, incorporating a spare bedroom for occasional visitors. The platform has been built at a height which allows you to walk comfortably underneath and still sit up in bed.

sleeping or for storage you will only need enough headroom in which to sit up. Don't forget to take into account the depth of the platform itself when making your calculations. If you plan to use it as a study space or a relaxing area, you will of course need rather more room.

When you are fitting a mezzanine into a room, it should span the narrower of the room's dimensions, and preferably be located away from the windows. Fit in a handrail, and a staircase for access. A spiral stair is elegant, but a simple ladder will save more space, provided that you are agile enough to use it.

Corridors

Corridors are generally a waste of space that could be put to more productive purposes as part of usable rooms. They can provide extra space for hanging pictures, and storing books

– but that is all. A successful house plan is one which minimizes the lengths of corridors by grouping rooms in the optimum way. In some types of house you may find it possible to exploit them by removing existing partition walls.

Staircases

Fitting a new staircase into a house to replace an existing one is a major undertaking, and rarely worth the effort unless it is part of a much larger scheme. However, if you are considering an extension at the back or side of your house, it may be possible to insert a new staircase to provide better access to the rest of the house and possibly simplifying any corridors that are needed. The building regulations are very strict on the subject of staircases, both in specifying the dimensions of steps, and the provision of handrails. The rule is always seek professional advice.

3 The top of a built-in wardrobe used as a sleeping platform, freeing the rest of the room for furniture other than the bed.

4 The top of a mezzanine needs a protective barrier – why not combine it with storage space for books?

5 A mezzanine installed as a half-level at the back of a tall room away from the windows is the traditional studio pattern. Recessed downlighters in its lower surface light the back of the room without encroaching on the limited headroom.

USING FURNITURE

Furniture can have a major part to play in defining the quality and character of a space. In large, open interiors, the furniture will play an architectural role, so that, for example, storage units could act as the visual equivalent of a solid wall. In a small space, folding tables, stacking chairs and sofa beds will help to make the best of what little space you have.

In either case though, when you are planning your furniture layout, you should consider its effect on your interior. The conventional three piece suite for example, with a bulky sofa and two matching armchairs, will often swamp today's smaller sized living room. It may make more sense to choose a seating system made up from modular units instead. These will not only be more compact in their design, but will require much less space around them for access. They can also be grouped in many more permutations than is possible with sofas and armchairs.

Lining up your furniture parallel with the walls will waste less space than positioning it at an angle across corners, and this arrangement can be just as intimate and informal. But pushing pieces like tables and sofas, or beds hard against walls may not be making quite such good use of a limited space as it appears at first sight, as you will be limiting your room for manoeuvre around each piece.

The classic use of furniture as a spatial element in a design is in the division of, say, a kitchen from a dining room or a dining room from a living room. In these circumstances a work-top counter can be more than just a useful place to chop carrots and store dishes. It will tend to create the demarcation line between homely kitchen chaos and dining room formality when there are no walls.

Even in a small bedroom which is used as a study or for a teenage sitting room as well, a cunningly located

wardrobe can help to create a sense that there is more than one separate area within the overall space. If there is room, move the wardrobe toward the door, so that you cannot immediately see right in. Put an easy chair, or a table and a chair in front of the wardrobe, and a bed beyond it, and you have divided the room effectively into two parts, each with its own character.

Where circulation routes, or corridors, cross living space, use bookshelves to provide a protective feeling around the sitting areas, screening them off from passers by. Do not be afraid to tailor furniture to specific architectural quirks within your interior – a sofa that fits exactly into an alcove for example, or a dining table placed against a chimney breast.

Try to use furniture to emphasize the best architectural characteristics of a room. It can be attractive to draw attention to its threshold for example by putting a large bookcase or wardrobe

next to the doorway, and at right angles to it, which will have the effect of making a dramatic entrance. Or if your dining room has a formal and symmetrical plan, respect that formality by arranging your furniture on the same axis. When there is some architectural feature of note in the ceiling, such as a skylight, or a rooflight, draw attention to it by placing a major piece of furniture beneath it. And in the same way reinforce the dominating presence of an attractive fireplace by focusing your furniture around it.

By the same token, it is possible to use furniture to camouflage some of the defects of a room. If you have a door that you never use, but you don't want to go to the trouble of blocking it up, don't waste that valuable wall space, instead push a bookcase across it. Household appliances such as refrigerators or washing machines can be used in a similar way.

1 In a large, open plan space, try using pieces of furniture as a way of subdividing the area into small, distinguishable 'plots'. The folding screen is a traditional dividing device and is very useful for creating a more solid barrier in the room.

2 Functioning as a corridor, this large scale piece of specially made storage is used to screen off the living area from people passing through to the rest of the house. But because the unit is punctured with holes and stops short of the ceiling, people in the sitting area can still enjoy a feeling of spaciousness that would be lost with a solid wall.

3 To mark the transition between kitchen and dining room, designer Colin Forbes fitted these purpose-built cabinets. By using the same materials — black tiles and solid timber facing — on both sides, a visual link is made between the two functions yet each side retains its individual character.

4 Bathrooms aside, there is not one permanent internal wall in Michael Hopkin's London house. Instead, Venetian blinds can be raised or lowered to define individual areas. The kitchen, for instance, can be opened up for sociability, or closed off when not in use.

HALLS

Resist the temptation to concentrate all your energies on decorating the main rooms of your house at the expense of the hall. It may not directly affect the way you live, but the light in which visitors see your home is determined very much by those first doorstep impressions. And even if you see your hall every day, a welcoming impression will make coming home out of the cold that bit more pleasant.

Often, the most minor elements have the largest part to play. The feel of a generously proportioned brass door knocker for example, or the style of the house number. Once inside, a more elaborate range of effects can be deployed to establish a welcoming atmosphere. But if you have an irritating door chime, people's minds will already be made up.

The hall need not just be a cosmetic curtain raiser, however, but designed in such a way as to earn its keep. It can be a useful place in which to put pictures, or to store books. And if it is large enough, and space elsewhere is at a premium, it can even be pressed into service as an extra room.

The front door has a crucial part to play in the architectural character of a house. Don't rip out original doors just to replace them with bland and inappropriate flush panel specimens unless you have a very good reason. Think hard also before you put in one of the mass-produced theme doors; whether they are watered down neo-Georgian or hacienda style, they very rarely look right. If your house is on the Government's list of protected buildings of historic, or architectural interest, you will need planning permission for this kind of change anyway. On the other hand, if you find that hardboard panels have been tacked over an authentically detailed period door, prise them off, make good the damage and repaint it.

1

1 A typical canalside Amsterdam house whose tiny front entrance opens into an airy hall cum dining area. Sealed old boards and glazed doors create a fresh and welcoming atmosphere.

2 Warm mellow brickwork perfectly sets off a richly coloured canvas in a delicate gold frame.

3 The classic proportions of the front door are echoed by the formal arrangement of pictures on the wall inside. Ahead, a glazed door tempts the eye further into the apartment.

4 The essence of the country house look: Yorkstone flags smooth with age, whitewashed brick walls and an old refectory table. Sophisticated modern lighting helps bring out the warmth of this hall, without interfering with its essential qualities.

MAKING AN ENTRANCE

Designing a bright, attractive and welcoming entrance hall can be one of the most satisfying parts of creating an interior. It can be a chance for design at its most theatrical, freed from constraints, and serving simply to create a good first impression. Both in a practical and a symbolic sense, the hall is a buffer between the home and the outside world. It should have a tough enough floor surface to cope with muddy boots and dripping wet umbrellas, and it should be designed in such a way as to screen the more private areas of the home from casual visitors and outsiders who call.

The fad in the 1960s for knocking entrance halls into all-in-one open plan living rooms rarely proved a satisfactory arrangement. Apart from the lack of privacy, there is the added problem of heat loss with no entrance hall to serve an airlock function.

The key to creating an attractive entrance hall is to satisfy all the practical needs in as unobtrusive a way as possible, and at the same time to create a space which is open and generously proportioned. In design terms you might like to provide a hint of the style of the rest of the house, or else you might opt for shock tactics and deliberately set out to create surprises.

Bear in mind the way that people will experience an entrance hall. If you live at the top of an apartment block with access along a series of twisting corridors and staircases, you might like to accentuate the difference between the communal spaces outside and your own hall. One particularly stunning London apartment achieves this with murals of giant grainy clouds. Even regular visitors never fail to feel a sense of release and surprise on walking in from the dark confined spaces outside.

In small homes, the hall can be a means of creating a more generous sense of space. Clear the walls, and paint them white. Banish the clutter, either to another, less conspicuous part of the house, or into well-integrated built-in storage cupboards. Select a single, attractive object or group of objects to hang on the walls, or position a single classic piece of furniture in a prominent position. It can all add up to a soothing counter balance to a series of overcrowded little rooms, packed too densely together.

A favourite theme for the entrance halls of houses both big and small is the country house look – lots of mellow quarry tiles on the floor, rows of Wellington boots and perhaps a dog basket or a well-stocked umbrella stand

on the floor. The colours would be appropriately based on so-called traditional shades, deep dark green perhaps, throwing pictures and objects on the walls into sharp relief.

If you do have to use your hallway as an overflow to the living room for reasons of shortage of space, don't let things get out of control. If you have to park the pram, store the bicycle, and keep the phone in the hall, try to control all the disparate elements, so that you don't simply end up with a messy dumping ground. Make the telephone table as attractive a spot as

possible, not just a species of phone box. Choose a really comfortable and attractive chair to accompany it; one that will look good simply standing by itself. Make sure that the hall is properly heated so that it is warm enough; a space that is cold and draughty will automatically be underused. Accommodating a pram can be a problem. Many modern houses just do not have the space to deal with them in the entrance hall. Bear in mind how much space you will have to store the pram indoors before deciding which type to buy.

1

2

4

1   A dark hall makes a sophisticated background for pictures and objects. Here the jungle greenery outside is echoed by recycled garden implements, transformed into wall decoration by a coat of paint.

2   Never neglect the space under the stairs. If you don't need it for extra storage, bring it to life with an interesting piece of furniture and a collection of well-chosen objects, and accentuate it with a dramatic spotlight.

3   A pair each of shrubs, shell light fittings, and garden chairs emphasize the solid, symmetrical proportions of this long slim hall without looking fiddly or inappropriate.

4   In a cramped hallway it's the simplest approach which achieves the best results. Attractive textures and a soft subtle colour throughout are all it needs.

3

THE PRACTICALITIES

Just how feasible it is in practice to use your entrance hall as an extra room will depend on its specific layout and its relationship with other rooms, as well as its sheer size. Before making up your mind, draw a floor plan of the hall area, showing in particular which doors open where, and see if it is possible to fit in the furniture you need with room to open and shut the doors.

Quite often a conversion will give rise to a potential extra room where the entrance hall is simply a square windowless space from which all the other rooms open. If it is large enough to take a table and chairs, it can make a very useful dining area. Folding chairs will probably help you to save space. You may find that you will need to take a door or two off their hinges if they open outward in an awkward position. Either reverse the door swing, or if it is not essential, leave it off altogether. Aim to be able to push the table to one side when it is out of use, and position a suitable light over the table.

If the entrance hall is tall and thin, it may be possible to install a mezzanine, by hanging timber beams with joist hangers from the two facing walls. When there isn't much headroom, use it simply as storage space. When it is tall enough to sit up in, it can become a spare bedroom.

The space at the top of a staircase can also make a useful extra room. A narrow desk can fit snugly into the width of a landing. Just add a desk lamp, a chair and a filing cabinet, and you can make yourself a study.

In decorative terms, your hall will seem much more spacious if you try to unify it, using one overall colour scheme that ties walls, ceiling and staircase together. Plain white, or a discreetly patterned wallpaper can look good. Strong colours will tend to shrink the apparent space available. Plastering the walls of the hall with collections of objects is not as popular as it once was, although groups of pictures are always effective. It's probably better to select just a couple of items, which could perhaps stand on a table or the floor. Properly lit and positioned they will look far better than a motley collection.

A letter box should be positioned in the front door at a convenient height; the postman does not want to lie stretched out on the ground to get your letters through. There should also be a set of readily accessible light switches just inside the door that will control not just the hall, but the stair lights as well. And there should be an adequate quantity of door matting. A generous area, stretching right across the doorway opening and a few steps into the hall will not only look better than a perfunctory 'welcome' mat, but it will also help to keep the whole house cleaner. A large mat should be recessed slightly into the floor, so that it is flush

1

2

3

1 It's a soothing climb up this light, cool, green staircase. Laying the carpet right across makes the stairs look wider and avoids strips of paintwork on either side which chip easily.

2 A small half-landing can be put to good use with the minimum of props. Full-length curtains and a pair of chairs flank the marble column and create a country house flavour.

3 Architects often use the staircase to make an emphatic design gesture. Here, the bold set of shapes makes enough of a statement without needing adornment.

with the floor finish in the rest of the hall. Any furniture you choose to put in your hall will depend of course on the space that you have available. In any case it will tend to be chosen more for its looks than pieces in more heavily used parts of the house. And there is scope for flower arrangements and so on.

Try to have a cupboard for keeping coats and boots out of the way if you want to create a formal atmosphere in your entrance hall.

The stairs

Installing a new staircase is a costly, time consuming and complicated process. If you do decide that it is necessary, you will want to gain the maximum advantage from it. By changing a staircase's position you may be able to make better use of your existing rooms, or it might take up less space and therefore free the floor area for other purposes.

If it is a question of cramming a staircase into as little space as possible, then a spiral will probably be the solution you opt for. But do bear in mind that spirals are not without their problems – it becomes extremely difficult to take large pieces of furniture up and down them. And though many graceful off-the-shelf spiral designs are available, their very geometry can make them an over-insistent element in an interior and not to everyone's taste.

There are other ways of using a more conventional staircase to save space. It is possible to build storage space underneath, or perhaps more elaborate types of accommodation, a bed alcove or a small study area. The precise details of staircase design are very much in the hands of local authority officials, who have the power to specify not just the permitted height and width of each step, but the type of handrail, and the width between bannisters. They can also insist that you do not have single steps anywhere in your home, and that handrails are provided even for just two steps, all much to the despair of many architects and designers who profess to find it an arbitrary and unnecessary cramping of their style. In general, the stringent regulations limit the form of staircases to a few well-known permutations.

In decorative terms, it is usually best to carry the design treatment that you have used in the hall up the stairwell. For example, if you have decided to fill every available square inch with lavishly framed paintings you should carry on doing so up the stairs as well. Arrange what you put on the walls of the stairwell to take account of the geometry imposed by the rise and turn of the stairs. Long horizontal rows of pictures will present more visual problems than if they are arranged in a series of vertical rows. The staircase itself will often be an important visual element, especially where it circles around the edges of a generously proportioned hall.

Remember before you commit yourself to a decorative scheme that stairs and hallways are areas in which the traffic of feet is likely to be particularly heavy. Carpets will need to be especially hardwearing; and the walls are likely to suffer damage from the knocks and scrapes of bicycles or prams and greasy fingers.

Lighting layouts can assume particular importance on a staircase. From a safety point of view you will need a good level of background light to make sure that people do not miss their step on the stairs. If you have pictures or objects on the walls you will also need to consider extra lights to show them off to their best advantage.

4 Building regulations in some countries prohibit staircases without handrails. In a house with children or old people a rail is obviously a sensible precaution, but stairs on their own make a striking piece of design.

5 These Piranesi engravings have stronger impact when lined up with great precision as a set than scattered at random over the wall.

6 The Victorians made much use of mirrors and polished mahogany. That era is lovingly evoked in this modern recreation which has all the splendour of a gin palace.

LIVING ROOMS

In recent years the role of the living room has undergone a change. As the kitchen has increasingly evolved into the family room, the living room has become an adult room, a cultural refuge, more formal than it was previously, where children are often discouraged from playing.

The 1980s have seen a retreat to the home. Eating, meeting and drinking are more likely to take place there than in clubs and restaurants. Television, video films and hi-fi – even music making – have, for many, supplanted the cinema and theatre as entertainment, and electronic games can also be played at home. Other rooms are rarely large enough for such pastimes with their sophisticated gadgetry, and the living room has come into its own as a place for leisure activity (of a fairly untaxing nature) as well as relaxation.

The new formality that the living room is now acquiring means that the old laissez-faire arrangements that went with open plan living spaces are no longer appropriate. As walls go back and divisions return between the main living areas of the home – hall, kitchen, living room, dining room – the most important of them, the living room itself, is gathering new distinction and style. Casual folksiness has become distinctly passé. Coupled with a greater feeling for comfort and ease, the new-found formality and order has much appeal, but needs corresponding order and careful planning to achieve.

Three other factors have changed the way living rooms now look and function. The first is a new wave of furniture designed and made in Italy. Quite different from the stereotyped designs, whether old or modern, with which we have furnished our rooms for so long, it is powerful and demanding and, like the sculpture it resembles in both price and appearance, requires careful positioning. It is exciting, intrusive, comfortable, and its impact on our rooms, even in watered-down versions, has been considerable.

The second important change is in the colour schemes which dominated the domestic scene for so long – bland and eventually dull creams, beiges and browns, or for the less cautious, bright cheerful primaries – have given way to a predominance of soft pastels, sometimes sharpened by a shot of brighter pink, green or yellow. With their subtle references to 18th century designs, these new colour schemes are perfectly in accord with the quest for formality. Certainly they have lent themselves splendidly to the vogue for decorative paintwork. Rather than hanging paper or vinyl which were popular for so long, many people now apply paint – or have it applied by trained craftsmen – with finishes such as stippling, dragging, marbling and ragging (see the chapter on Do-It-Yourself). It is a vogue which forms a background to both modern and traditional styles of furnishing.

Finally, there has been an influx of different materials which affects the way living rooms are furnished. Mainly of industrial origin and not always new per se, they are being put to unexpected domestic uses by architects and designers, often in their own homes. They include the studded rubber flooring which was developed for the factory and the laboratory but which did not take long to march across first kitchen and then living room floors; brightly printed plastic laminates which Italian designers have taken off kitchen worktops and plastered over some very unusual looking furniture; wood, now stained and lacquered in glowing pastel colours to meet the new taste; and steel – tubular or sheet – which has been fashioned into stylish and hard-wearing pieces of furniture. Fibrous plaster has been used to imitate columns, mouldings and other decorative features of the past, whilst chromed or plastic-coated wire has been made into visually light storage and shelving.

Mention of these few details gives an indication of the wide choice available and the many different styles which can be adopted. None is dominant however; a comfortable minimalism in one home is just as acceptable as lavishly swagged and draped luxury in another. Movements such as high tech and post modernism can be mixed and matched, diluted and adapted; within the contemporary formal framework, anything goes.

1

1 and 2 The traditional comforts of an Edwardian gentlemen's club can be recreated with a far from solemn effect. This leafy conservatory/living room has all the right elements, but not necessarily on the same scale. The billiard table, highlighted by the thick blue-green glass lampshade, gives the whole room an after-dinner glow. Tiffany shade, pub mirror and leather club armchair complement the lazy opulence of the room.

PLANNING

You have decided what your room is to be used for. Now you must resist the temptation to start buying, and plan, preferably on paper, the most comfortable and good-looking way in which the various activities can be accommodated. A scale plan is an indispensable aid.

Long or short term

If you are settling into a home you own and intend to inhabit for some years, your plan should be equally long term. Think first about structural alterations. Do you want to remove a wall or, if the formal style appeals to you, replace one, perhaps between dining and sitting rooms? Do you want to open up a fireplace which has been wantonly blocked by a previous owner, move a door to release a decent length of wall space, or enlarge a window? All these should be planned and carried out, shelves and cupboards must be built in, new lighting or power points installed, before you start on cosmetic work such as furnishing and decorating.

On the other hand, if you are in rented accommodation or a place you intend to occupy for a relatively short period, plan to exploit the existing structure to its utmost. Overlarge windows can be partially screened with curtains and blinds, ones that are too small, given more value by strategically placed mirrors; superfluous doors can be ignored and obscured by large pieces of furniture. Temporary shelving, which you can take with you when you go, can be installed, and ugly fireplaces diminished by applying paint or even using a plywood screen.

Sitting areas

The most important part of the room is the sitting area, and this should be settled upon first. Here you will talk, watch television, eat snacks, play games, read and relax, so it should have comfortable seating, but should also be planned so that aids to these pastimes are grouped nearby.

If yours is a small living room avoid huge, heavy sofas or armchairs that are rarely moved, and assume a rigid and fixed arrangement which will cramp your style when there is an above average number of guests. Remember too that a three-seater sofa eats space but is rarely used by three people at a time, for three-in-a-row is an unsociable configuration. Opt for small, light

1

2

3

1 A spacious living room has been created by knocking two rooms into one. With such a large open space to tame, furniture becomes a vital part of the interior. The tone it sets is cheerfully eclectic.

2 This generously proportioned double height space, with its huge window wall provides a dramatic setting. Over-elaborate contents would just be a distraction; instead the seating is unobtrusively built into the floor.

3 A clever variation on the conventional twin sofa layout, four huge armchairs are strategically placed, each pair with its own table. High enough to serve more useful functions than mere coffee tables, these pieces are not so large as to inhibit conversation.

furniture which can be swivelled and regrouped to accommodate a crowd. Conversely, in a large space have one or two heavy and fixed pieces, but with lighter weight satellites which can be grouped in various ways around them if the room is crowded. You want to avoid the situation where a large group is fixed in an immutable circle, and the versatility of modern furniture makes this possible.

Whatever the size, keep the seating area apart from traffic routes, as it is both irritating and distracting to have someone clumping across the room in front of you when you are trying to read, talk or watch TV. Make sure books, records, cassettes, video tapes and other leisure time paraphernalia are stored (in a visually pleasing way) within easy reach, and that there are low tables for glasses, ashtrays and magazines; but avoid placing these so they block off parts of the room. Supplement a pleasantly low overall artificial lighting scheme with sufficient direct spot lighting to make for easy reading and other close work.

Dining areas

A separate formal dining room may be difficult to achieve because you lack space (or even inclination), and in any case you may prefer to eat family meals in your living room. Unless you entertain a great deal, you may not want to devote so much precious space to a separate dining room.

Remember the old gate-leg tables? There are ingenious modern counterparts. Some look like slim console tables during most of the day (complete with bowls of flowers and framed photographs) but swivel open to accommodate a dinner party of six or more people. Others work exactly on the gate-leg principle but have slim modern lines, and fold down to a sylph-like 20cm (8 in.) depth. And some, generally custom made, are attached to a wall and fold flat against it when not in use. Modern dining chairs too can help with this parsimonious use of space by folding, stacking and even hanging on the wall when the meal is over.

If space is not a problem and you relish the idea of an all-in-one room, plan your eating area so that it is, nevertheless, quite detached from the sitting space, easily accessible from the kitchen, and preferably able to be concealed in some way when the eating is over. Individual lights can be extinguished or dimmed to throw the table into shadow, a free-standing screen can be used, or a permanent screen can be made which will partially obscure this part of the room as well as the debris and dirty dishes left after a good meal.

If there is insufficient space for furniture in which to store tableware and cutlery close at hand, a well-designed modern trolley will serve several purposes; as storage, transporter and serving table.

Other activities

Think about other activities which will take place in the room at planning stage, rather than cramming in things in a haphazard way at a later date. Work – study, writing, reading – is best done in a quieter place than the living room, such as one of the bedrooms. Likewise, major sewing operations do not really fit well into the family living room. But if it is to be used for such work at non busy times, keep a space that can be well-lit, undisturbed when not in use, and equipped with a strong table and its own chair which will not, frustratingly, have been taken off and left in another room when you need it in a hurry.

If the occasional guest is to sleep in the room, this fact should not be apparent; and sofa beds now are designed for discretion, though test them for ease of transformation, and for comfort in their sofa role, as some fail miserably. Store bed linen in a cupboard elsewhere.

FOCAL POINTS

The fireplace makes an obvious and good focal point in the living room, whether it contains an open fire or not. Some focal points gain piquancy from being off-centre, in a corner or otherwise away from the main part of the room. A fireplace does not. It should be situated in the centre of one of the room's long walls if possible, so that there is space for an ample group of seats in its vincinity, as well as for the accoutrements (fire irons, log basket, bellows etc.) which need to be kept nearby. Don't indulge in too strident a decorative scheme for the fireplace; in such a dominant position it could easily become boring, irritating or even stressful before you can afford to change it. Instead, settle for something which is good-looking but relatively unassertive.

You may not have a fireplace, or even want one. To avoid the bland sameness which can endanger a room where there is no change of emphasis, arrange some alternatives. You won't necessarily want to sit round them, but they will give your room a lift.

Instead of dumping pots of greenery around the room in an arbitrary way, group them together in profusion and light them artificially at night; this type of arrangement, unlike a fireplace, looks good in a corner where it will bring life to a dull spot. Or have a huge arrangement of dried or fresh flowers set against a large mirror where they will have a dual and dramatic impact.

Many light fittings are objects of intrinsic sculptural beauty. Choose one for its looks, place it in a prominent position and enjoy its light output as a bonus. Some uplighters of this type throw spectacular light and shadows onto the ceiling or walls.

Arrange a group of drawings and paintings for their concerted impact as well as for the individual pleasure they offer. If you have a particularly important or well-loved picture, give it a prominent and solitary position; have it dramatically spot-lit at night, preferably from a concealed source. An exceptional piece of furniture could be given similar treatment.

Exploit the often derided coffee-table books. Arrange your best and most beautiful in an eye-catching heap – on a coffee table, of course. Guests will undoubtedly finger and inspect them, and they will contribute to the interest and visual impact of the living room.

If you have a garden, plunder it without mercy and group together several small arrangements of flowers, in a variety of containers, to make a focal point. In winter, when there's a dearth of flowers, be imaginative about using branches, silver-shrub foliage, and evergreens.

If you are a collector of small objects, arrange them fastidiously (and rearrange them frequently) to make an

1 The visual focus here is not the fireplace as one might expect but the two armchairs in striking pink fabric. The simple outlines of the chairs and their insistent colour work well as a foil to the elaborately arranged objects on the shelves behind.

2 Partly an art object, partly a gently ironic touch of fun at the expense of over-precious table arrangements, this collection of half-smashed crockery is a slightly disturbing distraction in an unusual Californian living room.

3

unusual and interesting focal point: antiquarian books, pebbles, boxes, fine glasses, decoy ducks, jugs and lead soldiers are all obvious candidates for this type of treatment. But the more unusual the collection the more attractive it is as a focal point.

A first-rate architectural feature such as a graceful arch, fine 18th century pillars, beautiful mouldings and plasterwork or old ceiling timbers should be cossetted and kept in perfect repair to form a feature of the room, and never obscured by ill-placed furniture or dim lighting.

The best focal point is a beautiful view. If you are lucky enough to have one, chairs should be grouped to enjoy it to the full. A near view – a pretty terrace or courtyard – should be lit so that it can be enjoyed from inside the room after dark.

There is always a natural tendency for the television set to become the centrepiece of a living room, but TVs do not make good focal points, particularly when the screen is blank. It is also very difficult to accommodate other activities around the TV if it is sited bang in the middle of the main wall with all the furniture grouped around it. Some people wheel it away into a convenient cupboard when it is not in use. If this is not possible, try to place yours where it will be visible when in use, but not dominant in the scheme of things.

3 Artist Allen Jones' living area is based around an eye-catching rug. With the help of a fireplace, albeit non-functional, it creates a well-defined sitting space.

4 A patchwork quilt wall-hanging provides an attractive visual focus for a rustic room.

5 An industrial lampshade can make a room look alarmingly stark, without some object, like this carved doll, to distract the eye.

4

5

INSTALLING A FIREPLACE

There has been a marked volte face recently in attitudes to the fireplace, with many blocked flues being reopened. However warm a centrally heated house may be, the psychological comfort to be derived from an open fire is incomparable.

If your living room has neither fireplace nor flue, the expense of installation will be considerable but worthwhile. Employ an architect to ensure that the new flue is satisfactorily concealed within the house – behind a false wall or inside cupboards – or alternatively that it is featured in a handsome way, or, if it is to be on the outside, that this is done neatly and competently.

If you are reinstating an existing fireplace, investigate carefully before deciding to rebuild it. Hardboard has been known to conceal delightful antiquities, and even if what you uncover is of no particular architectural merit, a satisfactory and inexpensive revival job can be achieved by cleaning, painting, stripping or repairing. If the fireplace is beyond repair, you loathe it or its style clashes with your plan for the room, take care over the replacement. Hire an architect or designer for original thinking, visit scrap yards, antique shops and warehouses selling architectural relics if you are recreating a past style. Stand over your local jobbing builder to guide his every step if you are making a simple hole in the wall grate, because simplicity, proportion and scale mean different things to different people.

Look at the new imitation gas log and coal fires; the best are remarkably convincing. Their main advantage is that they provide the comfort of a real fire without the inconvenience of having to clear away ash and clean the grate, and unlike real fires they light straight away. Although they should not be relied on as your sole source of heating, they do throw out a surprising amount of heat. They are however twice as expensive to run as an ordinary gas fire, and you need to have a chimney.

If you have a huge room, consider a smokeless fuel or wood-burning stove. The best are reasonably well designed, and though not sophisticated enough for the most formal room, they are doughty performers.

Whatever your fuel, make tidy and ample provision for log baskets, hods and good-looking fire irons.

3

1 A mellow brick fireplace houses a woodburning stove and log store.

2 A fireplace can still have a role in an open plan setting.

3 A hole in the wall grate with minimal surround.

4 Even without a fire, a mantlepiece can be a focus.

5 Grate inset in glass.

2

4

5

DISPLAYING ART

The living room is a risky place for art that will depress you, inflame guests of strong political persuasion or clash with the colour scheme. So unless you are a knowledgeable and dedicated collector for whom art is a *raison d'être* before which all else pales to insignificance, try to keep pieces of a non-controversial and pleasant nature for this relaxing place. That being said, do not become too bland in your choice. Whether you have inexpensive posters and prints, good quality oil paintings, water colours, sculpture, photographs (the best are recognized as an art form), fine glassware or china, or a splendid combination of all these, choose them for positive delight. If you have chosen judiciously, you will get a stab of pleasure every time you enter the room.

Arrange your art works with care and rearrange them quite frequently. There is a danger that you will cease to see a picture, however fine, if it has hung in one place for too long. Hang low rather than high for this is generally more pleasing to the eye. Hang some things in groups, ranged close together and not scattered indiscriminately. Give others solitary prominence, and change the one singled out for this importance frequently. Arrange lights so that single pictures are directly lit and groups are flooded with light from uplighters or wall washers, avoiding reflections. Train a recessed ceiling spot or uplighter concealed behind a piece of furniture onto a large sculpture to gain maximum dramatic impact.

1 Group families of objects together to create one dramatic display.

2 A comic identity parade of pottery people lines the mantlepiece.

3 and 4 Two views of a living room in which the pictures have been displayed with precise symmetry to echo its formal lines.

5 Create an impact with one large painting hung at eye level.

DETAILS

1 A photographer's spun metal studio floodlight shade can make an effective fitting for a standard lamp which looks appropriate in this loft.

2 Zandra Rhodes shows off her collection of ceramics in an elaborately decorated glass-shelved case. It merges with the flowing paint lines on the walls and paint-spattered radiator to build up a riot of pattern and texture.

3 Frank Gehry's California houses all have this quirky, stripped-down appeal. Specially designed furniture made from unconventional materials reflects the apparently random openings in the walls and ceiling. Gehry's objective is to use familiar elements in a room to create a distinctly unfamiliar mood.

4 Built-in furniture, accommodating seating and storage, helps to make the most of space, especially when a home office has to be incorporated into the living room.

5 A well-located sofa serves to highlight the window alcove, together with the potted palms.

1

2

3

5

6

7

9

11

6 The minimalist approach: a view from the dining to the living area with its arresting fireplace.

7 A pair of symmetrically positioned palms on each side of this richly decorative period stained glass make an appropriate frame for the patterned sofa.

8 Loft spaces do not always have to be kitted out with high tech bric-a-brac. When you want to sub-divide space within a large area, classical columns, cornices on low partitions and even a grand piano can make effective divisions.

9 Storage units, used here in a monumental, architectural way, create a sense of enclosure.

10 A specially built work top makes the best of an unorthodox curving wall that would cause problems for rectangular desks.

11 An imposing standard lamp gives this entrance a ceremonial flourish.

8

10

FORMAL LIVING

The French have always been adept at arranging the formal living room, and though the British rightly demand higher standards of comfort than hard, upright French furniture traditionally provides, we can learn much from them about the advantages of formality.

Formal living rooms will preferably not cater for other activities. Dining will take place elsewhere, there are no overflowing tables where somebody has recently been studying for A-levels or cutting out a new shirt, and overnight guests are definitely *de trop*.

Television sets and record players will either be hidden in cupboards when not in use or built into an elegant storage unit of individual design which does its best to conceal their functional roles, and even books will be beautifully arranged in specially made cases; collapsing paperbacks stacked on DIY shelving have no place here.

For all that, whether it is furnished in a modern or traditional style, or in a judicious mixture of the two, this room is very comfortable, sometimes even sumptuous. Since its prime purpose will be for sitting, relaxing and talking, seating is of major importance. There

should be one or two sofas if space permits and several other chairs, all grouped in a formal way to facilitate conversation. In a big room there may be several such groups and when large gatherings take place, all will be in use. A scattering of lightweight chairs can be moved from one group to another as needs dictate, but the main groupings should be permanent and the furniture rarely moved out of position. Ample occasional and low tables must be carefully arranged with plants, large ashtrays, bowls of flowers and other visually pleasing objects, and even the cushions should have their particular positions from which they are not allowed to stray.

If there is a fireplace, it must be immaculate and tidy when not in use, and fire irons, whether modern or traditional, must be gleaming and methodically set out.

Curtains should be beautifully made from good fabrics such as silk taffeta or fine wool: hanging pure and straight in a modern room, swagged and draped and perhaps augmented by festoon blinds in a more traditional one. The floor should be of polished wood or

1 A classic European apartment interior: rich rugs, an antique bureau and dark oil paintings are used with conviction as part of a scheme that also includes Saarinen's low table and other modern pieces.

2 Strong colour contrasts need to be handled with care and confidence. A huge red canvas and vase of poppies combine to set off stylish gloss black furniture.

3 This muted grey and silver colour scheme is given a boost of energy by the decorative use of neon, seen reflected in the mirror.

covered in fitted carpet, and rugs must be arranged rather than scattered.

Decoration should be simple but carefully considered. You may have good quality wallpaper in a small, geometric pattern, richly coloured fabric with edgings of contrasting braid, glossy paint applied in many layers to achieve a polished, gleaming surface, or one of the fashionable paint finishes such as marbling, stippling, rag-rolling or dragging.

Pictures, whether modern prints covered in Perspex or gilt-framed oil paintings, should be hung in precise and carefully thought out arrangements, lit either by traditional picture lights or well-placed spots. Other lighting should consist of an overall scheme from recessed ceiling spots or strips concealed beneath shelves, as well as dramatic spot lighting from good quality table lamps and uplighters.

This type of living room is not for everyone; certainly it is impractical in a bustling household short of space. Yet it is surprising that despite so much rigidity and studied formality it is a look that is becoming increasingly popular among young home owners.

4 Gloss walls and the indirect lighting scheme play up the contrasts between light and shade. Low seating and a profusion of patterned cushions create an oriental atmosphere that is underscored by Japanese prints on the walls.

5 Marcel Breuer's chrome and leather armchair, the Wassily, squares up to Charles Rennie Mackintosh's masterpiece opposite. Furniture with as much presence as these pieces needs plenty of room to breathe. Other elements such as bookcases and flooring are deliberately low key.

URBAN LIVING

The urban living room may be the most taxing to contrive, but will often turn out to be the most striking and original when finished. This might be the place to recreate a cosy Victorian parlour or, at the other extreme, a room with a modern hard edge approach to exploit and flatter its often modest proportions.

Furniture, even of the well-stuffed period variety, should be small and adaptable enough to be easily rearranged. Have one small sofa at the most – there are many light modern versions, some on wooden or tubular steel frames – and furnish mainly with individual seats. Guard against over-furnishing, and arrange what you have so that it is not only comfortable but looks inviting and not just a jumble as you enter the room. Avoid a plethora of occasional tables, which will obstruct the floor space, and search out one really beautiful design in laminated plastic, glass or wood.

In a small urban living room as many possessions as possible – books, television, hi-fi, home computers, ornaments and even some lighting – should be arranged in an orderly and decorative manner in a comprehensive unit: shelves of perforated sheet metal and tubular steel or a range of flush-doored, barely perceptible cupboards along one wall in the high tech or hard edge room; a glass-fronted cabinet, for this old timer is back in favour in modern – often pastel coloured – dress; or, in the old-fashioned parlour it could be a small chiffonier or sideboard. Whatever you have, go for looks which contribute to your overall scheme, as well as for function.

This is a room where existing doors may be moved to make more wall space available, bookshelves built around and above doors to utilize every inch of space and a large fireplace surround redesigned in a less dominating and space-eating style, or even removed to leave a hole-in-the-wall grate. Imitation gas log fires are not always as kitsch as they sound, and can be convenient for such a room.

If you want to fit in a dining table, drape it with a heavy cloth to conceal its primary purpose in the traditional room; select one of the fold-down

varieties which doubles as a console table; or have a simple slab of wood or sheet steel, hinged to a wall at the kitchen end of the room.

Hang blinds – fabric, Venetian, paper or cane – at your windows in the pure, sparse room, taking care that they reveal and complement the window shapes and mouldings; rich fabric curtains are appropriate for the cosy type of room. Have translucent blinds or lacy sheers across the windows if you want to obscure a bleak view.

Urban rooms gather and display dirt

with consummate ease. Decorate accordingly. Cover walls in pale, modern versions of cabbage-rose wallpaper if cosiness is your style, in panels of laminated plastic, in pvc sheeting, air-brushed clouds on pale paint, washable gloss paint in a pastel colour, or mirror glass in sheet or tile form if you are more adventurous.

Floors should have one overall covering to increase the apparent size. Studded rubber, heavy duty linoleum and painted or polished boards would suit a minimalist approach, fitted

carpet (of the speckled berber variety, for example) if the aim is traditional.

Go for big, statuesque houseplants rather than a fluster of little pots. Select pictures and other accessories with care, for they will crowd in on you in a small space. And since city rooms often need artificial light during the day, aim for interesting effects: many table lamps, especially those from Italy, are sculptural pieces in their own right, and you can use uplighters – to create dramatic shadows or throw large-leafed houseplants into silhouette.

1   A handsome bay window – the natural place to put such an obvious scene-stealer as a grand piano. Individual blinds help to emphasize the slender proportions of the windows.

2   An architectural period piece, where panelling, cornices and woodwork are all 18th century originals. Subdued furniture looks as if it has always lived there.

3   A carefully restored terraced house, with shutters, and window panes still intact. Built-in shelving echoes the classical woodwork.

4   A contemporary interpretation of the traditional urban living room. The fireplace has a minimal surround, and the sofa is positioned to emphasize the striking semi-circular window.

2

3

4

RURAL LIVING

Whether it is large or small, the rural living room will have a greater feeling of space and relaxation than its urban counterpart. The inevitable focus is the fireplace and if this has been blocked up it should be reinstated forthwith. Have log fires in winter and huge, informal arrangements of wild flowers during the summer.

Keep furniture arrangements relaxed and comfortable. Deeply upholstered unit seating is appropriate if the room is large enough, with footstools and a mass of cushions to foster the relaxed and restful atmosphere. Occasional tables should be on a grand scale to take the jugs of flowers, tobacco jars and bowls of fruit which epitomize country living. Shelves should be broad, cupboards capacious and console tables long to take the welter of *objets trouvés* – cups won at gymkhanas, framed family groups, carved wooden fruit, and so on – which inevitably gather dust in rustic rooms.

If dining must take place in the room have a table big and sturdy enough to seat large groups of people. And in this room alone avoid such materials as plastic, chromed steel and (in any quantity) glass, for this will diminish the carefully cultivated rural atmosphere. It has to be wood or nothing.

Floors of natural materials are also well suited to rural living: quarry tiles, flagstones or bricks will be expensive but suitably mellow looking and long lasting, whilst wood flooring (much cheaper if self-layed in the new laminated strips) gives a traditional and warm gleam. In line with the general feeling of lavishness, rugs should be large and thick, with strong modern or traditional patterns. Coir or rush matting are inexpensive and appropriate materials in which to effect a short-term overall cover-up, as well as suffering dirty boots with equanimity. Fitted carpet is not so practical, but does not necessarily look out of place in this type of room.

Have good quality cotton curtains, full and heavy, in light, pretty prints or pale plain colours. Hang them from wooden poles but avoid the swagging, flouncing and festooning which have a definite metropolitan flavour.

Walls can be of unplastered,

fair-faced brick or stonework, but the strong feeling for formality – even in such a country room as this – makes light, painted walls a more appropriate choice, perhaps decorated with formal stencil designs in soft colours. Pale, tiny flowered wallpaper might be appropriate if dirty-fingered children are part of your household.

The country room should never be brightly lit. Dim corners and pools of warm lamplight are the very essence of this room. So avoid overhead lighting, stick to shaded table and standard lamps, and have candles in beautiful holders, or even the occasional oil lamp, in positions where they will not prove a fire hazard. They will not only provide a romantic light, but will be a godsend in the inevitable power failures that periodically hit the country.

Unless you want to over-gild the lily, avoid hanging pictures of bunches of flowers or country landscapes. Fine architectural line drawings, family portraits or strong modern abstracts will sweep away any faint hint of sentimentality that may have crept in.

1 A collection of old baskets and other rural implements dangling from the ceiling over a well-scrubbed table helps to give the atmosphere of a traditional country cottage. If you are going to try it, make sure you have enough objects: one shopping basket swinging in the breeze will simply look silly.

2 An antique stove, positioned in front of an old grate is a more efficient way of using solid fuel than an open fire, and can be equally picturesque.

3 Pretty pastel pink walls provide a good base on which to build up patterns, layer upon layer. The curtains, the loose furniture covers, even the tablecloth all help to create a genteel rural look.

4 Clutter needs to be handled with care if you don't want your home to turn into a junk shop.

MERGING WITH THE GARDEN

Rooms which are almost part of the garden have become popular, along with a growing interest in gardening and a fashion for landscaped areas near the house. This is certainly not confined to large country properties, and if anything the best examples can be seen in small urban back yards. People who have put a great deal of thought into the space around their home want to enjoy it to the full, and the outdoor/indoor living room is the result.

Keep a nucleus of static furniture in the room (cupboards, shelves, sofas and perhaps the dining table), but have it in pale wood such as beech, ash, oak or light paint colour to sustain the outdoor look; and stick to thin, washable fabrics for the upholstery. Aim to have some furniture which will be just as happy inside as out, and which is not too heavy to be easily transported. Cane furniture is perfect for this purpose particularly as there are excellent designs, often luxuriously cushioned, for armchairs, sofas and chaises longues. Look too for some of the pretty Lloyd loom chairs which are enjoying a revival. Canvas seated folding chairs (with the canvas in clear, bright pastels, for example) can be moved freely between the two areas, and be used for dining, as can trolleys and small occasional tables. Elegant folding tables, made of wood, or of steel lacquer or stove enamel in soft colours, would be an excellent choice for eating outside or in. If this is a dining/living room, keep the dining table static to avoid a total strip-down of the room on summer days; have a table outside which will survive summer showers.

Flooring should be hard and easily cleaned to accommodate the inside/outside activities: quarry tiles, brick or vinyl (of which good patterns do exist but are hard to find) would all be suitable. Thwart any suggestion of winter bleakness with washable, long-haired flokati rugs which are

1 **Architect Ian Ritchie designed this all-glass house at Fluy with its living room looking directly over the garden. Sitting inside feels just like being out in the open, surrounded by flowers.**

2

4

2 The feeling that the garden has crept right through the huge glass windows enlivens this narrow living area.

3 A new house should be sited to make the most of existing trees and shrubs. Here they form a major decorative element in the room – almost like a vivid green wallpaper. In these circumstances it's best to leave the walls plain white.

4 Even the tiniest of internal courtyards can be fitted with glass walls to bring in colour and sunshine.

3

available in colours as well as in their natural off-white.

Don't feel obliged to drape windows with great flower-patterned curtains to conform to the in/out theme: this is not a conservatory or a garden room. Instead, shop for large modern prints in soft colours which will invoke the garden in a much more subtle way, or consider folding wooden shutters as an alternative. They can be left in their natural state or painted a strong colour to give this end of the room presence when the garden has to be shut out. Walls too should be treated imaginatively. Reflect the precious outside view with strategically hung mirror glass. Bring the garden into the room with *trompe-l'oeil* decoration. Have a trellis for climbing houseplants. Hang textured paper to blur the line between inside and outside wall textures. But in all cases, keep the colours light, pale and fresh.

Keep ornaments and other accessories to a minimum or they will be left homeless when furniture moves outside. Concentrate on banks of healthy plants, some of which will move outside in the warm months, perhaps in one of the wrought iron jardinières which the Victorians loved; reproductions are now available from shops selling garden furniture.

There should be a high level of light, not only to keep the plants healthy but because this is inherently a bright, cheerful place. Hang pendant lights or train spotlights over your main plant arrangements, and use dimmers to keep lighting low when you are sitting inside but enjoying a floodlit view of the night garden. Have fat candles in glass containers for carrying inside or out, and keep an eye out for the new battery rechargeable lamps from Italy which will become cheaper as the idea is copied.

LOOSE-FIT LIVING

If your way of life is established and fixed, all well and good. Many of us, however, can see change in the near future, and then more change. People become increasingly prosperous, job prospects demand a move, children are born and grow up, life becomes less busy on retirement. Plan, at least a little for such changes.

Unit seating is a good buy; you can start with one or two pieces, add more as finances and the family grow, and rearrange what you have as family life changes. Some pieces can go to bedrooms when teenagers want privacy away from the family living room, others can be grouped in large configurations as entertaining takes a grander form – and so on.

Inexpensive carpet is judged a bad buy for rooms which are likely to suffer wear and tear. If that is all you can afford, use it anyway, but cover worn spots later with good rugs.

You may want expensive uphol-stered furniture right from the beginning, but are planning to start a family. Have loose covers to preserve it during the sticky-fingered years, then reveal it in all its glory when the home is more civilized.

Acquire a storage system gradually as your needs expand, and vary its arrangement, not only within the room but elsewhere in the home. For example: a new dining room can acquire some of the low level cupboards, so making space for another armchair in the living room; a writing table section can be moved to a bedroom where someone is studying for exams; more shelves can be added as your library grows. Think about your room in this flexible and open-minded way, then it will adapt to your evolving lifestyle.

The living room/bedroom
It may be that you need flexibility of a different order: that you want relative formality during the day but a place to sleep at night. You can either make it

1

1 When space is tight, or there is a pressing need to put an existing living room to other uses, a generously proportioned hall can make a valuable new living area.

2 A long narrow living room can be difficult to furnish. This one opens directly onto a dining room, and it is important to plan the two together. A pair of sofas face each other, defining the living area, while the dining table is positioned on the same axis through the archway.

3 Despite the inviting fireplace, this room has an air of ambiguity, its function deliberately undefined.

4 The work area in the corner of this living room is civilized by oil paintings on the walls and screened by the two striking Rietveld chairs.

2

perfectly clear to all that this is the case, or strive to conceal any hint of the room's dual function.

In the first case, make a bold statement of the sleeping arrangements. Build a sleeping alcove (from a wood or Dexion structure) which incorporates its own storage and lighting; make a sleeping gallery if the room is high; box off space in the centre if it is very large, as has been done in several warehouse conversions. Young people often sleep simply on a floor mattress or a Japanese futon; by adding cushions and shelves, you could make this a daytime conversation and lounging place in a less conventional style of room.

If concealment is your aim, avoid a cushioned divan shoved against a wall; this looks incurably like a bed-sitter. Some wall storage systems – expensive ones – have beds which let down with the greatest of ease, and of course there are in-built provisions for housing the sleeper's possessions. Sofa beds are totally discreet, but a capacious cupboard will be an essential for storing bedding (use a duvet for simplicity). A common or garden bed can be hidden from everyday life by a free-standing screen made of bamboo, perforated metal, wood and paper, or wood and cane. A more permanent structure could be faced with mirror glass, decorated as an extension of the adjacent wall, or hung with pictures, and should be designed to contribute to the room's general aesthetic appeal.

Multi-purpose living

Perhaps you simply want to use your living room for a particular purpose during part of the day: as an office or sewing room, for instance. Again, you can approach the matter in one of two different ways.

First, if you have the space, you can allocate a whole area of the room to this specific use. Arrange everything necessary along one short wall of the room, or in an alcove or chimney recess, and then make provision for it to be totally cut off when not in use.

It is surprising how much can be accommodated along even a short length of wall: a pull-down table for cutting out garments, a table to house the sewing machine with drawers below for patterns, scissors and threads and shelves above for bolts of material. Similarly, provision can be made to house the home office. In both cases make sure you have adequate artificial light shining directly onto the work surface, typewriter or sewing machine (not onto the worker), and if an outside wall is involved investigate the possibility of making a small window to enliven the working day. Everything can be shut away behind folding doors, sliding panels, pull-down blinds, a free-standing screen or, at worst, a curtain, when the working part of the day is over.

Alternatively, make a virtue out of necessity and organize your work space so elegantly that you would balk at the very idea of hiding it away when it is not in use.

Choose a desk or cutting out table which will, whether it is antique, modern or just plain traditional, stand in its own right as a handsome piece of furniture and select everything that goes on it, under it or above it for a visual as well as practical contribution. Typewriters, sewing machines, scissors, pencil holders, notebooks, telephones, desk lamps and filing cabinets can be very well designed objects and make a considerable aesthetic contribution to the impact of your room. You could choose to have the majority of things in one colour (or in complementary colours), and make sure that when they are not being used all the small objects are in immaculate order, rather like a still life. Box files could be colour co-ordinated, and neatly grouped on a shelf along a nearby wall; fabrics similarly arranged in perfect order and colour groups for their decorative appeal; cotton reels neatly stacked on wooden poles; and small plastic or metal storage towers fitted with castors so that they can be switched into any convenient position when not actually being used.

Making aesthetic demands of your working materials so that they do not spoil the harmony of your living room will become second nature after a while. Watch out though that this painstaking care does not assume obsessional proportions.

FURNITURE

Whether you choose antique or contemporary furniture for your living room, you will find that the range available for such essential pieces as sofas, chairs, coffee and occasional tables, bureaux and storage units is vast. This wide choice is matched by an equally wide price range, so before you go out and spend a fortune on furniture for your living room, consider the alternatives and shop around for pieces that will suit your own style.

Sofas and chairs

You must consider three things when buying sofas and chairs: looks, comfort and wearability, and the order of importance will vary according to your personal values and inclinations, and your lifestyle.

Looks Like most things nowadays, furniture design is extremely varied. Almost any style can look contemporary, though the following are still out in front:

1 Softly padded and puffed sofas and chairs whose structure is concealed.

2 The classic modern designs of many years ago. Most were conceived in the late '20s and early '30s by architects and are still being made. They include Petit and Grand Confort armchairs and a chaise longue by Le Corbusier; Charles Eames' lounging chair (from the '50s), Mies van der Rohe's Brno chair and many of Charles Rennie Mackintosh's turn-of-the-century designs.

3 Refurbished relics of the '30s, particularly the broad-armed, rather chunky style, then often covered in cut-moquette or mock leather, but whose straight lines look good in modern covers.

4 Blocks of foam cut to a variety of seat shapes, with padded covers for comfort.

5 Steel-framed furniture with its high tech allusion and – at best – reasonable comfort.

6 Wood-framed furniture with the emphasis almost entirely on pale woods such as beech, ash and oak which are sometimes stained in pretty colours. Upholstery has the fashionable puffed-up quality.

7 The quirky Memphis style, originating in Milan, which has only a toehold in Britain as yet, and comprises strange, asymmetric shapes, unexpected alliances of laminated plastics and conventional upholstery, plus strong, clashing colours and printed designs.

Comfort Opt for whichever style takes your fancy but insist on comfort. This may depend on shape rather than softness. Test sofas and chairs for the correct back height and seat depth. If your feet fail to make contact with the ground, or conversely if your knees come up to meet your chin, the seat depth is wrong. If a structural bar digs into a vertebra, or your head is thrust forward by a wadge of upholstery, or you feel your neck is not getting the support it deserves, the back has been designed incorrectly for your needs. Look elsewhere.

If knitting is a favourite pastime, choose a chair whose arms won't clash with yours. If you – or any of your visitors – are elderly or infirm, avoid low, deeply upholstered chairs which are difficult to drop into or rise out of. If you like to read or write in an armchair, make sure that your body has sufficient support to do so in comfort. If you want to curl up or sprawl out, look for low, deep-seated furniture.

Wearability Cheap furniture may be all you can afford (or want, for a temporary home). It will not normally be invested with the same wearing qualities, either in strength of frame or durability of covering, as more expensive products. With that in mind, choose upholstered furniture which has a strong – not wobbly – frame; printed or textured fabrics rather than smooth plain ones to conceal dirt (as additional protection have your fabrics sprayed with Scotchguard, a protective film against spills); removable covers for easy cleaning (or at the very least, zip-off cushion covers); and wooden or tubular steel rather than upholstered arms if your home is shared by wreckers such as small children and teenage tearaways. Tightly upholstered arms will show shiny grease marks and may easily fray within months of purchase. Many of the more expensive furnishing fabrics are pre-treated with stain repellent to cope with the rough and tumble of family life.

1

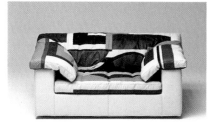

5

1 With all-glass walls breaking down the barriers between indoors and outdoors, unit seating helps to make the most of the view, without spoiling the spacious feel of this room.

2 Dining and living areas flow into each other here. But their individual character is clearly established by the consistency that is shown in the choice of a matching range of sofas and a contrasting design for the dining table and chairs.

3 Simple patterns for the covers on this unit seating help to set the mood for this relaxed little alcove, and at the same time to camouflage its awkward and cramped proportions.

4 Le Corbusier originally designed his Grand Confort armchairs in black leather upholstery. White gives them a very different look that helps to establish the sleek and sophisticated tone of this highly calculated post modern interior. With soft and diffuse lighting, the room exudes quiet glamour.

5 A modern variation of the traditional upholstered sofa from the Italian firm of Zanotta.

FURNITURE

1   Two more permuta-
tions on the ever popular
theme of the club
armchair from Zanotta.

2   A cheerfully relaxed
living room, in which a
whole range of contrasting
influences is at work – from
the 1960s revivalism of
the egg chair, to the svelte
grand hotel flavour of the
huge sofa.

3   Le Corbusier's black
leather Basculant chairs
and chaise longue
highlight the stylish
sophistication of this
interior. A striking
contrast is provided by
the 1950s parody of a
Sheraton table in pale
wood with exaggerated
Queen Anne legs.

4   Two bent plywood
armchairs designed by
Alvar Aalto, teamed with
his trolley give a
consistent theme to what
would otherwise be a
slightly stark,
conventional modern
interior.

5   Yet another applica-
tion for Le Corbusier's
ever popular chaise
longue. With a big, open
room like this, it is
possible to use the
furniture to define
different spaces.

frame; solid wood tables, many in the paler woods such as beech, ash or pine, some of which are stained black or, more fashionably, pale and pretty colours; and lacquered fibreboard tables, which achieve good looks at low cost.

The traditional oblong and rectangular shapes have been augmented by much less formal designs, often of Italian inspiration. There is for instance one table which is best described as a truncated version of a circular stairway, the treads floating outwards to form resting places for all the impedimenta normally accommodated on a coffee table. You might prefer a two- or even three-tiered table, with some of the tiers partially cut away to give an attractive stepped appearance, or a circular table (some of these are also two-tiered and may have part of the upper tier cut away).

Marble topped tables can still be found but most have, for some reason, assumed a somewhat passé character. Very large tables for the eye-catching type of arrangement are hard to come by; commission a designer to make one to your special requirements, or push several indentical smaller tables together, or, if you are penurious but handy, saw the legs off an out-dated dining table, strip it of varnish and paint, and lacquer or stain it to your personal taste.

Other occasional tables – sofa tables, consoles and those which lurk in corners to support pot plants, table lamps and television sets – are not available in quite such a plethora of styles. But, whereas low coffee tables were unknown until recent times, the occasional table, in a variety of manifestations, has been made for centuries. So search antique or junk shops. Simple modern console tables (some of which ingeniously convert into dining tables) are made in wood, or comprise a glass top set on trestles, or may consist of chipboard panels faced in matt laminated plastic. You can also find similar round, square or oblong corner tables. Battered round tables from a junk shop, or inexpensive chipboard circular tops on a simple base can be covered in floor length drapes to conceal a multitude of sins.

Wearability   Most modern wood furniture, treated with matt polyurethane lacquer, is mercifully immune to ring marks, and plastic laminates or lacquered surfaces are equally accommodating. Marble on the other hand is not and retains every wet mark or stain. Similarly, antique furniture must be protected from abuse, though less valuable second-hand furniture can be treated with a coat of matt or high gloss lacquer.

Watch for vulnerable edges and corners; a wooden lipping to a plastic table is more than just a decorative feature and will inhibit the chips likely to occur in the rough and tumble of family life. Champfered corners make damage less likely at another danger spot. Remember that glass surfaces, even when they are very thick or Georgian wired for strength, will rarely withstand an onslaught from the really determined child armed with a heavy instrument. Avoid them till family life is less hazardous.

Storage

Storage ranges, especially those incorporating cupboards as well as open shelving, offer an easy and tidy way of housing the paraphernalia which accumulates in most living rooms, and they can generally be bought or extended piecemeal as cash and needs dictate. Vastly diverse in styles and quality – pale and woody, glass and steel, perforated and tubular steel are all available – they are not difficult to find or select. But do not disregard other options. Individual, free-standing pieces of storage, whether a fine 18th century bureau, a tall narrow piece of lacquered furniture comprising shelves concealed behind a pull-down tambour shutter, or a zany, asymmetric Italian piece, have infinitely more character and will often be more appropriate in a carefully conceived living room.

If you are broke, think up some extemporization like several old-fashioned filing cabinets lacquered white and adorned with gleaming new chromed handles. If your space is limited, look out for occasional tables which incorporate drawers and perhaps even cupboards.

Tables

Looks and wearability must be your considerations when choosing the hard (as opposed to upholstered) furniture which will go into your living room. It is comparatively easy to buy, for whatever your aesthetic style and however low your budget, there is a broad selection available.

Looks   As with upholstered furniture, any style can look appropriate, such is the comprehensiveness of the current approach to design. Coffee tables can be chosen which, though made of chipboard, are smartly faced (legs included) in matt, laminated plastic; the fashionable pale colours, as well as many others, are all to be found, and at several small specialist furniture shops it is possible to have this type of table made to your chosen size and shape. Other choices include tables with glass tops set into a wooden or tubular steel

RELAXING

Whatever your style, and whether you live in town, country or suburb, the living room will be a place where you want to relax, either alone or with guests. With this in mind, have comfortable furniture, and be sure that it is not of the looks-good-but-feels-lousy variety. Comfortable seating is not necessarily the softest however, so test all chairs and sofas for back-support, ease of movement and leg room before you buy.

Unless you are an excessively orderly, adult family, do not opt for fragile decorations and furniture in this much-used room. Constant yelling at small children, muddy gardeners or people with newsprint all over their fingers to " be careful what you're doing" will send any hope of relaxation flying out of the window. Both furniture and decoration should be chosen for their ability to camouflage grime and withstand hard, daily knocking about. At the very least, furnishing fabrics, wallcoverings and carpets should be easy to wash or clean.

Think about your personal lifestyle. It would be crazy to have valuable ornaments if the family includes boisterous teenagers, nerve-racking to have polished floors and rugs if someone in the house is ageing and arthritic, a constant irritation if you lumber yourself with house plants which are on the verge of death because you are so often away or otherwise too busy to cosset them.

Make sure you have a soothing level of overall artificial light. But there must be adequate spotlighting for reading, sewing, piano playing and so on, unless eyesight and tempers are to be ruined. Similarly, unless you are deliberately ignoring and obscuring an ugly view, allow daylight to flood the room, unobstructed by dark blinds and heavy furniture. Have some chairs with their backs to a window for comfortable daytime reading, and writing tables or pianos placed so that daylight comes over one shoulder.

A strong, dramatic colour scheme is best reserved for a room in less constant use, such as the dining room. Anything too demanding will not only be a deterrent to calm and meditation, but may become positively infuriating

when you have sat with it just one evening too many. Soft pastels and misty greys, large washy prints and pale, plain fabrics will prove much more conducive to relaxation.

Aim for warmth (preferably through central heating) without stuffiness, and do not forget the therapeutic qualities of an open fire. Fix draughty windows, doors and fireplaces. Have too little furniture rather than too much, too few ornaments and pictures rather than too many. A cluttered, over-full room confuses the eye and therefore the mind, and can prove a minefield for the clumsy, disabled, elderly or just plain mischievous (not to mention the poor soul who has to clean the place). A room with minimal but comfortable furniture and few extraneous items in the shape of vases, pots, boxes and other mementos is, unless you are of an obsessively acquisitive temperament, likely to be the most restful and relaxing of all.

1

2

1   An old Paris factory is brought to life with fresh pastel colours, and a jungle of greenery. The bare bones of an old partition wall make a useful demarcation line between areas.

2   Book-lined walls and sober colours give this living room the relaxed calm of a study. Full of personal mementos, the shelves have been carefully arranged to show off books and pictures to their best advantage without looking contrived.

3   A collection of odd, even bizarre objects is successfully brought together to create a playful and informal living room, where every corner contains a fresh surprise.

4   Old floorboards, sanded, waxed and polished to a high gloss, with exposed brickwork and a flickering wood fire give a room a texture and atmosphere that are still unbeatable when it comes to creating a relaxing ambience.

3

4

TAMING THE HARDWARE

Whether you are about to go out in search of the most expensive and sophisticated high performance sound system that money can buy, or simply want to plug in an old black and white portable television set, stop and think about what you are doing first. Few such apparently trivial decisions can have so enormous a potential impact on the way that you end up using your home. Too often, even in otherwise meticulously planned interiors, the TV set or the hi-fi system are sited almost accidentally and without enough consideration paid to their implications for the rest of the design scheme.

Carelessly locate a giant and unwieldy colour television set in your living room, and it immediately puts down roots, ruthlessly making itself the unchallenged centre of attraction, forcing armchairs to swivel in its direction, dominating the lighting scheme, and dragging all the members of the household in to pay daily homage. Even if they don't want to watch the screen, the room with the TV set in it quickly becomes the most likely place to find other people in a home.

On the other hand, if you put the television in the kind of kitchen in which you already eat most of your meals, you will rapidly find the most comfortable of your easy chairs migrating there too, leaving the living room proper a dusty and under-used household backwater. It is a classic case of the tail wagging the dog.

An audio system doesn't have quite the same power as a television, unless it is a question of the sheer nuisance value of its potential noise output. But its physical presence can be even more disruptive. A mass of wires trailing like spaghetti over the floor seems to be an almost inevitable accompaniment to even the most sophisticated record player. And even such apparently minor details as the length of the cable connecting the speakers with the amplifier can determine the position of your bookshelves if that is where you want to keep your speakers. Sometimes even the position of so humble an element as an electric socket can become the main constraint on a room's design – governing the position of the record turntable, and so almost every other decision about the layout of a room and its contents. The solution to the problem at least is simple. Make sure you have as much flexibility as possible; that means plenty of power points, and lots of spare cable.

Audio hardware is slowly becoming more civilized; miniature systems are now available that are nowhere near as visually intrusive as their larger predecessors, but capable of giving equally good results. The fetish for component hi-fi has declined in favour of complete systems with each part made by the same manufacturer and visually complementing the rest. Best of all, rack systems are dispensing with cable spaghetti; but we are having to cope with more and more electronic equipment jostling for a place in our living rooms. Video recorders and games, and home computers have all made huge advances into the domestic interior in the last few years. And most of them are still designed by manufacturers who deploy the maximum of glitzy chrome and techno-flash to attract the purchaser's eye, which is all very well in a shop full of equally glittery competitors, but

1 Choose a low shelf for your TV set if you plan to keep it in the same place permanently.

2 A portable set is the least obtrusive way of putting a TV in the living room. Keep it under a shelf when not in use.

3 For enthusiasts, audio visual equipment can become the raison d'être for an entire room. There's no reason why it shouldn't be designed to look good too.

4 A steel and chrome hi-fi system can be a rude intrusion in pastel rooms like this one. It is best to hide it away.

5 A music system built into a storage wall should allow space to store records and tapes next to the playing equipment, and also room to position the speakers for optimum sound quality.

6 Architect Eva Jiricna designed this glossy black housing for a TV and video recorder to go with a Deco-inspired interior.

hideously out of place at home. Even the television set is only just beginning to come out of its equivalent of the Detroit tin tail fin and chrome phase, towards better looking and more subtle domestic styling.

However, dealing with all this equipment needn't simply be a question of avoiding the pitfalls and the disasters. With some thought and advance planning, it can be deployed in such a way as to become a positive asset to an interior scheme.

Start by thinking about audio and video equipment on a strategic level. Don't let them dictate the way you live: use them instead to help you make the most of all the space that you have at your disposal. If you have plenty of space to play with – in an older house or apartment, possibly a series of rooms of indeterminate function where it is

never quite clear what the drawing room, or the family room, will be used for when there is a living room available as well – think about the possibility of creating two alternative focuses. The main television set can be the draw for the living room, while the audio system, tape deck and records can be put in another room to act as a counterbalancing attraction. It might need to be reinforced by an additional focal point, perhaps a fireplace, or a wall of bookshelves or even the telephone. The result, if the strategy works, is that you end up with two distinct rooms, each with its own character, rather than simply putting all the electronics in one room and plunging the household into a continual struggle for screen time.

On a more detailed level, audio systems have been part of domestic life

long enough now for all but the enthusiastic few to take sound quality for granted, and to concentrate on selecting the system that looks best in the setting that you want, rather than on woofers and tweeters.

Discreet neutral black or grey finished systems will look more at home in a variety of settings than bulky chrome or teak faced units. Both audio systems and television sets in particular will look less intrusive if they can sit naturally on the furniture, rather than sitting square in the middle of a room, or piled up on a special storage unit like some household shrine. Building hi-fi systems into furniture on the other hand needs to be approached with caution. It is an idea that can easily end up looking like a kitsch piece of James Bond style gimmickery. Worse still it can make equipment difficult to

maintain, and even more difficult to replace when it needs upgrading.

Developments in audio in recent years have turned mainly towards miniaturizing systems. Even the record deck, once the largest sized component because of the need to accommodate albums, has been shrinking. There are now fold-out decks available with retractable turntables which can sit comfortably on top of amplifiers and tuners and, unlike the Perspex-covered variety, do not need any headroom for access. The compact disc players developed using laser technology are equally convenient to use.

If you want music on tap throughout the house, think about getting an amplifier powerful enough to drive more than just one pair of speakers. If you have a taste for gadgetry you can buy an elaborate infra red remote control handset to stop and start it as you move around.

Thanks to the Japanese, Italian and Danish manufacturers, who are now treating the design of the exteriors of their television sets with the same care they lavish on the cathode tube itself, TV sets are looking a great deal better. But home video equipment still has a long way to go before it is sufficiently civilized to look comfortable in a living room. Much of what is currently available looks bulky and aggressive and has even more straggling cable on show than the worst audio system. For the time being at least, it is probably best banished to a cupboard, if one can be found or placed close to the TV screen. Sony however have begun to produce a better alternative with their Profeel unified video system which includes a screen, a tuner, video and stereo speakers that are all designed to look good together, and can be built up step by step as modular components.

In a cramped room where space is at a premium, it is particularly important to keep the television in its place. A portable that can be moved to the bedroom or the kitchen is a useful alternative to the free-standing full size set. Or else put the set on a purpose made swivelling arm-stand bolted to a wall or piece of furniture, where it will take up less valuable floor space, and can be angled toward the viewer.

4

5

6

DINING ROOMS

Eating at home is not just a question of refuelling. Of course it can mean grabbing a snack on the run in the kitchen, or tucking into a microwaved sandwich whilst watching television. But it is also one of the most important forms of home entertainment in its own right, the ingredients being good food, wine and company.

Eating in provides the excuse for bringing old friends into the home, for consolidating new friendships, even for impressing the boss. It is a chance for food buffs to exercise their culinary skills on a captive audience of fellow gourmets, or simply for relaxed family gatherings. It is not surprising then to find that the dining room is assuming more and more importance. It needs to be tailored to cater for any or all of these functions, and to provide the background for these different styles of eating to take place. Just as gourmet food will not taste the same served on paper plates, so the atmosphere of a dining room will have a crucial effect on how a dinner party works, even perhaps on how good the food looks.

A dining room needs to provide an appropriate setting for a meal in the way that a stage set complements a play. It needs to be arranged and situated so that food can be served quickly and conveniently. But it should also have a sympathetic enough setting to encourage late night conversations over after-dinner brandies.

Depending on the size and shape of your home, a dining room can assume vastly different forms. It may be squashed into the corner of a kitchen, or else offer full-blown chandeliered splendour, with starched white tablecloths and silver. Interestingly, despite the fact that the ever-shrinking space of modern houses has forced the virtual disappearance of a room used exclusively for dining, more and more people are again trying to create proper formal dining rooms, an indication perhaps of how seriously food is being taken these days.

With careful planning and the judicious selection of furniture and accessories, it is still possible to create a real dining room, that will work well for other purposes too. A dining room can double as a spare bedroom for occasional use by visitors, or a place for children to do their homework. It could even fill in as a library.

There are also functional requirements to bear in mind; you don't want to be so far away from the kitchen that food gets cold on its way to the table, or that the cook feels isolated from the fun at dinner parties, but neither do you want cooking smells everywhere. And there are psychological factors at work too: colour, light and furniture can all be used to encourage intimacy or a sense of occasion according to your tastes.

This section looks at the way in which various styles can be used to create attractive dining rooms, what constitutes a formal dining room, and how to relate it to the rest of the house. The practical requirements of planning a dining room are also considered, together with ways of putting the room to other uses. There is also advice on choosing the right furniture, and the appropriate finishing touches, such as cutlery, glass and tableware, which are just as important.

3

1 The barest essentials for a dining room are a table and chairs, here chosen with care to produce an attractive café setting. An old kitchen table, resurfaced with a veined marble top, is complemented by the spaghetti chairs by Alias, while the tile finishes provide a stylish but functional background.

2 Architect Tom Brent's dining room has an air of faded, smoky opulence, created by layers of textured paint and stain finishes that spread over walls and table.

3 Cool white finishes, perfect for a summery dining room.

1

2

FINDING YOUR STYLE

Think about what makes a restaurant a success, and you will find that very often the same factors are at work in the domestic dining room too. Food has a great deal to do with it of course, but the surroundings in which it is consumed are just as important. Like a restaurant, a dining room can be kitted out in any style, from faded clubland traditional, to chrome and steel modern, with equal success, so long as the mood is right for the diners.

Just like a restaurant, a good dining room will be able to cope with different types of atmosphere and occasions. It needs to look sparkling when it is full of people, but it should not be intimidating when it is the setting for a dinner *à deux*. Otherwise, you will quickly find that your dining room becomes neglected and desolate.

Choose a style that is right for you. Your dining room should complement the way that you eat; if eating in is a casual, relaxed affair, then the room should be too. But if you enjoy experimenting with classic cuisine and drinking good wine, even dressing up for dinner, then why shouldn't your surroundings be designed to match?

Before choosing a style, you should think carefully about the character and proportions of the room itself. Equally, your dining room should be decorated in a way that is compatible with the rest of your home, so that you can, for example, redeploy extra chairs from the kitchen without them looking too obviously out of place.

The basic ingredients are simple; a table, of course, chairs, perhaps a sideboard. The style of the furniture you choose can be the dominating elements in your dining room, but much can also be achieved by thoughtful selection of lighting, colour schemes and accessories.

The key question is: what do you want this room to say about you? What do you want to put in it, either as ornament, for practical purposes, or to make it suitable for other functions too? Your choice will be influenced by a number of factors, not least the question of the particular purpose of the room. Is it going to be used solely as a dining room, or will it have other uses? It might even have to be shared with another function. Will it be in constant use as a family dining room, or will it be kept as a separate, more rarified sanctuary for entertaining only? If it is to be a general purpose dining room, how much special provision must be made for children?

The period of your house or apartment is important too. The better the architectural quality, the more appropriate it is to work within its style. Recreating the original panelled splendour of a Georgian dining room will be expensive, but very worthwhile. In an example of 1930s suburbia, a Deco dining room can be equally appropriate, and rather easier to complete the look. Victorian or Edwardian houses seem to adapt well to a variety of styles, and in post-war interiors you usually have a clean slate with which to work. The most important thing is to feel comfortable with what you have chosen, and to know that you can live with it.

Here we select four of the styles highlighted at the beginning of the book — country house, hard edge, eclectic and decorator — which particularly lend themselves to creating elegant dining rooms.

Country house

Just because you have a kitchen full of modern gadgets and a living room cluttered with jokey pieces of eclectic 1950s nostalgia, you need not be prevented from creating a flavour of the country house when you sit down to eat. The important thing however is not to overdo the style, especially if the house is modestly scaled and you do not intend to carry the theme through all the rooms.

A mellow old oak or pine table, scored and scratched, spotlit in the middle of a plain white walled room can be enough to give the relaxed informality that is the essence of this style. If the chairs are a motley mixture of stripped plain woods too, then so much the better. A Welsh dresser, or built-in cupboard with glass sliding doors containing a collection of pretty plates and cups could help. Sanded and sealed boards, or quarry tiles would be appropriate for the floor.

This is a practical and hard-wearing

FINDING YOUR STYLE

look, perfect for family dining, which, with a few extra flourishes, can be upgraded for more elaborate special occasions. Candles will always be a help, so will a vase of cut flowers caught in the middle of a spotlight. The characteristic of this look is a layering of patterns and ornaments: pictures arranged in groups, a clutter of objects on the mantlepiece. If you choose to apply the style to the whole house, you can really let rip with patterned wallpapers and curtains.

Folding wooden shutters on the windows, if you have them, are ideal. Otherwise, use heavy curtains to shut out the outside world at night. Try to include alternate light sources — perhaps a wide brimmed hanging pendant over the table for dramatic effects at night. But also have secondary sources to light up the walls for those occasions when you want to show off your pictures.

Hard edge

The hard edge look in the dining room is for tidy perfectionists alone. It is only for those who can live happily with glass and metal and rubber surfaces, who want a place for everything, who don't drop their food on the floor, who prefer simple shapes and plain colours — even monochrome — to busy patterns and cluttered informality. It has an air of purposeful efficiency — with chairs that are likely to fold and stack, or which are mounted on wheels, storage for cutlery and plates on open wire or plastic-coated racks.

Classic modern furniture is mixed in with high tech cult objects: mesh trollies, trestle tables and the like. This style is hopeless for children, unforgiving if you get it wrong, and likely to be noisy — cleaning plates away makes a terrible clatter on all the glass and metal — but when the effect does come off, it is stunning. In a monochrome colour scheme with nothing but hard, smooth finishes, the food on your plate will suddenly start to stand out like a work of art — provided your cooking can bear up to all the attention.

This is the look that appeals to people who own a pasta maker, who use a wok, who have a small machine that makes after-dinner espresso. It's monastic and expensive. Ideally the dining room will look as if there is nothing in it, bar the dining table — and even that might be a specially designed fold-down affair so that the room can be used for something else, very much in keeping with the high tech/hard edge ethic. Windows will be screened with Venetian blinds, floors will be covered in studded rubber.

Eclectic

The eclectic dining room is for those who do not take their eating too seriously, or who have a well-developed sense of period nostalgia. It is the jumble sale look made good, where furnishing is based on styles that used to be considered kitsch or plain bad taste. The characteristic look uses bright, brash colours and gritty, abrasive textures. Tables and chairs have splayed legs, the floor will be linoleum, colour schemes will involve a great deal of blue and red used next to each other.

It is possible to create this look in two ways. At the low budget end you can use real jumble sale furniture, bought piecemeal, or in lots at bargain prices. At the expensive end, you must be prepared to spend money on modern antiques, collector's pieces from the 1930s, '40s and '50s.

A '30s style dining room, for example, might consist of three-quarters pale oak panelling, and a solid suite of furniture in the same wood, including the sideboard. The finishing touches would be a parquet floor, peach, silver or cream paintwork, and a collection of appropriate memorabilia.

This kind of approach provides an opportunity to give your dining room a theme, and not only to put collector's pieces to practical use, but to display them in an appropriate setting.

Decorator

The decorator look applied to the dining room is rich and glossy, focusing attention on a simple but striking table, flanked by elegant chairs. The table might be light ash, or walnut, white Melamine and wood or glass. The chairs could be wood, tubular steel and leather, or even moulded plastic.

Background colours are predominantly white or neutral, allowing the furniture to stand out as art objects. Walls are adorned with prints, arranged in neat groups, or with large and flamboyant paintings. If your budget does not run to these lengths, framed posters will look just as good.

The floor could be polished wood, or possibly ceramic tiles, while plain coloured roller blinds might be the choice for the windows. Finished in pale colours these rooms will work well for daytime eating, while an appropriate lighting scheme will ensure that they translate for night-time use too. You might choose a modern classic pendant light over the main table in white, black or spun aluminium, with a floor-mounted uplighter to focus on another part of the room, for example.

1 Elaborately draped, full-size curtains emphasize the classic proportions of this room and provide a handsome setting for formal dining. An assortment of antique chairs complement one another and prove that it is not necessary to have a matching set.

2 Fifties revival is a well-established theme. Here it is given fresh emphasis with shroud-like curtains which echo the shape of the bent metal chairs and table legs.

3 Calculated eclecticism is achieved here by mixing Italian pop plastic furniture with Marcel Breuer modern classics and carefully selected Art Nouveau pieces.

4 Dark sombre walls are the perfect shell for an opulently laid table where eating takes place strictly at night time.

5 Revivalism meets post modernism; furniture and light fittings are brought up to date with a fresh, strong colour scheme.

6 The country style makes eating a relaxed affair. The ingredients are simple: pine dresser, a collection of crockery and a pretty tablecloth, which together create a comfortable, jovial mood.

THE PRACTICALITIES

No dining room, however attractive and inviting to the guests, will be successful if it is not also practical and functional for the host. Deciding how often and at what times of the day the room will be used, whether it will be wanted for other purposes as well, what size table you want, how food will be brought from the kitchen, where to keep all the necessary tableware and what sort of lighting will be most effective, all this must be done before rushing off to buy any furniture, materials or accessories.

Serving

If you are lucky enough to have a separate dining room, it should if possible be close to the kitchen. (The practicalities of dining in another room, such as the living room, are dealt with under Flexible Dining in this chapter; eating in the kitchen is covered in the chapter on Kitchens.)

The disappearance of the sideboard in many homes has meant that food is served instead in the kitchen or brought to the table and served from there. If the dining room has to be some distance from the kitchen a trolley may be handy for bringing the food and taking away dirty dishes. An electric 'hostess' trolley would keep dishes warm during the meal, and a less obtrusive hotplate on the sideboard does the same job.

Like the sideboard, a hatch connecting the kitchen to the dining room has lost popularity. Nevertheless it deserves consideration since it cuts out the bother of constant traipsing between the two rooms. The standard hatch needs to be wide and deep enough to provide space for dishes waiting on either side. It might combine with storage units below on one or both sides. Rather than double doors, consider a sliding cover for the hatch, possibly of glass so that it resembles a window.

Storage

The storage of china, cutlery and glass depends on how and where it is most used. If you do keep a dinner service for use on special occasions and want to separate it from your everyday tableware, then you may want to store it in a cupboard or sideboard in the dining room. It might, however, be more convenient to keep it in the kitchen where you have it to hand and can put it away easily after washing up. Precious wine glasses kept only for special meals are probably best kept in the dining room out of harm's way, as is the best cutlery. If you don't have a sideboard, some sort of storage unit — a neat chest of drawers or built-in cupboard — will be useful in the dining room for storing tablecloths, mats, napkins and so on.

Doors

The ideal dining room will share a communicating door with the kitchen. Consider one that is hinged to swing in both directions, provided that there is room enough on both sides. The door should not swing too violently so make sure that the return spring is gentle. A sturdy kick plate on the kitchen side will allow for ease of movement. The floor joint between the two rooms should be smooth and trip-proof — an aluminium or steel plate may help.

Another alternative is a stable door. This is a door split into two across the middle which provides a half screen but enables you to see into the dining area from the kitchen. It is particularly useful if you have small children about as you can keep an eye on them while shutting them out of a potentially hazardous area.

Walls and windows

Having decided on the most practical way of serving and clearing away an elaborate meal, your attentions can now turn to the decorations. Here, practicality need not be a prime consideration. Wear and tear is not as likely as in other rooms, and so you need to be less hesitant about using delicate finishes: walls could be painted white and hung with pictures, prints or posters; or they could be covered in fabric; or transformed into fantasy by a *trompe l'oeil* mural; windows might boast elaborate Roman or festoon blinds, or curtains of delicate lace or matt glazed chintz.

Dining rooms are often small, with little natural light available. If this is the case, steer away from dark walls; consider mirror tiles or *trompe l'oeil* paint techniques, such as marbling or a mural, to create an illusion of space. Blinds on the windows instead of full curtains always help a small room. As a general rule, wallpapers are best kept plain or simply patterned in a dining room; large dominating patterns tend to detract from the main focus: the beautifully laid table.

Floors

The flooring must be sensible, as well as in keeping with the style and atmosphere of the room. Wine will be spilled, and food trodden in, even in the smartest of dining rooms. Carpet, good-looking and warm though it undoubtedly is, may not be the best answer here. Consider some alternatives. Stripped and sanded floorboards, polished, painted or stencilled, look marvellous, especially against wood furniture, and are easy to keep clean. A more expensive, but very smart, wood finish is parquet. For a cheaper substitute, you could use pine, teak or cherry wood planks with cork backing and vinyl surface. Any of the more sophisticated looking kitchen floor finishes are suitable for the dining room: dramatic black and white vinyl tiles, for example, can be particularly effective with the right furniture.

Seating plans
All measurements are in centimetres.

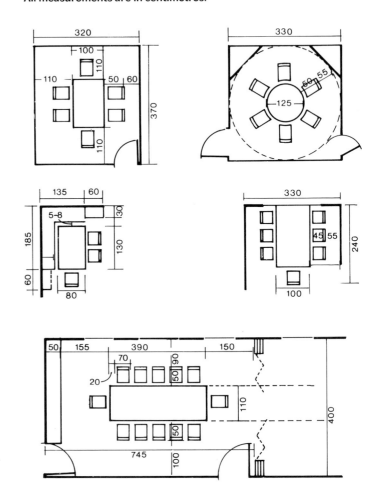

Lighting

A central light suspended over the dining table is often the best solution. It will look good even when not in use, and will flatter any table setting.

The height at which a suspended light is hung, however, is critical. You can work this out by seating two people opposite each other at the table. The shade should be neither so low as to obscure the other person's face, nor so high as to emit excessive glare. Use a rise-and-fall fitting if you want to adjust the height. The bulb should not be visible from any chair; choose one that is half-silvered to soften the glare. Additional or alternative lights should be carefully positioned. Lights are much more imaginatively designed these days and you can be more adventurous with your choice. An uplighter such as Arteluce's milk of magnesia blue 'Jill', for example, can look spectacular against a white wall without detracting from the table light.

Remember that a lighting scheme needs to help the room work for relaxed Sunday lunches, sparkling dinner parties and intimate suppers. Choose your fittings so that they offer a choice of lighting schemes: at the very least so that you can focus on the walls as well as the table. Spotlamps are very rarely as flexible as they appear at first sight. Consider instead a floor-standing uplighter which is much easier to move about, and has just as much impact.

Dining in comfort

Choosing the right dining table and chairs requires thought. Decide first the maximum number of people you will want to seat at one time. Then decide what shape of table you want: round, oval, square or rectangular. The diagrams will help you to choose the correct size of tables and chairs for comfort and to fit the room.

When you sit on a dining chair, there should be enough room to fit your legs under the table, and the chair itself should enable you to sit comfortably for sustained periods, with a supple seat and good back support. Space is critical, not only at the table, but also around it. You should allow enough room for each person to get easily in and out of their chair, and a wide enough passageway on all sides of the table.

1 This seemingly casual group of furniture has been studiously arranged to form a symmetrical still-life. The diverse collection of glass gives the table an aesthetic as well as a practical purpose.

2 Distinctive Art Deco dining chairs, a pretty flame stitch cloth and a simple flower arrangement ensure that this table looks as good when not in use as it does during meals.

3 The simplest of elements – bare painted walls, basic slatted folding chairs and black china are skilfully united by introducing a shiny foil cloth. The effect is to turn an otherwise plain room into one stylishly minimalistic.

FORMAL DINING

Any room that is used for entertaining needs to be something of a show-piece. If you are lucky enough to have the space for a separate dining room, then you have the chance to create a traditional focus for your home.

This will probably be the only room in your house that is used for just one purpose: dining. There should be no sewing machines hidden behind the door, no beds folding out of the wall, or piles of homework on the table. Your dining room is not a dumping ground. In order to achieve the appropriate air of formality, this room needs its own character that is separate from the rest of the house; and you can therefore be as uncompromising as you like about the style of decoration.

Achieving the look

The formal dining room need not be difficult to achieve — nor does it necessarily cost a lot of money. It does, however, require some serious planning and a little self-discipline. This is the one room where everything has its place, and, down to the last knife and fork, must justify its existence within your chosen scheme.

First decide, as far as possible, when you will be using the formal dining room. This will influence your choice of colours. Dark browns, rusts, terracottas and reds all look warm in candlelight, but can be harsh and unwelcoming in the cold light of day. Softer pastels, apricots and pink washes look very good at night and would probably be a better choice if you plan to use the room during the day as well.

A formal dining room should try as far as possible to be timeless. So avoid falling for the fashionable wall treatments. Instead, go for classic plain colours and smarten them by adding a frieze along the top of the wall, or by painting the dado rail and skirting boards a shade darker. A lighter effect is achieved with Regency striped wallpaper in pale greys or greens. And if you must, then a very subtle paint finish, perhaps bag-graining, would work well in a formal scheme, as long as the choice of accessories and furniture is kept plain and simple.

If you have a very small room, rather than attempt to make it seem

1 The essence of formal dining: mahogany table, candlelight, sparkling crystal, silver cutlery and perfect symmetry. The classical proportions are brought up to date with strong geometric patterns on the chair upholstery.

2 Do not be afraid to mix heavy china and antique chairs with contemporary details like silver Venetian blinds and a boldly patterned tablecloth when creating a formal look.

larger, try tenting the ceiling with a richly coloured fabric, and drape it down the walls, to create a warm Oriental cave, which combined with the appropriate furniture, looks very formal.

If you find painted walls too severe, then cover them in a lightly patterned fabric. Hang heavy, lined taffeta or wool curtains and steer clear of anything too fussy as this will detract from the formality. Brass or wooden curtain rails with rings can look effective. And if you are lucky enough to have original wooden shutters, paint them in a colour matching the walls, and you may find that you don't need curtains at all.

Lighting
Work out your lighting scheme in advance. No formal dining room should be without candlelight. But you must decide if you want to limit yourself to candlesticks, or whether to go all the way and invest in a candelabra with sconces for real candles, to hang above the table. The effect will be magical. If, however, you prefer to have electric lighting — a chandelier is very much in keeping — use a dimmer switch, thereby enhancing the glow of any candles on the table.

Furniture
A beautifully polished wooden table when laid with silver, crystal glasses and delicate china is hard to beat for formal dining. And it is worth investing in such a table — don't worry about matching chairs. If you don't own a table with a perfect surface then ensure you always use a crisp tablecloth. It is no longer necessary to match chairs to the style of the table, and even within the setting of a formal dining room, they should be comfortable.

Little other furniture is necessary in the formal dining room, although a corner cabinet, if you want to display objects, or even a sideboard for storage, would not look out of place.

Laying a formal table
The table should be the centre of attention. And the advantage of the formal dining room is that it is possible to lay the table well in advance of any meal. This means you can spend time planning it. Pick out one colour from your scheme, and match the tablecloth, napkins, plates and candles. Or cover the table with a sparkling white damask tablecloth, and lay it with crystal glasses, silver flatware, smart table mats and delicate china plates. Match your napkins and flowers. Glasses will make any table look formal if they are very slender, as will napkins, if they are beautifully folded.

There are endless colour permutations for your formal table setting — you could even match the food with the colour scheme — and it is worth bearing this in mind when choosing the colours for your dining room.

Finishing touches
Use the room to display favourite collections in carefully worked out groups. Arrange plates on the wall, or jugs, antique coffee cups, even glasses on shelves. Lining the walls with books — as long as they are not ragged old paperbacks, can look very good. One large picture on the wall as a point of focus for the diners, is probably better than lots of little ones. Avoid putting pot plants in the formal dining room. Invest in cut flowers when you need them, and never mix types of flower. One stark vase of irises or tulips looks much smarter than mixed flowers.

141

FLEXIBLE DINING

Although many homes do not have the luxury of a separate dining room, it is possible to improvise a dining arrangement in almost any room provided it has enough space. But it is essential to use whatever space you have at your disposal to its best advantage, and to be as flexible as possible; for example, folding chairs and tables are a good solution if space is tight and the dining area will only be used occasionally. Before buying any furniture, remember that when a room has a dual role, you must plan carefully what goes into it. Avoid overloading the room with furniture or you will end up with a confused area where neither of the room's roles is catered for properly.

Combined living and dining

This is a very familiar arrangement in many homes, and became popular when the vogue started for one large open plan reception room, as opposed to two smaller rooms. It is also an ideal combination in Victorian and Edwardian houses where two rooms have been made into one large area or are simply divided by folding doors. Where you do not have this natural division and there is less space for the dining area, you could move the table against a wall when it is not in use, and perhaps display photographs, ornaments or books to make it look more like part of the sitting room and less like a redundant dining table. The chairs can be dotted about the room until they are required for dining. On the other hand, if there is an alcove, the table and chairs might fit neatly into it, thus forming a dining area distinguishable from the rest of the room.

As a study

Dining rooms are often designated as rooms where children can do their homework. But they are also invariably little-used, rather cold and intimidating places. A warmer and more accommodating arrangement is to combine the study and dining room with furniture that subtly adapts for either use. The table could be any variation of a desk, drawing table or table with a practical Melamine or Formica top to cope with onslaughts from pens, crayons, typewriters and sewing machines, as well as hot dishes. An expandable table is a good choice if you don't always need a large surface on which to work. Folding wood, acrylic or polypropylene chairs are also a very useful alternative to regular dining chairs; even an attractive office chair would not necessarily look out of place at a dinner party. Cupboards and bookshelves are essential in a work room, so there should be plenty of storage space which can double for both study materials and dinner plates and cutlery.

As a guest room

This combination requires some clever thinking and space planning; beds are even further removed from the dining table than desks. Sofa beds are the obvious solution to this problem and would be quite appropriate in an informal dining room. Many shops now specialize in sofa beds and offer a large variety of styles and sizes. A cupboard will be almost vital in this room for storing both bedlinen and tableware — an armoire in mellowed wood, or similar antique cupboard, will look less out of place in the dining room than a modern wardrobe whose function would be difficult to disguise.

1 Two contrasting ceilings subtly distinguish the dining area from the work space in this room. The owner, who works from home, has created a dining area that can double as a conference room.

2 Kitchen, dining and living rooms are successfully blended into one in this informal area designed by architect Richard Rogers.

3

3 A dining area is cunningly created out of an alcove in the study. Bookshelves make an appropriate backdrop and office chairs double as smart dining chairs.

4 A specially designed glass table teamed with canvas folding chairs creates a gentle transition from dining to living room.

Making use of your hall

If it is spacious enough and not too draughty, a hall can make an interesting dining area. Provided that the space is not too narrow or an obvious thoroughfare, you can leave the table and chairs in place. If this is not possible, use folding chairs and a gate-leg table which can double up as a slim hall console table, a place for flowers, letters, or messages. Electric lighting is all important, especially if there are no windows. Light should obviously be focused on the table, but also, where possible, on another object in the hall to create further interest in an otherwise bare space. An uplighter in a corner for example, would do this effectively, or a downlighter focused onto a sculpture or a well-arranged vase of flowers.

The hall may already have stair cupboards, in which case storage for both dining purposes and general household clutter will be no problem. If there is no room for a cupboard, discipline yourself not to fill the hall with paraphernalia — people will not enjoy eating next to an overflowing coat rack or an umbrella stand.

4

FURNITURE

Dining room furniture seldom has to perform its primary function for more than a fraction of the day. For the rest of the time, your table and chairs will just sit idly. If you buy carefully they can be redeployed elsewhere in the house, or pressed into service for other purposes, such as sewing or homework. Keep all this in mind when you are choosing your dining room furniture. Can your table be moved easily? Is it too fragile to withstand the pounding of a typewriter?

Do not forget that dinner is a variable feast. Any number can take part, from one to as many guests as you can cope with. Your furniture ought to be comfortable with both extremes. This can be achieved with an adjustable table which has extra leaves or equally by bringing in another table and camouflaging the difference with a cloth. If you are buying a table with this strategy in mind, make sure that it is the right height: it is remarkable how frequently 'put-together' tables don't match.

Also consider the effect that the shape of your table has on conversation — if you have enough room to choose. Squares and circles bring people closest together, but round tables do not co-exist very easily with other shapes; long, thin rectangles are easiest to serve to, but do tend to limit people's conversations to their immediate neighbours.

If you are prepared to keep your dining room furniture out of action for much of the day, then you should certainly make sure that it looks as good when it is standing idle as it does when set up for a dinner party.

If on the other hand space is at a premium, choose your furniture with a dual role in mind, or make sure that it is designed to fold or stack up out of the way. A good cheap solution for a temporary table is to put a flush panel door on trestle legs — which will stack flat when it is not needed.

Remember that eating is inevitably a messy affair, so choose surfaces that will clean easily, or be prepared always to use a tablecloth. A glass table may look glamorous, but is seldom very pleasant to eat off — the inevitable stains are unpleasant, and the noise can be too disturbing for comfort.

Table legs present another practical problem, which is worth considering. Round tops with a single central support are the most flexible and convenient — there are no legs to get in the way. Trestles on the other hand eat into the available space for dining to an alarming extent. If you do plan to make a habit of moving your dining table around, choose light chairs so they can be moved easily too.

1 Glass is not always the most suitable material for the dining room, being difficult to keep clean and a noisy surface for plates and cutlery, but Le Corbusier's table, designed in the 1920s, has become a classic.

2 The Tangram table from Cassina is made up of a range of small, differently shaped tables which fit together like a jigsaw.

3 and 4 La Barca by Piero de Martini is an updated version of the drop-leaf, extendable dining table. As a rectangle it encourages conversation; extended, it forms a square suitable for large dinner parties or even a conference table.

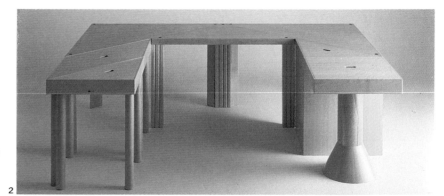

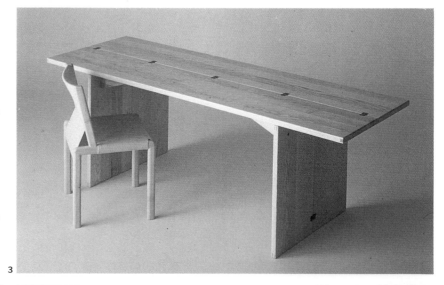

5

5 Inspired by the 1950s, this handmade table is designed by Oval 31; one of a number of younger, small-scale manufacturers, who offer the chance to buy purpose-made designs at affordable prices.

6 A variety of different configurations are catered for with this Alvar Aalto design using segments built up on a laminated timber base.

6

Tables

You must first decide whether your space demands an oval, rectangular, round or square table. If the area is very restricted, remember that the traditional dining table with fold-down, slide-under leaves has been happily superseded by a number of modern interpretations on the same theme, and for a small dining room you might prefer one of the several versatile designs around at the moment, which fold up or out into many configurations. The more imaginative designs hail from Italy and combine technical ingenuity with an exciting use of materials.

If you want a table that makes a virtue out of the folding principle by exposing its hinges, you might choose Cassina's solid ash or walnut rectangular table, La Barca, which has a simple folding top. Another unusual table that folds inwards to make a large square is Bonacina's Teorema. As the name suggests, the flaps fold outwards to form different geometrical configurations, again with the hinges exposed, and the practical white Formica top sits on beech gate legs.

Other tables which enable you to add or subtract are Cassina's multi-unit Tangram; Alvar Aalto's Artek 4-905, a very simple oval in laminated wood that divides into four and makes smaller round and square table shapes; and Oval 31 Design's triangle table, a Memphis-style design in varnished blackboard. Interesting designs are not always found in mainstream shops or design showrooms, and it is worth doing some research and hunting out the smaller studios and shops.

If you want to get away from solid wood, try glass which combines perfectly with steel as well as wood. Le Corbusier's classic LC6 table is imposing with its matt black, light blue or black and grey enamelled steel base. The top is also available in natural or ebonized ash. Magistretti's circular Pan table also comes with glass or wooden tops which perch artfully on the broomstick inspired legs. If you don't like being able to see through your table while you eat and want a more misty glass table top, Pallucco's Ponti d'acqua on white metal legs offers the perfect solution.

FURNITURE

Chairs

Dining chairs are one category of furniture where comfort really has to come first — far too many dinner parties have been blighted by those folding beech chairs that dig into the small of your back, and cause untold hours of squirming agony. Comfort is of course a subjective as well as an objective issue. It has to do with support in the right places, and posture, rather than overstuffed cushions. Think before you buy and always try a practical test.

The range of designs is as varied as the range of prices. Obviously solid natural wood or leather are going to be more expensive than cane, canvas or some plastics. Bear in mind when making your choice that although chairs do not have to form a matching set with the table, they should at least complement each other.

There is no shortage of modern classics in production, especially given the revival of natural woods; for example, Thonet's simple bentwood chair or Aalto's graceful Artek chairs in laminated birchwood. The Mackintosh high-backed black chairs look stunning but can be rather uncomfortable to sit on for any length of time. Whereas, the simple lines of the moulded plastic chairs designed in the '40s and '50s by Saarinen, Jacobsen and Eames not only look good but are very comfortable too.

It is also interesting to note how contemporary chair designs are reverting to basic principles: simple, classic shapes and pale, natural or neutral colours. Such chairs look good with a variety of dining tables. Bellini's Cab chair in light leather is one expensive but extremely elegant example or, in a similar style, the grey moulded plastic Selene by Artemide. There is a sculptural Pan chair to match the table of the same name and, also by Magistretti, the classic red or natural beechwood chairs with rush seats are a popular and economical choice. Chairs can look striking in white, black or grey metal: Hans Coray's classic aluminium chair would be an appropriate choice for a hard edge setting, as would the stunning tubular steel white and black chairs designed by Harry Bertoia.

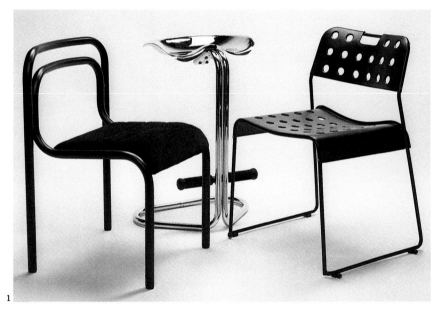

1

1 **High tech seating designed by Rodney Kinsman for OMK ranges from tubular steel to a perforated metal stacking chair. Even the original shape of something as simple as a tractor seat is considered a worthy base for this inspired stool.**

2 **Thonet's bentwood and cane seat – the classic café chair.**

3 **A singular, one-off design from Oval 31's imaginative workshop.**

4 **Too good to keep reserved for the office, these stacking chairs designed by Charles Eames use just two versatile materials – polypropylene and steel.**

2

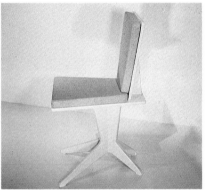

3

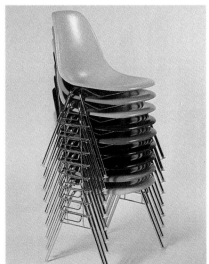

4

Antique dining furniture

Antique has become a flexible term these days, and in the dining room it can be applied to almost anything from a table made of fine veneers, designed and built by an individual master craftsman in the 18th century, which comes complete with the original set of matching chairs, to a machine made 20th century reproduction. In between these two extremes come the second-hand, the heavily restored and even the deliberate fake.

Antique furniture can, in fact, be an economical alternative to the highly priced modern classics, especially if you are fortunate or skilled enough to pick out the kind of second-hand furniture that will in due course turn into real collector's pieces. Equally an antique, or perhaps a more recent period piece, can serve as the starting point for the design of a complete room.

Like a historic piece of architecture, antique furniture needs to be sympathetically treated and cared for. Even utterly utilitarian second-hand furniture should never be submitted to the indignity of a coat of enamel gloss paint – a practice which nowadays is thankfully less common. Many potentially attractive period chairs and tables were sacrificed to the '60s mania for cheering things up. A stencilled pattern may sparingly be applied, or an utterly charmless specimen might be improved with the aid of a paintbrush, but think carefully first.

Sanding and stripping should be approached with almost as much caution. There is no going back once you have started, and the attraction of the finished result often fades. Certainly there is no question of such cavalier treatment for a serious antique, which may indeed be so fragile that it cannot even cope with the dehydrating effects of air conditioning.

The fact that you have chosen to use antique furniture does not necessarily mean that you have to design your dining room around it, or that you have to be consistent about using antiques that are all from the same period. The chief glory of old furniture is very often the mellow patina that comes from well polished worn and aged wood. It is a quality that can often be displayed equally effectively in a cool, clinical setting as it can amid Regency stripes.

When buying antiques that you intend to use regularly, rather than simply admire, you should bear in mind the same criteria of comfort and convenience you would apply to selecting modern furniture. Ancient tables may have an elaborate mechanism for extending themselves, so make sure they are still working. Check also that there is not a forest of legs lurking beneath the table top to trap the unwary. Chairs with cane or upholstered seats can always be repaired, but remember that a professional job can be very expensive.

5 The right ingredients for formal dining: a classic oak dining table, two dining chairs and two carvers combined with lace tablemats, silver goblets, candlesticks and a central flower arrangement.

6 Resuscitate an old box with stencilling and you have a perfect storage chest for table linen.

7 A formal dining room needs few embellishments. Additional frills would only detract from the impact of the furniture – chairs inspired by the Arts and Crafts Movement, and a beautifully glossy table.

TABLE SETTINGS

There is no point in bothering about a distinctive room set if the details that go with it don't get just as much attention. China, cutlery and glass do not necessarily have to match the style of furniture that you have chosen, but they should be appealing both to look at and to eat off.

It is obviously satisfying to have a complete dinner service but with a little imagination and flair you can mix a variety of plates and glasses very successfully. For example, you could present each course on different but equally pretty plates or bowls and on different individual serving dishes. The more simple the designs, the easier the plates will be to mix: classic white dining plates look good next to decorative plates of any period. Beautiful old plates handed down as family heirlooms or collected from a variety of sources — English, Mediterranean or Oriental — can look delightful on a perfectly laid table.

For really formal dining, a consistent set of china is important. Collecting a whole service can be a costly business; be sure to choose a design that will be easy to replace, and one that will stand up to a dishwasher. Try to choose dinner plates which are generously proportioned; food looks much better if it is spread out rather than piled up.

Choose the cutlery with the china in

1   The simplicity demanded by the post modern style produces a satisfyingly clean cut table setting. Pale grey rubber together with plastic mesh draining mats produce an interesting mix of texture and pattern. A pale pink, faintly stippled, dinner set made from the latest Bakelite, breaks up the dark colours and softens the sharp lines.

2   The rough-hewn oak refectory table is an unusual base for such delicate plates and slender bone-handled cutlery, but the country house props of chunky glasses and blue grid napkins introduce a fresh informality to the meal.

mind, for they must look good together. Traditional bone handled silver or stainless steel Sheffield knives and forks are unbeatable if you are lucky enough to inherit or find a set in good condition. There are now modern versions of this classic style which go well with most china and glass. Alternatively, there are several attractive modern designs in production, but as with all tableware, it is practicality as well as aesthetics that count; some are simply too heavy or angular, and not all of the best designs are dishwasher proof.

A beautiful table needs little embellishment and a tablecloth can sometimes seem an unnecessary camouflage. It's surprising though, how different tablecloths and matching napkins can alter the atmosphere of a room, so keep a few contrasting ones to ring the changes from time to time. A fresh white linen cloth shows the food and dishes off to best effect. Mats of some sort will probably be necessary, especially on a bare table top unless it is completely heatproof. A centrepiece finishes off any table setting perfectly — it could be a large hand-painted bowl filled with fruit or an arrangement of fresh flowers — a few stems of the same flower rather than a large mixed bunch looks best. You are then well prepared to dine in style.

3 An eclectic table setting can be as casual or as formal as you make it. Here a pretty collection of plates from different eras combine with a Regency painted glass and silver cutlery on a 1920s hand-embroidered cloth.

4 Matching china is essential on the formal table. Classic Wedgewood plates with rims to match the gold-plated cutlery affirm the formality. For that sparkle, simple glassware and damask tablecloth are vital.

5 For a fun look, make good use of primary colour co-ordination and materials such as plastic.

FINISHING TOUCHES

1

2

4

5

1 Candlelight is the subtlest, most flattering way of lighting any dining table. On a highly polished wooden surface, position groups of several candles together to take greatest advantage of the soft reflection in the wood. Alternatively, single candles on a crisp, white damask tablecloth will create a very sophisticated look.

2 There is almost always space for a dining area, even in this tiny apartment. The perforated metal table folds away and bench seats offer greater flexibility than single chairs. The area need not look like a temporary picnic. The red and black china, matching grinders and cutlery turn this into a smart formal table.

3 Remember that a bare dining table still has a strong presence in the room. Carefully positioned directional light makes it a point of focus, emphasized by simple objects placed on top.

4 Amongst the sleek shapes and lacquered surfaces, this grained dining table, worn with age, impresses the eye with its individuality.

5 If there is a centrepiece on the formal dining table let it be a statement. This spectacular bowl of well-arranged flowers picks up on the dominant yellow theme of the room.

6 A refreshing start to the day — pretty pastel colours co-ordinated without any self-consciousness. Pieces of blue and white china do not have to match to look good together.

7 Pale colours and simple shapes help to create an identifiable corner for eating in this Paris loft.

KITCHENS

Every culture makes the hearth the centre of the home – a gathering place for warmth and sustenance. Even today's highly practical kitchen is a social mecca, more than a simple food factory. Many people spend more waking hours in the kitchen than in any other room – especially people who care about food – and so the kitchen becomes the living room.

Common sense and personal tastes are the most powerful influences on kitchen design. But the ideas and points covered in the next few pages should stimulate and help you to follow a practical path, whether you are starting from scratch, overhauling or simply revitalizing. The basic principles involved will be the same for any household, but we all make different demands on the space, and when planning a new kitchen it's worth thinking about what you might expect – in the best of all possible worlds – and then perhaps take a few pragmatic steps backwards.

Aim for a successful marriage between function and style. You want an efficient space that makes necessary or monotonous chores as pleasant as possible, and at the same time is a comfortable, personal room – a place for creativity and enjoyment.

Beware the slavish dictates of fashion – no sooner have you finished your spanking new hard edge kitchen, bristling with chrome and glass, than magazines announce that natural

1 Architect Eva Jiricna's own kitchen, fitted into a minute space in her London apartment. It has all the well-ordered efficiency of a ship's galley.

2 Confined spaces mean it's possible to be much more adventurous with colour than in larger areas. Here yellow industrial storage trays contrast vividly with the green studded rubber on floor and walls.

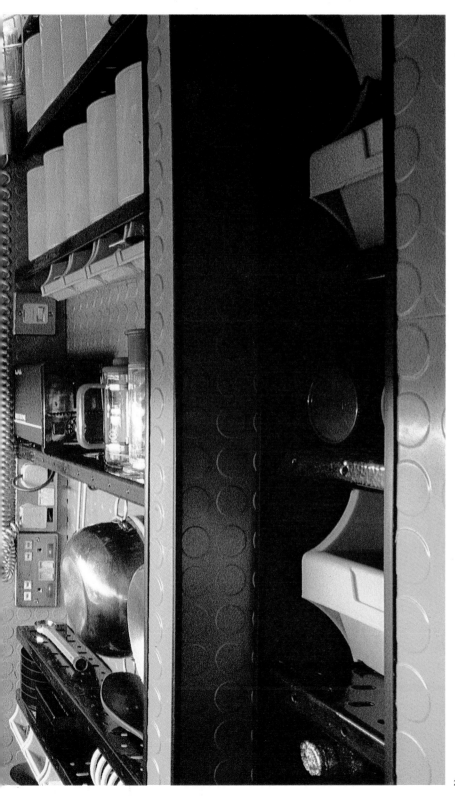

woods and pastels, or plastic primaries are the latest vogue. Trust your own taste and follow your inclinations. Search for the kind of materials and equipment you would most like to combine. Don't make do with second-rate designs because you can't find the cooker, lighting system or floor tiles that you are looking for – it may just take a bit of hunting. If you detest cookers with orange and brown control knobs, you won't be able to bear them any more easily in two or three years time. Study other people's kitchens.

What problems have they given themselves? What bright ideas have they had?

If finances won't allow the kitchen of your dreams, plan it so that elements are flexible and you have room to manoeuvre and upgrade your fittings. Allot a possible place for a future dishwasher, washing machine or freezer, and fill any gaping holes with as many shelves as possible which can easily be replaced with the large appliances you want when you can afford them.

PLANNING

Before you actually start mapping out the kitchen, ask yourself some basic questions, which should help you work out your priorities and the room's potential. What do you dislike about your present kitchen? Will your new kitchen be used for cooking only, or will it be a family and laundry room too? Will the cat or dog sleep there? Will you usually eat in the kitchen? What kind of cook are you – passionate, infrequent, convenience, family? Do you shop on most days, or do you visit the supermarket once a week to stock up? Are the shops close by? In other words, will you need a lot of food storage space or not? Are the supplies of power – gas and electricity – and water satisfactory? Does the kitchen get steamy, or is there sufficient ventilation?

Location

If you have a choice about where to put the kitchen, try and locate it in the most convenient place; any walk to a dining room should be minimal, preferably not involving stairs – carrying tureens of soup or stacks of dirty dishes up and down stairs is not only tiresome but courts disaster. Choose a room that enjoys natural light with windows facing south-east, south or south-west if possible.

Structural changes

The age and architecture of your house will, to a great extent, dictate the type of kitchen that is appropriate. Apart from the generous kitchens in country farmhouses and grand town houses, original kitchens are practically always too small for the equipment we expect to fit into them today. However, most Victorian and Edwardian terraces and houses built between the wars have a scullery, larder or small breakfast room that can double the size of the kitchen if you knock down the intervening walls and chimney breasts. But don't wield the sledgehammer before checking with the local building inspector or district surveyor, and ask former occupants where electric cables and plumbing pipes have been sunk into walls and floors. Keep a plan of any changes you make for future reference.

The ergonomics

Start planning in earnest by measuring the room in metric, and draw up a diagram on graph paper at a practical scale of say 1:20. The next step is to measure the appliances you already have, and anything you are planning to buy. Then cut out squares of paper (to scale) which will represent your appliances, and move them around on the plan until you have worked out an arrangement that suits you. Although everyone will have their own priorities, these points are worth bearing in mind:
1 The so-called 'work triangle', devised by researchers at Cornell University, concludes that the sink, cooker and food storage (fridge) areas are the most frequently used in the kitchen. So try and arrange these quite close together.
2 Since the sink is the most expensive element to move around – with all its associated plumbing – it is most economical to keep it where it is. And plumb in other appliances close by.
3 Most kitchen units and appliances are standardized in height, although tall and short people suffer terribly from this conformity. So work out what height suits you, and build an additional plinth under your units to raise them, or do away with the plinth altogether. The standard height for units, based, somewhat chauvinistically, on the average height of women, 1.66m (5ft 4in.), is approximately 900mm (3ft). Measure this height on a wall and see how it feels. A sink should ideally be about 75mm (3in.) higher.
4 Allow the worktop to project at least 19mm (¾in.) in front of the base unit so it's easy to sweep off rubbish.
5 Toe space is designed into standard units, so that you can stand comfortably close to the worktop. It should be at least 75mm (3in.) high and 75mm (3in.) deep. If you choose to have wall-mounted base cupboards – a good idea for people who are not of average height – keep these dimensions in mind.
6 Passage space between banks of units should not be less than 1.25m (4ft) if two people are likely to work in, or move around the kitchen, though in small 'single' kitchens it can be cut down to 760mm (2ft 6in.).
7 Position the cooker so that there is work surface on both sides where you can prepare ingredients or dishes.
8 Most appliances are well-insulated, but if you want to put the fridge next to the stove, it is a good idea to separate them with a chipboard panel.
9 Plan plenty of electric sockets for worktop appliances, such as the toaster, food processor, kettle etc – at least two banks of three sockets.

1 A well-conceived purpose-built kitchen unit with circular endpiece, which looks good, provides maximum storage space and makes a subtle and attractive room divider.

2 It's a long walk to the far cupboard, but this straight run of kitchen units provides maximum usable storage space.

3 Inspired by the layout of a caterer's kitchen, an effective and highly practical room is planned with a serious cook in mind. At its heart stands a huge island unit, incorporating sink, dishwasher, hot plates and storage space.

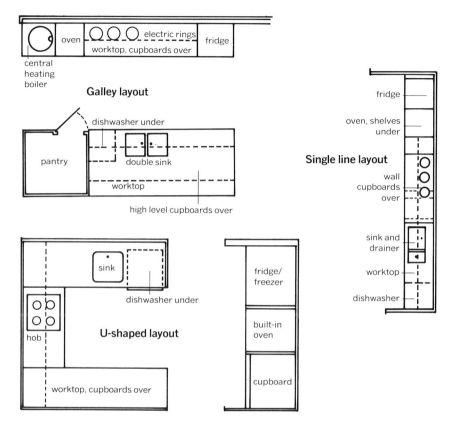

central heating boiler
oven
electric rings
worktop, cupboards over
fridge

Galley layout

dishwasher under
pantry
double sink
worktop
high level cupboards over

Single line layout

fridge
oven, shelves under
wall cupboards over
sink and drainer
worktop
dishwasher

sink
dishwasher under
U-shaped layout
hob
worktop, cupboards over

fridge/ freezer
built-in oven
cupboard

Worktops

The worktop is the most important element to a cook; it is the site of greatest activity, so its composition, height, depth and length are fundamental to the kitchen's design. The standard depth of 600mm (2ft) doesn't allow for any decent space behind the hob or sink, where it's very handy to store a jar of wooden spoons, the salt cellar, washing up liquid etc; you really need another 140mm (5½in.). A broader worktop also means that toasters, food processors, radios and other small appliances can be parked permanently without taking up too much valuable space.

Laminates The most economical covering for worktops, laminates are available in a great range of colours and varying densities. The laminate is stuck onto chipboard, blockboard or plywood (in ascending order of quality and price). Front edges are either post-formed, rounded or edged with timber lipping. Although easy to clean, laminate scratches easily so shouldn't be used instead of a chopping board.

Wood A sympathetic, attractive surface for worktops, but it must be hardwood. Beech and teak are excellent but expensive and need constant care and re-sealing. A small piece of wood cut across the grain can be let into another type of work surface to be used as a chopping board.

Stone Marble or slate tops are excellent for making pastry, although marble stains easily and, again, is expensive. A small piece can be let into a work surface or stood on rubber feet to anchor it to the worktop.

Stainless steel A sleek, good-looking surface, which is easy to clean and very hard-wearing. It can be polished or matt and made-to-measure in a continuous piece with integral sinks and a space cut out for the hob. Cut down noise by putting insulation board underneath.

Ceramic tiles These make a relatively tough and very handsome worktop, so long as you use strong sealants to avoid water penetration. The dis-advantages are the noisy clatter every time you put something down, and the ease with which they break if you drop anything heavy.

Storage

Vertical layout is as important as the floor plan. You can minimize bending by having a wall-mounted oven, fridge, and food and crockery cupboards, though avoid doing this at the expense of worktop area. If only one appliance can be wall-mounted, many people prefer it to be the fridge as it's the most frequently used piece of equipment. Bending and picking up heavy things from below the worktop is more tiring than stretching above, though wall cupboards should be at least 400mm (lft 4in.) above the worktop, to make the most of the work area.

The way you choose to organize your storage–off-the-shelf units, custom made or DIY shelves and cupboards, or a mixture–affects the look of the kitchen more than anything else. Good-looking, well-designed, mass-produced units are not the easiest to find, and the great sweeps of cupboards and drawers that manufacturers encourage us to buy can look monotonous and can easily depersonalize a kitchen. The better looking ones tend to be foreign (German or Italian) and thus rather expensive. They will rarely fit your kitchen exactly, but gaps can be used for storing trays or for a stack of wire baskets. Ugly trims on cheaper units can either be removed, or much improved with a lick of hard-wearing paint.

If the only units you like are hopelessly expensive, look into the costs of having cupboards, drawers and shelves made to measure, perhaps with a ready-made worktop. With a little planning and design on your own part, a good carpenter could install the hob for the same price, or less, and you will end up with a kitchen that really suits you. Alternatively, investigate the many self-assembly kits that are on the market, based on open shelves (including industrial metal and plastic designs) or traditional cupboards; plastic-coated metal grids with butcher's hooks make cheap, flexible hanging areas. In any arrangement make sure that your cupboards are sturdily built; have drawers with laminated or lacquered interiors for easy cleaning; sensible handles; and shelves that are well made and adjustable.

3

THE PRACTICALITIES

Four important factors to bear in mind when you're planning a new kitchen or revamping an old one are the lighting, ventilation, heating and flooring.

Lighting

Aim for flexibility and efficiency with kitchen lighting. By using several different sorts of lighting plus a few dimmer switches, the atmosphere can be changed instantly from functional work space to intimate dining room.

Worktops need to be well lit. Downlighters, spots or hanging industrial bulbs should be carefully sited so that you don't create a shadow to work in. Tubular or spotlights mounted behind a batten underneath storage cupboards are a traditional solution, though the flicker in fluorescent tubes bothers many people and tungsten tubes are much more expensive. An adjustable pendant light over the table creates intimacy for eating, and cuts off the rest of the kitchen at the same time.

To make the most of possible sources of natural light, glaze doors that lead into the garden, and make a skylight if the kitchen is a single storey extension. Even a small skylight makes an enormous difference as it will catch direct light from so many more points than a window. It's a good idea to double glaze skylights against condensation. If you want to have a large skylight that has to be specially built, check with your local environmental health department first to see whether there are any local fire regulations to be met. Some authorities will insist on wired glass or special fire-resistant materials.

To reinforce the natural and artificial lights in your kitchen, choose a light colour scheme. Dark colours absorb light and tend to make the room look and feel smaller than it is. But if your heart is set on pine green, paint the ceiling white or off-white so that it will reflect light down into the room.

Ventilation

Condensation is the worst enemy in the kitchen. It quickly damages timber and decorations, and is defeated only by adequate ventilation. Extractors work

1

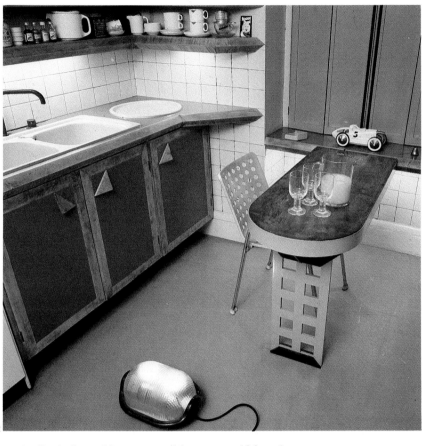

1 The conventional modern kitchen using tough hard-wearing materials for floor, walls and worktops. The room's location makes the most of natural light, but even with the windows, an extractor fan is still included.

2 Concealed under-shelf lighting illuminates the sink area while a quartz halogen floor light can be moved anywhere in the room. Vinyl flooring is easy to clean and now available in some very attractive designs.

3 Ideal for kitchens: ceiling spotlights which can be directed toward oven, work surface, or wherever a good light source is needed.

very effectively, wafting away cooking smells as well as steam. All cooking creates smells, and even though they are usually delicious ones, they become stale if allowed to hang around, particularly if they permeate soft furnishings; and although most cooking creates some water vapour, gas hobs produce even more.

Of the many types of extractor available, the most common sit above the hob and either recycle the air with an electric fan through a charcoal filter that must be changed regularly, or take air out of the room altogether through an outside wall. With extractors that are ventilated to the outdoors, it isn't so essential to have an electric fan incorporated in the system, which makes life much quieter, though a fan does make the process more efficient. It is also a good idea to have a fat filter in the extractor hood, so that the fan is protected from the dirt and grease in the fumes, and doesn't become clogged.

Although extractors are not attractive to look at, they can be hidden with a little invention; the easiest way to do this is in a suspended storage block over an island stove. Large industrial metal tubing, which can be painted either to camouflage or highlight it, makes a very smart, high tech extractor hood. Builders' merchants or good hardware stores should be able to provide you with the necessary tubing.

Opt for a model of extractor that has more than one speed and ask for a demonstration in order to avoid buying one with a deafening roar. If your cooker is against an outside wall or a chimney breast, an extractor fan can be let in just behind the hob.

Heating
Small kitchens rarely need any extra heating, as fridges, freezers, lights and cookers all produce warmth, either constantly or in bursts. However, a radiator near the table, if you eat in the

kitchen, makes life more comfortable.

If your kitchen is large and tends to double as a family living room, then here too, a radiator makes good sense. Invest in radiators with individual thermostats so that you don't toast in the kitchen and freeze in the bathroom. No doubt you will find that the kitchen radiator can be set quite low most of the time. If heat is needed very infrequently, perhaps a blast of warm air from a fan heater first thing in the morning and in the early evening could do the trick. Many models can be mounted on the wall for extra efficiency. If you plug your heater into a timer socket, it can switch on automatically so that the chill has been lifted by the time you go in to make the day's first cup of tea.

Flooring
For many people, finding a successful floor covering for the kitchen creates the biggest headache of all when it

comes to decorating a house. You may be thrilled with your choice when it is first installed, only to curse it later for a host of unforeseen reasons.

A kitchen floor has to take a tremendous amount of punishment. The perfect surface has yet to be discovered, but whichever type you choose, make sure that it is first and foremost hard-wearing and easy to clean. You may for example, opt for quarry tiles, which are tough but rather cold; or cork tiles, which you can lay yourself but can quickly look down at heel; or rubber, increasingly popular as a domestic floor surface, although the studded and ribbed types tend to trap food and dirt; or vinyl, which now comes in a wide range of designs, but can be easily damaged. It's a question of finding the one that suits you best from an aesthetic as well as a practical point of view. For the full choice, and the advantages and drawbacks of each type, see the chapter on Floors.

FAMILY KITCHENS

This type of kitchen constantly evolves and changes, but at all stages in the family's life the room needs to be particularly hard-wearing to cope with the onslaught of young children or hungry teenagers. Ideally the room should be large enough to have clearly defined areas so that homework can be done in relative peace away from the cooking area. All surfaces need to be easy to clean, including walls and tables. Flooring should be tough and resilient – preferably wood, lino or rubber.

Safety

Above all the kitchen must be as safe as possible especially when children are about. There are more accidents each year in the home than on the roads, and in the kitchen, the hob causes most of them. The safest position for the burners is in a row at the back of the worktop surrounded by a hob guard, so that it is difficult for children to pull saucepans down. It is also a good idea to have the controls out of reach. Fix a portable fire extinguisher or fire blanket to one wall so that everyone knows where it is. It's sensible to put some shelves too high for curious hands to reach, even when standing on a chair; but don't put heavy things on top shelves. If the kitchen leads into the garden, keep a direct line of vision between the two, so that you can keep an eye on the children without always having to be outside. (For more information, see the section on Safety, pages 232-233, Children's Rooms.)

Creating an atmosphere

If the kitchen is a good size, it will inevitably be a place where the family spends a great deal of time. Warm, natural materials – wood, brick, terracotta and stone – will make it an inviting and comforting room to be in. But beware the temptation to scrape the plaster off the walls to expose the bricks underneath. Although bricks make a very attractive, cheerful surface, the unevenness of the wall will collect dust and grease, and you will find yourself having to vacuum clean the wall – surely a chore no-one needs. Bricks, however, do make good low supporting walls for ceramic sinks, DIY shelving or for raising units.

Soft, but flexible lighting and the reassurance of a constant stove, such as a Rayburn or Aga, provide the basis for a countrified kitchen that can be efficient without being clinical. Plan to have several of your favourite things – collections or pictures – in the kitchen. Incorporate old tiles into a splashback behind the worktop, using

1

2

small plain tiles to space out your antique discoveries. Old stained glass can be refitted into existing windows, or take inspiration from Charles Rennie Mackintosh's work and design some simple glasswork of your own: you could let squares of glass into a wooden pelmet covering a curtain rod so that sunlight and streetlight shine through. Mackintosh also set simple glass shapes into the top halves of doors – squares, diamonds, hearts – adding decoration to a usually plain surface. Doors can also be given a coat of blackboard paint and be used for shopping lists or reminders. Alternatively attach a multitude of hooks to the back of the door for hand towels, aprons, satchels and handbags.

Labour-saving machines

Large families and keen entertainers benefit most from labour-saving machines such as dishwashers and freezers. At first, a dishwasher may mean that you have to increase your stock of crockery, cutlery and glasses, as a proportion tends to be permanently 'locked up' in the machine. But the advantages are many; not only does everthing come out gloriously clean but you can conserve energy into the bargain. Dishwashers use up less hot water than hand-washing and rinsing, and a large machine will allow you to accumulate at least a day's dirty dishes and then can be run overnight. Many models have low energy washing and drying cycles. The low energy drying cycle lets the dishes 'drip dry' at normal air temperature rather than switching on the heating element.

With a little care, fridges can also be made energy-efficient. They tend to be the single biggest energy-user in the kitchen – so choose one with the best possible insulation and site it away

1 The comfortable, lived-in kitchen. Tough, natural materials wear well and age beautifully and a solid fuel range is guaranteed to create warmth and homeliness.

2 Family kitchens have to be spacious, and in this small London house, the length of the ground floor has been opened up to create a combined kitchen and dining room which has lost none of its intimate quality.

3 Contemporary houses need not be excluded from having up-to-date versions of the traditional family kitchen, as here. Butcher block work surface, wood panel walls and an oak floor create a mellow background.

4 A high-ceilinged old living room, put to use as a comfortable and elegant kitchen. The new units do not interfere with the room's proportions and the oil painting helps to smooth the change of function.

FAMILY KITCHENS

1 An old barn has been converted into a relaxed, jokey, yet subtly sophisticated kitchen. The rough paintwork of the building deliberately contrasts with the expertly finished storage units and elegantly laid table.

from other heat-producing appliances, such as stoves, washing or drying machines, though all this equipment doesn't have to be squeezed into the kitchen. Freezers particularly lend themselves to living somewhere else – in an outhouse, garage, under the stairs or simply in a hall. New freezer owners may at first feel as if they have brought a greedy tyrant into the home, forever demanding more food. But you will soon get used to buying or baking five loaves of bread at a time, cooking three times as much pasta sauce as you need (in the same time) and buying up bushels of beans and spinach when they are cheap, to be enjoyed later.

Relaxing

Try and plan as much flexibility as possible into a family kitchen, although it's bound to grow around you in a slightly uncontrollable way. If you have enough space for a relaxing/reading/ television-viewing area with a sofa, cushions or easy chairs, it's even more relaxing to be able to close if off from the centre of cooking activities with Venetian or canvas blinds, a folding screen or hanging fretwork screen. You could easily make your own hanging screen with two pieces of long, strong dowelling and a large piece of material – sheer muslin, cotton or parachute silk. Hem the material top and bottom to make a sleeve for the dowelling and hang it from the ceiling.

When you want to open up the room, you can roll up the screen and tie the dowel rods together. Large banners and flags could also be used.

Any soft furnishings and upholstery covers should be easy to remove and clean – as they are bound to be the victims of food spills and children's scrambles. A cheap washable bedspread or length of material can be used to throw over a sofa and swiftly whipped off to the sink or washing machine if it meets with a bowl of tomato soup or glass of red wine. And plastic blow-up cushions, which children find great fun, only need a wipe clean.

If the hamster, goldfish or budgie *has* to live in the kitchen, everyone will be healthier and happier (including the pet) if its home is placed as far away as possible from the food preparing, cooking and eating areas. And if there is nowhere else for the cat's litter tray than in the kitchen, buy a top cover so that the cat can get in and out, but smells tend to stay in.

Giving your kitchen a facelift

Over the years your kitchen is bound to suffer from periods of heavy battering, and even if you have chosen hardy materials that don't wear out, everyone gets a little weary of colour schemes and materials after a while. The surfaces themselves are bound to start looking a little tired too. Rather than going to the expense of redoing the whole kitchen, you can give the units, floor or walls a facelift relatively cheaply, and without disrupting the overall scheme.

A coat of paint on all surfaces is an easy solution, as is a change of handles on cupboard and unit doors. Or, a little more drastically, laminate the doors with a wood veneer or one of the various plastics available. This is really a job for a professional as all the doors will have to come off to be worked on, and the task needs a practised accuracy. Change over to open shelves by taking off the cupboard doors altogether, and then you could paint the

shelves a contrasting colour from the rest of the kitchen.

For a happy compromise make or buy blinds to fit the shelf openings so that the contents can be open to view or not, as you like. To make your own: cut and hem pieces of lightweight canvas so that they are 1cm (½in.) narrower and 20cm (8in.) longer than the openings. Hem up the bottoms so that a piece of dowel can be threaded through and a handhold hole cut out, then attach the canvas to a roller from a kit. Dowel, flattened slightly on one side, can also be cut and screwed or glued to units to make inexpensive new handles.

A couple of new storage baskets or hanging rails, of butcher's hooks will be useful additions to your kitchen. Browse in catering equipment shops, usually to be found in established city restaurant districts. They are wonderful hunting grounds for outsized industrial equipment that can be used to great effect on a domestic scale too. All sorts

2

2 Simple fittings and uncomplicated shapes, enlivened by the recycled 1950s lampshade which sets off the vivid blue of the matching table and chairs.

3 The antithesis of the traditional family kitchen, yet still with its own brand of warmth and welcome. So well hidden are hob, oven and extractor fan that it would be hard to identify the room as a kitchen at all.

4 Redolent with nostalgia, this contemporary evocation of a farmhouse kitchen mixes antiques with junk shop finds – a Welsh dresser and refectory table with salvaged chemist's shop fittings. The dangling green glass shades inject a shot of colour into the predominantly mellow wood tones of the interior.

3

4

of wire baskets, intended for deep-frying or industrial dish-washing, are good for storing crockery, vegetables or cleaning materials. Giant ladles, colanders and mixing bowls may also be useful for large parties or family cooking at Christmas.

As the family grows up and starts either to leave the nest, or at least become slightly more responsible and sensitive, you may dare to bring some more precious belongings into the kitchen. Once the children can be relied on not to walk into the house covered in mud or to drop their food repeatedly onto the floor, it could be worth risking a good rug in part of the kitchen, or a new cover for the sofa in a more attractive, perhaps less practical material. And if you have an enormous kitchen table, designed to withstand even the messiest or most destructive of children, it could be replaced with a smaller more sophisticated one that would make eating in the kitchen a more intimate affair.

COOKS' KITCHENS

The term 'cook's kitchen' is really a contradiction – we're all cooks of one sort or another, whether our culinary repertoire stops at spaghetti bolognese or extends to the realms of *nouvelle cuisine*, but it must be said that some cooks are more passionate about the art than others, and for the chef *manqué*, cooking space is all important. Lots of work surface and storage for food is essential – as your local corner shop is unlikely to stock the pink peppercorns or dried cep vital for tonight's recipe. A large cooker and combination fuel hob will reap the benefits of both gas and electric cooking, as well as being an insurance against power cuts.

Dedicated cooks are often rather disapproving about gadgetry and swear by their favourite Sabatier rather than a Magimix. So plenty of cupboards for equipment are important to avoid under-used machines taking up precious worktop space. As the cook will spend many fruitful hours in the kitchen, the layout should be sociable rather than isolating. An island plan or turn of the units into the middle of the room allows the cook to look into the kitchen and socialize while working.

Planning

As keen cooks are usually happier in the kitchen than anywhere else, they will particularly enjoy planning their room, and will also have very strong ideas about what elements are essential and where they should be in relation to each other. If the budget allows, a largely made-to-measure kitchen is best. This type of cook is probably capable of designing the layout and directing the builders and joiners, so the cost need not be any higher than for an off-the-shelf design.

The proud owner of the cook's kitchen is involved as much as possible with every step of a meal's creation, from the buying or growing of the food, through its preparation and cooking, to serving and of course eating. The garden is devoted to vegetables, whether the growing area is limited to a window box of herbs or immaculate rows of mangetouts and purple-sprouting broccoli; seed catalogues are favourite bedtime reading. A freezer is an absolute essential for storing the annual harvest, along with valuable herbs, precious coffee beans, and mushrooms that can't be eaten fast enough during the limited foraging seasons. A larder is another basic necessity – or at least a ventilated cupboard in which to keep cheeses, fresh vegetables and usable leftovers.

For preparing food, plan a worktop with flexibility and a variety of qualities. Try to include a chopping board let into the surface near a sink and a marble or slate slab for pastry making. A slot in the surface with a waste bin below will make it easier to keep the top clean as you work. Two sink areas – one for washing up, the other with a waste disposal unit for vegetable preparation – will mean that these activities can go on simultaneously without queuing or risking soapy disasters. An island plan lends itself to such an arrangement, as the island can be devoted to preparation, with its own sink, equipment storage and waste bin. Suspended shelving above the island will give horizontal storage for spices, books, pots and pans, as well as vertical storage for hanging implements of all sorts within easy reach on butcher's hooks.

A large cooker, ideally catering size with six burners, would be most cooks' dream, plus plenty of heat-resistant setting-down space on both sides of the hob, so there isn't any need for constant rearrangement of pans in a frantic bid to have everything ready at the same time. Most 'foodies' have gathered an array of favourite pottery and ethnic cooking equipment, which is a joy to see, so allow some space for display shelving. Wines will need storage space too, whether under the worktop, in the larder, or in a treasured cellar.

1   For the single-minded cook, an efficient workshop in which to create culinary masterpieces. The central butcher block work surface allows plenty of elbow room, and is excellently lit.

2   The island unit principle on a large scale. Here sink, dishwasher and storage units are all contained within a solid brick rectangle, topped with a gleaming expanse of marble.

3   Architect Richard Rogers' kitchen in Paris. Culinary inspiration is helped by placing the island unit containing all necessary appliances in front of a superb view.

4   Conceived by designer Johnny Grey as a means of getting away from the severe lines and functional aura of most purpose-built kitchens, this gourmet's enclave is highly practical yet a pleasure to work in.

2

3

4

FUNCTIONAL KITCHENS

The 'functional', labour-saving kitchen must really work from day one. Owners of such a kitchen are probably professional people under a great deal of pressure who are forced to use their time efficiently. Unless cooking is their only form of leisure, they won't have any spare time to potter about in the kitchen, experimenting or indulging in lengthy preparation. All the elements of the kitchen need to be highly organized and designed into the room from the outset; this type of kitchen doesn't 'grow' in the way that others do. The layout has to be very practical, so beware of any decorative idiosyncrasies that could hinder the room's function. All units, shelving and worktops need to be made of good quality materials that demand little attention – laminates, metals and well-sealed woods. And a properly 'fitted' kitchen is the most suitable, with no nooks and crannies that will add five minutes to the time you spend cleaning.

Time-saving machines
Every detail can be thought of in terms of the time it will save or consume. First of all, you will need plenty of counter space, or special shelves, for the various helpful machines that make life run smoothly. For example, using a coffee machine in the morning leaves you free to sort out the rest of breakfast, rather than being tied to the filter pot, kettle in hand, waiting for the water to drip through.

A food processor is a must in the functional kitchen. A multitude of machines in one, it chops, slices, shreds, purées, mixes and kneads – so there's no need to cry over chopped onions again.

The microwave oven comes into its own in the functional kitchen – jacket potatoes can be cooked in four minutes, a three pound chicken roasted in around half and hour, even a Christmas pudding is ready in nine minutes. It can be a helpful tool for cooking and defrosting quick meals for people who are always rushed off their feet.

The most futuristic ovens also have a microcomputer that will set the oven, cook the dish and alert you when it is ready, after you have keyed in essential information about the type of dish and its weight. But if the idea of your oven winking and bleeping at you doesn't appeal, choose one that you can set manually, so that it will turn on and off automatically, cooking the lasagne without you having to leave your desk until supper time.

A dishwasher is essential in the functional kitchen; crockery, glass and cutlery cupboards or drawers sited nearby cut unloading time to a minimum. Rather than stacking cups and glasses on shelves, which tends to lead to chipping, store them neatly in shallow drawers. Make a grid of fine wood dowel to fit on the base of the drawer so that cups and glasses sit in their own niche. A stack of such drawers would form a kitchen plan chest, and if installed under a worktop that projected into the room, it could open on both sides – one side for loading up from the dishwasher, the other for unloading onto the table.

Details
The uncluttered atmosphere will be enhanced by a limited colour scheme. That doesn't mean that everything has to be hygienically white with a dash of dramatic black; brilliant yellow, battleship grey or pistachio green can be used to great effect. Efficient, relatively strong lighting works best in this sort of kitchen. Downlighters, recessed neatly into the ceiling are attractive and unfussy, allied with spotlights onto the work surface from above or under wall cupboards, or good quality neon strips hidden under the cupboards. Wipeable blinds for the windows need much less attention than slatted blinds or curtains.

Storage
Solid cupboard doors hide the visual jumble of jars and packets of food; any food on show should be decanted into a collection of smart storage jars. A trolley, which fits under the table or worktops when not in use, makes an extremely useful addition to the work space, and can of course be wheeled to wherever you need an extra surface. You can buy special kitchen trolleys with butcher block tops incorporating knife storage slots, waste bins and drawers, which are almost kitchens in their own right.

1   A tiny basement transformed into a light, efficient kitchen. The full height window doubles as a door to the postage stamp garden. Inside, a hard-wearing stainless steel worktop, and chairs which stack neatly away.

2   A 'fitted' kitchen with matching wall and floor units is the quickest way to create a functional area in which to cook and eat. Parquet might not be the most conventional type of kitchen floor, but if you can afford it, it is certainly one of the most practical.

3   One of the most efficient ways to prepare food: an island unit in the centre of the kitchen, with sink, oven and hob against the wall.

4   Stylish, but useful; grey ceramic tiles are used on both the floor and worktop and the decorative panel is continued across the dishwasher for a slick, streamlined effect.

DESIGNER KITCHENS

When style is a stronger influence than function, materials and the finished look give more pleasure than convenience. Such kitchens are usually designed by someone other than the cook – someone who doesn't mind bending, stretching and cleaning more often than could be absolutely necessary, in order to have the kitchen looking just right. But it's unfair to condemn the visually exacting. This type of kitchen designer takes time to solve spatial and visual problems in innovative ways that are then often taken up by magazines and manufacturers, and so our kitchen vocabulary grows.

Draining boards, clothes racks and off-the-shelf units may be banished along with other useful clutter, for the sake of aesthetics. In favour are industrial stainless steel and heavy-duty plastic borrowed from the factory floor, or clinically severe ceramics and expanses of glass – wired, frosted and clear. Always on the look out for new ideas, the design enthusiast rescues and utilizes under-used equipment from hotels, supermarkets, canteens or factories – glass-fronted cold chests, swing doors, tiles, taps, light fixtures, bar tops, china and glass.

The style doesn't wallow, however, in comfy nostalgia, but is a mixture of good design from any period. Contemporary products and materials will be major features. Every detail demands attention, from the cooker to the corkscrew. If everything has to be matt black or royal blue, it will take longer to equip your kitchen but it will be worth it (for you) in the end. It doesn't have to be an expensive venture; simple cheap solutions can be just as efficient and good looking, if not as status-raising as design classics from last year's Milan furniture show.

A dramatic impression created by the clever use of lighting and by repeating the slate blue finish throughout the kitchen. The only details to stand out are a single, elegant mixer tap and an immaculate display of pots and pans.

Equipment
Over the last decade, the design and function of cookers and white goods have improved dramatically. Straightforward, unfussy cookers (usually Italian or Scandinavian) in plain handsome colours are now available in good department stores at reasonable prices. Smart sinks – round, square, rectangular, or any combination – fit over or are let into worktops, and give endless scope to the tap enthusiast. A former blind spot, taps have recently been given new life, so that the choice in terms of shape, material and colour, has increased enormously. Choose from jolly yellow enamel to glossy chrome or no-nonsense utilitarian stainless steel.

Layout
Spatial arrangement is always important to the design conscious, so how rooms relate to each other – how one room looks from another – is a factor to be borne in mind. Floor colours and wall coverings should either sit happily with their neighbours or be vigorously and intentionally clashing.

TINY KITCHENS

If space is at a premium and the kitchen is forced into a tight area, which is often the case for people living alone, in a bedsit or small flat, planning is even more important. This kind of kitchen calls for custom-made fittings almost more than any other, since off-the-shelf units and worktops could greedily consume all the available space. In fact a judicious mixture of made-to-measure and mass-produced equipment is probably the best idea. Fit in as much work surface as you can by having it cut down to a narrower than standard depth. Shelves for pots and pans, plates or storage jars can be built underneath. Make them just wide enough to take their intended load so that you don't have to scrabble around in search of egg cups behind casseroles.

Saving space

There are many space-saving appliances available, from tiny fridges and washing machines to miniature dishwashers and cookers. But people with limited cooking space can be just as keen entertainers as family or 'foodie' cooks, so opt for equipment with flexibility. A double oven is a good idea so that you can use the smaller one when you just want a baked potato. And a hob with a cover will give you extra work surface.

Keep doors that open to a minimum in a small space; sliding doors on units are best, or open shelves, as you will probably be using crockery and saucepans often enough for them not to sit around gathering dust. A sliding door into the kitchen, or a blind will also save a few precious inches. And hang as many pans and utensils as possible on an overhead grid of hooks.

If there isn't room for a table to eat at in your kitchen, and you decide to have it in a living room instead, you can save valuable cooking space by keeping cutlery, glasses and even plates near the table. One solution is either to adapt a table top or have one made to resemble the outer covering of a slim matchbox; the internal cavity can hold a tray of cutlery, napkins, cups and plates, which will make table-laying a far simpler operation. To make the most of any square cubic inches of unfilled kitchen shelving, hang under-shelf mesh baskets for storage.

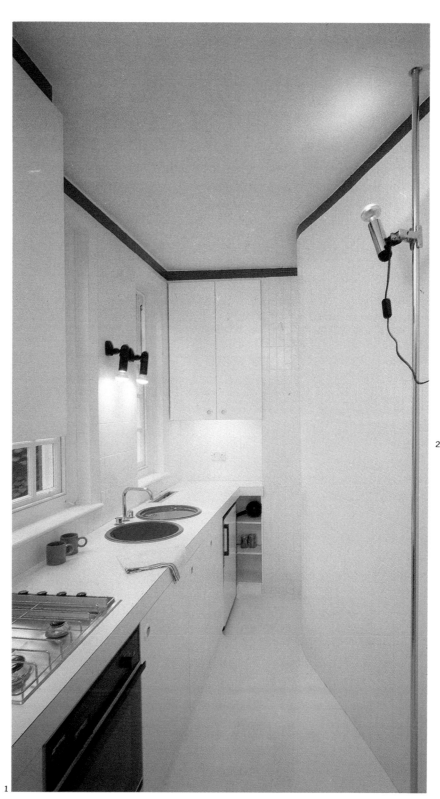

1 A tiny kitchen need not be a cramped nightmare. This sliver of space has been put to use with maximum effect. White tiled floors and walls are set off by two dashing red sinks, echoed by the single stripe of colour where walls meet ceiling, making the room look cheerful as well as efficient.

2 Squeezed into a mezzanine, this smart red and black kitchen still manages to tuck a breakfast bar along the edge of the sheer drop. A porthole window makes the space light and airy.

EATING IN THE KITCHEN

If your kitchen and dining room are one – or usually one – the arrangement is bound to be based on an open plan layout. Although this is sociable and informal, there can be several drawbacks. Cooks don't always want to be on show – in full view of everyone when they drop, taste or ruin something. Smells can hang over friends and family while they are eating; and washing up mounts into unsightly piles. So it's a good idea to make a spatial division between eating and cooking areas by bringing more units and shelves into the room (those cupboards that act as a partition could be accessible from both sides) or a row of Venetian or canvas blinds, or a moveable screen. A raised back on a room-dividing worktop will hide clutter when you are sitting and eating. An extendable table saves space when you are not entertaining, and a bench along one side of a rectangular table will enable you to squeeze in more people.

Separate lighting between work and eating areas – direct and efficient for the worktop, subtle and softer over the table – and ensure that a good extractor or natural air flow whisks away fiercer cooking smells before they dominate. Cut down tiring noise from kitchen appliances by mounting them on rubber pads. Cork or cushioned vinyl flooring stops sound reverberating better than tiles; wood worktops, shelves and panelling are quieter than stainless steel, laminate or ceramic, and open shelves absorb sound better than shiny cupboard doors.

1

2

3

1 If you have to put the dining table in the cooking area, make a virtue out of it. This specially designed one, more an art object than anything, sets the tone for the room.

2 A built-in kitchen unit with a low upstand screen on top hides the pots and pans and provides useful extra shelf space. Such a device makes a neat unobtrusive division between cooking and dining areas.

3 Eating in the kitchen doesn't have to mean snatching a snack on the run. Here, carefully chosen finishing touches – lamp, Hockney posters, smartly laid table, flowers – turn a functional kitchen into a seductive dining room by night.

4 A novel room divider: house plants encased in a purpose-built glass-fronted cabinet.

IDEAS

1

2

3

4

1 Drawers and shelves made of perforated metal are a stylish alternative to wood, as demonstrated by Eva Jiricna, designer of this galley kitchen.

2 Timber dowel, here let into the timber work surface: a good-looking and convenient way of draining crockery and glasses.

3 A sophisticated version of the well-worn serving hatch created in the space between a deep worktop and hanging cabinets above.

4 Glass-backed cabinets, supported on an island unit, provide storage space without shutting out the light.

5 A storage trolley on wheels fits neatly under the worktop when not needed elsewhere.

6 Industrial shelving system and handyman's plastic trays given a new domestic role in the kitchen.

7 Timber storage units are stained to provide a touch of personality which so many laminate kitchen units lack.

8 A cheerful and appropriate decorative touch; labels from canned foods.

EQUIPMENT

Essential appliances, such as cookers and sinks, are at long last becoming subjects of serious, good design. It seems extraordinary that such obvious household objects have been ignored for so long. Cumbersome shapes are giving way to more straightforward lines, thanks to European design influences, and awareness of the handsome, hard-working equipment in professional kitchens.

Cookers

Fuel may not be a matter of choice, but if it is try to back both gas and electricity with a gas hob and electric oven. Gas is more flexible for critical cooking – tricky sauces or perfect omelets – but electricity keeps its temperature more evenly for lengthier cooking. It is possible to buy a free-standing combination fuel cooker that will slide between units which is much more economical and less space-consuming than a split-level oven and hob. Split-level ovens do however have the advantage of saving your back when peering in at a soufflé, and being out of small children's reach.

Microwave ovens

These ovens work by agitating the molecules within the food and thus cooking it from the inside out. They are a boon to busy cooks, and parents who want to heat up small amounts of food quickly for grumbling infants. However it is difficult to cook food as appealingly as in a conventional oven as generally meat will not brown very well. Some ovens have both microwave and traditional electric power, and switch from one to the other for browning.

Sinks

Gone are the days of the simple stainless steel sink and drainer, when the biggest decision you had to make was which side to have the drainer on. Now the choice of shape, size, colour and materials is quite bewildering, to say nothing of the taps to go with them.

When buying a sink, remember that the largest thing you will probably want to wash in it will be an oven shelf. And beware architects and designers who want to banish drainers – unsightly as they may be in their eyes, a drainer

FRIDGES

Fridges are no longer mere randomly sized cool chests. The permutations of size and shape are multifarious and they now come in modular sizes to fit in with almost every kitchen design. Separate fridge and freezer units can fit side by side underneath a worktop, or one above the other. They range in sophistication from a 'centre' with different zones, each with a separate door, that can be turned from fridge to freezer to larder at the flick of a switch, to a mini fridge just 0.7 cubic metres (2.5 cubic feet) in capacity. Accessories extend to chilled drink and ice cube dispensers.

MICROWAVE OVENS

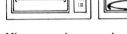

Microwaves have revolutionized the kitchen. There are now models that can heat and brown food at the same time. Some have turntables or a fan for even cooking.

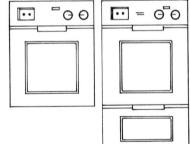

SPLIT-LEVEL OVENS

Ovens cater for every standard of cook, with models offering catalytic 'stay clean' backs and sides, defrosting devices, removable grease filters, and glass panels. Fan-assisted ovens are now sophisticated enough to crackle pork. Double ovens with a grill/second smaller oven are very useful for smaller meals, or heating up plates when the main oven is full.

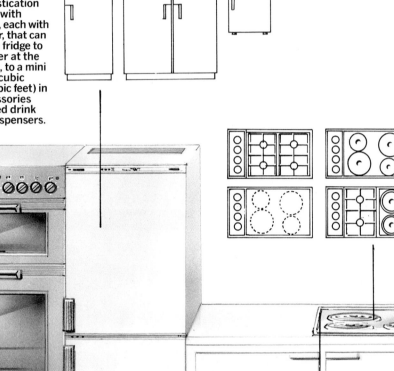

FREEZERS

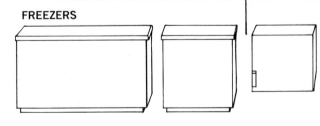

Whatever the size of your family, there are now many different sizes of freezer to cater usefully for any number from one person up. In different shapes of both chest or upright versions, the largest can store about 159kg (350lbs) of food, the smallest, a compact model, about 49kg (108lbs). Some models have automatic defrost and built-in drainage outlets included in each cabinet.

HOBS

Hobs now cater for all individual cooking preferences: from vitreous ceramic hobs which are easy to clean, gas rings, electric rings or a combination of gas and electricity. The latest hob is a mix of halogen and electricity, where three halogen lamps instantly become hot or cold at the turn of a switch. Together with two electric rings, the whole unit is housed under a ceramic top.

SINKS AND TAPS

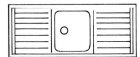 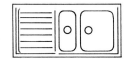 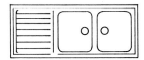 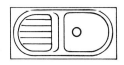

Sinks can offer combinations that seem almost tailor made to individual requirements. The material may be stainless steel or enamel, the

shape round, square, rectangular or half-oval, and the colour can be chosen from a spectrum wide enough to blend with most schemes.

Accessories that fit over the sinks make life easier – drainer baskets with integral plate racks, strainer bowls, chopping boards and flat drainer

trays have turned the sink from a place to wash up into an activity centre.

  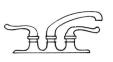

Mixer taps are a sensible choice for any kitchen sink. They are available in chrome, satin chrome and in a broad range of colours to match the

sinks. You can choose between having separate hot and cold taps or one single lever tap which operates force of flow, and alters levels of hot and

cold water at the same time. Mixer tap necks range in shape from angular to elegant swan necks.

WASTE DISPOSAL

This is what you don't see of your waste disposal unit. Some models have attachments which will drive vegetable peeler machines, or turn your sink into a mini washing machine.

is an invaluable piece of equipment – without one you will find yourself forever drying up. The draining racks that fit over some sinks are useful but rarely very generous. With wood worktops, runnels can be (carefully) carved into them to allow water to drain into the sink.

Taps
The enormous choice, particularly of handsome Continental designs, has created a new kind of fetish. While some swear by Danish taps, others will only contemplate having Italian ones. Whatever your inclinations, it's worth shopping around rather than putting up with what the builder orders. Beware fiddly plumbing involved in some designs. Mixer taps suit the kitchen sink best.

Dishwashers
When you have been spoiled by a constant supply of squeaky clean glasses, it's difficult to put up with the smears of hand-washing ever again. A dishwasher can transform your life and is totally addictive. Choose a model that's well-insulated so you aren't deafened by its sloshing, and one that can cope with pots and pans as well as fragile glass.

Fridges and freezers
Serious cooks, large families and keen gardeners would be lost without a freezer. They don't have to be enormous supermarket chests – upright ones will fit neatly under a worktop and are easier to keep organized. If you have a freezer, use it to make ice as well, then you will only need a larder fridge. Many fridges and freezers can have their doors hung on either side, so think about which way would suit you best, and whether you want ones which can be stacked on top of one another. Colour has invaded these traditionally 'white goods', but beware buying anything too vivid.

Washing machines
Another regular in the contemporary kitchen. Most will fit happily under a worktop, and if space is at a premium consider buying a combined washing/dryer design, or stack the machines.

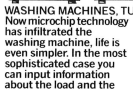

DISHWASHERS
Dishwashers now offer a choice of programmes including 'plate warming'; some will even wash dirty pans. Worktop models are now very sophisticated and efficient.

WASHING MACHINES, TUMBLE DRYERS AND SPIN DRYERS
Now microchip technology has infiltrated the washing machine, life is even simpler. In the most sophisticated case you can input information about the load and the

machine selects the programme. Front loaders are ever popular but top loaders are elegantly slimline. For greater control of wash and spin times and water

temperature, twin tubs are favoured. Tumble dryers now leave clothes crease free. Spin dryers leave your washing iron (not bone) dry, and rinse as well as spin.

APPLIANCES

Kitchen appliances often tantalize with promises of time or energy saving, healthier food or exotic new concoctions. Many are invaluable and improve the quality of kitchen living, as well as dining. But others will soon lose their initial fascination and be consigned to an early retirement. How handy it would be to visit a kitchen gadget 'library' where you could exhaust curiosity and consuming desires for more gadgetry, without permanently cluttering up your shelves.

Kitchen equipment departments in large stores are devoted to rows of the latest sandwich toasters, electric slow cookers, deep fryers and microwave ovens – most of which are extraordinarily ugly and hardly essential. A few, however, are rewardingly helpful.

Food processors

The ultimate in kitchen appliances, these chop, slice and grate vegetables, mince meat, whip desserts, beat cakes, knead dough and purée soups. The more sophisticated models have a vast range of attachments, making it possible to squeeze oranges, peel potatoes, grind coffee and even make pasta. An upright model takes up the least work space, though you still need storage for the attachments.

Slow cookers

These cook their contents of, say, lamb hotpot or Irish stew for hours. Using only as much electricity as a light bulb, they can be left to cook the supper while you are working. But they do not really save your labour as the meat and vegetables still have to be prepared and browned before going into the slow cooker.

Toasters

There is a large selection to choose from, including new sleeker, slimmer designs than the original bulky box shapes. Automatic toasters have a control which determines how well the toast is cooked. Some take four slices – ideal for large families – but most take two. Make sure that the slots are wide enough to take thick slices of homemade bread without burning them, and that the toaster has a removable crumb tray.

Top row: Sandwich toaster with five heat settings; sandwich toaster with thermostatic controls; traditional toaster; convenient hand-held blender for sauces, soups and cocktails; electric mixer with a variety of different whisks; spring balanced scales with two trays.
Middle row: The familiar Brown Betty teapot; heat resistant teapot which holds the tea leaves in a central mesh; espresso/cappuccino machine with two cup capacity; wall-mounted coffee grinder with variable adjuster for granule size; glass jug Cafetière which makes both tea and coffee; blender/

Kettles

The conventional shaped metal kettle has been joined on retailers' shelves over recent years by upright, plastic, even coloured versions of this essential appliance. Like taps, kettles have left the purely functional world to become as much of a visual accessory as anything else. The upright electric kettles, often made in tough plastics, are good because they are graduated in diameter so you only have to put in a cup full of water to cover the element, saving energy and water.

Coffee makers

Apart from the simple jug method, and Cafetière which is really a sophisticated jug, there are many ways of making coffee, each with its own devotees.

The drip filter method has been electrified into a useful machine, which heats the water and then drips it through a filter paper filled with coffee into a jug that sits on a hot plate to keep warm. The resulting coffee can be very good, but the hot plate tends to stew the coffee after a while.

The other mechanical method gaining popularity is for making espresso coffee. There are many domestic machines on the market to choose from, though the expensive Italian models are the most effective, as well as looking the most stylish. The dark, aromatic coffee, with its distinctive 'cream' top is produced by forcing hot water under pressure through highly roasted, finely ground coffee. Many designs also incorporate a steam pipe for heating and frothing milk for cappuccino.

Pasta machines

The popularity of all things Italian, from pasta to Pirelli, means that the country's cooking equipment is becoming progressively commonplace in our kitchens. Pasta machines can make the special treat of home-made pasta a daily event for the dedicated, though purists would probably opt for doing the whole process by hand – mixing, rolling and cutting the dough. There are domestic machines that will do everything for you, with a variety of discs to produce the different pasta types, from macaroni to fettucine.

liquidizer with half litre (one pint) capacity; pump and drink thermos flask; thermos jug designed by Eric Magnussen; microchip kettle which can boil as little as one cupful of water at a time or as much as 1.5 litres (3 pints); classic automatic kettle.
Bottom row: Rice cooker and steamer; cappuccino/espresso machine with a 20 cup capacity; filter coffee maker with heatproof glass jug; pasta machine with facility to make 20 different pasta types; food processor with Sabatier stainless steel blades and a variety of different attachments.

BATTERIE DE CUISINE

Accumulating a random personal collection of equipment is one of the joys of cooking, though stocking up is also one of the most pleasant parts of setting up or expanding a kitchen.

This list of tools is several steps above the bare necessities – a really good knife, spoon, chopping board and saucepan might be enough for some people.

Sharp edges

Go for quality; good knives are a cook's greatest friends. Superior tempered stainless steel with a high carbon content or carbon steel are best; both will hold a fine edge, though carbon steel needs more attention as it is corroded by acids in fruit and vegetables. Store knives carefully so their edges don't get battered by other occupants of a drawer. A knife rack or box will do the trick.

Saucepans

Different materials have different qualities and a variety of types will serve you well. Enamelled steel pans are basic and serviceable, but not as tough as aluminium or cast iron. Enamelled cast iron pans are particularly good for slow cooking on the hob or in the oven. Durable stainless steel won't react with acids or alkali, but doesn't conduct heat as efficiently as other materials. Aim for heavy gauge pans with strong heat-resistant handles. Solid topped stoves need solid ground based pans or you will waste fuel and time.

Utensils

Culinary fashions and holidays abroad lure us into buying all sorts of more exotic equipment, which can either be short-lived passions or radically change our diet. Wok cooking, for example, is fast food par excellence, and the wok quickly becomes a favourite pan, whereas an asparagus or fish steamer has such a specific function that only devoted cooks will want to give them a permanent home.

Left to right from top: Rubber ice trays; salt and pepper mills; wire mesh sieve; storage jars; conical grater; fruit press; measuring spoons; funnel; marble pestle and mortar; measuring jugs; collapsible steamer; single slice lemon squeezer; thermometer; lobster crackers; garlic press; egg wedger; tongs; nutcracker; rotary grater; nutmeg grater; salad shaker; mesh skimmer spoon; loop wire whisk; balloon whisk; tea infuser; can opener; corkscrew; potato peeler; scissors; potato chipper; flat grater; turner; apple corer, fish slice; perforated metal spoon; ladle; cooling rack; fish mould; petits fours moulds; pastry cutters;

Sharp edges

1 each of large, medium and small carbon steel or stainless steel general purpose cook's knives
1 paring knife
1 boning knife
1 Chinese cleaver
1 serrated bread knife
sharpening steel or carborundum sharpening stone
magnetic knife rack or knife box

box grater
mandoline
pepper grinder
coffee grinder (electric or manual)
food processor (Magimix)
Mouli food mill

Invaluable vessels

At least 3 aluminium or enamelled steel saucepans in a variety of sizes
heavy duty frying pan (enamelled cast iron or steel)
small enamelled cast iron frying pan for eggs
casserole (enamelled cast iron or ceramic)

large mixing bowl
nest of 3 mixing bowls
pestle and mortar
ceramic quiche/tart/pie dish, with fluted edges
soufflé dish

meat roasting pan
baking sheet
loaf baking tin
2 round cake tins
wire cooling rack

expandable fan steamer
wire sieve
metal colander
salad shaker

rubberized ice tray

glass or transparant plastic storage jars

La Cafetière, or Moka express, or filter coffee pot
teapot
electric kettle

marble slab; cutlet frills; pixie bun tin. From top: Beech chopping block laid with decorating knife, vegetable scoop, zester, pastry wheel, grapefruit knife,

butter curler; egg timer; mandoline; knife block; knife rack; ravioli rolling pin; revolving rolling pin; sharpening steel; oyster knife; parmesan cheese knife.

Knives from top to bottom: cleaver, bread knife, fillet knife, three general purpose cook's knives, boning knife, paring knife. pastry brush; wooden meat tenderizer;

fork; spaghetti spoon and slice; pepper mill; beech coffee mill; mezzaluna; cheese plane; sandwich slice; boxwood spoons; bamboo steamer; chopsticks.

BATTERIE DE CUISINE

For good measure
measuring jug
set of scales or balance
measuring spoons

automatic timer
all purpose cooking thermometer

lemon squeezer
wooden chopping/bread boards
marble or slate slab

Kitchen drawer
corkscrew (two 'arm' handle variety)
tea strainer
can opener
skewers
rolling pin
potato peeler
apple corer
garlic press
metal and wood spatulas
balloon and rotary whisks
nut crackers
kitchen scissors
individual tea-making spoon or egg
palette knife
Spoons: wooden spoons, various sizes
perforated metal spoon
metal ladle
wooden fork

Special utensils
These are either more specialized,
expensive, or electrically operated. The
scope, of course, is endless.

oyster opener
copper bowl for beating egg whites
salad spin dryer
chinois (metal conical sieve)
fish kettle
enamelled cast iron terrine with lid
wok
tempura pan
pressure cooker
asparagus steamer
rice steamer ball
two-tier aluminium steamer
Chinese bamboo steamer
pasta cutting machine
outdoor barbecue (Hibachi)
double wire grill
yoghurt maker
wine rack

Top row: Stainless steel roasting tray;
metal loaf tin; white ceramic soufflé dish;
copper bowl for beating egg whites;
white crinkly-edged flan dish; nest of
Pyrex mixing bowls.

Middle row: Three cake tins; cast iron
frying pan with wooden handle; one-
handled aluminium colander; metal
chinois; steel wok for high-speed Chinese
stir-frying.

Bottom row: Cast-iron casserole; stainless
steel omelet pan; double-boiler;
general cooking pan; asparagus
steamer and basket; white enamelled
milk pan; aluminium fish kettle.

Every home needs some sort of work space, whether it's a small desk for keeping the household accounts and writing personal letters, a larger space for needlework, a complete workshop for wood or metalwork or a serious business area for those who earn their living at home. In many cases very small and apparently unpromising alcoves, recesses or other little used areas can be adapted extremely well for efficient working. Thus, at one extreme, you could have a telephone in the kitchen, fixed next to a shelf for telephone directories, box files, notebook and pencil; and at the other, the traditional spacious, book-lined study with a calming atmosphere for reading or writing in peace.

In between come various solutions suited to the shape of the house and the requirements of the people living there. Needs for homework, for instance, may simply be met by a study area in the student's own room or a space at the kitchen or living room table, while there is a whole range of miscellaneous activities which, though they don't need a room to themselves, would be more pleasurable to do if there was somewhere specifically set aside for them: needlework, model making and cleaning shoes, for example.

What all these activities need in common is a large enough work surface at the correct height, comfortable upright seating (also at the right height), adequate and suitable lighting and unlimited storage. Even if your finances won't stretch to the library/study you can still aim for something bright, welcoming and efficient which will draw you to work there. Such spaces must be warm, well ventilated and attractive, otherwise, no matter how well organized they are in theory, they will simply not be used.

Spaces for work need more disciplined planning than spaces for leisure, and you should plot your requirements in detail before deciding on the site and the arrangement of your work area.

Think carefully about how much space you will need. Allow for more storage than you think you require including shelves, cabinets, pinboards and specialized storage for equipment, such as sewing or tool boxes, the telephone and any machines (such as a sewing machine or typewriter).

How much privacy will you want? Gregarious people work best with others around, but some activities, such as business telephoning, are better undertaken in peace. If the work in progress requires deep concentration over long periods, try to find a separate room or a space that can be screened off when necessary.

What services will you need? All activities will require adequate lighting and heating and therefore electric current with sufficient power sockets to take whatever equipment you intend to use. Some will require water and drainage too (a dark room or a pottery, for instance). Carrying pipes from room to room and power cables to a garage or shed can be expensive. If the activity is a serious, long term one, you could probably justify the expense but get one or two estimates before deciding.

In many ways the kitchen would seem an excellent place for hobbies, having water and power laid on, plus good work surfaces and cupboards, but it can be very unfair on the cook. Activities which are noisy and unsociable really need to have a room of their own. The garage, a garden shed or a dry, well-lit basement are good places, or failing that a ground floor room next to the kitchen would be perfectly suitable.

The safety of your work space should be planned at an early stage, when a number of dangers can be foreseen and eliminated. Doors should be lockable; all dangerous substances and tools kept out of reach of small children; socket outlets installed at chest height with on/off switches where they will be most convenient for the machinery so that cables will not trail about the room (this applies to telephone cables too). Make sure all appliances are earthed and keep power points away from conductors such as metal pipes, radiators and sinks. Avoid open fires, gas fires and electric radiant bars if you are going to be using inflammable materials and if you use a butane burner keep this away from any storage areas, rags and other flammable materials.

A study carved out of the corner of a living room can still have the flavour of the country house original on which it has been modelled. Among the ingredients are an antique desk, a Windsor chair and a student's lamp. A Persian rug covers the bare wood floor.

THE TRADITIONAL STUDY

Lucky indeed is the home that can afford a room specifically set aside for reading, writing and study. Traditionally such a room was for people with leisure, essentially the man's domain, and sometimes called the smoking room. It had purpose-built bookcases ranged around the walls from floor to ceiling, deep, comfortable leather-covered armchairs, an open fire, a desk overlooking the lawn, standard lamps and velvet curtains.

A modern family with academic, musical or literary leanings would find a room in which books take precedence a great bonus, and would use it constantly; in some cases such a space could even take the place of the conventional living room. Certain compromises to modern living would have to be made, such as making room for a television set, perhaps a home computer and its accessories. The important thing is that it should be equipped for serious but, at the same time, pleasurable study.

The basic plan

Study is the emphasis, so storage for books is important. Cover as many walls as necessary with purpose-built or built-in bookcases with adjustable shelves; or use a more elaborate storage system which may include wall-hung cupboards as well as shelves. Bookshelves should be divided at intervals to provide support for the books. The shelves themselves should be supported at not less than 1m (3ft) intervals because books are heavy and the shelves should not sag. The thicker the shelves, the better they will look: 13mm (½in.) is the minimum, 19mm (¾in.) is better. Large books, records, and the television set should have a specially tall shelf space created for them near the floor. Unshelved walls are best painted in a positive plain colour, or papered in a traditional Jacobean flower print, or (in a Georgian house) in Regency stripes.

Furniture, as opposed to built-in fitments, suits the traditional study well and can play an important part in creating the right atmosphere. There should be a desk with pigeon holes for papers and drawers for filing. Good quality furniture can grow old gracefully, so second-hand furniture would be better than something cheap trying to look traditional. Reproduction furniture will look better when it's been allowed to live a little and acquire some honourable scars. Flooring is traditionally wood block with Persian rugs, but fitted carpet will look good and help to keep the feet warm. Lighting should be discreet with spots or picture lights directed onto the books and paintings. There might be wall lamps for background light and maybe a standard lamp, and an Anglepoise or other desk lamp to work by.

The traditional study would have had a fireplace with an open grate, but if this is unrealistic, perhaps a gas log or coal fire, or a wood burning stove would give visual appeal while supplying warmth.

1 A well-organized working area — perfect for keeping the household accounts in an unfussed way. Victorian details — the shelf brackets and glass-fronted cabinet — match the desk and carved chair.

2 A modern evocation of the country house library. Dark colours set off rich book spines and a 20th century version of the leather club armchair. Glints from the table lights add an attractive finishing touch.

3 Taming the work place: a pretty relaxed room, where technology is not allowed to swamp the setting. A table rather than a desk, an armchair not an office chair, help to create an ideal atmosphere in which to face the bills.

Windows

Make the most of the windows, either as a light source or as a feature. You can build shelves on either side with a built-in window seat and if the window is rather high in the wall, put storage beneath it with the window seat a little higher. If the windows are placed so there's no opportunity to put shelves next to them, you can still use the space by putting a sofa or chaise longue there to enable you to read in good light.

Doors

A solidly made and well fitting door will help to soundproof the study. In general, unless restoring a period house, it is best to avoid fancy or reproduction door handles and to choose instead from the many simple, brass or porcelain classic fittings now on the market.

If you can't spare a complete room, folding doors, which slide neatly out of the way, can divide the library portion of a room from a more lively social area.

A modern alternative

An alternative to the traditional look is the high tech library. Here the shelving would be glass, chrome or some other industrial system, the chairs modern, brightly covered foam or tube framed, the floor sanded and sealed or stained, and scattered with kilim or other rugs. There might be a desk made up of trestles or low filing cabinets with a glass or wooden top, as well as modern track lighting, and if the room is tall enough, a platform of brightly painted scaffolding on which to support a desk for quiet study. Modern brightly coloured plastic door furniture would particularly suit this approach.

In essence the problems and solutions are the same; the difference is in mood. The modern version would suit a young family, and would probably be cheaper to set up than the more traditional one which must carry that solidity of materials and workmanship and an aura of permanence which is characteristic of the past.

THE OFFICE

E very home has to be 'run'. Even at the simplest level, bills must be paid, plumbers found, the house stocked with supplies and forms filled in, yet there is seldom any provision made for this. Instead papers are kept in various places; the telephone is in one room, message pads in another; unpaid bills lie on the table where they were opened.

For the basic minimum of housekeeping and family organization, a corner of the kitchen may be the most convenient place to work. A wall-hung telephone, with a shelf next to it for directories, notebook and pencil, a folder for papers, an adjustable kitchen stool and a lamp over the shelf or worktop are all that would be needed to provide an efficient work station without losing too much kitchen space.

For people who write many letters or are involved in part-time work, on committees and so on, a little more may be needed in the way of both space and planning. Sometimes a half-used room (a dining room or spare bedroom) can double up as a working space. Visitors will not mind sharing for a short time an orderly, well managed work room, and if the bed is a simple foldaway no 'worker' is going to mind sharing the room with the occasional guest. A good guideline is the very economical and imaginative type of student study/ bedrooms designed for modern universities, which manage to combine room for sleeping, storage and working in minute spaces.

The arrangement

To save space it is probably best to range everything against the wall, leaving the middle of the room free. If you are using a spare bedroom, keep the 'office' section distinct from the bedroom section as much as possible. A folding sofa bed can be used as seating for visitors. If you want to divide the bed and work area, construct a simple screen to act as a pinboard on one side and a bedhead on the other. For the house guest, fix hooks to the back of the door for coathangers, and provide a very small chest of drawers or a bedside 'box'.

For the office section, fix adjustable shelving to the walls, adding more as it

becomes necessary, but don't be inhibited about the amount you install initially; you can never have too many shelves. Some shelving systems are made with modular units which can be useful for certain types of storage. And some makers of fitted bedroom furniture include desk modules in their ranges so that it is possible to co-ordinate the bedroom and office sections of the room. Co-ordinating colours can also be used, but on the whole colours should be kept simple: there will be enough pattern created by the fact that it is a work space.

Storage units should not protrude further than the width of the working surface. There should be background light from the walls, a working light at the desk and a reading lamp by the bed. Central heating would be ideal but failing that a fan heater will warm up a small room very quickly.

Equipment
The home office requires carefully chosen equipment if it is to work efficiently. Consider the work you do, make a list of the equipment you use then sort out your priorities.

For simple household filing all you need is a small concertina file or a large box file with specially marked compartments. For more comprehensive filing, cabinets are available in bright colours, not just office grey and green, and the two-drawer versions can be fitted into quite a small space or even used as bases for a desk. Moulded plastic trays are available for pens, drawing pins, paper clips and so on.

Communicating
You may find that a wall-mounted telephone is best in the kitchen or hall, where space is scarce; that a desk phone is more appropriate in a concentrated work area; and that a cordless one will suit you if you wander round the house while working. An answering machine is vital if you rely on the phone and are not always at home.

Writing
A typewriter should be an essential piece of equipment for all who write letters. A very basic electric portable is quite adequate for housekeeping work or personal letters and will take up very little space. A more sophisticated

machine would be required by anybody typing for a living, and a word processor is invaluable for many small home-based businesses. Seek expert advice from a range of sources before settling on any machine and make sure the after sales service will be adequate. Allow a large enough worktop space for the machine and its printer and for other desk work as well.

Light
The recommended level of light for work areas is about 400 lux (lumens per square metre). Daylight is still the best, so exploit it. It is generally better to work sideways onto a window than facing it, to avoid glare from the sun, although adjustable louvred blinds would help to prevent this. Fluorescent tubes give excellent general lighting at two or three times the efficiency of tungsten bulbs. They should be suspended well above eye level, again to avoid glare; choose colours that simulate daylight. Lighting track is easy to install and will take spotlights which can be angled in various directions to give the light you need where you need it.

Furniture
The minimum essentials are a table and a chair. The table should be at elbow height for writing and reading but about 100mm (4in.) lower for typing. The best solution is to have two worktops at right angles to each other, one low, the other higher, and a chair which will swivel to face either. Unless you are going to have your furniture built in as part of a shelving system or of a co-ordinated whole, the best furniture for working on is that designed for the purpose — office furniture. Modern office furniture is flexible, tough and good-looking. Typists' chairs are designed specifically for people sitting at desks all day and modern ones can be very attractive as well as supportive.

Heating
Sitting still all day tends to make you feel cold. You will need your room temperature to be between 20° — 22°C (68° — 70°F) unless you get up and do exercises every hour or so. If you have no central heating, a fan heater of at least 2kW and preferably 3kW will be necessary.

1 The drawing board has been specially chosen to double as a desk in this light, spacious studio.

2 This thoughtfully planned U-shaped work room makes use of the maximum desk space and allows the owner to turn from one task to another with the greatest of ease.

3 Working at home from a cramped terraced house need not be a problem. Well-chosen antiques, enlivened by OMK stacking units, create a schoolroom atmosphere.

THE WORKSHOP

The obvious place for a workshop is the garage or a garden shed, though it is quite possible to adapt a room within the house if it is on the ground floor or basement and doesn't create too much noise or nuisance. What you can't hope to do is make it double up with another unrelated activity. Workshop activities are noisy and dusty, so choose a room as far away as possible from the living areas. A simple home workshop can be quite satisfactorily sited in a long narrow space, where the worktop can run along one wall and the opposite wall can be used for storing materials. The bench should be solid, though in a very small workshop you could probably begin with a portable workbench.

Storage

Tool storage is particularly important, not just so that you can find something quickly when you need it, but because workshop tools are delicate and expensive instruments and storing them carefully will help to preserve them. Keep them above the workbench on a pegboard with the outline of each tool painted on it so you can see what's where and what's missing. Screwdrivers, chisels and similar tools can be hung in specially cut grooves in wooden battens mounted on the wall. Holes drilled into a wooden block will hold spare drill bits.

Shelving is necessary for all the miscellaneous accessories such as glue, varnish, nails, tacks, screws, polish, cloths and so on. Sets of plastic drawers available from DIY stores are useful for very tiny bits and pieces such as tacks and drawing pins.

Store large sheets of materials upright against the wall opposite the workbench with a wooden batten nailed to the floor to hold them in place. Industrial metal systems such as Dexion can be put together in different combinations to create storage of all kinds including very wide shelving.

Provide a big waste bin next to the workbench in which to sweep offcuts and other bits. The space under the workbench is good for bulky objects, for instance the sawhorse.

Lighting and heating

Provide general lighting with fluorescent tubes, then add spotlamps over work surfaces and machines. Constant background heating is important or the tools will get rusty, but the room temperature need not be high, since working itself requires a lot of physical activity and generates heat.

Flooring

Choose a hard floor covering which you can sweep easily. Vinyl sheet or tiles are excellent and cleaning will be even easier if this is carried 200mm (8in.) up the wall to give a coving. A gloss paint is probably best for the walls, though modern eggshell paints are quite easy

to wash, and less clinical to live with.

Safety

Follow the obvious safety rules: avoid clutter and be disciplined about putting things away as you use them; connect electrical tools to power points near them so there are no trails of flex (a continuous power track on the ceiling is very safe in this context); avoid fires with open flames and keep a dry powder extinguisher within easy reach of where you work, and a first aid box prominently marked.

Specialist needs

Certain hobbies demand special facilities in order to be pursued seriously, particularly if they are noisy or require a lot of space. Be prepared to devote a whole room to your hobby and to equip it properly.

Model making

Seal the door against fumes; muffle engine-testing noises by building test boxes out of a dense material and lining them with fibreglass blanket; fit engines with silencers. These rules apply whether the room is in the house or in an outhouse. The models can be suspended from the ceiling for storage

so a high room would be ideal, otherwise you will need a deep rack or cupboard. A loft space is perfect for this sort of workshop because of its height and because you can use the floor space next to the outside wall for storing models where the ceiling is too low to stand up.

Printing and dyeing

You need a fairly large room with its own water supply, and a table in the middle so you can work all round it, though if necessary one end could be against a wall. The table should be 150mm (6in.) larger all round than the largest print and for printed textiles should be not less than 1800mm x 1200mm (6ft x 4ft) and its height should be about 200mm (8in.) lower than the elbows. Other worktops should be as long as the space allows, up to 900mm (3ft) wide for screen printing but only about 400mm (16in.) wide for block printing, and are best ranged against the wall. A specialized rack system would be the best solution for storing prints because vertical drying is essential. But an old-fashioned kitchen pulley, if the ceiling is high enough, or a plan chest, are both useful for storing prints. For the rest, brushes, bottles

1 Every spanner and screwdriver has its place in this well-designed workshop. Combining practicality with good looks, this room not only provides space for carpentry, but also a worktop and typist's chair for the paperwork.

2 Started in the corner of the kitchen, this home wine-making operation has expanded into the workshop, the perfect place to accommodate it.

3 This full-blown domestic workshop is equipped with no-nonsense finishes such as the hard-wearing tiled floor. Joe Colombo's bobby trolley provides mobile storage.

4 A New York loft combines a soothing living area with a concentrated work space.

and tins can be stored on the ubiquitous upright-and-bracket adjustable shelf system, which is probably the cheapest and most convenient solution.

Pottery

You will need a supply of cold water, and a waterproof floor which is easy to clean, with, if possible, a central or side gutter so you can sluice it down. Clay is a heavy material so all the furniture and fittings should be solid and sturdy. Old kitchen or garden tables, or old sewing machine tables would all work well. Taps should be high enough to fill a bucket in the sink. Clay and prepared slip and glazes can be kept in large plastic bins with fitted lids. Use different coloured buckets for slip and glaze. As always, you will need plenty of shelf space for storage and also for drying pots. A 'damp' cupboard can be useful to store work in progress. Custom-built damp cupboards are lined with zinc and have sealable doors but you could make one by covering the shelf of any cupboard with zinc and laying a layer of plastic over the floor.

Heating should be versatile since sometimes a potter works quite hard physically, and at other times the job involves sitting still for fairly long periods. If the kiln is in this room, keep it carefully locked with an isolating switch mounted on the wall at a high level. The same applies to an electrically operated wheel.

Photography

Setting up a really good dark room can be expensive and it is not always easy to find the right space. It will need a cold water supply fed from the cold tank, not from the mains; a second bathroom or small bedroom with a basin would do. You will have to have a special wooden frame made to fit the window exactly and cover this with black felt or velvet to exclude all light. Make sure the room is ventilated either by allowing the door to let in air but not light, or by mechanical ventilation. The room should be divided into wet and dry areas, one containing the sink and developer, and one the enlarger, the paper, masking frame, glazing sheets, guillotine and dryer.

If possible, the room should be just big enough to reach both sides without having to walk backwards and forwards. Dark rooms should be kept at a fairly constant temperature, but not too hot; keep a thermometer on the wall. Melamine or ceramic tiles can be used to protect the walls round the wet areas from chemical splashes. The floor should be asphalt or vinyl. Walls and ceilings should be white, but the wall finish round the enlarger should be matt black.

THE LAUNDRY AND UTILITY ROOM

The kitchen is usually considered the right place for laundry equipment but it is not really the most suitable. Dirty washing and food preparation do not go well together and the kitchen is often too small to accommodate laundering comfortably anyway. A separate room off the kitchen or downstairs bathroom would be a much better answer; sometimes the garage can be satisfactorily adapted. An old scullery, passage or an extension out into the garden would be suitable too.

Obviously you will want a hot and cold water supply, space for a washing machine and dryer and a waste outlet, some form of storage for dirty clothes, a worktop for wet clothes as they come out of the machine, and high shelves for bleaches, washing powders and so on. If you can afford to heat this space and paint it becomingly you can use it for ironing as well.

The room should be on the ground floor if possible, with a waterproof and easily cleaned finish since it is in the nature of washing machines to flood from time to time. If you want to box in your appliances so that they look like cupboards, make sure the maintenance man can reach inside when he comes to service the machine.

The cleaning cupboard

A utility room is a good place to store the cleaning equipment for which it is always so difficult to find room. A cupboard with a well-planned interior should include shelves at a high level, with wire baskets and drawers to hold miscellaneous and oddly shaped items. Hanging storage is useful for window cleaners, cobweb brushes, other brooms and vacuum cleaners and you can use bulldog clips for cloths, rubber gloves and so on, which will dry while hanging up and be easy to locate. The more you can fix to the wall, the more space you will leave for sorting washing and standing an ironing board. Run your waterproof floor finish right into the cupboard, which will make it easier to clean and easier to wheel heavy objects into.

Don't put up with the usual single light bulb hanging from the centre of the ceiling, but install a light track for several spotlights which can be angled

as you wish. Fluorescent strip lighting will be effective, if you choose one of the warmer colours. Ventilation is important, so if necessary install an electric extractor fan.

The sewing room

A sewing area can often be set up in a part of the home where other activities take place. Certain sorts of sewing such as embroidery, darning or patchwork can be happily worked on in the living room, since they are sociable activities, provided that suitable storage is made available: a drawer or two for materials, a sewing box and somewhere to put buttons.

If the sewing machine is going to be used frequently, it would be better to set up a work area in a less commonly used room such as the dining room or a spare bedroom, although it might be possible to turn a landing or a large alcove into a workmanlike space. You will need to allow space and storage for all the processes used in sewing: preparation of the material (i.e. cutting out), machining, fitting and ironing. So you will need a large amount of worktop or usable floor space for the cutting and arranging of the materials,

worktop space for the machine and for the fabric alongside it, also room for a tailor's dummy or for the live model to stand in front of a full length mirror. The ironing board and the iron could be kept out of the way by mounting them on a wall when not in use.

Plenty of storage and plenty of work surface are the first essentials: chests of drawers or large shelves for fabrics; shelves for books, magazines and patterns; a pegboard for scissors and sticky tapes; a pinboard for ideas, notes, memos, addresses and fabric samples. The ideal height for the working table is the same as for a typewriter, about 100mm (4in.) below the elbows. An adjustable chair such as a typist's chair is the best form of seating. Try to plan the room so that you don't have to put away the table and hang up the ironing board every time you finish work — it will be best if everything is ready to hand and you can begin work again at a moment's notice. If space does not allow for this then a table hinged to fold out from the wall could be useful.

Many of the accessories designed for office workers are just as invaluable for people who sew. Plastic tidies can hold

French chalk, pins, pens, buttons, hooks and eyes; an old cutlery canteen makes an excellent box for cotton reels; a hanging rail, either as part of a wardrobe or on its own is good for hanging garments on (if space is limited hang them on a bentwood hat rack instead). There should be shelf space for bottles of various kinds: cleaning fluid, starch, fabric finisher and so on. Try to provide space for the sewing machine to be permanently at the ready. Otherwise a fitment can be bought which swings it up and over from a shelf below. Bales and lengths of fabric can be kept on open shelves or in drawers. The absolute rule is that everything should be to hand, easily accessible and ready to use. Most people's sewing fails to be completed because of the chaos surrounding the unfinished work, hidden in cupboards and lost around the house.

Lighting should be much the same as for an office environment except that daylight is rather more important for looking at and comparing colours. A room temperature of between 18° — 22°C (65° — 68°F) is best, as sewing is a sedentary occupation, although ironing warms you up quickly.

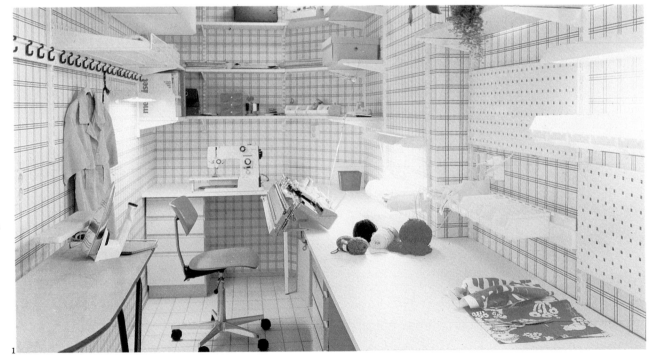

1

3

2

4

1 A functional yet cheerful sewing room with plenty of storage space and a long worktop, where sewing and knitting machines can be kept out. An ironing board and pegs are handy for pressing and hanging the finished article, and a typist's chair prevents backache.

2 Set aside a whole room for household activities if you have the space. But it shouldn't look drab or industrial. Attractive floor tiles and a trompe l'oeil blind will help to brighten up your chores.

3 It's possible to create a utility corner even in an open plan interior. The floor is practical and hard-wearing, and you are not cut off from the rest of the house.

4 Extra wide corridors can provide the space to make a laundry. A washing machine, dryer and ironing board are all concealed in the cupboards.

BEDROOMS

While the heart of the house is usually the kitchen, the bedroom is the place to indulge in personal fantasies. The days when bedrooms were designed only for sleep are gone. Born out of the '60s trend for one-room living and the need to make every inch of space pay its way, the bedroom increasingly accommodates other activities. No longer is it automatically designed around a bank of built-in cupboards and the central reason for its existence – the bed. Furniture usually associated with the sitting room now appears as a matter of course in the bedroom. Individual pieces, such as armoires and chests of drawers, frequently replace the hidden storage solutions of the last two decades, all combining to make a room with character.

Once, decorating a bedroom meant deciding on a colour scheme and finding curtains to match. These days, it means choosing a look. The possibilities are unlimited, from lacey romantic flounces to a sparse minimalist approach. You simply have to decide which aspect of your character you want reflected in this very private room.

1 Architect Rick Mather completely rebuilt his London house so he could see more of the garden. With skilful reworking of floor levels, both inside and out, he was able to bring the roof terrace within view of his vast bedroom window.

2 This town house bedroom renounces all but the most feminine of looks. Pleated fabric at the walls, softly ruched blinds, and a full table-cloth give the impression of a room soft and sensual.

1

In a period house, the opportunities for creating a particular atmosphere or reproducing a specific style are more open than they may be in a modern house or apartment. Victorian mouldings and ceiling roses can trigger off inspiration for a lace-and-frills romantic style, while a floor of beautifully seasoned boards might suggest a rustic English or an American colonial bedroom. A fireplace, which ten years ago would probably have been boarded up to make an extra wall for the bed, might now become the focus for a booklined room with the feel of a gentlemen's club. You only have to decide which particular look to create.

You may already have certain pieces of furniture that you will want to accommodate in the bedroom, and these may limit your options. In a modern house you could be starting with a blank canvas, which can make the choice harder. Will you follow the lead of its modular design and go for an easy-to-run industrial-look high tech room? Or will you create an unexpected surprise by filling it with strong colours and highly patterned fabrics for an exotic or even eastern effect?

Once you have settled on your theme, you must work out to what uses the room will be put. Will you keep all your clothes in the bedroom? Will personal things like make-up and brushes be kept here or in the bathroom? Is the room to be used for other activities like sewing and typewriting? Will telephone, television or stereo be stored here? These questions should help you to define how much storage space you will need, whether you have enough electric sockets and if they are well-sited, whether you want to create different areas within the room for your other work, and how much you need to consider sound insulation.

FINDING YOUR STYLE

The privacy of the bedroom can make it the natural place for rather bolder design than would look comfortable in more public parts of the home. If you have always wanted an Arab tent, a Victorian parlour or a beachcomber's hut, the bedroom might be the right place to recreate it. Because it is out of sight and because conscious use is limited to a small fraction of each day, such themes will not become as oppressive as they might be in more heavily used parts of the home.

Remember that artificial light will have a major part to play in the design of any style of bedroom. Obviously it is important to establish early on whether you are interested in creating a room that is designed to be seen at night, or one which makes getting up and rushing off to work a less painful experience. If your strategy is to banish natural light as much as possible and create a night-time atmosphere, you will need to add the sparkle of rich colours and glossy finishes. If on the other hand you choose to create the kind of room in which you can pull back the curtains and let the morning sun come flooding in, you will need to work with bolder, tougher elements –stronger shapes, brighter colours and more textured fabrics–that can stand the exposure.

The elements available to create style in a bedroom may be rather more restricted than in your other living rooms. If space is limited, you will probably only have a bed, a table, a chair and the walls, floor and ceiling to work with. At the other extreme, when you have the space and the inclination to turn the bedroom into a place in which to dress, and to start the day at a leisurely pace with a cup of coffee and the morning mail, it may be possible to create several different focuses in the room. If you do opt for a theme, carry it out with conviction, not on a half-hearted scale.

The type of bed you choose, and where you put it are always key decisions. Some people prefer to draw attention to it, to make it the unchallenged focus of the room, either by its position, or by selecting the type of four poster, or brass bedstead that naturally steals the limelight. This

approach can work in several different styles. For the rustic look use an antique French, simulated bamboo, carved or English pine bedstead. Set it off against a natural wood floor, natural coloured fabrics with contrasting textures and weaves for the cushions, chair coverings, curtains and quilts. Paint the walls white or off-white, and strip the doors and window frames. Other accessories could include marble washstands, samplers, rag rugs and rush or coir matting on the floor. A hanging converted oil lamp would complement the look.

Nostalgia on a grander scale can also be focused on the bed. A four poster topped by a bold print fabric gathered into frills and furbelows, teamed with full curtains pulled in to either side of a pelmeted window by heavy braid cord, will go a long way to create the atmosphere of a grandly proportioned Victorian room. A chaise longue or an armchair upholstered in rich velvet would also be appropriate in this setting.

With a brass bedstead, it is possible to soften the glossy highlights of the brass by piling the bed with assorted cushions of contrasting lace finishes. Have a lace bedspread and lace-trimmed pillows and sheets; blousy festoon blinds, or swathes of cotton net would look good at the windows, along with a lace tablecloth draped over the bedside table, pale wall to wall carpet, and ribbon-threaded pleated paper lampshades.

The alternative to focusing on the

1 Traditional Victorian furniture and swagged chintz curtains combine well with the proportions of this bedroom to create the city traditional look.

2 Wilful post modernism: a platform bed is flanked by a pair of uplighters which match the colour of the architraves and beading perfectly. The same shade is picked up in the distressed paintwork, giving a subtle lift to the two-toned colour scheme.

3 The purest form of high tech minimalism is achieved not only with few pieces of furniture but by keeping them low. Sleeping in the middle of the room is for extroverts only – most people seek the security of a wall.

4 Piers Gough's jokey eclectic bed and bathroom studiously subverts conventional good taste.

5 The smallest of rooms can carry off the grandeur of the country house style if the look is put together with complete authority. The striped wallpaper is a perfect background for the architectural prints, and the room is crowned by the chandelier heirloom.

bed, is to minimize its impact. This can be accomplished in a variety of ways, by screening it off from the rest of the bedroom with furniture or a low partitioned wall, or by choosing a design of bed that is as minimal as possible. At one extreme you could use a roll-up futon mattress; at the other extreme you could build the bed itself into the room.

A chic, hard edge approach to a bedroom would involve making the bed seem to disappear simply by having a soft mattress set almost flush into the floor. Storage would be contained in minimally detailed units, perhaps hidden by floor to ceiling mirrors. Venetian blinds would be an appropriate window covering. Other furniture would be kept strictly to a minimum,

perhaps a single wheeled bedside table to take an immaculately crafted reading light, and a high tech alarm clock/radio. On a fine morning with the sun filtering in through the blinds, the effect can look sensational. But keeping the look fresh depends on high standards of tidiness. It is possible to create a slightly less daunting version of the same look using greys and whites, blinds and a simple low bed.

The decorator look – glossy walls, stark sculptural pieces of furniture and dramatic lighting schemes – can be tailor-made for a bedroom. Don't be afraid of trying out a variety of different positions for the bed. With the right supporting furniture, placing it in the middle of the room can work just as well as backing it up against a wall.

DETAILS

The walls, ceiling, floor and windows of your bedroom give you the opportunity to establish your own particular look right from the start. There has never before been such a vast and exciting choice in wall and floor coverings and window dressings, but this richness can be bewildering, and it is essential to avoid having too many different elements in what should be the most restful room in your house. The following offers a few pointers.

Walls

We have become much bolder in our use of paints and wallpapers. No longer do we feel that we always have to play it safe with a choice of wallpaper or paint that tones with or brings out some tint in our curtains or furnishing fabrics. The huge range of paint and wallpaper that is now available makes the possibilities for decorating endless; and the bedroom is the best room in the house in which to experiment – if it's not a total success, at least no-one else needs to be shown the result.

Wallpaper   Most paper collections are now designed to co-ordinate through several different patterns with borders, friezes and fabrics. The one link is the colourway that you pick as your starting point. Having settled on that, you have the option to use up to six different patterns in one room – and cleverly done that can look very striking. For instance, if you have a large, high-ceilinged room, you can create greater intimacy by reducing its height visually with a strong frieze at the top of the walls. Bring the room in even further by running a complementary border in dado-rail fashion round the middle of the walls. But first between the ceiling and dado border lay a paper of one design, then on the dado (the area from the border to the skirting board) a different paper but of co-ordinating design. Hang a contrasting material at the windows and on any furniture. Bring it all together by picking out one constant plain colour for your cushions.

There are equally effective, but less theatrical co-ordinations. The print on the paper may be repeated on the contrasting fabric, but with another pattern imposed upon the basic design.

Chintzes have seen a strong revival, given a new twist by being printed over simple geometric backgrounds that are the design of the co-ordinated paper. Some of the foreign imported papers – admittedly at some expense – transform your room into an exotic oriental fantasy. Paisleys have seen a great revival with French designers, printed in deep purples, rich crimsons, dark greens, lifted with lines of gold. The initial expense of the papers may be high, but classic designs such as these are less likely to become tiring than some of the brash, jarring geometrics that defined the '60s.

Borders and friezes are useful both for adjusting the dimensions of a room and for emphasizing different areas. Think about running them *down* the wall, as well as across it, framing a chimney breast, or windows and doors. They work well too, when used on walls painted in a colour echoed or picked out in the frieze. An elegant look can be achieved by pasting across fitted cupboard doors like paper beading.

An alternative to wallpaper, if your surfaces are absolutely sound, is stencilling. On a small scale, for an American colonial effect, a stencilled border could run up or around the walls, repeated on chests of drawers and cupboard doors. For a more ambitious decorator, many department stores and large stationery and home improvement shops now stock a hard machine with a rubber roller that blocks a pattern onto the wall. There are more than 50 designs to choose from, and these are transferred with a thinned emulsion onto a contrasting colour background, to produce a pleasing hand-printed wallpaper effect.

Paint   We have become much more adventurous in our use of paint, exploring avenues of paint technique that were previously considered the province of the specialist. Home decorators have begun to realize that 'distressed' – that is to say, broken - colour can be more restful and interesting than flat colour. With patience and care, special effects can be achieved by the amateur (for more information, see the chapter on Do-It-Yourself).

If your room is too small, or its ceiling is too low to take a patterned

1

wallpaper, consider deceiving the eye by painting and dragging the walls, an effect which will add height to a room, but should only be attempted on absolutely sound walls. Alternatively, distract the eye from the room's proportions by sponging the walls – a quick and easy method – or marbling or even creating a tortoiseshell effect, both of which are more difficult to achieve. If you are not a competent painter, or your walls are in too bad a condition to paint, almost every one of these looks is available on wallpaper in a wide range of colours and in some cases on other textures such as vinyl.

If you have a room with a mean window onto a poor view, or a room whose proportions might have seemed different had there been other windows or a French window leading into the gardens, why not paint a *trompe l'oeil* to give that impression.

Floors

Your first thought must be for the room below your bedroom. If you live in as apartment, it will not help relations with your neighbours if you stomp about in clogs on a wooden floor. If you expect to play music in your bedroom, however softly, think about carpeting. People in other rooms will find waiting for the next chorus as disturbing as waiting for drips from a leaking tap.

Floorboards   It may tie in better with the theme of your room to leave your boards bare. But check their condition first. Reboarding can be as expensive as laying down good carpet in a wood-look tobacco colour, and they won't keep the room as warm as fitted carpet will. If, in a futuristic bedroom, you want to lay an industrial sheeting floor, the boards will also have to be in sound and regular condition, or your new covering won't lie.

1 It took a few simple details to turn this little attic bedroom into one with a Victorian flavour. The brass bedhead, floral decorative frieze and two glass lamps are put together for maximum effect.

2 Use the floor as a decorative element in the bedroom. This minimalist room acquires much of its character from the mellow grain of polished wood.

3 There is a bold hand behind the choice of fabrics in this bedroom. Matching bedspread, curtains and tablecloth are emphasized against a contrasting backdrop – a device which cunningly softens the effect.

DETAILS

Carpet Because this is the room with the least wear and tear, you can opt for a light coloured carpet and even a relatively cheap one (though it is generally said that this is the room where you can go out and out for the most luxurious and expensive you can afford). A cheap carpet, often a bad investment in living areas because they show wear so quickly, will receive less knocks in the bedroom. And you can change it when you change your decoration with fewer qualms about wasting money.

Ceilings

Since you spend more time staring at the ceiling in this room than in any other, it is wise not to make too much of it, or you will quickly tire of any clever decorative effect. If you have ceiling roses and mouldings, decide whether you want to emphasize them by picking them out in a strong colour from the spectrum in which the rest of the room is decorated, or to lose them in a toning one. Picking out details in contrasting colours is probably not a good idea unless your bedroom is large enough to bear attention being drawn to the

mouldings. Whether your ceiling is painted in a lighter or darker colour than your walls depends on whether you want to raise or lower its height.

If you have a penchant for tents and canopies above your bed, give some thought to what your bedroom overlooks. If a main road runs beneath your window, concentrations of dust will collect on the drapes and they will soon look jaded.

Windows

Sometimes the amount of fabric you would need for curtains is simply going to cost too much for you to consider them. And sometimes they just aren't an appropriate window dressing for your room theme.

Blinds are an obvious solution, but they don't help insulation problems. If your budget can't stretch to double glazing yet your room needs extra protection, consider having a pair of internal shutters made to fit. Some period houses still have them in place. But most joiners can build them to any design that you want. Not only do they fit in with most interior designs, but will also cut down on outside noise.

1 Small details in a large room can get lost. In this loft, with its plain walls, the detail comes from the ceiling. The foil-backed insulating material is a stark contrast to the rough hewn beams, and it is high enough not to become overbearing.

2 Resist the temptation to install a characterless picture window. A lovely feature is made of this window by dividing it into three to create a screen-like shape which is no less effective at taking in the view.

3 Delicate lace hung at the window, or on cushions and bed-spreads, may simply be a finishing touch, but instantly makes a room look pretty and feminine.

It is vital to have decent storage space in the bedroom, particularly if you have little or no room for storage elsewhere in your house or apartment. And if the room is to have more than one function, it is especially important that it shouldn't appear a permanent clutter of untidy bits and pieces. But do be on guard – junk generally expands to fit the space available for storing it. If something disappears into an overhead cupboard, then it will probably stay there until you move house. It is a good idea to go over the things you have packed away once a year to see if you can't throw them out and make way for new treasures.

The first thing to look at for its space-saving possibilities is the bed. It may be worth your while to buy or build a new one if the one you currently own is taking up too much floor space without offering anything·more than a place to sleep. Immediately under the bed there is a useful area to fill. Some divan beds are sold with fitted below-bed drawers. If you build your own onto an existing bed, remember to drill a good many holes in the mattress base board so that air can circulate. Otherwise, simply sliding boxes under the base is a good solution for things that are in constant use, like toys, shoes and sports equipment – even blankets, sheets and pillowcases. Sturdy plastic boxes in bright colours with wheels attached even look good when they are left out in the room.

Stacking beds might be appropriate in a small house where there is no formal guest room. The top bed can still be slept on with the other one beneath it. Equally there are some handsome and reasonably priced sofa beds around. The simple, covered foam types are the most quickly converted into extra spare bedding and are useful in teenagers' rooms as seating. The more robust sofa beds fit perfectly happily in a formal sitting room.

If you are considering buying bunk beds, choose an interlocking type that can be converted back into single beds as children grow up. Probably the most productive space-saving idea is the bunk bed with storage space underneath. It comes ready-made or for self-assembly, the latter often giving

you the chance of choosing separate parts that make up into the best use of the space for your own special needs. There are systems which offer a wardrobe, desk and drawers, or open hanging space plus desk and drawers, some on permanent fixtures, some that can be changed about as your needs alter. Depending on the style of your room, you can choose systems in painted scaffolding, plain varnished wood, white Melamine, painted wood, or metal slot-in click systems in bright primary colours.

A built-in solution, perfect for a high-ceilinged room, is to construct a platform for a bed or work area above a bank of cupboards. Thus the ground floor becomes a permanent sitting room, while the sleeping zone stays hidden above. This effectively increases the ground floor space by almost half again, but check that you will have enough room to stand up on the platform. The platform need not be restricted to one end of the room. If the room is large enough, it can extend

along two or even three walls. The full height of rooms is often wasted, yet ingenious use of space need not spoil their proportions.

Storage space can be created by unblocking a boarded-up fireplace, opening it out to its full extent and building cupboards or open shelves inside. The most obvious place for built-in cupboards is on either side of a chimney breast, and sometimes it is a good idea to diminish the size of the room slightly by building out and right across it to fit in two cupboards and a drawer and dressing table unit between them. But investigate whether you might remove the chimney breast entirely, supporting any weight above with an RSJ. Once gained, the 22.5 cm (9 in.) that a chimney breast intrudes into a room can radically alter your placing of furniture and fittings and increase the feeling of space.

Since floor to ceiling cupboard doors in a small room will make it look even smaller, why not store clothes in open-fronted drawers with a lower lip

than back, like those used in department stores? In a room with alcoves or a chimney breast, shirt, jersey and underwear drawers on runners can be built into one side, and a cupboard faced with louvred doors to echo the open look into the other side.

The simplest of all storage systems is shelving. Change the proportions of a long, thin room by building shelves right across one end, with a desk and drawer area beneath. Whatever is stacked on the shelves becomes a part of the room's decoration.

Often the problem in very small bedrooms is the lack of space to open doors of cupboards without having to squeeze around the end of the bed. Change doors for roller blinds and, in a pattern or colour that echoes the decoration of the room, they will add to its style. Remove the door that opens into the room and fix a door that slides on the outside in its place. The space that was needed for the sweep of the door can then accommodate a small chest of drawers.

1 Bedroom storage that makes the most of its decorative possibilities. A drawing office trolley serves as a bedside table, red plastic storage trays on shelves make an ideal home for shirts, socks and underwear, and a restaurant kitchen unit on wheels stands in as a wardrobe. Perfect in a restricted space, this type of flexible storage keeps your clothes tidy and accessible.

2 Two hanging cupboards, one cupboard of shelves and a set of drawers all contained within one large, versatile and stylish unit. It incorporates solid shelves and plastic racks and hanging space for both long and short clothes. It can either be combined with other storage units from the same range, to provide a run of fitted cupboards, or used as a single free-standing unit.

BEDS

Buying a bed may feel like a once-in-a-lifetime investment, but you should aim to change your base or mattress at least once every 15 years. Beds take a major slice out of your furnishing budget, and if they are to last that long, you must be able to hand over your money convinced that the choice you have made is the right one.

Choosing the right bed

Make it a basic principle - whichever type of bed you choose - to buy the most expensive that you can afford; you will quickly regret a phoney bargain. The prospect of paying a great deal might be daunting, but dividing the sum by the number of nights you will spend in it over 15 years eases the agony. And you will never regret buying a comfortable bed.

Comfort depends on the ability of the mattress to keep the spine in its anatomically normal position. If a bed gives too much, the heaviest parts of the body sink below the rest; too rigid a bed and the lighter parts are forced to bend to the level of the unyielding surface. If you have a back problem, an 'orthopaedic' bed won't necessarily cure it and an arthritic condition may even be aggravated by too firm a bed. If you do have a bad back and are planning to buy a new bed, discuss it with your doctor first.

When you are buying a bed, try and lie on as many different ones as you can for at least ten minutes each. You will soon begin to feel the difference between them. If you are buying a double bed, both partners must test them together. There are manufacturers of single beds and mattresses that zip or slot together to meet the demands of couples whose needs are incompatible.

Points to watch for

A bed should be 15cm (6in.) longer than the tallest person sleeping in it. Check the *middle* of the bed since the edges will be taut anyway. There is no standard definition of 'firmness'. Obviously every manufacturer wants to sell his own brand. So if you are buying in a large shop or department store, ask the sales assistant if he is employed by the store or earns commission from a specific

manufacturer. Don't buy the first bed you see. You will be sleeping on it for years, so it is worth spending time on your choice.

Bed bases

Beds come in two parts - the mattress and the base. There are a number of different types on the market, so take care over your choice.

The traditional sprung bed   Typical of our grandparents' day and rarely made now, the sprung bed was an iron frame with a dense wire web stretched over the springs. Today beds are usually straightforward wooden divan base structures with a degree of springing to support the mattress.

Firm edge base divan   This type of bed base contains the springing inside a wooden frame, which is particularly useful if the bed is also used as seating.

Sprung edge divan   In this divan the springs are mounted onto a straightforward base and tied to each other above, while the flexible edges of the springing are lashed together by wire or to a bamboo cane. As the coils extend right up to the edges and provide consistent support for the mattress over the whole bed, this type offers a larger sleeping area if space dictates a small bed. Although some osteopaths see no reason for having springs in a base at all, since modern mattresses can be supportive enough for the spine on their own.

Slatted wood base   A wooden base generally has no springs, though it is often made from pre-sprung timber. Standard in densely forested Scandinavia, it has found favour with Britain's knotty pine buffs. Always check the jointing methods: a good mortise and tenon joint is the most likely to stabilize the wood as it settles.

Solid base beds   Often termed 'orthopaedic' beds, solid base beds obviously have no springs at all, although some are sold with a thin layer of foam on the base.

Water bed   An almost extinct symbol of the swinging '60s, the water bed was only effective if filled to exactly the right tension.

Camp bed   An osteopath's nightmare, camp beds should be avoided at all costs. Even if your needs for one are

1

only temporary, it would be better to sleep on a mattress on the floor.

Pallet base with futon   The Japanese tradition of unrolling a futon - a natural fibre stuffed mattress - is catching on fast, particularly with people who need to use their bedrooms as living areas during the day. The mattress should be placed on a slatted or solid wood base designed to be sold with it. If you lie directly on the floor, air can't circulate and the futon will quickly become stuffy, particularly if it is to be rolled up during the day.

Mattresses

A mattress is like a sandwich - it is the quality of its contents that affect its

price. Over and above the springs comes the padding. The minimum consists of a layer of hessian on the springs, then a layer of coarse fibre padding, next to a layer of soft fibre or foam padding, and finally the ticking or outer cover. A mattress with a core of hair sandwiched by fleece is very warm, while one entirely stuffed with hair is cool.

The type of ticking on the mattress is important. It is linked to the layers inside by special stitching or tufting buttons. Whether or not it has air vents in the sides is not crucial, since the mattress will breathe through the fabric. Ideally the ticking should be made of a natural fibre like linen or

1 Simplicity, both in form and colour, is essential in the modern bedroom. The metal frame bed has no headboard and relies on the zig zag strip underneath for embellishment. The diagonal stripes on the duvet echo the harsher horizontal lines of the Venetian blind.

2 A contemporary reworking of the curtained four poster, which is more a lush, opulently extravagant tent than a bed. Don't skimp on the material.

3 Two futons covered in black glazed cotton completely fill this tiny bedroom. Perforated steel shelves take up the high tech theme, and drama derives from the bright blue cushions. The proportions are confused by the Marlene Dietrich doll reclining on the bed.

cotton. Man-made fibres might come in prettier designs, but they are sweatier, slippery and bedclothes will slide about on them. Who sees them once the bed is made anyway?

When choosing a mattress your most important consideration must be the springing. There are three shapes of spring – cylindrical, barrel and hourglass – and three sorts of springing systems, which are described below.

Open coil or traditionally sprung This is the most common system, and comprises rows of springs joined together along the top and bottom by a continuous small spiral spring. The gauge of wire governs the resilience of the spring: the higher the gauge the thinner – and

therefore more giving – the spring.

Pocket sprung This type of mattress uses nearly three times as many springs as a traditionally sprung bed. Each one is slotted at the top and bottom into a fabric pocket sewn onto a hessian backing which dampens any noise. Barrel-shaped springs are held together by twine at the waist, while cylindrical springs are joined at the top and bottom by metal clips or twine; so although both types are connected to their neighbouring springs, they can move independently. Such mattresses are more expensive than the open coil variety, are considered more flexible, and give more support.

Continuous springing An overall knitting

of supple steel wire, making an interwoven springy web, similar to an old iron frame bed.

Foam Some mattresses offer a combination of springs and foam. Others simply have foam at each corner or along the edges. There are also mattresses made from 100 per cent foam, which many osteopaths recommend. These can come in two or three different densities – reconstituted polyether foam on the bottom, latex foam in the centre, and soft polyether on the top – to accommodate the shoulders and hips where more give is needed. Less expensive foam mattresses are usually made entirely from polyether. Some may have holes

moulded into their undersides.

General care
How long your mattress and base will last depends on your treatment of them. Bed manufacturers reckon on a life expectancy of 10-15 years, though you could buy a reasonably priced bed and change your mattress every few years. If you turn the mattress regularly it will wear more evenly. But if you have a foam mattress, check with the maker's instructions on this. Most are designed to be lain on in one direction only. Never put a new mattress on an uneven old base or the mattress will quickly develop the faults of the old.

THE SOFTWARE

Deciding on what sort of bedware you will settle for is almost as difficult as the decision on how you will decorate your bedroom. First, the range is now enormous, and second, how will you most effectively echo the theme you have chosen for the room?

Duvets

It is hardly more than a decade since the continental quilt, now better known as the duvet, was introduced into this country. Yet since their late '60s arrival, they have been adopted in almost half of Britain's households. Their appeal is that, in an attractive cover they offer warmth without weight, they look good even without a bedspread and are great time savers when it comes to bedmaking. But be careful about checking the filling of the duvet you want before you buy it. Since it is impossible to have a direct look at what is inside, it's wise to know what the categories on the label mean.

Natural fillings These must be either down or a mixture of down and feather derived only from waterfowl, normally duck or goose.

Pure down is the best and most expensive duvet filling. It comes from the breast of the bird, has no quill shaft, and is able to absorb and hold air better than any of the alternatives.

1 All the fun of a duvet – and none of the bed-making work. Sheet sets are now designed in endless permutations for changing the look at a toss of the duvet.

2 An adaptation of a 19th century American patchwork quilt. The traditional Meadow Lily design is printed on cotton, then quilted.

3 A strictly masculine, business-like bed is achieved with dark, striped pillowcases and sheets folded over a navy, blanket.

4 Black satin is a familiar cliché, but this comforter is in on the joke with pillows jazzed up by festive stripes.

Down and feather is a mixture in which the down content is predominant and the feathers used are small and curly. *Feather and down* is a mixture in which the feather content is predominant. *Feather* offers an economical but reasonable filling, as long as the feathers are only from small waterfowl. Beware a label that says a quilt is filled with curled feathers – this means poultry feathers.

Man-made fibre fillings The advantage of man-made fibres is that they are non-allergenic and therefore suitable for asthma and hayfever sufferers. They are also easily washable. Go for a dependable manufacturer or brand-name fibre producer. Trade marks like Dacron, Diolen, Terylene and Trevira cover reliable fillings. Cheap unbranded synthetic quilts are best avoided. Unless their covers are of particularly closely woven material, their short staple fibre fillings will probably filter through the fabric, especially when they are washed.

On any quilt, for the same reason, a knitted material or nylon covering won't contain the contents. But if the synthetic cover is thick enough to prevent this, it will probably make you sweat. Covers on quilts which have natural fillings must be made of cambric to keep the feathers and down intact. Most manufacturers sew an inner wall into the seams of the channels that run down the quilts to stop heat escaping.

THE SOFTWARE

1 and 2 The epitome of romanticism; this style of bedlinen looks as pretty rumpled after a night's sleep, as it does before. White polycotton sheets and pillowcases with scalloped edges threaded with pink satin ribbon, are perfectly set off by the matching pink wool blanket and handmade lace bedspread.

3 The soft colours and geometric pattern of this comforter make it a flexible choice. It could be mixed with pretty, flounced pillowcases and sheets or used in a masculine, minimalistic bedroom, both with equal success.

4 Striking ice cream shades are used on this comforter, in a different pattern on either side. The subtle sheen of the embroidered flowers on both pillowcases and sheet add a pretty lustre to the already delicious-looking bed.

5 The last word in hedonistic software. This ivory satin bedspread with gold brocade borders, and matching crescent and square pillows looks better suited for play than for mere dreaming. Not a choice for the practically minded.

Tog rating This is a guide, devised by manufacturers in conjunction with the British Standards Institute, to the expected warmth of a duvet. It ranges from 4.5 to 13.5 in 1.5 steps, with the average single blanket the equivalent of 4.5. If you sleep in a draughty room with no central heating, you will probably need a tog rating of 13.5. If you turn your heating off at night, 10 to 12 should do. If your room is always warm, choose between 4.5 and 6.5 togs.

There have been occasions when the tog rating system has been abused and

want to have sheets and blankets. Flatter and more dense than an eiderdown, they are used in conjunction with a sheet, in place of blankets. They are usually made in attractive materials, designed to match sheets and pillowcases. If you put extra and unusual shaped pillows – bolsters and continental square pillows – on the bed, you won't need a bedcover in a bedroom that is also used as a sitting room.

Bedlinen
If you still prefer to slide between crisp white linen and pull an eiderdown up under your chin (on the whole still the most luxurious way to sleep), then there is more white linen to choose from now than ever before. It is the most expensive type of bedware (though costs can be trimmed by choosing a reasonably priced base sheet) and generally needs a good deal of looking after. Most bedlinen is now made of polyester and cotton mix which can be drip-dried and needs little or no ironing. But pure cotton, Irish linen or Egyptian percale sheeting needs proper ironing to look and feel good. And, the frilled, flounced and laced pillowcases, so pretty in white, can't go straight onto the bed from the tumble dryer. But if you are prepared for extra work, a sumptuously romantic look can be achieved by mixing different shades of white. Take a plain base sheet, add a scalloped top sheet embroidered white on white, and cover different shaped pillows with frilled, lace or cut-work cases. White satin trimmed cellular blankets continue the softness of the look. An elegant alternative that the French consider very English is to fold a white linen sheet over a blanket of a strong colour, like burgundy, navy or forest green.

A flexible scheme is to keep to a flat colour for the bottom sheet and choose printed fabrics in contrasting colours for the top sheet and pillow cases. These should be bold in pattern or colour – the teeny weeny sprigs of flowers in faded shades can look tired nowadays. If you want prettily feminine floral sheets, plain white linen or cotton embroidered along the top border in different coloured silks is a successful, classic design.

Striped sheets and pillowslips on plain bottom sheets look good – thin and light stripes for a fresh style, thick and dark stripes in a masculine bedroom. Some department stores now make up their own bedlinen in this design, so it is not expensive to change to this look.

American and American-influenced bedlinen, now produced by British designers, offers a stunning choice of sheets, duvet covers and quilts in colours and designs so striking and subtle that bedcovers are not necessary. With some of these ranges, the most impressive effect is achieved by mixing as many different prints within the same colour spectrum as have been produced to co-ordinate.

Bedspreads
If you prefer to hide your bed under a spread, it should not be the cosy old candlewick. Despite attempts to give it a new lease of life by producing it in fashionable burgundies, greys and cold blues, it will never quite achieve glamour status. Thin quilts designed in the West and made in India are now hugely popular and not too expensive. They are available in both strong and pastel colours and in a variety of large and small prints. A characteristic of all these spreads is the small size of the triangular and square sewn shapes that have taken over from the hexagonal cut-outs of the handmade American quilts, on which they are based.

It is still possible to find old lace bedspreads or ones that have been hand-worked in cotton yarn, though their price in antique shops is usually high. A cheaper solution for an old-fashioned or romantic bedroom is to buy a modern copy of a lace panel designed for Victorian windows. With a plain valance added, these will fit a double bed. Made by specialist companies, major department stores can usually order them if they don't already hold stocks.

A beautiful rug (well-cleaned in advance) can look good on a bed. Silk Chinese or Middle Eastern rugs, too delicate to lay on the floor, look especially rich in a room of restrained and subdued colouring, while a thin kelim works well in a room decorated in hot spice shades.

has not provided a true guide to the warmth potential of the duvet described. So it is always wise to buy from a reputable brand name.

Size A duvet should measure at least 45cm (18in.) wider than your bed. For tall people, there are quilts available, which are 217cm (87in.) long; quilts are also made for bunk beds, generally 115cm (46in.) wide, and for cribs.

Covers Some duvets made with patterned materials give the impression that they don't need a loose cover. But, this is misleading; we lose 0.9 litres

(1½ pints) of liquid each night (an awesome 57 gallons a year), so a removable and washable cover is a hygenic necessity. It also increases the effective insulation of the duvet.

Quilts and comforters
A new idea in bedlinen is the cotton mattress quilt from America, a flat, thin quilt that lies on top of the mattress. It is less likely to ruckle up than an under blanket and is washable.

Comforters are a useful compromise for those in warm bedrooms who don't

THE FLEXIBLE BEDROOM

Frequently only used at night, the bedroom lends itself to performing a dual function – perhaps as a sitting room, or even a study. Deciding what additional role you want your bedroom to fulfil is the first step in planning your furniture and storage arrangements.

As a sitting room

This double role often prompts people to try to squeeze small sofas, chaise longues or armchairs into the room regardless of space. Unless your bedroom is large enough for the sitting room zone to be set apart from the bed and focused around another piece of furniture – a television, coffee table or fireplace – then it will be the bed that will be sat on and the other seating ignored. And why not? It is, after all, the comfiest place to relax, particularly if it is 'de-bedded' during the day with cushions and an interesting bedcover. What will give the room a sitting room feel is your approach to the rest of the furniture. If, instead of built-in bedside units and cupboards, you aim for free-standing pieces, at once you will alter the tone of the room. If, for example, you covered two round tables either side of the bed with a striking fabric to the floor, and on each stood,

not a bedside light, but table lamps; if you installed chests of drawers, armoires, corner cupboards and bookcases, then you will have created the feel of an elegant and soothing sitting room.

Don't sacrifice your storage needs for the sake of design, however. Should they be too great for anything other than fitted units, then there are a number of different treatments you can give to fitted cupboard doors. In a futuristic room they should be left blank, and unless you can find handles of an utterly minimal design, fit spring catches. In a more formal bedroom, add beading details to each door. In a primary-coloured children's room the slats of louvred doors could each be painted in a repeating sequence of red, blue, yellow and green; in a Mediterranean style room plain or louvred wood doors could be left bare under a polyurethane seal. Plain doors can be papered, but fabric covering is outdated. If your run of cupboards does not cover the entire wall, use the side at the end to build bookshelves.

A useful storage and seating idea is to build cushioned units at the same height as the bed round the free walls and a wide shelf or small wall-hung

cupboards above. If you need further storage, you could lay your mattress on a base of storage cubes, in which case it should sit first on a board well drilled with holes so that air can circulate.

In a small room that has to double as a sitting room, the best solution is to build the bed on a higher level. There are a number of systems on the market for self-assembly constructions with the bed above and a sofa below. These come in wood, in metal, and in scaffolding. Alternatively you could build a large sleeping and sitting platform, reached by a small flight of steps, and use the area below for hanging and storage.

As a study

This is a less congenial partnership, particularly if the room is shared territory, unless it is for a teenager or student. In a large room, however, you could separate the study from view with screens or shelves fixed to floor and ceiling battens which would provide space for books and files. Alternatively, a made-to-measure Venetian blind hung from the ceiling makes an effective and adjustable division, while free-standing metal grid shelving offers a high tech look and a

1 A space for sitting created off the bedroom by knocking two rooms into one. The colour scheme becomes warmer and the furniture arrangement cosier in the sitting area.

2 The dark sombre colours of a club library used to great effect. Richard Sapper's angular Tizio light and a mirrored wall ensure that this room, where sleeping and working can take place equally happily, doesn't look too stuffy.

3 Stunning colours and an imaginative table lamp give this bedroom/ study a stylish post modern look.

1

2

3

movable solution. The whole work area can even be concealed behind cupboard doors. In a small room the best solution is to use self-assembly systems with a desk and filing cabinet below the bed structure.

Extra storage is always useful in a dual-purpose room and can be pieces designed for other uses. A stacking plastic vegetable rack in a bright colour could accommodate make-up and brushes, or clothing accessories; shop hanging rails and display racks could take the place of formal cupboards; tough cardboard filing boxes and plastic stacking boxes could store children's toys; tin trunks could be painted and covered with cushions for storage seating. With these kind of ideas you can create a room that is not only practical but fun and attractive as well.

BED AND BATHROOM

If you want to make a bathroom out of the open bedroom, the first point to remember is that it cannot include a lavatory, which must be separated from any living area by a door. Look closely at how well the room can be ventilated, because clouds of steam are undesirable in a bedroom.

On the most simple level, putting basins in your bedrooms can make all the difference to queues for the bathroom and early morning tempers. Choose a wall which allows the waste pipe to be connected to existing drains with the shortest possible stretch. There are so many different styles of basins these days, you don't need to feel reminded of a boarding house by the sight of one in a bedroom. Whether designed to fit onto a pedestal or to be fixed straight onto the wall, basins now come in a vast range of shapes, sizes and designs, from small floral patterned wall-hung porcelain shells for a romantic or feminine bedroom, to bowls of beaten brass for an exotic Arabian nights' scheme, or free-standing space-age shapes for a futuristic room.

In a room with limited space, drop a basin into an extended unit and not only will you create extra storage, but the bathroom fitting will look less functional and more an integral part of the room. If the room has a run of fitted cupboards built against a wall with access to a draining pipe, consider altering one section of the wardrobe to accommodate a small, walk-in wash room. Mirror line the entire area and it won't feel pokey.

Once you have decided to extend existing water supplies into the bedroom, you might find that it pays to go one step further and install a shower cabinet at the same time as adding a basin. It can be disguised behind whatever style of panelling covers the cupboard doors. Abut a free-standing cabinet onto the end of a built-in basin unit in a teenager's bedroom and the main bathroom will once again become your territory. Lay a sheet of mirror on one or more of its sides and you add space, light and a good-sized looking glass to the room.

In an L-shaped room, a bathroom can easily be tucked away and, being partially invisible to the rest of the room, even decorated as a separate entity.

However, if it is an integral part of the bedroom, it must be able to blend in with the whole and not appear an intrusion. Tiling the bathroom area from the floor to basin height and carrying either all the tiles or only the top two rows right into the main room will link the different areas.

In a rectangular room, the bathroom can be partitioned off by a half wall wide enough to act on the bedroom side as a bookcase. If the room is large enough, open shelving could be built above the partition base to the ceiling. Build the bath into a tile-covered fitting at least one tile width away from the walls, and the ledge will form a shelf for bath accessories and decorations.

Stylize the bathroom area with good-looking furniture and you won't need to separate it physically from the bedroom at all. Take the same carpet right through from the bedroom up to the bath; place a steamer chair, a rocking chair or chaise longue in the bathroom area; put a table, an antique wash stand, or chest of drawers there too, and you will have successfully integrated the bath and basin without any building expenses.

Bathroom fittings will look less functional and more an integral part of your bedroom if they are built-in. This will also give you storage space for make up, medicine and towels.

In a large bedroom, floor to ceiling fitted cupboards can act as the divider between bedroom and bathroom. To provide a more interesting break in the solid line of surface, place the entry into the bathroom area anywhere but at either end of the wardrobes.

With a bedroom that leads off a corridor or landing, you could block off a part of the landing to create a bath or shower room, knocking through the internal wall to make the entrance. There may already be a lavatory on the landing outside your bedroom; if so, consider turning it into a bathroom.

If you have a large stairwell that rises through the centre of your house, space can be made for a bathroom by building across the stairwell on the upper floor, cutting into the bedroom on one side to create a new landing and new bedroom wall. Note that if a bathroom contains the only lavatory in the house, it must be constructed so that it can be entered without having to pass through a bedroom.

If you don't have enough space for a full length bath and you dislike showers, then consider installing a sitting bath (see the chapter on Bathrooms). These make up in depth what they lack in length. A basin plus bidet combination is a good compromise solution where there is limited space.

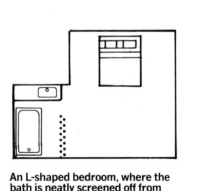

An L-shaped bedroom, where the bath is neatly screened off from the rest of the room.

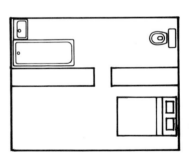

Fitted cupboards make a practical division between bedroom and bathroom, with a central opening.

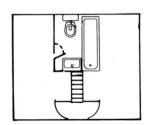

Part of the corridor borrowed to create a shower room.

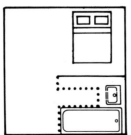

A low tiled wall divides the two rooms, and the tiles are repeated in the bathroom for a sense of continuity.

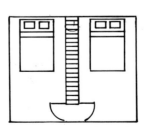

A house with a central staircase is a candidate for a bathroom built across the stairwell on the upper floor.

1 Lack of space is no excuse for failing to install an en suite bathroom. A shower was ingeniously blended into this attic bedroom by using white tiles, and keeping evidence of shower curtains or doors hidden.

2 Shielded from the bedroom by frosted glass windows, this bathroom still remains a strongly integrated part of the room.

3 and 4 An unconventional version of the en suite bathroom. A free-standing glass structure in the middle of the room gives hazy privacy and allows an interesting view of blurred bathroom fixtures from the bedroom.

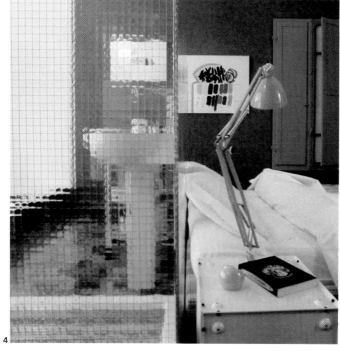

BATHROOMS

Until not so very long ago, the British bathroom was characteristically a cold, damp, drab room. No-one was ever encouraged to enjoy their ablutions, and suggestions that the bathroom was a place for relaxation were considered suspect and self-indulgent. When you remember the importance placed upon bathing in comfort by those ancient Greeks, Romans and Egyptians so respected by our forefathers, you would think we might have avoided the puritan approach to washing that we suffered for so long. Perhaps post-war prosperity and the gradual conversion in most houses to central heating and better water heating systems has altered the general view of bathrooms. Once a fixed radiator has been installed in a bathroom, it is a small step to increasing the suggestion of comfort by laying fitted carpet or rugs, instead of enduring those cold floors and damp bathmats of old. All at once it becomes natural to include the bathroom in decoration plans, instead of stopping outside its door; so that even in houses and apartments without central heating, it is reasonable to make the bathroom as comfortable a room as any other, within the limits of your budget.

Depending on your budget, a bathroom can be the most expensive room in the house to design – or the cheapest. Before you start decorating you must first sort out the practicalities. If you are living in rented accommodation, or if you have only a small amount of money to spend, then clearly you must work around current installations and not include any building work in your plans. If you are planning a bathroom in a new house, you must ask yourself several questions. Are you happy with the present fittings, or will you be starting from scratch? How many people are going to use the bathroom? Is it for anyone very old or very young? How large or small is the space? Will it be used for anything else? Do you want to build in storage space?

As with any other room in the house, you must also consider the mood you want to inspire. If you enjoy lingering long in the bath with a book, your decorating plans will clearly be different from those of someone who prefers a brisk rub down.

Now that we have come to accept that there is no shame in enjoying a self-indulgent bathroom, one that has been well-planned and coherently decorated will add considerably to the value of the house without necessarily having cost you any major outlay. Just because the bathroom may be the smallest room in your house, there is no need for it to be the dullest.

1

2

1 A modest sized bath-room can still evoke a feeling of stateliness. Horizontal grooves along the walls visually increase the sense of space. The marbled and coved cornice, period light fitting and solid taps enhance the classical yet traditional mood.

2 A Californian design which upsets all conventional ideas about what the bathroom should be like. The galvanized steel bath is in fact an industrial tank. Free-standing in the middle of the room, it looks more like a piece of furniture than a bath-room fitting.

PLANNING

Planning a bathroom is very often a question of squeezing as much as you can into as little space as possible, treating it as a functional production line, rather than a room in its own right. When money is tight as well, it becomes important to minimize the distances you have to run the pipework connecting the sanitary fittings in your bathroom to the main drainage pipe linking your home to the public drains.

If you are starting from scratch, you should locate the main soil stack of the house before you decide where to put your bathroom. It shouldn't be hard to find; in older houses it is very likely to be an 11cm (4½ in.) cast iron pipe tacked to an outside wall. Otherwise it will be in a boxed duct inside the house. Try and site your bathroom as close as possible to the stack. If you are carrying out a wholesale remodelling of the house, it may be necessary to put in a brand new soil stack, which is governed by elaborate regulations about the number of appliances, venting and so on. The location of the pipework should be determined by the position of the nearest possible link with the public main drain, which will in turn help determine the optimum position for the bathroom.

Other factors to bear in mind when locating the bathroom or bathrooms are the need to avoid walking through other rooms to reach it, and the possibility of using it as a sound barrier between quieter and noisier parts of the house, for example between a bedroom and a living room.

Remember that each of the main elements in the bathroom, the bath, lavatory and basin, will need to be linked to the stack. The simplest and cheapest way of doing this is to line them up in a straight run along one wall. Thus the optimum minimal bathroom will be as wide as the bath is long, with the basin and lavatory (in that order) pushed together along the other wall. The door, opposite the lavatory, can either open outwards, or be a sliding model to avoid eating into the minimal space inside. An alternative layout would be to place the basin and lavatory opposite each other, with access from the wider wall.

The building regulations insist on a

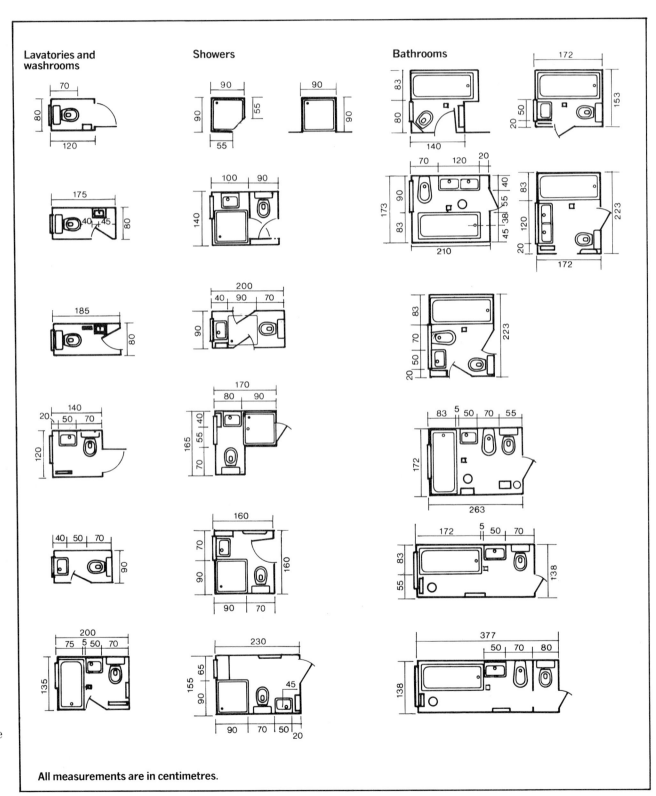

Lavatories and washrooms

Showers

Bathrooms

All measurements are in centimetres.

minimum number of air changes per hour in the bathroom to avoid condensation problems. This can be achieved either with a window of the specified size, or with a mechanically operated fan. These are best linked to the light switch and fitted with a time delay device which keeps them running for a specified period. Bear in mind that the fan must vent to the outside air, so it should be positioned against an outside wall, or fitted with a duct that runs in a straight line to an outside wall.

The more generously proportioned the space, the more possible it is to create a pleasant and comfortable environment. According to architects, bathrooms are gradually turning into a very different kind of space, in which a much wider range of activities takes place, and in which privacy may not always be as essential as it once was. It can be the place to put the washing machine and the tumble dryer, the scales and the laundry basket, to do the ironing and your exercises. In these increasingly narcissistic days, it is the place to carry out what might be called body maintenance – everything from applying make-up to taking medicine. If that view is correct, then the minimal bathroom is likely to become rapidly obsolete. If you do have the space, it is worth considering a more elaborate bathroom, possibly one that is linked to a bedroom, and equipped with a window or windows. It is still sensible to keep your drainage runs short and simple. So the major fittings will be in a straight line, but the run can be expanded to include a bidet and shower at the very least. They can be incorporated in a continuous run of work surfaces – a layout very much like that of a modern kitchen, with the washing machine pushed up against the far wall.

For a very different kind of bathroom, it is possible to place the bath in the centre of the room – provided it is self-supporting.

1 Studded rubber originally intended for factory floors covers the walls of architect Eva Jiricna's tiny bathroom. It not only conceals any imperfections, but is also totally waterproof. The entire bathroom is only the width of the bath.

2 A bathroom tucked into the corner of a living room, the bath screened off by a low wall.

3 A cool, sophisticated bathroom created out of a minimal space with white tiles.

THE PRACTICALITIES

Although bathrooms are bound by quite specific building regulations, they are free from the minimum ceiling height specification of 2.3 m (7ft 6in.) which applies to other rooms. So it is perfectly possible to place a bathroom under the eaves, or even below stairs if there is room and little distance to the external waste pipe. Although it cannot open directly into any room other than a bedroom, if it contains the only lavatory in the house it must be constructed so that there is access to it from somewhere other than just the bedroom. Any room that includes a lavatory must either have an opening window or skylight of at least one-twentieth of the floor area or a mechanically operated extractor fan. And if you have a windowless internal bathroom, the size of the fan, the length of time that it operates and the size of the duct are all governed by building regulations. Whether or not the room includes a lavatory, a fan is useful to help dispel the steam. It is important to have some means of getting rid of it as quickly as possible before it turns to condensation. Lingering steam forms droplets on walls and ceilings and will eventually turn into mildew if it is not able to escape. Wallpaper will begin to peel and a musty smell will gradually build up. The simplest thing is to open a window, if you don't have a fan. A steady heat in the bathroom will also help to dispel steam. But make sure your radiator is connected to the hot water system, not the central heating; otherwise there will be times of the day or seasons of the year when the system is switched off and the radiator is cold.

Lighting

The first rule is not to have any free-standing light anywhere in the bathroom. According to regulations, bulb sockets have to have an extended cover to stop contact with the live part. Preferably all lights, even those above basins, should not have to be turned on with direct contact to the switch. The combination of wet or even damp hands with electricity can be lethal. The safest position for the light switch is outside the bathroom. Inside, lights should be operated by a cord connected to the switch. If you have children, remember that the cord should be long enough for them to reach.

There are two approaches to bathroom lighting: the view that it should be strong and bright enough to be invigorating, or that it should be moody enough to conceal and cosset. If you run your lighting on a dimmer, you can please both parties at once.

The most common form of lighting is a central ceiling fixture. However several cylinder downlighters sunk into the ceiling at well chosen spots create a more intimate atmosphere. If the bulbs are concealed behind a lens or baffle, they will give a more general spread of light and not glare into your eyes when you lie back in the bath. Fix spotlights in corners and direct the beam upwards for a soft effect that involves minimal electrical alterations. If you have an internal bathroom and want to create a sensation of daylight, you could consider putting lighting behind a false floating ceiling of opaque glass. Good lighting round shaving and make-up mirrors is important. Some are equipped with their own lights, but a strip light with a shaver socket is a popular solution; the fittings are now available in colours other than institutional grey or pampas. A better light is provided by bulbs set at intervals round the three free sides. Like those in stars' dressing rooms, they create a particularly dramatic effect round mirrors that are set into a recess above a basin. In any style of bathroom the amount of light can be increased by clever positioning of mirrors to reflect natural light from a

1 **Bathrooms are bound to get wet. So floor and wall tiles are a far more practical proposition than, say, carpet or wallpaper.**

2 **An ingenious location for a basin. It saves space and allows both basin and bath to share a plumbing outlet.**

3 **Thoughtfully designed cupboard units fit together to create a mirror wall, increasing the feeling of spaciousness in this fairly small room.**

4 **Flattering star's dressing room lights complement the old-fashioned free-standing tub and recycled Edwardian taps.**

5 **Special waterproof quilted fabric provides an unusual, but practical, wallcovering in architect Jan Kaplicky's London bathroom.**

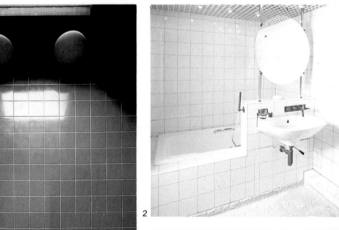

window or to throw artificial light across the room.

Heating

Cold bathrooms are dismal. Nowadays centrally heated houses automatically have a radiator in the bathroom. But that means that when the system is switched off, the bathroom stays cold. If your bathroom is not far from the hot water cylinder, you can link your radiator to that instead. Other but less powerful options include, on the smallest scale, a wall-mounted fan or infra-red heater which must be switched on well before you use the bathroom. An electric towel rail can supply a limited amount of heat to a small room, and at least it offers a guarantee that your towels will be warm when you spring from your bath. If the room is cold physically, decorate it so that it looks warm. Pick cheerful colours for the walls, hang fluffy towelling at the window instead of

5

curtain material, lay a thick carpet on the floor, pin posters of sunny country scenes on the walls.

Floors

Before you lay anything down, check that your flooring base is waterproof and properly sealed so that any dramas with water won't affect the ceiling of the room below. Whatever flooring you settle for, make absolutely sure that you carry out the manufacturer's instructions correctly.

The cheapest flooring is linoleum, which now comes in a wide choice of styles and colours, in sheeting or in tiles. But beware how you clean it. A cleaner with built-in polish will create a slippery surface. Equally don't lay down rugs or bathmats that are not backed by foam or rubber, or they will slide too. Vinyl tiles are another cheap option, and rubber stud flooring looks good in a bathroom with a modern, functional feel; carry it up one or more walls for a striking effect that is waterproof too. Cork tiles make a room look warm, but unless you buy the more expensive vinyl-coated tiles, you must seal them with several coats of polyurethane. Quarry tiles, ceramic, marble, or earthenware tiles are, of course, completely waterproof. But they are expensive, heavy and can be slippery. They must be laid professionally, on a properly prepared floor. If you decide to lay tiles, run coving some way up the wall to seal the join between the floor, bath and units.

Alternatively, carpeting, if you feel it is practical, need not be expensive, and it certainly gives an air of luxury to a bathroom. Careful searching among offcuts at carpet retailers will often produce just the size you need at a reasonable price. But cheap or expensive, the carpet must be rubber backed, or it will rot.

Walls

The cheapest decoration is paint. If you have a problem with condensation, stick to emulsion. Gloss will make the situation worse–use it only on woodwork and pipes. If you want to brighten your bathroom with the minimum expense, you can create a tremendous effect by painting your

walls in one colour and deliberately focusing attention onto all the woodwork, piping and mechanics by painting them in a different and stronger shade.

Vinyl wallpaper, a practical finish for bathrooms, now comes in a more attractive range of colours, textures and patterns than ever before. If you prefer to have conventional wallpaper, paint it over with a special glaze to seal it and give it a longer life. Papered rooms must be free from condensation or damp problems.

The cheapest tiles are in plain white, and are thinner than floor tiles. Think about running them right up to the ceiling and filling them in with coloured grouting. This is made by adding a powder, available in strong primary colours from most hardware stores and builders' merchants, to standard grouting powder. If the size of the room is going to raise the total cost of the tiling, lay them only to waist or three-quarters height and paint the area above and the ceiling in a colour that matches the grout.

Tongue and groove woodwork hides piping effectively. It is more unusual to lay it horizontally than vertically and it will make a small room look wider. Coloured stains are now available in pretty shades if you like the look of natural wood but want to avoid having a bathroom that resembles a sauna. Laminate panels can be hung on walls and round built-in basins and baths. Choices range from marbling in real and fantasy colours to stark white textured finishes. Have a look at designs intended for kitchen use before making your final choice. In a small room, size can be visually increased by clever use of mirror tiles. Even more effective–though expensive–is to use mirror sheeting. Hang it not only on the walls but on the ceiling too for real drama. The hidden price you have to pay for either is extra work keeping them clean.

Storage

Bathrooms can become cluttered with things from towels and toys to bubble bath and bars of soap, all of which you want in the bathroom, but not lying about in disarray. There are certain

items that must be stored in the bathroom: towels, toiletries and medicines, for example. The last two are best hidden, both from a safety and a tidiness point of view. Towels, however, can contribute to the decoration of the room. If your bath sits in an open alcove, you could have open shelves at one end of it for towels and pretty jars of bath beads, lotions and oils. In a large room, open shelving for these and other things can act as a room divider. In a small room, back your shelving with a mirror.

In a large bathroom, the entire floor around the bath could be built up, with steps rising to the now sunken bath, and the false flooring that has been created could be designed to accommodate deep drawer space for linen, or hinged-lid storage or under-floor cupboards for suitcases.

If there are things that you use each bathtime and don't always want to have to put away afterwards–a range of loofahs, brushes and sponges, or a mass of children's bath toys perhaps–storing them in a coloured wire vegetable basket hanging from a ceiling hook above the bath looks appealing.

In an apartment without access to an outside drying area, make a virtue of the need for somewhere to dry clothes. Either run a wooden curtain pole above the bath, fixed to handsome wood brackets, or paint up a traditional clothes airer and hang it from coloured yatching cord to keep above the bath.

When you are considering boxing in exposed pipes, think big. Instead of just covering the area where they run, and creating no more than a shelf often only a few inches from the floor, build a proper cupboard around them. A wall that supports both the basin and the lavatory carries enough piping to justify boxing in the entire wall from waist height to the floor. Don't stop there, either: build a series of small cupboards right up to the ceiling all along the wall apart from the area above the basin which you can completely fill with a mirror.

Cupboards for medicines, spare razor blades and scissors should always be equipped with childproof locks. Even if you don't have children of your own, they may come to your house.

THE BATHROOM AS A ROOM

If you have enough space, there is no reason why your bathroom should only be used for bathing. A warm carpet, long curtains at the window, a bookcase and a chaise longue add up to a relaxing room where you could happily retire with a good book. Even a small room could be given the atmosphere of a boudoir by adding a small chair in pastel painted cane or covered with soft towelling, hanging a festoon blind at the window and plastic-lined curtain fabric or net across the bath, caught dramatically by cords at either side.

Adding personal touches to the bathroom can make it into an intimate place. But because bathrooms are natural magnets for clutter – those half empty bottles of lotion, boxes of tissues and bits of make-up – any collection on display must be a disciplined one or it will simply look a mess. A wall of family photographs going back several generations to the days of sepia creates an Edwardian atmosphere, particularly if you emphasize it with period pieces, like a washing jug and bowl, or a collection of old bottles filled with coloured water or bath oils. A large conch filled with treasured shells or pretty pebbles sits well beside pots of plants. If the bathroom is well lit, it is the one room in the house where specific greenhouse plants can thrive. They will not lose their visual appeal so long as you look after them, and put them in good-looking containers rather than standing them on slimy saucers. In this room you could display a collection of cigarette cards, old postcards, early advertisements, cartoons or other treasured ephemera, whereas elsewhere in the house they may just amount to a mess. Paint them over with several coats of a glaze once they have been stuck in place to protect them from steam and condensation.

1 Bathrooms don't have to be harsh and antiseptic. Dark colours, heavy slatted wooden blinds, a carefully displayed collection of prints and photographs and discreet recessed downlighters give this bathroom the air of a smart gentlemen's club. **1**

2

3

4

2 An attic bathroom – the perfect place to conduct a leisurely morning, reading the paper, opening the mail and relaxing in the tub.

3 The pine-panelled double bath, blue and white china, antique light fittings and brass taps highlight the rural flavour of this bathroom. Floral wallpaper which co-ordinates with the fabric used in the bedroom provides a link between the two rooms.

4 A bathroom which doubles as a dressing room. The shower is banished to a corner, allowing the centre of the room to be used for dressing, with mirror fronts to the cupboards.

If you are a fitness enthusiast, and you have a large bathroom, this is where you could set up a permanent gymnasium. Blondwood exercise rails along the walls double up as hanging space for towels. Fit chunky no-nonsense tops on a white stream-lined basin and bath, build an open-fronted shower at one end of the bath, hang a huge floor to ceiling mirror on one wall, swop small scales for a proper chemist's weighing machine, paint the room white, and have lights spaced around the room.

A room undisturbed by children could even accommodate a library of books, a writing desk or table well-stocked with stationery, a sofa or an armchair. Painted or papered in deep colours, any modern fittings boxed in with dark wood panelling, the bathing area hidden behind a fabric-covered screen, the room can have a soothing, dignified appeal.

A large room can act as a dressing room, too. Free-standing or built-in cupboards positioned in alcoves, a dressing table and chair partitioned off with floor to ceiling shelving, or screened from the rest of the room by a good-looking divider can make a positive area out of unexploited space. But if you are planning to accommodate clothing, then particular attention must be paid to eliminating condensation and to keeping the room well aired.

FINDING YOUR STYLE

Including a shower in the bath tub is always a problem, not least because of the difficulty of finding a shower curtain that does not rapidly become a limp rag of an eye-sore. A strong piece of geometry – the oval curtain rod, and the clear plastic curtain avoid all that.

Plumbing fittings are long lasting and expensive to change; new wall-sized mirrors and suspended neon tubes are a more economic way of giving this bathroom a fresh look.

Just because it's the bathroom you don't have to limit the choice of objects on display to mugs full of worn out toothbrushes.

The bathroom can be the best place to keep house-plants that will thrive in a hot steamy atmosphere.

Tiled floors can be slippery traps for pools of water: mats will help.

The bathroom as an exotic, escapist fantasy, a retreat from the troubles of the world. All the functional, mundane elements are hidden away behind a thick coating of gilt, mirrors and tiles, just the place for a long soak in the tub.

If you have the space, its possible to recreate the beaded and fringed splendour of the Edwardian country house. Dark wall colours help make white fittings stand out.

Ornate display cabinets – more like sweet shop containers than the stark clinical fittings of the modern bathroom. They can still be practical.

Handsome, generously proportioned tap fittings are an essential complement to the bulky proportions of the basin and bath.

The traditional bath tub, complete with lion's claw feet, often to be found camouflaged behind layers of panelling.

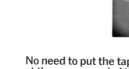

No need to put the taps at the narrow end of the bath – putting them at the side offers the chance to lean back at either end.

The post modern approach to the bathroom. The shapes of the fittings are all-important – the angled bath set off against the unorthodox metal shower booth.

BATHS AND SHOWERS

There is an enormous range of bathroom fittings, in every sort of colour, shape and design.

Standard baths

Baths are made in four different materials:

Enamelled cast iron   Enamel takes well to cast iron, and these are the most hardwearing and good-looking baths. They are, however, extremely heavy and the thickness of the cast iron tends to cool down the heat of the water.

Pressed steel   This resembles enamelled cast iron but is far cheaper and lighter in weight.

Acrylic   The cheapest type of bath on the market, available through do-it-yourself shops and light enough for one man to carry away. Not as rigid as glass fibre baths, they do scratch easily, though light surface scratches can be polished out with metal polish once the bath is dry.

Glass fibre   Usually made from cast Perspex sheeting reinforced with glass fibre and polyester resin. The material is versatile enough to offer a wide range of finishes, including metal, pearl and sparkle effects.

Fitting

The standard length for a bath is 1680mm (5ft 6in.) by 711mm (2ft 4in.) wide, but there are baths made to fit any space or shape. In restricted areas you could either fit a smaller traditional bath, 1380mm (4ft 6in.) by 680mm (2ft 3in.), or a sit-up bath 530mm (1ft 9in.) deep at the tap end and 1070mm (3ft 7in.) long by 710mm (2ft 4in.) wide. You should allow at least 710mm (2ft 4in.) in space on the open side of the bath for drying or bending over. But there is no reason why you must step over the long side of the bath to get in and out. If you have nowhere else for a bathroom than corridor space, place the taps and plugs against the outside wall of the room, or fit them as separate fittings into a side wall, and step into the bath from the butt end.

Exotic baths

If you have lots of money and plenty of space, there are now hydro-massage baths, whirlpool systems, baths with under-water jets of bubbles, steam baths, spa baths and hot tubs. The ultimate in luxury must be the built-in environmental enclosure, which gives you the sensations of sun, soft rain, steam and warm breezes to the sound of your favourite music while you lie and relax. Only slightly less exotic are baths for two, hexagonal baths, triangular baths, circular baths and sunken baths. Copies of Victorian claw foot baths, whose outer casing is prepared for painting up, make a fine centrepiece for the traditional type of bathroom, which will need very little more in the way of decorative touches to complete the look.

Colours

All baths, whether exotic or standard, are available these days in a wide range of colours. To today's bathroom

2

1   **Glass blocks and marble used to create an imaginative bath, which is an intrinsic part of the architecture.**

2   **More like a space capsule than a bathroom fitting, this delux shower has a place for everything, but at a price.**

3   **Simple tiles form the basic shower room. But the skylight makes all the difference on bright sunny mornings when you feel like singing under the spray.**

4   **A traditional Edwardian style bath, complete with lion's claw feet. Painted black outside and white inside, the bath echoes the theme of the rest of the room.**

1

3

4

Showers

Many people nowadays prefer a shower to a bath. Certainly it is cleaner to wash in running water. And despite the fact that the water comes in a continuous flow, you still only use about one-fifth the amount that goes into a bath, so there is less water to heat. Even more appealing, from an energy and cost-saving point of view, is that showers can be supplied by a wall heater that takes water direct from the mains and warms it up only at the instant you turn on the tap.

Equally attractive is the space-saving advantage that a shower offers. Excluding the drying area needed outside an enclosed cabinet – the same as you would plan for a bath – all it takes up on the floor is 900 sq. mm (3 sq. ft). An open tray shower with only one or two sides of the tray enclosed takes up the same floor space but less space is needed outside the tray for drying – approximately 400mm (1ft 4in.) would be adequate.

Types of shower

Shower cabinets can either be a built-in structured part of the house, or installed as self-contained units bought complete from a bathroom retailer. Unless you are planning a wall-hung water heater, your water cistern must be at least 1m (3ft) above the shower head to produce adequate shower pressure. The most unrestricted way to shower is in a wet room. This is a completely waterproofed room, with tiling all over the floor, ceiling and walls, coving wherever the floor meets other fittings, such as bath, bidet, lavatory or basin. It is not a room for storage units. The floor slopes towards a central, unplugged outlet, so that water from the wall-fitted shower head immediately drains away. The entry to a room such as this must be protected by a waterproofed lintel, or else you should have steps leading down into it.

A prefabricated unit only needs attaching to existing hot and cold water supplies and a nearby waste outlet. Some are sold as one-piece units. One of the most futuristic is a round Perspex cabinet with primary coloured back supporting the snaking chrome

fittings. Others come in self-assembly parts. Trays are made of the same materials as a bath. You can of course build your own in tiling. Always try to accommodate the largest tray you can – a cramped shower is not something you will enjoy indefinitely – and make sure that all the walls and the join between shower tray and floor are absolutely waterproof. If you buy a deep enough tray, it can be used to bath small children. In this case, choose a tray that is fitted with an overflow system. Notice that this and the position of the plug outlet alters with different makes and styles. So choose one whose siting means it can be connected to your draining system with the minimum amount of new pipework.

There is nothing worse than a shower constantly affected by the change in water pressure. One minute you scald, the next you are freezing to death. It is worth investing in the expense of a thermostatically controlled mixer valve, particularly if children use the shower.

The bath shower

The simplest form of shower, of course, (notwithstanding the detachable rubber hosing type), is a shower spray with flexible pipe that is part of the bath tap fixture. The shower head can either be hand held or slotted into brackets fixed to the wall while you stand beneath it in the bath. The only drawback with this type of shower is that of containing water splashes. Shower curtains only keep water trapped if they are draped inside the bath, and if they are, they can quickly start to smell stale and even develop mildew if they are not regularly washed and dried. A strengthened glass or Perspex panel can be fixed on the top outer ledge of the bath at the tap end, but it makes reaching for the taps to run the bath and cleaning the bath more difficult. Walls of a bath shower must be protected. If the area is not tiled, consider fixing a Perspex panel all the way up to the ceiling. Each edge must be sealed with a non-hardening mastic or water will penetrate behind it. The ceiling, too, should be well protected against a build-up of steam and beads of condensation.

designer, 'Avocado' is no more than a vegetable and 'Pampas' a dated garden plant. Strong colours now transform the bathroom from the discreet and genteely drab place it used to be into a much more refreshing place to face first thing in the morning. But the most appealing colour of all is still white. It is the only shade that doesn't limit your design possibilities when, in a few years' time you want to move on from your current decoration.

Revamping an old bath

Do you need a new bath? If your perfectly good one is merely suffering from staining or chipping, there are

products on the market that can give it a new lease of life – a much cheaper solution than buying a new one that might not be such good quality as the old. There are companies offering total resurfacing services listed in the Yellow Pages. The Council of British Ceramic Sanitaryware Manufacturers offer advice on how to look after old bathroom fittings. And there are paint-on products on sale in do-it-yourself shops, hardware, bathroom and department stores, from small bottles for touching up little chips in enamel, to special paints for completely altering the colour of your bath, basin and lavatory.

BASINS, BIDETS AND LAVATORIES

It is not just the bath that has begun to appear in new shapes in recent years. Basins, bidets and lavatories are now available in an enormous range of shapes and sizes, so shop around until you find what appeals to you most.

Basins

There are three styles of basin: pedestal, inset and wall-hung. If you are placing a basin against an unsound wall, choose a pedestal type. This will not only support the bulk of its weight (they must also be bracketed into the wall), but the pedestal also has the advantage of hiding the pipework. An inset basin dropped into a vanitory unit saves the bother of disguising pipes — they are all concealed by the cabinet. The vanitory unit gives you extra surface space for bathroom accessories, as well as storage below for medicines, towels and other bathroom things. A wall-hung basin has the advantage of leaving the floor space below it free, which might be vital in a small room. But the wall which is to support it must be sufficiently strong to carry the weight. In a very small space, a wall-recessed basin might be worth considering, though it is far less practical.

Latest designs The most clean-lined futuristic shapes of the moment are the pedestal basins from Italy, large imposing structures in white. British manufacturers have come up with their own very angular geometric alternatives and some have even commissioned exclusive Italian designs for manufacture over here. Some are even larger than 750mm (2ft 6in.), though part of that area combines wide splashback and surround for soap and washing accessories. These basins are generally enamelled cast iron or vitreous china.

Basins designed to sink into vanitory unit tops are available in materials as exotic as beaten brass, marble, or humble acrylic and glass fibre. One Italian designer has produced a range of oval vanitory unit basins in vitreous china with a sparkling glitter finish, against which he offsets chunky taps and plug surrounds in strong primary colours.

Other vanitory basins come in hexagonal shapes, in circular shapes, and even plain round kitchen sinks in grey steel have been set into bathroom units in very modern settings. A marble look has been contrived for wall hung and vanitory basins, in shades of sand, moss and slate. Other wall-hung basins come in hand-painted, shell-shaped porcelain, and there is a wide choice of pretty floral wall-hung and pedestal basins. Whichever you choose, you must pick your taps and plug surrounds at the same time. The wrong taps will make the right basin a disastrous mistake.

Fitting When you pick your basin, think about the amount of space you have to put it into. Think also about how many people will be queuing to use it: it may be worth your while installing two. These could be set on either side of a centrally placed bath, or dropped side by side into a long vanitory unit.

A rim height of 750mm (2ft 6in.) is fine for family use – 1m (3ft) if it is only to be used by adults. 800mm x 600mm (31½in. x 23½in.) is a convenient size. You must allow at least 700mm (2ft 4in.) standing space in front of a basin and (3ft 3in.) width for elbow space, particularly if you use the basin for hair washing or washing clothes. Basins for small separate lavatories or cloakrooms obviously can afford to be much tinier. In principle you should get the largest basin you can afford and have space for, with plenty of lip room for soaps.

Bidets

As more people travel to the Continent and confront bidets in their hotel bathrooms, their popularity increases in this country. They cannot be included instead of any other bathroom fitting, but if there is room, they do complement other washing facilities. They don't take up any more floor space than a lavatory: 700mm (12ft 4in.) from the wall to the front of the bidet, 325–400mm (13–16in.) in width and 375mm–600mm (15in.–2ft.) in height. You should allow a further 700mm (2ft 4in.) in front and at either side as clear room for manoeuvre.

There are two types: those with an over-rim supply of water are easier to install. Water is delivered either from separate taps mounted over the rim or through mixer taps, and the bidet is

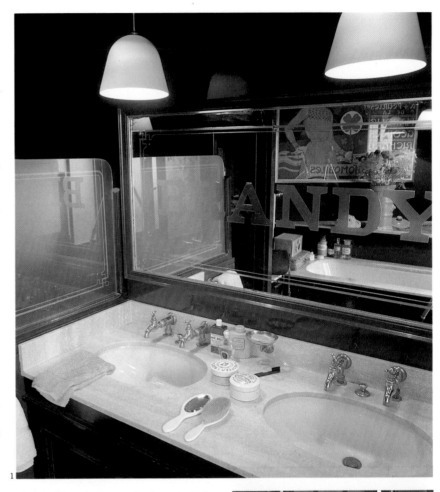

plumbed in exactly as a basin or bath is. A bidet with a through-rim supply and douche has water passed under and round the rim to warm it, before it flows into the bowl. The water can be forced upwards by pulling a lever that sits between the taps and into a spray nozzle, through a pipe connected to the waste outlet. If the bidet is not supplied by a cold water storage tank with a base at least 1.8m (6ft) above the level of the bidet inlet, there is a risk that dirty water can siphon back into the plumbing system.

Lavatories

If the lavatory is part of the bathroom, regulations for new housing stipulate a separate additional lavatory. This doesn't apply to old houses.

There are two main types of lavatory flushing systems, each

3

4

1 Double oval basins dropped into a honey-coloured marble sink unit fit perfectly with an old pub mirror, brass taps and mint green glass light shades. The overall effect makes for a gentle start to the day.

2 Kitchen worktop principles applied to the bathroom. This basin is sunk into a laminated unit.

3 Twin basins in Tom Brent's Art Deco extravaganza of a bathroom.

4 Tiny, but well thought out, the basin and Vola taps can be hidden from view by a simple, but smart, roller shutter.

5 Lavatory and bidet, side by side, with a handy shelf in between for essential reading matter.

5

operating on a different plumbing principle. The most common and least expensive is the washdown flush, in which two gallons of water rushes from the cistern down the flush pipe, to wash around the bowl and force the contents into the outlet pipe. The second system, the siphonic, has two variations, but both work on the principle of using the flushing water to create a vacuum in the pan and atmospheric pressure to force the contents into the outlet. Both come with cisterns 1.8m (6ft) above floor level as high-level suites, or with the cisterns just above the level of the pan yet separate from it as low-level suites, and as close-coupled suites, with the cistern and the pan forming a single unit. These last are the most standard.
Fitting A lavatory takes up the same floor space as a bidet. Space allowance should be made for at least 775mm (2ft 7in.) from side to side and 600mm (2ft) clear in front of a lavatory. High level cisterns are streamlined in design these days and low level cisterns are made in plastic and are so slim that they only project a matter of 114mm (4½in.) from front to back. Both cantilevered lavatories – those fixed to the wall and supported by invisible brackets which go behind the wall and under the floorboards – and lavatories which barely rest on the floor and are secured with wall fixings must have their cisterns concealed behind false walls. You must be able to provide easy access to them. A false wall that projects only half way up provides shelf space for books, plants and bathroom paraphernalia. If you want a Victorian looking bathroom, you could box in the lavatory, adding a wooden seat.

DETAILS

If you want to create a stylish room in which to bathe, the small details are every bit as important as the bath, basin and lavatory. They must be right for the style: you won't succeed in creating a period bathroom if, having spent a lot of money on a claw foot bath, you don't abandon your chrome geometric shaped towel rail. You could indeed produce a room with period character by details alone: keep whatever bath is currently in place but add touches like a free-standing wooden clothes horse for your towels, stencilling on the bath panel if it is boxed in, a marble-topped washstand for a display of period objects, a wooden lavatory seat, brass taps, or a bevilled glass mirror in mahogany frame.

Taps

If you are buying a new bath and basin, you must choose your taps at the same time. They should tie in with your decorative scheme and complement your choice of fittings. Not all taps look right with all bathware. Copies of traditional brass taps, plugs and chains are the natural choice for traditional basins destined for a formal bathroom, or for florally decorated, and shell-shaped basins. The new austere streamlined styles of bathware demand the modern bright coloured or white nylon plastic coated fixtures with their swan neck mixer tap – a good shape for washing hair under. Well-designed plain chrome-plated taps look good too. If you want the low level mixer tap shape, but would like to be able to wash your hair in the basin nonetheless, think about fitting it with a taps and shower combination made for baths.

Odd-shaped vanitory basins will have had taps specifically designed to go with them: hexagonal tap heads match hexagonal basins; brass ball heads go with beaten brass basins.

Lavatory seats

If you expect ever to sit or stand on the lid, or have children who will bang the lid up and down, buy the most rigid plastic lavatory seat you can find. They come in a broad range of colours. Wooden lavatory seats, in mahogany or pine, are expensive, but perfect for a period bathroom, and warm to sit on.

Also warm, and witty too, are brightly coloured seats in padded plastic.

Towel rails and soap racks

Towel rails, linked to hot pipes, or free-standing electrically heated ones are designed in interesting shapes and colour coatings. You cannot have too much space for hanging towels, so why not run a towel rail the entire length of one wall? If you prefer to stick with standard length rails in brackets, fix three, one above the other on the wall.

Soap dishes and racks which stretch across the bath have also come under the designer's scrutiny. They are now made in wood, ceramic, metal and bright plastics, in new simple styles.

Mirrors

Mirror glass can be cut to size to fit above basin recesses and in awkward shapes. If it is not possible to have a wall mirror, consider a circular double-sided mirror mounted on an expanding chrome arm – both stylish and practical. Technology has been commandeered to tackle the problem of steam and has come up with an electronically controlled mirror that is steam sensitive and prevents condensation from forming on the glass – at a price however.

Shelving

Open shelving in a modern bathroom can look good in self-assembly metal track systems made in bright colours. For the smaller bits and pieces, you could fix up a wire grid wall hanger coated in nylon plastic to which other grid baskets and racks can be hooked.

Tiles

Tiling was common in the bathroom long before it was adopted in kitchens, dining rooms and modern living areas. There are hundreds of different designs now, some hugely expensive, some hand-made – often unevenly and therefore difficult to lay – but most are mass-produced and reasonably cheap.

Marble is probably the most expensive sort of tiling, but in shades of blue, acqua, eau de nil or grey it has a fresh, marine feel which looks good in bathrooms. You can cut the cost without losing the effect if you face

your unit panels with white or complementary coloured tiles and save the marble only for surfaces and walls. Tiles printed with a marble-graining pattern are a cheaper variation.

If you cannot afford patterned tiles, or feel you might tire of them too fast, plain tiles can be laid to great effect with a little thought. Take the time to plot your layout on a piece of graph paper. Explore the possibilities of breaking the flat colour with a band of tiles in a contrasting solid shade, or a line of patterned tiles. Coloured rows could be set diagonally for a diamond effect, run in a border parallel to the ceiling or in large rectangles, or in a Greek key pattern. There is also no reason why tiles have to be laid square. They can run diagonally across the

wall, so long as you have a sharp tile-cutter, patience and plenty of spare tiles to slice across to produce the triangular shapes for your border.

Rectangular shapes make a change. They can be laid brickwork fashion, horizontally on top of one another to widen a room, or vertically to add height. Mosaic shapes are unusual, too. A small bathroom covered all over (ceiling as well) with mirror mosaic would create a stunning effect, especially if accessorized in chrome.

Tiling whole walls can be very expensive, even with the cheapest tiles. So think about only partial tiling, with paint or paper carrying on up to the ceiling. A witty idea is to continue the suggestion of tiles by hanging square patterned paper that creates a *trompe*

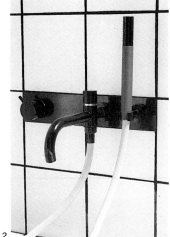

l'oeil effect. If you plan to paper, hang it before you tile, so that it comes under the last row of tiles you place.

Windows

Windows need careful thought. Is the bathroom overlooked? If it is, are you going to fill the frame with opaque or moulded glass, or will you hide behind curtains or blinds? Vertical louvre blinds are more practical than horizontal Venetian blinds because they let the light in through the slats even while they are closed. Bamboo or matchstick blinds are fun and look warm; café curtains bordered with white cotton broderie Anglaise are pretty. These are hung from a rail fixed a quarter or half way down the window, so that the sky can be seen over the top.

You don't have to be limited by conventional materials in a bathroom. In a sleek, modern room, why not use PVC in black, white, or the primary colours for a blind or very long curtains? Towelling makes cosy curtaining and in white can look particularly chic; you could border it in a band of strong colour. Gauzy festoon blinds add a touch of glamour, old lace panels a touch of romance. If there is no view outside worthy of looking at, why not pane the window with mirror instead of glass. If you have an internal bathroom but would like a view – and a humorous touch – paint a *trompe l'oeil* mural on one wall, frame it with red curtains or a blind, and fix a window ledge below for plants and decorative bottles and jars.

Furniture

Bathroom furniture has recently had a facelift. Elegant, yet versatile pieces have supplanted the ready-made storage units and dressing tables of the past. An Italian range includes a chrome-framed cheval mirror on wheels, across whose back is slung a linen pouch for make-up, cotton wool, or soiled underwear. Well-cushioned seats in white or primary coloured plastic lift to reveal storage space for bath oils, shampoos and soaps. One of the best inventions for bathroom clutter is a small plastic trolley on wheels of stacked partitioned boxes which swivel out from a corner rod. Everything can be sorted into its own compartment, taken out and slung back, then closed to hide the contents.

The sort of detritus that accumulates in bathrooms always looks unpleasant lying about in wastepaper baskets. In a modern room, add a brightly coloured lidded plastic bucket, or a chrome pedal bin. In a more formal room, consider fixing a kitchen bucket to the inside of a cupboard door whose lid is raised by the action of opening the door. The space needed to accommodate the bucket is not wasted – behind it at the back is where you can store the bottles of bathroom cleaners and disinfectants that look ugly outside. Other ideas can be usefully transported from the kitchen: plastic vegetable racks make useful shelving inside a vanitory unit or out in the open for towels and soaps that are attractive to look at.

1 A purpose-built bath, using marble slabs and incorporating old-fashioned taps and a useful shelf.

2 High tech mixer tap and shower attachment from Vola, who offer a complete range of bathroom fittings in co-ordinated shapes and colours.

3 Towel rails positioned over the bath – handy for grabbing a towel when you're in the tub.

4 Black tiles used on the floor and walls inverts the usual colour convention for bathrooms, but with white fittings still looks functional and smart.

5 A circular mirror on an expanding arm is a practical and good-looking detail.

6 Salvaged Victorian tiles make a pretty period background, into which modern taps have been cleverly and unobtrusively incorporated.

7 A kitchen worktop counter contains the basin as well as hiding the plumbing and drainage runs for the bath and lavatory.

CHILDREN'S ROOMS

When preparing a room for the first baby there is a tremendous temptation to create a darling of a room, frilly and small in keeping with the spectacular smallness of the infant. At all costs, unless you are very well off, resist this. By the time your baby is about eight months old, he will already be crawling around, throwing things across the room, spilling biscuit crumbs and juice all over the floor and soon afterwards bumping the babywalker into the furniture and scribbling all over the walls.

Although your child will be the smallest person in the house for some years, don't necessarily choose the smallest spare bedroom as the baby's room. Remember that a child makes much more use of his bedroom than you do yours — in time he should be able to sleep, play, work and entertain in it, so try to make as large a space as possible available for him.

Looking ahead

Having chosen the room, look to the future when considering the decoration and furnishing. The basic decoration should last for some years so choose one which will suit the needs of the toddler as much as the newborn. A suitable flooring is one which will be warm and comfortable to crawl on, smooth enough to build bricks on and not so babylike that later on a child will be ashamed to live with it. Walls should be easy to clean and preferably they should be suitable for repainting so that grubby finger marks and scribbles can be obliterated.

Furniture too should be adaptable to the growing child as well as suited to his present circumstances. You may choose not to have an expensive cradle but make do with a wicker basket, the top half of a folding pram, or even a well-lined drawer taken from an old chest. There are many cots and other pieces of furniture on the market which are intended to convert or extend so that they last longer into a child's life. Don't allow the furniture to eat up too much space.

Arrange for more storage space than you will need at first; even if it is underused for a few years it will all be needed in time.

Where to play

When a child is very young it is sensible and often necessary to allow him to play in the living room or the far end of the kitchen if it is large enough, where the parents can keep an eye on what he's doing. As children grow older and have, first of all a mass of large and bulky toys, and later homework and their own friends, their own music and their own lives to lead, it becomes desirable to find a room to which they can escape. It is also essential for the parents to be able to have some time away from the children. Without a special – and inviting – room to contain them, children are likely to take over the house completely.

Unfortunately many homes are too small to have the ideal basement room where the children can make as much noise and mess as they like without disturbing the rest of the house. Many people are forced to give up, say, the dining room, but they find it a worthwhile sacrifice. It may need some determination and imagination to find space for, say, a darts' board, a small snooker table, a place to play cards or charades or just to loaf around in comfortable chaos, but it's certainly worth the effort.

Suiting the child

One sort of child will want, very early on, to have a pretty room with small ornaments, pictures, flowery curtains and wallcoverings, floor cushions for friends: a social centre. Others will need space for model making and storage of materials for hobbies, or for sophisticated stereo or computer equipment. If, early on, you can create a basic space where any of these things can take precedence, you will be well on the way to providing a suitable environment for growth, pleasure and harmony in the home whatever your child's interests turn out to be.

The specific needs of children at various stages in their development are outlined in the next few pages. One important guideline is that the room belongs to the child and not to you. Even though you can create the possibility for industry and neatness or noise and sociability, it is the child who must decide which pattern he fits into.

1

Nobody can prepare a parent for the momentous change a new baby brings into their life. First of all he will take up an astonishing amount of time. Feeding, changing, bathing, clearing up and burping seem to occupy 24 hours a day. But though you cannot imagine the emotion, you can prepare for the event in a practical way by envisaging all the processes the new baby will require and arranging the most comfortable, satisfactory and cheerful surroundings.

The basic shell
You will not want to keep repainting, repapering and laying new flooring as the child grows up, so choose finishes and floors which will stand up to the ravages of babies and time. Eggshell paint is tough and washable and more pleasant to live with than gloss. In many respects a plain colour is more practical than patterns, because inevitably there will come a time when a child brings home all sorts of bits and pieces from school and from friends, which will clutter the room so that any background pattern on the walls and floor will just add to the confusion. However, there are some truly pretty washable papers and, if a dainty background seems right for something so delicate as a new baby, you can

always cover just one wall, or paint or paper over it with something more robust later. Too many swags and drapes tend to get dusty however, so avoid them unless you enjoy washing and rehanging.

Carpet is warm and comfortable but will soon be littered with bits of cotton wool and rusk unless you are a meticulous parent — and, in the practical light of parenthood, floors do get dirty and things do get spilled. Remember too, that your child will want to build bricks, run cars around and spin tops, activities which a smoother flooring is better at coping with than carpet. Vinyl is a practical material, and cork is excellent, available with a thin veneer of vinyl which makes it easier to clean.

Heat and light
A new baby should be kept in a uniform room temperature of 65°–70°F (18°–21°C), so some form of reliable heating is essential. A thermostatically controlled central heating system would be best, but failing that a thermostatically controlled electric convector heater is satisfactory.

If you are having the room rewired put in plenty of socket outlets — though you may not need them all now,

they will be useful later on when the children want to use more electrical equipment. It's safer by far to have plenty of sockets than to use double and triple plugs from one socket outlet.

For lighting the room, reflector spot lamps or wall lamps will give a much softer background glow than one central light, and angled lamps can be used for specific purposes such as nappy changing. You will find that a dimmer switch is very useful so that you can peep at your baby when he's asleep at night, and it can be used as a night light when he reaches the age of being afraid of the dark.

Basic equipment
The shopping list for a newborn baby is inevitably long and daunting, and needs careful consideration before the final choice is made. Instead of a crib, you may choose a Moses basket or carrycot which have the advantage of being easily transportable.

Between three and six months your baby will need to move to a cot; instead of blankets a brightly patterned cot-size duvet is practical for the mother and cosy for the baby.

Fitted storage is best in a baby's room as it takes up less valuable floor space, but a chest of drawers for the endless possessions a baby acquires from the moment of birth is essential.

Changing
You will need a table, bed or support of some kind to change the baby on. The greater part of the day seems to be spent stooping, which is one of the reasons parents get backache. You can buy a special nappy changing table; or alternatively a narrow table or chest of drawers is acceptable while the baby is still tiny. Never turn your back on the baby, though, in case he rolls off.

1 In this room for three, lighting and surfaces are attractive and practical, storage is prodigious, and the use of colour gives each child a sense of identity.

2 A nursery designed to suit both mother and child to a tee.

ROOM TO GROW

From the time your baby starts to become an independent person you will need more storage and to become more disciplined about using it. Children acquire so many toys and treasures that unless you impose some order smaller items will get lost or broken under larger ones. When he's still a toddler, much of your child's playing will be done not in his own room but in the living room or part of the kitchen, if large enough, where you can supervise. Nevertheless his bedroom can be the store room for most of his belongings, and you can keep a large basket or box where he plays in which to put all the toys at the end of the day. The bedroom will undergo many further changes while your child is growing so rapidly, so flexibility is the key consideration.

The basics

Give up all hope of a neat and orderly room. Children need to be stimulated, to practise and experiment. They need lots of variety, different sorts of toys and materials. The most practical background is the kind you find in nursery schools and playgroups: a simple setting with painted wall surfaces or cork to pin things on, floors which can be cleared, swept and mopped easily, and a large waste bin (perhaps an old log basket).

If you are adapting part of a spacious kitchen for the child to play while you work and keep an eye on him at the same time, the best finishes are probably already there in the form of excellent kitchen surfaces. Floor surfaces should be smooth and if possible feel warm. Wall surfaces should be washable. A wall kept specially for scribbling on acquires an interesting character of its own, and can eventually be repainted. Alternatively, blackboard paint can be used on part of the wall for this purpose. Children love colour so don't be afraid of slapping deep cheerful coloured paint on at least one wall of the child's room.

Storage

Children of pre-school age are growing very fast and are very anxious to do things for themselves. The articles that a child will want to be able to fetch and carry for himself must be within easy reach or you will find him climbing on chairs and trying to grasp things just beyond him. Better to concentrate on installing low shelves which the child can easily reach. Again, the more fitted shelving you can install the better. The best is probably the upright-and-bracket type found in most DIY stores. This can be added to from time to time, and the shelf heights and widths can be adjusted as the child's interests change and he acquires more belongings. This sort of storage also has the advantage of being quite robust and will hold heavy equipment such as a TV set as well as books, rows of toys, boxes of bricks and so on.

For this age group box storage is also extremely useful. A built-in box with lift-up lid could run along one wall, perhaps under a window. When the lid is closed it doubles up as a bench which the child can sit and play on. Inside, the box should be compartmented so that teddies don't obliterate plastic soldiers, and muddy boots can be kept apart from precious dolls.

For clothes a little wardrobe or fitted cupboard with a rail and shelves is useful. When space is limited rails and shelves can be installed very simply minus the cupboard fronts; this gives the illusion of more space. If you want to hide the mess, a pretty curtain does the trick. A chest of drawers is probably still necessary; there are always items which are safer in drawers, and socks and mittens, vest and pants are less likely to become divided from each other if they have their own compartments.

While your child needs to be kept safe in his bed, a drop-sided cot is the obvious answer. Some cots are specially designed to convert later into a bed; otherwise a small divan would do. A

1 **Bunk beds with a difference. The beds are timber, with metal mesh panels sprayed blue. The steps double as bedside tables and pink felt lines the walls.**

2 Pretty and practical: a combined work surface and storage unit runs beneath a childproof window. Below, box storage for toys and a toddler's chair can be pushed out of sight when not in use.

3 A cosy corner designed to coax even the most recalcitrant child into bed. An L-shaped platform provides a base for a low divan for sleeping, as well as plenty of extra space for lounging.

4 Plain walls and floor for practicality; a bright and beautiful quilt for fun.

practical alternative is the Japanese futon bed: the mattress, either on a slatted base or placed directly on the floor is useful in small spaces. During the day it can be rolled up for seating.

For two children in a confined space, bunk beds have become the traditional solution. There are many on the market to choose from, but a handyman could easily make a set to fit the room. Check that the child in the bottom bunk will be able to sit up comfortably to read and play without fear of hitting the top bunk, and that each child has a reading lamp. And even if you only have one child don't rule out bunks: the lower bunk can save space by providing a valuable storage area.

Tables and chairs

You may think your children never sit still, but given miniature chairs and a table, they can often be found quietly absorbed in hosting a dolls' tea party, or drawing, or poring over a book. Unfortunately child-size furniture often seems horribly expensive, since — as with most items for the very young — it must be exceedingly robust.

Windows

Bedroom windows must be safe. They could be non-opening windows with ventilating discs or louvres, or you can fit wooden or metal bars. For young children roller blinds are better than curtains, which can be swung on. Make sure the child can't lean out of the window or play with the catches.

3

A ROOM OF THEIR OWN

In the same way that toddlers are constantly experimenting with different shapes and textures, so teenagers experiment with being grown up, airing their own points of view, and discovering their own interests. At this stage a room of their own can become an important tool in defining their personality and tastes. They may quite deliberately choose decorations and colours opposed to the tastes of their parents, and take a perverse pleasure in being as untidy as possible. The room is theirs, however, not yours, so if they really want black walls and red light bulbs, perhaps you should let them. One proviso is that, unless you have a separate one available, the room should be practical for other purposes: suitable for model making, homework, music making, dressing up and making up, lounging and hobbies of various kinds. If, in the past, you had planned with foresight, all this could be accomplished without having to put in any expensive fitments or furniture.

Homework and hobbies

Many children have to struggle with their homework in the kitchen or living room, trying to compete with the television, the chattering of other people, a table at the wrong height and inappropriate lighting. If you can provide your teenager with somewhere pleasant and satisfactory to work, you will be doing him a great service. This is where the upright-and-bracket shelving installed for the small child's room can really come into its own by being extended to cover a much larger wall area. You could put in a very wide shelf at working height as a work surface. Standard desk heights are usually between 650mm (26in.) and 750mm (30in.), but an easy rule of thumb is to make them elbow height when the child is sitting down. A comfortable chair, preferably a typist's chair, can be adjusted to the child's own height. Attach a reading lamp to the wall, stand a desk lamp on the work surface or clamp one onto a shelf. An adjustable angled lamp is probably the most versatile and satisfactory. A couple of second-hand filing cabinets or small chests of drawers under the working shelf provide storage for

1

paper, envelopes, reference material and so on.

Homework is not the only kind of concentrated activity your teenager may need to be provided for. Model making, sewing, drawing and electronics are all popular pastimes. The working shelf you have created will be suitable for any of these and the drawer storage beneath will hold materials for most hobbies. Box files, small chests of drawers from DIY shops and small compartments from office furniture stores can all be used for the storage of very small items.

Electrical and electronic equipment

Music is a basic ingredient in a teenager's life. Mercifully, the advent of headphones has eased the parental headache caused by teenagers' desire to play their music so terribly loud. You should provide adequate storage for the equipment and paraphernalia that goes with modern electronic music. Records and tapes are delicate and need looking after, and they also take up space. Properly compartmented racks will help to protect them.

Count up the number of appliances your child is likely to want to run off the mains: perhaps a fan heater, possibly a TV set and/or computer, a sewing machine, record player, tape deck, hair dryer, working lamp, bedside lamp,

2

3

1 Running the length of a wall, this work station takes up minimal space, leaving plenty of room for extra seating and important electrical equipment.

2 A room ideally suited to work, rest and play. The rather spartan tongue and groove panelling is enlivened by brightly coloured paintwork.

3 A raised platform is a clever way of creating a separate sleeping area as well as providing ingenious space for storage and radiators.

4 The perfect place to entertain friends: simple banquette seating with storage lockers below, bright cushions and rug, and plain white walls — the best background for favourite posters.

4

occasionally even a vacuum cleaner. Work out where these might be needed, given that a child may rearrange the room from time to time. Then make sure there are outlets for two or three of these pieces of equipment to be run simultaneously and that they are placed where they can be conveniently reached without tripping over yards of flex.

Entertaining

A child often finds it easier and more fun to entertain friends in his own room than to have to share them with the family and its preoccupations.

A low, simple bed such as a divan is ideal for sitting and lounging on. Extra sitting space can be provided by huge floor cushions depending on the numbers of your children's friends and the size of the room. Some sort of table will be useful for putting mugs on, though if the room is small, the worktop desk will be enough.

Clothes

In the view of their parents, teenagers may dress in a curiously eccentric way. Within their own age group, of course, they are very conformist and looking right is of the utmost importance to

them. They will have mounds of garments, and the mounds will grow mountainous as the child grows older.

It will be necessary to extend the wardrobe accommodation, though not necessarily with a fitted cupboard because in a smallish room this can be a dominating feature. You could suspend a long rail in an alcove or right along one end of the room, perhaps boxed in at either end but without doors. If the child collects clothes seriously, a double tier of rails could be fixed, with shirts on one rail and longer clothes on the other one. Parallel rails on wheels, such as are used in clothes shops, are a good idea, and a supplementary form of storage is a bentwood pine hat rack, not just for hats, but for clothes hangers, holding shirts, scarves and so on. A battery of hooks on the wall can be used for jewellery and a panel of pegboard, chipboard or cork can be used as a pinboard for postcards, messages, beads and other bric-a-brac. Most teenagers will appreciate a full-length mirror, fixed to the wall or inside a cupboard door. Shoe racks or bags hung inside the wardrobe keep the trainers from getting underfoot. A dressing table where girls can make up will be appreciated.

PLAYROOMS

The family which has space at home for a separate playroom for the children is lucky indeed. Such a room has enormous and lasting value, from the moment a child can play by himself, right through to his teens. In many spacious modern homes, particularly in the United States, the playroom has become an integral part of a family house, often situated in the basement where loud noise won't disturb the rest of the family or the neighbourhood.

What is a playroom?
Whether you call it a den, a rumpus room, a recreation room or a playroom, such a space gives children a chance to work off their surplus energy, and to play and relax without restriction. It also gives an opportunity for parents and children to carry on their own lives without imposing on each other. Adults can talk to friends in the living room without cramping their children's style, and children can congregate and make a noise and a mess without constantly being found at fault.

Ideally a playroom should offer the possibility of several different kinds of leisure activities from reading peacefully to dancing to disco music. The larger the room, the more scope there is. While the children are still toddlers, the main priority is plenty of floor space for building Leggo and driving pedal cars. Later on, it should have some comfortable seating, plus perhaps a table for playing board games or cards,

a darts board, even a snooker or ping pong table. You might consider facilities for making coffee or a small refrigerator for soft drinks.

Choosing the room
Many houses and apartments are too small for a purpose-built playroom, and a bedroom or living area has to be denied, but with ingenuity however it is often possible to find a place for some sort of separate activity room. The problem is tricky because one of the attractions of such a room is the chance to make a noise. One excellent site, if it can be spared, is the garage. It should be possible to put in a few electric socket outlets and some form of heating. And it will not matter if the children have to go outside to get to it. The basement, if there is one, may be suitable with a bit of damp-proofing, and again, extra electrical socket outlets, better lighting, and some form of ventilation. Then there's the roof space. This may require a loft conversion, but even under a sloping roof, it is possible to create a pleasant and workable space. Indeed, the more unusual the hideaway, the more exciting the children will find it.

Equipping the room
If you are lucky enough to have a large space, equipment for many different activities can be fitted in; if not, you will have to decide which activity you want to concentrate on.

1 Plenty here to keep both toddlers and teenagers amused, from building blocks and miniature kitchen to stereo and model boat. Dark sisal matting is a good choice for flooring — it's tough and doesn't show the dirt.

2 and 3 The garage as a playroom: during the day the car is in use; when the kids go to bed it comes in for the night.

4

6

4 Tucked under the eaves, a child's paradise.

5 Homework is quickly abandoned in favour of a visit inside this marvellous walk-in dolls' house.

6 Getting the taste of a businessman's life: this young entrepreneur has all the office equipment he could wish for — including Smarties.

5

Don't be tempted to make this space a storeroom for unwanted furniture. There's nothing less relaxing than an overcrowded room with no space to play in and nothing comfortable to sit on. The ideal furniture would be a voluminous sofa with soft cushions, one or two easy chairs, and a large table for cards, board games and jigsaw puzzles.

If yours is a musical family, you could fit acoustic tiles on the ceiling and perhaps the walls as well to contain a little of the sound. True soundproofing requires new walls to be built. If listening to, rather than making music, is the important thing, don't fit acoustic tiles which are inclined to deaden sound. A system of scheduled listening hours and/or a set of headphones may be necessary if other people complain of the noise. TV is one of the worst noise nuisances, so the playroom is a good place for children to watch television, play television games and fix up their computer.

Easy-to-clean surfaces are less critical here than in babies' rooms since hygiene is not so crucial for older children, the playroom is not anybody's

permanent bedroom, and the children can also be expected to do a certain amount of tidying up and cleaning themselves. A row or two of basic shelves for books, games and so on is essential. The lighting should be adequate and suitable: overhead lighting is best for games, while wall lights give a pleasant background light, and angled lamps or well-placed spots for reading should be enough. Ventilation is important too, particularly if the room is in the basement. Where there are no opening windows, an extractor fan will be necessary.

Although this room is the children's domain, the adults should oversee it from time to time to check on the safety of the sockets and plugs, to collect up mugs and cups and make sure the lights and heaters have been turned off at night. Otherwise the charm of such a room is that it need not be tidy or especially clean, and that it is a place where the children's standards apply, rather than the adults', though ideally adults will not feel excluded from the room and will enjoy relaxing in it too.

FURNITURE

It's always better to have too little furniture than too much, because children need plenty of floor space to play on. Everything in the room should have a purpose, even two purposes, and as much of the furniture should be fitted as possible, making it more likely to be of use as the child grows older, taking up less floor space, and being less easy to topple.

There is plenty of interesting children's furniture available, much of it well designed to be flexible and practical. You might, however, consider making your own, which will be tailor-made to fit the child's room and may be substantially cheaper.

A simple door with holes drilled in it for ventilation, placed on supports, even on storage chests, may be more convenient and cheaper than the most elaborate child's bed. Equally, a door placed on two chests of drawers may make a better desk than a small free-standing one.

Furniture for sound sleep
A child's bed should be firm and comfortable without being too soft. Very small babies have a wealth of choice in Moses baskets, carrycots, wooden cribs and rocking cradles. The baby will, however, grow out of a crib in a very few months, so the wise thing

would be to buy something cheap and spend more money on the next stage of bed which can be made to last until the child is well into the teens.

You can invest in a drop-sided cot and then move the child later into a bed. Or you can buy a convertible cot which extends into a bed. A foldaway bed may be necessary if space is at a premium, but the trouble here is that the bed has to be cleared of toys and bedclothes every morning, and the child can't creep into it during the day to have a little snooze. Futons can be used as sofas during the day and unrolled as bedding at night, though the rolling and unrolling requires a certain amount of discipline and tidiness. Another possible form of bed is one which houses another or even two underneath it. These secondary beds can be pulled out at night, either for a second child or for visitors. Many divan beds are available with drawers beneath them for bedding or toys.

Storage
You cannot have too much storage in a child's room. Not only does a child acquire a huge number of varied possessions, but to be used and appreciated they must be kept separate. There are plenty of standard types of fitted cupboard units available

which will allow the maximum clear play space on the floor, and will leave no gaps where objects can get lost and which are awkward to clean.

Full height units are often fitted with shelf storage, as well as hanging storage, using an adjustable system so the shelf heights can be altered from time to time. Some of these are designed so that you can add sections as necessary. This sort of storage allows for change of use, so that a cupboard used originally for toys and clothes for a young child can be used later as a work space or desk area just by changing the interior arrangement.

Shelves for books will be needed too. Widely available are three-shelf folding, stacking bookshelves which can be added to from time to time, eventually covering quite a large wall area. These are cheap but not so sturdy or versatile as uprights fixed to the wall and used with brackets at adjustable heights supporting chipboard or wooden shelves.

Bookshelves can be part of a modular storage system, usually in pine. Don't forget the ubiquitous kitchen cupboard unit; such cupboards can make very good nursery storage.

Storage boxes can be ranged under a window, along a wall or stacked to form a sort of unit in themselves. This

form of storage, perhaps with a chest of drawers, will accommodate most of the toys, sports equipment, clothes, shoes and writing things a child accumulates. Sliding doors take up less space but often get in the way of each other. It might be best to do away with doors altogether and keep the equipment on open shelves, or in open box storage so the child can identify and grasp objects quickly and put them away easily.

Suppliers of school and nursery school equipment have excellent furniture and storage which, although expensive initially, are flexible, reliable, tough and usually good to look at. There are trolleys on wheels, storage boxes, batteries of drawers and so on. Second-hand furniture such as the Utility furniture made during and after World War II in Britain is often a better buy than new, somewhat flimsily made objects.

Sitting comfortably
There are various types of high chair on the market, some adaptable into low chairs with their own tables. Plastic and chrome are popular but there are some good-looking wooden ones around too. As we have said, miniature chairs and tables are much appreciated by toddlers and perfect for tea parties.

1 A sturdy wooden box with compartmented inner shelf keeps fiddly pieces of Leggo in some semblance of order.

2 A large solid desk, repository for many treasured possessions.

3 There is a sedate approach to this top bunk, by ladder, but this Tarzan prefers a more energetic climb — and the metal scaffolding can take the strain. Painted bright blue and extended to make shelving as well, it looks as good as it is strong.

4 Built-in cupboards maximize much-needed storage space as well as creating, in this case, a cosy berth.

Very young babies who can't quite sit up on their own yet are often happiest in a bouncing chair which gives them an excellent view of the world around. From about three months onwards some babies get the greatest fun out of a baby bouncer attached to the doorway or the ceiling. When the baby can sit on his own, a circular baby walker on wheels is also usually much enjoyed and helps to strengthen his legs and encourage walking. Plenty of space is needed though once the baby gets the hang of it.

Working furniture

Even small children need somewhere to sit and draw or 'work'. (The sooner they learn that learning is interesting the better.) For school children a work space is absolutely essential. A fitted work surface, especially if combined with a shelving system, will make less demands on the space and can be tailored to fit the room. It can occupy a whole wall, and with storage beneath and above, will take care of all the storage needs of the working child. This is perhaps the most expensive way to do things, but in some ways the most attractive. Some children prefer to do their homework on similar furniture and in similar surroundings to those which they have at school, in which case your child may prefer a separate desk with a traditional lifting lid and inkwell.

Lighting

Good lighting is vitally important. There should be good background light either from a central fitting, though this is frowned on as being harsh and unfriendly, or from wall lights. There should also be a bedside lamp for reading and a working lamp by the desk or work surface. For working, an angled lamp is probably the best, attached to the wall or clamped to a shelf, or standing on the worktop. Night lights which give a comforting glow in the dark are available in all sorts of shapes and sizes from owls and rabbits to little gnomey houses.

231

SAFETY

Toddlers and the elderly are more frequently victims of accidents in the home than any other age group; and more under 15 year olds are killed by accidents at home than by any other accidental cause — including cars.

Small children are at risk all the time. They are unsteady on their feet and likely to trip up or knock into things. They are curious and will touch or taste anything they see and can reach. Obviously every danger cannot be eliminated and in any case a child must build up his own sense of self-preservation, but it is possible to remove the most obvious and deadly dangers, and teach him to tackle others in the safest possible way. First make yourself aware of potential danger traps.

Windows
Windows which reach near floor level should have bars fixed in front of them, close enough together so the child cannot get his head between them. Large expanses of window should have safety glass put in.

Electricity
If a room is being rewired, it is useful to put socket outlets at a higher level than normal so that a crawling baby cannot put his fingers into the holes. Alternatively, safety socket covers can be bought. Electrical leads should not be allowed to trail all round the room, and the same is true of telephone cables. It goes without saying that leads should be unfrayed and checked from time to time to see that they have not become twisted, and that there are no bare wires. Try to site any electrical equipment as near to its socket as possible, and if you can put it out of reach of the child so much the better. Irons should never be left on while you go to answer the door and the hair dryer should not be left, even if switched off, where the child could possibly reach it.

Fires
Any fire or stove which becomes too hot to touch or which has an open flame or a heated element must be guarded. You can buy metal fireguards at baby shops and though they are not the most beautiful objects in the world they have

other practical uses. You can and should teach your baby about heat. Once he's introduced to the idea, he will have a healthy respect for things hot, but there's still a chance he might trip and fall onto the fire so the fireguard is essential. Always keep a fire extinguisher in the house, and a fire blanket in the kitchen with which you can suffocate a fire caused by fat catching alight in the pan.

Stairs
All stairs must have solid bannisters in good repair with steps that are not too slippery and on which any carpet is not frayed. If the child's room is upstairs, it is wise to have a gate either on the door of his room or at the stair head so there's no chance of him falling. You should teach your child to negotiate stairs (coming down backwards on hands and knees) as soon as he can walk or even crawl. See that lights on the landing do not cast shadows so the steps are difficult to see.

Poisons
It goes without saying that no household cleaner or weed killer, or any other product which might be harmful, should be left where a young child could get hold of it. Many everyday household chemicals are highly poisonous and all such products should be kept on the tallest shelf or in a locked cupboard and very tightly closed. Children will drink red dye out of a Ribena bottle, weed killer out of a lemonade bottle. After it has happened it's all so obvious; the important thing is to think ahead and prevent it happening. This applies just as much to household medicines: aspirin, cold cures and so on, which should be kept in a child-proof cupboard in the bathroom. There's nothing easier than for a child to take out a bottle from his mother's handbag and sample the contents.

Sharp implements
Scissors, knives, safety pins, razor blades, all in everyday use, should be kept well out of reach of small children. In the kitchen, knives can be kept in a drawer out of range, or on a knife rack on the wall, preferably not a magnetic

one which may lose its force if it gets grubby. Hooks on the wall can be used to hang scissors. A work-box with pins and needles in it should be taboo.

Sleeping
Bunks should have a good ladder with wide rungs and bars at the sleeping end so the child can't fall out in his sleep. Small babies should never be given soft pillows which might suffocate them. If you are using a second-hand cot, check that it is in good order and the bars are sensibly spaced.

Animals
Cats have been known to curl up on a sleeping baby: so when they are too tiny to fight back, babies should be protected while sleeping in their prams by a cat net. Your pets' plates should be washed separately from the rest of the dishes to prevent any chance of the baby catching worms. Don't leave pets' plates on the floor for the baby to play with and don't let your animal lick your baby's face.

Bathtime
Never leave a young child alone in the bath, even for a second. Babies can drown in a very short time and in very shallow water. The bathroom should have a non-slip floor and you should have a baby bath at a raised height for a new baby, rather than using the big bath; that way it is easier and safer for the parent to reach the baby and lift him up. Non-slip bath mats are invaluable when the baby is at the sitting stage.

Rugs
Rugs look pretty and make a hard floor more comfortable to crawl and play on, but certain rugs may ruck up or slip causing a young child to trip or fall. Rugs should either be thick and heavy enough for this not to happen, or alternatively you can fit them with non-slip backings.

Furniture
Furniture presents two main dangers. A child can manage to pull over even a heavy piece of furniture, which is one reason why fitted furniture may be a better solution. Or he may climb inside

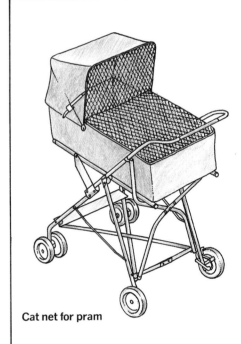

Cat net for pram

Safety cupboard catch

and inadvertently lock himself in. Door catches should be easily opened from the inside and close fitting doors are not necessarily the safest.

Furniture with very sharp corners should be avoided. Little babies stagger and hurt themselves quite badly if they catch the side of their heads on the sharp corner of a table, chest, or worktop.

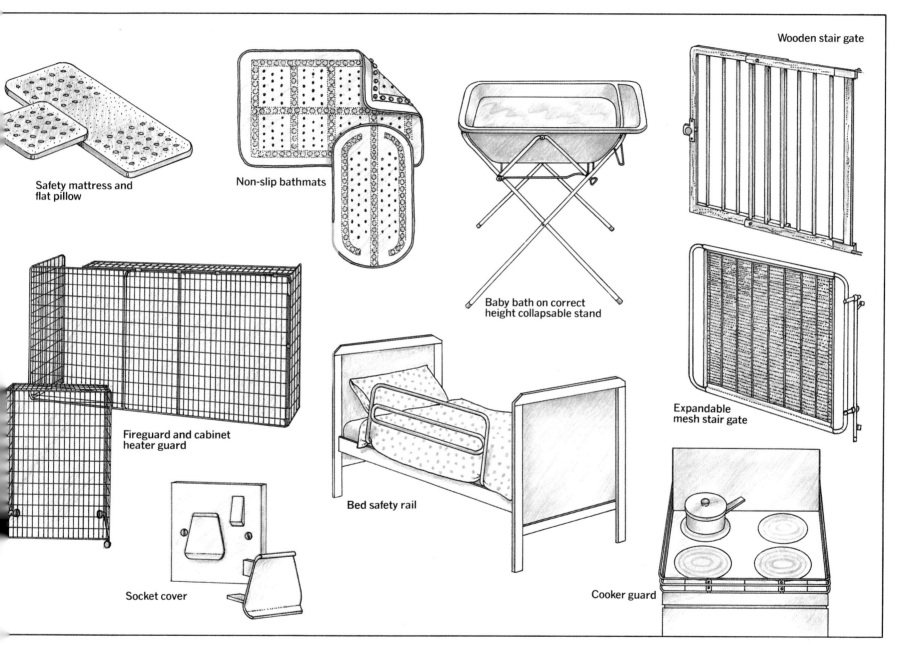

Safety mattress and flat pillow

Non-slip bathmats

Baby bath on correct height collapsable stand

Wooden stair gate

Fireguard and cabinet heater guard

Expandable mesh stair gate

Bed safety rail

Socket cover

Cooker guard

First aid
Accidents do happen, but you can diminish their seriousness by having the right first aid equipment to deal with disasters on the spot. This should be kept somewhere obvious and inspected from time to time to make sure it still has all the necessary items in it: sticking plasters, antiseptic, scissors, crepe bandage, cotton wool and painkillers. Keep it out of reach in a lockable bathroom cupboard or on a top shelf of the kitchen or the children's playroom. The list of numbers next to the telephone should include the chemist and the doctor's surgery. You should have a simple first aid book and read it before you need it, so that the information does not seem new to you when you need it in an emergency.

Keep the book in a convenient place so that it is always to hand.

Common sense
Safety is, in the end, largely a matter of common sense. A parent will soon learn what particular danger to look out for and to guard against it. Some children are always swallowing things and will put anything into their mouths, others are daredevils, always taking flying leaps from the top of a chair, some are simply clumsy and fall over a lot, yet others are ever-curious, always poking and prying into odd holes and corners. A natural instinct for your child's preservation, an ever-watchful eye and plenty of common sense will go a long way towards preventing accidents in the home.

ONE ROOM LIVING

In the last ten years one-room living has become an increasingly popular option for many people, regardless of age, income or personal style. It need not just be a matter of economic necessity; one room can mean anything from a vast converted warehouse space to a tiny bedsit. But even the smallest home of one's own offers privacy and independence. And at last developers, aware that people are living in single spaces out of choice, are providing one-room devotees with purpose-built blocks of studio apartments which have become the chic alternative to bedsits.

Transforming one room, no matter what the size, into a real home should take as much thought and planning as organizing a whole house. But instead of choosing different wallpapers for the living room, dining room and bedroom, you will have to work out how to highlight or disguise different areas to best effect.

The selection of decorating materials is expanding. Manufacturers are more readily taking up new ideas and trends while continuing to improve their existing products. Special tools now come to the home decorator's rescue in the form of stencils, and the pattern-embossed rollers which, with little effort, can liven up a dull wall, ceiling or door.

Furniture is much more flexible, both in design and price. Many people are more at ease with adaptable systems and lightweight materials in place of the solid wood furniture of the past. As a result the style rules that once existed have been broken or changed. Witness the growing amount of laboratory stainless steel basins, shop fittings and garden furniture, for example, being incorporated into domestic interiors.

But unless you are experienced in translating what you think is chic or stylish into the confines of a single room, complete chaos is likely to ensue.

The result may well be a conglomeration of clashing styles, or a tired reproduction of a much imitated design style to the extent that the space looks like a catalogue room set.

How you make your chosen look work for you is just as important. Lack of space is predictably the main grumble voiced by those who live in small bedsits or studios. This complaint is totally understandable if setting up a foldaway table means blocking out the kitchen door, or letting down a double bed means you have to shift an armchair before you can hang your clothes in the cupboard. Conversely, what to do with space once you have it is a common problem for people who live in a huge loft or warehouse.

This chapter looks at the practical aspects involved in a one-room lifestyle and at the different forms it can take, whether it be a tiny studio, a huge loft or a bed-sitting room in a shared house.

1

2

3

1, 2 and 3 Extra high ceilings provide room for a highly unconventional version of the familiar mezzanine: a bed platform – like a circus tent in its striped fabric – juts out over the living area as if it were hanging in space. Floor to ceiling radiators flank the windows; mustard coloured studded rubber unifies the whole area; the mezzanine handrail doubles as a storage unit. Tucked into a corner: the kitchen and dining area.

PLANNING AND PRACTICALITIES

Unlike living in a house or apartment where each room has an individual function, one-room living means compacting your whole home into a single space, so that living room, dining room, bedroom and kitchen are incorporated into what might not be more than a 4 x 4m (12 x 12ft) room. The problem is not simply how to fit everything (including the kitchen sink) into a small space, but how best to organize your room so that a multitude of different activities can co-exist happily within four walls. This is just as important a consideration in enormous lofts where the problem is often how best to use the space.

First things first

Ask yourself several obvious questions. What kind of life do you lead? Will you be at home for most of the time or are you never in? What will you need to use your room for? Do you entertain a great deal, need good cooking facilities, or a place to study? Will the space be occupied by you alone or will you be sharing it with a partner, or friends? Or will your room be part of a shared household? Will you have to find basic equipment and furniture or do you have these already and if so, do they fit in? Perhaps the room is already furnished and decorated, in which case will it need altering, adapting or revamping?

Thinking along these practical lines will mean that your lifestyle in one room can be ordered and easy-to-maintain, you will not waste time shifting armchairs to make way for the fold-down bed, or moving tables to get to the wardrobe. Heath Robinson inventions are definitely not feasible in a single space.

Taking stock of your requirements in both furnishing and lifestyle before you move in will enable you to keep a realistic grip on any decorating you do. Think first of the walls, floors, ceilings, windows and lighting as these provide the initial framework around which everything else revolves.

When you are starting from scratch think about the function of each area in relation to the others. You will probably want the service areas – kitchen and bathroom – at the other end of the room

from the living and bedroom areas. If you are installing plumbing make sure that both the kitchen and bathroom can work off the same system, and when it comes to the electrics that there are enough sockets in the right places. Trailing flexes between the bedroom and kitchen area should definitely be avoided. If there is only one source of natural light, you will have to decide whether you want to centre your working, eating or sleeping areas around it. Or you might need overall artificial lighting on the whole time; if so, install a system which can accommodate the new energy saving light bulbs.

Your room might be large enough to put up partitions and high enough to make another room by constructing a platform, but you will have to check that the supporting structure can take the additional weight, and that any area underneath the platform is lit effectively to use for some other

activity. If you live in a larger space and want to install a room within a room make sure that it does not look too overpoweringly solid; a more flexible device of screens or curtains would offer the same privacy and affect the size of the room less.

The basics

Take your time before rushing off to buy fixtures and furnishings. Ultimately this will save you time and expense, no matter how quickly you want to have a room decorated to your taste. A major priority when you move into any new home is to work out your budget, making one list of essential furniture and equipment, and another of the necessary building work (see the chapter Be Your Own Interior Designer).

You may find when you move in that certain fixtures, such as radiators or doors, may not be to your taste. But unless you have unlimited funds, try

disguising rather than replacing them. Radiators could be stippled or dragged; painted to blend in with the colour of the wall; even boxed in. Beading can be stuck onto flush doors to give an impression of panelling.

Furniture

Once you have made any structural improvements and redecorated, you will need some basic furniture. Consider designs which can double up for other activities; and so reduce the amount of clutter that can accumulate in a small space. An obvious starting point is the bed which, with a little dressing up can become a sofa during the day. Have cushions which can double up as pillows at night. Should you want to disguise the bed or if space is too restricted to be taken up by one at all, invest in a sofa bed. There are now some very good inexpensive Italian designs which come in a range of bright colours. Futons from Japan are

also popular with people who live in one room and are now available in patterned fabric as well as the more traditional plain canvas covering. Avoid the foldaway bed, as inevitably you will have to move a piece of furniture every time you want to go to bed and, when stored in an upright position, it makes an imposing wall which is difficult to disguise.

For seating, in addition to the sofa bed, think in terms of foldaway upright chairs which can be stacked or stored. The usual impulse to cover one area of the room in cushions or low seating has the effect of making everything happen at a low level so that even a normal height ceiling can seem farther away than it really is. Upright seating takes up less of your valuable floor space and is also easier to sit on when you want to eat.

When choosing a table (especially if you have limited space), go for a round one which has no corners to bump into and can seat more people than a small rectangular one. But whatever the table you eventually decide on, it should be positioned fairly near if not next to the kitchen area; you don't want to trail hot dishes of food from one end of the room to the other.

Storage
An obvious necessity in any home, storage is more difficult to get right in a small space where it can be obtrusive. Easy-to-assemble, free-standing shelving units are often the best solution as they not only hold more than any cupboard and take up less room, but they can also act as an effective room divider.

Adaptability
When you move into a room which has been tailor-made to suit a previous occupant, take a positive attitude and use what is already there to your advantage. The same applies to your existing furniture, which you may feel has dated. Rather than throwing out good pieces, let them inspire you to use them in a different role. Use matchstick, roller or Venetian blinds to divide a space instead of hanging them against a window; make cushions out of old bedspreads; dye existing covers and buy smart aluminium or coloured frames for posters.

Wit, ingenuity and a few basic tools can give your room a new look in much the same way as a fresh coat of paint. It's a mistake to think that all changes have to be major ones. Details in a small place can enhance a room and make uniform white walls, ceilings and window frames stand out rather than being a bland background. With decorative paint techniques currently in vogue you could treat your otherwise plain walls to a dado, panelling or a frieze without having to know anything about the origins of such grand-sounding additions. Adding cornices – these are available from any builders' merchant – and moulding has the illusion of lowering the ceiling and adding a pretty, decorative touch. This is especially effective if you have a platform loft from which the moulding is easily visible at close quarters. Mirrors are the standard way of making a small room seem bigger. They are expensive however and can, if used on a large scale across one wall, give the effect of making the room look busier than it actually is. Mirror tiles are a good way of creating a glass effect without being as costly.

Whether you adopt the rather English notion of letting a room grow up around you or the more American one of everything being tailored to suit your purpose, plan the practicalities of your room well in advance. Making plans, budgets and lists of requirements and priorities will help you to find your own style within the framework of a single-room existence.

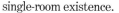

1 A Paris studio, tamed and civilized for one-room living with a new hardwood floor. A trestle table doubles for work and eating, while the bed makes no bones about being just that. The vast window and sloping glass roof become the dom-inating element, and would swamp any pic-tures on the walls. Cane, basketwork and bamboo furniture create a summery effect. Alcoves in the wall provide storage space that doesn't protrude.

2 A large turn of the century Edwardian studio converted into a single space home/office by architects Julia and Peter Wilson. A mezzanine complete with a pediment hides the sleeping area with an architectural flourish, and the room's original cornice is left intact. A low level screen provides a support for the work surface and shelters the dining table from the front door.

THE HIGH LIFE

Loft living is a much glamorized variation on the conventional one-room existence; so much so that it is now an expensive trend in most major cities of the world. These up-market lofts are usually converted from the individual storeys of old disused warehouses. A large open room with the appearance of unlimited space combined with a light airy feel and, where the warehouse is on a river bank, stunning views, offer an attraction that many people cannot resist. It was a way of life that started in Paris in the 1930s, and fired the imagination of artists and gallery owners in New York in the '60s and architects and property developers in London in the '70s.

The kind of people who choose to take on a warehouse or loft are usually tired of living in a conventional, standard shaped house, apartment or room and want the change of lifestyle and challenge a loft involves. Whether you want to move into a loft which has been converted already, or have the impetus to convert a loft yourself, the initial problem, as with living in a single room, is space. Here however the problem is not how to enlarge but scale down the space to suit your needs and lifestyle. Originally used as light industrial spaces, sweatshops or storage areas, lofts can have the appearance of a factory floor if you are not sure how to adapt the space. The following suggestions should prevent this from happening and make your loft even more dynamic than it already is.

Converting your warehouse

If you are scouting around looking for a warehouse to convert yourself, take heart when you do eventually find one; the space itself will probably look as though a team of factory workers has just moved out leaving all their equipment and mess behind. The first positive move is to get a skip for all the rubbish. Check whether the lift works or if you need to lower rubbish down the side of the building.

Grimy windows can be easily cleaned with hydrochloric acid, but take very special care not to get it on your skin or your clothes.

If you have wooden floors and want to keep them natural, you can hire an

industrial sander to remove the top surface of grime. You could be in for a pleasant surprise and find that the floor is maple. If you do not want the effort of polishing vast expanses of wood floor, then cover it with linoleum, which is the cheapest solution when it comes to a large floor area.

Brush down any beams, flaking paintwork or rusty radiators with a wire brush. Having cleaned all these surfaces you may want to leave them in their natural state, so make sure you seal them properly.

Heating

A large space requires more than just a few fan heaters to maintain a pleasant temperature. An industrial heating unit can be installed and, if you do not want a breeze wafting through the loft, it can be ducted through a series of pipes along the floor, or on the ceiling. Any form of heating which demands chimneys should be checked with a surveyor first as often, in old buildings, the risk of fire is a major concern. In a large space a sensible and very effective energy saver is to insulate the roof with foil-backed insulating fibre which will prevent a great deal of heat loss and look good.

Putting in the services

When it comes to electrical equipment and plumbing, it is best to consult an architect who will tell you where you can feasibly build a kitchen or bathroom, or install your lighting. Once the plumbing has been installed, building a kitchen and bathroom is not as difficult as it sounds. Any wall you build can contain services such as pipes and the electrics and, if you do not have lighting directly above the work-space in your kitchen, the wall can provide a surface on which to attach a track of spotlights.

High lights

Lighting a large space, especially if it is not on the top floor and there is limited natural light, can be a strain on any budget. Rather than have all the lighting on one switch, economize by having different areas of lighting which can be turned on when you want them. Spotlighting is best for kitchens and bathrooms. If, as is usually the case in warehouse lofts, the ceiling is fairly high, drop lighting will involve infinite lengths of flex. A better idea might be uplighters or lamps. The lighting will play as big a part in dividing a space into different areas as any wall or

screen. Once you have worked out your basic floor plan, lighting will highlight individual parts of the space without having to construct different rooms.

Creating separate areas

Even though you may like the style of the loft as one big open space, you might want to build some kind of room to sleep and dress in. The easiest way of building walls is to make a wood frame and secure this to the floor, then fix plaster board to both sides of the frame, plaster and paint it.

If the idea of dividing the space with walls reminds you of living in a conventional house, you can still have your own private space by running huge screens across; or a rail from which you can hang a dramatic expanse of cloth. Depending on your budget and personal taste, garage doors are an interesting variation on standard screens. Invest in metal roller doors – they make a striking contrast to natural wood. Or you could use less solid, free-standing screens if you prefer to maintain the sense of space. Rather than employing straight screens, think about the effect that curves have on the rigidity of a large square space.

3

1 A working artist's studio apartment created out of an old Paris factory. Banks of houseplants used to make informal partitions and a new floor help to tame the ruggedness of the interior.

2 Swinging high in a New York loft. Sliding sash windows, albeit vast, lend a domestic look, while fine carpets and furniture make a surreal contrast to the original workaday environment.

3 Michael Baumgarten's loft helped bring the taste for warehouse life to London.

4 An old Victorian school becomes a spectacular one-room interior. Any subdivision would ruin the character of the heavily beamed ceiling.

Alternatively, if you want to add a touch of fantasy to your room think about building a Japanese style pagoda or pavilion, and construct it in the centre of the space rather than against a wall, or have it at an angle jutting out into the space, so that it will then act as a screen between two different areas.

If you are lucky enough to have a high ceiling and beams, use the beams as support for a platform. Use chipboard for the floors and plaster-board for any walls. A good way of building a wall which continues right up to the ceiling is to construct a trellis or chicken wire screen from floor to ceiling, and cultivate climbing plants, which grow quickly in a light space.

Furniture

It is the furniture you choose that will most impose your character upon the space. First make a floor plan of where you want to put everything. While you might favour a look where pieces stand in no particular relation to each other, this can be annoying if you have to carry dishes of food between a kitchen at one end of the loft to a dining table at the other, so working out what space is for which function and how they interact is as vital as the decoration.

You can afford to be bold with furniture and fittings, and use things that would have no place in a normal sized home. One large piece, such as an enormous sofa, or huge refectory table, will look very imposing and make you more aware of the loft's dramatic dimensions than a group of tiny pieces.

Details

In addition to the furniture you bring with you, if you don't want to spend any additional cash, rummage round dumps, skips and markets for unusual objects to add drama to the space. Use huge water tanks, and chimney stacks instead of conventional pots for plants. Install pillars if you don't already have them, and use them as a focal point for delineating space. If noise is not too much of a problem, if the loft below has an insulated roof for instance, invest in large trolleys, which can also be used as storage. In keeping with a non-conventional space take a hint from your local supermarket or shop and buy shop display and storage units to keep all your clothes, books and objects in.

Once the basic necessities of heat and light have been installed, loft living is said by its devotees to be the most exhilarating form of town dwelling.

4

STUDIOS

Call them claustrophobic or cramped, for many people studios have become a way of life, especially in cities where spacious apartments command a high price. Modern studios should not be confused with that most romantic of homes, the artist's garret. They are essentially an updated version of what one-room living used to be all about – the bedsit.

Whereas single units were formerly only for rent – and the bane of a student nurse's life – property companies have at last caught on to the fact that more people are actively choosing to live on their own (rather than sharing with friends), and there are now some very smart purpose-built blocks consisting purely of studios. Some can be moved straight into without having to lift so much as a paintbrush.

General layout

If you have bought a studio which needs restructuring and decorating from scratch you will need to think along the following lines. Usually the best plan is to have the service areas – kitchen, bathroom and storage – around the main entrance. There is something satisfying about walking through a short corridor or under an archway and on into what then appears to be a large room. You must then consider whether the area is light or large enough to put up physical room dividers. Where the room is not big enough, divide the space into separate visual areas, by using different lighting, floor surfaces or rugs, and colours. Ask yourself if you would prefer to eat, sleep, work or cook where there is most natural light and in which areas you could effectively combine dual, even multi-purpose, functions. To live successfully in a small room, you will need discipline, neatness and above all imagination. Pleasurable studio living is an attitude of mind above all.

Adding a level

One of the most impressive ways of delineating various areas is to create different levels. If you have the height, build a bed platform. Rather than employing a ladder to get you to the top, have a narrow but long flight of steps going up one side of the wall.

These can also form a series of cupboards or drawers and when there are too many people to have sitting down, they make an effective tier of benches – keep a few cushions or flat seat pads handy. The area under the platform can either be used for the 'service areas' – such as bathroom and dressing room, or if these are in a separate room, use the alcove for the kitchen, or dining area.

If the idea of plastering and carpentry is too ambitious but you like the idea of a platform, simply construct one from a Dexion kit. Like Meccano, it's kids' play to put together and can form a compact free-standing structure to house a bed, storage, or dining table.

Floor surfaces

The type of flooring you have can contribute to an illusion of grandeur. Avoid heavy patterns which clutter a room before you have even put in any furniture. Tile the kitchen area or paint the floor a rich colour. Keep the rest of the floor covering to neutral colours, taking it right to the walls if it is carpet. Alternatively, if you want a more modern, sophisticated look, which is also practical, run rubber studded flooring throughout. If you choose to lay heavy industrial canvas as a floorcovering, make sure it has a good underlay and that it has been treated with a water-resistant coating. Run it up the walls as far as the window sill to conceal what is often an awkward gap between the floor and window.

Windows

If windows are fairly close to the floor, a crafty idea is to raise the floor height to the window sill making the room appear larger and the view outside even more dominant. Windows in a room where light is precious are obviously important and should be highlighted. If it is structurally possible, think about lengthening your windows from floor to ceiling to give an impression of French doors. Where a room is very exposed, use sugar glass in the lower half of the window. Avoid if possible placing radiators under the windows – not only is precious heat lost through the glass, but you might lose valuable wall space where a low sofa or storage box would be better positioned.

Walls

Plain wall surfaces need not be dull. Paint effects such as rag rolling, dragging and stencilling have become ubiquitous, and give a sense of richness without distracting attention from paintings or decorations you may want to hang on the wall. In a small room, choose wallpapers with soft, subtle patterning. Large, formal designs unless used parsimoniously tend to overpower everything in the room. For a plainer look, instead of resorting to conventional wallpaper consider hanging lengths of fabric interfacing against thin panels of softboard, which can look extremely pretty.

Furniture

The kind of furniture you choose for your studio is also important. Foldaway beds, unlike collapsable tables and chairs, do nothing but emphasize the fact that you are in a tiny room. Furniture which incorporates various functions, free-standing or at least easily movable, is easier to live with. Futons make excellent beds and sofas; brightly coloured mattresses which fold in two and store under a low table are a good alternative. Double beds do not always have to be pushed up against a wall so that there is somewhere to lean; they can simply be a focal point. Cover the bed in a plain bedspread and lay two bolsters of the same material, across the middle to provide not one sofa but two.

Brightening up a rented apartment

When you are living in rented studio accommodation, some of these ways of imposing your own style will not be possible. But rather than put up with a dreary room, there are invariably small-scale improvements that can be made.

Light fittings are usually the most unimaginative item in a rented room; often just a nasty nylon shade and a miserly length of flex. Take down all such fittings and replace with your own (the original fitting can be stored and put back in place if you want to leave the room the way you found it). Those with a modicum of electrical knowledge could extend the flex, loop it over to the darkest corner and suspend the light from a hook in the ceiling. Uplighters are also a good solution for dark corners and can be plugged into normal plug sockets. Clip-on lights are fun, especially if you have a long flexible lead, in a bright colour, to run up a bare wall. When you cannot repaint the walls but want to jazz them up a little, paint the skirting or dado rail a shade darker or lighter than the wall colour.

Giving a room depth can easily be achieved. The favourite method, for one-room dwellers is by using mirrors. Hung in a particular place, mirrors will reflect a window or the whole room.

When you cannot take up a shabby carpet, cover it with lengths of coloured cambric and staple it into place. The staples are easy to remove and will not damage the carpet.

For instant zing, amass plants on window sills and shelves, and spotlight them at night.

1 A bright and cheerful studio which was decorated on a shoe-string budget. Coloured tissue paper, sealed into place with clear varnish, creates a unique flooring. Industrial palettes make cheap seating that converts easily into beds.

2 A tidy mind and a pale colour scheme keep order in this office studio. A flush panel door slung across two filing cabinets and rush matting keep the costs down.

3 Space is tight in this study/bedsit, but a calm colour scheme and matching lightly patterned bedspread and curtains give a more relaxed feeling than the dimensions would suggest.

SHARERS

Sharing your home, whether it is with best friends, relatives or total strangers, can either be the best or the worst living arrangement of your life. It is a potential minefield for human relationships, when major arguments can be caused by even the smallest issue – a long telephone conversation, or the washing up left unwashed.

Flexibility, consideration and understanding will go a long way to making a success of a shared household, but the climate you create in your own private space is equally important. No matter how well you get on with the other inhabitants, you will still want the privacy of being able to shut the door of your own room and relax in your own surroundings.

Whether you are preparing a bed-sitting room in your own house – for an elderly relative, grown up child, au pair or lodger – or whether you are yourself living in a house divided into bedsits, remember that a flexible approach to both the room and to the people you share with makes for a household which is friendly and open.

Planning a shared house
While a house shared by friends might appear uniformly nondescript in appearance to the outside world, the various bedrooms will differ enormously in taste and style. Whatever style you choose to stamp on your room it will have your signature written across it. Whether it's rented property or your own, first consider the overall plan of the house; where the rooms are situated; which ones can be used as bedrooms; and, if you have the space for a living room, where it should be situated. Make sure the kitchen and bathroom are easily accessible to everyone – you should not have to walk through someone else's bedroom to have a bath or midnight snack.

Try to avoid a living room which doubles as a bedroom, as you will inevitably get the situation where one member of the household wants to go to bed and another is holding a party in the same room. Where possible do not position a bedroom by the front door; bikes being brought into the hall or late night chats can be just as annoying as a party in a house where soundproofing may be minimal. When there is space for a communal living room, make sure it is close to the kitchen; often the kitchen itself is not big enough for a table and chairs, and the living room can double as a dining room. When this is not possible and the household is forced to live in the kitchen, plan the space carefully to accommodate everyone at once if necessary.

Renting a room
As a tenant of someone else's property you may well want to make minor, but significant, changes to your rented room. Consider, in this case, altering paintwork and floors. Keep to white or light colours if you have a dark room, but remember that if you are trying to conceal a heavily patterned wallpaper you will require quite a dark paint. Scatter lots of rugs and mats on the floor to hide ugly or worn carpeting. Build your own shelving system out of planks and bricks and then paint them in whatever colour scheme suits your room. Throw some bright cushions onto your bed during the day if you need extra seating in the room. When you are faced with furniture that is not to your taste – an old armchair perhaps that has seen better days – throw over some pretty lengths of fabric and tie them down at the feet and back, or tuck them in.

Storage space is often limited. Milk crates and orange boxes make good storage, lined up or stacked, for shoes,

1 A corner of privacy in a shared studio space. The bed is camouflaged by purpose-built shelves, and becomes a sofa during the day.

2 When your bedroom also has to be a sitting room, it is important not to cram too much in. A bed, cupboard, table and chair are all you really need.

3 Avoid wasting valuable space with a large, ungainly wardrobe that hogs so much room in many rented apartments. Discard it if you can, and hang clothes from the picture rail. It looks decorative and helps you keep things tidy too.

books or clothes. Cardboard tubes are also good for storing old bits and pieces. Lay them flat and build a pyramid, thread them together with string, tying a knot at either end to prevent them rolling apart. When there is no cupboard stand a clothes rail across a corner of the room. This also makes an effective screen to dress behind as well as keeping your clothes. Invest in one with castors for mobility. Alternatively if you are lumbered with a large and imposing cupboard you could remove the doors and substitute lengths of bright fabric hung with double-sided tape to conceal the clothes.

Replace existing curtains with your own, either by fitting them to the curtain rail or tying them to it with pretty little bows. Or, if you prefer, tie a matchstick blind to the curtain rail. A blanket trimmed to size can make an excellent curtain – choose one which does not look too makeshift.

Catering for an au pair or relatives

If you are providing a room for someone in your house such as a granny, au-pair or teenager, it's a good idea to install some basic washing and, if practicable, some kitchen facilities, to give them the feeling of independence while maintaining the status quo in the rest of the house.

Where an elderly relative is concerned make sure the overall design, decoration and layout is not so intimidatingly modern that it cannot accommodate the prized possessions or antiques that can make the difference between feeling at home and existing in the spare room. All foldaway space saving furniture should be avoided; the last thing a grandparent wants to do is shift things across the room, pull down beds or lift-up table flaps.

Don't use furniture with sharp corners which can be bumped into; a round table is often better. Position the bed so that it is projecting into the room rather than against the wall – it will be easier to make. Where a youngster is concerned, say a lodger or your own teenage child who is making a bid for independence, the more flexible you make the living arrangement, the better. Take a screen on castors, right across the room so that the space can become more interesting. Build shelves, cupboards or use systems that include alcoves and desk space to punctuate what might otherwise be a rather monotonous length of wall.

4 A bare but effective room, decorated in primary colours, where everything, except the bed, can be packed flat into a suitcase for a quick getaway.

5 A kitchen in a bedsit doesn't have to be a squalid affair. This compact, well-lit kitchen has been fitted into an unobtrusive corner, making the best possible use of a minimal space.

6 If you don't have the luxury of a dining room, at least give yourself a corner in which to eat.

SPACE SAVING IDEAS

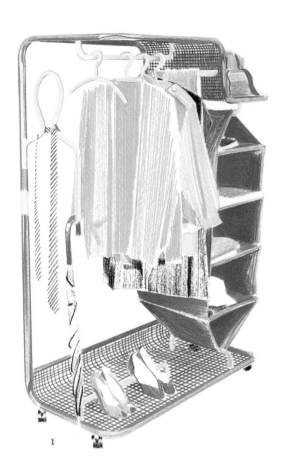

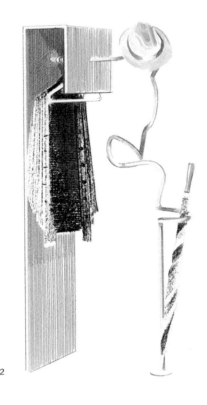

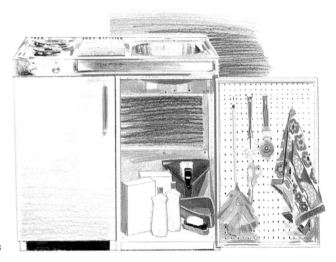

1 Lightweight storage units on wheels claim less space and are much more flexible than heavy traditional wardrobes.

2 A hat stand supports a hanging rail – a jokey and economical way of fitting in storage space.

3 The barest minimum – a kitchen comprising a hob, sink, fridge and cupboard, all crammed into a single unit. Several manufacturers now provide these mini-kitchens.

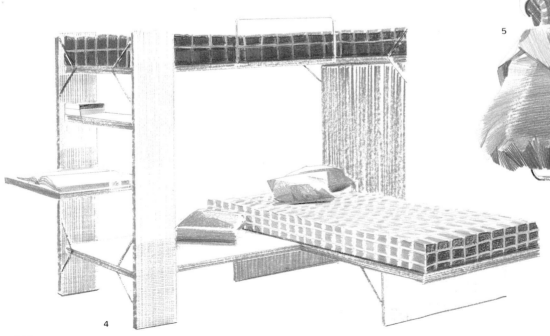

4 When you're short on space, large pieces of furniture must earn their keep. Make your bed double as a desk top and storage unit, as well as providing an extra bunk.

5 The sofa that becomes a bed is an old stand-by for one-room devotees. Modern methods make them much easier to convert.

KITCHENS AND BATHROOMS

With the possible exception of warehouse lofts, one-room living means that space is at a premium, and that means that kitchen and bathroom facilities must be fitted into a very small area. The intricate planning of these two areas is essential, because when it comes to fitting everything into a tiny space, plumbing and electrical mistakes can be easily made. The following suggestions should help you avoid any common pitfalls as well as to make your tiny kitchen or bathroom a pleasant place to cook or wash in.

Planning the kitchen

People who live in a single room rarely have the luxury of a separate kitchen and often find they are restricted to cooking and washing up in a tight corner. However the illusion of a separate area can easily be created, and working in a confined space need not be as impossible as it sounds. In fact it has the advantage of turning any cook into a disciplined worker and of ensuring that all your equipment and ingredients are close at hand.

In a tiny kitchen every inch of space has to work. It makes no difference whether you are planning to cook the odd omelet or prepare extravagant dinners, the basic requirements of fridge, sink and cooker still have to be fitted in. Rather than try to squash standard size kitchen units into what little room you have, choose from the smaller ones on the market. Look for the single sink design which comes with a slide-over chopping board and drainage rack. Instead of installing a full scale cooker choose a smaller two-ring gas hob, with a lid which covers the burners when not in use, thus creating extra work space. Ovens can be wall-mounted which makes them easier to work from in a small space, and leaves room underneath for a unit of drawers. Fridges come in every size but if there is no room for one in the kitchen area, take a line from plush hotels and keep it outside the kitchen dressed up as a drinks cabinet.

Planning the order of fittings is the main concern in a small kitchen. A good plan should make a tiny kitchen run like a ship's galley where everything is to hand and not under your feet. Whether

An old London basement, converted into a one-room studio. The marble top for the work surface is a practical luxury that makes the kitchen seem less of an intrusion in the dining area.

the kitchen is a straight line against the wall, or in a nook under the stairs, ideally the running order should be: drainer, sink, workspace, cooker. Site the hob as far away as possible from the most used part of the kitchen so as to avoid knocking over saucepans. Electrical equipment – coffee grinders, kettles or mixers – are best kept to a minimum and given storage space away from the valuable worktop. Small narrow shelves are good for this, above the worktop but below existing storage; these shelves are also useful for items that need to be at hand – herbs and spices, salt and pepper, and so on. Avoid door handles which catch onto pocket or sleeves every time you walk through.

A well thought out plan will mean

you can prepare food and keep an eye on what is cooking at the same time.

Storage

Storage, and how you organize it in a small space will determine the way your kitchen works. Cooking pots and towels littering the worktop are dangerous as well as unsightly. Even if the kitchen itself is nothing greater than a cupboard, you can store more on shelves, hooks and racks than into swing-door cupboards and pull-out drawers. There are some good ranges of metal shelving either free-standing or which can be bracketed to the wall. If you have a high ceiling but don't want to lose valuable space or light, hang a grid rather like a lower ceiling complete with meat-hooks for hanging pots, pans

and baskets. Make sure that it's low enough to reach but not so low that you bump your head on the hanging objects. Plastic Dexion toolboxes (which are easy to clean), or individual baskets lining open shelves can make pretty alternative storage for crockery, cutlery, vegetables and other culinary necessities. Mobile trolleys under a worktop or table can be used for paperwork, and books as well as storing tins. If you want to conceal open storage, run a rail of PVC or shower curtain material, roller blinds or even washable chintz across the whole area.

If cupboards are a necessity, remember that sliding or roller doors make good alternatives to swing-open doors, and take up no space when open.

245

KITCHENS AND BATHROOMS

Cupboard doors made of perforated hardboard are useful for hanging mugs and the odd string of onions outside or in. A shelving unit on castors which slides under the worktop is handy as an additional work or table top. Windows, whilst an aesthetic bonus, take up valuable space. Line them with shelves – glass or white ones are best so as not to reduce the light drastically.

Ventilation and lighting

Good ventilation is essential if you are cooking and living in one room; the smell of cooked food, however delicious to eat, is not particularly pleasant when you are lying in bed. There are some attractive fold-down extractor units, including Vent-Axia's small, unobtrusive and inexpensive ones which now come in a wide range of colours.

Equally important in this small area, is the method of lighting you choose. A track of spotlights on the ceiling can be positioned to light up different work areas. In cases where these are impossible to install, make a feature of a single fitting. Fix, hang or clip a light with a coloured flex onto cupboards and shelves making sure the flex or

power points are not in the way. Or, if you want to conceal your lights, there are non-fluorescent strip lights for bathrooms which can be hidden underneath shelves and cupboards, or, on a larger scale, light fittings which can be raised and lowered from the ceiling over your table or counter. Whatever form of lighting you choose, remember that it will reflect off the walls, ceiling and floors, so lurid colours should be avoided. Stick to light airy, plain colours, which are by far the most pleasant for kitchens, particularly where light is at a premium.

Floors

Avoid, at all costs, flooring which demands elaborate cleaning. On the kitchen floor area, you could use washable plastic sheeting (which can be stapled into place), or you might choose to strip the existing floorboards, which must then be sealed and varnished. Alternatively cover the floor with lino, rubber sheeting, plastic, cork or ceramic tiles. The last two are the most expensive but are very suitable finishes for a small space. Failing all these, a temporary solution would be to cover

the floor with several non-slip rubber mats. There is a wide range of colours from which to choose.

Dining in a small area

You must also consider where you are going to eat. Rather than carrying endless trays of food across the room or feeling that you have to resort to meals on trolleys, fold-down tables are clever space-saving devices, particularly if combined with a rack of folding chairs. Pull-out tables from shelving units are also useful.

Hiding the kitchen

Having the kitchen running exactly as you want while working in it, should not affect the way it looks for the rest of the time or how it appears to waiting guests. Hiding it completely is one solution, either with sliding doors or a solid line of cupboard doors. A simple Venetian blind makes a temporary screen. A sheet of glass positioned across the kitchen also creates a barrier from cooking smells and noise, but allows the cook to keep an eye on the rest of the room. A kitchen worktop with a bar counter in white or

coloured Melamine or in stainless steel is another good way of having a room with a view without having to see the aftermath of a meal.

The unfitted kitchen

When space is so tight that your kitchen is simply a converted cupboard, you might think of investing in one of the ranges of mini kitchens available. These are now a good deal further advanced than the bedsit Baby Belling and consist of a base unit with two electric rings, a tiny sink, drainage board on top and a small fridge below. Ones on the market can be as small as 600mm deep x 1m long x 1m high (2ft x 3ft x 3ft), and designers are continually producing smaller ones. All they need in the way of services are a couple of power sockets, water supply and waste pipe. For additional storage the doors can be used to hang mugs and cooking utensils, and the whole kitchen can be as compact as a glamorous caravan camper. These mini kitchens are so versatile that, if you like the idea of a free-standing kitchen, they can be positioned as a central unit in the middle of the room.

1 Kitchen appliances, work and eating surfaces and storage units are cleverly incorporated in a single architectural element. Once through the hatch, everything is immediately to hand.

2 White tiles give this slit of a kitchen an ordered and airy look. A recessed downlighter provides a flattering light over the sink.

3 When space is at a premium every last inch needs to be pressed into use; here the space above the bath has been commandeered for the airing cupboard.

4 An attic corner, otherwise unusable, is just wide enough to accommodate a bath.

3

4

Planning the bathroom

With one-room living, just as you can expect a tiny kitchen, you may also be faced with an equally miniature bathroom. Whether you regularly pamper yourself, or rush in and out without looking in the mirror, the bathroom is the one room where a little extravagance does not go amiss – even if it is simply in the form of a thick floor carpet, or a heated towel rail. But whether you demand luxury or not, the bathroom may still require attention.

First decide what you are using your bathroom for. It is unlikely to be big enough to dress in, or for two people to use at the same time. Depending on how much money you have to spend and whether you want a luxurious atmosphere with a deep bath or simply a functional room with a shower installed, even the smallest, drabbest bathroom can be transformed.

A quick face-lift

If you want an immediate and cheap solution to a gloomy bathroom; put up large mirrors on the walls and fit a higher watt light bulb. Cover the walls with a coat of washable paint, and box in any exposed pipes. Old cracked tiles can be camouflaged by painting with yacht paint and covering in gloss. If the bathroom is papered, strip off the peeling sections and repaper or face the walls with clear or coloured Perspex which will give you easy to clean and maintain surfaces. Old and chipped baths and basins can be retouched with enamel restorer, or if you love old architectural pieces, you can replace all the fixtures and fittings with antique ones. Take care when it comes to plumbing them in however, as old bathroom fittings were not made to the same scale as modern ones.

Starting from the beginning

If your bathroom needs more than just a touch-up, and you are starting from scratch, the ideal space-saver is a shower. There are some exciting new circular and oval shaped shower designs available in brightly coloured or transparent perspex, where the exposed pipes are curled up below the taps. If you do have room for a bath, remember to add a shower attachment – it is a good energy saver. Doors which open inwards can be rehung or replaced with sliding or folding doors. If there is no lavatory in the bathroom (and privacy is not an objective) you could even do away with doors altogether and hang washable fabric across the entrance instead.

Creating the illusion of space

If your aim is not only to save space, but to make your bathroom seem larger than it is, white tiles with brightly coloured accessories will make a space seem bigger without creating a clinically cold atmosphere. Recess all your fittings such as lavatory roll holders and soap trays so you do not keep bumping into them. A neat solution to the tiny bathroom is to abandon the idea of a shower tray and instead to use the entire room as a giant shower, where the water drains down a hole in the middle of the floor. If the floor area of your bathroom is only as big as the average shower tray, sink the tray into the floor and cover with a metal grill or wooden slatted frame.

The makeshift bathroom

If you are totally without bathroom facilities and the only place to wash is a bowl in the kitchen sink, install a shower attachment to wash your hair, or at least have a single jet tap high enough to get your head under.

Antique wash stands are a good substitute for those who share a bathroom and just want the privacy of a quick splash in the morning or a place to clean their teeth. There are also some exciting Italian stands which come in brightly coloured plastic or metal with mirror and toothbrush holders included. It is now quite possible to install free-standing baths in any room, which have almost sculptural qualities when they are positioned in a corner. Or if you need something purely functional a bedroom shower unit might be very useful.

People who live in one room say that having a dressing room is almost as important as having a bed. If you feel this way, either tack a piece of gauze or muslin to the ceiling and drape the material back when you don't want the partition.

Storage

Better than vanitory units, which contain storage but look unattractive, are the trolleys or canvas laundry bags on castors. These are ideal for hiding away towels, soaps, even bedlinen and clothes. Some are fairly tall and would act as a screen for a free-standing bath unit. Not only are these collapsible for storage but the bags are detachable and can be used for taking the weekly wash to the laundrette.

Whatever style you prefer in your tiny bathroom, remember that if you want to make it appear larger choose bright, airy colours; if you like the thought of capitalizing on its cosiness, pick rich, warm colours and low, gentle lighting.

CONVERSIONS AND EXTENSIONS

Adding an extension, whether that means converting a loft space, or building on at the back, may be the perfect solution when your home becomes too small. Of course, you could 'trade up' and move somewhere else; but many people find that these days moving creates far greater problems than extending and staying put.

Why stay put?

People who opt to make more space out of what they already have generally do so for both personal and financial reasons. You may feel that you have arrived at a place which suits you and those with you. You may like the area, have lots of friends nearby. There may be convenient shops, transport, parks. Perhaps the local school is good and it would upset your children to have to start afresh at a new one. Maybe you've spent years getting the garden into order and you can't face the idea of starting from scratch with another jungle or worse, the detritus of other people's half-baked ideas. Some people have a psychological need to move on as soon as they've made a place habitable; but others view the process with dread and would much rather stay put.

Then comes the crunch. The children are growing up and demanding their own rooms. You've started to work from home and the dining-room table just won't do. The kitchen is tiny, the bathroom's worse. You would appreciate it if the children *didn't* bring their friends in to play under your feet in the sitting room. And then in the back of your mind there's that long-term plan of having your parents or grandparents living with you – but they must have separate quarters for both your sakes.

Of course, not everyone is necessarily pushed for space when they decide to expand; you might want to add, say, an independent flat which could be rented out or kept for visiting friends and relatives. After all, the extra space is certainly going to enhance the value of the property if and when you eventually do sell it.

Move out and pay up

This brings us to the hard financial factors involved in a move. It costs

money – a great deal of money. The amount varies according to how lucky you are and how much of the legal side of things you are prepared to take on yourself, but most people will find themselves paying fees to estate agents (or for advertising if you sell privately), to solicitors, or other people who can do the conveyancing, to a building society or a bank for valuing the new house, to a surveyor for thoroughly inspecting it for faults, and to banks or other financial sources in interest on bridging loans and overdrafts as those vast sums of money swirl about. Then – assuming the deal doesn't fall through, in which case you will incur many of these charges again when you try next time – there's the cost of physically moving yourselves and your possessions. Add it all up and it comes to several thousand pounds – and that can significantly reduce the profit you've made on the value of your current property.

In periods of low inflation and a stagnant property market, moving costs can be a big worry. In boom times they're proportionately less important but there's a greater risk that you'll be gazumped and so have to pay many of the costs twice or several times. Obviously, all this doesn't deter most people; and expanding your existing home is not necessarily a bed of roses.

Employing an expert

New spaces – at the back or side, on top, in attics, spanning alleys, sitting on top of existing, lower parts of the house – need to be designed. One of the greatest delights of giving yourself room to move in this way is that it allows you to flex your muscles as a designer. But before you go too far in this direction, it's advisable to take on an expert, preferably an architect with experience in this type of work. The worst extensions and roof conversions frequently result from someone going to a jobbing builder and saying, "I want something like this", in the mistaken belief that such a direct approach will save money *and* achieve the desired result. All too often it does neither.

You will have to pay an architect's fees. But for your money the architect

will turn your ideas into something that will work, something that will pass planning permission and building regulations, and that will look good into the bargain. He will also obtain the most realistic tender for the job from a number of builders and will supervise the work as it proceeds to make sure that things are done properly and in the right order. (See the chapter on Dealing with the Experts for further advice.)

Untangling the red tape

An architect will also guide you through the regions where you may be completely ignorant – the laws surrounding house conversions and extensions. You know that approval is needed for your plans. What you may be unaware of is just how many different types of approval are required. (See the chapter on The Paperwork for more details.) But for now, bear in mind that the local council will want to scrutinize your plans if the extension is above a certain size and type. Building work will have to conform to the national building regulations. And you will have to tread particularly carefully if your house is listed as being of architectural or historic importance, or is in a special zone such as a conservation area.

The following pages set out your options for expansion. How much space do you have available at ground level? Have you considered the potential of your attic? Is there a use for that flat roof you overlook from the landing window? You may find that your house can be expanded in all these areas. Each will yield exciting spaces, and each will be of a different character. Consider what you want to use the new room for. The planned use may suggest the location. But don't be disheartened if at first it seems that you are already stretching your house and its land to the limit – the chances are, you're not.

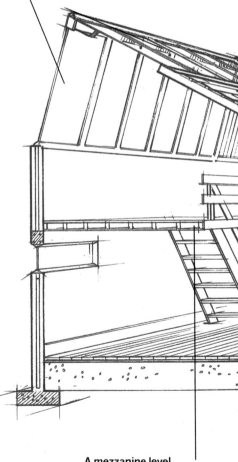

Rooflights are a good compromise if you don't have the money or the headroom to go up a full two floors.

A mezzanine level platform gives you extra space without encroaching too far on your existing space.

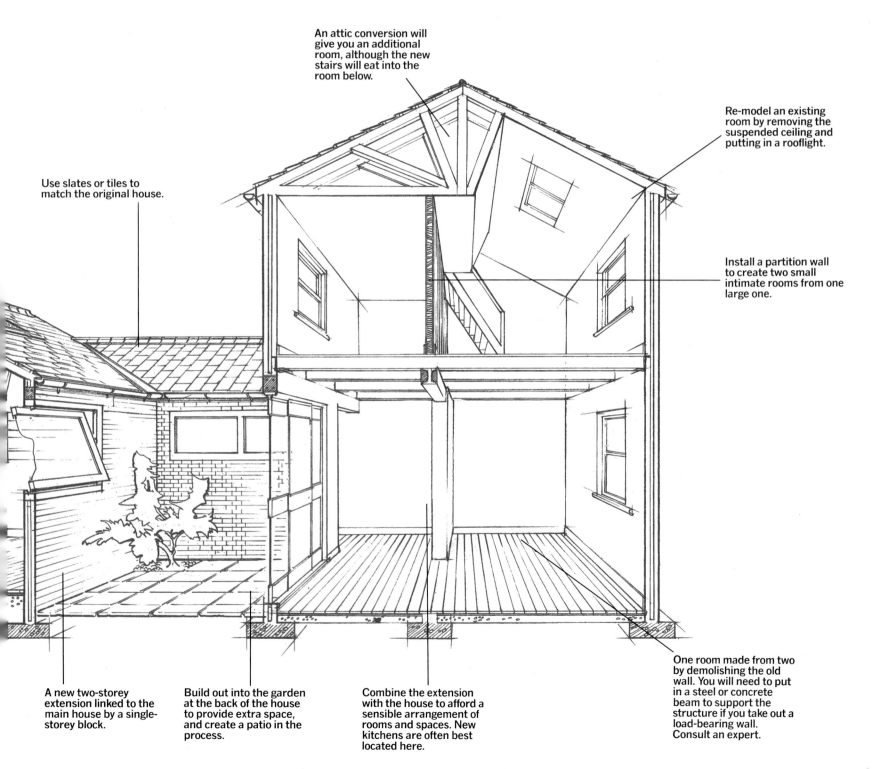

An attic conversion will give you an additional room, although the new stairs will eat into the room below.

Re-model an existing room by removing the suspended ceiling and putting in a rooflight.

Use slates or tiles to match the original house.

Install a partition wall to create two small intimate rooms from one large one.

A new two-storey extension linked to the main house by a single-storey block.

Build out into the garden at the back of the house to provide extra space, and create a patio in the process.

Combine the extension with the house to afford a sensible arrangement of rooms and spaces. New kitchens are often best located here.

One room made from two by demolishing the old wall. You will need to put in a steel or concrete beam to support the structure if you take out a load-bearing wall. Consult an expert.

CONVERTING THE ATTIC

The most tempting way to make more space for yourself is to convert the attic. Most houses have them, but they are generally just so much wasted space apart from the cold water tank and the inevitable old boxes of junk. The last time you were up there – squeezing through that tiny hatch to find out what was causing the water overflow – you probably noticed how warm it was and vowed to get it insulated. You may have thought that the space was too small to make much of. You were almost certainly wrong.

Attics are attractive because the space is already there, enclosed by walls and a roof; a back extension involves building a new shell from scratch, maybe taking up rather more of the garden than you would like. The character of an attic room is very different from that of a ground level extension. Apart from its often distinctive and attractive shape, it tends to be quiet by virtue of its position, with no thunder of feet passing by. It can be a room to escape to. As a relatively cheap space-making exercise, opening up into the attic has a lot going for it.

1 An outwardly conventional house has been totally transformed inside by replacing all the old rooms with a single space that uses the whole height of the building, punctuated by several mezzanines. Only the fireplaces remain floating in free space as a reminder of old rooms.

2 A bedroom fitted into the rafters.

3 Gutting an attic can provide a new self-contained apartment.

4 Top floors can be opened up into the rafters by removing the ceiling to create a distinctive new room.

5 A gable wall which has been entirely glazed.

6 Skylights are the simplest way of bringing light into an attic room.

Is the attic suitable?

The steeper the roof pitch the better, is a basic rule of thumb. Generally anything with a pitch of more than 20° will convert well without the need for costly roof-raising exercises.

Before you start, steel yourself for the inevitable disruption. There will be a great deal of dirt and noise with building materials being carted up and down stairs. Even with the most basic type of attic conversion, there may be times when holes are knocked through the tiles and maybe through gables for windows, and your house is protected from the elements only by flapping plastic sheets.

Opening up from below

Where the attic does not offer enough space for a complete new room or even a mezzanine, you can still exploit it to raise the ceiling of one or more of the rooms on the top floor of the house. Imagine the ceiling removed so that you are looking straight up at the rafters. With windows placed correctly, you can catch the sun and bring light flooding in. The whole emphasis of the room is changed and you can use the vertical possibilities to the full in a new decorating and lighting scheme. Such an opening-up could be confined to a key room at one end of the top floor, or carried through right the way along.

Mezzanines and platforms

These are, literally, the next step up. You have a greater volume of space to play around with, but still not enough to make a full-blooded extra room or rooms. The constraints are these: that the height of any space classed as a living room or bedroom must be a minimum of 2.25m (7ft 6in.) over at least half of the existing unobstructed space; and that such habitable rooms will generally need a proper, permanent staircase, not too narrow and not too steep, leading up to them.

You can fiddle the height problem in a number of ways – see the following pages for details – but you may well find that there is only a comfortable height available in certain small areas of the roof space. This is where mezzanines and platforms come in. At its simplest, a platform might take little more than a bed. At its grandest, a mezzanine might, as its name suggests, form a half-floor overlooking the one below. It's the old concept of a minstrel's gallery, put to more everyday use.

Quite apart from height restrictions, you may prefer the idea of the mezzanine for a specific function – such as a more private study or reading area which is separate from a main living room without being isolated. Such areas can be created at the tops of other rooms or storage units, can straddle retained horizontal tie-beams or even be entirely free-standing on legs from the floor of the room below.

Using existing timbers

It can be very effective to leave as much of the existing timber of the old ceiling and non-load-bearing wall partitions as possible when installing platforms or mezzanines. Many timber-and-lathe walls will respond well to being exposed in this way, helping to create a pleasing tracery that serves the function of defining spaces. If the house does not yield such materials, the effect can be created – screens rather than walls according to the degree of privacy you want – visually and accoustically.

Where two rooms on the top floor of a house are opened out into one *and* the roof space is opened up, the 'skeleton' partition between the old rooms can remain and a sleeping gallery be installed above one of the old rooms. Thus you get a double-height space in one part and a gallery overlooking it – without losing the 'memory' of the original layout.

New rooms within the roof

Although the mezzanine arrangement may be the most spectacular thing you can do with your roof space, there's no doubt that the attraction of complete new rooms under the roof is a powerful one. For more ambitious schemes which involve breaking through the roof with dormer windows, forming terraces, and even building on an extra storey, see Raising the Roof. Here we are concerned with the construction of rooms entirely within the existing roof, using windows that scarcely interrupt the profile of the roof from inside or out.

Even inside a steep-pitched roof, not all the space will be inhabitable. You will have to allow a margin around the edges – this is particularly true of hipped roofs, which have sloping rather than vertical ends and generally sit on top of the house like a hat. Vertical brick gable ends obviously afford more headroom from end to end of the attic. The Georgian-style mansard roof with its double slope affords the maximum usable space – but for this reason most houses from this era were built from the start with roof rooms – often the servants' quarters.

The space round the edges can however be put to good use for storage.

You will almost certainly want to move your existing water tank out of the way – under a low part of the roof, where it can be screened off.

Making the most of your headroom

You don't want to keep banging your head – nor will the building regulations allow it. In a roof space you must have an average headroom of at least 2.25m (7ft 6in.) over at least half of the clear floor space – although you are spared this constraint if the rooms are non-habitable spaces such as kitchens and bathrooms. You can fudge this a bit by such tricks as reducing the floor space with built-in cupboards around the edge. More drastically, you can lower the attic floor at an edge to give yourself the headroom.

Remember too that not only will you need a proper permanent staircase leading to the new rooms, but that there must be sufficient headroom at the top of the stairs.

Roof windows

In the roof itself, flush windows are readily available in a range of sizes which can be fitted to most pitches of roof. They come complete with the appropriate flashing – the weather sealing round the edges – for various types of roof.

Generally flush with the roof, these windows are an excellent source of light – which in summer also means heat. They open usually on a centre pivot and can be fitted with internal or external blinds.

Windows for the new attic rooms may be installed in the vertical gable ends of the house. As with other external works, new window openings will require planning approval.

Insulation

It is unlikely that you will be able to re-use any insulation already existing between the floor joists in the attic. Insulated boards between the rafters, with appropriate air gap and vapour barrier, are the usual solution (see the chapter on Heating and Energy). Your new attic rooms can be as energy efficient as the rest of the house – but don't block up vital ventilation openings in the process.

RAISING THE ROOF

Once the decision to use the roof space has been taken, you have to decide just how far you want to go. In the last section we dealt with the spaces you can create within the existing roof structure, with windows following the roof profile. This section deals with the physical growth of your house – upwards.

Breaking through the roof and adding new parts to the house structure is naturally a more complex exercise than simply opening up from below. Apart from the structural implications – minimal in the case of a dormer window, clearly very important when it comes to adding a complete extra storey – planning and building regulation officials like to take a closer look than they do for more minor works. Allow more time for getting the various approvals and make sure your architect or other qualified designer is getting the process rolling. It is often more difficult to obtain planning permission for alterations to the street frontage of a house than for back extensions (see page 262).

Sideways shifts
Space in the attic is frequently confined because you only have clear headroom right in the centre, underneath the ridge of the roof. Much depends on the profile of the roof – the angle of the pitch. Steep roofs may have ample headroom in the middle but have a constricted floor area. Shallow roofs, if used intact, can mean wasting a lot of space around the edges and can make it hard to see out of Velux type windows unless they are raised at the top edge.

The most common answer to these problems is to install dormers, which have the effect of lifting a flap in the roof and propping it open permanently to give you room to move. A dormer window is placed vertically in a sloping roof and so has a roof of its own – either flat, or with its own pitch.

Older houses, particularly in the countryside, have different angles of pitch to their roofs: steep at the front, shallow at the back is a common configuration which allows you to make discreet use of the rear roof to install dormers. In this way almost a complete storey can be added without going above the roofline at the front.

Window-only dormers
These are the most traditional type of dormer window – often occurring in a row along the front roof of a big old house with decorative 'pediments' or gable flourishes on top. They are essentially only as wide as the windows they contain, which is space enough for a person to stand in and look out of, but which does not provide much extra room by today's standards. Nevertheless, such a row of small dormers can result in a very dramatic space inside, as well as enhancing the outside if properly handled. They also allow you to bring more light in by glazing the sides and top of the dormer as well as the front.

Dormer rooms
Today, it is more common to merge the dormers into a strip and so maximize the floor space within the roof. Windows need not run the length of the strip — the visual impact of the new big dormer can be reduced by cladding parts in materials sympathetic to the existing roof.

To give the effect of a normal room, with no particular attic characteristics, dormers can be installed at the front and rear and a uniform-height ceiling placed across. This is a good idea where there is little height left to the roof ridge.

Slicing in
Another, more complex way to create vertical windows in a roof is the 'inverted dormer'. Instead of poking out, these are recessed. The advantages are that they are less obtrusive and provide the opportunity for hidden balconies and roof terraces. The disadvantages are that they provide less internal space and create the problem of draining an external flat floor. If your attic space is large, or if you have gone so far as to add an extra storey, they can be an excellent idea. Be warned, they will cost considerably more (see page 256).

Adding a storey
Some dormer exercises have the effect of literally raising the roof. In bad examples, an attractive pitched roof is practically replaced by a flat one as a result of over-large dormers being installed. It doesn't have to look that ugly. Maybe it's best to acknowledge that what you need is, quite literally, an extra storey. The approach you will then adopt is quite different from simply squeezing space out of an attic.

Here more than anywhere, you must have an architect's help.

Adaptable terraces
If your house is in a terrace, and the terrace has cross walls which stand proud of the roof, probably also containing chimney flues, then an extra storey may well be relatively straight-forward structurally without being over-obtrusive. Georgian terraces of the smaller kind often lend themselves to this type of upward extension, particularly if they have a parapet at the front as well as the cross walls. The extra floor can follow the 'mansard' profile of many such Georgian roofs, behind the parapet and between the cross walls. In many instances, the cross walls will have to be raised, but not to any great extent. If your house is in a conservation area or listed, be sure to contact the planners right at the start to find out whether your alterations are acceptable or not.

Less adaptable terraces
In smooth-roofed terraces, where cross walls end beneath the roof tiles, an extra storey could well just look silly – and you will have to carry out a lot of new building work. In such cases, the compromise of a large 'dormer room' in the roof to the rear may be the only alternative.

It can help if several house owners work together. Extra storeys in a common sympathetic style look good and save on unit building costs.

Semi-detached houses
Again, carrying out such drastic work in your half of a semi-detached house may not be allowed, and in many instances quite rightly. Semis tend to have 'hipped' roofs, sloping towards the ends as well as to front and rear. Where this is the case, a dormer at the back or side – or both – is often the acceptable compromise. There are few semis

1 The ceiling in this top floor room has been removed and skylights inserted in the roof. Daylight from two directions will always give a room character.

2 A room created in the space over a garage built beside the house.

3 Architect Rick Mather cut through each floor of his house from ground to roof to create an intricate set of inter-locking spaces.

4 All-glass walls give this rooftop outcrop of a room the feeling of a greenhouse.

5 An attic wide enough to become a properly proportioned room.

6 A full height dormer window with sliding glass doors provides access to the newly created roof terrace.

which justify the removal of the roof for the addition of an extra storey. Apart from visual objections, the roof space is generally sufficient for you to try a lower-key approach.

As with terraces, it helps enormously to have like-minded neighbours. A big dormer at the front of your roof will upset the house's symmetry – but where it is matched by an equivalent on your neighbour's side, the problem is resolved.

Detached houses

Because your house stands alone, don't think that there's no need to consider the neighbouring houses. If they are the same type of building – or even if not – you can run into trouble with planning permission. The same constraints will apply to the side which faces the public domain.

Quite a few detached houses have lower wings, in an L-shaped or T-shaped plan, which can be raised to insert an extra storey. Where possible, raise the roof ridge of the lower section

so that it corresponds to the taller parts, and insert the floor beneath. This course of action, taken in conjunction with dormer windows in the roof, can give you a lot of extra space without ruining the appearance of your house.

Home within a home

In all cases of attic conversion and extension, access to the new spaces must be of a high standard. For living rooms and bedrooms, building regulations set out the minimum requirements; but if the rooms are to be extensively used, you may need more than the minimum. New rooms on top can act as separate apartments for your family or as separately rented accommodation. In this case, remember that you may not want too many people tramping up and down your stairs.

External stairs – or in some cases a separate internal staircase – may be what you need to make a self-contained apartment truly self-contained.

A BRIGHTER OUTLOOK

Two rewarding aspects of a successful attic conversion are the new views which are opened up and the light which comes flooding in. Windows should not be an afterthought, but an integral part of your design: remember that they have a major effect on the way your house is seen from the outside, as well as the way you see out.

Skylights and lanterns

Skylights have always been useful: set high in the roof lighting a stairwell, or providing light with privacy for a bathroom or lavatory. Nowadays skylights have advanced considerably but still perform the same function – the difference is that skylight-type windows can now be used at quite a low level, to see out of as well as to catch the sun.

Partly as a result of the popularity of attic conversions, opening lights such as these – Velux is probably the major manufacturer – now come in all shapes and sizes. They may be pivoting, top- or side-hung, sometimes with integral blinds, possibly remote-controlled when they are in awkward locations. For the basic attic conversion, they can be all you need. For more ambitious jobs, they can still play a part.

Lanterns – glazed framed structures to let in light from above – can be beautiful and dramatic. They also have to be purpose-made.

Gable windows

The gable end of a house, often neglected, is ideal for special windows. Depending on the proportions of the wall at your disposal, you can use the gable end for circular, semi-circular, arched or triangular windows, or combinations of these shapes with the usual rectangle. You can even build a small balcony outside.

2

1

3

Dormers

When glazing the dormer windows, remember to keep them in character with the other visible windows in the house. Although small 'window-only' dormers can be treated as specials, larger dormers need to be visually integrated. Think of the tops and sides as well as the front: it's possible to create a mini-conservatory effect.

Picture windows

Reaching to the floor and acting as a door as well as a window, sliding picture windows – or more traditional French windows – can be used in a roof space as access to a terrace or balcony.

Terraces and balconies

As suggested above, one way to maximize a special gable window – even, in the right circumstances, a completely glazed gable – is to construct a balcony outside it. In the roof itself, a more private open area is made possible on the 'inverted dormer' principle where a wedge is taken out of the room and the window/door is installed from the top edge down to the attic floor, so leaving a portion of the floor outside.

The paving and weather-proofing of such a terrace so that it does not leak into the rooms below demands strict attention to detail – it's certainly not a job for an amateur. The terrace floor can be raised above that of the attic and a railing put round its edge. Or you can leave it fully recessed so that the roof itself becomes the parapet.

Greenhouse in the sky

As with dormer windows, a roof terrace can be used as an elevated mini-greenhouse. Fully glazed, it can have sliding glass panels in the roof to open up in summer. It looks very pretty, but again – watch out for the weather-proofing. An expanse of glass at roof level needs protection against the wind.

1 A skylight cut into the roof space brings light slanting down into this impressive corridor.

2 The pitched roof of this old industrial building has been glazed and the roof timbers cut back to let in maximum light.

3 New circular windows inserted into a stairwell.

4 The old loft in this barn has been opened out to create a single space – lit by a new semi-circular window over the door.

5 A new bathroom of traditional simplicity installed in the eves; a skylight has been fitted neatly in between the rafters.

6 A half-moon skylight which cleverly echoes the shape of the spiral staircase below.

BUILDING AT THE BACK

The potential of your house for expansion is not necessarily confined to roof or to ground level. If you are pushed for space outside your house as well as inside it, the answer may well be to extend at first floor level or above. Such an exercise might mean a modest bay or several extra rooms. Which you opt for depends not just on your purse, but on the potential of the house and its layout.

As with attic rooms, explore every possibility before you decide on one particular course of action. Space can be created in the most surprising places – who would have thought, for instance, that there would be any point in extending stair landings rather than a room?

Roofline

Don't forget to consider the roof if your first floor extension goes high enough to meet the roofline. The happiest solution is to continue the line of your pitched roof out across the top of the extension, so blending it with the character of the house.

Expanding landings

It's by no means for everyone, but where the staircase runs up the back of your house, you can make rooms out of the landings by building on a bay all the way up. Such quirky extra space can make an enormous difference to the feel of the house; plants can be grown there in profusion, and chairs grouped for people to sit. It's a trick of which Victorians were particularly fond.

The ground floor extension is the most popular way of making more space. Its advantages are manifold: building work takes place largely outside the house, so there is less disruption to the household routine than on a major attic conversion; scaffolding is kept to a minimum; the strength of the house's existing structure is not important; visitors and estate agents alike are impressed; the extra space is on a level where most of the house's activity occurs – a particular advantage where children are involved.

Of course the picture is not all rosy. Consider the mess in the garden, the expense of foundations and poured concrete floor slabs, the necessity of a damp-proof course, the need to make it as secure against burglary as the rest of the house. But there is a logic and attractiveness about building at ground level which, most people consider, transcends these problems.

Do it properly

Many firms have cashed in on the house extension market by offering quick-assembly kits, and they will often put them up for you as part of the cost. Some of these kits are quite good in an unimaginative way; others are flimsy structures with cheap roofs that are little more than glorified garden sheds – and look like it.

As with everything else, you pay for what you get – unless you are fooled into paying too much for an inferior product. Kits are generally timber-framed, and the more solid ones have brick infill panels. Back in the energy-wasteful days of the 1960s and '70s, the value of insulation was scarcely considered, and even in these more energy-conscious times, some manufacturers still don't seem too concerned. The result is not just high fuel bills, but uncomfortably cold and draughty spaces that you never want to use except in high summer.

Some kits have certainly improved, and some are quite sophisticated pre-fabricated structures of a fairly durable nature. The lifespan of such extensions varies according to their materials and quality. If you are eager to enhance the value of your property, don't get talked into a cheap kit.

From the aesthetic point of view, don't go for an off-the-shelf extension *at all*. It's far better to do the job properly and employ an architect with experience in this kind of work who shows some signs of flair. (For details on employing an architect, see the chapter on Dealing with the Experts.) Using a good architect for a purpose-built extension will give you something unique and valuable. His fees can even be covered by the money he saves you through effective management of the building process. Of course, there are bad architects – who can easily be avoided if you take the right precautions – but there are many more unscrupulous jerry builders.

1

What are its uses?

Before you start to plan, consider carefully what use you want to put the new space to. Think not just of the immediate need – such as a playroom for the children – but of the long-term need. By opting to build an extension you have effectively decided against moving house, at least for the time being. Adding to your house in this way gives you the opportunity to achieve exactly what you want, rather than making the best of existing spaces.

A playroom has a limited usefulness – children grow up, and the daytime room may have to become a bedroom or study. Whatever its original use, the chances are that it will change. Be careful not to saddle yourself with a room which is so rigidly designed for one purpose that it cannot be adapted for another. Sun rooms don't make good bedrooms and must be considered separately (see Conservatories).

You may want to draw up what the architect will call a 'brief' – fairly exact instructions from you to the architect. Alternatively you might prefer to carry out this brief-making process in consultation with your architect. That's not a bad idea, because by involving a professional right from the start you can become aware of possibilities you might otherwise have overlooked. Unlike most other people in the building process, architects are creative as well as practical – so simply handing over instructions without consultation is wasting the talent you're paying for.

2

3

4

1 A new brick extension, built out over one and a half storeys, transforms the house on the inside with a minimum of visual intrusion on the outside.

2 and 3 An ingenious and individual extension by architects, Benson and Forsyth. Although in a totally different style from the rest of the house, it is made to feel an integral part of it, not an afterthought, by the judicious provision of new openings in the old walls.

4 Built onto the back of a tiny one-room wide cottage, this three-storey glass and steel extension into the garden provides twice the original space.

5 Making the most of what was once a dark and dingy basement. The garden has been cut back far enough to create a terrace which also lets the sun in. An original window has been enlarged into all-glass sliding doors.

5

BUILDING AT THE BACK

Looking for modest growth

Once you've analysed your needs – and your bank balance – you may decide that you don't need even one completely new room, but do need more space in the ones you've got. If your kitchen is on the ground floor but you have to eat at a table squashed in one corner, or use the living room instead, then a small-scale extension outwards can give you all the space that you require.

In many houses, particularly older ones, the ground is lower at the back than it is at the front. You can take advantage of this when you set about creating, say, a dining area off a kitchen. Building steps down from the food preparation area to the food consumption area is one neat way to distinguish between the two spaces. Different flooring materials and colour schemes will emphasize the change. Such 'half rooms' are best left open to their parent room, but in some cases a light, perhaps moveable, partition can be justified. If there is no change in level but you want to make a distinction, a screen or a low wall studded with plants may serve the purpose perfectly well.

Depending on the land available outside, such add-on spaces can be narrower or wider than their parent room. The most satisfactory solution is often to go for a narrower space which allows you to install a bay window. This will give you a different viewpoint and will make the whole room lighter.

Don't make the mistake of thinking that it's summer all the year round. Pleasant though it is to sit and eat in a glazed sun trap during the summer months, such areas can be freezing cold in winter because of the extent of glazing and general thinness of construction. It doesn't matter so much if the area is big enough to be closed off for the winter, but if it isn't, then heat from the rest of the house will escape. Anyway, there's little point in spending money on something you can use only for a few months in the year.

With regard to insulation, treat semi-extensions as part of the main room. If there's a lot of glass and you intend to use the extension all the year round, consider double-glazing. Otherwise, make sure that walls and roof are well-insulated and that there

1 and 2 An intricate mixture of old and new extensions at the back of this Victorian house. A glass-roofed conservatory, tacked onto the side of the old extension, leads into a new L-shaped building beyond. In the process, an outside wall becomes the interior of the conservatory.

3 If you have the financial resources, your back extension can incorporate two storeys, not just one, for very little extra work.

4 A stylish, neat and practical way of making the transition between indoors and out, without eating up too much of the garden.

3

4

aren't any gaps for draughts. *Never* try to save money by putting on the sort of translucent corrugated plastic roof used in garage lean-tos. It looks horrible and heat is quickly lost through it.

Using existing materials

You may be able to save time and money on the foundations of a full-size extension by cannibalizing existing outbuildings. Older houses in particular often have a clutter of buildings which served as scullery, kitchen, outside lavatory and so on. Consider losing some of these to form the base of your new extension–some or all of their existing foundations may be usable. A few of the existing walls may be incorporated into the new part to make an organic whole. Alternatively, the demolition of such small ancillary structures may provide you with enough in the way of original building materials to build the new extension entirely. Don't waste old paving setts, good timber or sound window frames if you can make creative use of them. In the process you will save money and end up with an extension that looks entirely natural.

Getting the right angle

Whether or not you are able to use existing materials, ask yourself if you can get away with building just two walls by fitting the new room or rooms into an outside right angle. In houses where the two sides of the right angle are long enough, a dramatic new space is possible by constructing just one wall across it to make a triangle. Developments of this theme are possible in a T-shaped house where such triangles can be introduced to either side and even jointed through the middle. Such a solution is an elegant and economical way of using limited space.

By using the external corners of a house in this way, you can save on building materials and on energy costs–because the less the surface area of any structure, the less heat is lost through it. If there are no such useful angles to play with, remember that the principle still applies: the more of the existing wall of your house you can use, the better from an energy and building materials point of view. The most wasteful way to build an extension is to build straight out from the wall of your house on a slim rectangular plan, with the connection through the narrow end. Far better where possible to turn it round so that the long flank is against the house. Then less of the garden is wasted as well.

Foundations

Buildings need foundations, and the heavier the building, the deeper the foundations need to be. Putting in the foundations for your extension may mean that you have to re-route some of the pipes and drains that service your house. It all depends where these services run. It might be worth siting your extension to avoid them, if you can, and so save time and money. If you wish to put a bathroom or lavatory in the new building, extra work in the ground will be needed. And in almost every case, some form of drainage will have to be laid–even if only a soakaway–for rainwater from the roof.

Take care also that the new works do not slice through existing land drains–simple clay pipes–in the garden, or you may end up with a morass where before you had a beautifully drained lawn.

Suit the style

How you choose the appearance of your extension will be influenced to some extent by the dictates of the planners. Beyond that, bear in mind that the larger the extension is and the more rooms it has, the more assertive it becomes in relation to the whole house, particularly if it is more than one storey in height.

Selecting the style is a highly subjective matter. As a generalization, small extensions can be more brazen in their appearance than large ones–rather like people and their clothes. Once the extension is half the size of the existing house or more, the entire nature of the combined building changes. Planners may demand a say in its appearance well below that scale. The decision has to be made whether to choose materials and details that match or are sympathetic to the existing building, or whether to acknowledge the newness of the extension with a very different style. Either way, it is the appropriate image which is important–it is a big mistake to go for a non-style, a bland appearance, in the hope that it will please everyone. The most such structures usually inspire is bored indifference.

Level pegging

Finally, make full use of the floor levels and ceiling heights that an extension allows you. It's quite likely that the ground level will suggest steps down into the new rooms. This may give you the opportunity to raise your ceiling and make a lofty, double height space, perhaps with a mezzanine floor or balcony, without blocking off windows on the first floor of the main building. The change in level is one of the things that can make the extension into a special place. A flat roof can be turned to advantage by the simple expedient of making a door through onto the new roof from the main house's first-floor level (the roof will have to be properly paved and drained). It's a worthwhile extra feature at a small cost, resulting in a spectacular roof garden.

CONSERVATORIES

Remember that conservatories are not just greenhouses. They are not merely for plants, or for people potty about plants. Rather, they are habitable rooms which have been specially adapted to allow delicate and exotic plants to thrive.

Originally an adjunct to many of the best mansions in Europe, the conservatory reached a peak of popularity in Victorian England when relatively modest – though still substantial – houses were graced by them. Sometimes they were called 'winter gardens', because their function was just that – to provide a garden environment when the rigours of the English winter precluded the use of the real thing.

After World War I their popularity declined. Many were not maintained properly and were removed. Today, they are undergoing a great revival. They can still be grand, but increasingly it is the small examples which are providing the new impetus. The traditional Victorian designs are once again popular, though the concept

1 A modern conservatory, designed as an integral part of the house. Bare boards painted white make a smooth transition from carpets to paving.

2 Overhead trellis and frilly festoon blinds give this conservatory a self-consciously period flavour, reinforced by the oil table lamp, ceiling fan and hanging basket.

3 A cane chair recalls the traditional elements of a conservatory in this steel and glass lean-to.

4 A timber-framed, glass-walled extension tacked onto the back of a Victorian house to create a leafy living area.

5 Constructed of glass and slim structural posts, a new room which feels completely open to the sun.

has been upgraded with new materials. They now face competition from crisper architectural forms made possible by better glazing techniques.

The size and type of conservatory you choose will depend greatly on how you see yourself using it. Will it be in constant use by most of the household – perhaps for eating in – or will it be largely one person's private domain? Do you intend to use it all year round? If so, allow for proper heating and secondary-glazing in your budget.

Glazing
There are various kinds of glazing materials available nowadays. The cheapest is a form of double-walled translucent plastic which adapts well to curves and provides a basic form of insulation but which you can't see through. It does however provide enough light for most plants. As well as ordinary, breakable glass there is car windscreen type toughened glass. It's expensive, but useful for vulnerable areas such as doors.

If you or your neighbours are in the habit of throwing stones, you could opt for a completely non-smashable conservatory in polycarbonate glazing. Better than glass in some respects, polycarbonate sheet is also expensive. There are now new forms of glass which have an invisible coating on the inside to prevent radiant heat from escaping. Such material must be used with caution in conservatories because it can lead to overheating.

How much to glaze?
Greenhouses need the maximum of glazing. Conservatories do not, and for your own comfort you may not want too much glass around you. A fair proportion of solid wall allows you a degree of privacy, and helps to even out temperature fluctuations, as well as enabling you to install a stove easily and to put up shelves and pictures.

Choosing the site
A conservatory will be successful in temperate climates so long as the sun can reach it for a reasonable period in any day. This means that a south-

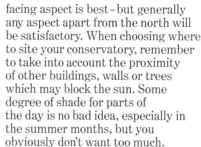

facing aspect is best – but generally any aspect apart from the north will be satisfactory. When choosing where to site your conservatory, remember to take into account the proximity of other buildings, walls or trees which may block the sun. Some degree of shade for parts of the day is no bad idea, especially in the summer months, but you obviously don't want too much.

Many of the locations suitable for a ground-floor extension will lend themselves as sites for a conservatory, assuming that there is enough light. Consider especially the angles of L- or T-shaped houses, and the suntrap possibilities of a high garden wall. Your conservatory can be free-standing in your garden – but you will probably use it only as a summer house. Or it can be attached to your house. The advantage of a mainly glazed structure is that it does not appear bulky; a quite sizeable conservatory can be acceptable against a house where the equivalent size of solid extension would seem overbearing.

Consider too, a conservatory in the sky – perched dramatically on top of a flat-roofed back extension at first or second floor level. If you own an upstairs apartment in a house and you can persuade the neighbours and the freeholder, you can achieve an extra room that doubles as a garden.

Free-standing or lean-to
The simplest form of conservatory to adopt is a rectangular box with a sloping roof against a wall of your house, placed for instance around a back door so that there is direct access through. A lean-to can look a trifle primitive, but if well designed, with good materials and interesting glazing patterns, it can be useful and attractive. More immediately pleasing are the neo-Victorian types with round or polygonal ends projecting out from the house, sometimes with their own bays and L- or T-shapes. The angled corners reduce the available floor area slightly but also provide more facets for the sun to shine directly through.

Off-the-shelf or tailor-made
There are a number of good firms who make conservatory elements, including

glazing to your specification, which fit together however you want. Conservatories tend to consist of a number of repeated parts and this makes the kit approach attractive. Some companies give design advice, which means that your conservatory need not look exactly the same as your next-door neighbour's.

Up and out
Some of the most dramatic conservatories have been achieved by enclosing more than just the ground floor of a house. A cascade of glass coming right down the house, with balconies or access at each level, is the most extreme form – a space that might almost be called an atrium. The vertical emphasis allows you to use trailing plants at each level as well as the usual ground-based plants and pots.

Some of this effect is possible on a modest scale by giving the humble lean-to conservatory the extra height needed to take in the first-floor. Even a small sun-room of this type can easily include a balcony at the upper level. Apart from the visual effect, such mini-atria can favourably influence the energy performance of the house, acting as a buffer zone and sun trap. As with all conservatories, there must be enough easily operated openings at the top to control excessive heat build-up.

Decorating
Conservatories have always inspired the eccentric and frivolous in people. Despite their name they should be anything but conservative places. Aim to create a light and airy feel – carpet and furniture which too obviously belongs to the living room will look out of place here – punctuated by amusing and eye-catching objects – junk shop busts or urns full of plants perhaps. Garden furniture looks well in the conservatory, and can be moved outside when necessary. Or consider Victorian, or reproduction, white painted cast iron work with rich decorative patterns. In contrast to the walls and roof, the conservatory floor should be tough and heavy. Black and white marble tiles are the ideal; but concrete screed covered with rush matting looks perfectly good.

5

BLENDING OLD WITH NEW

Adding new space to your house is bound to affect the way it looks, outside and inside. You have to be very careful about both. Something that works well in terms of interior spaces may make your house an eyesore in the rest of the street – that is, if the planners allow it in the first place.

From adding a small dormer window in the roof to building a major extension, it's important to respect the appearance of your house, and to consider how it fits into its surroundings. It's a matter of form and scale as well as materials, and it's always best to get advice from a registered architect before you let the builders loose. There are almost certainly several different ways to achieve the sort of extra room you have in mind. Some will be much less obtrusive than others.

Private versus public

The most sensitive part of your house is the frontage onto the street. If there's no street frontage, then it's the main elevation that counts – the side of your house that people see as they approach. In a sense it's part of the public domain because it impinges on the vision of passers-by. So it's here that any new works must look right – in the context of the houses round about as well as in the way it affects the look of your property.

In the private domain – the parts of your house that only you and a few others see, such as where it backs onto the garden – you will want to get the appearance right for your own satisfaction. Depending on the attitude of the local planners and whether the house is listed or in a conservation area, national park, or suchlike, you are likely to be able to do more at the back than at the front. Some parts of the walls or roof may be completely invisible from ground level. If you can create space without it being too apparent so much the better.

Brickwork

If you decide to build an extension in brick to a brick house, see if you can obtain an exact match in colour and texture. This may be difficult – in the case of older houses in particular. One solution is to re-use old bricks, and

some builders keep stocks of them from demolition sites for this purpose. You may have outhouses or a lean-to built of the same material as the house which can be demolished to provide the bricks.

Where a match is impossible, it's better to cement-render the extension and paint it to distinguish it from the house. Contrasting bricks can work — particularly if details such as string courses are copied to give harmony with the rest of the house.

Tiles and slates

As with bricks, so with roof materials. New synthetic slates – and even new genuine slates – will look odd next to rough but serviceable old ones. Second-hand tiles and slates are available to help you over the problem. If you can't get hold of the right sort, and you want to roof, say, a wide dormer window at the front of the house, you could use existing slates from a less visible roof, probably at the rear. The front of the house will then look consistent and you can use new tiles or slates at the back where it will matter less. Flat roofs to dormers can be acceptable, preferably using lead or a modern alloy equivalent rather than roofing felt.

Windows and doors

Study the existing apertures in your house before you rush to order the windows and doors for your extension or attic conversion. If you have timber sliding sash windows elsewhere, it makes sense to fit new ones of the same type. A number of firms have standard or made-to-measure ranges.

The same is true of other types of windows – unless the existing ones are totally unacceptable. Then, you might consider renewing the whole lot, at any rate on the front. Again, match them up.

Many houses have had their original windows replaced with entirely inappropriate ones. A glance at the other houses around you might give the clue, and the pattern to follow when you set about restoring the original appearance. Avoid wherever possible overlarge areas of plate glass – it gives houses a blank eyeless look. Smaller panes allow better ventilation as well as generally looking better.

2

3

4

Doors, too, will help a new extension to fit in. Try moving the existing back door to the outside of the new building. If that's not possible, try to get a door of the same type as the rest of the house. Again, make sure your existing outer doors are original before you start replicating them.

Show sympathy

The use of sympathetic materials and forms, no matter what the age of the building, does not have to be a question of craven imitation. The important thing is to respect what's there and take it into account when adding to it. The proportions of the main building can be echoed in the new work without the need to copy every little detail. Timber and glass can be successfully used against a brick building because they are visually lighter; a pure, uncluttered shape can work very well in the context of ornate Victorian details – so long as it remains subordinate.

The inside view

One of the rewards of extending your home is that the spaces you create can have very special characters. You may decide that you want the new room, or rooms, to feel very much part of what's there already, and will fit them out accordingly. But often the most rewarding thing you can do is to emphasize that these are deliberately *different* places. A spiral staircase up to an attic room defines it as being special; a partition between rooms in the form of the timber framing from the old wall does the same.

The entrances to spaces serve to define them – a door may not be strictly necessary, but can be installed for this purpose. Changes in level, changes in the materials on the floors, sharply contrasting colours and different means of lighting, are all ways of making the new parts of your house exciting. Think how the new rooms will affect the way you use the rest of the house – and be inventive.

1 A glass and steel extension with a faintly nautical flavour doesn't interfere with the Georgian character of the original house, but is obviously a modern addition.

2 In the extension to his own house, architect Piers Gough has employed the style of the 1930s in keeping with its suburban setting.

3 and 4 Once memorably described as resembling a crashed airliner in the back garden, Gareth Wright's extension to a Georgian London house makes no concession to period details. A new glass entrance at the front of the house hints at what lies in store at the back.

GARDENS

If you have grown up surrounded by a garden, played hide and seek in it and lazed there on hot sunny days, then you will have a fair idea of how to create a garden of your own. If on the other hand you are meeting your garden head on as a complete novice the initiation can be daunting.

Of course the scale of the problem depends largely on what you inherit when you buy your home; it may be that it has been lovingly cared for by the previous occupants, supporting a wonderful array of trees, shrubs and flowers, but all too often that is not the case. It could equally be a barren space, uncultivated and deserted, appreciated only by builders as a suitable place to toss all the rubble out of the house whilst it is being converted. Unwanted bricks and plaster, splintered wood and bits of wire, rejected cable and plumbing, dried out cement and ballast, broken bottles and retired gym shoes all combine to give whatever soil there might have been a heavy dose of depression. In the following pages we assume that you are starting from scratch.

If you are moving into a new home, you will probably want to get the house organized first, but don't forget when budgeting your expenditure to leave something in the kitty for the garden. Have it cleared of debris before wallpapers are hung or carpets laid, especially if the only point of access to the road is through the house. If you know what basic materials you are going to need – soil, paving stones and so on – get these in and stacked until you are ready to start work. If the garden is at least cleared and tidy it can sit fallow for a while without depressing you at every glimpse through the window.

When you are ready to tackle the problem of your garden, try asking yourself a few rudimentary questions. Gardens work best when there is a cohesion of ideas, a sense of direction and a plan of attack. Even if the work is not all done at once, the overall aim should be decided at the start.

What do you want?
What do you intend to use your garden for? If there are young children then the garden must be planned with them

in mind; grass is better for falling on than paving stones. Sandpits, swings and climbing frames need to be incorporated into the plan at an early stage; remember too not to include plants that scratch or poison. Maybe there's a disabled or elderly person living in the house who enjoys the therapeutic values of gardening, in which case raised borders and beds will help them, with steps replaced by slopes or ramps with textured surfaces to minimize slipping. Do you intend to use your garden primarily as a space for outdoor activities, or will it be devoted lovingly to the cultivation of plants and shrubs? Most people want to find a happy compromise between the two, but you must decide in advance just what your requirements will be.

Bear in mind the amount of time you will be able to give your garden. Even the smallest ones can be very time consuming, so if you only have the odd weekend, don't be too ambitious at

the start; you may begin with the best of intentions, but later wish you had created something a little simpler. Certainly part of the fun of a garden is the cultivation, but part is the simple pleasure of being in it, and relaxing.

How long will you stay?
If you know you will be moving on in a few years you will want to make the garden as effective as possible for a minimum outlay. Plants must be chosen carefully, maximizing on quick growing, or you should allow for the expense of mature plant stock. If on the other hand you fully intend to stay put for many years, then the planning process can be more leisurely, giving greater thought to detail. Time is on your side, and it is much better to let the garden progress at its natural pace, evolving as the seasons change, mellowing as it gets older, the bricks and stone weathering and the plants showing middle age spread.

What is the aspect?

Locate the north point.
It would be fruitless to incur considerable expense constructing a garden, only to discover that the sun merely winks at it briefly before you get up, deserting it for the rest of the day. Some plants are sun worshippers, others grow without fuss in the shade, but neither types will thrive if they are planted in the wrong place. A southerly or south-westerly aspect is the ideal, but don't despair if your garden faces north – a surprising variety will grow there.

Look at your surroundings, noting which trees or tall buildings might obscure light, and which plants are doing well in neighbouring gardens. Note the access points from the street to your garden if there are any, and establish locations for dustbins, clotheslines and a garden shed.

View from the inside

Remember that the garden is an extension of the house, and as such is often enjoyed from inside as much as out, so keep in mind the screening of unsightly views, using trellis and climbing plants or suitable trees. The eye naturally wanders to a focal point, so make sure you create a pleasant one. Diligent placing of a sculpture, ornaments, or large pots of plants will keep the view under control.

Consider the windows of your house – large sliding glass doors mean that much more of the garden will be visible, so don't make an eyesore of the compost heap or garden shed. Also remember the view from upstairs.

Learning the art

Research other gardens and read about plants as much as you can before making your final selection. Hundreds of plants can be bought through mail order, and the dark cold days of winter are the perfect time for catalogue browsing. Most of the home and garden magazines carry advertisements for the seedsmen, nurseries and growers, while the more esoteric journals will reveal some of the more exotic species.

Garden centres allow you the chance to wander round their selections of plants, as well to see their ranges of garden buildings, furniture, tools and other accessories. With luck you should find someone to assist you with your enquiries, especially if you avoid weekends. Alternatively you may consider employing professional help.

1 **Concrete blocks laid at single pace intervals make a charming and inexpensive path.**

2 **A bungalow crowned by flowers.**

3 **Never be daunted by your limitations; a garden can be created anywhere.**

4 **Just as an interior should be a personal expression, so should your garden, whatever the style.**

THE BUDGET

Undeniably the most prosaic part of gardening is budget planning. Nonetheless it should be tackled before you start any creative work. Grandiose plans are liable to wither like plants without water when costings are made and estimates totted up. So before we draw up a plan let us look at the finances.

First decide on the figure, affordable and realistic, that you are prepared to spend on the garden. As a rough guideline, you might allow approximately 10 per cent of the cost of the renovation or refurbishment of the house. Certainly don't be tempted to spend more on the garden than you would be able to recoup in increased property value when the time comes to sell. Whatever figure you finally arrive at, it will be affected greatly by your intention or otherwise to tackle the work yourself.

A new patio or terrace would probably be the most expensive item on your budget, but fencing, trellis, lawn, shed, lighting, terracotta pots and top soil are all costly. In fact the only components for a garden with relatively low price tags attached are the plants themselves, but so many are needed that their cost soon mounts up.

If you are considering whether to commission a garden firm to undertake the work, with or without plans supplied by you, ask them first for some basic estimates over the phone such as the cost of a square metre (one square yard) of turf laid on a cleared surface, and likewise for stone or paving, be it reconstituted or brickwork. The firm should also be able to estimate for garden fencing, if you know its length and height, as for trellis and other forms of screening. If they are unable to give you this sort of information, beware of them. In addition to these estimates, ask the garden centre for their price list and keep a check on how much you spend from the mail order catalogues. With the help of a calculator, add all these figures up, and soon you will have an idea of the final cost.

If you intend to have a lawn, consider the cost of a mower. Very cheap electric types tend to be a false economy unless your lawn is pocket handkerchief size; anything larger and they soon tend to burn out. A slightly more expensive electric, rotary or cylinder mower will probably save you money in the long run.

If you need to hire a skip for clearance remember that you should obtain a licence if it's parked in the street and that it must be lit at night.

Large, expensive equipment such as ladders, rotavators, hedge trimmers and chainsaws can be hired, but don't forget smaller but nonetheless indispensable items – peat, bonemeal, training wire, stakes, canes, secateurs, spades, etc – which all add to the cost.

When budgeting for the plants themselves, remember that mature ones – or species as they are called in the trade – are expensive. Try limiting yourself to just a few, strategically placed. Annuals are tempting to buy, as they bring instant colour, but they need replacing every year. Keep them mainly for pots, containers and window boxes, and for padding out small areas of border. Trees are comparatively inexpensive if you buy them young, while shrubs vary in price.

Finally, don't forget essential equipment for yourself, namely, a good pair of gardening gloves – there are plenty of stings, prickles and scratches in store for you.

1 It's not necessary to spend vast amounts to get pleasing results. Here inexpensive paving, fencing, table and chairs are set off by climbers and well-stocked borders.

2 Mellow old bricks follow the curvaceous lines of the border.

3 A corner of a mature country garden-where flowers and shrubs are carefully planned for a stunning display of colour.

4 Established trees are always a good investment. They add instant maturity to a newly laid out garden.

5 Roof terraces need careful planning too. Here a framework of metal pipes makes an unusual and airy enclosure.

6 If your budget is tight, think about concentrating on just one focal element. Here a stunning pool has been created in the centre of a dull concrete expanse.

Here is a checklist of items you will need to take into account when preparing the budget and initial plan for your new garden.

Clearance
Skip (hire)
Wheelbarrow
Rotavator (hire)
Chainsaw (hire)
Builders' bags
Shovel
Spade
Fork
Clippers
Gloves
Bucket
Rope

Materials
Rockery stones
Terrace paving
Wall bricks
Fencing panels
Trellis
Pergola
Top soil/peat
Fertilizers
Gravel
Turf

Tools
Fork
Half-moon edgers
Spade
Dibber
Rake
Hoe
Hose
Watering can
Secateurs
Clippers
Mower
Trowel

Sundries
Training wire
Stakes and canes
Pest sprays
Hammer
Nails
Spare plant pots
Sprayer
Rubbish bags
Seed trays

Plants
Trees
Shrubs
Climbers
Annuals
Perennials
Alpines
Ground cover
Roses
Bulbs
Herbs
Vegetables
Seeds

Containers
Terracotta pots
Tubs
Hanging baskets
Window boxes
Jardinières

Extras
Lighting
Furniture
Shed
Pond
Fountain
Climbing frame
Sandpit
Cloches
Greenhouse

THE PLAN

Depending on your skill at drawing, the basic plan of a garden can range from a doodle on the back of a brown envelope to a full-blown architectural presentation, but a compromise between the two is probably best. Equip yourself with a pad of paper, pencil, rubber, ruler and tape measure, and venture outside.

First draw a rough outline of your garden against the base line of your home. Measure the house walls, noting the position of windows, doors, gates and drains. Mark the north point. Check the condition of party fences and walls, neighbouring trees or shadows caused by surrounding buildings. Next measure the length and width of the boundaries, and mark in manhole covers, trees and any stock worth keeping, even if you want to reposition it later. Fill in your sketch with as many measurements as you think necessary. Back inside transfer your measurements onto graph paper with an easy scale such as 2.5cm to 30cm (1in. to 1ft). It is not necessary to be totally accurate. The function of this plan is mainly to help you work out how much space you have to play with.

Having achieved your outline drawing keep it as a master and, using a tracing paper overlay, start marking in the components. This gives you the opportunity to experiment with ideas. Having marked in, for example, an area of terrace, you can calculate the square yardage and check with suppliers the cost of the materials you will need to order. If the cost is too much, simply alter your plan accordingly. The same principle applies to lawns and borders, as well as to lengths of fencing, walling, trellis etc.

The foundations

Having drawn up your plan, and cleared the plot of debris ready to start landscaping and planting, take a brief look at the bare foundation of your garden. There will be soil, and boundary walls or fencing, probably little else.

Strictly speaking, party walls or fences should not exceed 2m (6ft 6in.) in height. If they need replacing it's worth talking to neighbours about splitting the cost of replacement. Generally the right hand boundary is your responsibility and neighbours can insist that you pay attention to its condition.

As for the soil in your garden, don't worry too much about its PH level. Small gardens can have a good, well-balanced loam made up by adding peat and bonemeal, fresh top soil and organic fertilizers. If the garden is bigger, the type of soil is more important to understand, and a reading should be taken with a soil-testing kit, available from garden centres or chemists. It will reveal the level of acidity or alkalinity in the soil.

One other point to consider before you start: is there an outside tap? Even if you have easy access to a kitchen or bathroom tap, you will soon appreciate the value of an exterior one when work begins and muddy feet are about.

KEY TO GARDEN PLAN
1 Hostas
2 Bamboo
3 Hebe speciosa
4 Phormium tenax
5 Ivy canariensis
6 Cornus kousa chinensis
7 Solanum crispum
8 Sedum maximum
9 Euphorbia
10 Pittosporum
11 Genista hispanica
12 Beech hedge
13 Buxus
14 Espalier fruit tree
15 Alyssum
16 Garrya
17 Cotinus coggyria
18 Potentilla
19 Cytisus kewensis
20 Paeonias
21 Box hedge
22 Rosa mermaid
23 Philadelphus
24 Pinks
25 Santolinas
26 Pieris
27 Nasturtiums
28 Catmint
29 Marigolds
30 Pyracantha
31 Herbs
32 Climbing hydrangea
33 Annuals (e.g. geraniums, petunias, ageratums, lobelias, etc)
34 Salvia superba
35 Astilbe
36 Hibiscus syriacus
37 Skimmia
38 Acer (deep red)
39 Choisya ternata
40 Honeysuckle
41 Mahonia
42 Cineraria
43 Fuchsia
44 Ceanothus
45 Hypericum calycinum
46 Kerria
47 Iris
48 Weeping cherry (prunus)
49 Hellebore
50 Viburnum tomentosum
51 Lavender
52 Lysimachia punctata
53 Clematis montana

A landscape gardener's ground plan for a typical long, slim south-facing urban garden. Right, the finished product in all its glory.

THE COMPONENTS

Sorting out all the components needed for a new garden and deciding where they should go is rather like putting a jigsaw together. Just like a jigsaw, it's immediately obvious where certain elements – a beautiful shrub or a statue – should be sited, whereas with others it takes careful consideration of many factors till the right choice is made. The resulting picture, of course, should be of a balanced and harmonious garden.

For the sake of simplicity, all the components of a garden can be divided into four categories: the necessities, the useful props, the luxuries and the plants themselves.

The necessities
No garden will work properly or look right without certain essential elements.

The terrace An important paved area, which changes the texture and breaks up the layout between the garden proper and the house, controlling the mud coming into the home, and providing a hard base for garden furniture and children's bicycles.

Fencing and walling Not only do fences and walls enclose the boundaries of the property, but they serve to frame the overall effect of the garden. Don't be tempted to build walls too high or they will look heavy – about 1.2m (4ft) with 75cm (2ft 6in.) of trellis above is ideal. The same applies to fencing panels.

Lawns Providing an inexpensive way of covering the area, lawns are marvellous for children to play on and soften the feel of the garden. They also make a good contrast to the borders.

Borders These are beds for plants – an obvious and essential feature of every garden. Their size must depend on the time you are able to give to their maintenance.

Raised borders Giving prominence to the flowers, and helping to define the lines of the garden, a raised border also provides a useful seat. Excellent for gardeners with bad backs or for the elderly.

Level changes Whether natural or specially created, a change in the level of the garden adds interest. Steps up to the new level can become a focal point.

Trellis A device to increase the height of party walls or fences without blocking out the light. It acts as a support for climbing plants, and can be used decoratively for arches and screens.

Plants and soil For plants to grow successfully they must be nurtured with a well-balanced loam, so fresh soil and organic fertilizers must be imported. Carefully plan the selection of trees, shrubs and flowers using our listings.

The props
Whatever kind of garden will suit you – be it a place where children can play safely, or a beautiful showpiece – there are a number of props which can help you achieve your aim.

Ponds A pretty focus for attention, the movement of water in a garden is soothing and attractive, and darting fish, water plants and a fountain all add charm.

Sandpits A joy for young children. Use silver sand from builders' merchants and have a cover to keep animals out.

Lighting Floodlights bring the garden to life at night as well as doubling as a security asset.

Barbecues Cooking outside is always popular when the weather is kind, either for a spontaneous meal or a planned party. Build your own or buy a portable one.

Focal points If there is no natural focal point in the garden – central steps, a pond or rockery for example, use

1 A full size neoclassical statue makes a grand and romantic gesture in any garden, however modestly proportioned.

2 A small incline is transformed into a spectacular level change simply by employing old railway sleepers and plenty of gravel.

3 In town gardens the contrast between soft flowers and hard man-made surfaces is an important highlight.

4 If your conscience is troubled by the extravagance of flood-lighting don't forget that it not only looks good – it deters burglars too.

5 However tiny, a pond, with its attendant plants and fish, adds an attractive and cooling element.

6 Even small gardens need not be deprived of the luxury of a gazebo, provided that it is carefully positioned, as here within a simple circular clearing.

statuary, ornamentation or a spectacularly planted large urn or pot to attract the eye.

Sheds However small your garden, a shed is invaluable for storage of tools, garden furniture, ladders, seed trays, the lawn mower etc.

The luxuries

If you haven't spent all your money achieving the basics in your garden, why not indulge in something a little more frivolous?

Swimming pools and jacuzzis Installing and maintaining a swimming pool or jacuzzi involves lots of money, work and fun. Their inclusion should be planned at an early stage.

Murals Wonderful for brightening up dark corners, and, in the case of *trompe l'oeil*, for giving an illusion of space.

Gazebos and summer houses If your garden is large enough, one of these makes a pretty focal point as well as a

5

6

perfect place to sit and relax.

Follies Non-functional, nonsense buildings, follies are frivolous and good conversation pieces.

Tennis courts Whether grass or hard, you will need an area roughly 33.6 x 15.6m (112 x 52ft) for a tennis court.

Ornaments and statues A traditional part of garden decoration, used to create focal points. They might be antique or reproduction.

Planting out

This list of plants is intended merely as a useful working guide, a basic selection from which to choose stock for your garden. All these plants should be readily available through local nurseries or garden centres. However, selected reading and research will help you to discover many more plants, both unusual and exciting.

Apart from its preference for sun and shade, remember to take into account the type of soil a plant prefers, its ideal siting, and the ultimate height to which it will grow.

Climbers which thrive in shade or partial shade

Hydrangea petiolaris
Jasmine
Lonicera (honeysuckle)
Parthenocissus (Virginia creeper)
Cotoneaster
Hedera

Climbers which thrive in sun

Actinidia
Campsis
Clematis
Lathyrus
Passiflora
Polygonum
Roses (climbing)
Solanum
Vitis
Wisteria

Shrubs which thrive in shade or partial shade

Aucuba
Berberis

Camellia
Cornus
Deutzia
Euonymus
Forsythia
Fuchsia
Garrya
Hamamelis (witchhazel)
Hydrangea
Hypericum
Ilex
Kerria
Laurus
Mahonia
Paeonia (tree paeony)
Pernettya
Philadelphus (mock orange)
Pieris
Rhododendron
Skimmia
Symphoricarpos (snowberry)
Viburnum

Shrubs which thrive in sun

Arundinaria (bamboo)

Berberis
Buddleia
Caryopteris (blue spiraea)
Ceanothus
Chaenomeles japonica (quince)
Chimonanthus (winter sweet)
Choisya (Mexican orange)
Cistus (rock rose)
Cytisus (broom)
Daphne
Elaeagnus
Genista
Hebe (veronica)
Hibiscus
Lavandula (lavender)
Magnolia
Phlomis
Potentilla
Spiraea
Weigela

Trees to plant in the garden

Acer (maple)
Aesculus (horsechestnut)
Arbutus (strawberry tree)
Cercis siliquastrum (Judas tree)
Crataegus (hawthorn or may)
Ficus (fig)
Juniperus (juniper)
Laburnum
Magnolia
Malus (flowering crabapple)
Prunus (flowering cherry, plum etc.)
Salix (willow)
Sorbus
Syringa (lilac)

Annuals and biennials

Ageratum
Alyssum
Antirrhinum (snapdragon)

Begonia
Calendula (pot marigold)
Callistephus (aster)
Centaurea (cornflower)
Chrysanthemum
Clarkia
Convolvulus
Dahlia
Delphinium
Digitalis (foxglove)
Gaillardia
Godetia
Gypsophila
Helianthus (sunflower)
Iberis (candytuft)
Ipomoea (morning glory)
Lathyrus (sweet pea)
Lavatera
Lobelia
Matthiola (stock)
Mimulus (musk)
Nemesia
Nicotiana (tobacco plant)
Nigella
Papaver (poppy)
Petunia
Phlox
Rudbeckia
Salvia
Scabiosa
Tagetes (marigold)
Thunbergia (black-eyed Susan)
Tropaeolum majus (nasturtium)
Verbena
Zinnia

Alpines which thrive in shade or partial shade

Ajuga
Dodocatheon
Geranium (cranesbill)
Lysimachia (creeping Jenny)
Omphalodes
Pachysandra
Pulmonaria
Saxifrage

Tiarella
Vinca
Waldsteinia

Alpines which thrive in sun

Achillea
Aethionema
Arabis
Armeria
Aubrieta
Dianthus (pink)
Dryas
Erinus
Erodium
Genista (broom)
Helianthemum (rock rose)
Iberis
Potentilla
Pulsatilla
Satureia
Sedum
Sempervivum
Silene
Thymus
Veronica (speedwell)

Herbaceous plants which thrive in shade or partial shade

Aconitum
Ajuga
Astilbe
Bergenia
Calamintha
Campanula
Doronicum
Digitalis (foxglove)
Epimedium
Euphorbia
Geranium (cranesbill)
Helleborus
Heucherella
Hosta
Hypericum
Iris
Lamium
Lysimachia
Pachysandra
Polygonatum
Polygonum
Pulmonaria
Salvia
Saxifrage

Tradescantia
Veronica
Vinca (periwinkle)

Herbaceous plants which thrive in sun

Acanthus
Achillea
Althaea
Anchusa
Anemone
Aquilegia (columbine)
Aster
Centaurea (cornflower)
Chrysanthemum
Coreopsis
Cortaderia (pampas grass)
Delphinium
Dianthus (pink)
Geum
Gypsophila
Helenium
Hemerocallis (day lily)
Kniphophia (red hot poker)
Lupin
Oenothera
Papaver (poppy)
Phlox
Prunella
Pyrethrum
Ranunculus (buttercup)
Verbascum

Bulbs

Allium
Anemone
Colchicum
Convallaria (lily of the valley)
Crocus
Eranthis
Fritillaria
Galanthus (snowdrop)
Gladiolus
Hyacinthus
Iris
Lily
Narcissus (daffodil)
Nerine
Scilla (bluebell)
Tulip

DECORATIVE EFFECTS

Plants are probably the single most decorative feature in any garden, but they need by no means be the only ones. Just the odd inspired touch will help to give a garden character and identity. As the decorations we choose in our homes give clues to our personality, so they do in our gardens.

Painting

A naturally dark garden will benefit from a coat of paint on the walls, but beware of painting straight onto old walls. The pointing must be in good condition or the brush will rub out the crumbling cement leaving holes that no amount of paint will fill. If repointing is too tedious, the alternative is to render the wall (cement plastering). This base should then be coated with an appropriate sealant and paint can be applied. Use oil-based or exterior paints.

Painting and patterning can be carried onto flower pots, tubs and containers, garden buildings and trellis. Experiment on timber offcuts or broken pots. Search junk shops for a wealth of objects to paint and plant up: old basins, jugs, colanders, pots, pans and buckets will all come alive with a splash of paint. Plant them up with bright annuals and hang them from walls, put them in a group or, if they are dramatic enough, stand them on their own.

Topiary

Great skill and patience is required for the traditional art of clipping hedges into whimsical and wonderful shapes. The classic plant for topiary is yew, but it is slow growing. Box and cypressus are quicker growing and can be clipped and trained to produce the same effect.

Mirrors

Double your space, create light, reflect your plants and watch yourself gardening. The use of mirrors should only be confined to a small area in the garden, however; too much is tiring.

Balustrades

Add a little pomp to your garden. Traditional balustrading is now reproduced by several garden ornament firms and illustrated in their catalogues. They are available in sections and in a variety of sizes. In the same vein consider Doric columns and even temples of Diana.

Textures

Don't forget the possibilities of achieving attractive and interesting patterns and textures from the materials you use on the ground. Railway sleepers that form an edge to the lawn or even gravel, moss covered bricks or small water pools can all have a part to play. A garden with a variety of textures will be of more interest than one which sticks to all lawn or all paving.

1 A floral fantasy enlivens a drab window and provides a fitting backdrop for the garden.

2 Topiary can take many forms, always to great effect. Here, a hedge is cut with artless elegance, its gently curving lines lending distinction to the simple corrugated facade behind.

3 Decorative fencing and trellis make an unusual boundary and a beautiful frame for plants.

4 A cool spurt of water splashes into a stone trough from the gnarled old head of a carved lion.

5 Singly, these old pots would be lost. Grouped together, they make an attractive decorative effect.

GARDEN FURNITURE

Little has changed in the basic designs of garden furniture over the years. Deck chairs may be available in brightly coloured and patterned canvas as well as the traditional old stripes, but they have retained their old shape; and indeed why change something that works so well and is comparatively inexpensive? Pub tables made from plastic coated aluminium have appeared, making them lighter to handle, if less attractive; the classical teak garden bench maintains its position as a best-seller with matching table and carver seats. Directors' chairs, the folding type traditionally used on movie sets, are both cheap and practical. The average collection of furniture at any garden centre leaves little to be desired, but if you are prepared to pay for it, some more exciting designs are available from other sources – department stores and so on. Good garden furniture is expensive, and, after all, not often used. Consider, therefore, buying furniture which will look equally good indoors – in a conservatory or garden room – as well as out, thereby serving a useful dual purpose.

If you want a lounging chair, try one of the French makes, upholstered in soft, deep-buttoned cushions with well painted frames. Tables, either glass-topped, timber or metal, are available from department stores and garden centres, in an assortment of shapes and sizes. Add a parasol or huge umbrella for a romantic touch. Swing seats are comfortable and relaxing; as they take up a fair amount of space, they lend themselves better to a larger garden. A tree will make a pretty central setting for tables and chairs built in a circular fashion around it. Alternatively, two obligingly spaced trees will make the setting for a hammock, the simplest and most comfortable of all garden furniture. Hammocks are also available on frames if there are no suitable trees.

Consider carefully whether to buy your outdoor furniture in wood, plastic or metal. Wood is really the best, as it can be left outside and will last a long time, while metal rusts if exposed to the elements. Folding plastic furniture has practical advantages, as it can be redeployed in the house.

1 Directors' chairs – cheap, practical, good-looking and now available in a wide selection of colours.

2 Sturdy and dependable, a traditional white painted wooden bench, with matching flower tubs.

3 These perforated metal chairs may not be entirely weather-proof but they have the advantage of looking as good indoors as out.

4 Al fresco dining in style. Any meal would be a pleasure under this huge stripey sun umbrella.

ROOF GARDENS

Not everyone is lucky enough to own a garden, but that in no way means the pleasures of gardening need be denied them. Roofs, terraces and balconies, windowsills and walls all offer space for you to practise this gentle art.

Some people manage to create a roof garden in the most inaccessible spots. They squeeze past chimneys, and edge along gutters, nimbly carrying their watering cans. For others, life is a little easier with comfortable access through a large window or door. Whichever, roof gardens come with their own package of problems.

Before you decide to create a garden on your roof, ask the advice of a professional about weight. Most roof gardens support several people standing on them at one time, so a selection of pots and assorted containers should be perfectly safe. Don't, however, start building brick walls or laying stone floors. Keep to light materials: use decking on the floor, or light tiles. Make sure the surface is sealed with a bitumen and don't drill any holes into it without sound knowledge of your roof's load potential; there could be a serious possibility of cracks and strains appearing, causing permanent damage. They may not show immediately, but their lasting presence might well emerge when a surveyor's report is produced for a potential purchaser. Strengthening your roof may be a major undertaking and should be considered at an early stage if you are renovating the house.

Plastic grass, although dismissed as tacky by some, has a surprisingly good effect on roof gardens. Choose pots in plastics, fibreglass or wood, and use vermiculite peat and light composts in them. Wind will be a problem and trellis, securely fixed with a small mesh is the best answer. The effect is to minimize the wind's strength by allowing it to flow through the trellis, thus avoiding turbulence or a build-up of pressure. Hang pretty half pots on the wall and use hanging baskets. Judicially trained climbers enliven walls and can be trained over canopies. Keep garden furniture to a minimum – use folding chairs and light tables.

Balconies

Weight and wind problems are again present, but as the space is likely to be much smaller, the concern need be less. Don't plant everything on the ground; draw the eye upwards by fixing boxes to the railings, filled with trailing plants and annuals. Plant a small ornamental tree (e.g. *malus* golden hornet) in a large pot and train climbers up the wall. Foldaway canopies lend a Mediterranean ambience as well as providing shade. Gravel on the ground or wood shavings (cedar) give a Japanese feel especially with the use of bamboo and a couple of sandstone rocks. Bird baths or feeding tables add interest. Paint the walls and railings in bright or pastel colours. If your balcony is large enough, keep some attractive, but weatherproof, furniture permanently outside.

Window boxes

Even the dullest of views from a window can be enhanced by a box of flowers; and it is inexpensive to install, and undemanding in maintenance – just keep an aerosol of insecticide handy.

Kitchen windows are the perfect spot for herbs; remember mint dominates so don't mix it with the others such as sage, parsley, thyme or rosemary. On windowsills outside less frequently used rooms, try something a little more unusual like wild grasses or ground cover plants, e.g. *pachysandra* or *lamiastrum*; they will look after themselves apart from watering. Make sure fixings are secure, and use a hook and eye to avoid boxes slipping off the ledge. Drill drainage holes into the bottom of the box. Install broken crocks over the holes or fill with 15mm (¾in.) pea shingle.

1 New York roof garden with a spectacular view. Furniture is civilized enough to look good indoors and out.

2 Italians have a strong tradition of creating delightfully lush roof terraces. Thickly planted, with a framework for trailers, they provide privacy even in a city setting.

3 Ingenuity is the essence of the urban roof garden, putting to use all sorts of forgotten corners. Tubs provide the soil for plants, and timber decking is a workable alternative to lawn.

4 Don't turn up your nose at artificial grass. On the roof it looks surprisingly effective.

5 A miniature garden in the sky. All the elements are there: border, planting boxes, sitting out area, a corner protected by an awning.

6 Window boxes are an easy way to transform a dull exterior. Here a mass of trailing geraniums spill over the window ledge.

INDOOR PLANTS

For those of us denied the space to grow plants outside, the ever widening availability of houseplants is a great boon. Indeed for everyone, indoor gardening is becoming more and more popular, both as a hobby and as an important decorative effect. This new awareness of the importance of plants has been inspiration for dozens of books on the subject, and a spate of new shops.

Inevitably some plants are more obliging than others, apparently willing to struggle on with poor light, dry soil, draughts and pest attacks, and bullied by too much central heating. Others take this lack of attention personally and promptly pass out. This can be disconcertingly expensive and dispiriting. Thus the choice of plants must be studied. Consider the sort of life you lead, whether you are away a lot, and have friendly neighbours who can pop in and water them for you. Do you have time to pander to their needs, or are you prone to forget about them a bit,

overlooking the fact that they are alive and not inanimate? All too often plants are bought for their decorative value, then placed, without thought for the conditions, as if they were a piece of furniture or sculpture.

Decorating with plants

The first step is to decide where you want to place your plants, what sort of size you require, and the type of foliage, be it dense or light. Then look at the situation you've chosen, checking the amount of light available and how much draught there is. With this knowledge, you will be able to eliminate some of the more unsuitable characters when you research plant lists.

When using plants for decoration, decide whether you want just one dramatic plant, standing alone, imposing itself on its uncluttered surroundings, or large groupings of several types of plants, in varying heights, shapes and colours. Arrangement of several large plants can look heavy, so balance the

foliage with the pots and the stands or pedestals they sit on. Trellis screening used for training climbing plants and to divide the room is effective. Staircase wells or awkward alcoves need a large plant to fill the space – a staghorn fern or monsteria is ideal. Remember that climbing plants don't like to be treated as trailing plants. The warmth of kitchens and bathrooms permits you to display more exotic plants such as maidenhair ferns or mimosa. If there is plenty of direct light try, for example, training an allamanda up the wall.

The conservatory

This is not just a room for plants, but a place for peace and relaxation, perhaps for eating with an exotic backdrop of jungle greenery. Whether your budget allows just a simple lean-to or a classic Victorian conservatory, it will undoubtedly add value to your property, as well as providing pleasure and interest, and extra space.

Arrange plants on different levels:

1 A recreation of the classic Victorian conservatory. The symmetrical arrangement of the plants echoes the pure lines of the room.

2 Indoor plants used to create a ceiling of greenery. The tropical effect is achieved by grouping, amongst others, spider plants and maidenhair ferns in hanging baskets.

3 A bank of plants on different levels from floor to ceiling looks effective in this garden room.

4 A tropical oasis created by strategically placed palms.

have hooks for hanging baskets, shelves for smaller pot plants and seed trays, and containers on the floor for larger plants. If you decide to grow a vine, plant the root outside and bring the leaders in through a hole at ground level. Investigate automatic irrigation systems, great time savers, which allow you to go away without worrying about the watering. Feed plants with concentrated humus every fortnight during the growing season.

This is an ideal place for ceramic cachepots and Victorian bowls and pedestals, too precious to put outside. Light wickerwork or bamboo chairs are best - easily portable furniture is useful if you want to take it outside in the summer. Keep colours to pastels and pale shades for a feeling of airiness.

Maintenance

Whilst certain plants are more demanding than others, the application of a few basic rules should keep most of them happy. Good plant care is essentially common sense; whether you have 'green fingers' or not depends purely on your desire to provide plants with what they need, and on your devoting enough time to them.

In general, water indoor plants a little and often, rather than over watering them at infrequent intervals. Keep soil damp, not wet or dry. Feed with five drops of bio to 0.5 litres (1 pint) of water every two weeks. Most plants enjoy a misting: use an atomizer with a fine nozzle and spray twice a week.

Check leaves, on both sides, for tiny enemies. Red and black spider, meally bugs and other little mites can be controlled with suitable sprays of liquid Derris or Melathan. If they have really taken hold, destroy the plant before they spread.

Gently prick the soil on the topped up surface every month; this aerates the soil structure and allows water to permeate better. Every spring repot your houseplants into containers one size larger.

FLOORS

Floors take constant punishment. Not only do they have to withstand the weight of furniture, and the constant abrasion of feet, but they have to resist dirt and spills. And apart from the practical aspects, the floor is important from a decorative point of view since it must both be an attractive element in itself and harmonize all the disparate elements in the room. Choose with care –mistakes, though seldom irreversible, can be costly.

The subfloor
To start with, you need to check the existing floor or subfloor to make sure it is in good condition and damp-proof. There are basically two types of floor construction.

Suspended timber floors   These are found upstairs in most properties and on many pre-war ground floors. They are usually floorboards (frequently tongued and grooved), supported on timber joists, which are in turn connected to the walls of the house, or held up by brick walls laid over a concrete foundation. Joists may be less sturdy than they should be in some older properties, particularly upstairs, and the boards may well be thinner, so these should always be checked before a heavy surface (ceramic or quarry tiles, marble, terrazzo etc) is laid on top.

Solid concrete floors   These are laid over the foundations and found in most post-war properties. They may then be finished with a screed, and may well have tiles, woodblock or other permanent or semi-permanent flooring on top.

Tough and easy to clean, quarry tiles make an ideal floor surface for a hallway, where mud and dirt will inevitably be brought in from the garden on boots or bicycles. More practical for outside, paving stones have been used on the patio.

Initial considerations
Before you reach a decision about what flooring you are going to use, think about your budget realistically. You should always buy the best floor you can possibly afford, as it needs to stand up to hard wear. If you have any problems, call in the expert. Always ask for advice when buying, and don't be tempted to lay a floor yourself if it is beyond your capabilities, or is a flooring which should really be professionally laid.

Preparation
All floors should be level, clean, smooth and damp-proof before any new flooring is installed or laid on top. Sometimes it may be necessary to put a floor-levelling compound (sometimes called a screed) on top of the existing floor. These are mixed on site and poured over the floor, and are self-levelling. They may be professionally laid, but there are some do-it-yourself types available. One type can be 'feathered' at the edges and is particularly suitable when a subfloor is very uneven, or where there are likely to be problems at skirtings and doors.

If the floor is in very poor condition (after the removal of old ceramic tiles for example) or after damp-proofing, it may need to be re-screeded. There are various types available, from a basic cement sand screed, to a special tough mixture (more frequently used in commercial properties), and some of the compounds are classed as screeds. Screeds are best professionally laid.

Old floorboards, and some other floors can be covered with hardboard, chipboard or plywood to make them smooth, level and draught-proof. These should be of flooring grade and the hardboard should be tempered – lay the shiny side down, rough side uppermost as this provides a better grip for the new flooring. They should be screwed down to existing floorboards, or may be stuck down in some situations, to prevent movement, and the joins should be sealed. These boards can all be decorated, and used as flooring, softened by rugs.

Damp-proofing floors
If the subfloor is damp, this must be cured before any new flooring is laid on top, otherwise the damp could affect the new surface, or, in the case of some hard flooring, may creep up the walls.

Installing a proper DPC (damp-proof course), if there is none, is the most effective method. Some houses (pre-1920) were built without a DPC, but in old properties the damp-proof course may simply be in a poor state and need professional attention. Any old, damp, crumbling or rotting floors will have to be removed and replaced.

There are various damp-proof membranes which can be put down. Some are poured on as liquid and left to harden; others are in sheet form and some are painted on. There are also various vapour barriers available, which are recommended for use with some floorings (e.g. rubber).

Damp-proofing should be professionally done, so call in the experts, but remember to discuss with them the type of flooring you plan to install, so you get the correct damp-proof membrane laid first.

HARD FLOORS

These are the most durable floor types, and stand up to wear and tear and heavy traffic. Many properties already have good hard floors in situ, such as floorboards, ceramic or quarry tiles, stone, parquet or woodblock, old flagstones, slate, even marble.

Most existing hard floors can be refurbished if necessary. Wood can be stripped, sanded, stained (if need be) and re-sealed. Ceramic and quarry tiles can be replaced carefully (old cracked ones may be difficult to get out) and re-grouted if necessary. Most ceramic tiles have a permanently glazed surface, but some quarries are porous, and can be sealed. Slate may need a special dressing – badly scratched marble can be repolished. Old flagstones and brick may be crumbling, but it is a pity to lose their texture and quality, so only seal (or paint) if absolutely necessary. Some of these floors are not very practical to install from scratch because of expense.

New hard floors must be laid on the correct subfloor, which must be smooth, level, clean, free from bumps and indentations and damp-proof. All hard floors can be covered with rugs, rush matting, etc, so think carefully before covering them up. Don't polish underneath rugs on a hard surface, and make sure they have a non-slip backing if necessary.

Some cement/concrete floors can be painted (as can floorboards) to make them look attractive. It is best to use a special industrial floor paint, or a boat (deck) paint.

Bricks/paving bricks

Not used for indoor floors nowadays, but may be found in some older properties on the ground floor in the hall/kitchen/utility area, where they may have been laid directly on the earth. More usually found outside, for patios and paths; or can be used to floor greenhouses, conservatories and garden room extensions. The bricks come in a variety of tones, so patterns may be laid (border effects) using several different colours, and as they are usually rectangular (brick) shaped, it is possible to lay interesting patterns such as herringbone. Nowadays it is more usual to bed in mortar, and as bricks are heavy, the subfloor must be firm, dry and level. Brick and paving bricks can be handled by the amateur.

Cleaning Bricks are porous, so may be sealed, in which case they can be mopped over with a damp mop. Unsealed bricks simply need sweeping. Some people polish brick, but it seems a pity to spoil the texture in this way.

Ceramic and quarry tiles

These are hard, cold and noisy underfoot, but stand up to heavy wear exceptionally well. They are impervious to water and most chemicals, so spills can be mopped up immediately – ceramics can be slippery when wet.

There is a wide range of colours and designs available, many of them imported from the Continent (especially Italy) and some are made in interesting, interlocking shapes. Size and thickness varies, but floor tiles are always thicker and heavier, and often larger than wall tiles. Always make sure the tiles are flooring grade before putting them down – some manufacturers make a universal tile which can be used for both.

All tiles are heavy, so must be laid on a solid concrete floor, or on specially reinforced suspended timber floors (they can be covered with flooring grade chipboard, screwed down). The subfloor must be perfectly flat (otherwise the tiles could move when walked on, and crack), damp-proof and clean. If you plan to lay heavy tiles upstairs check that the joists are strong enough to take the extra weight.

Most tiles can be laid by an amateur, but this is only wise if you are fairly experienced. It is best to call in the expert, as ceramic tiles are expensive, and many suppliers quote a price which includes laying.

If you plan to use ceramic or quarry tiles in a conservatory, where there is a lot of glass, and the temperature is likely to be extreme, consider using frost-proof tiles. These *must* be used on outdoor patios – some manufacturers will frost-proof any of their flooring tiles to order, and some have special frost-proof ranges.

Cleaning Most ceramic and quarry tiles only need mopping over. Some quarry tiles are porous, so may need cleaning with a proprietary cleaner. They can be 'dressed' or sealed to make them less porous, or may be polished with a special tile polish. Use the manufacturer's recommended treatment.

Floorboards

Most properties already have well-fitting floorboards, upstairs and downstairs (in pre-1940 houses). These are hard and can be noisy underfoot, but stand up to wear and tear so long as they are properly sealed. It is important to make sure there are no gaps or cracks between the boards, otherwise they can be draughty. Most sealed boards are fairly impervious to water and stains, but spills should be mopped up immediately.

Old floorboards can be sanded professionally or by the amateur (sanders can be hired). They are then stained if necessary, and sealed, or they can be treated with a stain-and-sealer in one, although this may need more than one coat. There are some very attractive and subtle coloured stains available, which can be used to stencil floorboards, or pattern them in interesting ways. Floorboards can also be painted, using a good quality paint or a special floor or boat paint. Or they can be treated decoratively by the various techniques such as marbling, tortoiseshelling, etc, and can also be painted to simulate a carpet or rug design. If a gloss surface is not required, a coat or two of matt wood sealer can be used over the top of the paint.

If the boards are in good condition, this is an economical way of flooring a room, and rugs or rush matting can be used to deaden noise and give a warmer, softer effect (make sure they won't slip).

Cleaning Sealed wood can be wiped over with a damp cloth. Floorboards can be polished (take care not to make them too slippery) or just sealed. When they get very dirty, old polish/seal will have to be removed and the boards re-sealed and/or polished. In very bad cases, the floor will have to be sanded back to the original wood.

Marble

Though not used very much for flooring today, as it is very expensive, marble is a superbly elegant and hard-wearing surface, impervious to water and stains. Most marble has its own built-in shine (pre-polished before laying) although some is polished after laying.

Like ceramic and quarry tiles, marble is very heavy so needs a strong subfloor, and should be laid on a solid concrete screed, which is perfectly smooth and level.

Some marble comes in square blocks, in a variety of sizes and thicknesses, but it is also available in strip and shaped form, so inlaid patterns can be created. Some slabs have special ribbed backs to make laying easier, but it is not a DIY

HARD FLOORS

job-call in the professional. Marble is cold and unyielding underfoot, although it can be combined with underfloor central heating which takes the chill off (but remember if the heating system goes wrong, the floor may have to come up). Marble floors can be softened with rugs, but again make sure they have non-slip backs.

Cleaning Marble should only need wiping over with a damp floor mop, but it can be cleaned with a special proprietary cleaner if very dirty. Never use harsh abrasives. Very badly scuffed marble can be re-polished professionally.

Mosaics

Traditionally made of glass or sometimes marble. There are also some ceramic mosaics available, both glazed or porous (terracotta type). Individual mosaics are usually small – about 2.5cm (1in.) square and are slightly irregular in shape. The design possibilities are endless, because of the wide range of colours and textures. You can create a picture with mosaic because it is such a flexible material, and there are specialist suppliers who will do the design work, pre-cast the mosaics into sections, and then install them on site.

Mosaic tends to be rough underfoot, fairly harsh and inflexible, but very hard-wearing. It is fairly heavy, and needs a good level, damp-proof subfloor – usually mosaic has to be laid on concrete or on a specially treated latex subfloor.

Some mosaics come on a paper backing. But this is less flexible and not very easy to handle. There is also a mesh backing, which allows room for manoeuvre, but does not allow for such

interesting design possibilities. These can be self-laid.

Cleaning Usually only needs sweeping and occasional wiping over with a damp mop, but can be washed with water and a mild detergent. The glazed type should not be polished – the porous type can be sealed and/or polished.

Slate

A natural material, usually greyish-green in colour, although there are some other tones available (mauvish and reddish brown). Like marble and tiles slate is very heavy, so needs a firm subfloor. It can be quarried in random shapes, but is more usually sold as square or rectangular paving slabs.

Slate is hard-wearing, though cold and inflexible underfoot, but it can be softened with rugs or matting. Professional laying is recommended. It may be left natural, polished, or have a riven (textured) finish to make it non-slip, as it can be slippery when wet, and is impervious to water – any spills should be mopped up immediately.

Slate must be laid on a cement or concrete base, and may be sealed, if necessary (not the pre-polished type) after laying with a special sealer, or water-based emulsion polish.

Cleaning Usually only needs sweeping, but it can be polished, or it may be treated with linseed oil.

Stone

Hardly ever used for domestic interior flooring nowadays, although some older properties may have stone floors in the kitchen, basement or hall area. If using stone outside, check that it is frost-proof. Stone comes in many different natural and local types – York stone, Portland stone, sandstone, granite,

limestone etc, and there are many reconstituted paving slabs available, as well as stone or granite chippings mixed with cement to form a slab. There are different colours, shapes, sizes and thicknesses. Square and oblong are the more usual shapes, but there are some decoratively shaped and interlocking ones available.

Stone can be very hard and inflexible underfoot, but is extremely hard-wearing, and most types are impervious to water, although the porous type can crumble away unless properly sealed. An ideal material for patios, paths, greenhouses and conservatories, but may also be used in porches and possibly entrance halls.

Stone is very heavy, and needs a strong subfloor. It is usually laid on a concrete subfloor, or in a bed of cement. It need not necessarily be professionally laid, particularly outdoors.

Cleaning Sweeping, washing, even scrubbing are all ways of cleaning stone, and if it is used outside, cleaning with an anti-fungicidal product may be necessary occasionally. If the porous type is to be sealed, use a proprietary sealer, but it may change the colour so check on a spare slab first.

Terrazzo

A material which is heavy, hard-wearing and fairly inflexible underfoot. It usually comes as large slabs or tiles, made from marble chippings and dust set in cement, coloured and ground smooth. There are also

polymeric terrazzos made from marble aggregate set in a polyester resin which is a slightly more flexible material and so softer underfoot.

Terrazzo comes in a range of colours – traditional marble shades, pastel and deep tones, as well as some metallic effects. Conventional terrazzo must be laid on a screed subfloor, but some of the lighter weight polymeric types can be laid on a suspended floor as long as it can take the weight, and is perfectly smooth and flat, otherwise movement could cause cracking.

Terrazzo laying is a specialist job, particularly as expansion strips may have to be installed round the edge of a room, or where two areas of flooring meet, and it also has to be professionally polished after laying.

Cleaning Sweep, mop with a damp cloth or wash with a mild detergent. If terrazzo becomes pitted or scratched, it may need repolishing professionally.

Wood surfaces

Most of these surfaces, whether wood block, mosaic, hardwood strip or parquet, are warm, and fairly resilient underfoot, but can be noisy. They stand up to heavy traffic and, like floorboards, are fairly impervious to water and stains, so long as they are sealed and/or polished. Spills should be mopped up at once, as they can cause wood to warp, and may cause water-marking or staining.

There are many different types of decorative wooden flooring available, and price varies enormously, according to quality and finish. Many are interlocking, and different patterns can be made – and various coloured woods of the same flooring grade can be used together to create

SEMI-HARD FLOORS

a more interesting finish. The colours are mostly natural, but there is a wide range of woods from which to choose, including some stained (coloured) floors.

Some types should be professionally laid, and may need a complicated finishing process once down, but there are many DIY kits (including self-adhesive) which are not too difficult for the competent amateur to handle.

The subfloor must be sound, level and free from damp, but this type of flooring can be laid on top of floorboards, so long as no movement is likely to take place, which could cause the warping of the new floor (latex compound or flooring grade chipboard may be used first). Some types must be laid on a solid concrete floor (usually the professional type). Wooden floors look very effective when decorated with rugs but make sure they have a non-slip backing or alternatively don't polish underneath.

Cleaning Once laid and sealed, sweeping and mopping may be all that is needed, but re-sealing and/or polishing may be necessary. If this type of flooring becomes very stained or pitted, it may be possible to strip and sand smooth, but not on very thin grades. Always avoid the use of harsh abrasives.

Although not as durable as truly hard floors, semi-hard surfaces will stand up to fairly heavy wear and tramping feet. They are usually fixed to the subfloor, so are not easily removable, but more so than any of the hard floors.

In some cases, it may be possible to cover a semi-hard floor with a different type of flooring – either loose-laid, stuck down, or pinned into position, or it may be advisable to cover a semi-hard floor with a latex compound before putting another type of flooring on top. If in doubt, seek expert advice. As with any type of flooring, the subfloor must be clean, smooth, level, dry, free from bumps and indentations and damp-proof before the semi-hard floor is laid.

The subfloor
Poor boards and some other subfloors can be covered with flooring grade chipboard, tempered hardboard or flooring grade plywood, before a semi-hard floor is laid. In most cases they should be screwed down to the original floorboards, or stuck to the subfloor, to prevent any movement, as this eventually works through the top layer of flooring causing it to crack.

Hardboard and ply flooring
These flooring grade boards can also be used on their own as semi-hard floors. Make sure the joins are sealed, always lay hardboard rough side downwards, and finish any of these materials for permanent use by painting, sealing with a polyurethane varnish (gloss, semi-matt and matt); they can be stained before sealing, in natural or bright colours. Polish can also be used after sealing and they can be softened with rugs, matting or carpet squares.

Cork tiles
These are warm and fairly bouncy underfoot. They stand up to heavy traffic so long as they are properly sealed, and they provide natural insulation and are quiet to walk on.

Most cork tiles come in natural golden-brown and gold tones, but there are some coloured corks available, where a coloured base 'grins' through the top sliver of cork; there is also a pastel white tile with a milky look and cork texture.

Cork tiles come in a range of sizes, and some different shapes, but are usually square or rectangular. They can be laid to form a pattern, using different colours and tones.

When properly sealed, cork is impervious to water and spills, although they should be mopped up immediately. The pre-sealed type are best for kitchens and bathrooms where water spills are inevitable – the seal-after-laying type are suitable for other areas. If cork is not properly sealed, water causes it to swell and the tiles push up.

The floor is usually slip-resistant, even when wet, and can be softened by rugs, carpet squares or matting. It should be laid on a smooth, level, dry subfloor, and is usually stuck down using a special adhesive. If floorboards are uneven, they should first be covered with hardboard or flooring grade chipboard, otherwise the movement of the tiles will eventually cause them to split.

Cork can be easily laid by the amateur, and cutting round objects is simple with a small file and knife or pair of scissors.

Cleaning Cork should only need mopping over – never saturate with water. A special dressing may be applied occasionally and tiles can be re-sealed if they begin to look worn and tired, although all the old seal will have to be removed first.

Linoleum
Considered old-fashioned for some time, linoleum is now making a comeback. It is immensely hard-wearing, flexible, fairly quiet and bouncy underfoot. It is available in a good range of muted colours, mostly with a marbled effect. It also has the advantage of design possibilities, as individual patterns, motifs and border effects can be cut in, creating an inlaid design.

There are several thicknesses (gauges) available, and the thicker the material the harder wearing it is, and the quieter. It comes in sheet form, in several widths, and also as tiles. The sheet form, particularly in a wide width, can be difficult to handle and is best professionally laid. The tile form (which should also be stuck down using special adhesive) can be easily laid by the amateur.

Lino can be slippery when wet, and although it is water- and stain-resistant, spills should be mopped up at once. It needs to be laid on a smooth, dry, level subfloor; floorboards, which move, can cause the linoleum to crack, so the floor should be covered with hardboard or flooring grade chipboard. It can be sealed and polished, but make sure they are non-slip or the floor is not polished underneath them.

Cleaning Mop over occasionally, wipe if necessary with a mild detergent. Re-polish (with wax polish) if necessary or seal with a special dressing, supplied by the manufacturer.

SEMI-HARD/SOFT FLOORS

Rubber

A combination of natural and synthetic material, rubber is becoming more popular in domestic situations, although it is still predominantly used in contract and industrial work.

Rubber comes as tiles, in sheet form, and with interesting textures which make it very tough and non-slip. Stair nosings and narrow tiles are also available, so staircases can be covered with rubber. Rubber is hardwearing, bouncy and quiet underfoot, and stain-resistant; any spills should be mopped up at once, because water causes rubber to perish – it is also affected by oils, acids and very strong sunlight.

Rubber is available in muted and strong colours, sometimes with a slightly marbled effect – the heavily textured studded or ribbed strongly coloured form is particularly suitable for high tech interiors.

Rubber must be laid on a smooth, level, damp-proof subfloor, and ideally with a built-in vapour barrier, otherwise any condensation could cause the tiles to push up. Welded rubber makes a particularly practical seamless floor, but there must not be any damp underneath, so a vapour barrier is essential. It should be laid by a professional.

Cleaning   Can be washed with a mild detergent, but it should never be allowed to become saturated, or it will perish and push up. The clean floor should be re-sealed with a special dressing, made by the manufacturer, or it can be buffed. Avoid harsh abrasives.

Thermoplastic tiles

There are two types of thermoplastic tiles – the thin, brittle and fairly harsh underfoot type and the slightly more flexible type which crack less easily. They tend to be fairly noisy. Cracked or broken tiles can be replaced, although this is not an easy job. They are often found throughout the ground floor in newly built properties (although less frequently these days). They are stain- and water-resistant, but can be slippery when wet. Spills should be mopped up immediately.

Colours are usually muted and the tiles generally have a slightly marbled effect, with streaks of white, grey or black. Sizes vary, and there are several thicknesses available, although they tend to be very thin. The large type are usually laid by builders, but the smaller tiles can be laid by do-it-yourself enthusiasts.

The subfloor should be smooth, dry, firm and flat, and the tiles are stuck down, using a special adhesive. In some cases it is recommended that they are laid on a vapour barrier, so they will be put down on a bitumen screed. They can be laid on floorboards, so long as any movement is controlled by covering the floor with flooring grade chipboard or hardboard first.

Cleaning   Most thermoplastic tiles can be mopped regularly, scrubbed if necessary, and then sealed. They can be polished or treated with a special dressing. Build-up should be removed occasionally and the surface will have to be re-treated.

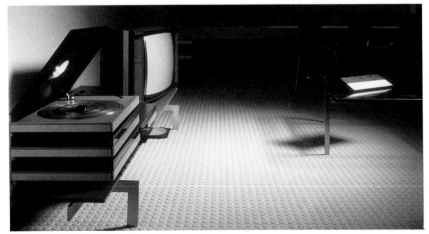

Soft floor coverings come in many types, shapes and sizes, and are frequently laid on top of hard, semi-hard or semi-soft floorings. Some are loose-laid, but others (such as fitted carpet and carpet tiles, and some mattings) can be fully fitted directly over the subfloor, so long as it is smooth, clean, dry, level and damp-proof.

Most popular is carpet, which comes in a wide range of types, styles, colours and prices. Some carpet is woven, but other types are tufted, and some are 'felted'. Carpets are also made in a range of different fibres and mixtures of fibres, and it is the pile fibre (or blend of fibres) which affects performance and wear. Some carpets are produced as 'squares' (which are rarely square, usually rectangular) with bound or fringed edges, for loose-laying. There are also carpet tiles which are made in as many different ways as carpet. Rugs are discussed separately on page 286.

Carpets

Carpets come in many different types with wide-ranging price tags, and can be constructed in several different ways. They can also be made from several different fibres, or blends of fibre. Carpet should be chosen for the situation in which it will be laid, and the type of wear it will receive. Generally speaking, the more expensive the carpet, the greater will be the density of the pile; and the more natural the fibre (wool or a wool and synthetic blend), the longer lasting and harder wearing it will be – but not always. As a guide to carpet buying, always look on the back – the label (if the manufacturer is a reputable one) will tell you the grade (A,B,C,D,E,F) and performance rating. It will also tell you the fibre content, method of construction and widths available, and some may give laying instructions. All carpets produced by members of the British Carpet Manufacturers' Association will carry this type of label.

With any type of carpet, always buy the best quality you can possibly afford, for the situation for which it is intended, and use the hardest wearing quality for the areas of heavy traffic – the hall, stairs and landing and

family living rooms in most houses.

Some carpets should be professionally laid, and this includes most fitted carpet, and particularly stair carpet (unless you plan to use stair rods or grippers), but some of the tufted, felted, cord and carpet tiles can be laid by the amateur. If you are having a carpet professionally laid, always insist on an itemized estimate, to ascertain whether underfelt is included or not. Also discuss where the seams should fall to avoid heavy wear.

Never, ever be tempted to lay new carpet on old underfelt, or on top of an old carpet – the previous wear pattern quickly shows through the face of the new carpet.

Carpet types

Traditionally carpets are woven.

Axminster carpet   This is usually patterned, with a wide choice of colours within the design. The pile yarn is seen only on the surface and the carpet will have a jute or hessian backing, which may be strengthened by polypropylene. Widths vary up to broadloom 5m (16ft 5in.) but Axminsters can come as carpet 'squares' and rugs too. Fibre

SOFT FLOORS

content can be all wool, a wool and synthetic fibre blend or all synthetic.

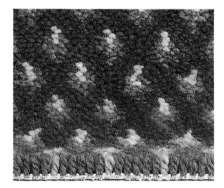

Wilton carpet Usually plain, although some patterned Wiltons (with a restricted number of colours) are produced. The pile is close-textured, and can be smooth and velvety, looped, looped and twisted, or a combination of pile textures creating a sculptured or 'carved' effect. Any yarn not used on the surface is woven into the backing to give added strength and thickness. The backing is as Axminster, and fibre content can be all wool, wool and synthetic fibre blend or synthetic.

Widths are available from 67.5cm (27in.) to 1.8m (6ft) which usually have to be seamed to fit a room fully, but broadloom widths of up to 3.6m (12ft) are also produced, and there are some Wilton 'squares' available with bound or fringed ends.

Tufted carpet Now the most commonly used type of carpet, which comes in a wide range of colours, textures and fibres – and blends of fibres. The tufts are woven into the backing and then anchored into position with a latex (or similar) solution. The carpet is then given another backing such as good quality foam (so an underlay is not necessary) or a traditional woven kind. Many rugs and special carpet designs are made this way by hand, with a hand-tufting 'gun'. Widths vary from 90cm (3ft) to 5m (16ft 5in.).

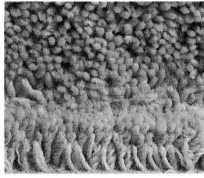

Bonded carpet This type is made face-to-face like a sandwich. The 'filling' is the carpet pile, held between the two specially treated woven backings. When the pile is sliced through its middle you get two bonded carpets. All the carpet pile is on the surface, and this type of carpet is usually hard-wearing. Fibres can be of any type, but are usually synthetic. Widths are

usually broadloom, up to 5m (16ft 5in.). Bonded carpet is generally plain with a velour texture.

Needlefelt or needlepunch carpet Made by needling a fibrous mass by machine into a strong backing, this type of carpet can be plain, textured, mottled, or printed with a design, and the backing is usually foam. The surface looks like dense felt or very fine corduroy. Widths vary, and this method is often used for making carpet tiles.

Carpet fibres

Nowadays there are many different fibres and blends of fibres used in carpet construction. They all give their own distinctive character to the finished carpet, and affect its durability and resistance to staining. Many synthetic fibres, for example, are very hard-wearing and stain-resistant, but they lack natural resilience, and so tend to flatten after a few months. This is why many carpet manufacturers now blend a natural and a synthetic fibre together to give the best of both worlds – an 80/20 mix of wool and nylon for example, is a very popular blend.

Natural fibres

Natural fibre in carpets generally means wool, although occasionally it can mean cotton

Wool Hard-wearing, soil- and flame-resistant, easy to maintain and resilient, wool has a natural warmth and good acoustic and insulation properties.

Some carpets are made up from 100% wool pile – others may be a blend of wool and synthetic fibres in various proportions.

Cotton This is rarely found in carpets (except occasionally as part of a blend), but is found in some imported carpet 'squares' and rugs, but it is often long, looped and twisted. It is hard-wearing, easy to maintain and washable.

Synthetic fibres

There are several different types of synthetic fibre used in carpet production. They may be used alone, or blended with a natural fibre, or several synthetic fibres can be used together. Most synthetic fibres do not absorb liquids readily.

Acrylic fibre This has the characteristics which most closely resemble wool, so it is popular as a carpet fibre, as 100% Acrilan pile, or occasionally in a blend. Carpets made from this fibre are easy to care for, hard-wearing and, because acrylic fibre dyes well, come in some rich and beautiful colours. Acrylic fibres do stain, but can be specially treated to resist soiling.

Nylon Used under many brand names, nylon is very durable and easy to clean. It has good abrasion resistance, is now soil-resistant, and can also be specially treated to resist staining. It is frequently mixed with wool in carpets.

Polyester A fibre generally used for light weight and medium wear carpets. It soils fairly quickly and cannot always be restored to its original appearance if allowed to become very dirty. It is best used in a combination with other fibres, such as nylon.

Polypropylene Fairly hard-wearing, stain-resistant and easy to clean, is found in cords, twists and velours as well as being used for needlefelt carpets and carpet tiles. Can feel rather harsh and tends to look shiny.

Viscose and modified viscose Not very hard-wearing, unless it has a very dense pile. It is sometimes blended with other fibres to give a soft, silky texture. It can stain and flatten, but is easy to clean.

Carpet tiles

Carpet tiles come in a range of sizes, and are usually square, plain-coloured or patterned. They can be made in any of the same ways as carpet and from the same fibres or blends of fibres.

Most carpet tiles are loose laid, although it may be necessary to stick them down round the edge of the room and at doorways. This can be done using a heavy-duty double-sided tape, especially intended for carpet laying. Some people prefer to stick the tiles down, which can be done with adhesive as well as with tape, but this rather defeats the object. They can be moved round to even out wear, and can be taken up individually for cleaning. Carpet tiles can be easily laid by the amateur. There are special carpet tiles available for use in kitchens, which will withstand grease and oil spills, but it is still wise to buy a few spare tiles.

SEMI-SOFT FLOORS/RUGS

Although there are some very hard-wearing vinyls available, some of these floorings may be less durable than harder ones. Some are stuck to the subfloor, but other types can be loose-laid, and are called 'lay flat' products. Some are lightly fixed at doorways or round the perimeter of the room, and in certain cases the flooring can be stapled down.

As with any flooring, the subfloor must be smooth, level and damp-proof, but most of the flexible semi-soft floors will mould themselves to the subfloor and so movement is not crucial, and a rigid surface is not essential. They are all resilient underfoot and fairly quiet which makes them good for use upstairs as well as down.

Cushioned vinyl

Because it has little air bubbles trapped between the wear layer and the glass-fibre reinforced backing, cushioned vinyl is bouncy underfoot. It comes in sheet form, although there are a few tiles available, and in several widths which allows for a completely seamless floor, in all but the largest rooms. It is warm and quiet underfoot.

There are many different colours, designs and effects available, from modern graphic designs, to simulated ceramic and woodblock, and some have a built-in shine. Most vinyl can be laid by the amateur, although very wide widths can be difficult to handle, so professional help may be necessary.

Some types should be stuck to the subfloor, but others are 'lay flat', and only need fixing at doorways, or round the edges, and at joins – also sticking down is recommended where heavy appliances are likely to be moved around frequently.

There are several different grades of cushioned vinyl, from very inexpensive to fairly costly. The most expensive is a very durable quality, specially formulated for heavy wear areas.

This flooring is waterproof and resistant to oil, grease and most household chemicals, and the cushioned type is not slippery when wet, but spills should be mopped up at once.

Cleaning Mopping or wiping over with a damp cloth regularly keeps the floor clean, but it can be washed with a mild detergent. Any scuff or black marks can be removed by rubbing gently with a fine nylon scouring pad moistened with polish. An acrylic polish can be used as extra protection.

Sheet vinyl and vinyl tiles

There are several different types of sheet vinyl and vinyl tile. The most popular sort is the cushioned vinyl (see above) but there is a thinner, non-cushioned form available as sheet and tiles, which tends to be rather more brittle.

Sheet vinyl and tiles are less bouncy underfoot than the cushioned type, more slippery when wet, and in some cases less hard-wearing. The sheet type comes in a wide range of colours and patterns, and is available in various different widths.

Vinyl tiles come in a very wide range of types, styles and sizes; some of the more expensive quality ones have interesting textures and simulate brick, terrazzo and ceramic. There are good ranges of plain colours, mostly flat colour, but with a marbled or stippled effect.

Some sheet and vinyl tiles should be laid by the professional as they always need sticking down on a level, smooth, clean, damp-proof floor, but there are several DIY types available, including tiles with a special peel-and-stick backing, and 'lay flat' sheet vinyls.

Cleaning Mop over regularly with a damp cloth, and wash when necessary with a mild detergent. Tiles and sheet form can be sealed with a special sealer – be guided by the manufacturer – and an acrylic polish can be used as extra protection.

Covering a complex and diverse range of cultures, materials and patterns, rugs can bewilder and confuse the uninitiated.

At the simplest level rugs provide decoration for the floor, breaking up the flatness of a plain carpet or other floor-covering, providing a point of focus and defining small areas in large rooms. Here, the choice of rug is often based upon aesthetic preferences – you might, for example, opt for the pretty pastel colours of an Indian dhurrie or feel that a pile rug is warmer than a flatweave. New rugs, in this case, are cheaper than their antique counterparts, and many shops now import wide ranges of modern dhurries, kilims and other eastern rugs. Sometimes these are in traditional patterns but increasingly can be found woven to incorporate western design influences – not always very successfully.

Rugs should always be laid over a non-slip underfelt which not only eases their wear, but will help to avoid accidents on slippery floors. A few of the more commonly found rug types are as follows.

Persian rugs Made of silk or wool, these are knotted by hand on to a firmly woven base. They are considered to be some of the finest and most beautiful examples of rug making ever produced, and have been revered by the western world since the 15th century. Much of their fascination might be attributed to the fact that they are the expression of an attitude to life which is almost totally alien to our own.

There are many different areas of origin for what are collectively known as 'Persian' rugs, but even for a novice, they are instantly recognizable; the rich colours, classical designs and high density of knots to the square inch set them apart from almost every other type of rug.

Kurdish kilim A brightly coloured flatweave rug, woven by nomadic tribes from wool; often soft and blanket-like. The most common form of weaving technique is the slitweave, formed by wefts of differing colours. Each time the colour changes a slit is formed in the rug – in older examples where the weave has become looser, this produces an almost lacey effect.

Often the designs in the Kurdish kilim are embroidered over the top – a technique known as Soumak. In modern examples the traditional designs – mihrabs, trees of life and lozenges – are sometimes enlivened at the weaver's whim with the addition of buses, cars and curious little animals and figures.

Afghan kelim These are woven, like the Kurdish kilim, in wool, but are generally tougher, thicker and more hard-wearing. The colours are sombre, making great use of rust, magenta, yellow, brown and blue, and there tends to be less pattern than in the Kurdish kilim – the Afghans are not afraid of producing rugs with a plain ground.

Coming from two distinct regions, Baluchistan and the northwest of Afghanistan, they are easily distinguished. Rugs woven by the Balouch tribes are decorated with exceptionally intricate embroidery work. Rugs from the northwest are woven by Turkoman people, often with the slitweave technique, and are brighter in colour with a mix of orange and purple and green.

Dhurrie Exclusively from India, a flat-weave rug made entirely of cotton. It has seen an enormous revival in popularity recently, so much so that modern dhurries are now widely available in pretty pastel colours, and at relatively inexpensive prices.

However, none of these modern examples are as fine as the late 19th century dhurries with their bold geometric designs and use of few colours. The decision by the Indian government, effectively banning the exportation of antique dhurries has increased not only their attraction but their worth.

Berber Also called Hanbels, these are tribal rugs from the Atlas mountains in Morocco. Although woven by the Berber tribes, who nominally fell subject to Islam about 1200 years ago, these rugs are quite distinct from the mainstream of Islamic influence. Used as floor coverings and communal family blankets, the rugs show a vitality of colour, pattern and texture that makes them quite easily recognizable. The choice of colours – usually scarlet, yellow, blue and green – stems from the vegetable dyes available to each tribe.

1 In a rustic house, where the only wall decoration is an impressive collection of flatweave rugs, a Monestir rug from Turkey hangs above the bed.

2 On a gable wall, another Turkish rug.

3 On the opposite wall, a pale brown and blue Thracian rug.

4 A fringed Turkestan rug.

5 Hung horizontally and close to the floor, a beautiful Bachtiari rug.

6 In contrast to the traditional patterns of the wall-hung rugs, this cotton dhurrie, in a completely different setting, has been made by similar craftsmen but to a western design.

WALLS

Walls, like floors, can form a visual backdrop for furnishings and fabrics, but they are no less significant in determining the character of a room. They not only define the space, but also present the largest surface area in the room, and therefore what you cover or colour them with is important. Whatever decoration you choose for your walls, it should stand up well to wear, and not be so hideously expensive that you cannot change it occasionally as tastes alter.

Paint and wallpaper are still the quickest and most common methods for redecorating old rooms and giving new ones a touch of style. But these are by no means the only two solutions; numerous alternatives exist, especially in the guise of wallcoverings which, until recently, were restricted to factory and contract use. Paint effects, such as dragging, marbling, rag-rolling, sponging, stippling and tortoise-shelling, are currently fashionable and easy to achieve without being too expensive. (See the chapter on Do-It-Yourself for information on these techniques.)

Before rushing into any decisions, live in the room for a while to get the feel of it and think how you can make the best of its proportions. If you are unable to decide what covering or colour will be most appropriate for the room, try painting the walls off-white or one of the wide range of tinted whites now available. A neutral background for your furniture, fabrics and pictures is often a good step towards reaching a final decision.

When considering the walls, don't exclude skirtings, mouldings, architraves and ceiling roses, which you might want to play down or alternatively to emphasize. They are particularly useful if you need to adjust the room's proportions visually; if, for example, you wish to give the impression of lowering a very high ceiling, adding height to a low ceiling, or widening a narrow room.

1 Painting the door, skirting and wall the same shade of pale pink makes them all appear to recede, highlighting the oak beams and rich colours of the oil painting.

2 Sue Ridge's cleverly positioned and beautifully executed mural, giving a real sense of being able to walk outside.

3 Corridor walls painted a neutral colour and used as gallery space for a series of colourful, large-scale canvases.

4 A mixture of rough textured walls — achieved by painting over tissue paper — and delicate paint tones provides a cheap transformation.

As with floors, practical considerations must come before decisions on colour and texture.

Condition of existing walls

Before you start your decoration programme, first check whether your walls are structurally sound, and if not, undertake any necessary building work at this stage.

Damp Make sure that any property you buy is properly surveyed; a surveyor should locate damp if it exists. But it is worth your while to double check every wall (even inside cupboards) to see if they are dry.

If you are having a conversion or alterations done, this is the time to sort out any damp problems rather than tackling them later or covering them up and pretending they don't exist. Staining on a wall or ceiling is the clue for damp. If you are lucky the stain will be an old one and the problem already solved. But find out what the underlying cause is before trying to deal with it.

All new plasterwork must be allowed to dry thoroughly before you cover it with anything.

Types of walls

The type of covering you choose for your walls – and any treatment they may need before decoration – depends on what kind of walls you are dealing with. Are they brick, new plaster, old plaster, plasterboard or wood panelling?

Brick Check brick carefully for damp. Also look to see whether the mortar needs pointing. Brick walls, like floors, can be sealed, painted, or panelled.

New plaster Leave new plaster untreated and allow it to dry thoroughly before paint or any type of wallcovering is applied. Ideally plaster in a new house should be allowed to dry for a year. Small replastered areas can be painted with emulsion after three to four weeks.

Old plaster Usually suitable for paint and most wallcoverings, old plaster must, however, be checked for cracks, damp, and places which need replastering entirely. You can tell if plaster is 'floating' by tapping the wall with your knuckles. A change in the

sound from a dead noise to a hollow one indicates an area of plaster that is coming away from the wall. Uneven plaster can be covered with lining paper to provide a smoother surface for paint; this should be butt jointed.

Plasterboard This must be sealed and then primed or treated with a combined primer/sealer, before it is painted or wallpapered.

Wood panelling The possibilities offered by wood panelled walls are greatest of all. They can be stripped, sanded, sealed, stained or painted. Make sure there's no grease, dirt and old varnish that should be removed first.

Materials

When buying materials, don't just think in terms of initial outlay; whatever you buy, make sure that it is good quality – poor materials will only need replacing or require constant maintenance, costing you more in the long run.

The vast range of DIY products available may be tempting in terms of cost and labour-saving, but products do vary in standard. Find the best to suit your needs. Painting the walls yourself with good quality paint, which has more covering power, will save money on labour, and if you want to splash out on expensive finishes, why not restrict them to one area where they will be most appreciated both aesthetically and practically? Cash is not always the key factor. You may live in rented accommodation and be unwilling to spend money on or put effort into what you can't keep or take away with you, or you might like to ring the changes with your decoration fairly often.

Certain rooms' requirements are different from others and should be taken into account when it comes to decision time. Bathrooms, for example, tend to steam up, so use washable wallcoverings, such as ceramic tiles, mirror, vinyl, seamless plastic or plastic

1 Bare brickwork and beams, combined with contrasting clean white paint and highly finished gilt picture frames, give a warm, attractive finish to a country style room.

2 A mirrored alcove serves to increase light in a dark corner.

laminate (sometimes referred to as wallboard). Steam also builds up in kitchens, where there is the additional problem of grease, which forms particularly on ceilings and above cupboards where it is difficult to reach, so use tough oil-based paints or plastic emulsions, rubber, vinyl, ceramic tiles, or tongue and groove boarding. It is also more practical to use washable paint or wallpaper in corridors and children's rooms, where walls are particularly prone to stains and dirty finger marks.

Quantities

Measuring quantities for paint and wallcoverings can be tricky; sizes and amounts vary. Having measured the room, wall by wall, take account of the doors, skirtings, windows and ceiling. Make a room plan, and consult the instructions on the side of the paint can for coverage (also see the chart on page 292).

WALLCOVERINGS

Papers, tiles, laminates and panelling are the principal types of wallcovering. Their main advantage is that they add a textured finish to walls, giving them a depth that cannot be achieved with plain paint. However, not all coverings are as attractive as paint effects, and if you are undecided about which to use, opt for paint as it's easier to cover up if you find that you have made a disastrous mistake.

Wallpapers

The most common form of wallcovering, wallpaper comes in all kinds of patterns, textures, colours and finishes. Most wallpaper is made from a simple paper construction, and usually comes in standard rolls. If you have chosen a patterned paper, when measuring up, allow extra for the pattern repeat. Wallpaper is available both unpasted and ready-pasted.

Anaglypta   Made from wood pulp, Anaglypta is an embossed paper and as a result, provides a good, strong surface for covering cracked walls and ceilings. It usually needs to be painted. Decorative Anaglypta is also available, but the designs tend to be rather overblown. Other trade names of similar textured designs include Supaglypta, made from cotton linters, Vynaglypta, a paper-backed vinyl, and Worley Permabos, a blown vinyl. The vinyls are much easier to strip than Anaglypta or Supaglypta, although once painted, stripping becomes more difficult.

Foil   Silver-sprayed polyester on paper backing, it comes in rolls and is effective if you want to make small spaces seem larger without the expense of mirror.

Ingrain   Otherwise known as woodchip (or surveyor's nightmare) ingrain paper has a knobbly texture, and will hide cracks but not serious defects. It has to be painted with emulsion or oil-based paint, and once on is extremely difficult to remove.

Lincrusta   An embossed paper which simulates wood panelling, decorative plaster and tiles, etc. The relief patterns are embossed on a putty-like substance that's bonded to a paper backing and then allowed to harden. It needs to be painted with gloss or eggshell paint.

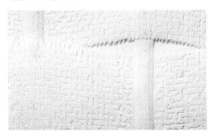

Lining paper   Although it won't cover up conspicuous defects, lining paper is the answer if your wall surface isn't perfect enough to paint directly. There is a special ceiling paper available for hiding hairline cracks.

Moiré silk paper   Giving the effect of this luxurious fabric, but in paper form.

Standard printed paper   Although unwashable and not as tough as washable or vinyl paper for example, standard wallpaper is available in a vast range of different designs, both manufactured and hand-printed (in which case it tends to be fiendishly expensive). Many manufacturers are now producing paint effect wallpapers, which create a similar impression, but with less effort involved.

Vinyl paper   Wallpaper with a vinyl surface is both waterproof and grease-resistant, and therefore ideal for kitchens and bathrooms.

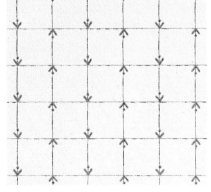

Woven textiles   These wallcoverings include cotton, flax, hessian, jute, silk and wool. The easiest to hang are backed with paper and ready pasted with adhesive. A boon in practical terms, they can be lightly cleaned with a sponge or vacuumed. Vinyl imitations of these effects are also available.

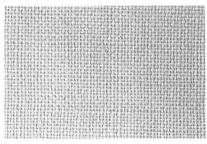

Tips

1   When working out how many rolls of wallpaper you need, remember to take into account the pattern repeat, if there is one.
2   Avoid cheap wallpaper as it will not wear well.
3   Always check the batch and shade numbers on rolls of wallpaper, as colours and patterns tend to vary slightly.
4   All wall surfaces must be fully prepared as with paints.
5   Always follow the manufacturers' instructions.

Alternative wallcoverings

A move in recent years towards using less conventional materials to cover walls has resulted in a situation today where there is practically no limit to the types of wallcoverings around from glass fibre to wood panelling.

Ceramic tiles   The second most popular wallcovering after standard printed paper, ceramic tiles are produced in a correspondingly large range. Hand-made or manufactured, textured, plain or patterned, glazed or unglazed, they are most suitable for areas that are bound to get wet, such as bathrooms, showers and kitchens, and especially for splashbacks. They are also made in different shapes and sizes, with matching border tiles, and in families of patterned and plain tiles.

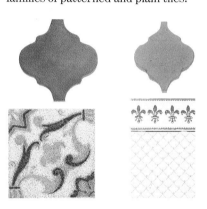

Cork   Available in tiles or sheets, and now in bright colours too, cork has many advantages. It doesn't show the dirt, but in any case is easily wiped down; it is a good insulating material, and also creates a feeling of warmth. If it has no protective coat, the cork will usually need to be sealed with polyurethane or wax polish.

Fabric   An increasingly popular wall-covering which embraces all types of fabric from plain canvas to highly patterned weaves. It has the tremendous advantage of concealing defective surfaces without the need for the wall to be made good or old wallcoverings to be stripped off. There are three main methods of fixing the fabric to the walls: pinning the fabric directly to the wall with a staple gun; covering panels of medium board or plywood with the fabric; and setting the fabric on battens–a slightly more involved process than the other two, but probably the best method for pattern matching. Make sure that the fabric you use is not likely to shrink or distort. It can be vacuum cleaned.

Felt   Tacked to softboard panelling that has been pinned to the wall, felt looks particularly good in children's rooms and can double as a pinboard. Use white ironing backing material for a more sophisticated effect, which is especially appropriate in studies. Some felt is paper-backed and can be hung like wallpaper. All felt is difficult to wash, and must be vacuumed down as it collects dust.

Glass fibre   Used to reinforce the wall surface, glass fibre gives a tough, durable finish. After the surface has been primed, an adhesive must be applied and then the lengths of glass fibre. It gives the impression of a woven textile.

Mirror   The most effective way of making a small room seem larger, mirror looks good if it covers a whole wall, especially in a bathroom or at the end of a narrow corridor. Mirror sheeting is heavy, so it has to be screwed into place, and expensive. Mirror tiles, which can be stuck with adhesive, provide a cheaper alternative. The only problem with these is that the wall needs to be completely flat, otherwise the image will be distorted. Usually you will have to line the walls with 18mm (¾in.) plywood, set on battens. Cheaper than either sheeting or tiles, however, is mirror film, which is applied like a vinyl wallcovering with adhesive, and has the same effect as mirror; it is also very light.

Plastic laminates   Corian and Formica are two of the most widely used plastic laminates. They are bought in rigid sheets and must be fixed by battens in the same manner as wood panelling. In small areas, adhesive can be used.

Polystyrene   A useful insulation material both for sound and heat, polystyrene is available in tiles and sheeting, and can be painted. It must be stuck on with non-flammable adhesive, as it is not always flame resistant.

Rubber   Nowadays made from synthetic materials, rubber makes a resilient and tough wall finish, which comes in numerous colours and several textures. Strips of rubber are effective for splashbacks.

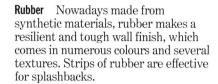

Vinyl   Being water resistant, vinyl tiles or sheeting are appropriate for bathrooms and kitchens. Vinyl sheeting can be a good substitute for wallpaper, particularly where the wall is uneven.

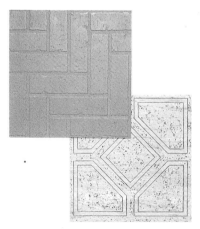

Wood panelling   The most common type of wood panelling is stripped pine tongue and groove. As with tongue and groove flooring, the panelling needs to be treated and sealed. It is fixed onto battens at ceiling and floor level. Oak and plywood panels are alternatives to pine; but these are often thin veneers on a laminate sandwich backing.

PAINT

Paint is one of the simplest and easiest decorating products to use, and will bring about a total transformation at the flick of a brush or run of a roller. But, as with any form of interior decoration, the paint is only as good as the surface to which it is applied, so this means proper and thorough preparation is always essential. It is also important to choose a new paint which is right for the job you want it to do, and to be sure that it will go on successfully over a previously painted or papered surface.

Preparation

On woodwork and metal – old, perished and blistered paint must be totally removed, either with a blow torch, a hot air stripper or one of the many chemical strippers now available. The surface may then need priming or patch-priming with the appropriate primer, then undercoating before the final coats are applied.

If the paintwork is not perished, it will need washing down and de-greasing with sugar soap or another proprietary paint cleaner. Gloss paints may need 'keying' (rubbing with abrasive paper) to roughen the surface slightly, providing a key for the new paint. Cracks, holes etc will have to be filled and smoothed.

On walls and ceilings old paint will not need removing unless it is flaking; simply wash them down and de-grease as above. If the walls have been papered and previously overpainted, or you plan to paint over existing wallpaper, simply check that the paper is sticking firmly to the wall. Slash any bubbles and restick. Stick down any peeling patches and check seams. Make sure that no adhesive is sticking to the front of the paper, as this can 'break through' new paint. Fill any cracks and holes and rub down to a smooth finish. NOTE: If you plan to paint over wallpaper check that it is colour-fast. Some silver and gold patterns in paper cannot be overpainted, so check an area of wall (or piece of spare paper) first.

Coverage

Some paints cover better than others, depending on the type and the porosity of the surface. If you are changing from a dark colour to a light one, then you will need to use more coats of paint, than changing from a light colour to a dark. Most paint manufacturers give a guide to coverage on the can, so measure up the room, try to work out how much you need, and buy it all at once, otherwise there could be some variation in colour if you have to buy a second (and third) batch.

An approximate guide to paint coverage per litre		
	sq.m	sq.ft
Gloss	17	55
Non-drip gloss	13	42
Lustre/Eggshell	12	39
Undercoat	11	36
Primer (depends on type of walls – read can)	6–15	20–49
Masonry paint (depends on type and state of walls)	5–10	16–33
Matt emulsion	15	49
Silk emulsion	14	46
Non-drip emulsion	12–13	39–42
Multi-purpose paint (depends on surface)	13–15	42–49

Choosing paint

Most paint is sold in cans of various sizes, or plastic drums, and the choice of colours is usually shown on a colour card, or on special colour chips. These show the actual paint, sprayed onto the chip, but the cards may be printed, and so the colours are less accurate. As both cards and chips are fairly small, it is difficult to judge the finished result. Remember pale colours will look much weaker and lighter over a large area, and strong, bright ones will appear much bolder or darker.

A few manufacturers make small sample pots, which you can try out at home before you buy. The cost of the sample pot is refunded against the cost of your final paint purchase.

With some of the more sophisticated paint mixing systems (called tinting systems) where the paint is shaken, rather than stirred for you in the shop, larger samples are available, and the paint can be tried on a spare piece of card or paper once it has been mixed. With this type of paint it is essential to buy the correct quantity (and a little to spare for touching-up) at the outset, as a second batch could be a slightly different colour.

Some paint manufacturers operate colour services, where they give individual advice on colour schemes. Some of these are run on an in-store basis – others are a postal service, where you fill in a form (available from the manufacturer or stockist) giving full details of the room and items to be incorporated in the scheme, enclosing colour samples where possible. The manufacturer will send you a total scheme, complete with samples, for a minimal fee, which in some cases is refundable against the cost of the paint.

Application

Paint is usually applied by brush, roller or pad. The size will depend on the area to be covered – it is foolish to try and paint a large wall or ceiling with a two-inch brush, and it is equally silly to try and paint delicate beading on panelling or windows with one that is too wide.

There have been several developments recently, all intended to take the pain out of painting. A spray paint for example, is becoming more popular, and this is sold in aerosol cans, and is usually a gloss finish. It is rather expensive, so is best used in small areas, or for furniture, stencilling, or touching-up. It is also an ideal way of painting radiators, and some manufacturers sell a special paint, which contains a heat-resistant element.

An emulsion paint has been introduced in a box (like wine in a box) with an easy-to-pour spout at the bottom. This can easily be transferred to a paint kettle or a tray for use with a roller. A 'solid' emulsion paint, the consistency of cream cheese, is now available in its own rigid plastic tray, ready for roller application.

A special painting machine was developed a few years ago, which has a lightweight container for the paint that can be attached to a belt. The paint is fed to the painting head (brush, roller or pad) by means of a transparent tube, which works by a simple soda syphon bulb – a push-button controls the flow. This system is especially practical for exterior painting and for coping with ceilings and large areas, as both hands are left free for holding ladders etc when climbing. Originally this tool could only be used with one type of paint, but an adaptor is now available which enables some other types to be put into the machine.

Paint types

Paint is sold under many brand names and may also have different descriptions, so read the small print on the container to make sure you buy the right type.

Basically there are two main types of paint, for interior and exterior decorating, which are chemically

1

formulated in a different way – oil-based (sometimes called resin-based) and water-based. However, a new type of paint has recently been produced which, although oil-based, has many of the properties of water-based paints (brushes may be washed out in hot water for example) and might be best called multi-purpose paint. It includes silicone and polyurethane in the ingredients, so the name 'silthane' is often synonymous with this paint.

Oil-based paint This may be gloss, non-drip gloss, lustre or eggshell, and also includes the range of primers and undercoats. Basically it is used for decorating metal and woodwork indoors and out (the lustre or eggshell type is only suitable for interior decoration), although it may also be used for walls and ceilings in rooms like bathrooms and kitchens where a tough, washable surface is required.

Gloss is shiny, tough and stands up to hard wear both indoors and out. It mostly comes as a ready-mix paint, and will normally need a suitable undercoat; the manufacturer usually recommends a suitable one (and colour) on the can.

Non-drip gloss is the same as gloss, but is a thixotropic or *gel* paint. It should not drip, because of the jelly-like consistency, unless the brush is too loaded or the paint is 'brushed out' or worked till it thins. It is easy to handle and should not make sags or runs on the finished surface, so it is an ideal paint for the beginner to use; professional and more experienced decorators tend to prefer the conventional gloss paint.

NOTE: This type of thixotropic paint should not be stirred, or it will lose the jelly-like consistency and become a runny gloss. Should this happen, leave the paint, with the lid firmly on the can for several hours until it re-sets.

Lustre/Eggshell is similar to gloss, but has a semi-sheen or almost matt finish. It needs to be used with the recommended undercoat and is not usually considered suitable for exterior use. It comes as a free-flowing or as a thixotropic or *gel* paint.

Multi-purpose is oil-based, and can be used on all surfaces, including walls, ceilings, woodwork and metal, although it is not recommended for exterior use. The advantage with this type of paint (apart from the fact brushes can be washed out with hot water under the tap) is the ease of application, particularly for a beginner. You don't need to have any joins as all the surfaces can be covered with the same paint. It can be gloss or semi-gloss, contains silicone and polyurethane which makes it flexible as well as tough and washable, and it is not necessary to apply an undercoat.

Primer comes in several different formulations, depending on the surface to which it is to be applied. It is used on new, bare wood and metal to seal the surface, and also on surfaces which have been stripped or burnt off. A 'universal' or all-surface primer is suitable for most jobs, but some surfaces will need a special one. Galvanized iron and aluminium should have a special metal primer; new wood needs sealing with aluminium wood primer; chromate and bitumen-coated surfaces should be sealed with an aluminium primer; some porous or crumbling surfaces may need a stabilizing primer.

NOTE: Some resinous wood will need treating with a 'knotting' (a special wood primer) to prevent the sap in the knots from leaking through the newly painted surface. Use this first, under the primer.

Undercoat should be applied to woodwork and metal before the final oil-based topcoat (or coats). Always use the undercoat as recommended by the manufacturer, to go under the gloss, lustre or eggshell paint of your choice. A suitable colour should be suggested on the tin of topcoat, and it is wise to use both paints made by the same manufacturer.

1 Paint doesn't have to be applied as a flat, seamless surface of solid colour. Here the brush-strokes are deliberately left visible, and colour is applied as it would be to a painting on a canvas, gradually building up to full strength in the middle of the walls and petering out towards the edges. The same technique is applied to the skirting and ceiling, affording a curiously abstract decorative effect.

2 Climb into the clouds; a favourite theme of the muralist – dreamy clouds in a sky blue background.

The cornice is real, but the crown capitals are fake — created with a marbled paint effect. Mouldings on the door panels have been picked out in different colours; the top cupboards have no mouldings, but have been painted to match. A bold and effective combination of techniques that loses nothing from its simplicity and the obviously less than perfect state of the woodwork.

In some cases, one undercoat is recommended, followed by the topcoat, and the surface should be lightly rubbed down between the coats. In other cases, two undercoats (rub down between the coats) are suggested, with one topcoat; or one undercoat and two topcoats. Follow the manufacturer's recommendations, and remember, the better the preparation and the more coats, the tougher the surface will be.

For areas which take hard knocks (skirting boards, doors in family rooms, exterior metal and paintwork) it is wise to use at least three coats – either two and one or one and two, as above. With thixotropic paint, if the previous surface is in good condition and the wear is not likely to be too hard, it may not be necessary to use an undercoat. NOTE: Many oil-based paints (particularly light coloured ones) used to contain lead. Very few do these days,

but if you are planning to paint furniture, woodwork or metal in a room to be used by a child, make absolutely sure that the paint is lead-free.

Water-based paint This is usually sold as emulsion these days (distemper and water paint being a thing of the past), and is available as a matt finish or with a slight sheen (usually called silk). It is called by various names, of which vinyl matt emulsion and vinyl silk emulsion are the most common. *Emulsion* is normally used for walls and ceilings indoors, although there are exterior emulsions available for brickwork etc. It is available in a wide range of colours and as both a free-flowing paint and as a thixotropic or *gel* paint. Emulsions do not need a special undercoat – they can be applied direct to a clean, smooth, dry wall. An initial 'size' or undercoat can be applied – this is a coat of the emulsion

thinned down with water. In the case of a very porous, chalky or powdery surface it is wise to use a coat of stabilizing primer first. If there has been a problem with damp, or the wall is an exterior one where there may even have been problems with algae, use a stabilizing primer which contains an anti-fungicide.

NOTE: New emulsion can go on over old, so long as it is washed down, but walls and ceilings in older properties may have been painted with water paint or distemper, not emulsion. As flaking distemper and water paint cannot be covered with any other type of paint, it will be necessary to strip or wash this off, and to re-line the area before repainting. Sometimes washing down thoroughly, followed by a coat of stabilizing primer will seal the original surface sufficiently for repainting. *Masonry* is a tough emulsion paint,

specially formulated to protect as well as decorate outside walls. Most contain a mould and algae inhibitor, and can be smooth-textured, so that dirt particles are not trapped easily. Some contain sand, granite chips or other materials to give added strength and covering power – the result is a rough-textured masonry paint. The smooth textured ones are kinder to brushes and rollers.

Masonry paints do not need primers if the wall surface is in good condition, but if there has been a damp problem, or the brickwork is in a poor state, it may be necessary to use a stabilizing primer, or one which contains an antifungicide, or an alkali-resistant primer. In some cases, the wall can be treated with ordinary household bleach. If using a primer, make sure that it will be compatible with the topcoat, and follow the paint manufacturer's recommendations as to suitable primers.

Solid emulsion is a new paint, specially formulated for easy application, as it is non-drip. It is a thixotropic or *gel* emulsion, the consistency of cream cheese, which has to be applied with a roller. Just like all *gel* paint, if it is 'worked' too much, it will become free-flowing and will drip. It is sold in its own special container, and at the moment the colour range is restricted. It is only suitable for interior use. *Textured emulsion* comes as a very thick paint, almost like plaster, and can be moulded into various textures and finishes. This type of paint is intended for cover-up jobs, where the wall or ceiling is of poor quality and really needs replastering, or after tiles have been removed and it is not possible to get a totally smooth surface. The effect can be attractive, but these textured paints are very difficult to remove, and heavily textured surfaces can hold dirt and grime very easily.

New exterior finishes A modified paint has been specially formulated for exterior use. It appears under a variety of names – opaque stains, breathing paints or micro-porous paints. They are solvent- or water-based, and may be matt, lustrous or glossy. They are specifically intended for use on exterior woodwork, and have a flexible finish. They do not need an undercoat.

PAINT EFFECTS

Sophisticated 'distressed' paint effects are currently very fashionable even though they have been in existence for a long time. They are often more flattering than an expanse of unbroken colour as they give a room depth rather than shrinking it.

The effects described below are quicker to apply than conventional paint, cheaper and more elegant. You don't need specialized equipment as you can improvise, and they are not difficult to achieve with the exception of *trompe l'oeil* and murals. All 'distressed' finishes look best over a base of flat to mid-sheen oil-based paint. Before attempting a whole wall, try experimenting on a small area. (For a guide to achieving paint effects, see the chapter on Do-It-Yourself.)

Colour-washing
A water effect which has the feel of Mediterranean washes, colour-washing used to be done with distemper, but nowadays a glaze of thinned flat oil-based paint or undercoat over an eggshell oil-based paint is used. Latex paint gives more visible brush strokes, but take care not to let it dribble.

Dragging
The effect is of finely graduated lines, irregularly spaced and closer together in some areas than in others. Dragging gives a very dignified appearance and fits in particularly well with the city traditional style. A decorative development of wood graining, dragging can be done in different layers of colour either in the same direction or the opposite direction. It gives the impression of making rooms look larger.

Graining
This gives the impression of woodiness without necessarily being wood coloured. Effects can be rippled, blurred, wood-lined or knotty.

Lacquer look
The effect of lacquer look is a rich surface glossiness and a very dense colour finish. It can be fairly tiring to look at in large areas, and also needs a perfect wall surface as imperfections tend to show through. It can be created with various colours and tinted glazes.

Marbling
This paint technique falls into two categories: highly skilled professional marbling which aims to deceive everyone that it's real, and an effect which merely creates an impression and which anyone can do. There are at least seven different types of marble – travertine, serpentine, brecciated, alabaster, laminated, variegated and statuary. Practise marbling on a small surface first as a huge fixed marble pattern can be rather dull and tomb-like, whereas in smaller blocks it will be lively and fun.

Mural
If you're not an expert, try making a grid which you can paint onto. Only attempt two-dimensional objects as perspectives are difficult to achieve successfully. Or employ a professional muralist to paint a more complex scene.

1

2

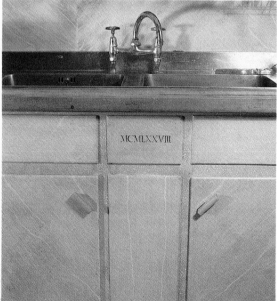
3

1 This mural brings the outside world into a room that lacks a view, making the most of the awkward shape created by the arched dormer window.

2 A marble paint finish, professionally applied, transforms a plain basin and splashback, and is almost indistinguishable from the real marble on the walls. A matt emulsion ceiling is suitably low key in contrast.

3 Marbling techniques used on the walls and units give a classical feel to an otherwise quite obviously 20th century kitchen.

PAINT EFFECTS

1 Soft, remarkably realistic marbling – a highly skilled technique that lends dignity to the humblest of interiors.

2 Keep stencil patterns simple and bold. A strong pattern is much more effective than a failed attempt at elaborate perspectives.

3 A spectacular piece of trompe l'oeil painted by Alan Dodd. Reproducing architectural details in paint is a traditional part of interior design, and Dodd excels, both technically and in the wealth of period detail he deploys, from Gothic fan vaulting to classic Greek key motifs.

4 Not an entirely flat surface – the rail really is three-dimensional. But various stippled paint finishes are used to suggest three-dimensional stone blocks, grooves in a flat column and, higher up, woodwork. The effects are built up in layers, alternating brushwork with glazes and washes.

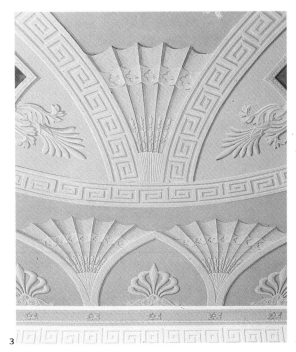

Rag-rolling or ragging
This effect originated with stippling, and is done with a scrunched-up rag, pressed into a wet glaze with a rolling movement that shouldn't be too regular. This is a good effect for large empty expanses of wall in confined spaces such as corridors and staircases. Its striking effect often looks better in soft colours or toning ones used together.

Scumbling
A typical 1930s design, related to stippling, scumble is an opaque coat painted on top of a bright base coat.

Sponging
This is very quick and easy to do with varying effects, depending on the type of sponge you use and the number of colours. Unlike most other effects it is sponged *on* for effect giving a cloudy impression. Two-colour sponging produces a marbled finish.

Stencilling
This is very versatile, fun and cheap; you can make your own stencils or buy ready-made kits. Try them out on a small area first where you can decide on your base colour. Stencilling is particularly effective for making architectural features stand out, for borders, to decorate chair rails, and large stencils make pretty dados. Metallic stencils – gold and silver – on dark lacquered backgrounds look sumptuously dramatic.

Stippling
The effect of stippling is of softened colours rather like an impressionist painting. This method means you don't see any brush marks and makes for a soothing unassertive background. The paint is applied with a brush or a pad.

Tortoiseshelling
The colours are laid in the wet varnish and the resultant spreading is curtailed by alternative direction brushstrokes. Tortoiseshelling creates a very rich effect and looks good in small spaces. Colours can range from blonde-red to brown-black.

Trompe l'oeil
Fun three dimensional jokes, which range from faking another wall surface, such as tiles, to depicting French windows opening onto a secret garden, can only be effective if expertly done.

When contemplating whether to put up picture rails, dado rails, cornices or mouldings, look carefully at the type of house you're dealing with. Although simple coving and architraves will complement even the most modern of houses, a fussy Victorian cornice will look totally out of place unless in its appropriate setting. On the other hand if you have an old house, where the original features have been ripped out, reinstating dado rails and ceiling roses can make a world of difference to the character of your rooms. How you choose to decorate such features is essential.

Architraves
Available in many different moulds, architraves give doorways and windows a decorative finishing touch.

Cove cornices
At the point where the walls join the ceiling, cove cornices give a finished effect. They can be painted either to blend in with the ceiling or to highlight it. To emphasize details in the cornice itself, you can pick them out in a different colour; otherwise they can easily become lost, especially if your ceilings are high.

Mouldings
Ceiling roses, pelmets (which resemble flat columns) and plinth blocks are available. Ceiling roses used to be made from wood, but are usually plaster now. Panels and panel moulds can be made to match other mouldings, and fitted on apron panels, either between the skirting and dado rail, or above this but below the picture rail. Smaller panels are used for doors. If the panels are made of softwood, you will need to prime them before painting as the wood is often fairly knotty and brown stains tend to show through.

Dado rails
Dado or chair rails were devised to prevent the backs of chairs damaging the wall, and are about 90cm (3ft) up the wall. They make an attractive visual break, particularly in a high wall, and offer opportunities for using a combination of colours and textures in the decoration. The dado – the area below the rail – is traditionally covered with Anaglypta. Where a visual dado rail is preferred to a functional one, a stencilled paint border makes a particularly good substitute.

Picture rails
Fixed to the wall about three-quarters of the way up, and originally designed to hang pictures from, picture rails, like dado rails, form a decorative motif in their own right. If made of hardwood, they are not usually painted, but simply varnished. Plate rails which are slightly wider are fixed at the same height.

Skirting boards
Skirtings, which come in various sizes, prevent damage to the walls at ground level, so need to be tough. Softwoods are usually painted and primed, and have various moulded profiles.

Ceilings
In decorating, ceilings should be treated as walls. The paint you use must have good adhesive qualities, and should be easy to maintain as you won't want to wash it down every week. There are special ceiling papers to hide defects in the plaster, and a quick way of putting up a ceiling these days is to use Artex, which looks like textured plaster. Vinyl sheeting is also suitable for ceilings as long as there are no ugly seams; this is especially the case in bathrooms, where the steam might cause paper to peel off.

Creating visual effects
To give the illusion of lowering immensely high ceilings, paint them a darker colour than the walls or graduate the colour up the walls – becoming darker nearer the ceiling. Do the opposite to add height to low ceilings. Stencil borders can also be used to lower high walls visually, and if you have a pokey room, vertical stripes will make it seem more spacious.

Fabric looks particularly beautiful on ceilings as it is unobtrusively stylish. Make sure that there are no ceiling roses and that any light fittings can be accommodated. The decoration of mouldings should complement your colour scheme rather than competing with it. Brilliant whites are rather overpowering next to a matt finish or textured wallcovering. But white paint tinged either with warm colours – reds, yellows or pinks – or cold colours – blues or greens – is available.

Endless coats of unbroken, flat paint shrink a room, whereas paint effects will give it depth. Also remember what type of floor surface and colour you have chosen – not everything will look good against bright yellow studded rubber, for example. Try and keep the style of a room homogenous; don't have the latest high tech surfaces as a backdrop for Chippendale furniture, or a grand wallcovering if you only have shabby second-hand furniture.

Above all, walls and ceilings have to be lived with, and if you're not sure what decoration to choose, play it safe with neutral paint or wallpaper and let your furnishings create the interest in your rooms.

Paint used to great effect on an exceptionally ornate cornice. The combination of dark natural wood pediments and rich paint colours enhances the luxuriant, traditional quality of the room. Different colours have been used to pick out the various details in the cornice. A light colour highlighting the most decorative plasterwork, which, at this height, would be lost if painted a dark shade. Both subtle and fashionable, a band of stencilling carries on the theme.

WINDOWS

It is easy to forget that there are two ways of looking at a window. As far as the look of the house is concerned, the view from the outside is critical. The windows are one of the most important elements in giving a house its character. Their size also controls how much of your interior you put on show to the outside world, and this should be borne in mind when you are thinking about privacy. From the inside they provide a view, ventilation and daylight, and become a decorative element when dressed with curtains, blinds or shutters.

The view from the outside

There are three fundamental elements to a window, each of which needs to be considered in turn.

Firstly, there is the structural opening itself, and its position in relation to the other windows. If you are inserting a new window into an existing wall, you should weigh the impact that the new opening will have on the overall pattern and proportions of the facade.

Secondly, you must consider carefully the shape of the new opening, and the relationship of its height to its width. If for instance, all your windows are rectangular, and built to the same proportions, then a square addition will strike a jarring note. Don't forget also that walls have a depth. How far back your window is set in the wall affects its external appearance much more than you might think.

Thirdly, there is the frame by which the window is fixed to the wall. This can be made of timber, aluminium, and even plastic. Builders' merchants stock a wide variety of types and sizes that are designed to fit directly into the standard range of window dimensions. But if you opt for an unusual shape, or you want a window frame that matches the details of your existing windows, it is possible to have specially made window frames. Depending on your choice of materials, this need not be as expensive as it sounds, and is very often the best answer.

Resist the blandishments of door-to-door salesmen offering to rip out your existing timber windows and replace them with 'modern, maintenance-free' aluminium double glazing. It is expensive, and in most cases, the styles are totally removed from the character of the house. A house built with windows which have delicate glazing bars, small panes and deep frames, will be permanently disfigured by crude metal windows.

1 Decorative fringes of scooped lace on all the ground floor windows form a discreet and attractive part of the house's character.

2 A Georgian fanlight, its delicate ironwork painted white, set in a rubbed red brick arch.

3 The view from the outside can always be embellished by window boxes and hanging baskets or flowers, as here.

4 Flat, simple architectural shapes relieved by the frilled blind inside.

5 Traditionally windows were embellished by their boundary edges where they fitted into the wall; here the stone surround contrasts against the yellow stucco. The canopy of trailing plants adds a softening touch.

6 You need a steady hand, or a professional painter to pick out white stripes in the glazing bars like this, but the results, reminiscent of Dutch architecture, are worth the trouble.

7 Ivy used architecturally as part of the facade.

8 Robust Victorian plaster mouldings are best painted in colours that tone sympathetically with the brickwork.

9 Replacement windows needn't spoil an old facade as long as they are chosen with care, and perhaps prettified with a bright display of flowers.

THE VIEW FROM THE INSIDE

There are both technical, and aesthetic considerations to be taken into account when thinking about the effect your windows have on the interior of the house. A poorly fitting window will allow the penetration of damp. Its frame will deteriorate at a rapid rate if it is not made of high quality materials and properly maintained. And if it does not close tightly, it will allow the penetration of dust and draught into the house. Although double glazing is not a very effective way of providing thermal insulation when measured against its cost, in particularly noisy areas, acoustic double or even treble glazing can be a very valuable addition. For homes close to airport flight paths or urban motorways, it is essential. But acoustic double glazing is certainly not cheap. The two panes of glass need an airgap of at least 15 cm (6 in.) between them, as well as sturdy, properly fitted frames. Bear in mind the impact of a window's position and shape on the interior of a room. Windows in two different walls, especially in adjacent ones, can ensure that you make the most of sunshine throughout the day, and if it is worth exploiting, can give you a panoramic view.

But a window does not only effect the interior in terms of light and outlook. The different designs offer numerous advantages and disadvantages from a technical point of view – security, ventilation and even in the way they disturb a curtain or blind when they are opened.

The traditional window in Britain is the sliding sash, where both top and bottom halves can be opened independently. They slide up and down, counterbalanced by weights within the wallspace for ease of movement. The glazing bars allow for small panes of glass, which are cheap to replace. Room ventilation can be carefully adjusted

1

2

3

4

1 A check patterned roller blind is neatly fitted into the kitchen window frame.

2 Edwardian stained and patterned glass: best unadorned by curtains to preserve the original character of the house.

3 A new twin arch setting for the original rectangular window, emphasized by symmetrical lights and blinds fitted in the new inner wall.

4 Fitted above a round-headed window, a roller blind won't interfere with its attractive lines.

5 A teasing variation on the roller blind. Mounted at the bottom of the window, it blots out the worst and keeps the best of the view.

6 Not the usual type of curtain rail, but a metal bar makes an effective contrast to flimsy drapes.

7 An Art Nouveau screen builds up a layered effect against the window with its net curtain and shutter.

8 Plants naturally thrive at windows and can be just as decorative as curtains and blinds.

9 Turn of the century mixture of painted, stained and patterned glass set off to advantage in a plain cream frame.

7

8

9

with variably sized openings at top and bottom; and the opened window does not interfere with curtains, blinds or shutters, nor does it disturb any ornaments or books on the window sill. Security fittings can easily be inserted into these sliding sash windows. It is an established yet sophisticated design.

Modern window types come in all shapes and sizes. Broadly speaking they allow for larger areas of glass in the home, and consequently improve the light and view. Their emphasis is likely to be more horizontal than vertical. Often these modern designs dispense with glazing bars altogether, having just one large sheet of glass. They can be hinged, either at the top or the sides, or pivoted, again at the top, bottom or the sides. Either combination will get in the way of any curtains or blinds you want to hang and will severely cramp your freedom to use the window shelf either for display or extra storage space.

301

CURTAINS, BLINDS AND SHUTTERS

Just as important as the window itself are the curtains, shutters or blinds that are hung on the inside. These will particularly affect the look of your home at night, serving to filter and colour the light, to create interesting patterns, as well as providing privacy. The basic purpose of any window fitting is to help control the environment, particularly in saving energy and in reducing noise from the outside world. But often their most important role is as a decorative element in an interior design scheme.

Shutters

These have come back into their own. From a time when they were considered as little more than a quaint historical throwback, with as much relevance to contemporary living as a gas lamp, they are now seen as a valuable asset for the house. If you find that your house still possesses shutters, you should certainly keep them. It may be necessary to have them rehung, and stripped of the layers of paint that will probably prevent them from opening.

As far as decorative treatments are concerned, stick to plain, pale paint schemes. The painted murals which had a brief vogue in the 1960s now simply look twee; and picking out the panelling in a different colour looks unnecessarily obtrusive.

Fitting shutters to a new window from scratch is difficult, and rarely done. You need to have a considerable depth of wall to accommodate the folded back shutter neatly and unobtrusively, and this is very rarely present in modern houses. An attractive alternative is a folded louvre shutter. These are lighter than traditional shutters, their rigidity coming from just top and bottom rails and the frame. Accordingly they are less trouble to fit, and hang, and the hinges and screws can all be lighter than would be needed for full shutters. The strongly geometric pattern of the louvre blades can become an over-powering element, so in a small room use them sparingly. With a large window, they are best deployed in a bold way, perhaps used full height from floor to ceiling across the window.

Roller blinds

Though these blinds are a cheap, neat looking window covering, by themselves they do little more than screen out direct sunshine, and offer minimal privacy. As far as energy saving is concerned they are useless, and it may be sensible to use them in conjunction with conventional curtains.

Their popularity is more due to the fact that they do look attractive, bringing a splash of colour to any interior, and can serve to emphasize the character and proportions of a window. They look particularly effective when used in twos and threes in a room. If you use the right kind of waterproof fabric, roller blinds can also be useful in kitchens and bathrooms where curtains might be inappropriate.

Because rollers use so little fabric, they are a cheap altenative to curtains. Buy them ready-made to your measurements, or get a kit, but either way follow the directions carefully; it is easy to break the spring mechanism contained in the ends of the roller which is intended to roll the blind up when you tug gently.

If your window frame is deep enough, you can fit the blind inside it, flush with the outer edge. If not, mount it on the outer frame.

An interesting alternative to fabric blinds is to use pinoleum – split slats of very thin wood, rather like long matchsticks. They look particularly good when the sun shines through, splitting the rays like a prism.

Venetian blinds

These are a more expensive alternative to roller blinds, and are available with plastic, metal or wood blades. Metal blinds perform better than fabric roller blinds at keeping sunshine out. They will reflect a lot of the heat and, especially in summer, can be a useful way to protect large expanses of window from building up to much heat inside.

Venetian blinds are fitted with two cords, one which raises and lowers the blind, the other which swivels the blades into open and shut positions. The mechanism is more complicated than for a roller blind, and needs a smooth flat surface for its fitting.

Venetian blinds can be a strongly

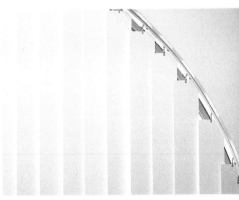

architectural element in an interior. They introduce a bold pattern into a room, which can be accentuated by the shadows cast by the sun filtering through half open blades.

Think carefully about your walls and floor before hanging Venetian blinds. A simple plain background complements them best.

Wooden Venetian blinds are much more expensive than metal or plastic, but give a mellow, opulent light to a room, redolent of *Casablanca* and lushly tropical interiors. Consider using them with cane furniture, fringed lampshades and potted palms to build up a complete look.

Curtains

Using fabric curtains is both a practical way of insulating your home from heat, cold, and noise, and a major decorative element in an interior. You need to consider not just the pattern, texture and colour of the fabric itself, but also its length, the mechanism by which it is supported, and the way the curtain will look in both open and closed positions.

In general, curtains look their best when they are full and generous. This means using a plentiful quantity of material, and dropping the curtain if not to the floor, then to the bottom edge of the window. Save if you must, on the quality of the material, never the quantity. Fabric can always be used to give it that heavy, deep-folded quality of expensive curtains. Conversely, skimpy, mean looking curtains never look good, however costly the material.

Curtain fabric should be chosen as part of the overall design scheme for the interior, not in isolation. Try to pick out colours used elsewhere in the room and relate them to the curtains. The same pattern for upholstery and curtain fabric can be effective.

Don't forget the impact that the curtain design will have on the proportions of the windows themselves. Tall, full length windows will look good hung with individual curtains; don't use horizontal stripes–they will spoil the effect. A length of window along one wall will be unified and dramatized by a small drop of material.

Billowing, swagged and elaborately folded curtains set the mood for a nostalgic, romantic interior. Heavy dark velvet ones will look effective at night in intimate candlelit dining rooms; as will softly ruched festoon or Austrian blinds. In a more down-to-earth room the flat folds of a Roman blind look particularly smart.

The look of a curtain is also determined by the way in which it is hung. The tape sewn to the back of the curtain, into which are inserted the curtain hooks, will determine the shape and size of the pleats. Pinch pleats look attractive with heavy, simple floor to ceiling curtains. Pencil pleats are tighter, run continuously along the length of the top of the curtain, and are intended for use with lightweight material. Gathered headings are a compromise between the two. They can look ungenerous in their use of fabric, and may best be hidden by a pelmet.

The simplest way of attaching the curtain to the wall, or the ceiling, is by means of a large diameter wood or brass curtain rod. Large rings fitted with eyes take the curtain hooks. With elaborate antique ends, brass rods can strike a particularly ornate note in a florid country house style interior. Curtain track on the other hand is intended to be a discreet, even invisible way of fixing a curtain.

1 A window with a limited view, best served by a plain roller blind, which allows the ethnic sculpture to take the limelight.

2 Pleated blinds, the cheapest solution of all, look attractive when let down and fold away into nothing.

3 If you are lucky enough to find shutters intact, make them a feature of the room.

4 Tracked hanging strips trimmed around a curve.

5 The belt and braces approach: net forms the first line of defence, backed by ruched blinds and conventional drapes to give a layered, '50s look.

6 With the aid of a mirrored alcove, distinctive Roman blinds have been taken across the whole wall to give the impression of a much larger room.

7 A variation on the pleated theme, with a deep dropped heading to frame the window.

WINDOW DRESSING

1 A stark, simple wooden house, its only ornament the original hand-made window frames.

2 Rambling leaves, and this carefully positioned selection of pots and garden ornaments form an effective contrast to the strong geometric pattern of the glazing.

3 The gentler touch: a broderie anglaise curtain.

4 Generous sweep of fabric, elegantly waisted, a suitable embellishment for a stately window.

5 When the streetscape is as pleasant as this, floor to ceiling glazing, with the front door set into the middle, makes a superb house front.

6 A window box, as pretty as its contents.

Never be tempted to consider lighting as a mere technical afterthought. The way in which a room is lit is in fact one of the most fundamental elements in interior design; both because of the strictly functional role it has to play in ensuring that it is possible to read or sew, for example, without straining the eyes, and also because of its aesthetic character. A single 100 watt bulb dangling at the end of a frayed and dusty cord in the middle of a room covered by an unsympathetic shade, can completely destroy the impact of what is otherwise the most attractive of interiors. A well thought out new lighting system, on the other hand, can

be the quickest, cheapest and most effective way to bring out the best in a room, emphasizing the attractive points and camouflaging the blemishes.

When planning a new interior, the way in which it will be lit should be just as much a part of your thinking in the early stages as colour schemes and furniture. Providing lighting from more than one source will help to accommodate a variety of different moods, and will always enhance a room. The light from an indirect source is much more flattering than that from a single overhead source which produces a distracting glare, and a flat, harsh look to the room.

There are two different aspects of

the problem to think about. There is of course the effect of the light source on the room. An uplighter which bounces light off the ceiling to give a diffuse soft light will create a very different effect to a strongly directional spotlight which will produce harsh shadows. And both will be affected by the physical characteristics of the room itself.

Just as important is the look of the fitting, both when it is switched on, and when it is not in use. Light fittings are becoming more and more like pieces of domestic sculpture in their own right, offering a huge range of alternatives to the traditional central fitting hanging from the ceiling, and equipped with an exotic array of new types of bulb.

1 One of the remarkable flood of imaginative new lights from Italy. Alberto Fraser's Nastro light designed for Stilnoro looks just as good off as it does on; intended for desk use, the brightly coloured flexible wire base supports a quartz halogen bulb.

2 Fabric drapes create a soft romantic light. Yet grouping the four together provides enough light to work at the desk by. Make sure you fit low wattage bulbs, which don't get too hot, and provide ventilation in the shades.

1

2

THE BASICS

The way in which a room is lit should be planned to work in conjunction with its basic characteristics, rather than struggling against them. Fittings should be compatible with the architectural style of the interior, not necessarily by choosing pseudo Regency striped shades and brass wall fittings for a classical interior; plain modern fittings can be much less intrusive. But don't go to the other extreme and screw an insensitive track of spotlamps across a delicate ceiling.

Technically your fittings should also be compatible with the characteristics of the room. It is futile, for example, to rely on direct uplighters for background lighting if you have very dark, matt ceilings and wall finishes; almost all the light will be absorbed, rather than reflected back into the room. Uplighters work much better with light, gloss walls.

The essence of natural light is its continuously changing quality. It comes from different directions, and varies in intensity throughout the day. There is evidence that its fluctuating nature is conducive to visual concentration and comfort. And it is important that an effective artificial lighting scheme should have these qualities too. Flexibility both in the amount of light and in its direction allows us to cater for different moods and tasks.

The practical way to achieve this is to provide a general level of background lighting, which gives you an overall light to cater for moving around a room, and to supplement it with accent and task lighting, directed at particular parts of the interior, which may be brought into use as and when necessary. The former gives you most of the light you need. The latter provides the shadows and highlights that make a room look interesting.

In a dining room, for example, the background lighting could come from a couple of standard lamps, or even from a number of downlighters recessed flush into the ceiling, with accent lighting provided by a pendant fitting with a broad brimmed shade low over the table to bring it into dramatic focus.

In a living room, there will usually be more than one focus to deal with, and each one will need to be catered for. Background lighting need not be the

traditional dead centre pendant fitting. It could be located off centre, or brought lower into the room. Localized lighting should help to reinforce the visual focuses in a room – narrow-beamed spotlamps to pick out art on the walls for example, or desklights directed onto a vase of flowers. If there is a central sitting area, standard lamps can help to define it with the low pool of light they cast at night. And special task lighting may be needed next to the television and audio.

In the kitchen, the traditional light source has come to be the neon strip light. This is still the cheapest way of lighting a room in terms of electricity consumption. But in the past the quality of light given off has been much harsher than the yellower, warmer light of the tungsten bulb. New techniques have greatly improved the quality of light from neon tubes, and it is worth asking for technical advice in your lighting shop to make sure you get the right kind of tube. But consider other types of lighting in the kitchen too. The neon look goes well with a clinical, stark kitchen, but you may prefer a softer, more domestic look created by a row of small pendant fittings hung low over the worktops.

1 Glass-walled houses, dramatically lit both inside and out, look most impressive at night.

2 Bare bulbs, the starkest of light fittings, are appropriate for this minimalist kitchen.

3 Lace-up lighting; a jokey touch for an eclectic interior.

4 Attracting attention to a display of objects, this ceramic-based table lamp almost looks part of the collection itself.

5 Lit from below, a tree becomes a work of art.

6 A mixture of lantern and candlelight produces a romantic glow to accord with a rustic setting.

7 A strongly focused point light source brings a vase of grasses to life.

LIGHTING SYSTEMS

The past few years have seen a dramatic diversification in lighting systems. Before committing yourself to a specific type, allocate time to careful planning of the effects you want and how to achieve them.

The electrics

A fundamental requirement for an effective lighting scheme is an up-to-date and well thought out electrical wiring layout. In older houses where the wiring has not been modernized, it is impossible to install a full new lighting system without overhauling the electrics too. Where this is not feasible, for example in rented properties, you can achieve considerable improvements with a cosmetic facelift; perhaps simply with new shades. In the long run, however, safety considerations alone will dictate rewiring.

In the meantime, the most common deficiencies of older lighting systems are too short a drop of flex from ceiling pendant fittings, and an inappropriate location of the ceiling rose. Both of these drawbacks can be tackled fairly simply by anybody who knows how to change an electric plug, by extending the length of flex. A couple of extra feet will bring the light down far enough to give a more sympathetic effect. More spare flex will allow you to reposition the light altogether by coiling the wire over a new ceiling hook. To carry out this operation, first be sure to turn off the power source at the mains. Next unscrew the ceiling rose, where you will find a junction box connecting the lighting flex with the mains. Remove the old flex, and screw in a new length according to your needs.

An alternative is to rely on the electric sockets in the skirting of a room to power light sources. These can be either desk or table top fittings which provide localized sources of light, or standard lamps on the floor which provide a general light throughout the whole room.

Sockets and switches

When planning a lighting system from scratch it is important to allow as much built-in flexibility as possible. Generally this means having as many power points, sockets and lighting outlets as you can afford. You probably won't need them all at once, but it is much simpler to install them all in one go, than to carry out messy piecemeal alterations later on. Think carefully about the position and location of the switches too. Locate switches for background lighting sources conveniently near the door of a room so that you can find them in the dark. Make sure that you can light the whole of a staircase or a corridor from the front door, and also put in switches along your route so that you can turn off the lights behind you as you make your way to bed.

Dimmer switches are worth consideration too. They are more expensive than conventional switches, but allow you to cut down lighting levels to suit different moods, and of course they save energy.

Don't forget to take into account how the siting of your switches will affect the look of a room. Out of keeping, or insensitively sited switch plates can stick out like sore thumbs.

Track-mounted ceiling systems

Originally devised for use in architectural installation – primarily shops and art galleries – track-mounted ceiling systems started to become widely available in domestic versions during the 1960s, in response to the need to provide more flexible lighting sources. In practice the flexibility turned out to be rather less than was originally promised. Certainly you can use track-mounted spotlamps to light a variety of furniture arrangements in a room or to show off different configurations of posters and pictures on the walls. But this system will only be effective if you have both sufficient lighting track and spotlights. One 1m (3ft) length of track and two spots hardly qualify. And when you do have a decent length of track, you find yourself with an intrusive, potentially dominating piece of hardware on your hands that will look totally out of keeping in many rooms.

One ingenious variation on the track lighting theme is to couple it with the shelving supports of a storage system, allowing for the inclusion of small desk lights simply clipped into position on the metal brackets; this is a neat and useful option.

A track-mounted lighting system is only as good as the light fittings

1 and 2 Lighting designers are becoming progressively more adventurous and playful in producing table lamps that are as much pieces of sculpture as they are practical light sources. Essentially they all work on one of two principles. Either they hide the bulb and allow the lamp to emit light that is filtered through a variety of different types of shade — glass is particularly popular — or they create a light source which is adjustable and can be moved in any direction you want. In this case, the point is to try and provide as stable a base as possible that takes up the least room.

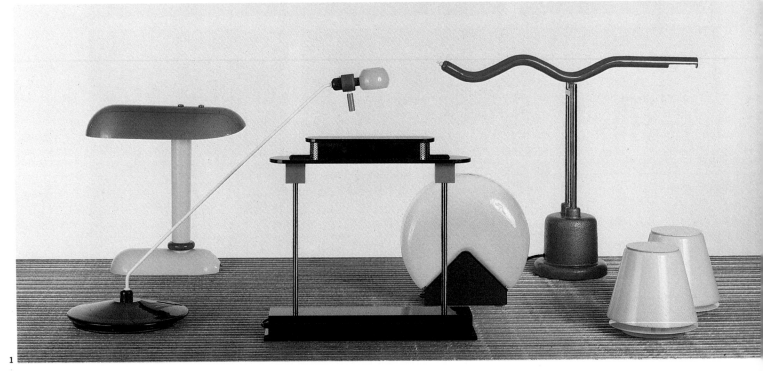

1

themselves. They must be designed to be easily adjustable, so that the angle at which they direct their beams of light into the room can be changed and the spots relocated anywhere along the track quickly and simply. Many of the domestic track fittings available do not meet either of these requirements, and in addition give a harsh, unsympathetic glare. On the other hand, in certain types of interior, the sparkle that one or two discreetly positioned spotlamps provide can give a particularly attractive lift to a room.

Alternatives

As far as flexibility is concerned, standard lamps, perhaps equipped with two or three spotlamps, or else a simple uplighter can offer just as much flexibility as a track system, and as an added bonus are much simpler to install, and to pack up and take away if you move house.

A rise and fall fitting for a pendant light may be a useful addition to a system, doubling as a background light in its upright position and a local accent light when lowered over a dining table or work surface.

Light fittings

Light fittings are becoming the focus for a remarkable outpouring of creative design effort – of the kind that used to be lavished on chairs. This has resulted in a huge range of fittings which not only produce light that is attractive in its quality, but which look good in themselves. They can be used not simply for practical purposes, but to help establish the character and style of a room too. All manner of new materials are being used for both the fittings and their shades, from ground glass to plastic and perforated metal. And the new types of bulbs now on the market are being deployed to considerable effect.

The problem with all light fittings is to get the balance right between producing enough light to allow the eye to carry out the tasks that it is set, but not so much that it experiences glare which can be both uncomfortable and, in some cases, so strong as to make it impossible to see at all. Imagine, for example, trying to read a newspaper in bed on a sunny morning, with sun streaming directly onto the surface of the paper. The glare would be so

powerful that it would prevent you from being able to focus.

Glare is partly the result of looking directly at too bright a source of light, and partly to do with contrast. If you are reading at night by the light of just one desk lamp in an otherwise darkened room, you are much more likely to experience glare than if you have another source of background light in the room. At the same time you will find it easier to concentrate if the surface of the paper is a bit brighter than its surroundings – a matt surface will help reduce distractions. You will also be likely to experience glare – and to strain your eyes – if you watch television at night with all the lights off. Avoid these kind of problems by having a background light on.

Localized lighting will be particularly useful beside the bed. Lights can be clamped to the bedhead, positioned on bedside tables, or free-standing on the floor. For double beds it is important to have a light on each side to avoid eye-strain and arguments.

Certain types of task light can also provide background lighting – use several, and angle them to bounce light

off the walls and ceiling. The earliest task lights had their origins in strictly functional applications – Anglepoises and their heavier equivalents, manufactured in France, were intended for use at the workbench, on the shopfloor or at the drawing board. They now make attractive domestic lights too. But their present-day descendants are much more sophisticated. The classic Tizio light, for example, designed by Richard Sapper, has a built-in dimmer switch, uses a tiny, but very powerful quartz halogen bulb, and is equipped with elaborate counterweights to make it stable, despite having a minimal base so as not to encroach on desk space.

Currently new crops of lights are coming out with the frequency of annual fashion collections, and the trend is steadily in the direction of pure art objects.

Bulbs

The business end of any light fitting is its bulb – known confusingly in the trade as the lamp. It is the bulb which actually produces light. In a tungsten filament bulb, a metal wire becomes hot and glows when current is passed

In this collection of recent Italian lamps, four are in the diffuser category — the second, third, fourth and sixth from the left — and all, except Ettore Sottsass's perforated metal design in the middle, are made of glass. The remaining two provide adjustable sources of light.

LIGHTING SYSTEMS

1 and 2 From left to right: an adjustable table lamp fitted with a quartz halogen bulb, which emits an intense, bluish tinged light, is very powerful for its size and usually has a built-in dimmer; a new flat-topped version of the original Anglepoise, which was designed to be moved like a human arm to give a smoothly adjustable, easily controlled source of light; a simple glass disc which provides a soft, diffuse light; a desk lamp with translucent hood which partly reflects light downwards and partly diffuses it out into the room; increasingly light-weight quartz halogen bulbs allow desk lights, like this one, to have smaller bases without toppling over, making more room on your desk for papers; a decorative version of the adjustable table lamp; a pendant lamp that reflects most of its light upwards to diffuse into the room through its glass core, and so avoids creating a distracting glare.

3 Placing a light source on the floor to shine up the curtains creates strong patterns and accentuates contrasts between light and shade. A bulkhead wall light was the inspiration for this design.

through it. In a neon tube, the passing of electric current in the neon gas inside the tube sets off a discharge of light. These two types of lamp have very different properties. The tungsten bulb will give off a warmer, yellower light that will generally flatter rooms and more accurately show off the colours within them. Neon light is bluer and harsher – although it is now possible to get tubes which give a better quality of light. Neon uses considerably less power than a tungsten bulb, and is therefore cheaper to run, although it is more expensive to buy in the first place.

Tungsten bulbs get hotter than neon, and you will need more of them to achieve the same level of light – a point worth remembering if you are thinking about using many spotlights close to a wall or a ceiling. You can easily end up with a whole row of blackened scorch marks unless you position the lights very carefully.

Light reaching the eye directly from a naked bulb will tend to be too dazzling for comfort. The glare, or contrast between the bare bulb and its much darker surroundings is too much to take for any length of time. The primary purpose of a shade is to reduce that contrast, by hiding the bulb itself from the eye, and letting light filter through or around the shade into the room. Glare can also be overcome in part by using opalescent or even silvered bulbs.

In recent years a host of ever more exotic permutations of these types has become available for domestic use. The quartz halogen bulb gives off a far more

intense and powerful light than the conventional tungsten bulb. It is much too dazzling to be used for direct lighting, and is generally employed for uplighters that bounce light off the wall and ceilings and thence back into the room again. These bulbs are very expensive, but will last far longer than the conventional bulb. They should be treated with care; handling them without gloves will be enough to stop them working.

Several manufacturers have now produced miniaturized versions of a neon tube – notably Thorn's 2D lamp – which are small enough to be used in conventional decorative fittings.

Task lighting

Delicate tasks – darning, reading small print for long periods of time, chopping fine ingredients in the kitchen – are all hard on the eye, and require a great deal of light. And the older we get, the more light we need; one study shows that a 60 year old will need roughly twice as much light to carry out the same task as a 30 year old. During the day visually demanding tasks are best carried out by a window, preferably one which faces north to avoid the glare of direct sunlight. After dark, general background lighting should be supplemented by an adjustable light source that can be used to bring light directly to bear on the work surface without casting shadows, or causing glare. The Anglepoise lamp, with hinged sprung joints, originally derived from the suspension system of an early military tank, is still the standard by which all other task lighting is judged.

4 Vico Magistretti designed his table lamp to look as if the top is about to fall off the base.

5 Lighting can be fun; a handful of coloured balloon lights are an amusing touch in a child's room, or even at parties.

6 Putting cables in wall-mounted conduits is a cheap and tidy way of wiring up lights.

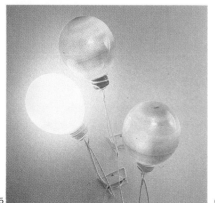

LIGHTING SYSTEMS

Uplighters

The standard lamp has seen a major revival since the quartz halogen bulb became generally available. The more powerful light source has made it possible for the standard lamp to become the means of providing general background light – dispensing with ceiling fittings, complicated wiring and any need to put cables inside walls altogether. From being a clumsy, heavy-shaded affair, standing uncomfortably in corners, the standard lamp, or uplighter as it has become known, is now the mainstay of contemporary lighting schemes, suitable for use in a variety of styles of interior.

These lights generally have a strong sculptural presence, tall, elegant and geometrically pure. In large open plan interiors they can be used to help differentiate one area from another and, by their positioning, to indicate circulation routes.

They work either by screening their bulbs altogether, and bouncing light off the ceiling, or by allowing their light to diffuse through translucent shades, or a combination of the two. Other refinements that are now generally included are an adjustable hinged head, which allows the beam of light to be angled in any direction, and a foot-operated dimmer switch.

1

2

1 The 1950s feel of this room is reinforced by the standard lamp, a nouveau antique with two translucent coloured tops on curved brass stems.

2 Variations on a theme: the uplighter on the far left has an adjustable top so that you can angle light back down into the room. The others either hide the light source with varying degrees of elegance, or expose it, allowing light directly into the room, rather than bouncing it back off the ceiling.

3 From left to right: adjustable track-mounted spotlamps which can be used both vertically and mounted on walls or ceilings; floor-mounted standard lamp with angled top and anti-glare baffle; vertical neon tube in a neatly profiled fitting; unfussy steel light with adjustable top and quartz halogen bulb; totem pole light, originally intended for garden use; series of lights suspended between two wires; giant glass cone, a soft light source best positioned against a wall; uplighter which directs all its light up onto an adjustable disc which then reflects it out into the room.

4 A traditional standard lamp, the forerunner of today's flamboyant sculptural uplighters.

5 The effect of an uplighter is to emphasize the ceiling and upper part of the walls at the expense of the floor. It also provides a restful source of background light.

STORAGE

Before you plan exactly what kind of storage to opt for, think clearly about how each room is used. In design terms, it's all too easy to envisage continual well-ordered perfection with not a book out of place; in practice a good storage system must cope with the everyday essentials of life – the papers, clothes, records, pots, pans and so on. Unless these are all given a proper home, they will inevitably swamp what may initially seem the tidiest of interiors with distracting clutter. There are people who, self-disciplined and tidy, feel happy clearing up as they go along, discarding or re-allocating the sea of assorted objects acquired during the course of a day. But most of us need copious storage, where we can hide all the clutter, and find necessary household items when we want them.

Don't fall into the trap of making storage a last minute afterthought; by that stage it is much too late to do more than the basic minimum. To incorporate storage most effectively into an interior scheme, it should be considered early in your plans, so that it is possible to make the most of limited space, by integrating the storage with any furniture, and architectural features.

The method of storage you choose should take into account the character of the room, the people who use it, and what they will use it for. It is worth compiling a checklist of the items you plan to keep in each room to help you decide how much storage to install – you will be surprised by the length of the completed list. It is impossible to have too much storage: shelves, walk-in cupboards, and wardrobes will all be used eventually.

Decide at the same time as planning your types of storage, where you will want to keep things; the options are often wider than you may think. Books, for example, can be just as suitable on shelves in a bedroom as they are in the living room or the dining room. Pots, pans and food would be best stored in the kitchen, but if space is scarce, you may think about keeping items such as plates or glasses in wheeled floor-standing units that can be moved around easily from room to room. Clothes may equally well be kept in a damp-free bathroom cupboard, as in a bedroom wardrobe.

The major practical consideration in determining the type and location of the storage that you need is the frequency with which you will require access. Once in a lifetime items – prams, cabin trunks, archives and the like – can go into the attic, or into underfloor compartments, secure in the knowledge that although the disruption needed to recover them will be severe, it is not likely to occur very often. Everyday items, from cutlery to clothes, will need to be positioned for more readily convenient access. Fuel, bulk purchases of tinned food, and similar items will be in an intermediate category where instant access is not quite so important.

Think carefully about storage when making any initial changes to the internal layout of the house. A complete storage wall of shelves, or a mixture of shelves and modular cabinet units can be the neatest and most effective means of providing the maximum storage in the minimum space. But every partition wall that you demolish, and every radiator that you hang against the length of a wall reduces your chances of achieving it.

Consider also the possibility of using storage units in an architectural way. A free-standing shelving unit, for example, can act as a useful room divider, defining two individual spaces within a larger room. Wardrobes can be used to screen the bed in studio apartments from being the first thing that you see on entering the room.

Bear in mind not just the sheer capacity of your storage, and its location, But also the effect it will have on the look of your interior. Far from being unobtrusive, built-in units which may cut unsympathetically into attractive cornices, mouldings and skirtings will not only look instantly wrong, but end up making a room seem smaller than it really is.

Free-standing wardrobes or cupboards will look more appropriate in such a setting. Try to use odd corners on long corridors, or the otherwise useless headroom in very tall narrow passages to fit in extra storage space by building a platform to act as a supplementary attic.

3

4

5

6

1 Inspired by the geometric aesthetics of Gerrit Rietveld, architect Robert Barnes designed this storage system for his studio. Rather than blending in as a functional background, the bold dividing struts turn the storage fitting into a major element of the room's design.

2 Old chemist shop drawers bring out everybody's magpie instincts. Attractive pieces of furniture in themselves, they are very useful for storing all those small treasures that in anything bigger would only get lost.

3 An inventive piece of design foresight. Space was allocated right from the start, in this tiny dining room, to store away all the folding chairs, when not in use.

4 Not content with 'storage on show', this do-it-yourself totem pole positively screams for attention. The metal framework is equipped with cheerfully coloured industrial storage bins and mounted on wheels so that the television can be conveniently moved around.

5 Providing a dual role of storage space and room divider, there are several off-the-shelf storage systems now available offering tables, shelves and cupboard space in matching finishes and styles.

6 Storage space can be used with architectural emphasis. The free-standing cupboards not only help to separate living room from kitchen, they also act as a buffer to shield the small apartment from facing directly onto the front door.

SHOWING OFF

Storage does not necessarily mean you have to hide things away. Often the contents of a kitchen cupboard, or a bookcase can look good in their own right, an asset to the atmosphere and the appearance of a room, simply by being left on show in an attractive way. Neat rows of paperback books, or professional looking pots and pans hanging down from the ceiling can be effective decorative elements while at the same time being stored conveniently. But it does depend on how tidy you are prepared to be if you are to show off your storage to best advantage.

Sometimes the best answer is simply to put a few items out on show, a matching pair of glasses on a shelf for example. In other situations, it looks more effective to do things in bulk – a stack of wine bottles in several racks, not just one, for example, looks purposeful, especially if you light it well.

1 A series of metal grids strung together with butcher's hooks provide a handy storage surface for lightweight items.

2 Modular storage systems can be built up piece by piece. With a variety of different fronts and interior fittings, you can choose what to show or hide.

3 An office on show, particularly in a domestic setting can look very colourful. Mesh is set within a Dexion framework and the tough industrial finish is brightened up with carefully chosen primary colours.

4 Storage skilfully turned into a work of art. A Perspex structure with the ghost of a pediment allows a collection of ceramics to appear to float weightlessly in space.

There are many different ways of displaying storage for show, from the traditional kitchen dresser sporting a cheerful row of plates and mugs dangling by their handles, or an antique glass-fronted cabinet in the living room, to a high tech metal grid on the wall of the study, providing a framework on which to hang small implements and stack letters.

Wall-mounted shelves

Don't forget that the storage system itself can look attractive, whether it be an antique wardrobe, or a tubular steel shelving support. Choose yours for simplicity and robustness as well as flexibility. Wall-mounted shelves look best when deployed in quantity. A whole stack of them running from floor to ceiling will look better than a single lonely specimen. And where possible have them running the full length of a wall, or else fit shelves to coincide with

some natural division in a wall; such as the alcoves on each side of a chimney breast, or beneath a window.

With any type of wall-mounted system, you will need a smooth perpendicular wall surface. Be sure that the wall is strong or in good enough condition to take the load. With modern plasterboard partition walls this is not always the case – stick to outside or party walls in these circumstances, or find the timber studs within the internal wall, and fix shelving supports directly to these.

Proprietary shelving systems

These come in many different forms, both wall-mounted and free-standing. Typically a wall-mounted system will include metal upright pieces, which are fixed to the wall, and brackets which clip into the uprights to support the shelves. The distance between uprights is determined by the weight of the

storage that you plan to support. With some systems you can fit shelves at any point on the upright, others can only be positioned at pre-determined points.

Remember that wall-hung storage units are not always as flexible as they seem. They are always harder to take down and relocate than you expect, and if you are re-planning a room, or moving out, it is impossible to move them without leaving an unsightly scar in the plaster work.

Free-standing shelving

This form of storage takes up slightly more room, but is much easier to dismantle and take away when you move. It is, if you choose the right type, more flexible too. It can be pushed hard up against a wall, or moved toward the centre of a room to help define different areas. It can also provide a work surface, or a desk unit, if you include deep shelves at the right height.

Free-standing shelving can mean either an individual piece of furniture, or a modular system which can be expanded in stages to provide as much or as little storage as you need, by linking basic components together. Tubular steel or timber are the most common materials. The latter is more likely to need bracing of some kind to give it stability, which makes it not quite so useful as the metal variety which can be approached from both sides of the unit.

5 Consider the textures of what you are displaying. Mellowed leather book spines make an intriguing contrast against the harsh modern brick pillar and glossy red shelves.

6 Floor to ceiling storage such as this is as much decorative as it is practical.

HIDING AWAY

Not all storage looks good on show. If you are trying to achieve a cool, calm interior with simple shapes, and minimal distractions, it is best to hide untidy clutter away. Even more important, when you are trying to make a room perform a variety of functions, hiding the basic props in unobtrusive cupboards will allow you far more scope. In a bathroom, for example, you might hide the washing machine and ironing board in a walk-in cupboard. If you want to use a bedroom or a corner of the living room as a study, then full height closing doors concealing built-in shelves, will allow you to hide all your papers and files instantly, without having to tidy everything away each time you want to stop work.

Concealment can be achieved with nothing more elaborate than a roller or Venetian blind positioned across the front of a tier of shelves. It may be a sliding door across one whole side of a room, or a wall of elaborate built-in cupboards – expensive and permanent.

The latter also becomes a major element in the design and furnishing of a room, and has the potential to alter its proportions radically. Handle with the same care and attention to detail as the rest of the room. If you have architectural elaborations such as cornices and mouldings, then think about matching them in the treatment of built-in cupboard doors, and choose appropriate handles too. Or else make the whole installation as unobtrusive as possible, using drawers and cupboard doors that open smoothly without handles, and minimizing the gaps between opening leaves. Make this kind of storage work as hard as possible for you – it is after all a major investment that you will be unlikely to take with you when you move. If you are using it in a bedroom or a bathroom, consider facing the doors with mirrors.

When choosing the wall on which to locate built-in cupboards, think about the potential for improvising sound insulation between rooms. Make sure that you have a sufficient range of different types of storage provision inside, both hanging and shelf space of the appropriate size and shape.

Consider also the possibility of using unfamiliar types of storage, perhaps installing the same system in both kitchen and dining room. Or you might prefer industrial wire racks in the bedroom as a useful way of storing folded clothes.

Remember, if you are buying off-the-shelf units, not to be put off by small details – it is easy to replace an ugly handle, or respray an unsightly strip of fake teak, and in this way you can make substantial savings by buying the most basic of units.

1

2

1 With dramatic, almost Oriental simplicity, this cupboard has the capacity to hide a multitude of sins. A custom-made variation on the traditional wardrobe, two banks of shelves mounted on hinges swing out to reveal a serving hatch beyond.

2 Any awkward space can be turned into effective and discreet storage by fitting a door across. Michael Baumgarten designed these units in his London loft to echo the shape of the staircase.

3 Robert Barnes designed his kitchen in Mondrian red, white and blue squares. The units do not register as cupboards but, more subtly, as flat decorative wall panels.

4 Getting maximum use out of built-in storage can be tricky, if you are not to end up with too many cupboard doors all banging against each other, or with inaccessible corners. Here, a combination of sliding shelves and hinged cupboards held in place with magnetic catches is neat and unobtrusive. The effect of such well-ordered geometry is emphasized by the carefully positioned mirror.

5 The warm, wood-panelled atmosphere redolent of an Edwardian library, is evoked by designer Colin Forbes with his finely detailed storage units. The chrome finished twist-and-pull handles are neatly inlaid into the timber facings.

6 When you cannot obtain colour and pattern from the objects you display, take note from architect Ian Ritchie. He designed this wall of storage units using a range of colours to stop it becoming too bland an element in the interior.

FIXTURES AND FITTINGS

We experience an interior at two levels. First impressions are made by the overall effect and depend on colour schemes, textures, furniture and lighting. These elements blend together, layer upon layer like a collage to create a single look. But just as important are what we find at close-up level – the details: all the door handles, window catches, hinges, switches and gadgets that make an interior actually function. If the view seen through half closed eyes is not attractive, then an interior will never look right. But unless the details work as well, then the favourable first impression will quickly be dissipated.

Getting the details right depends on choosing the appropriate fixtures and fittings. They have to work well as a group, and they have to fit in, unobtrusively, with the overall intentions of the interior scheme.

In general therefore, these elements should not be skimped on. Relative expense is a measure of quality, though that doesn't mean you have to go overboard with gold and onyx taps. It can make good sense to opt for a relatively cheap, simple range of kitchen storage units, and elevate them by selecting your own special handles. This small touch will upgrade the feeling of quality of the whole product, not necessarily because the handles are ornate, but because they feel right.

1 Jan Kaplicky has designed a special bracket to support a television in high tech style.

2 A doormat lined up neatly with the grid of the floor tiles.

3 Getting the details right is a matter of bringing together a host of different patterns — produced here by the carpet, tiles, blind and underfloor heating vent — in a way that looks as if it is intentional, not an accident.

4 A real porthole recycled as a bathroom window. The chrome finish echoes the sponge rack.

5 Make sure that electric sockets match the dimensions of your tiles. Lining them up looks tidy, and means that you don't have to cut too many tiles.

6 An original touch: a curved door, in which the designer has taken the trouble to recess the area around the handle.

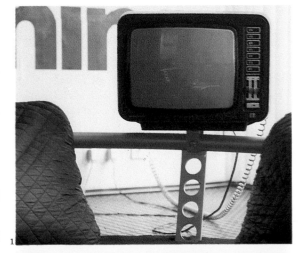

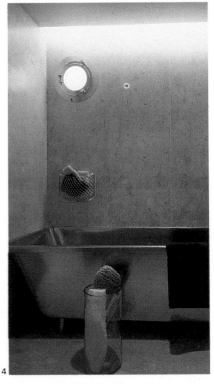

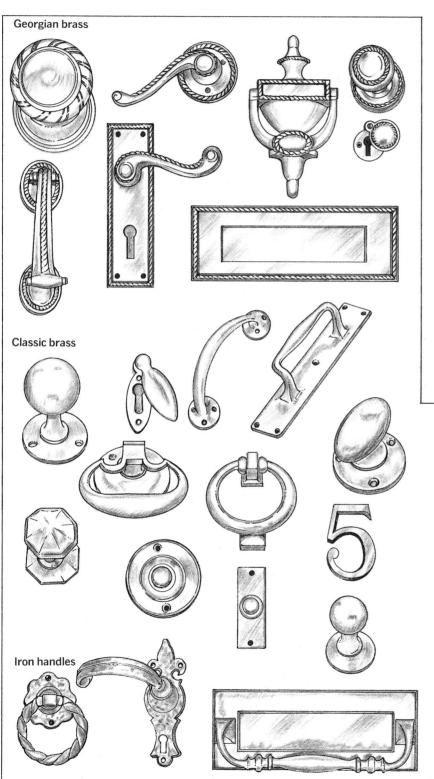

Georgian brass

Classic brass

Iron handles

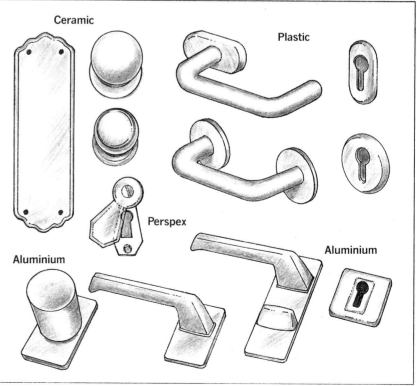

Ceramic

Plastic

Perspex

Aluminium

Aluminium

Door furniture

In the past the importance of the fixtures and fittings in an interior was acknowledged by the care which architects would lavish on the design of special ranges of door furniture, taps and hinges, even cutlery for their more elaborate buildings. In the mass produced climate of the present, this practice has almost disappeared, and we must rely on a careful selection of off-the-shelf products, leavened by a few recycled second-hand fittings.

If you are content to leave the selection of door furniture to your builder, just one insensitive choice – crude handles on the doors, or clumsy catches on the kitchen cabinets – may disrupt the harmonious impression that you had planned. With care it is still possible to work towards a single consistent look throughout a house; one can select families of handles that match with hooks, mirrors, catches, taps or keyholes. But, as with so many other elements of an interior, it is important to use hardware that is appropriate for the style of the house. In an unsympathetically modernized house for example, you would immediately notice the jarring effect of unpleasant plastic door handles, substituted for the original brass. Together with hardboard tacked over panelled doors, they were the DIY devices of the 1960s, applied in a naive attempt to achieve the sought-after simplicity of the style of that era.

If you are going to make the effort to rip off the hardboard, try to get door furniture that fits in with the original design: brass will always look fine. Good manufacturers now offer straight-forward contemporary versions of the ornate Edwardian originals; second-hand shops may stock more economic alternatives. Door handles, knobs, pulls, knockers, numbers, letterbox flaps and bell pushes should be all of a matching set. Differently scaled doors will of course require differently proportioned furniture, but there is no reason why they cannot all come from a consistently designed family of products.

Electrical fittings

Inside the home, similarly close and careful attention needs to be paid to the choice of electrical fittings; the switches and switch plates, the power points and sockets, the ceiling roses and so on. With these, the question of getting the period style right is rather more problematic than it is for handles. After all, many houses were designed long before electricity was generally available for domestic purposes, but installing electric light fittings that look like melting candles in an attempt to recreate that era, will just look foolish.

Switches

Georgian style chased metal switch plates can look almost as inept a compromise as melting candle lights. But a plain, polished brass switch plate would look appropriate in both contemporary and traditional settings.

It is particularly important to get the positioning of electrical fittings right. Don't cut into door frames or panelling to place switches. And make sure that your electrician positions the switches with some thought for the look of the finished interior. If you want to minimize the impact of your switches, then opt to have them sunk flush into the plasterwork. On the other hand, if you are after a high tech industrial look, use exposed metal conduits to carry the cables, and install bulky metal power points and switch boxes proud of the wall.

When choosing your switch fittings, don't simply opt for the cheapest or the most basic products; the choice is wider than you may think, varying from plastic to metal in a variety of finishes. If you are planning to use dimmer switches the choice becomes still wider, with varying sizes of rotating switch. Some dimmers can emit an irritating buzz when they are in use. It is worth testing them for noise if it is likely to disturb you.

Electric sockets

Power points can be an even more intrusive element in an interior than light switches. The simplest way of rewiring is often to run plastic conduit around the skirting boards, and tack on the power points at the same level.

However this can look unsightly, especially when you have a few fittings plugged in, and cables running everywhere. Equally, positioning your power points in the middle of a wall can look like a crude afterthought. To minimize the intrusiveness of a power point, sink it flush into the wall, or even the floor, where it can be covered with a special hinged flap. Group sockets in twos and threes for neatness. This can be especially important in a kitchen, where sockets will be close to eye level, and will need to be carefully positioned to fit in with the module of the tiles backing the work surfaces.

Bathroom fixtures

In the bathroom, the range of fixtures and fittings expands to include mirrors, trays, dishes and soap holders, and toothbrushes as well as towel rails and special power points for shavers. It is therefore even more important to keep the visual clutter under control by choosing compatible fittings. It's possible to choose pieces from a range that includes everything from taps and shower heads to lavatory handles and soap holders. They come in an assortment of colours, are dimensionally co-ordinated with the standard tile sizes, and, by using similar shapes and materials, are designed to look like part of a single family.

The key to dealing successfully with fixtures and fittings depends on the ability to recognize these elements – the visual equivalent of white noise – which are usually taken for granted in the general mêlée of an interior, and to civilize them, either by choosing more attractive fittings, by positioning them in the least obtrusive way possible, or even concealing them altogether.

Radiators

Among the least attractive, but most essential fixtures, radiators present problems in decoration. If yours are the bulky old-fashioned models, your best course of action might be to conceal them behind a cover, which allows the heat to escape, but can still look attractive. Slim modern radiators are far less intrusive, and could be decorated to match your walls – marbled or stippled, for example.

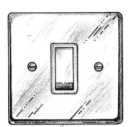

Brass wall switch

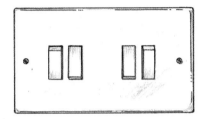

Plastic two pair switch

Georgian brass double dimmer switch

Brass triple dimmer switch

Plastic dimmer switch

Brass double wall socket

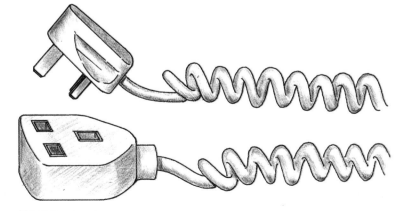

Movable extension socket and plug

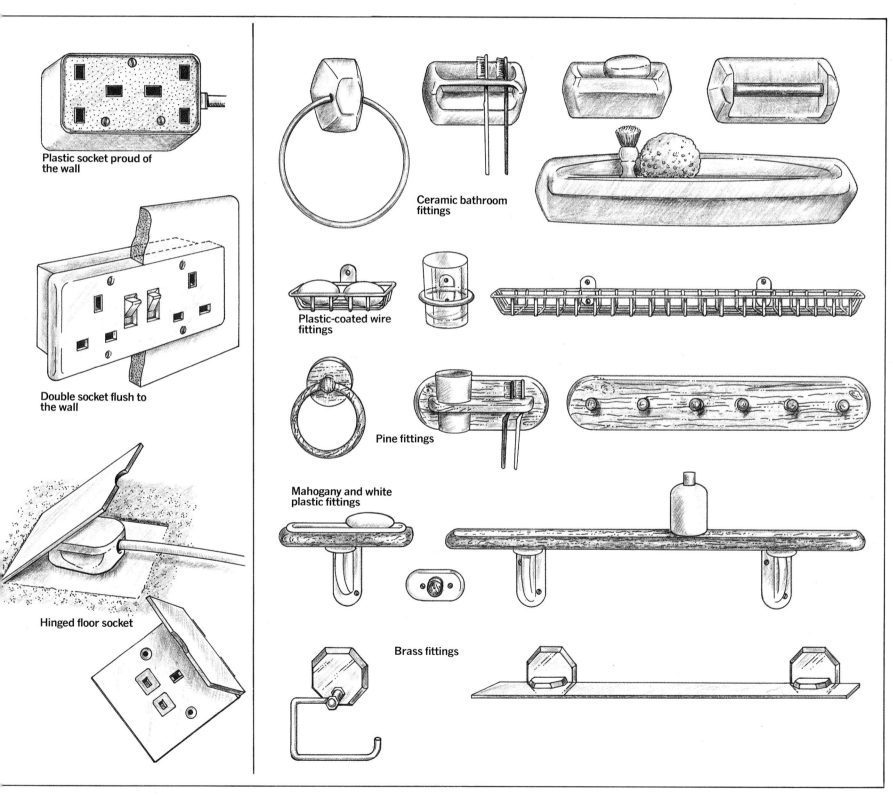

Plastic socket proud of the wall

Double socket flush to the wall

Hinged floor socket

Ceramic bathroom fittings

Plastic-coated wire fittings

Pine fittings

Mahogany and white plastic fittings

Brass fittings

SECURITY

No lock, bolt or chain will ever make your house completely burglar proof. Even alarms, surveillance cameras and grilles across the windows are not invulnerable. Of course adequate insurance cover is an essential protection for your valuables, but this does not mean that you should neglect the quality of the security fixtures with which your home is equipped – in any case no insurance company will give you full cover unless they are satisfied you have taken reasonable precautions.

Protecting your property should start with a proper analysis of your home's weak points, and the potential threat. It is worth contacting your local police station for advice from their security expert. The main risk is from casual walk-in thieves who are after easily portable valuables: video cassette recorders, television sets, cash, jewellery and so on. Most such crimes are committed in broad daylight, so these thieves will not want to spend time forcing locks in public view. And in the nature of things they believe in a quiet life, so why bother to spend the ten minutes it may take to circumvent a mortise dead lock when they know that next door they can walk virtually straight in? Don't make things easy for them.

Door locks
In most homes it is always possible to improve protection against unwelcome visitors. The conventional rim latch, with which many doors are fitted, presents no obstacle at all to even the least expert of housebreakers. The latch can be slipped with a penknife or even a piece of celluloid. And since the latch is fixed to the inside of the door, not let into its edge, there are only the screws which hold it in position to stop a hefty shoulder pushing it in.

The strongest device for protecting the door is a proper mortise lock, fitted into the door itself, with its plate set into the frame. You have to unlock and lock this as you go in and out, but it is a small price to pay for the extra security.

There is no point in strengthening the security fittings, if the door itself is still vulnerable. If you have an all glass door, the strongest mortise locks will be useless, unless you fit Georgian wired glass. Equally, if a door's hinges are exposed, a determined burglar can work these open.

Other easily taken security measures for your doors would be bolts, chains and peepholes, to ensure that you know who you are opening the door to. Even if you live off the ground in a block of apartments, you should still protect your front door. Multiple occupancy apartments with entryphone remote door opening systems are rarely very secure.

Window locks
You need to get a balance between the fitting and the kind of door and window openings you have. Don't expect a well guarded front door to be of much use, if a burglar can slip around the side of

Mortise deadlock

Front entrance mortise deadlock

Rear entrance mortise deadlock

Security bolt for glass doors

Door chain

Spy hole

Patio door lock

your house, and find a louvred glass window – a type which is impossible to protect, and which should never be fitted on the ground floor. Similarly don't forget to protect the back door, or easily reached upper windows.

Ground floor windows can be even simpler than doors to open. A penknife slipped in between two sliding sash windows is all it takes to push back the catch. It is important to protect all your ground floor windows with toughened bolts that screw into the frame, and remember to screw them in tight every time you go out.

Garage locks

If you have a built-in garage which opens into your house, don't forget to protect the garage door too. If the up-and-over frame doesn't have the strength to take a mortise lock, you should concentrate on protecting the door from the garage into the house itself.

Deterrent systems

For most of us locks will be an adequate measure to provide the minimal extra protection required to deter casual thieves. But for high risk crime areas – which tend to be the wealthier rather than the poorer neighbourhoods – and for people who have irreplaceable objects for which insurance will be no adequate recompense, more elaborate protection may be necessary. Unfortunately many of these devices will have the effect of turning your home into one that is not only protected like a fortress but which looks like one as well. Sliding security gates across ground floor windows always look unattractive. A less intrusive option might be to use steel shutters that look like traditional wooden ones. A very useful form of protection when you are out, is to have a time switch fitted to your wiring system which can switch lights on and off while you are away, giving the impression that the home is occupied.

Alarms

A variety of automatic alarm systems are also available, ranging from the kind with an alarm box mounted on the outside of the house which provides a psychological deterrent, and drives your neighbours to distraction when it is triggered accidentally while you are away for the weekend, to sophisticated systems that are linked to phone lines to the local police station or security firm.

The simplest of these systems sets off an alarm when electric circuits are broken by opening wired up doors or windows. The most elaborate kind uses infra-red light to detect an intruder.

You must decide, when protecting your home, how far you want to sacrifice the pleasure of open windows, and a relaxed atmosphere, in the desire to hang on to your possessions. It can be very irritating when granny comes to stay, walks through three infra-red beams on the way to the larder, and is then forced to share her midnight snack with half the local police force who have raced to the scene.

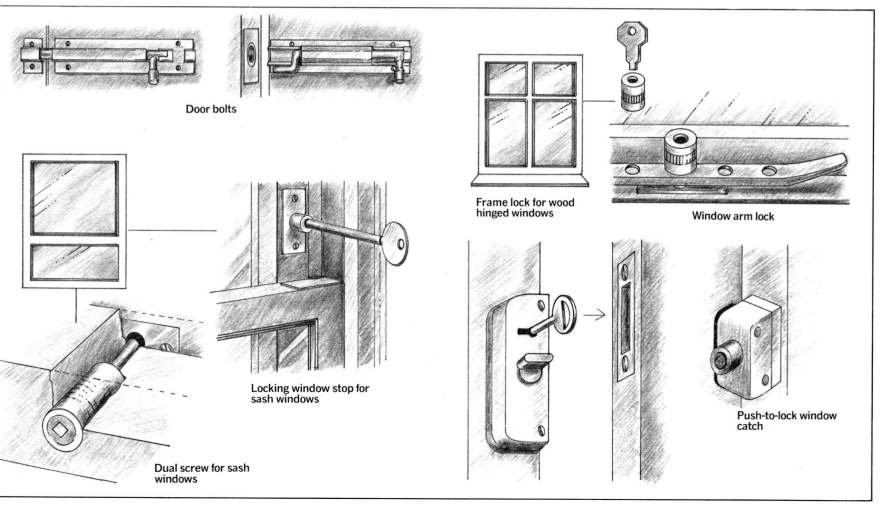

Door bolts

Frame lock for wood hinged windows

Window arm lock

Locking window stop for sash windows

Dual screw for sash windows

Push-to-lock window catch

HEATING AND ENERGY

Since 1973 the cost of heating oil has soared by a factor of six, electricity and coal prices have risen by 400 per cent and the average householder now spends about £6-8 per week on fuel, light and power, compared to £2 per week in 1973.

Britain's total fuel bill is currently about £35 billion a year, of which approximately £20 billion is spent on heating and lighting all its buildings. Of this figure roughly half is consumed by heating, lighting and domestic appliances in the home. Various estimates have been made on how much of this vast amount of energy could be saved every year. Most experts agree that it is fairly simple to save about 20-25 per cent of the energy used in the home. Others reckon that a concerted effort could halve most fuel bills. If all the homes in Britain adopted energy conservation measures it would save the same amount of energy as 30 million one-bar electric fires would use running continuously throughout the year. The scope for saving energy is therefore enormous.

What types of fuel do you use?
Energy is supplied to the home using many fuels – coal, gas, electricity, oil, paraffin to name but a few. In the 1950s and '60s coal was by far the most popular household fuel, claiming around 75 per cent of the total. Households using gas, oil or electricity as their main energy source were then quite rare. Today the situation is very different with the four main fuels – coal, gas, oil and electricity – each taking a roughly similar proportion of the total energy cake. Over the last few years both gas and electricity have been given a boost thanks to natural gas finds in the North Sea and the growing trend towards electricity generating nuclear power stations. Oil has fallen in popularity due to price increases.

It is difficult to predict future trends, but as North Sea gas reserves become exhausted it's likely that gas will be scarcer, more expensive, and consequently less commonly used in the home. Electricity will probably hold its own, while coal may well show signs of a recovery, especially as there are underground reserves still available.

How we measure energy
Although coal, paraffin and gas are totally dissimilar, it's fairly simple to transform the energy content of each of the common fuels into a single standard unit. These days we use the kilowatt-hour (kWh). A kilowatt-hour is best visualized as the energy consumed by a one-bar electric fire burning for one hour. A two-bar electric fire, burning for an hour would therefore consume 2kWh. A 1cwt bag of household coal provides about the same energy as 435 one-bar fires burning for an hour (435kWh), while a litre of paraffin would provide the equivalent of ten one-bar fires burning for an hour (10kWh). A cubic foot of natural gas would be equivalent, in energy terms, to a one-bar fire burning for roughly 20 minutes.

How do we use our energy?
For an average three bedroom house with a weekly energy bill of £8, roughly £6 of this is needed to provide background heating in the home, about £1 goes on providing hot water and the rest is consumed by the cooker, lights and domestic appliances. Heating for the home is therefore by far the biggest consumer of energy, and consequently anything you can do to cut back on this big portion of the bill will reap the most obvious savings.

Energy wastage
The first area to concentrate on is energy loss. In a typical home energy is lost through the walls, windows, roof and floor. Energy is also wasted due to draughts and through inefficent boilers and chimneys which vent heat directly to the outside. The other main energy waster is your plughole – every gallon of hot water you pour out of your bath is a potentially valuable source of energy.

In round figures about 20 per cent of all your energy goes up the chimney, about the same goes through the walls, and a similar amount through the windows. Draughts account for about 15 per cent of all heat losses, followed by the roof (about 10 per cent), hot water down the drain (10 per cent) and losses through the floor (roughly 5 per cent).

Saving energy
Clearly it makes sense to begin any energy saving campaign by concentrating on those parts of the home responsible for the main energy losses – check draughts around windows and doors, wall and roof insulation, and your heating system to make sure it isn't losing energy up the chimney. Your hot water cylinder, unless it is already fitted with an insulating jacket, would also be another good candidate for early attention. Once you have tackled these key areas you might then consider fitting proper controls to your present heating system to make it more efficient, insulating existing solid walls, providing insulation under floors and fitting secondary glazing.

Draught stripping
Most homes leak badly, thanks to a combination of poor seals around doors and windows, gaps between floorboards around loft hatches and pipe inlets, and inefficient flues and chimneys.

There are two main types of draught stripping material for use on doors and windows – wiper seals and compression seals. The former tend to be more durable and are often made of a blade of copper or rubberized fabric. Compression seals are cheaper and easier to fit but they don't last as long.

It is usually best to use the more durable wiper seals around doors as they are opened and closed so often. At the base of a door a brush wiper is the simplest answer. For new doors a weather bar is usually provided with a built-in draught stripping device.

It is not easy to generalize about the best type of draught stripping for windows, as there are so many different ones. Wooden casement windows are easiest to cure with self-adhesive compression seals; special wiper seals can be used to remedy the notoriously draughty sash window, and a special chaulking gum usually works best on older metal windows. With new pvc or aluminium frames, nylon brush seals can normally be fed into place where the originals need replacement.

Old suspended timber floors present another draughty problem. Laying hardboard over the top is usually the best solution. Papier-mâché squeezed into the cracks is really the only other answer if you want to keep the boards open to view. Loft hatches should be sealed using self-adhesive compression seals, and the gaps between window or door frames and the walls, or around pipe inlets, should be sealed with flexible mastic. Letter boxes can be sealed using a two-brush seal and keyholes can be fitted with a flip cover. Automatic door closers are also worth considering, as are removable covers for fireplaces not in use.

Porches are a very wise investment as they provide an air-lock between the cold exterior and the warm interior.

Controlling ventilation
Good, controlled ventilation is, of course, essential for both health and safety. This is especially true with heating appliances. If you have any type of fire or boiler with a flue it is essential that this is never blocked. These appliances need a supply of air to burn safely and efficiently.

In some parts of your home you may find, particularly in winter months, that opening a window is rather a crude way of controlling the ventilation. Several types of 'trickle' ventilator are now available that are designed to fit into window frames or the glass of a window. These offer far greater control of ventilation, and are particularly well-suited to kitchens and bathrooms, where condensation may be a problem.

Insulation
Having eliminated the draughts the next priority is insulation. The easiest parts of the home to insulate are usually the hot water cylinder and the roof. Wall insulation is more complex and costly, particularly if your existing walls are solid all the way through.

Hot water tanks It is a very easy task to fit a ready-made insulating jacket to a hot water cylinder tank. Use a jacket that is at least 8cm (3in.) thick and be sure to choose one that bears a British Standard Kitemark. A properly fitted jacket will pay for itself in a matter of weeks, so is an extremely worthwhile investment.

Roofs An uninsulated roof space will usually account for at least ten per

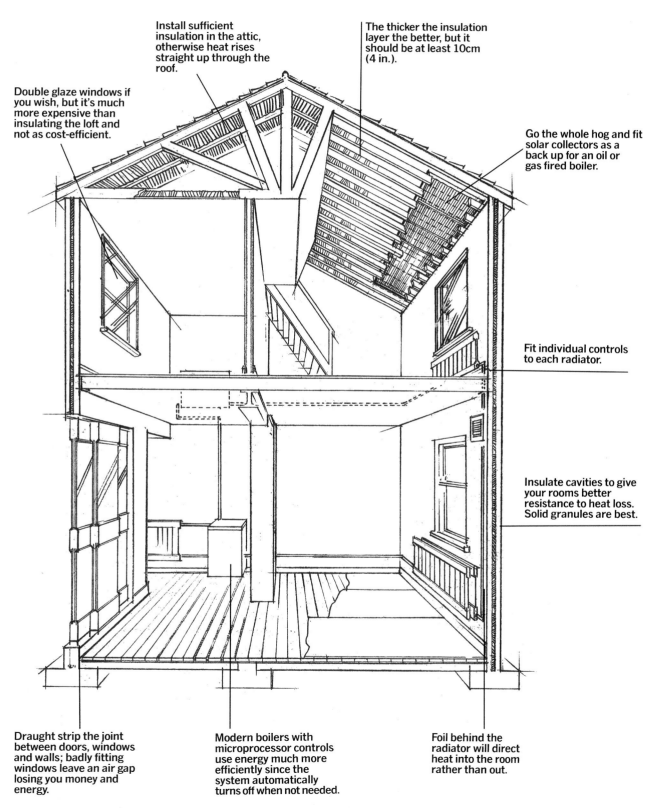

Install sufficient insulation in the attic, otherwise heat rises straight up through the roof.

The thicker the insulation layer the better, but it should be at least 10cm (4 in.).

Double glaze windows if you wish, but it's much more expensive than insulating the loft and not as cost-efficient.

Go the whole hog and fit solar collectors as a back up for an oil or gas fired boiler.

Fit individual controls to each radiator.

Insulate cavities to give your rooms better resistance to heat loss. Solid granules are best.

Draught strip the joint between doors, windows and walls; badly fitting windows leave an air gap losing you money and energy.

Modern boilers with microprocessor controls use energy much more efficiently since the system automatically turns off when not needed.

Foil behind the radiator will direct heat into the room rather than out.

cent of all heat loss from a home and, in exceptional cases, can be responsible for as much as 30-40 per cent of the heat wasted. Insulating a roof is a fairly simple do-it-yourself job and costs comparatively little. And if you haven't already tackled it you should be eligible for a grant towards the cost from your local council. If you apply for a grant remember you cannot begin the work until the council approves your application (see the chapter on The Paperwork).

If your home possesses a conventional accessible loft space, putting in insulation is a quick and simple matter. There are many different types of insulation available: in rolls, as fibre, in slabs and even as little balls. Whatever type you choose ensure it's at least 10cm (4in.) thick.

Insulation is usually placed between the joists, leaving a small gap near the eaves to allow for continued ventilation in your loft space. If you block out all the ventilation at the eaves you may get condensation problems in the loft. Don't forget to insulate the top of the loft hatch (this is easiest using a little insulation in a plastic bag that is then taped to the hatch) and carefully wrap up all cold water pipes and cold water tanks in the loft. This is very important as once you have insulated your roof space it becomes colder, and pipes are therefore more likely to freeze. Remember always to use gloves and to wear a dust mask if you are using a mineral fibre insulation to avoid skin and lung irritations.

If you have a flat roof or an attic room that needs insulating it is usually simplest to use slabs of foam insulation, fitted between the rafters.

A sheet of polythene to act as a vapour barrier, and a layer of plasterboard are then applied. Again, to avoid problems with condensation, ensure there is at least a 2.5cm (1in.) air gap between your insulation and the tiles. Flat roofs can be treated in the same way, or can be insulated on the outside by applying a layer of special water-resistant foam insulation. This is a complex process, so it's best to seek professional advice.

Grants towards loft and hot water cylinder insulation are available from local authority environmental health officers. They usually stand at around 66 per cent of the total cost. For elderly people and those on low incomes, grants of 90 per cent of the cost are available.

Walls and floors   There are three basic types of wall construction; solid walls (common in older houses built before 1935), cavity walls (often comprised of an outer layer of brick then a 5cm/2in. cavity and an inner skin of blockwork) and timber-framed (common since the 1960s and made up of a brick outer skin, a gap and a timber inner frame that is usually filled with insulation).

You can insulate solid walls from either the inside or the outside. From the inside it involves attaching 5 x 5cm (2 x 2in.) timber battens to external walls, applying 5cm (2in.) of insulation in the gaps, carefully sealing with '6 mil' polythene sheeting to act as a vapour barrier. Finally plasterboard and skim over all. Alternatively all-in-one insulation and plasterboard can be used which you can glue or fix direct to the outside wall.

External insulation methods are more expensive and less cost-effective. They are also inappropriate if they are likely to mar the look of your home. There are two main techniques: one involves applying battens, insulation and weather-boarding to all exterior walls; the other uses polystyrene panels that are fixed to the wall, reinforced with a metal mesh and then rendered.

For internal insulation, there are three common materials used to fill cavities in walls: urea-formaldehyde foam (cheap, but some health worries have been expressed, and it has now been ruled unsuitable for timber-framed homes); expanded polystyrene (blow-in resin-coated beads and granules); and mineral fibre (most expensive and again blown-in). This is not a do-it-yourself job, so make sure the contractor you appoint is using a method and a material that complies with the British Standard, or has an Agreement Board certificate.

Suspended timber floors can be insulated by 'hanging' insulation slabs between the joists using netting. If you have enough crawl space under the floor you can insulate without ripping up the whole floor up. With solid floors the best method is to arrange a layer of expanded polystyrene onto the original surface, cover this with polythene sheeting and then fix a tongued and grooved chipboard floor above.

Heating controls

Most energy experts agree that the installation of good heating controls is very cost-effective. In most cases it ranks as a high-priority task, alongside draught stripping and loft insulation.

The simplest form of heating control is the basic boiler thermostat. Try experimenting with yours to see if you still feel comfortable with it turned down a notch or two. You may have got used to very high temperatures at home, perhaps as high as 22°C (71°F), and always walk around in shirt sleeves. Wear warmer clothing and you will probably feel just as comfortable at a temperature of 19°C (67°F). Setting your thermostat back just a few degrees will save you many pounds a year.

More and more homes are now fitted with a time-switch or a central heating and hot water programmer. These are used to ensure your heating and hot water systems are only operating when they are really needed. Some have special features that will take account of your different heating requirements at weekends. Others can be used to activate immersion heaters, night storage heaters and other devices at night, when cheaper rate electricity is available.

Hot water cylinder thermostats are a fairly recent innovation. They limit the temperature in the tank to a pre-set level; consequently the water never becomes scalding hot.

Room thermostats are also a fairly recent phenomenon. These are able to sense the temperature in the room, compare it with a pre-set level, and shut off the heating system if the room is already adequately warm. Most homes only have one thermostat fitted in the hall. A far better solution is to install thermostatic valves to all your radiators. This will give you individual control of the heating level in each room, so you can have, say, just background heating in little used rooms or the bedrooms. The savings that can accrue from controlling the use of energy like this are quite dramatic, and fitting better controls to a heating system is usually quick and simple.

Glazing

Contrary to popular belief the fitting of double glazing is not ordinarily a priority item. Of course it does often help to cut down on draughts, but it is not usually a very cost-effective measure, and often takes 20 years to pay for itself.

If you are determined to fit secondary glazing, the cheapest technique involves securing a layer of flexible plastic sheeting to your window frame using double-sided adhesive tape. Do-it-yourself shops also supply plastic strips in which you can mount glass panes and then clamp to wooden frames. Both these methods are simple, but will not last indefinitely.

Do-it-yourself kits are also available for full secondary glazing, along with an ever-increasing number of systems offered by double glazing contractors. Finally there are sealed double glazed units, some of which use special types of heat-retaining glass. Sealed units normally come complete with a new window frame, though it is possible to buy sealed, double glazed panes just to replace existing single glazed panes.

Two words of warning: make sure your contractor is reputable and his price equates with those of his competitors (the double glazing business attracts many 'cowboys'), and ensure that the new windows don't conflict with the style of the rest of your home. Many modern replacement windows look crude and completely out of place when fitted to a fine Victorian building. Some councils now have local planning bylaws that outlaw architecturally insensitive replacement window systems in older homes.

Good interlined curtains, when closed, can work just as well as double glazing. And the old idea of fitting internal insulation shutters has recently been rediscovered. But for curtains or shutters to be effective it is important that they fit well.

Household appliances

Roughly 20 per cent of all the energy used in the home is consumed by cookers, lighting and other domestic appliances. While this may seem like a relatively small proportion of your total fuel bill it is still quite easy to record considerable savings by choosing your domestic appliances with care, and using them sensibly. Cookers are the biggest offender, so shop around for those with energy conserving features like economy rings for small saucepans, fan-assisted and well-insulated ovens. When you use your cooker remember to keep the lids on your pans, avoid vigorous boiling (it doesn't really speed up the cooking process, and impairs the flavour of food) and consider employing a pressure cooker more often.

Grilling food, though healthy, is an energy wasteful exercise, as most of the heat misses the food. Roasting, frying and boiling are more energy efficient ways. Thus making toast under a cooker grill works out much more costly than using an electric toaster. And if you only want one cup of coffee don't fill the kettle to the brim.

The other big consumers of energy are washing machines, dishwashers, tumble dryers, irons and freezers. To maximize your energy efficiency, always try to use full loads in washing machines, dishwashers and tumble dryers (or if your washing machine has a 'half load' setting make use of it). Some appliances are plumbed into a cold water supply only, and heat up the water internally. This can be rather expensive, so if you already have a supply of cheapish hot water (from a back boiler perhaps) try to choose a machine with a hot and cold water inlet. Irons use a significant amount of electricity, so don't leave them on longer than necessary.

Lights, and appliances like TVs, stereos and radios, use little energy. However, significant savings can still be made by opting for the new types of fluorescent light fitting. These only use 20 per cent of the energy of a conventional bulb and last five times as long. Some of the new, small fittings are very attractive. The snag, of course, is that the capital cost of the bulbs is very high.

Choosing a home heating system

Because each of the main fuel industries vie with each other to sell their own particular energy source, it is very difficult to discover (from their information) which fuel and home heating system offers you the best economy. In recent years, as the price of gas has risen in relation to electricity, the clear-cut case for gas has not been so obvious, and many of the fuels are now fairly level pegging.

The easiest way to cut through the complex tangle of figures is to obtain an excellent and impartial publication from the Energy Efficiency Office at The Department of Energy. Called "A Guide to Home Heating Costs" it is available free of charge from Citizens' Advice Bureaux, local offices of the Department of Energy, and most gas and electricity showrooms.

It is impossible to generalize about which fuel and heating systems will be the most economic for you; it depends on where you live, what fuels are available, type of house and the degree to which it has been insulated.

However, for the typical three bedroom semi, the figures suggest that all-electric heating and hot water systems that make good use of the Economy 7 tariffs are a good buy (about £1,330 to install and £240-330 per year to run). This compares with a mains gas installation costing about £1,520 to fit and between £230 and £320 a year to run, and a solid fuel (anthracite beans) room heater and radiators package costing £1,580 to fit and £310 to £370 a year to run.

What this doesn't take into account is the appearance of the installation and the likely price changes in the rule in coming years. Predicting fuel price rises is a notoriously risky business, but it's likely that gas and oil will continue to increase in cost, while coal will get cheaper, since there are more known natural reserves of coal. Future electricity costs are more difficult to predict, but may well rise, as electricity generating power stations are not proving to be the fantastic source of cheap electricity that was once claimed for them.

When it comes to appearance there's little to compare with a good old-fashioned fireplace. The romantic appeal of logs burning in an open hearth is strong, and certainly leaves floor- and wall-mounted boilers, radiators and portable heaters looking bland by comparison. Fireplaces act as the focus of a room and come in an almost infinite variety of styles. Open fireplaces are, however, very inefficient burners of fuel. A good compromise might be a solid fuel hearth boiler, which gives the attractive warm glow, and can also provide lashings of hot water for a string of radiators and the hot water tank.

Alternative energy sources

Over the last few years a small band of architects and designers have been experimenting with several of the so-called 'alternative' energy sources like solar power, wind power, gases from human waste and water wheels. The results of these experiments are still inconclusive, though it does appear that solar power may prove an energy contributor in homes of the future.

Solar power is harnessed in two main ways; via 'active' solar collectors, and 'passive' solar design features.

'Active' solar collectors usually consist of a device that looks rather like a black painted radiator mounted on the south facing roof of a home. The collector is warmed by the sun's rays which heat up a liquid inside the collector. This liquid is then usually ducted or pumped through to the hot water tank to help boost the temperature of the water it contains. Various active collector systems are already available, but few are likely to last any significant time and most are difficult to justify from a cost-effective point of view.

'Passive' solar energy appears to offer more potential. Typical passive measures include south facing conservatories (which trap hot air and then feed this into the home), larger than normal south facing windows (which work in the same way) and heavyweight floors and walls (to help store the free energy provided by the sun). Conservatories are an especially attractive idea, as they also provide extra living space for a good proportion of the year.

Running Costs of Common Electric Domestic Appliances

The table below shows you how much 'work' or time you would obtain from common household appliances for one kilowatt hour of power. In 1984 one KWh of electricity cost, at daytime rates, approx 5½-6p.

Appliance	Output
Cooker	One meal for family of three
Washing Machine (automatic)	One day's washing for family of three
Dishwasher	About a third of a load
Freezer (3 cu. m/10 cu. ft)	About 12 hours
Fridge	About 24 hours
Tumble Dryer	About 30 minutes
Spin Dryer	About 5 weeks' laundry
Toaster	70 slices of toast
Vacuum Cleaner	2-4 hours
Television (black & white)	14 hours
Television (colour)	12 hours
Stereo System	8-10 hours
Radio	Over 20 hours
Kettle	12 pints of boiling water
Iron	Just over 2 hours
Food Mixer	60 cakes
Food Blender	500 pints of soup
Can Opener	About 6000 cans
Coffee Percolator	75 cups of coffee
Tea Maker	35 cups of tea
100W Tungsten Filament Light Bulb	10 hours
Low Energy Fluorescent Equivalent	50 hours
Standard 5ft Fluorescent Tube	10 hours
Electric DIY Drill	4 hours
Hair Dryer	3 hours
Under Blanket	One week
Shaver	Nearly 2000 shaves
1 kw Infra Red Heater	1 hour
2 kw Fan Heater	30 minutes
3 kw Radiant Heater	20 minutes

Running Costs of Domestic Gas Appliances

The Gas Board sells gas by the therm (a therm of gas is equivalent to 29.5 kWh of electricity). In 1984 one therm of gas, inclusive of a proportion of the standing charge, cost about 38p. The table below shows how much time you will obtain for one therm.

Appliance	Output
Cooker Oven	36 hours on Mark 2, 20 hours on Mark 7
Cooker Grill	7 hours
Cooker Hotplate	9 hours on high, 133 hours on low
Gas Fire	5 hours on high, 10 hours on low
Fridge	One week
Freezer	5 days
Hot Water	8 baths, 32 showers or 82 bowls of washing up

THE PAPERWORK

Britain's planning system is something of a minefield, so it is always advisable to visit your council's planning department well before you start any improvement work just to check what the local position is.

For many home improvements planning permission is not required, whilst for others, even apparently quite minor things like replacement windows or decorative wall claddings, do need to win planning approval before you can begin. However, there is a piece of legislation called the General Development Order which gives 'automatic' planning permission for many types of home extension provided that:

1 The extension is no greater than 70 cubic metres (230 cubic feet) or 15 per cent of the original volume of the house, whichever is the greater, subject to a maximum limit of 115 cubic metres (373 cubic feet).

2 The extension, or any other improvements, do not make the house any higher.

3 The extension, if more than 4m (13ft) high, is no closer to your boundary than 2m (6½ft).

4 The extension or improvement doesn't project further forward than the front of the house in any way.

5 The extension doesn't result in more than half the garden area being built on.

This makes it all sound relatively simple. In practice, of course, it never is. For example if you live in a conservation area, an Area of Outstanding Natural Beauty, a National Park or your house is in a terrace, the permitted extension is restricted to 50 cubic metres (162 cubic feet), or to 10 per cent of the original house volume. If you are planning a porch you are automatically given permission if the floor area is less than 2 sq. m (6 sq. ft), and it is no more than 3m (9ft) tall – but only if it is not within 2m (6ft) of the road. Garages are treated as house extensions if they stand within 5m (16ft) of the house. If they are required to stand further away gaining permission will be more complicated, but will still be granted without too much fuss, provided they are no more than 3m (9ft) high (4m/12ft for a ridged

roof), that they do not cover more than half the garden, and that they do not project in front of the house. For those who live in a listed building the rules are far more rigorous: even a new coat of paint for the front door will need to be approved.

Whatever type of house you live in, the rule is *always* check with the local planning department before embarking on any work.

How to apply for planning permission

If, after checking with your town hall, you discover that your proposals do require planning permission, you will have to brace yourself for some extra bureaucracy. Every planning application requires a set of plans and elevations showing the proposed work and construction details, a site plan (usually to a scale of 1:1250 or 1:2500), details of the materials proposed and a form filled out in triplicate. You also need to complete a certificate to indicate that you own the property (or the owner knows what you are up to).

The planners will also require a fee for processing your mountain of paperwork and drawings. Theoretically they will evaluate your proposals and either approve or reject them within eight weeks of submission. Quite often, however, there are delays, so be prepared for a longer wait.

Should your proposals be rejected you can appeal to the Department of the Environment's Planning Inspectorate. Appeals must be lodged within six months of refusal and are usually heard via written submissions from both sides to an Inspector. Preparing a good submission can be expensive and most housing appeals are dismissed, so be sure that you have a very strong case.

Your chances of winning planning consent in the first place are usually greatly enhanced if you have an architect working for you (see the chapter on Dealing with the Experts).

Building regulations

Building regulations have got nothing to do with planning permission; their purpose is to check that what you are planning to build will stand up, and is properly constructed to meet health

and safety and modern thermal and noise insulation requirements. The current legislation fills a fat document and goes into great, and often baffling, detail. Unless you are familiar with the basics of the building industry it is not very easy to 'read-up' on the building regulations to ensure that you comply with everything that is demanded of you. Professional advice is nearly always worth considering.

To obtain building regulations' approval you need to submit detailed plans, elevations and sections showing all the proposed work, and constructional details, together with a site location plan. You also need to complete a form and pay a fee.

Building regulations' approval usually takes about six weeks. Once it is yours, the council issues a batch of postcards one of which you have to send in to the town hall whenever significant stages in the building work are completed – for example, when the drains are ready for inspection, or the foundations have been built. The council's building inspector will then visit the site to ensure the work has been completed to a satisfactory standard, and if it has, he will give you the go ahead to proceed to the next phase. If it is not up to scratch he will demand that the work be put right. At the end of the job he will make a final inspection. You can ask for a letter to confirm the work was completed to building regulations' standards, but these are not normally issued unless specifically requested.

Improvement grants

The drawback to obtaining a grant towards improvement on your home is that the council will demand that the work be carried out to its set standards – standards which might well be way above yours. They might also demand that other improvements be undertaken to ensure the whole house is brought up to scratch. You may well decide that it's not worth incorporating the long list of additional improvements just so that you can qualify for a small grant on the work you require. On the other hand, if you are planning across-the-board improvements involving plumbing and electrics, insulation and heating, the

total improvement grant could run into thousands of pounds.

There are two main types of grant aid that you could be eligible for: intermediate grants and improvement grants. Intermediate grants will contribute towards the provision of basic amenities like a bath or shower, inside lavatory, wash basin and hot and cold water. If these facilities are lacking, you will generally have the right to a grant for this type of work. There is, however, a long list of conditions attached.

Your house must have been built before 1961: it must have a rateable value of less than £225 (£400 in London) per year (except in designated housing action areas); and you are required to live in the house yourself for at least five years after the work has been done. This final point is, however, not always insisted on, and it is very rare for a council to demand its grant money back if you move on, say two years later.

Improvement grants are awarded at the discretion of your local council and will go towards work such as enlarging kitchens or bathrooms, or structural repairs. Exactly how much you are entitled to as part of an intermediate grant depends on several factors. The Government sets 'eligible expense limits' for the fitting of items such as lavatories and baths, and you will never get more than this. You will also only ever get a percentage of this total 'eligible expense limit'. What percentage you will qualify for depends on the area you live in and your personal circumstances.

Since improvement grants are awarded by your local council, your entitlement quite often depends on how much money the council has in its purse. At the end of the financial year the supply may be completely exhausted, so it's worth considering making an application in the late spring or early summer when the council's coffers are usually at their fullest.

The only way to obtain full details of what you might be liable for is to pay a visit to the local environmental health department at your council offices. The alternative is to employ an architect to do all the intricate paperwork for you.

Even the most competent handyman will have to resort to employing skilled craftsmen from time to time, or will need the services of a professional architect or surveyor. But finding the right people to help you is often a difficult task, and ensuring the work is completed to the standard you desire is even harder to achieve.

Very few building projects are completed without at least one dust-up between the owner and his builders or professional advisors. But if you plan carefully from the very beginning and ensure everything is properly recorded and understood before you start, the chances of acrimony can certainly be reduced.

The first thing you need to do is get a clear idea of exactly what you want from your home. Do you really need an extension? If you enlarged the living room and knocked the dining room into the kitchen could this work just as well? How will your needs change over the coming years, as say, your children grow up and leave the home? Will you then be left with a rarely used and expensive-to-heat extension you wished you'd never built?

Before you do anything sit down with all the members of your household (and even the neighbours if they are likely to be affected) and consider your options. Think laterally, and think ahead. Prepare a rough plan of your present accommodation and doodle away until you think you've come up with the optimum solution. Don't go overboard; almost all building work is expensive. Equally, don't cut corners and skimp too much; an extension that needs to be adapted or enlarged a year later will cost you dearly.

Architects

Having got to this stage the next thing to do is to seek some professional advice, usually from an architect or surveyor. Don't assume you can do without professional help. Remember, you would almost certainly use a solicitor for legal advice and a doctor for medical help; so approaching an architect for design guidance is just as logical. Architects spend years learning how to translate your ideas into a really workable solution, and this expert skill is usually worth every penny of their fees. They know all the technical requirements of the building industry; they usually know what improvement grants are available and how to get the maximum from them, and they know their way round the notoriously confusing planning system.

A good architect will not try to transform your modest ideas into a grandiose scheme that will win him design awards and send you to the bankruptcy courts. He should listen to your ideas and make a careful note of your needs. It may well be that his suggestions are on similar lines to yours; in other cases he may be able to apply another dimension to your ideas and produce a much more workable solution that you can implement for a fraction of the cost. Whether he just casts a watchful eye over your proposals and endorses them, or comes up with a different solution, his advice is almost always worth seeking.

The easiest way to track down an architect is to approach the Royal Institute of British Architects, which runs a free and impartial Clients Advisory Service. The Yellow Pages will provide you with details of the local RIBA offfice. The Clients Advisory Service's sole function is to match your needs with an architect who specializes in that kind of work. If you live in London, it's probably worth visiting the RIBA's Clients Advisory Service offices in Portland Place, where you can look through a selection of photographs and brochures of suitable architects' work before preparing a shortlist of candidates to approach.

The RIBA also publishes a Directory of Practices which lists every firm of architects in the UK, together with details of their specializations. Most good libraries will stock a copy.

Architects are now allowed to advertise, so your local papers may be another good source. A word of warning however; always check that your 'architect' is genuine. Only properly qualified people are allowed to practise as architects and all have to be registered with the Architects Registration Council. This body produces an annual Register of Architects, and most libraries will have a copy. A 'cowboy' architect could cost you dearly, so be warned. Approach each of the architects on the RIBA's list and explain your needs. Ask them what experience they have had of this type of work in the past, and if they will send you details of similar jobs already completed that you can take a look at. Also quiz them about their fees. Most charge an hourly rate for the initial design guidance stages, though it is becoming increasingly accepted that this initial advice should be provided free of charge – in the hope that you will like their ideas and come back for the full service. If you decide to use an architect to do all the design work and to select and co-ordinate the builders right the way through to completion, fees are usually based on a percentage of the total building cost.

For a one-off house design the architect's fee might work out at about six per cent of the total value of the project – say £3,000 with a new £50,000 home. Work on extensions is usually more fiddly, so they tend to charge a higher percentage – perhaps 10-12 per cent of the total cost of the building work. This includes the initial 'ideas', the preparation of full plans and specifications, the placing of tenders to secure the best value builder and full site supervision to ensure the builder doesn't cut any corners. For a £10,000 house extension you might therefore end up paying an extra £1,000-£1,200 to the architect. If you don't want the full service but just want him to prepare proper plans and a specification, the cost might be nearer £500-£700.

A good relationship with your architect is vital. Try to find someone who's on the same wavelength as you and who has special skills in the sort of work you want done. A personal recommendation from a neighbour who has already been through the process and was well pleased with the service offered by their architect is often very worthwhile.

Surveyors

Surveyors come in various guises, each performing different tasks. Most estate agents have a valuation expert who will survey your home and tell you what it's worth. Then there are quantity surveyors – a special breed who know about the detailed costs of all types of new building work. Architects will occasionally go to a quantity surveyor to get a detailed breakdown of the cost of complex building works. Armed with this breakdown, it's sometimes possible to see where savings can be made.

Finally there are building surveyors or structural engineers. These experts are skilled in gauging the structural integrity of existing buildings and in calculating what will be needed to hold new ones up. Some building surveyors also 'draw up plans' suitable for obtaining planning permission and building regulations' consent. Surveyors also now offer an energy survey as part of a general valuation which assesses where your energy is currently being consumed, and indicates simple measures that can be taken to remedy unnecessary waste.

The Royal Institution of Chartered Surveyors in London offers an impartial and free service that will provide you with a list of three suitably skilled surveyors in your area. The Institution of Structural Engineers, also in London, runs a similar service and has a register of about 1,000 qualified structural engineers who specialize in domestic scale work.

Final decisions

Having assembled your professional advisors, and discussed your requirements, you should be able to prepare an outline design that fits your needs and your bank balance. Before giving the go-ahead for full detailed drawings to be prepared, think carefully about the outline design. Check and double check that it will work in practice. Provided everyone is happy, detailed drawings and a written specification of the work required can then be prepared for presentation to the council for planning and building regulations' approval (see the chapter on The Paperwork.)

Builders

At this stage your architect (or you) can draw up a list of local builders and ask them to quote for the work, based on the plans and the specification.

Finding a good, reliable, reasonably priced builder is no easy task. The rate of bankruptcies in the building trade is alarming, 'cowboys' are rife and jerry building is all too common.

There are three basic ways of going about the process, but none of them are foolproof. The best bet is a personal recommendation from someone you trust, say your neighbour, who has had first hand experience with a building firm; your architect, if you have used one; or a tip (unofficial of course) from the council's building surveyors section.

Secondly there's a free service offered by the Building Employers Confederation (formerly the National Federation of Building Trades Employers). Anyone enquiring at their London office will be furnished with a list of reputable local building firms capable of doing the work you have in mind. Most of the BEC's members specialize in complete new buildings, but a new guarantee scheme has now been introduced for smaller works, like home extensions. Anyone employing a BEC member covered by the guarantee can reclaim losses caused by bankruptcy or unsatisfactory building work.

Thirdly the Federation of Master Builders, also based in London, offers a similar free referral service. With 20,000 members, mostly specializing in smaller home extension type work, the Federation of Master Builders is generally a good bet for a set of reasonable, recommended contractors.

To join the Federation, builders have to get their work passed by other local members, so 'cowboys' are usually kept at bay. The Federation also operates a warranty scheme that provides insurance cover on home extensions to ensure the work is completed to a satisfactory standard. Only long established firms with a good record are accepted on the Warranty scheme. However, you will be charged an extra one per cent on the cost of the building work for the insurance cover.

Once your shortlist of recommended builders has been assembled each should get exactly the same set of plans and the same written specification. They should be given a set period (usually a few weeks) to prepare a detailed written estimate, and you should ask for a programme detailing when they could start and how long the work will take.

Once the estimates have all been returned you can then make your choice (usually with guidance from your architect) of the builder offering the best value and service.

Assuming your plans have been approved by the local authority, the next hurdle is the drawing up of a suitable contract between you and your builder. According to the Office of Fair Trading there should always be a written contract between a home owner and his builder, even for the most minor works.

Several simple forms of building contract can be acquired off-the-shelf. These specify all aspects of the proposed building schemes, how and when money will be paid, and what penalties the builder will incur if there are delays over completion. A builder who knows he's going to lose £100 for every week he takes over and above his original completion date is generally more likely to finish on time.

If you are employing an architect he will be able to advise on the best type of building contract to use. If not, contact the Building Employers' Confederation or your local solicitor who will give you advice.

Work in progress

You are now ready to begin on site. Typically, it will have taken you two or three months to get to this stage – perhaps even longer.

Once you know when your builder is due to descend on you, get all your valuable antiques and family heirlooms well out of his way. Establish a place for storing his materials and tools and set aside somewhere for his workmen to brew up. Remember too that they will probably want access to a lavatory, so put newspapers down to avoid damage to carpets on their way to and fro. It's also worth checking out the builder's insurance cover. Most firms will have full employers' and public liability cover; but make sure beforehand, otherwise you might find yourself out of pocket if a tile falls on your neighbour's head.

Acting alone

If you are determined to prove your ability at do-it-yourself you could, of course, organize the whole project yourself; designing it, getting approval and then acting as your own main contractor. This can save you money, but only if you do everything right. Any mistakes could cost you dearly, and ultimately devalue your property.

The order involved is basically the same as it is when you involve the specialists. The first step is to measure up the part of your home you are planning to tackle and prepare a reasonably accurate drawing. If you use graph paper you should be able to get an exact end result. You can then begin to analyse the existing spaces and what it is you feel you need. It might be a good idea to photocopy your graph paper 'master plan' and use these extra copies to doodle on and try out alternative layout ideas and arrangements. Discuss your ideas with the rest of the family; find out what they would like to see and what practical improvements they want.

Don't overstretch yourself. If you only have £5,000 to spend don't begin on something that will eventually cost £7,000. It's very easy to convince yourself that you can make big savings

by doing it yourself. Building work is expensive and quickly mounts up; the last thing you want is a half completed job without the resources to finish it.

Once you are sure of what you want, sound out the council's planners and building control people to check that everything is basically in order. Make any amendments required to comply with the planning and building regulations and then submit suitable drawings, with the necessary fees, to the council. Once you have got all the necessary consents you can then begin to plan the actual construction phase. But before you can do this you will need to get a good idea of the order of building work. Put simply, this usually begins with digging the foundations and laying the drains, followed by the construction of the solid floors and the main brickwork. The 'first fix' timber work then goes in – stud partitions, door frames, roof timbers etc – and the roof tiling is tackled. The plumber and electrician then do their 'first fixes', followed by the plasterer. Once he has finished the carpenter, plumber and electrician return for their 'second fix' – the details like skirtings, door architraves, radiators and light switches etc – followed by the glaziers and finally the decorators.

What you must ensure is that the right tradesmen are brought in to do the work at the appropriate time. If the schedule goes awry you will have people tripping over each other because they are all there at once, or twiddling their thumbs because they can't do anything until, say, the plasterer arrives.

Once you have worked out the approximate scheduling, track down suitable tradesmen, preferably by personal recommendation, and ask them to quote for their particular element of the work. You will probably need to show them drawings and prepare a detailed written specification for their portion of the project. It is important to shop around as the estimates will probably vary considerably.

Some tradesmen are only prepared to work at a daily rate, because they say it is too difficult to produce a reliable all-in estimate for the work, possibly because the job could turn out to be more complicated than it seems on the surface. This is not the best way of employing someone, but it may be your only option, particularly when the job in hand is a refurbishment which is difficult to assess. If you are forced to follow this path get a clear idea of daily rates before you start, and make regular spot checks to ensure time isn't being wasted with long breaks (that you are paying for). Only use daily rate workers as a last resort.

Supervising the work

Having assembled all your estimates and selected the tradesmen offering best value you are then ready to begin on site. As the work proceeds, you will be constantly called upon to sort out

on-site problems, so if possible arrange to be accessible. Check progress regularly and don't stand for any nonsense; a builder who recognizes a soft touch will often take advantage.

Most tradesmen will want interim payments for the work they are doing, so work out who will want what, and when, and make available suitable funds to cover this. Don't pay any cash out before work has begun, and never pay the final element until you are entirely happy with the workmanship.

At the end of the day, cutting out the professionals and adopting a do-it-yourself approach will save you 20-30 per cent of the total cost. People who like a challenge thrive on this approach; others reckon it's worth the extra cost just to off-load the responsibility onto someone else. The choice is up to you; either way you will almost certainly feel very relieved when it is all over.

BE YOUR OWN INTERIOR DESIGNER

You don't have to be a professional to design a successful interior, but you do have to have a professional approach. Apart from that, you need neither experience, nor spending power, not even a detailed idea of the look you want to achieve. If you did, all you would have to do is go shopping for it. On the contrary, a successful interior design ought to work so well that it has dimensions which you didn't even know you wanted. Be under no illusions however: designing your own interior is not easy. People who make a living from designing other people's houses find their own home the most difficult commission they have ever had to face.

Forward planning

Take your time and keep your eyes open. Long before you start work on your house, begin to amass design ideas that appeal. Scrutinize other people's interiors, analysing which elements work and which fail. Note the names of fabrics and paint colours which catch your eye, together with clever storage ideas, attractive floor coverings, light fittings, door handles, anything that could fit into the jigsaw puzzle of your own home.

Store these ideas in a roomy box file – not just a skimpy folder marked 'dream house', but a receptacle large enough to hold pictures cut from magazines, fabric samples, paint cards, manufacturers' brochures, charts showing fridge, freezer and washing machine sizes, indeed all the minutiae that go into making an interior design.

Index your filing system alphabetically and go on adding to it whenever you come across something new. The point is not to develop a crib sheet or shopping list of ideas to be squashed willy nilly into one impossibly hybrid design, rather, by building up information on what is available, to meet your problems with a strategy, instead of a series of impulsive decisions. When you finally do start thinking about a particular interior – when buying a new house, or changing the look of your existing home – you will have a head start.

A successful interior cannot be judged on looks alone; many other factors are at work. It must be durable, adaptable, and practical for the needs of your household. So, as well as collecting design ideas in advance, think about the way you live. How do you like to entertain? What times of the day is each room most in use? Are you uncompromisingly untidy? Huge open plan interiors are not for you if you are. Is it important to you to have separate rooms for eating, cooking, relaxing and working in? Do your requirements clash with those of other members of your family? Does your idea of good taste clash with theirs?

Think about long term strategies. Is the family still growing? Will you want to accommodate new additions by altering your existing home, or will you sell up and move on – in which case the scope of alterations you should carry out now will be fundamentally different. Often there will be no definitive answers to these questions, but by keeping them in mind it is possible to start looking at homes in an organized way.

First impressions

The temptation when looking at a house or apartment for the first time is to take it at face value. It is all too easy to assume that because there is brown lino in the hall, a multi-coloured synthetic carpet in the living room, and a lingering odour of cabbage everywhere, it would always be an irretrievably unattractive place to live. Your first, and perhaps most difficult task, is to ignore what you see before you and look for potential.

Professionals are able to find the potential for a house or apartment very quickly. A rapid visual survey will tell them whether a warren of little rooms can easily be knocked into one, whether a kitchen could be enlarged, another bathroom put in, a dark and gloomy room be lightened and so on.

The master plan

Learn to think about the layout of your interior in a three-dimensional way, working out how a 3D jigsaw puzzle of rooms fits together. This might be especially complicated in older properties where frequent changes to internal arrangements have been

made. It's important to be aware of how an interior functions before you start your decorative scheme, or the effect will be flat and stilted.

To get to grips with the problem, you will need a scale plan, or possibly a series of plans, one for each floor, and, if you are up to it, a cross-section through the building. If there isn't an existing set available, you will have to draw one up yourself. Use graph paper, clipped to a board to do your survey, a long steel measuring tape and a folding ruler for taking vertical measurements.

If you are drawing plans for more than one floor get the overall dimensions of the ground floor – length, front to back wall, and width – and then simply trace off the others as you go up. Mark the positions of windows, doors and fireplaces, including those that are bricked up. Mark also the thickness of the walls, and any drainage runs. Choose a scale that allows you to show enough detail, but will fit neatly onto a single sheet of tracing paper: 1:50 is good, 1:20 may be needed for doing schemes for individual rooms. Don't aim for great neatness and perfection when making your plan; that would be a difficult and painstaking task, and if you are only planning decorative changes a fairly rough sketch plan – provided the basic elements are right – will suffice.

Once drawn up, your plan can be used as the basis for the rest of the drawings you will need to carry out your design. Use it to explore alternative layouts and positions, to decide on finishes and colour schemes, to place furniture and appliances, and to work out your lighting scheme.

The brief

A professional interior designer attempts not only to solve the functional problems of running a well-ordered household, but aims to create an appropriate atmosphere and mood as well. He should make a home feel comfortable, provide its own individual style, camouflage any architectural shortcomings there may be, and enhance the best of its essential character. In order to fulfil these criteria he must reflect the personality,

needs and wishes of his clients. And so, just as a professional would take a brief from his clients, do the same for yourself. Consult, of course, anyone else who is going to have to live with the results of your work. Try and set out on no more than a couple of sheets of paper exactly what kind of place you want to end up with. Should it be traditional or high tech in character, intimate or stark? Do you favour many small individual rooms, or do you prefer one large multi-functional space? How important will the kitchen be? How many people do you expect to cater for at dinner parties? How much storage and where? All this can of course be tailored to apply to any scale of design from just one part of a bedsit to a whole house. And it is important to specify the budget you have available.

You will find thinking about the problem in these terms a useful way of focusing on it. A good brief is an essential first step in any design – even if it isn't always written down on paper first. It should act as a checklist for all the elements you will need to include.

A working method

A successful interior will integrate the functional aspects of design with the decorative ones. Designs which are co-ordinated throughout work better than those in which every element of an interior manifestly clashes with every other.

With your basic sketch plan as a starting point, shuffle round the various functional divisions – kitchens, bedrooms, living rooms and so on – to see how different arrangements work. If you find you can work with just a pencil and a vivid three-dimensional imagination, so much the better. Or you might prefer to start using simple three-dimensional models made out of card and glue. But at the same time that you are playing spatial chess with all these pieces, you should be beginning to think about how individual details will be treated in decorative terms too. Prepare checklists of finishes for walls, floor and ceiling, and of furniture, lighting, power points and heating for each room. Attach to your checklist little colour and texture samples of each of the finishes you

choose, to give yourself a clue as to how things will look.

Before your design can become properly finalized, you must introduce the reality of cost and time into your thinking. As you begin to weigh the merits of, for example, one carpet against another, you will need estimates of costs from manufacturers and installers. If you are planning to include any specifically designed features, such as worktops in the kitchen or sliding doors, these will have to be submitted for quotations from manufacturers. The same applies for carpentry, and you will need to adjust your design appropriately once you have the costings. You may find yourself having to make savings in the same areas, specifying cheaper tiles in the bathroom for example, in order to splash out in other areas – on beautiful curtain fabric for the living room, for example.

Think about timing too. Firstly, if you are planning to employ a conventional building contractor, you will have to set yourself a cut-off date by which to finish your design, and after which you should allow yourself no further changes without the risk of incurring all kinds of extra charges by the builder. And because very few thorough-going interior schemes can ever be achieved in one go, you should begin to think about the sequence in which work will be carried out. The rule is obvious really: do the messiest and most disruptive work first. But it is curious how often this is overlooked, and people find themselves ripping up newly installed carpet in order to put down cables under the floor a few months later when more money becomes available.

As you begin to firm up on the functional aspects of your design, you should be working on the decorative ones too. You might begin by trying the effect of different colour schemes using soft coloured pencils, or poster colours if you feel up to it. Alternatively you could use coloured paper cut-outs in your 3D cardboard model. But you should remember that these will only give an indication; you must allow for scale and texture to work on a much larger scale in reality.

Choosing your decor

Decoration is not an exact science. People are fond of saying that it is a personal, subjective issue, which is true as far as it goes, and it is certainly not the sort of subject which lends itself to a codified set of rules. On the other hand very few people really ignore what the rest of the world will think of them when they are planning their interiors: it is a spectator sport, and they do want to put some sort of message across. To do that there are guidelines which can be followed to achieve certain results. Even if you are going to flout them deliberately, it is worth being aware of what they are.

Conventional interior design wisdom has it that colour schemes should be co-ordinated, with accents and highlights in contrasting colours, and that harmonious tones should be used everywhere from the wallpaper to the cushion covers. Really, though, it is a question of what *you* want to achieve. Colour can be used in quite different ways (see the chapter on Working with Colour). Using a pale colour throughout – grey, white or cream for walls, ceiling and woodwork – will go a long way to creating a unified design which maximizes the sense of space. On the other hand you may choose to treat each individual room as a colour composition in its own right to create a range of spaces each with their own special character, and playing up the contrasts between them.

Don't be afraid, incidentally, to change your mind about colour once you have started work. If you have only seen paint in the tin, it's very hard even for an expert to judge its effect at the scale of a whole wall, especially when paint batches may vary greatly from the manufacturers' colour charts. Buy one small tin of paint to begin with (making sure that there's more of the same batch available), and don't be afraid to change it if it looks wrong when tested on the wall. Some manufacturers now make small testers especially for this purpose.

The finishes you specify for walls and floors are only one element in an interior. The proportions and shape of a room or space are equally important in determining its character. Once these have been fixed it is difficult to do much more than camouflage their effect: relocating a window for example, will be beyond most people's resources if it is simply an aesthetic decision. So it is very important to bear in mind the character of the spaces you are creating when you start planning to slice up old rooms into smaller new ones – or equally opening them up. New partition walls that split existing walls in two are very unlikely to do that. Tall thin corridor-like rooms with the window squashed into one corner are likely to look like forced compromises.

Decorative treatments can have a part to play in modifying the character of a room. Strong patterns will break up a room's proportions, masking its blemishes – or destroying its proportions – depending on which way you see it. Floors can be raised – in a tall room bringing the floor level up towards the bottom of the window can create an attractive sense of spaciousness. *Trompe l'oeil*, if done well, and in a style that is appropriate for the architectural character of the house can have a role to play too.

Dealing with the services

The services in an interior, the wiring, pipework, central heating and so on, can present real problems from the decorative point of view. It is always an attractive option to try and hide them completely away, burying pipe runs in plasterwork, or inside unobtrusive ducts. The problem of course is that if you need to get at them again, to carry out maintenance, or to make changes to the system, it will play havoc with your decorations. In any case, the location of the services is crucial for the overall plan of an interior. It will affect in the minutest detail where the kitchen and bathroom should be located for maximum economy. At an early stage you should plot the existing power points, boilers, soil stacks and drainage runs on your plan. It should quickly help you make up your mind where to place all the highly serviced rooms. If you are lucky there may be a choice of suitable positions. If you are not, you may have to make costly extra provision, such as installing new main drain runs.

Furniture

When you are assessing the merits of alternative layouts for the interior as a whole, you should begin thinking about the contents of each room, and the way in which furniture, appliances and fittings will complete the picture. How these fit in depends very much on the kind of room you are dealing with, and of course on what you already have, and how much you decide to purchase from scratch.

Professional interior designers are notorious for their "let's get rid of it all" attitude. Doing it yourself will at least give you the chance to decide what you want to keep in the way of furniture, and even to structure the interior around your most treasured pieces.

Remember that the more furniture you want to include in a design, the more your freedom of action will be limited. Sofas and dining tables are both hungry users of space, commanding far more floor area than one might expect from looking at them. Space has to be kept clear for access around and to them. In many modestly sized houses you will find only one way of accommodating, for example, a three piece suite in the living room. If that is what you want, fine. If you want to maximize the space in the living room, however, think about other furniture solutions. You may for example be able to put storage in the base of a seating unit. Think about bringing in chairs from other rooms when extra seating is needed. Tables might be special foldaway designs.

Write down all the furniture you require on your checklist, and then prepare scale paper cut-outs of the pieces you have selected for each room. Test these on your graph paper plans in a variety of configurations until you find the best solution. You may find that you revise your original choice of furniture very quickly on the basis of what you discover.

Preparing boards

Once you have begun to firm up your overall design, you should prepare definitive plans for each room. The professionals' approach is equally appropriate for amateurs: each room is allocated a board which will include a simple plan locating windows, doors, heating and power points. It will also contain cut-outs to indicate the furniture and its rough positions. Attach to the board fabric and paint samples to indicate the different finishes you have chosen and how they will work together. Go back to the original brief you drew up to see how successfully, in design terms, you have answered the tasks you set yourself. As you study the problems you may find your priorities shifting, so don't necessarily expect to find that your original brief remains inviolate.

Your boards should provide you with a checklist of all the components you will need to order – including names and addresses of suppliers and installers, trade names, colour codes and ordering numbers. They should also help you gauge the effect of your designs by placing the samples side by side. They can act as a salutory demonstration of the dangers of trying to do too much in too little space.

At the same time as your individual boards, work on a less specific set of boards which chart the house as a whole, floor by floor. These can be to a larger and less detailed scale to keep track of the way finishes run through the house. Even if you favour a cellular style of interior, with lots of small rooms each attempting to have an individual flavour of its own, this approach will be valuable. In reality you will experience these rooms as part of a series of spaces, moving from one to another. It is important to be aware of the effect on the eye of that vivid carpet behind the door as you move from one room to another.

The floor by floor boards will also allow you to focus on those very important, but often ill considered areas like staircases and halls which play a large part in creating initial impressions of an interior.

Adding the details

To explore some elements of the design, you may find that you want to sketch internal elevations, or even three-dimensional perspectives. This can be the best way of getting an idea of, for example, how windows will fit in and the effect of curtains or fabrics.

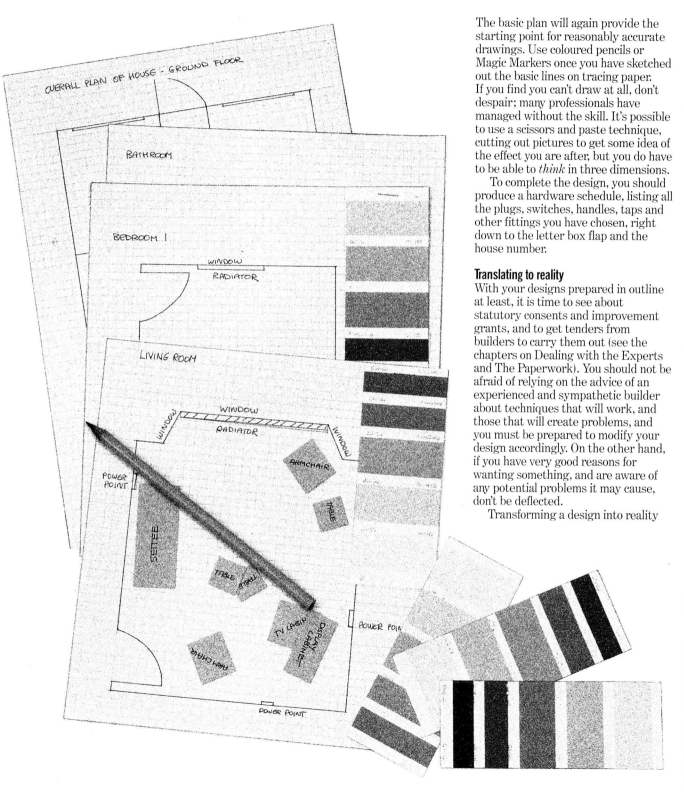

The basic plan will again provide the starting point for reasonably accurate drawings. Use coloured pencils or Magic Markers once you have sketched out the basic lines on tracing paper. If you find you can't draw at all, don't despair; many professionals have managed without the skill. It's possible to use a scissors and paste technique, cutting out pictures to get some idea of the effect you are after, but you do have to be able to *think* in three dimensions.

To complete the design, you should produce a hardware schedule, listing all the plugs, switches, handles, taps and other fittings you have chosen, right down to the letter box flap and the house number.

Translating to reality

With your designs prepared in outline at least, it is time to see about statutory consents and improvement grants, and to get tenders from builders to carry them out (see the chapters on Dealing with the Experts and The Paperwork). You should not be afraid of relying on the advice of an experienced and sympathetic builder about techniques that will work, and those that will create problems, and you must be prepared to modify your design accordingly. On the other hand, if you have very good reasons for wanting something, and are aware of any potential problems it may cause, don't be deflected.

Transforming a design into reality can be the most difficult part of the process, and to get what you want, you must expect to play a full part in overseeing work as it is carried out to ensure that all your original intentions are respected.

It is very often only possible to make decisions while work is in progress. You may for example suddenly discover that a wall which appeared to have the consistency of papier-mâché when your engineer looked at it, turns out to be fist deep in structural steel and is holding up the whole house in the opinion of the local authority's expert. You may find that opening out a blocked up fireplace reveals an attractive chimney piece which you would like to incorporate into your design, or that as walls begin to disappear you quite like the open feeling and change your mind about partitioning it all up again.

The text books will tell you that this is all highly unprofessional. But in fact it is just what the professionals do all the time, and there is a lot to be said for the intuitive approach, and for ad-libbing a response to an aspect of the design as the opportunity arises. You must, however, know what you are doing, and in what direction you want the design to go.

Fast footwork can be even more important in the completion of a design. Many of the most successful colour schemes are devised on site, or altered to accommodate last minute extra acquisitions. But don't forget there can be cost penalties, especially when delivery times come into the picture. Ordering special finishes and shades takes time, and can keep other tradesmen waiting to start on their part of the contract.

An interior is *never* finished. The glossy magazine photographs tend to give the impression that they are, but they only capture a totally artificial and highly contrived moment of perfection after which reality rapidly becomes a disappointment. To treat interiors like that is to turn them into a species of flower arrangement, fragile and transient. If the interior you have created is truly successful, it will be able to grow and mature as it is put to real use.

DO-IT-YOURSELF

Those who are not keen on DIY, or are completely inexperienced, often have the frustrating feeling that they are unable to create the type of home they really want. Of course, a decorator could be employed, but it's an expensive alternative and the results may not be exactly what you had in mind. The simple answer is not to fight shy of carrying out the work yourself. While it is obvious that many people will tackle far more complicated projects, the following pages describe the sort of essential tasks increasingly undertaken by those with just a modicum of DIY skill, in the hope that there will never be cause to call in the decorator for such minor work again.

These basic skills of painting, wallpapering, carpentry and the like are not difficult to master. Imaginatively applied, you may even surprise yourself at just how good the finished job is. But don't be too ambitious at first. Keep schemes to manageable proportions. Careful planning and preparation are absolutely essential – skimp on these at your peril – and take your time; nobody is expecting you to work as quickly as someone who does the job professionally.

Clothes
Wear old comfortable clothes which allow you ease of movement. Don't wear woollen jumpers, the hairs have a habit of getting onto wet paintwork. Roll up floppy sleeves as there is a danger of them catching in power tools as well as drooping into materials you're using. Overalls, dungarees or a carpenter's apron are ideal, with useful pockets to keep one or two tools readily to hand, but *not* knives unless the blade can be retracted into the handle.

If you do a lot of work kneeling down then buy, or make up, some knee pads which you strap to your legs. They may look silly, but you'll be thankful for wearing them at the end of the day, and they are more convenient than a mat or cushion.

Care of hands
Gloves will keep your hands relatively clean and protect them from blisters and cuts. As an added precaution rub in barrier cream before starting work to stop your hands from drying out and to

make it easier to clean them after you have finished, particularly if there is paint on them. Use a proprietary cleaner such as 'Swarfega' or 'That Stuff' which contains solvents to dissolve decorating 'dirt'. White spirit will do, but it isn't as kind to hands.

Working off the floor
Many jobs can be completed from floor level, but you will need some form of raised support to reach the tops of walls and windows, and the ceiling. Apart from comfort and safety, working at the correct height is essential for doing a good job. You can't work accurately if you have to stretch.

A sturdy chair, or better still a hop-up, will do for many situations. But good quality step ladders are better, giving more flexibility to the height at which you work. Some have a small platform at the top for resting paint cans and tools. They are made of wood, which has a reassuringly solid feel to it, or lightweight, maintenance-free aluminium. The types with wide treads are the most comfortable to work from.

The most versatile pattern of steps for indoor work is a three-way combination ladder which can act as an ordinary step ladder, an extension ladder and a stair ladder.

Ladder safety

ALWAYS…

1 check the treads of a ladder before using it. Don't use it if even just one tread is damaged or loose. You will probably forget which one it is when concentrating on decorating and this could lead to an unpleasant accident.
2 use stepladders in the fully open position.
3 check combination ladders to ensure they are correctly assembled in their various positions and that the safety locks are on.
4 site ladders on a firm surface. If you lean them against a wall make sure the treads remain parallel to the floor. Set the base 300mm (12in.) away from the foot of the wall for every 1200mm (48in.) the ladder extends directly upwards. By doing this they won't fall backwards on you.
5 put a batten across the feet to stop them sliding outwards. And wrap cloth round the top to prevent wall marks.

NEVER…

1 have more than one person working on the ladder.
2 overstretch – you could lose your balance.
3 stand on the very top tread of step ladders.
4 work from the bottom section of a three way ladder when working on stairs. And never climb above the pivot point where the two sections of ladder meet.

A raised platform
For painting and papering ceilings and putting up cornices and coving it is best to work from a raised platform. Construct this by laying a scaffold board (which you can hire cheaply) between the rungs of two step ladders, or over trestles. Alternatively, use the bottom section of a scaffold tower if you have room. You will be able to move this round more easily.

Working over a stairwell
Use ladders, step ladders and scaffold boards strapped together to form a working platform. How you do this depends on the configuration of the stairs. The diagrams give some

possibilities. Or again, you can hire a scaffold tower that can be set up to work over stairs.

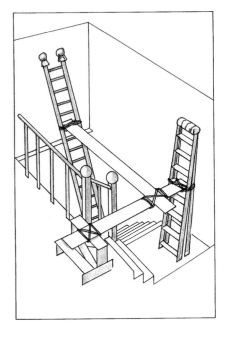

Safety with power tools

ALWAYS…

1 use the nearest available socket to prevent the flex trailing needlessly across floors.
2 unplug equipment before changing bits, saw blades and sanding belts, discs and drums.
3 make sure flex is well clear of treads when using a piece of equipment up a ladder.
4 pull an extension cable completely out of its drum housing before using, otherwise the heat generated by the current may melt the PVC sheathing.
5 connect the plug of an extension connector to the tool's flex and the socket to the extension lead.
6 check the position of electricity cables and gas and water pipes before drilling into walls and floors.
7 keep well away from cutting blades.

NEVER…

1 pick up a piece of equipment by the flex.
2 put a tool down until it has stopped operating.

PAINTING

Before starting a major painting job take carpets and as much furniture as possible from the room. Stand the remaining furniture in the centre of the room and you should be able to work over and round it. Cover everything left in the room with dust sheets.

Preparing the woodwork

Remove door handles, key hole covers (escutcheons), rim locks and automatic door closers.

Unless paintwork is in very poor condition – badly chipped, soft or crazed, or if countless layers of paint have obscured mouldings, you don't need to strip back to bare wood. Where the wood, often the architrave round doors, is itself damaged, this should be replaced.

Remove flaking and blistered paint with a scraper. Then wash down with detergent or sugar soap solution to remove dirt and grease. Rinse with clean water.

Sanding   For paintwork in good condition lightly sand with fine glasspaper wrapped round a sanding block to provide a key for paint. Alternatively use 'wet-and-dry' paper. Allow paintwork to dry, then wipe off any dust.

For paintwork in poor condition, you will need to use a medium grade glasspaper first and then a fine grade one, in order to remove bumps and rough patches, and to smooth the edges where paint has flaked away. Spot-prime areas of wood that have become exposed and allow to dry. Fill in cracks and holes with stopping or cellulose filler, working it well in with a filling or putty knife. Cellulose filler is available in powder form (follow the instructions on the box) or made-up in tubs. Let the filler harden before sanding to a smooth finish. Finally wipe down the paintwork to remove dust.

Preparing new wood

Wipe down with a damp cloth rinsed in detergent, sugar soap or household cleaner to remove any greasy finger marks. Go over the surface again with a cloth rinsed in clean water and allow to dry. Then sand with fine grade glasspaper to give a smooth finish. Brush on a white or pink wood primer, or an acrylic primer. When dry fill any cracks in the surface with cellulose filler. Let this harden before smoothing off with fine grade glasspaper.

Sealing gaps   Particularly when a new skirting or architrave has been fitted, there may be a narrow gap between the woodwork and the wall. This can be filled with ordinary cellulose filler, but as this might be subjected to vibrations (a door being slammed for example) use flexible painters' caulk instead, which can be bought ready to use from a tube. Run the nozzle against the gap pressing the filler into it. Smooth off with the end of a pencil (or a piece of dowel rod) dipped in water. Leave for 24 hours before over-painting.

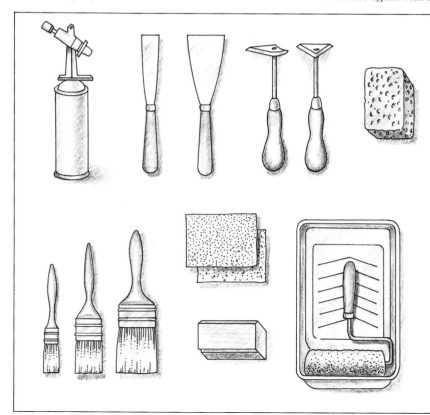

Preparing walls and ceilings

After plastering, a traditionally built house needs about a year to 'dry out' thoroughly. As you will want to decorate within this period, you can coat the new plaster with emulsion paint after three to four weeks. Emulsion still allows the walls to breathe, so be prepared for a white, crumbly efflorescence to appear from time to time. This is nothing to worry about: it's just surface salt which should be rubbed off with a dry cloth.

Before applying the emulsion top coat, key all surfaces with medium grade steel wool. This operation is important: try coating plaster finished to a hard shiny surface and the paint will run off. Next, prime the wall with diluted emulsion paint or alkali-resistant primer.

Don't use gloss or eggshell paint on the walls or ceiling for the first 12 months as this will prevent them breathing and drying out properly.

If you have had some replastering work carried out in a house which is more than a year old, the issue of drying out doesn't arise. Decorate the plaster as soon as it has dried – about two weeks. Small plaster repairs can be painted over in four to five days.

Preparing previously painted surfaces

Before carrying out any work, check that the walls are free from penetrating and rising damp. Rectify the situation if they are present, possibly calling in a specialist contractor to do the work.

Emulsion paint   If it is in good condition, wash with detergent or sugar soap, working from the bottom of the wall upwards to prevent tears of dirty water running down the surface, or they could show through the new paint coats. Rinse with fresh water and allow to dry. Fill cracks and holes with cellulose filler. On hairline cracks use fine surface filler, which you can buy ready made-up.

If the emulsion paint is in bad condition, wash, then scrape off loose paint and repair holes and cracks. Flaking paint can also be brushed off with a fairly stiff banister brush. Lightly sand around areas where a paint layer has come off to avoid a lip showing when the walls are repainted. If the wall remains powdery, coat the surface with a stabilizing primer.

Gloss and eggshell paint   Sand down to give a good key with 'wet-and-dry' paper or a flexible sanding block wetted in detergent or sugar soap. Fill cracks with a cellulose filler.

Wallpaper

Lining paper, and relief coverings (Anaglypta, Supaglypta, etc) are made specially to take paint. Provided they have been well hung they should be no problem to recoat.

To paint over ordinary paper that is in good condition, first coat a test patch to see if any of the wallpaper colours will bleed through the paint. This is a particular problem if gold is present.

Brush down the surface and wipe off grease marks, commonly found around

PAINTING

light switches and doors. Use a damp cloth wrung in detergent or sugar soap. Stick down any lifting seams. If colours will show through apply an aluminium primer/sealer followed by one (possibly two) coats of emulsion. Don't worry if the paper bubbles up in places, it normally flattens out again when the paint dries.

Washable and vinyl papers cause more of a problem when being applied with paint because of their waterproof surface. It's usually best to strip them completely.

Metal surfaces
Surfaces in good condition, such as already painted radiators or new radiators that have been primed, should be wiped with white spirit to remove grease and lightly rubbed down with fine glasspaper to provide a key. Treat bare iron, steel, aluminium, copper and brass with a rust-inhibiting zinc chromate primer.

Where surfaces are rusty, remove rust with a wire brush or steel wool, then treat immediately with zinc chromate primer. Very badly rusted surfaces can be cleaned up with a wire cup brush attached to an electric drill.

Types of paint
Thanks to the tremendous advance in paint types and painting products, applying this form of covering is no longer the messy and arduous chore it once was.

Vinyl emulsion paints
You can buy these with a washable matt or silk finish, the latter having a pleasing sheen, and in non-drip (thixotropic) and 'runny' form. Because they are easy to apply by brush, roller, pad and spray gun, they are most often used to cover walls and ceilings. Thinned down with water, they act as their own primer on bare surfaces. Special undercoats, as for gloss, are unnecessary.

Emulsions can be applied over woodwork, but they do not provide such a hardwearing finish as solvent-based paints. Always use good quality emulsion. As it is water-based, it is all too easy to cut the price drastically by increasing the water content. The result is a thin cheap paint, which means extra work in putting on more coats to get a good solid coverage. The cheaper 'white' emulsions are less 'white' than their more expensive counterparts. Remember that the colour you are covering over will also affect the number of coats required.

Solvent based paints
Traditionally, gloss paints have been used to give a durable, shiny surface to woodwork. They are now available in non-drip form and some have polyurethane or silthane added for extra toughness.

Ideally, apply solvent-based gloss over a solvent-based undercoat of the recommended colour. Similarly, apply water-based acrylic gloss over an acrylic primer/undercoat, but this won't give such a tough finish, and water-based gloss tends to lose its colour more quickly.

Gloss paint can also be applied to walls and ceilings – be careful here, it has a habit of showing up imperfections. It's best to brush it on rather than use a roller.

If you prefer a lustre, as opposed to a shiny finish, use eggshell paint.

Applying paint by brush
Brushes can be used to apply paint to all surfaces. Buy the best you can afford. Pure bristle gives an excellent finish, the longer the better. In fact length is more important than the thickness of the bristles.

You will need a 25mm (1in.) wide brush for skirtings and architraves, and if you are careful these can also be used for window frames. Otherwise use a 15mm (½in.) brush and a cutting-in brush for getting close to the glass. A

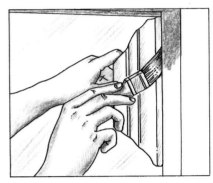

50mm (2in.) brush is suitable for doors, and 75mm (3in.) brush for walls and ceilings. Larger brushes are available but are unwieldy until you've had practice with them. They are also more awkward to dip into cans of paint.

When possible don't use a new brush to apply a top coat of gloss. Wear it in first on the primer and undercoats. This will help to round the bristle ends which will then give a smoother finish.

Before using any brush, work the bristles back and forth in your hand to prise out dust and loose bristles. With new brushes a few may still come out while painting – another good reason for not using them immediately for top coats.

When applying paint follow closely the instructions on the tin.

Stir the paint if necessary. If you have a large tin of paint, pour some into a paint kettle as it's much easier to work from this. Small cans can be stood in the kettle.

Hold the brush with your fingers pressing against one side and your thumb on the other. The handle should rest between the thumb and forefinger like a pen.

Load the brush generously so that about a third of the bristles are covered in paint. Wipe off excess (this is unnecessary with non-drip paint) on a string tied across the kettle. Don't squeeze the bristles against the rim as paint will eventually trickle down the outside.

Flex the brush so that the loaded bristles come into contact with the surface you're covering. Make smooth up and down strokes in one direction then cross these at right angles to ensure paint is well distributed before 'laying off' in the original direction.

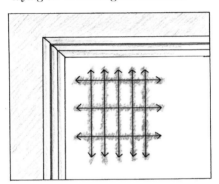

Don't over-brush non-drip paints, they are made to go on in a fairly thick coat which flattens as it dries.

Applying paint with a roller
Rollers are suitable for covering large flat areas; you will still need a small brush to get into corners. Various sleeves (the part of the roller that applies the paint) can be fitted depending on the surface to be covered. Beware of cheap foam sleeves: as they are rolled, air is forced out of them causing minute bubbles on the surface which dry to a pitted finish. These rollers are also prone to drip and produce a fine fall-out ('spray') which can land on other decorations – so dust sheets are essential.

Choose a synthetic or sheepskin roller instead. The general rule is short pile for smooth surfaces, long pile for rough, as this will be able to penetrate the crevices.

To apply the paint, pour some into a special paint tray. Gently dip roller into it and then roll it backwards and forwards on the sloping grid to disperse the paint evenly round the sleeve.

Work the roller on the surface to be coated in different directions to ensure good coverage. Gently lift away when the paint has run out, reload and repeat the operation.

Aerosols

Aerosols, although relatively expensive, are particularly useful for radiator panels and metal ventilation grilles as well as small items of furniture.

Order of painting

For best results always try to paint in natural light.

Tackle ceilings first When using a roller for most of the work, first use a brush to paint a 25mm (1in.) strip at the wall/ceiling join and round the light rose. Start above the main window and work away from the light in parallel bands 750-1000mm (30-40in.) wide.

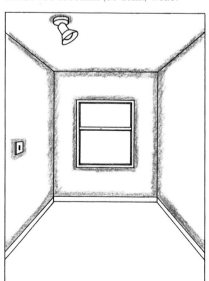

Work at a steady pace so you can feather into the previous band before it has a chance to dry.

Walls next Start from the top and paint down in 750-1000mm (30-40in.) strips again joining them up before the previous one has had a chance to dry. Similarly, work away from the light.

Windows Follow the sequence in the diagrams for painting the different types of window. Remove stays and

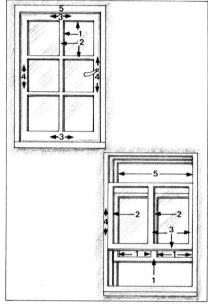

latch if possible. You can mask off the glass or use a paint shield – a George. But you should be able to get a straight edge without these by resting your brush hand against the glass or supporting it with your free hand. Remove any paint from the glass once it has dried with a razor blade held in a special holder.

Doors Follow the sequences shown in the diagrams.

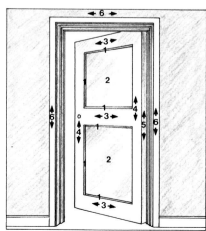

Architraves and skirting Take care with these particularly when painting near

to the floor – it's easy to pick up dust, so lay out some newspapers. Don't over-apply paint on decorative ogee moulding as drips can run from the grooves.

Painting radiators

For the most satisfactory finish use special radiator enamel applied when the radiator is cold. This gives a tough covering that will not discolour when it gets hot. For this reason don't use emulsion paints. Gloss and eggshell paints, however, are suitable.

An ordinary 25mm (1in.) brush is all you need to apply the paint, but a radiator brush with a small angle head set on a long wire handle will allow you to paint down the back as far as the eye can see. Also use it to paint down the wall behind and in between a double panel radiator.

Caring for brushes

As soon as you have finished painting clean out the brushes and rollers. If you've been using emulsion or other water-based paint wash brushes and rollers out under a tap.

With solvent-based paints wash out the easy-clean type in detergent and hot water. Other solvent-based paints should be worked in proprietary brush cleanser or white spirit, then washed out in detergent and hot water.

Special paint effects

You can add extra interest and depth to a painted surface by using one of a variety of methods to 'distress' or 'break-up' the paint. Alternatively, you can paint on a mural or use stencils to create a design. In either case, make sure the surface is clean and sound before you begin. In the final stages, to protect your work, apply clear, matt polyurethane varnish when the paint has dried.

Sponge stippling

This works particularly well using pastel shades with each coat being slightly darker than the previous one. Use a matt emulsion paint for both base and top coats or eggshell for the base and thinned eggshell or transparent oil glaze known as 'scumble' glaze for the top coats. You can colour a

scumble glaze by tinting it with artist's oil colour or universal stainer. Dip a sponge (it must be a real marine one) into water until it expands and then squeeze it out thoroughly. Lightly dab the sponge into the mixed top-coat paint, then press it onto a scrap of lining paper until you've got the paint density you want. Sponge onto the dry

base coat, refilling the sponge as required, so you get regular speckles all over. When dry, repeat with next colour. Note: to thin eggshell paint or scumble glaze, add equal parts of white spirit. Try out the diluted glaze on a test area first to see if it's the right consistency (this applies to the other paint finishes described as well).

Stippling

You can buy a special rectangular stippling brush but these are expensive so try an old clothes brush provided the bristles are of an even length. Paint diluted eggshell or scumble glaze over a dry eggshell base then go over the wall with the stippling brush quite hard to even out the wet paint. Make sure you hit the wall square on to stop the brush skidding. Go over again for a finely textured effect.

PAINTING

Ragging-on

Use the same types of paint as for sponge stippling but apply the top coat(s) with a folded rag. Dip the rag into the paint and then, after testing the effect on scrap paper, dab the rag

onto the surface, leaving an even space between each impression. Using the rag folded in the same way all over will give a regular pattern, but it's easier to create an irregular one; for this, refold the rag as you work.

Rag-rolling

Ideal for a formal setting, rag-rolling gives a look rather like crushed silk. You'll need a plentiful supply of soft, fine cotton rags cut into pieces about 300mm (12in.) square. Brush a top coat of eggshell onto scumble glaze diluted with equal parts of white spirit. Don't cover too wide an area at a time or the paint will dry before you get to it. Bunch up a rag into a sausage shape and roll it over the wet paint, refolding

the rag and changing direction as you go so the pattern is not too insistent.

342

Bag-graining

For a fine-textured, crushed velvet look (particularly effective on a white base coat), bag-grain a top coat of either emulsion paint diluted with an equal amount of water or eggshell thinned with white spirit. Paint a thin coat on a section of wall about 600mm (24in.) across using a wide brush. Take a polythene bag half-filled with rags and

securely tied at the neck and press it into the paint, overlapping each imprint slightly. Continue painting and graining in sections.

Splatter-effect marbling

This looks good on a white or off-white ground with the decoration carried out in two or more glazes, either in toning colours or shades of the same colour. After the base coat has dried, rub on a coat of thinner mix (three parts white spirit, one part linseed oil and a drop of liquid driers) and apply a glaze of colour with a 25mm (1in.) paint brush, rolling it on in a random fashion. Repeat with a second colour. Dab on a piece of marine sponge to distress the pattern. Flick on another colour by running your finger across a brush which has been dipped in glaze. Flick on white spirit to open up the pattern and then, if you wish, methylated spirits, to open it up further still.

Stripping paintwork

Whatever method you use, stripping paintwork is not a particularly pleasant job. It's messy and it takes a fair amount of time. However, if you're intending to repaint there's no need to go right back to the bare wood. Taking off two or three layers may be sufficient to remove original surface defects and to provide a sound, smooth surface for recoating. Spot prime bare areas and then apply undercoat and top coat as necessary.

Chemical strippers

They are relatively expensive compared with other methods, but they do save time. The strongest will remove virtually all coverings including gloss and emulsion paint and polyurethane varnishes. You can buy them in liquid, gel, paste and powder form.

Lay down plenty of newspaper to protect floors and the surrounding areas. And make sure you work in well ventilated conditions, as some products give off unpleasant fumes. Remove doors and work on them outside. It is essential to wear gloves to prevent burning your skin.

To apply, follow the instructions on the packaging. Pour the stripper into a metal container (or something similar which won't react with the chemical) and brush onto the paintwork, working it well into mouldings. Sometimes a second coat is needed after a few minutes. Pastes often have to be covered with a plastic blanket, and left for the recommended time, which could be anything from a few minutes to several hours, to allow the stripper to penetrate and soften the covering. The fact that the paint doesn't always bubble or wrinkle does not mean the stripper isn't working. Use a scraper to lift off the paint. The flat edges, points and curves of a combination shave hook are essential for awkward corners and curved surfaces. Otherwise use medium grade steel wool.

Some pastes form a skin which you peel off – the ideal type to use on balusters as the circular spindles are particularly difficult to scrape without scratching. Others are designed to be scrubbed off.

Finally neutralize the bare wood by

wiping it over with white spirit to remove any traces of stripper.

Hot air strippers and blowlamps

Use a hot air stripper in preference to a blowlamp if you want a natural wood finish; it's almost impossible to scorch the surface with one of these. Blackened patches caused by a blowlamp cause untold problems. Sanding doesn't always remove them, and the only alternatives are then to paint over or replace the run of wood.

The idea isn't to burn the paint away. To use these tools, play the heat

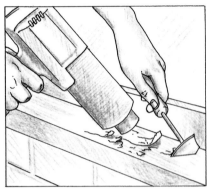

gently onto a small area of paint and scrape it off when it becomes soft.

Sanding

Large flat areas can be sanded to remove paint with an orbital sander.

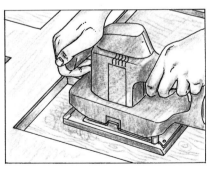

Start with medium grade glasspaper and work down to a fine grade. Finish off with a belt sander or a sanding block in the direction of the grain, if you're working on wood. Try using a drum sander on curved surfaces. Avoid disc sanders as it's so easy to gouge into the wood until you're fully used to handling them.

WALLPAPERS

It is a confusing business choosing wallpaper. The different types available today are myriad, and although your final choice will usually be based on aesthetic preference, many of the papers do serve specific functions; it is worth knowing what they are before making a final decision.

Lining paper
This is usually used as a base for other coverings. Hang it horizontally rather than vertically. If hung well on walls in a reasonable state you can paint over it. Avoid the cheapest papers, they are very thin and tear easily when pasted. Use an all-purpose adhesive or the same one as used for the final covering.

Ingrain (woodchip paper)
Available in various grades. All give a textured surface, but they won't hide defects in a wall. They need to be painted over with an emulsion or solvent-based paint. They're difficult to strip, as the woodchips stick to the surface when the paper is pulled away. Use an all-purpose adhesive.

Relief/embossed papers
These give a patterned, textured surface to a wall or ceiling, and will hide defects. There is a wide variety of designs available. They mostly need to be painted (use vinyl silk emulsion), which makes them difficult to strip. Look for the following trade names:
Anaglypta - made from wood pulp.
Supaglypta - made from cotton linters.
Vynaglypta - a paper-backed vinyl. Can be coated in gloss or eggshell paint as well as emulsion.
Worley Permabos - a blown vinyl that's soft to the touch, but hard-wearing. Again, this can be coated in gloss and eggshell paint.
All are fairly easy to hang. Use all-purpose adhesive for the first two and fungicidal paste for the others. You may have to match patterns.

Standard printed paper
This is available in a wide variety of patterns and is not very expensive. It is not washable, so is unsuitable for bathrooms and kitchens. Nor is it particularly hard-wearing. Avoid getting paste on the surface when hanging as it may stain. (Expensive hand-printed papers are also available, often in non-standard rolls.)

Washable wallpapers
Fairly cheap, having the advantage that they can be wiped clean. But don't press too hard or you will rub through the plastic waterproof coating or wear away the inks.

Vinyl wallcoverings
The range of patterns is enormous. They are very hard-wearing, don't fade and can be scrubbed. Use them in all areas of the house, especially bathrooms and kitchens where they are resistant to condensation and steam. Generally vinyl wallcoverings are good value.

Hang with a fungicidal adhesive and use a latex adhesive where the vinyl surfaces overlap in the corners. Many rolls come ready pasted. It's easy to strip as the vinyl surface pulls away to leave the backing, usually paper, ready for covering over.

Foil coverings
A metallized film bonded to a paper backing. Gives a shiny surface with printed patterns and can produce striking results. But don't use on uneven, lumpy walls as it shows up imperfections. It can be tricky to hang. Use a fungicidal, ready mixed PVA adhesive.
Important The metallized finish has the potential to conduct electricity, so cut round light switches and sockets and don't tuck the covering under the face-plates.

Alternative finishes
Apart from these readily available coverings, there is an extensive range of more exotic finishes to choose from.
These finishes include hessian, jute, sisal, grasscloth, felt, textiles (e.g. wool and silk) and even cane.
For ease of hanging go for the types bonded to a paper backing. This also helps prevent stretching which can distort a pattern.
Prepare wall surfaces as for ordinary coverings (see below). Cross-lining is advised – leave for a day to dry thoroughly. Mix up the paste as recommended by the manufacturer, unless it comes already made up, and apply this either to the wall or to the backing paper (as per instructions). Then offer up covering, being careful not to get paste on the surface – remove any with a damp cloth immediately. Some finishes are butted together, others overlap. Cut round electrical fittings as for ordinary coverings.

Buying wallcoverings
Most coverings are sold in a standard roll measuring 10.05m (32ft 8in.) long by 520mm (20in.) wide. Use the chart to estimate the number of rolls you'll need for the room you're decorating. Ignore door and window openings when taking measurements. The chart takes into account pattern matching, but you may need to buy an extra roll if the pattern drop is particularly large. The shop where you buy the covering should be able to advise you.

Always make sure that the batch numbers on the labels of the rolls tally. Shades may vary from batch to batch. The differences are conspicuous when the covering is on the wall.

Use the chart to interpret the symbols found in pattern books and product literature which describe the basic properties of the covering, the method of hanging and how it should be looked after.

Preparing the walls and ceilings
If the ceiling is to be left painted continue the colour down the wall 25mm (1in.) to help conceal gaps between wallcovering and ceiling caused by overtrimming.
New plaster This must be dry. Brush off any efflorescence. Lightly sand with medium glasspaper then size. Either brush on a special size preparation or further water down the adhesive you are using for the covering. Size blocks up pores in the plaster surface and so provides greater adhesion for the paste. It also allows the covering to be slipped into position more easily.
Emulsion-covered surfaces If they are in good condition and not flaking, wash them with detergent or sugar soap, then sand with medium or fine glasspaper to provide a key.
Scrape powdery or flaking surfaces, wash, then apply a stabilizing primer. Leave for two days to dry. Hang lining paper horizontally (i.e. cross-line).
Gloss-painted surfaces Wash thoroughly, then key with coarse glasspaper before cross-lining.
Covered surfaces Strip back to the original wall or ceiling surface. Don't paper over existing covering as the new one may pull the old away leading to peeling and bubbling.
To strip lining paper and ordinary printed papers soak the surface with a

WALLS Ceiling to skirting height IN METRES	HOW MANY ROLLS													WALLS Ceiling to skirting height IN FEET
	Perimeter measurement of room including door and window openings													
	IN METRES													
	9.1	10.4	11.6	12.8	14	15.2	16.5	17.7	18.9	20.1	21.3	22.6	23.9	
2.15–2.30	4	5	5	6	6	7	7	8	8	9	9	10	10	7–7½
2.30–2.45	5	5	6	6	7	7	8	8	9	9	10	10	11	7½–8
2.45–2.60	5	5	6	7	7	8	9	9	10	10	11	12	12	8–8½
2.60–2.75	5	5	6	7	7	8	9	9	10	10	11	12	12	8½–9
2.75–2.90	6	6	7	7	8	9	9	10	10	11	12	12	13	9–9½
2.90–3.05	6	6	7	8	8	9	10	10	11	12	12	13	14	9½–10
3.05–3.20	6	7	8	8	9	10	10	11	12	13	13	14	15	10–10½
	30	34	38	42	46	50	54	58	62	66	70	74	78	
	IN FEET													
	Perimeter measurement of room including door and window openings													
Ceilings	2	2	2	3	3	4	4	4	5	5	6	7	7	Ceilings
Add 1 roll to final total if paper has a large pattern drop.														

WALLPAPERS

solution of wallpaper remover, then scrape off. You need to score washable papers and those covered in paint (including woodchip) before applying remover. Novamura just peels off. And vinyl coverings can also usually be dry peeled. The backing paper stays in place to act as a lining for the next covering.

After removing the wallcovering, sand and fill any cracks which often come to light around window frames and architraves. Use cellulose filler or painters' caulk. Wash and size.

Papering ceilings

Always paper ceilings first, then walls. The techniques involved are basically the same as for papering walls, except that the job is made more difficult because you have to work off a scaffold board platform and above your head. Gravity is working against you tempting the paper to fall away from the surface you are trying to fix it to. Only tackle the job if you're confident of success. It helps to start with a small ceiling first.

Lay the first strip above and parallel to the main window and work back across the room from here. To fix a line against which you lay the first run of paper, measure in from the corner the width of the roll less 15mm (½in.). Mark this point on the ceiling. Repeat in the other corner. Coat a length of string in chalk and pin it taut between the two points. Gently pull the string down and allow it to 'ping' back against the ceiling to mark a gauge line you can work to.

Cut the paper to length allowing for 15mm (½in.) waste at each end. Paste, folding it into a 450mm (18in.) concertina as you work. Use a roll of

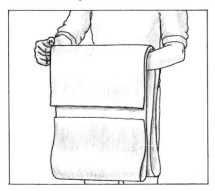

paper still in its plastic wrapping to support the folded length. Get up on the platform, open out the first fold and slip the paper in position so that it

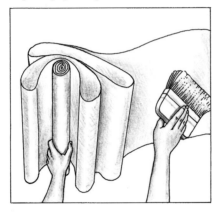

aligns with the chalk line and overlaps the side and end walls by about 15mm (½in.). Smooth down the paper with a brush gradually working to the other side of the room. Let the folds fall out of the concertina as you progress. Some people find it preferable to get a second person to support the paper over the head of a clean, soft broom. This leaves them free with two hands to work on the paper.

The last strip you have to apply may only be quite narrow, so cut it down before pasting to reduce the amount to be trimmed off at ceiling level.

The easiest way to deal with a ceiling rose is first to turn off the electricity, disconnect the flex and replace the cover. When papering take the paper right across it. Pierce a hole

and cut star-shaped segments enabling the rose to poke through. Trim neatly with scissors or a sharp knife. Refit the flex and restore the electricity.

Papering walls

Start where your eye first travels to when you enter the room. Usually it is the corner by the main window. Work both ways round from here to the door where the differences in the pattern matching won't be noticeable. If there is a chimney breast and recesses, and you are hanging a large patterned paper, centre the paper on the chimney breast and work out from here.

Stairwells can be awkward because of the long lengths you will have to hang. Start with the longest drop. Check where the other drops will fall and move the starting point if necessary to avoid fiddly cuts.

Marking the starting point On the starting wall, measure the width of a roll from the corner less 25mm (1in.). Use a plumb line to draw a vertical line and hang the first length against this so that it just laps round the corner.

On a chimney breast find the centre by measuring. Measure half the width of a roll to one side and draw a vertical line – the start line.

Measuring and cutting Accurately measure the drop on the wall. Decide where you want the pattern (if any) to start on the wall and measure out the drop on the paper from this point. Allow 50mm (2in.) above for trimming. Similarly allow a further 50mm (2in.) at the bottom.

Now cut all the drops you need, making sure the pattern matches between each one. Remember, when going clockwise around a room you have to match the pattern to the right hand edge of the previous strip. When going anti-clockwise you have to match to the left hand edge.

Mark and number the top of each drop so you can maintain the correct sequence.

Pasting Mix up the recommended adhesive for the wallcovering you're hanging, although you may have to use a ready mixed paste. Allow the adhesive to stand for 15 minutes before using.

If your pasting table is wider than the wallcovering, lay all your lengths face down on the table in sequence with number one on top. Pull this across towards you so that the table is completely covered by paper. This

means you don't have to keep repositioning a single length over the edges of the table as you paste to prevent adhesive getting on the top.

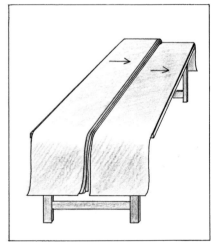

With this system it doesn't matter if paste gets on the next sheet as it has to be coated anyway.

Paste from the top to the bottom of the drop. Paste down the middle and then spread out towards the edges so there is a complete and even coverage of adhesive. After pasting about a half to two-thirds, turn the top over on itself, finish pasting and make a smaller fold at the bottom.

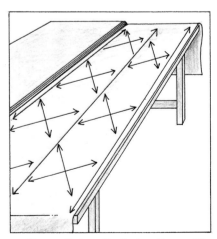

Depending on the instructions with the covering, either leave it to soak so that it's fully stretched when you come to hang it, or hang immediately. If you have to wait don't waste time, paste the next couple of drops.

Hanging the paper With the first length, open out the long fold in the drop and position the paper against the wall so that it aligns with the vertical starting line and there is a 50mm (2in.) overlap on the ceiling. Brush across the top and into the join with the ceiling, then brush down and outwards to remove all air bubbles. Ensure the overlap tucks neatly into the internal corner.

Unfold the bottom of the paper and work down with a brush to form a crease against the skirting. Mark top and bottom trim lines lightly with a pencil. Pull the paper gently away from the wall at top and bottom and cut off waste with scissors. Brush the paper back into position. Butt the next drop up to the first so that the patterns match exactly. Sometimes undulations in the wall cause small gaps to appear, but normally there's enough stretch in the paper to ease the edges together. On flat coverings use a seam roller to ensure that the join is well stuck down. If necessary, gently lift the edges and brush on some more paste.

Where the paper turns the corner suspend a plumb line down the edge of the overlap. If it isn't vertical, i.e. the corner isn't square (it's rare if it *is*!), gauge how much the drop on the new wall will have to overlap this. Pencil where the overlap will be and mark a roll width from this. Plumb a line here to hang the drop against. Then continue to hang in the normal way.

Use a similar procedure for going round internal corners which come in the middle of a drop. Measure the distance from the last complete drop to the corner in several places. Take the longest measurement and add 20-25mm (¾-1in.). Cut the paper to this width, paste and hang, so that it laps round the corner a short distance. Set a plumb line against the edge of the overlap to work out how much and where the offcut has to overlap this so that it can be hung to a vertical. Mark the position of the overlap. Measure the width of the offcut at the top and transfer the measurement to the wall using the edge of the paper or an overlap line as a starting point. You can now plumb and mark where the outer edge of the offcut should go. Paste the paper and hang.

Deal with external corners in a similar way. Cut the first drop so that it laps 25-50mm (1-2in.) round the corner. Then re-plumb and hang the offcut so that the pattern matches as accurately as possible.

With relief papers which are going to be painted, pattern matching isn't so vital. To stop a ridge forming where the drops overlap at corners, tear down the edge of the drop underneath to feather the edge. Don't use a seam roller. All this will do is flatten the relief resulting in a conspicuously smooth band.

Dealing with doors and windows Where the architrave is flush with the wall, simply cut round. If this means an awkward 'L' shape cut away most of the waste before pasting. Then hang and trim on the wall. If the window or door is in a recess (see diagram), continue across

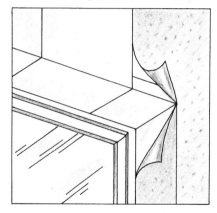

the top, and in the case of a window the bottom as well, and flap round the reveals. Patch the top corners of the underside of the recess and any gaps on the reveals where the paper hasn't met the window frame.

Behind radiators These are awkward obstacles to paper behind, particularly where a drop meets a bracket. Turn the radiator off and mark the approximate position of the fixing brackets with tape on the face of the panel. Hang the paper in the normal way, but let it rest over the radiator. Using the tape as a guide, cut out sections of paper where necessary to enable the paper to be manoeuvred round the brackets. Use a radiator paint roller or brush to smooth the paper down the back. Trim at the skirting board in the normal way.

Fireplaces Treat these as you would an architrave fitted flush with the wall surface. An extra problem arises if a shelf extends beyond the width of the surround. Cut slits in the paper and gradually remove the waste until you get a good fit.

Light switches and sockets Let the paper fall over the fitting. Pierce a hole with scissors at the centre and cut to the corners of the faceplate (if it's round, cut star-shaped segments). Smooth

down paper with brush and crease segments where they meet the faceplate. Cut along these with a sharp knife for a neat finish.

Alternatively, turn off the electricity supply. Cut a hole in the paper slightly undersize. Unscrew the faceplate, manoeuvre it through and refix so that its edges rest on the paper.

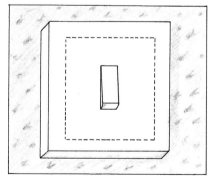

Important: never use this technique with foil wallcoverings.

Ready pasted papers
Cut the paper to the length required and lightly roll up from the bottom with the pattern side inwards. Immerse in a trough of cold water at the foot of the wall and leave for one minute. Then pick out of the trough and offer up to the wall. A string across the length of the trough will help remove water from the surface of the paper as it rubs against it. Hang as ordinary paper, and keep some paste handy to apply to edges that lift.

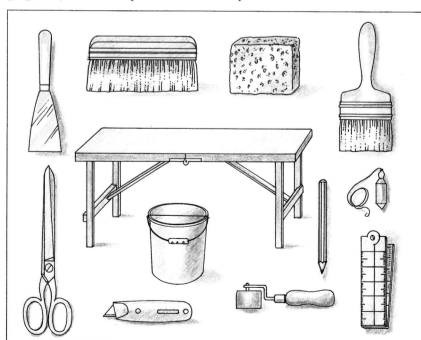

TILES

There are many alternatives to wallpapers, and in certain areas of the house, the bathroom and kitchen for instance, it is worth considering a more practical covering: ceramic or cork tiles, even sheet cork.

Ceramic tiles

Tiles are available in an extensive range of shapes, sizes and finishes, patterned and plain. Very small tiles can be built up into a mosaic, but if you want to use tiles this size, it's far easier and quicker to use those already mounted on mesh backing panels.

Planning is all important. Work on graph paper or a scale drawing of the wall(s) you're going to cover. Mark on the windows and doors. Then count up the number of tiles you will need, not forgetting the ones you will have to cut. You can sometimes buy tiles with a mitred edge to go round external corners, but these are only useful when you start the tiling from this corner. Avoid using patterned tiles where you have to cut them to fit round a corner. The break of pattern can look conspicuous. Instead plan out a design using a combination of plain and patterned tiles, making sure the plain ones go to the corners. Remember that tiles don't just have to be laid horizontally, one above the other. Rows can be staggered or set at an angle instead.

From your plan you will also be able to estimate the amount of adhesive you require. Because of the situations where tiles are most often used – as splashbacks to sinks and basins, on bathroom walls and in shower cubicles – always use a waterproof adhesive when tiling. If you're tiling a small area, say, a splashback you'll probably find it more economical to use a combined adhesive and grout mix to stick the tiles and seal between them. On wall areas grout the tiles as a separate operation after the adhesive has set. Before buying tiles, check if they have lugs on the edges which butt together to provide consistent spacing between the tiles. If they have lugs on all four sides you will need separate edging tiles with glazed edges. More commonly now you will find lugs on two sides and glazed edges on the others. Some tiles have no lugs at all – space these with matchsticks, cardboard folded over or proprietary plastic spacers.

Preparation Tiles can be fixed to virtually any flat surface. Mosaic sheets can even be taken round curves. The surface must be sound and clean. Strip wallpaper. Bare plaster and plasterboard should be sealed with a PVA sealer/adhesive suitably thinned or coated with emulsion. If in doubt about the state of the walls fix battens to it, clad with marine plywood and tile on this. Key ceramic tiles and painted walls in good condition with glasspaper. If paintwork is flaking, scrape off and coat with primer/sealer, or strip off all paint with a paint stripper. Use primer/ sealer over distemper.

Marking the walls Plan the tiling to minimize cutting. You will find this easier to do if you first make a tiling rod. Use about a 450mm (18in.) long 50 x 25mm (2 x 1in.) batten and mark tile widths and grout spaces along its length. Hold a spirit level against it to make sure it is horizontal, vertical or at 45° when you're moving it around on the wall.

If you're half-tiling a wall, perhaps in a bathroom, try to fix the height in whole tiles. If you can't, aim to trim at the floor. Likewise when going from floor to ceiling make the cuts at floor level. But if the ceiling slopes then you will have to cut top and bottom.

Similarly, when deciding on the lateral position of the tiles, plan so that the cuts into the corners are about the same on each side.

If the wall has a window or a door, centre the first tile on the opening, in the case of two windows centre the tile between them. Then work your laying and cutting pattern outwards to the corners.

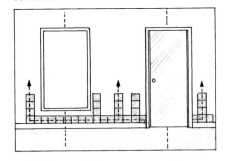

To tile a window recess, use tiles with glazed edges for the front of the sill, reveals and top. You may have to cut them to tie in with the bonding pattern of the rest of the wall. These tiles should project out a tile thickness so the tiles on the facing wall can be cut flush to them. You will probably have to cut 'L-shaped tiles at the corners of the recess.

Once you have decided how to arrange the tiles, using your tile rod as a guide, nail a horizontal batten to the wall on top of which the second row up of tiles will be laid. Mark the exact position of the tiles on it using the tile rod. Then use a plumb line or spirit level to position a vertical batten which will mark the side edge of the first whole tile in the row.

Starting to tile Use the comb supplied with the adhesive to cover about a square metre (a square yard) of wall, starting in the 'L' made by the battens. Firmly press the first tile into the

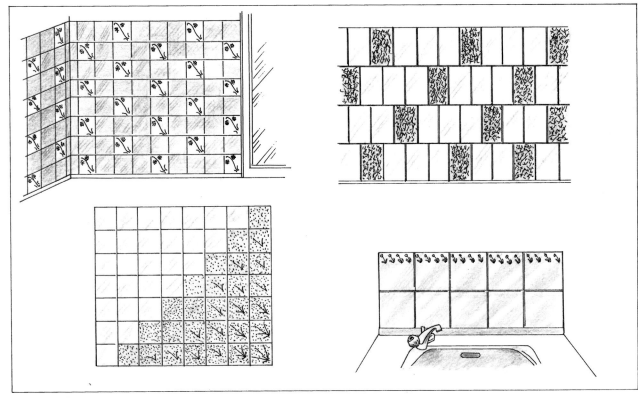

corner where the battens meet. Lay tiles along the bottom batten, using spacers if necessary, until you come to the end of the adhesive bed. Similarly, lay tiles against the vertical battening, then fill in diagonally between battens.

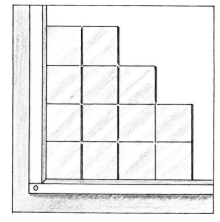

Apply more adhesive and continue to work upwards and outwards until all the whole tiles have been positioned. The cutting comes afterwards. But don't remove the battens for 24 hours – the cuts here will have to wait. Never leave the bottom edge of a cut tile unsupported. Tack a couple of nails or a small piece of batten underneath until the adhesive has set.

Cutting tiles Accurately measure the gap to be filled at each end and transfer the dimensions to the tile. Score along the surface with a special tile cutter so that the wheel tip or scribing point breaks through the glaze (you will hear a crackly noise). Pay particular attention to scoring the edges.

Position the tile, glaze uppermost, so that the score line rests over a couple of matchsticks. Press firmly down on each side of the score line and the tile will neatly snap in two.

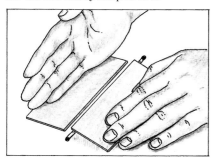

Alternatively, snap the tile in a special tool which you operate like pliers. If you're going to do a lot of tiling it's worth buying a measuring and cutting machine which clamps the tile while you mark and score it. To snap you just press firmly on the clamp.

Curved and 'L' shapes can be cut by scoring the glaze and then nibbling away with pliers or tile nippers. Otherwise use a tungsten carbide rod saw blade set in a hacksaw.

Grouting Although coloured grouts have been known to stain the face of some tiles they are very popular. Grout comes ready mixed (as part of the adhesive) or in powder form which you mix with water to a smooth paste. Press into the gaps between the tiles with a damp sponge and clean up tile surfaces immediately. When the grout has hardened, but is not fully dry, run a rounded stick (a pencil will do) over the grout lines to give them a

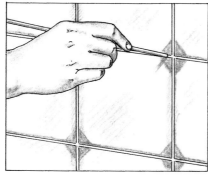

smooth, slightly depressed profile. Finally, buff up the tiles with kitchen roll paper.

Tiling round electrical fittings Turn off the power and unscrew the faceplate. Cut the tiles to go round box and refit faceplate so that it rests on top of them. You may need to use longer screws.

Tiling round obstacles When tiling round a sink or bath, nail a second horizontal batten above it so you can continue to lay all the whole tiles. Later remove the batten and cut down onto the top of the fixture.

If tiling a splashback use whole tiles only. Make sure glazed edges show on the perimeter. Unless the basin has a curved back you probably won't need to fit a horizontal batten. Just start the tiling against the top edge.

Accessories Soap dishes, toilet roll holders and towel rings, etc, are made to take the place of one or several tiles. Strap them against the wall until the adhesive has dried.

Seal the gap between bath/basin/sink and tiles with flexible, silicone mastic sealant. Alternatively, for baths, bed quadrant edging tiles on mastic.

Laying mosaics

This is very much the same operation as for ordinary tiles. Again arrange the sheets to minimize cutting, and set out the battens as described above. Cutting mosaic pieces can be tricky. You may find it easier to score and nibble away waste. The backing mesh can be cut easily with scissors to produce smaller segments. If you have to insert a single line of tiles, add spacers between each to maintain a uniform gap for grouting.

Apply waterproof adhesive and press sheets into position. With some mosaics there's a protective paper sheet stuck over the face of the tiles. Allow adhesive to set, sponge over and peel off.

Cork tiles

Leave cork tiles in the room for a few days to acclimatize to the environment.

Prepare the walls as for ceramic tiles. Painted walls can be keyed with glasspaper. For best results cross-line first. Similarly, plan out the tiles to minimize cuts. Pencil your starting lines on the wall – some people prefer to start in the centre of the wall and work outwards – or use the batten method.

Apply the recommended adhesive to the wall with a notched spreader and carefully press on tiles, butting them closely against each other. Work round the edges with a seam roller to make sure they are properly adhered. Use a damp cloth to wipe off immediately any adhesive that gets on the face of the tile or roller.

Finish laying the whole tiles then make the cuts with a sharp knife and a straight-edge. Hold the tile to be cut over the last whole tile in the row. Then position a second tile so that it butts against the wall and overlaps the first one. Pencil down this edge, remove tiles from the wall and cut down the line to

give a tile section that will fit the gap exactly.

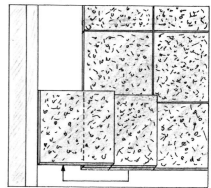

To tile round electrical fittings, you can make up templates from card, trace onto cork and cut out segments as necessary.

The neatest way, however, is to switch off the electricity and to detach the faceplate completely. Tile across the mounting box as though it wasn't there, then use a knife and straight-edge to cut a hole. Refit the cores of the supply cable into terminals of the faceplate and screw back to the wall with the edges resting on the cork. Restore the power.

Seal the tiles with polyurethane varnish or wax polish (if you haven't bought the factory sealed type) or leave in a natural state. You can hide the cut edges at the corners, ceiling and floor with wood beading.

Sheet cork

This usually comes on a roll either with a natural or printed colour finish. Cut drops exactly to length before hanging. Make cut-outs for electrical fittings, or deal with them as suggested above. Work out the position of the drops so that you have to cut into the corners on each side. Avoid having to cut slivers.

Plumb the first complete drop, apply the recommended adhesive and press sheet into place. Work over it with a paint roller to remove air bubbles. Hang all the full drops first, then the corner drops. To get a good fit take measurements for the width at a number of places to allow for the fact that the corner may not be square. Seal or leave the cork natural and finish off with wood beading.

FLOORS

If you had to lay flooring in a simple rectangular room there would be no problem in fitting virtually every form of covering. But it is never as easy as that. Chimney breasts, hearths, fitted cupboards and doorways mean that coverings have to be cut to fit, and this is where costly mistakes can arise.

So there's much to be said for sticking to some form of tiling and leaving the sheet materials to the professionals. Unless you've got the knack, large rolls of covering are unwieldy to handle. Carpet laying is often included in the price of the carpet. And hessian carpet has to be stretched with a knee kicker and hooked onto battens round the perimeter of the room – a job that requires skill and experience.

Tiles have a number of advantages. They are easy to lay and if you cut one incorrectly, you can try again on another without ruining the whole covering. It's also a simple matter to replace or swap round tiles that become damaged or show signs of wear. Consider using tiles in awkward areas where you would normally have to cut away a fair amount of sheet covering in order to get it to fit – with tiles there's little waste. So your options are: vinyl, cork, ceramic and quarry tiles and mosaic wood panels.

Preparing the floor surface
Flooring must always be laid on a dry, firm and flat foundation, otherwise the unevenness will show through and lead to unequal wear and patches developing. Floor coverings are also much more difficult to lay on a poor surface.

Concrete floor Lift old floor coverings and check for damp. If there are signs of damp, take professional advice. You may just need to brush on a liquid damp proof membrane or more drastic action may be required involving resurfacing the whole floor.

If the floor is dry and flat, wash down. If the surface is powdery, brush on a stabilizing agent. Fill any cracks with mortar and correct any general unevenness by applying a self-levelling compound: the most common are water based. Prime the floor with a PVA adhesive watered down following the

instructions. Then mix up the compound. As it sets quickly work in small sections. Pour the fairly runny liquid onto the floor and trowel out to a thickness of 3-4mm (⅛in). The trowel marks disappear as the compound dries. Repeat the operation until the defective areas have been dealt with. Self-levelling compound can also be applied over ceramic and quarry tiles to give a flat surface on which you can lay some other form of covering. Once dry, temporarily cover the floor, leave for two weeks, then put down the covering.

If vinyl tiles have been bonded to the floor ideally these should come up. Use a scraper and a hot air stripper to soften the surface. But if they are very firmly fixed you can brush on a special primer and then apply a coat of latex-based self-levelling compound. When using adhesive later on to stick down the new flooring check that it won't react adversely with this.

Timber floor Remove old floor coverings and any adhesive that has stuck to the boards. Then scrub with detergent. Make sure all the boards are nailed down. Use oval or cut nails to fix loose ones. Fill gaps with thin strips of wood planed down to floor level with a Surform. If the boards are old or uneven, coat with a latex compound that will fill the gaps and cover nail heads and then clad the floor in hardboard (shiny side up), chipboard or plywood. Tell the timber yard what you want to use the sheeting for and they will give you one of the right grade. It should be water resistant. If you choose this method ensure that there is good underfloor ventilation.

If you use hardboard soak the rough side with water and then allow it to dry in the room where you are going to use it for at least two days. Use 6mm (¼in.) plywood when overlaying ceramic and quarry tiles. These are quite weighty so you should also check that the floor can take the extra weight. If the original floor gives when you walk on it take professional advice.

Use the sheeting as big as you can handle it. Stagger the joints and make sure they are flush, then secure the boards with nails or screws driven in at 150mm (6in.) centres.

Planning
Draw out the room on graph paper, marking the door and the chimney breast if there is one. From this plan you should be able to calculate fairly accurately how many tiles you're going to need. It will also give you a chance to design any patterns you want to create with, say, different coloured carpet tiles. The exact laying position will have to be worked out on the floor.

For best results, vinyl and cork tiles should be laid from the centre of the room outwards. Wood panels and ceramic and quarry tiles are laid from one of the corners furthest away from the door – you work back to this point as your escape route.

The marking out method, however, is very similar for all types of tile. First chalk a length of string and stretch it between the centres of the two shortest sides. Snap it onto the floor to leave a chalk line. Measure to find the mid-point of this line and then use a try square to draw a line at right angles.

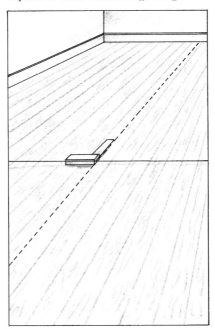

Set your chalk string directly over this and then snap a line which runs between the two longest walls.

Now make a dry run to check the size of the border tiles. Lay out the tiles, either butted together (vinyl, cork, carpet and wood panels) or

spaced to allow a grouting gap (ceramic and quarry), from the centre along the guidelines to the four walls. If the tile at one end is a thin strip and at the other almost a whole tile, adjust the position of the tiles in a row so the border tiles are nearly equal in size. If both border tiles are very thin, remove a tile from the row and make them larger. When you have fixed the positions redraw the guidelines.

To fix a starting position in a corner all you have to do is continue to dry-lay tiles up and across from the ends of the lines you've previously laid until they meet in the corner. In the case of wood panels, pencil round the outside edges of the corner panel to fix the start. In the case of ceramic and quarry tiles temporarily pin battens in the gap between the tiles and the skirting so they butt against the outside edges, i.e. the battens will form an 'L' shape. Once the starting positions have been marked all the tiles can be lifted up.

Vinyl tiles
It is easiest and far less messy to use self-adhesive tiles. Start at the centre, peel off the backing paper and align with two of the guidelines forming one of the quadrants you have marked. Make sure you lay any pattern in the right direction. Then 'build' into the quadrant tightly butting the tiles.

If you don't use self-adhesive tiles, apply adhesive with a notched spreader over a small area, allow to become tacky and press the tiles into place.

To cut tiles to fit at edges: lay a whole tile directly over the last whole tile in the row and butt a second one up to the skirting so that it overlaps the first. Pencil along the edge onto the tile underneath. Cut down the line with a sharp knife guided by a straight-edge, peel back the paper from the segment and fit it into the gap. To go round corners use the same procedure, but you will need to mark the tile from two directions from the adjacent walls.

Cut awkward shapes – around door architraves, basin pedestals and lavatories – by first making up a template made of card and then tracing the outline onto the tile.

Apply a bead of silicone mastic between the wall and tiles in a bathroom to stop water seeping down the inevitable minute gap that will be present after you have cut the tiles.

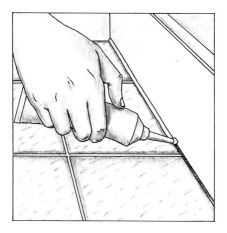

Cork tiles

Leave them in the room where they will be laid for a day or so before carrying out the work. Lay as for vinyl, but you will have to apply the adhesive separately.

Some tiles are already sealed, others need a polyurethane varnish finish brushed on. Thin down the first coat with white spirit to act as a primer, then apply several top coats. Also seal factory finished tiles when laid in a kitchen or bathroom to stop water penetrating the joins.

Fit a wood or metal threshold bar at the door opening to prevent scuffing.

Ceramic tiles

Once you have decided on a starting point and have fixed the battens, use a notched spreader to apply the recommended adhesive to about 1 sq. m (1 sq. yd) of floor. Position the first tile in the 'L' made by the battens and press firmly into the adhesive. Lay the next tile alongside and butting up to the batten. Use a thick piece of card, or the spine of a spare spreader to gauge the grouting space between the tiles.

Lay a complete row of tiles, then hold along spirit level or straight-edge on top to make sure the tiles are level and at the same height.

Continue to lay all the whole tiles, checking that they are evenly spaced and that they are flat in all directions.

Leave to dry for at least 24 hours before standing on them. When they have set, cut the border tiles.

Ceramic floor tiles are harder to cut than wall tiles because they are thicker. Measure the gap at both sides and transfer the measurements to the face of the tile. Score as deep a groove as you can in the face, then hold the tile in pincer-like snappers and break the tile in two – this is easier than it sounds. As some of the cheaper tile breakers are a bit flimsy, reduce frustration and anger to a minimum and hire a floor tile cutter which saves time and unwanted breakages. Curves and angles can be cut by scoring the face (having first marked it from a template) and then chipping away along the mark with pincers or tile nips.

Finally grout between the tiles. When nearly dry run a stick over the lines to produce a smooth finish. Wipe the tiles clean, but don't wash them for about ten days to allow the grout to harden fully. Mosaic tiles bonded to mesh backing sheets are laid in the same way.

Quarry tiles

These are very similar to ceramic tiles to lay. But with some types the individual tiles vary in thickness and shade, so make sure they are well mixed and be prepared to vary the width of the grouting lines to keep even rows.

Tiles can be butted up to the skirting, but because they are quite thick, you may want temporarily to remove the skirting and door architrave, take the tiles up to the wall and then refit the woodwork. Alternatively fit special skirting tiles. Lipping tiles are available for the front edge of steps.

The tiles can be set on a mortar bed, but you will probably find it easier to use adhesive, a 6mm (¼in.) bed being required which can be applied to the back of the tile or the floor. With the occasional thinner tile apply a thicker load.

Cut by scoring along the surface and then tapping the back over the score line. For curves and angles, score and then nibble away the rest with pincers.

Grout with mortar. Clean and leave, seal with polyurethane or wax.

Mosaic wood panels

As with cork tiles, it's a good idea to unpack and spread out the panels in the room where they are going to be laid a few days before fitting so that they can get used to the environment.

Lay the tiles as you would ceramic tiles. Start in a corner (battens aren't strictly necessary) and spread enough bitumen adhesive on the floor to cover one panel. If you get any of this tacky substance on your hands or the face of the panel wipe it off immediately with a damp cloth. Don't slide the panels together when butting up as this will encourage adhesive to ooze through the join. Continue to lay all the whole tiles and allow the adhesive to set before dealing with the cuts.

Use the same method as for vinyl to do this, but allow for a 12mm (½in.) gap between the cut panel and the skirting to accommodate any slight expansion in the wood. Cut the panels with a tenon saw. Either fill the gap with cork strip or cover with quadrant moulding.

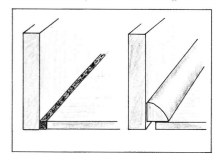

When finished, sand the floor with fine glasspaper, vacuum brush and wipe clean with a damp rag, then apply several coats of special sealer, sanding between each one.

Sanding floors

If the floorboards in a room are in reasonable condition and free from woodworm and rot it's surprising how, just by cleaning and sanding, they can be turned into an attractive decorative surface.

Once the old covering has been taken away, check for old fixing tacks and remove with pincers or a claw hammer. Clean off any traces of adhesive stuck to the boards with white spirit or petrol (but be careful how you use the latter).

Fill any gaps between the boards with long strips of wood, planing them down to floor level with a Surform. Drive in fixing nails with a punch so they are 5mm (about ¼in.) below the surface. You may have to take out screws and drill small holes (counterbores) into which you can sink the heads. This stage is important, don't skimp it, otherwise you will tear many sanding sheets to shreds.

Hire a floor sander to deal with the

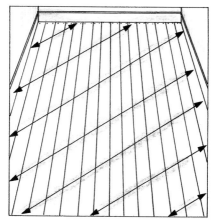

main floor area and an orbital sander to get into the corners and along the skirting where the larger machine can't reach. You will have to buy the abrasives. Follow the instructions that come with the floor sander closely. Fit a coarse grade abrasive to the drum first and work across the boards diagonally. Take the sander back and forth over the same strip then move to the next one. Never let the machine rest in one place or you will gouge the boards. When you have finished working diagonally, go over the floor again with the grain. Repeat this operation with medium and fine abrasives. Then use the orbital sander to clean up the edges. In all you will probably remove about 3mm (⅛in.) of wood from the top of the boards, hence the need to ensure the fixing nails are below this level.

Before finishing, thoroughly sweep/vacuum the floor and then wipe over. You can then simply apply clear polyurethane varnish for a tough matt, satin or gloss finish. Otherwise, bleach and varnish, or apply a stain to change the colour and then seal this with polyurethane varnish.

MOULDINGS

One of the keys to successful decorating is to make the most of original features. On older properties, in particular, ornate cornices, ceiling roses, panel mouldings and dado rails give a room much of its charm and character if well treated. But so often they are not fully effective for want of some basic renovation.

Renovating old mouldings

The most common problem is likely to be the countless coats of paint that have clogged up the delicate relief. To remove them is a painstaking job that must be done with care. You may have to try different methods. First soak with water and then use a small fairly stiff brush (an old toothbrush will do) or a screwdriver to prise out the paint. If the paint doesn't soften, try working in some paint remover, but don't forget to wash away all traces afterwards. Repair small damaged patches with cellulose filler or plaster of Paris. Mould to shape using glasspaper. Larger sections can be replaced by recasting the moulding using a length in good condition from which to form a mould – it's a job for a specialist firm.

Mouldings can be painted the same colour as walls and ceiling or they can be contrasted. Or the relief details can be picked out in a separate colour. For something slightly different try an antiquing effect to give an old and worn look. Coat the moulding with white eggshell paint and then brush on a scumble glaze. Stipple over with a stiffer brush (e.g. a stencilling brush) and then wipe with a lint-free cloth. The scumble left in the crevices will help to throw up the relief of the moulding.

Fitting new mouldings

These features can be added to more modern properties. But be careful, for unless chosen in sympathy with the style of the house they can look totally out of place.

Mouldings are made from a variety of materials including plastic, polystyrene, glass fibre, plastic foam, plaster, fibrous plaster and wood. Many are available off-the-shelf, but the most expensive (and most intricate) are made to order. Apart from the 'cornice

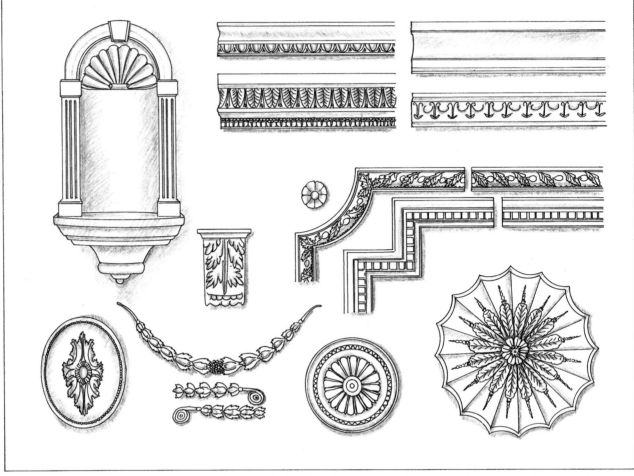

on a roll' which has to be formed into a curve at the ceiling/wall join, all other mouldings can be stuck straight into position. It's essential to use the adhesive recommended by the manufacturer. Some you have to mix up, others come ready to apply. With some mouldings contact adhesive is used. Install before other decorative work is carried out.

Cornices

Apply to wall and ceiling surfaces, not over wallpaper. Measure the length of the wall, allowing extra at external corners to cut mitres. Cut mitres using the template provided with the cornice, or use a mitre block. If the cornice is 'soft' enough, drive pins into the top of the wall leaving about 12mm (½in.) protruding. Apply adhesive to the back of the cornice and press into place over

the pins which will lend support until the adhesive hardens. Alternatively, drive pins at intervals through the face of the moulding to hold it in place. Punch below the surface or remove and cover holes with adhesive.

Ceiling roses

Again these are stuck in place, with pins for support. Drill a hole through the centre to take the light flex. Dealing with the electrics may cause a few problems, so consult an electrician before buying any type of rose.

Panel moulding

Accurately mark panel on the wall, then stick sections along guidelines. You may have to mitre corners, although special corner pieces are available. Butt join lengths together.

You can also apply panel moulding

to flush doors. Wood and plastic moulding is best.

Niches

These can be recessed into a wall, but it's far easier to use the type that is stuck onto the surface. The extra weight means they should be well supported while the adhesive dries.

Dado rails

Use wood moulding, set at a height between 750mm (30in.) and 900mm (36in.). It can be pinned into place, but screwing will give a firmer fixing.

Fireplace surrounds

These are decorative details and it's important that they are not exposed to direct heat. Some are screwed into place, others require adhesive and pinning.

BASIC SHELVING

Shelves can be made from solid timber, veneered- or Melamine-coated chipboard, plywood, blockboard or ordinary chipboard. In some situations you can also use glass. All but Melamine (and glass) should be treated with a protective finish, to ensure they can be easily wiped clean. For a natural look apply polyurethane varnish – clear or coloured – or a plastic coating, which will provide a tough surface with heat-resistance. Wax polish and various oils give attractive finishes but are easily marked. Otherwise paint with a gloss top coat for a tough surface.

The cut edges of veneered boards need to be covered with a veneer strip to conceal the chipboard core. If using blockboard, plywood or ordinary chipboard, lip the front and sides (if to view) with plain beading or decorative moulding to give a neat finish.

A simple shelf

On an open wall use 'L'-shaped brackets, choosing a style and finish to match the location.

Decide where you want to put the shelf, then test the wall. If it is solid brick or block there's no problem about fixing. With plasterboard stud partition walls, and lath and plaster walls, which normally have a lighter, hollow 'ring' to them, the brackets must be screwed to the upright studs. Even with cavity fixings, the wall surface is not strong enough to support the weight of a loaded shelf. Locate the stud by tapping the wall until the tone changes to a deeper, less resonant, sound. In practice this is not so easy to discover, particularly if the wall is insulated. So test by pushing bradawl into the wall. Check that you're not directly above, below or to the side of an electrical fitting so you don't strike into cables. Also check the path of water pipes. Once found, it then depends on the spacing of the studs as to whether they are suitable for fixings. In the end you may have to resort to a free-standing bookcase for shelving.

Spacing brackets The key point here is that the shelf should never sag. Consequently, spacing depends on the shelving material and the use to which the shelf is being put. But this doesn't take into account misuse, so go for a strong fixing. As a general rule space brackets at 600mm (24in.) intervals. You can set them a further 150mm (6in.) apart, on 18mm (¾in.) plywood and timber but on 12mm (½in.) chipboard it's best to keep brackets separated by about 500mm (20in.). Brackets should also be set fairly near to the ends of the shelf, which may mean you will have to introduce a third support even if the new spacing is a lot less than the minimum required.

Fixing the shelf First fix the brackets to the underside of the shelf at the correct spacing. Note it's the shorter arm of the 'L' that's screwed down. Then hold the shelf up to the wall with a spirit level resting on top.

When perfectly horizontal get a helper to mark the position of the bracket fixing holes on the wall. Remove the shelf and drill and plug the holes if working on brick or block. On other walls, drill through the plaster and just into the timber upright. Reposition the shelf and fix with 38mm (1½in.) No 10 screws.

If you are fitting several shelves on top of one another, check with the tallest object you intend putting on each that you are leaving enough space between them.

Shelves and alcoves

Use 50 x 25mm (2 x 1in.) battens to support shelves here. For a good solid fixing, run battening along the back wall as well as down the sides of the recess. Stop the side battens 50mm (2in.) short of the front of the shelf and

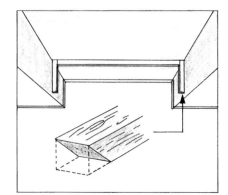

chamfer the ends to make them less conspicuous. Apply a finish to the battens and shelf prior to fixing.

Pre-drill fixing holes 50mm (2in.) in from the ends and then at 300mm (12in.) centres. Secure the back batten first. Position on the wall at the correct height (i.e. the height of the shelf less the thickness of the board) and set a spirit level along the top edge. When

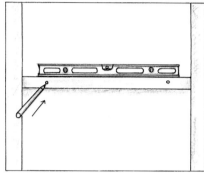

you've got the batten horizontal mark through the pre-drilled holes, drill and plug the wall and screw the batten into place with 75mm (3in.) No 10 screws.

Butt the first side batten up against the rear batten and rest a spirit level across the corner to check that the side

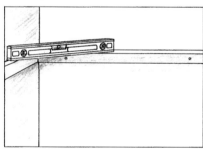

batten is also horizontal. Mark and fix as described above and repeat the operation for the remaining batten.

Screw plastic corner fixing blocks to the middle of each side batten and 75mm (3in.) from the ends of the rear batten so that they are flush with the top edges. Lay the shelf in place and screw up through the blocks to keep it in position.

Rather than battens, you can also use a less conspicuous metal angle strip to support the shelf. This too is an ideal means of supporting glass, which should be 6mm (¼in.) thick, plain or tinted, and get the glass merchant to burnish the edges so you can't cut yourself on them.

Making your own adjustable shelving

If you can adjust the height of shelves you have a far more flexible storage system. You can buy proprietary systems (see below), but it's very easy to make your own, especially if you set it in an alcove. All you need are four lengths of 50x25mm (2x1in.) timber to make the uprights and material for the shelves.

Clamp the four uprights together (face-to-face) and drill holes the diameter of a 6mm (¼in.) dowel rod completely through them at, say, 100mm (4in.) intervals. Drill fixing holes at 300mm (12in.) centres. Set the first upright in position on the side wall at the back of the alcove. Push a piece of dowel rod 40mm (1¾in.) long into one of the holes. Hold the next upright vertically in place on the same side wall at the front of the shelf, and put another piece of dowel into the corres-

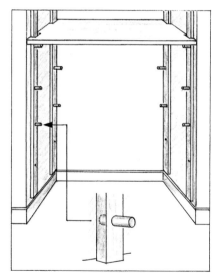

ponding hole. Rest a spirit level across them to check that they are in the same horizontal plane, then mark the fixing holes, drill and plug the wall and screw on the upright. Follow the same procedure to ensure the holes on the uprights opposite match up.

Then fit dowel rods into the holes where you want to fit shelves and rest the boards on top. You can also use proprietary plastic studs in the holes (there's a type suitable for supporting glass) or two-part metal studs for taking heavier loads.

CURTAINS AND BLINDS

Professional-looking curtains are well within the scope of even a complete novice. Start by deciding the style of curtain heading before buying the fabric as the heading governs the amount you need. Standard gathers need material one and a half times as wide as the track; pencil pleats need material two and a quarter times; and for pinch pleats, the amount of extra material required depends on the amount of pleats per inch and the width of the fabric. Remember also to add extra for matching patterns and for shrinkage. Never skimp on the amount of fabric allowed for fullness.

Most curtain fabric is 1200mm (48in.) wide; curtain lining is a little narrower so that it does not have to be trimmed.

Measuring for curtains

Install tracks and rods before measuring for curtains. They are fitted in different positions depending on the window shape and the style of curtains.

Inside the window recess Spring wires, rods and tracks for net and sheer curtains are generally fitted inside the window recess, A, and should be close to the top. Multiply measurement A two and a half or three times (depending on the style of curtain heading) for the fullness of the curtains. Take measurement B for the length and add about 200mm (8in.) for hems.

Outside the window recess Where possible, a wall-mounted track or rod should extend a little to either side of the window to allow for maximum daylight when the curtains are open.

For sill-length curtains take measurement C and multiply according to the type of curtain heading. Take measurement D for length and add about 25mm (1in.) to prevent wear along the bottom.

For floor-length curtains take measurement C, and multiply for fullness, and measurement E, adding on 200mm (8in.) for hems. They should clear the floor by about 25mm (1in.).

For floor-to-ceiling curtains, the track can be fixed to the top of the wall or to the ceiling. Neat, unobtrusive ceiling tracks are obtainable, but they must be fixed securely. Measure the length of the track C and multiply for fullness; measure from track to floor and add about 200mm (8in.) for hems. With ceiling tracks use a tape with pockets at the top; special hooks may also be needed, depending on the style of heading and weight of fabric.

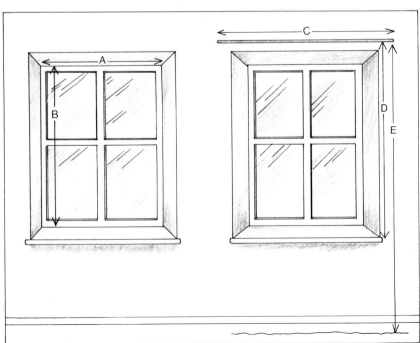

To make simple unlined curtains

Measure the window according to the shape and length of curtains required and cut fabric. Turn in 12mm (½in.) double hem down each side of curtain, snipping any selvedges, and baste. On most fabrics the hem can be machined, but hand-sew satins and velvets. At the bottom edge press up a 12mm (½in.) turning and turn fabric up again to form a double hem. Stitch by hand or with large machine stitch. Slip stitch folded edges at hem corners.

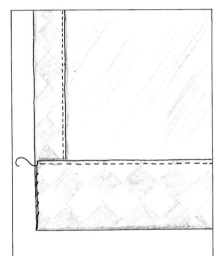

For a crisper look, stiffen the top of the curtains with iron-on interfacing. Cut interfacing 25mm (1in.) narrower than the intended depth of the top hem and iron it on to WS (wrong side) of fabric 12mm (½in.) from raw edge. Do not overlap ends on side hems. Turn down the 12mm (½in.) over it and turn down, pin and baste hem.

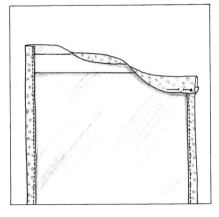

Gathered headings

Allow at least one and a half times the track length for fullness. Work a row of gathering along top of curtain, about 25mm (1in.) above turned-down edge, and another row 25mm (1in.) below. Draw up threads until the curtain is the right width and

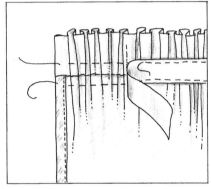

distribute gathers evenly. Pin, baste and machine ordinary 25mm (1in.) tape along rows of gathering over edges of top hem. Remove gathering threads and insert hooks in tape.

Pencil Pleats Allow two and a quarter times the track length. Turn down top hem 20mm (¾in.). Draw out 40mm (1½in.) of cord at both ends of tape; knot cords at one end only. At this end, trim off surplus tape and turn under. Place tape close to the top of the hem and attach.

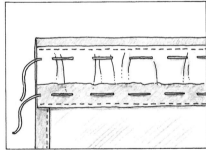

To hem

Hang the curtains for about two days before sewing the hem. All curtains, except very heavy ones, hang better if the bottom hem is weighted down with weighted tapes – small pieces of lead enclosed in a fabric tube. They come in various grades, and are passed through the bottom hem when the curtain is finished. Hem by hand or machine.

Blinds

An economical and easy way of covering small windows, blinds are traditionally made from holland, a coarse linen fabric, but canvas, printed cotton, linen union and many of the medium-weight synthetics as well as pvc-coated cottons can be used.

Roller blinds

Roller blinds with spring roller are the most popular type. They are available in kit form, with instructions and all the necessary fittings and screws.

Measuring Only two measurements are needed, the width, A, and length, B. Roller blinds are usually fitted inside the window recess. If there is no recess the blind should not extend too far beyond the edge of the window and should not drop below the sill.

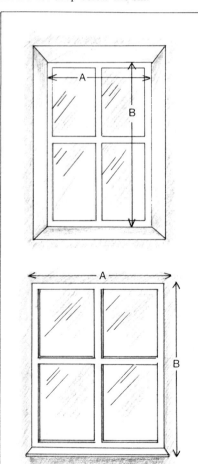

Making-up Buy a roller blind kit to measurement A or longer. Remove the metal cap from the end opposite the spring and cut off surplus on the wooden part of the roller. When the cap is replaced the complete roller should be 25mm (1in.) shorter than the width of the recess. Trim batten to fit.

Cut fabric on the straight grain or the blind will hang crookedly. The fabric should measure B plus about 300mm (12in.) by A, if fabric needs side hems. Cut fabric 25mm (1in.) narrower than A if stiffened or pvc-coated so the sides will not need stiffening.

Turn up and stitch a double lower hem to take the batten. Insert the

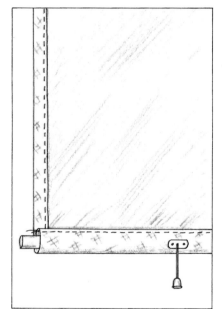

batten. Turn the top of the fabric over the roller, glue and tack down. On WS attach the cord to the batten centre with fitting provided. Place the roller on its brackets and work to adjust spring tension.

Roman blinds

This type of blind folds into soft pleats as it is drawn up by cords, and hangs straight when down.

Making-up Cut two pieces of dowelling the length of A. Cut fabric measuring A, plus 25mm (1in.) by B, plus 300mm (12in.) joining fabric lengths if necessary. Fix brackets at either side of window recess.

Turn in double hems down the sides and stitch. Press under 12mm (½in.) along top and bottom edges and then turn in the hems wide enough to take

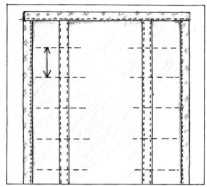

the dowelling, or, at the top, a brass rod. On WS about 100mm (4in.) from each side of the blind, stitch two lengths of narrow tape vertically between top and bottom hems, sewing down both edges of tape.

Work out width of pleats, 100mm (4in.) is average width. Mark pleats, fold fabric at marks and press pleats one by one. Mark both pieces of tape at

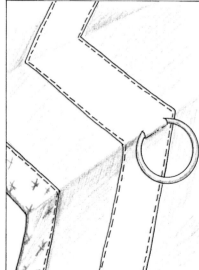

back edge of each pleat and push a small split brass curtain ring between tape and fabric at each mark, inserting last two rings at top edge of bottom hem. Fit two lengths of dowelling into top and bottom hems. Slip stitch bottom hem ends together.

Fix two screw-in eyelets or pulleys, A and B, to the top of the window recess in line with rings on WS of blind and one, C, at top of one side of recess. Hang blind. Thread a cord through C and B down through the rings on one tape and up through those on the other.

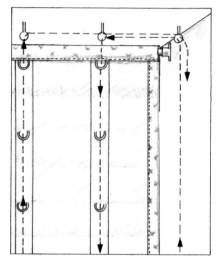

Take cord through A, back through B and down through C. Adjust the ends, cut level and pull both together to raise the blind. Attach the pleat to side of recess near bottom of cord and wrap cord ends round it.

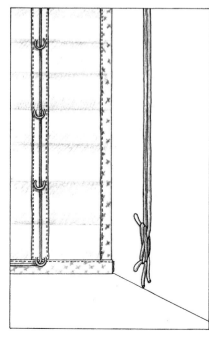

INDEX

Page numbers in *italic* refer to captions and illustrations.

A

Aalto, Alvar, 24, 71, 145, 146; *70, 128, 145*
acrylic carpets, 285
aerosols, paint, 341
Agas, 158
alarms, security, 325
alcoves, *28, 289*
alpine plants, 271
alterations: constraints on, 88
aluminium chairs, 71; *70*
Anaglypta, 290
annual plants, 271
answering machines, 183
antiques, dining furniture, 147
arches, 111
architects: conversion work, 256
dealing with, 331-2
extensions, 248, 256
architecture, 74-85
evolution of the house, 75-80
the historic house, 82-3
the terraced house, 81
the unorthodox house, 84-5
architraves, 297, 341
Art Deco, 44, 47, 49, 50, 58; *32, 132*
Art Nouveau, 44; *71, 136*
Artek, 145, 146
Arteluce, 139
Artemide, 146
Arts and Crafts Movement, *147*
attics, *94*
converting, 90, 250-1
sloping ceilings, 88
windows, 251, 254-5
audio equipment, 132-3
children's rooms, 226
Austrian blinds, 303
Axminster carpets, 284-5

B

babies, *see* nurseries
background lighting, 306-7, 309
bag-graining, 342
balconies, 255, 259
plants on, 275
balustrades, in gardens, 272
barbecues, 270
Barcelona chair, *71*
barns, converting, 85, 88; *16, 85, 160, 225*
Barnes, Robert, *315, 319,*
Barragan, Luis, 62-3
Basculant chairs, 70, 128
basements: converting, *257*
playrooms, 228
workshops, 184-5
basins: bathrooms, 218

bedrooms, 204
see also sinks
bathrooms, 206-19
basins, 218
baths, 216
in bedrooms, 204; *205*
bidets, 219
boxing in pipes, 211
colour, 69, 211
condensation, 210, 213
country houses, 15
dressing rooms in, 213;
eclectic style, *52*
environmental enclosures, 216
fittings, 220-1
fixtures, 322
flooring, 211; *209, 214*
heating, 211
lavatories, 218-19
lighting, 210
location, 88, 208
one room living, 247
planning, 208-9
showers, 217
storage, 211, 318
studios, 240
walls, 211, 289
warehouse conversion, 238
baths, 216
colour, 216-17
exotic, 216
fitting, 216
revamping old, 216
showers in, 217
batterie de cuisine, 176-8
Bauhaus, 20, 70; *36*
Baumgarten, Michael, *239, 319*
beams, exposed, *91*
bedding, *198-201*
bedlinen, *201*
bedspreads, *201*
comforters, 201; *200*
duvets, 198-9, 200-1
pillowcases, 201
quilts, 199, 201; *198*
sheets, 201
bedrooms, 188-205
bathrooms in, 204; *205*
carpets, 192, 194
ceilings, 194
children's, *see* children's rooms
city traditional houses, 30
colour in, 190, 192, 194
country houses, 15
curtains, 190, 192, 194
decorator style, 191
flexible, 202-3
floors, 192
high tech, *191;*
lighting, 309
location, 88

offices in, 182
paintwork, 192
period houses, 189
shared houses, 242
as sitting rooms, 202; *242*
storage, 195
studies in, 203
style, 190-1
wallpaper, 192
walls, 192
windows, 194
beds, 190-1, 195, 196-7
bases, 196, 197
brass, 30, 190; *193*
bunk, 195, 225
camp, 196
children's, 224-5, 230
choosing, 196
cots, 224-5, 230
divan, 73
foldaway, 237, 241
fourposter, 15, 30, 190
futons, 73, 125, 191, 196, 225, 236, 241
high tech, 19
mattresses, 196-7
platform, 125, 195, 202, 235, 240; *95*
sofa beds, 109, 125, 142, 195, 236-7; *242, 244*
storage under, 195
studios, 241
water beds, 196
bed-sitters, *see* one room living
bedspreads, 201
Bel Air chair, *73*
Bellini, Mario, 73, 146
Benson and Forsyth, *257*
bentwood chairs, 70, 146
bentwood furniture, 70
Berber rugs, 286
Bertoia, Harry, 146
Biba, 47
bidets, 204, 219
biennial plants, 271
blinds, 302
Austrian, 303
children's rooms, 225
dining rooms, 138
festoon, 28
kitchens, 164
living rooms, 118
making, 353
Roman, 353
as room dividers, 203, 237; *91*
for shelving, 318
trompe l'oeil, 187
Venetian, 24, 203, 302-3; *91, 97*
blowlamps, 342
Boffill, Ricardo, 36-7
Bonacina, 145
bookcases, *16, 27, 29*

bathrooms, 212
bedrooms, 204
as room dividers, 87
books, 68, 110, 141, 180, 314; *27*
bathrooms, 212, 213
bookshelves, 118, 132, 180
children's rooms, 230
colour, 68
as room dividers, 96
borders, garden, 270
Botschi, Pierre, *25*
brass bedsteads, 30, 190; *193*
bread ovens, 82
Brent, Tom, 75; *48, 49*
Breuer, Marcel, 20, 70, 72; *71, 117, 137*
brick floors, 281
brick walls, 289; *12*
brickwork, 78-9
extensions, 262
briefs, design, 335
Brno chair, 126
brushes, paint, 340, 341
builders, dealing with, 332
building regulations, 88, 330
extensions, 248
staircases, 95, 105
building work: acting alone, 333
architects, 331-2
builders, 332
supervising, 333
surveyors, 332
built-in furniture, 73; *114*
bedrooms, 195, 202
bulbs, flower, 271
lighting, 309-11
bunk beds, 195, 225
burglar alarms, 325

C

Cab chair, 146
camp beds, 196
cane furniture, 70, 122; *12*
cantilever chair, *71*
carpets, 284-5
Axminster, 284-5
bathrooms, 211
bedrooms, 192, 194
bordered, 285
carpet tiles, 285
colours, 67, 68
covering, 241
dining rooms, 138
en suite bathrooms, 204
grades, 284
halls, 105
high tech rooms, 23
living rooms, 124
natural fibres, 285
needlefelt, 285
nurseries, 223
rural living rooms, 120

stairs, *104*
synthetic fibres, 285
tufted, 285
Wilton, 285
Cassina, 145; *144*
cast iron work, *83*
castles, 84
ceiling roses, 297, 350
ceilings: bedrooms, 194
decoration, 297
heights, 210, 251
high, 87, 90, 94-5, 297; *109, 159*
painting, 341
papering, 344
preparing for painting, 339
raising, 250
sloping, 88
tented, 28-9, 141, 194
textured, *31*
Cesca, 70
chairs: bentwood, 70, 146
children's rooms, 225, 230
city traditional houses, *26*
contemporary, 70-2; *70-3*
deck chairs, 273
decorator style, *43*
dining rooms, 135, 139, 146, 147
directors', *273*
eclectic style, 50
folding, 73, 104, 122
home offices, 183
living rooms, 126
one room living, 237
study/dining rooms, 142
see also seating
chandeliers, 16; *15, 27*
chapels, 84, 85; *85*
chemical strippers, 342
children, safety in kitchens, 158
children's rooms, 222-31
beds, 224-5, 230
bunk beds, 195, 225
choosing, 222
entertaining in, 227
floors, 223, 224
furniture, 222, 227, 230-1
hobbies, 226
homework, 226
lighting, 231
looking ahead, 222
nurseries, 223
playrooms, 228-9
pre-school, 224-5
seating, 230-1
storage, 222, 224-5, 227, 230
suiting the child, 222
teenagers, 226-7
walls, 222, 224
chimney breasts, *93*
removing, 90
chimneys: barns, 85

evolution, 75
china, 141, 148
churches, 84, 85
circulation routes, 95, 96
city traditional style, 26-31
cleaning cupboards, 186
climbing plants, 271
coal, heating, 326
coffee makers, 175
coffee tables, 110, 129
collections: bathrooms, 212
   city traditional houses, *31*
   display, 15, 113, 141; *29*
   eclectic style, 49, 50; *51*
   as focal point, 110-11
   in halls, 104
   in kitchens, 158-9
   lighting, 15
colour, 64-9
   architectural role, 69
   bathrooms, 69, 211
   baths, 216
   bedrooms, 190, 192, 194
   bricks, 78-9
   choosing a scheme, 67-9
   city traditional houses, 29
   complementary, 65
   cool, 66
   country, 15
   decorator style, 43; *45*
   dining rooms, 140
   eclectic style, 50; *48, 51*
   effect of, 66-7
   fashion and, 67
   Georgian town houses, 83
   halls, 102, 104
   high tech rooms, 23
   kitchens, 69, 156, 164
   living rooms, 106
   natural, 69
   post modernism, 34, 35, 38; *36, 37*
   primary, 64-5
   relaxation and, 130
   secondary, 64-5
   spectrum, 64
   unified rooms, 93
   walls, 67, 288
   warm, 66
colour-washing, 295
columns, post modern, 36
combing (paint effect), 28
comforters, 201; *200*
complementary colours, 65
concrete floors, 348
condensation: bathrooms, 210, 213
   kitchens, 156-7
conservatories, 30, 260-1, 329; *12, 107*
   decorating, 261
   glazing, 261
   kit form, 261
   plants in, 276-7

siting, 261
contemporary furniture, 70-3
conversions, 248-63
   attics, 250-1
   raising the roof, 252-3
   see also extensions
cookers, 166, 172, 328
   slow, 174
   see also hobs; ovens
Coray, Hans, 71, 146; *70*
Le Corbusier, 20, 78
   seating, 70-1, 72, 126; *25, 38, 127, 128*
   tables, 145
Corian, 291
cork sheeting, 291, 347
cork tiles, 157, 168, 211, 283, 291, 347, 349
   laying, 347, 349
cornices, 30, 237, 297, 350; *38*
   unified rooms, 93
corridors, use of, 95; *187, 288*
   see also halls
cots, 224-5, 230
cottages, 12, 82; *83*
country houses, 12-18
   dining rooms, 135-6; *137*
   living rooms, 15-16
country mansions, 85
cove cornices, 297
Crump, Nigel and Midori, 56-7
cupboards, 314, 318; *319*
   bathrooms, 211, 213
   bedrooms, 195
   children's rooms, 224, 227, 230
   cleaning, 186
   kitchens, 155, 160, 164, 168
   living rooms, 129
   one room living, 245-6
   pottery, 185
   see also storage
curtain rods, 28
curtains, 303; *304*
   bedrooms, 190, 192, 194
   children's rooms, 225
   city traditional look, 28
   country house, *18*
   dining rooms, 138, 141
   high tech rooms, 23
   living rooms, 116
   making, 352
   rooms near gardens, 123
   rural living rooms, 120
   see also blinds; windows
cushions, 236; *31*
cutlery, 141, 148-9

D

dado rail, 140, 297, 350
dados, 30
damp: rising, 81
   walls, 289

windows and, 300
damp cupboards, for pottery, 185
damp proof courses (DPCs), 81, 82, 280
damp proofing floors, 280
dark rooms, for photography, 185
Day, Robin, 72
decorator style, 40-5
   bedrooms, 191
   dining rooms, 40, 136; *41*
de Martini, Piero, 144
desk lamps, *33*
desks, 125
   children's rooms, 231
De Styl, 49, 70
dhurries, 286
dimmer switches, 123, 308, 322
   nurseries, 223
dining areas: bed-sitters, 246
   halls, 143
   kitchens, 168; *169*
   living rooms, 109
dining rooms, 134-49
   antique furniture, 147
   chairs, 146, 147
   choosing a style, 135-6
   colour, 140
   combined with living room, 142
   comfort, 139
   country houses, 16, 135-6; *137*
   curtains, 141
   decorator style, 40, 136; *41*
   doors, 138
   eclectic style, 136; *137*
   floors, 138
   formal dining, 140-1; *151*
   furniture, 135, 136, 139, 141, 144-7
   as a guest room, 142
   hard edge style, 136
   lighting, 136, 139, 141, 306; *151*
   one room living, *243*
   serving in, 138
   storage, 138
   as a study, 142
   tables, 144, 145; *144, 145*
   walls, 138; *137*
   windows, 138
dishwashers, 159, 164, 173, 328
display: decorator style, *45*
   kitchens, 158-9; *31*
   see also collections
distemper, 294
divan beds, 73
Dodd, Alan, 296
do-it-yourself, 338
   basic shelving, 351

blinds, 353
curtains, 352
designing, 334-7
flooring, 348-9
mouldings, 350
painting, 339-42
tiling, 346-8
wallpapering, 343-5
door mats, 104
doors: automatic closers, 326
   bedrooms, 202
   development, 80
   dining rooms, 138
   draughts, 326
   extensions, 262-3
   fittings, 321
   front, 100; *101*
   glass panels, 80
   into halls, 104
   locks, 324
   painting, 341
   panelled, 80
   relocating, 90
   sliding, 93
   studies, 181
dormer rooms, 252
dormer windows, 252, 255; *250, 253*
'inverted', 252
double glazing, 298, 300, 328
dragging, 28, 295
drainage: bathrooms, 208, 209
draining boards, 172-3
drapes; country houses, *18*
   see also curtains
draughts, 326
dressing rooms, 213
   in bed-sitters, 247
duvets, 198-9
   covers, 201
   size, 201
   tog rating, 200-1

E

Eames, Charles, 20, 72, 126, 146; *21, 38*
eclectic style, 47-52
   dining rooms, 136; *137*
Egyptian motifs, *29*
electric sockets, 308, 322
   children's rooms, 226-7
   kitchens, 155
   nurseries, 223
   papering around, 345
electric switches, 104, 308, 322; *27*
   bathrooms, 310
   dimmers, 123, 223, 308, 322
   papering around, 345
   time switches, 325
electrical appliances: running costs, 329
   saving costs, 328

electrical fittings, 322
electricity: heating, 326, 328
electronic equipment, children's rooms, 226-7
embossed papers, 290, 343
emulsion paint, 294, 340
   cleaning, 338
en suite bathrooms, 204; *205*
energy: alternative, 329
   heating, 326-9
environmental enclosure, 216
ergonomics, kitchens, 154-5
espresso coffee machines, 175
estimates, obtaining, 332
Ettedgui, Joseph, *21*, 58-9
exercise areas, bathrooms, 209, 212
extensions, 90, 248-63
   adding a storey, 252-3
   back of house, 256-9
   brickwork, 262
   conservatories, 260-1
   dormer rooms, 252
   expanding landings, 256
   foundations, 259
   kit form, 256
   levels, 259
   raising the roof, 252-3
   style, 259
   sympathetic, 262-3
   kitchens, 156-7
extractors, bathrooms, 209, 210

F

fabrics: on ceilings, 297
   colour, 67
   country house, 15
   decorator style, 43
   eclectic style, 50
   high tech rooms, 23
   wallcoverings, 241, 291
fans: bathrooms, 209, 210
   kitchens, 156-7
Farrell, Terry, 38
felt wallcoverings, 291
fences, 266, 268, 270
fertilizers, 270
festoon blinds, 28
Fields, Dougie, *52*
filing cabinets, 183
fireplaces, 116; *112*
   bedrooms, 189, 195
   city traditional houses, *26*
   country house, 15-16; *17*
   evolution, 75
   as focal points, 110, 120; *32, 46*
   as heating systems, 328-9
   installing, 112
   living rooms, 118
   papering around, 345
   removing, 90

stone cottages, 82
studies, 180
surreal, 38
surrounds, 350
fires: country house, 15-16
    gas, 112, 118
fitted units, bedrooms, 195,
    202
fixtures and fittings, 320-5
flat roofs, 78, 81
flokati rugs, 122
floorboards, 82, 281; *27*
    bedrooms, 192
    dining rooms, 138
    direction, 88
    sanding, 349
floors, 280-7
    bathrooms, 211; *209, 214*
    bedrooms, 192
    bedsitter kitchens, 246
    brick, 281
    carpets, *see* carpets
    changing levels, 87
    children's rooms, 223, 224
    colour, 68
    concrete, 280, 348
    conservatories, 261
    construction, 280
    cork tiles, 157, 168, 211, 283,
        291
    country house, 15
    damp proofing, 280
    dining rooms, 135, 138
    draughts, 326
    finishes, 15
    floorboards, 82, 88, 138, 192
        281, 349; *27*
    halls, 102
    hard, 281-3
    hardboard, 283
    high tech, 23
    insulation, 328
    kitchens, 157, 166, 168
    laying, 348-9
    linoleum, 211, 239, 283
    living rooms, 118
    marble, 281-2
    mosaic, 282
    plywood, 283
    preparation, 280, 348
    rooms near gardens, 122
    rubber, 19, 157, 284; *209*
    rugs, 120, 122, 286; *27, 287*
    rural living rooms, 120
    sanding, 349
    semi-hard, 283-4
    semi-soft, 286
    slate, 282
    soft, 284-5
    stone, 15, 282
    studios, 241
    subfloors, 280, 283
    suspended timber, 280
    terrazzo, 283

thermoplastic tiles, 284
unified rooms, 93
tiles, *see* tiles
vinyl, *see* vinyl
warehouse conversions, 238
wooden, 120, 283, 349
workshops, 184
flowers: arrangements, 110,
    141, 149; *17, 27*
garden, 271
flues, 112
focal points: fireplaces as,
    110, 120; *32, 46*
    in gardens, 270-1
    living rooms, 110-11
foil wallpaper, 290, 345
foldaway beds, 237, 241
folding chairs, 73, 104, 122
folding screens, 96; *43, 87, 91*
follies, in gardens, 271
food processors, 164, 174
Forbes, Colin, *97, 319*
Formica, 291
Fortuny umbrella light, *58*
foundations, extensions, 259
four poster beds, 15, 30, 190
France, post modernism, 36-7
Fraser, Alberto, *305*
freezers, 160, 173
fridges, 173
front doors, 100; *101*
fuel, heating, 326-9
fun, *see* humour
function, in modernism, 33
furniture: architectural role, 73
    bathrooms, 221
    built-in, 73; *114*
    children's rooms, 222, 227,
        230-1
    city traditional houses, 30; *28*
    conservatories, 261
    contemporary, 70-3
    country house, 12-14, 15
    dining rooms, 135, 136, 139,
        141, 144-7
    eclectic style, 49
    finishes, 15
    garden, 273
    halls, 102, 104-5
    high tech, 19, 20; *21*
    home offices, 183
    and interior design, 336
    living rooms, 106, 116, 118,
        120, 122, 126-9
    living with, 73
    one room living, 234, 236-7
    in open plan spaces, 96
    relaxation and, 130
    size, 108-9
    as spatial elements, 96; *109*
    studios, 241
    warehouse conversions, 239
futons, 54, 73, 125, 191, 196,
    225, 236, 241

G

gable windows, 254
galleries, 94-5
    sleeping, 125
garages: building over, 253
    locks, 325
    planning permission, 330
    as playrooms, 228
gardening: on balconies, 275
    indoor plants, 276-7
    window boxes, 275
gardens, 264-77
    aspects, 265
    balustrades, 272
    budget planning, 266-7
    city, 30
    decorative effects, 271
    furniture for, 273
    lighting, 123, 270
    living rooms and, 122-3
    mirrors in, 272
    painting, 272
    planning, 268
    plants, 271
    roof gardens, 274-5
    texture, 272
    topiary, 272
    viewed from inside, 265
gas appliances, running costs,
    329
gas fires, 112, 118
gas heating, 326
gazebos, 271
Gehry, Frank, *114*
General Planning Order, 330
Gilardi, Francisco, 62-3
glass fibre, wallcoverings, 291
glassware, 141, 148
glazing: conservatories, 260
    double, 298, 300, 328
gloss paint, 293, 340
Gough, Piers, *191, 263*
graining, 295; *49*
Grand Confort, 71, 126; *127*
grants, improvement, 330
grass: plastic, 274; *275*
    see also lawns
grates, country house, 16
Gray, Eileen, *23, 59*
Grey, Johnny, *162*
Gropius, Walter, 78
grouting, 347
guest rooms: dining rooms as,
    142
    offices in, 182
gutters, 81
gymnasium, in bathrooms, 212

H

halls, 100-105
    city traditional houses, 29
    colour, 102, 104

decoration, *18*
dining areas, 143
lighting, 105, 143; *101*
removal, 102
see also corridors
Hanbels, 286
handles, 321
handrails, 105
hard edge style, 19-25
    bedrooms, 191
    dining rooms, 136
hardboard, flooring, 283
hatches, serving, 138
Hayward, Birkin, 60-1
heating, 326-9
    bathrooms, 211
    choosing, 328-9
    controls, 328
    country houses, 15-16, 17
    halls, 102
    home offices, 183
    insulation, 251, 256, 291,
        327-8
    kitchens, 157
    nurseries, 223
    potteries, 185
    relaxation and, 130
    saving energy, 326
    warehouse conversions, 238
    wastage, 326
herbaceous plants, 271
Hicks, David, 40
hi-fi equipment, 132-3; *39*
high tech style, 19-25
    bathrooms, *214*
    bedrooms, 191
    dining rooms, 136
    electrical fittings, 322
    kitchens, 19-20, 23, 24
    libraries, 181
historic houses, taking on, 82-3
hobbies: children's rooms, 226
    and the kitchen, 179
    workshop areas, 184-5
hobs, safety, 158
home offices, *see* offices
homework, 142, 226
Hopkins, Michael, 20, 75; *97*
hot air strippers, 342
hot water tanks, insulation, 326
hotplates, 138
houses: barns as, 85
    castles as, 84
    chapels as, 84, 85
    churches as, 84, 85
    country mansions, 85
    evolution of, 75-80
    historic, 82-3
    industrial buildings as, 84; *85*
    local materials, 78
    medieval, 74
    railway stations as, 85
    school conversions, 84; *91,
        239*

stone-built cottages, 82; *83*
    terraced, 81
    timber-framed, 78, 82-3; *91*
    unorthodox as, 84; *85*
    watermills as, 85
    windmills as, 85
humour: eclectic style, 47, 49,
    50
    in post modernism, 34, 38;
        37, 39

I

improvement grants, 330
indoor plants, 118, 123, 276-7;
    169
    in bathrooms, *214*
    decorating with, 276
    maintenance, 277
industrial buildings,
    converting, 84
industrial materials, 106
inglenooks, 82
ingrain paper, 290, 343
insulation, 291, 326-8
    attic rooms, 251
    double glazing, 298, 300, 328
    extensions, 256
Italian design, 35-6, 72-3, 106

J

Jacobsen, 146
jacuzzi, 271
Jencks, Charles, 36, 38
Jiricna, Eva, 58; *209; 59, 132,
    152, 171*
joists, 82, 88
Jones, Allen, *111*

K

Kaplicky, Jan, *320*
kelims, 286
kettles, 175
kilims, 286
Kinsman, Rodney, 73; *146*
Kita, Toshiyuki, *73*
kitchens, 152-78
    appliances, 159-60, 164,
        174-5
    batterie de cuisine, 176-8
    built-in units, 30; *31*
    ceiling heights, 251
    city traditional houses, 30
    colour, 69, 156, 164
    cooks', 162
    cookers, 172
    country houses, 12, 158; *17*
    creating an atmosphere,
        158-9
    decorator style, 40
    designer, 166

eating in, 168; *169*
equipment, 172-8
ergonomics, 154-5
for the family, 158-61
floors, 157, 166, 168
functional, 164
heating, 157
high tech, 19-20, 23, 24
hobbies and, 179
ideas, *170-1*
island units, 162; *165*
knives, 176, 177
laminates, 155
lighting, 156, 164, 307
location, 154
noise, 168
one room living, 245; *243, 244*
planning, 154-5
position of, 87
post modern style, 38
relaxing in, 160
safety, 158
saving space, 167
shared houses, 242
sinks, 154, 162, 166, 172-3
space restrictions, 90
storage, 20, 155, 160, 162, 164, 167; *31, 152-78 passim*
structural changes, 154
studios, 240
taps, 173
tiny, 167
units, 154, 155
ventilation, 156-7
wallcoverings, 289
warehouse conversions, 238
window boxes, 275
worktops, 155, 156, 162; *171*
'work triangle', 154
knives, kitchen, 176, 177
knobs, 321
Kron, Joan, 19

L

La Barca, 145; *144*
Lacey, Robert and Sandi, *31*
lacquer look, 295
ladders, safety, 338
laminates, 106, 211
  kitchens, 155
  in post modernism, 36
  wallcoverings, 291
lamps: desk, 33
  standard, 139, 307, 309, 312; *114, 115*
land drains, 259
Landi chair, 71; *70*
landings, 104
  expanding, 256
lanterns, 254
laundry rooms, 186; *187*
lavatories, 218-19

and en suite bathrooms, 204
  lavatory seats, 220
  location, 88
lawn mowers, 266
lawns, 266, 270, 272
  plastic grass, 274; *275*
leather, as decorative element, *27*
legal constraints, 88
  see also:
  building regulations;
  planning permission
letter boxes, 104
light switches, *see* switches
lighting, 305-13
  background, 306-7, 309
  bathrooms, 210
  bedrooms, 309
  bulbs, 309-11
  chandeliers, 15; *16, 27*
  children's rooms, 231
  clip-on, 241
  country houses, 15, 16
  decorator style, 40, 43; *42*
  desk lamps, 33
  dining rooms, 136, 139, 141, 306; *151*
  electrical layout, 308
  fittings, 309
  gardens, 123, 270
  hall/dining areas, 143
  halls, 105; *101*
  high tech, 19, 24
  home offices, 183
  kitchens, 156, 164, 307
  living rooms, 109, 110, 118 306-7; *114*
  localized, 307
  natural, 306
  neon tubes, 307, 311
  nurseries, 223
  oil lamps, 121
  pictures, 112, 113
  playrooms, 229
  relaxation and, 130
  rise and fall pendant, 309
  rooms near gardens, 123
  rural living rooms, 121
  saving energy, 328
  sewing rooms, 186
  soft focus, *12*
  spotlights, 15, 110, 139, 210, 238, 308-9
  studios, 241
  task, 311
  track, 183, 308-9
  uplighters, 16, 110, 139, 306, 312
  warehouse conversions, 328
  work areas, 125
  workshops, 184
Lincrusta paper, 290
lining paper, 290, 343
linoleum, 211, 239, 383

living rooms, 106-33
  as a centre of leisure, 106
  city traditional style, 29
  colour, 106
  country house style, 15-16
  dining areas, 109, 118, 120 142
  focal points, 110-11
  formal, 116-17
  furniture, 106, 116, 118, 120 122
  and the garden, 122-3
  lighting, 109, 110, 118, 306-7; *114*
  loose-fit, 124-5
  planning, 108-9
  post modern, *36*
  rural, 120-1
  seating, 108-9, 116, 118, 126
  shared houses, 242
  shelving, 108, 118, 120, 129
  sitting areas, 108-9
  storage, 109, 118, 120, 129
  tables, 120, 129
  urban, 118
  work areas, 125; *124*
Lloyd loom chairs, 38, 122
load-bearing walls, 88, 92-3
local authorities: building regulations, 88, 95, 105, 248, 330
  grants, 330
  planning permission, 330
locks: doors, 324
  garages, 325
  windows, 324-5
lofts: converting, *94*
  playrooms, 228
  warehouses, 238-9
loose covers, 124, 126
louvre shutters, 302
Lucchi, Michele de, *34*

M

Mackintosh, Charles Rennie, 126 146, 159; *71, 117*
Magistretti, Vico, 72-3, 145, 146; *311*
Mallet-Stevens, *59*
mantlepieces, 136
  city traditional look, *26*
  country house, 16
marble floors, 281-2
marbling, 295; *294, 296*
mathematical tiles, 80
Mather, Rick, 188, 253
mattresses, 196-7
medieval houses, 74
Memphis, 35-6, 73, 126
mezzanines, 56, 94-5, 104, 250-1, 259
  kitchens, *167*
microwave ovens, 164, 172

Mies van der Rohe, Ludwig, 41, 70, 126; *71*
Milan, *34*
mills, converting, 85
minimalism, 33, 54, 118; *115*
mirrors, 38; *41*
  in bathrooms, 220; *221*
  decorator style, 44; *43*
  in gardens, 272
  hallways, *105*
  one room living, 237, 241
  wall facings, 38, 291; *29*
Mlinaric, David, 40
model making room, 184
modernism, 33-4
  bedrooms, *191*
moiré silk paper, 290
mortar, brickwork, 79
mosaics, floor, 282
  laying, 347
mouldings, 297, 350; *294*
  fitting new, 350
  renovation, 350
moving costs, 248
mowing machines, 266
murals, 295; *288, 295*
  external, 271
  see also trompe l'oeil
music, 132-3

N

Nastro light, *305*
needlefelt carpets, 285
neon tubes, 307, 311
niches, 350
noise: double glazing, 300
  kitchens, 168
  model making, 184
non-drip paint, 293
nostalgia, 26, 47, 190; *49*
nurseries, 223
nylon carpets, 285

O

offices, 182-3
  on landings, 104
  in living rooms, 125
  see also studies
oil-based paints, 293
oil heating, 326
oil lamps, 121
OMK Designs, 73, 146; *183*
one room living, 234-47
  adaptability, 237
  au pairs, 243
  bathroom areas, 247
  kitchen areas, 245-7
  planning, 236-7
  relatives, 243
  sharers, 242-3
  space saving ideas, 244
  storage, 237

studios, 240-1; *237*
  warehouse conversion, 238-9
open plan spaces, 88
  removing walls, 82, 86, 87, 88, 92-3
Oval, 31, 145; *146*
ovens: microwave, 164, 172
  split-level, 172
  see also cookers

P

Paimio armchair, 71
paint: application, 292
  choosing paint, 292
  coverage, 292
  distemper, 294
  eggshell, 293
  emulsion, 294, 338, 340
  gloss, 293, 340
  lustre, 293, 340
  non-drip, 293
  oil-based, 293
  preparation, 292
  primer, 293
  textured, 295
  types, 292-4, 340-1
  undercoat, 293
  water-based, 294
painting, 79, 292, 340-2
  aerosols, 341
  bag-graining, 342
  brushes, 340, 341
  combing, 28
  dragging, 28, 295
  methods, 340-1
  new plaster, 289
  order of, 341
  preparations for, 292, 339
  rag-rolling, 296, 342
  ragging-on, 296, 342
  rollers, 340-1
  special effects, 295-6
  sponging, 296, 341
  stencilling, 28, 147, 192, 296, 297
  stippling, 28, 296, 341
  stripping, 15, 342
  walls, 288, 291-7
  wood graining, *49*
  see also individual paint effects
paintings: city traditional houses, 30
  displaying, *113*
  living rooms, 110, 117
  trompe l'oeil, 28, 38, 123, 138, 192, 271, 296; *18*
  see also pictures
paintwork: bathrooms, 211
  bedrooms, 192
  in the garden, 272
  nurseries, 223

studio walls, 241
Pallucco, 145
Pan, 145, 146
panel moulding, 350
pantiles, 80; *78*
Panton, Verner, 72
partitions: erecting, 93
    removing, 92-3
pasta machines, 175
paving brick floors, 281
paving stones, *280*
Pawson, John, 54-5
pediments, *38*
peg tiles, 79-80
pelmets, 28
Petit Confort, 126
pets, in kitchens, 160
photographic dark rooms, 185
picture rails, 297
picture windows, 255
pictures, *101*
    background to, 69
    city traditional houses, 29,
        30; *26*
    country houses, 15
    dining rooms, 141
    displaying, 113
    living rooms, 110, 117
    rural living rooms, 121
    stairwells, 105
pillowcases, 201
Piretti, Gian Carlo, 72
planning permission, 330
plants: in bathrooms, *214*
    buying, 265
    garden, 271
    indoors, 118, 123, 276-7;
        169, 214
    living room, 110, 118
plasterboard, 289
platform beds, 125, 195, 202,
    235, 240; *95*
platforms, 250-1
playrooms, 228-9
Plia chair, 72
plywood flooring, 283
plywood furniture, 71; *70*
police stations, redundant, 84
polyester carpets, 285
polypropylene carpets, 285
polypropylene chairs, 72
polystyrene wallcoverings, 291
ponds, 270
Ponti d'acqua, 145
pool house, 62-3
pools, garden, *266*
porches, 326
post modernism, 33-9
pottery, 185
power points, 308, 322
    children's rooms, 226-7
    kitchens, 155
    nurseries, 223
    papering around, 345

power tools, safety, 338
prams, storage, 102
primary colours, 64-5
primer paints, 293
print and dyeing rooms, 184-5

Q

quarry tiles, 157, 211, 281
    349; *280*
quilts, 199, 201
    patchwork, *198*
    see also duvets

R

radiators: bathrooms, 211
    disguising, 236
    painting, 341
    papering behind, 345
    thermostats, 157
rag-rolling, 296, 342
ragging-on, 296, 342
railway buildings, converting,
    84, 85
Rayburns, 158
refrigerators, 159-60
reinforced steel joists (RSJs),
    82
relatives, sharing house with,
    243
relaxation, 130
relief papers, 290, 343
revivalism, 36
Rhodes, Zandra, *114*
Ridge, Sue, 288
Rietveld, Gerrit, 70; *21, 71,
    124, 315*
rising damp, 81, 82
Ritchie, Ian, *122, 319*
Rogers, Richard, 142; *162*
Roman blinds, 353
roof gardens, 274-5
roof space: attic conversions,
    90, 250-1
    converting, *94*
    playrooms, 228
roof terraces, 255, 259; *253,
    266*
roofs, 79-80
    flat, 78, 81
    insulation, 326-8
    pitched, 78
    terraced houses, 81
    windows in, 251
room dividers, *169*
    blinds, 203, 237; *91*
    bookcases as, 87
    cupboards, 168
    furniture as, 96
    shelving as, 168, 237
rubber flooring, 19, 157, 287
    bathrooms, *209*

rubber wallcoverings, 291; *209*
rubbish skips, 266
    rugs, 120; *27*
    Afghan kelims, 286
    Berber, 286
    dhurrie, 286
    flokati, 122
    Kurdish kilims, 286
    Persian, 286
rural houses, 12-18
rush seated chairs, 73

S

Saarinen, Eero, 146; *116*
safety: children's rooms, 225,
    232-3
    kitchens, 158
    ladderwork, 338
    power tools, 338
    work spaces, 179
    workshops, 184
sanding: floors, 349
    woodwork, 15, 342
sandpits, 270
Sapper, Richard, 309; *54, 202*
sash windows, 80, 300-1
saucepans, 176, 177
schools, converting, 84; *91, 239*
Scott, Fred, *72*
screens, 125, 160, 168, 203, 238
    folding, 96; *43, 87, 91*
    window, *91*
    see also room dividers
scumbling, 296
seating: bathrooms, 212, 213
    bedrooms, 190
    children's rooms, 227, 230-1
    comfort, 126
    garden furniture, 273
    living rooms, 108-9, 116,
        118, 126
    loose covers, 124, 126
    modular units, 96, 124
    one room living, 237
    wearability, 126
    see also chairs; sofas
secondary colour, 46, 64-5
security, 324-5
    alarms, 325
    deterrent systems, 325
    door locks, 324
    garage locks, 325
    windows, 301, 324-5
Selene, 146
self-contained flats, 253
serving hatches, 138
sewing areas, 125, 186; *187*
sharing, 242-3
sheds, 271
sheets, 201
shelves, 314, 316-17
    bathrooms, 211, 220
    bedrooms, 195

bookshelves, 180
children's rooms, 224, 229,
    230
    free-standing, 317
    home offices, 182-3
    kitchens, 168; *171*
    living rooms, 108, 118, 120,
        129
    making 351
    playrooms, 229
    post modern, 38
    proprietary systems, 317
    room dividers, 168, 203
    wall-mounted, 317
    workshops, 184
Shire, Peter, *73*
showers, 217; *216*
    in bedrooms, 204
shrubs, 271
shutters, 136, 302
sideboards, 138, 141
Sinbad chair, 73; *72*
sinks: kitchen, 162, 166, 172-3
    location, 154
    skips, 266
skirting boards, 30, 140, 297,
    341
skylights, 156, 254; *255*
slates, 79, 80; *78, 262*
    see also tiles
slate floors, 282
Slesin, Suzanne, 19
sliding doors, 93
slow cookers, 174
smoking rooms, 180
sockets, *see* electric sockets
sofa beds, 109, 125, 142, 195,
    236-7; *242, 244*
sofas, city traditional houses,
    30; *28, 31*
    contemporary, 70
    living rooms, 126
soil, gardens, 268, 270
soil stack, 208
solar power, 329
Sony, 133
Sottsass, Ettore, 73; *34, 309*
soundproofing, playrooms, 229
space, constraints on altering,
    88
    decorator style, 43-4
    furniture as spatial elements,
        96
    and post modernism, 35
    restructuring, 90
    working with, 86-96
spare rooms, office in, 182
spiral stairs, 95, 105
sponging, 296, 341
spotlights, 15, 110, 139, 308-9
    bathrooms, 210
    country houses, 15
    warehouse conversions, 238
stackable chairs, 72

stained glass windows, 159
stairs, 105
    to attic rooms, 253
    handrails, 105
    high tech, *25*
    new, 95, 105
    regulations, 105
    space under, 105; *103*
    spiral, 95, 105
stairwells, working over, 338
standard lamps, 139, 307, 309,
    312; *114, 115, 313*
statues, garden, 271
stencilling: bedroom walls, 192
    furniture, 147
    walls, 28, 296, 297
stippling, 28, 296, 341
stone cottages, 82; *83*
stone floors, 15, 282
storage, 314-19
    attic rooms, 251
    bathrooms, 211, 221, 318
    bedrooms, 195
    bedsitter bathrooms, 247
    children's rooms, 222, 224-5,
        227, 230
    cleaning cupboards, 186
    dining rooms, 138
    expanding systems, 124
    high tech, 20
    home offices, 183
    kitchens, 20, 155, 160, 162,
        164, 167; *31, 152-78
        passim*
    living rooms, 109, 118, 120,
        129
    mezzanines, 94
    nurseries, 223
    one room living, 237, 245-7;
        244
    post modern style, *38*
    print and dyeing rooms,
        184-5
    sewing rooms, *187*
    studies/dining rooms, 142
    studios, 240, 241
    under stairs, 105; *103*
    work areas, 179
    workshops, 184
stoves, 15, 112
    country house, 15
stripping woodwork, 15, 342
structural alterations, 82
structural constraints, 88
studies: in bedrooms, 203
    in dining rooms, 142
    high tech, 181
    on landings, 104
    on mezzanines, 251
    traditional, 180-1
studio stoves, 15
studios, 240-1; *237*
styles: city traditional, 26-31
    country house, 12-18

decorator, 40-5
eclectic, 47-52
hard edge, 19-25
individual, 53-63
meaning of, 11
minimalism, *115*
modernism, 33-4
post modern, 33-9
revivalism, 36
subfloors, 280, 283
summer houses, 271
surveyors, 332
swimming pools, 271
switches, 104, 308, 322; *27·*
bathrooms, 210
dimmer, 123, 223, 308, 322
papering around, 345
time, 325

T

table settings, 141, 148-9
tablecloths, 141, 149
tables: bedrooms, 191
children's rooms, 225
city traditional houses, 30
coffee, 129
decorator style, *43*
dining areas, 109, 118, 120, 122
dining rooms, 139, 141, 144, 145
folding, 73
garden furniture, 273
home office, 183
kitchens, 161; *168*
living rooms, 120, 129
nurseries, 223
one room living, 237
post modern, *72*
print and dyeing rooms, 184
studies/dining rooms, 142
wearability, 129
Tangram, 145; *72, 144*
taps: bathrooms, 220; *214, 221*
kitchen, 166, 173
outside, 268
task lighting, 311
telephones, 102, 182, 183
television, 132-3
as focal point, 111
storage, 116
tennis courts, 271
tented ceilings, 28-9, 141, 194
Teorema, 141
terraced houses, taking on, 81
terraces, 266, 268, 270
roof, 255; *253*
terrazzo floors, 283
textiles, *see* fabrics
textured paint, 295
textured wallpaper, 290, 343
textures: decorator style, *42*
eclectic, 48

in the garden, 272
halls, *103*
rooms near gardens, 123
thatch, 79; *79*
thermostats, 328
Thonet, Michael, 70, 146
three piece suites, 96
tie rods, *78*
tiles, 79-80
bathroom, 211, 220; *221, 320*
carpet, 285
cleaning, 281
concrete, *79*
cork, 157, 168, 211, 283, 291; *347, 349*
cutting, 347
en suite bathrooms, 204
floors, 281, 348-9
grouting, 347
halls, 102
hanging, *79*
mathematical, 80
pantiles, 80; *78*
peg, 79-80
quarry, 157, 211, 281, 349
roofing, 262
thermoplastic, 284
utility room, *187*
vinyl, 286, 348-9
wall, 291, 346-7
see also slates
timber-framed houses, 78, 82-3; *91*
time switches, 325
Tizio light, 309; *202*
toasters, 174
tog rating, 200-1
tools, storage, 184-5
topiary, 272
tortoiseshelling, 296
towel rails, 211, 220; *221*
town houses, 83
track lighting, 183, 308-9
trees, 271
trellises, 270
trompe l'oeil, 28, 38, 123, 296; *18*
bathrooms, 221
bedrooms, 192
blind, *187*
dining rooms, 138
gardens, 271
tubular steel furniture, 70-1
tufted carpets, 285
tumble dryers, 209, 328
tungsten bulbs, 308, 311
typewriters, 183

U

undercoat paint, 293
upholstery, wearability, 126
uplighters, 16, 110, 139, 306,

312; *313*
utensils, kitchen, 176
utility rooms, 186; *187*

V

Van Gogh, Vincent, 64
van Heyningen, Jo, 60-1
vanitory units, 218, 247
Velux, 254
Venetian blinds, 24, 54, 203, 302-3; *24, 91, 97*
ventilation, 326
bed-sitter kitchens, 246
kitchens, 156-7
Victoriana, 49
video equipment, 132-3
views, 111
vinyl flooring, 138, 157, 168, 286
bathrooms, 211
nurseries, 223
tiles, 286, 348-9
vinyl wallcoverings, 291, 345
vinyl wallpapers, 211, 290
viscose carpets, 285

W

wallpaper, 288, 290, 343-5
Anaglypta, 290
bathrooms, 211, 290
bedrooms, 192
behind radiators, 345
buying, 343
ceilings, 344
country houses, 15
dining rooms, 138, 140
foil, 290, 345
haning, 345
ingrain, 290, 343
Lincrusta, 290
lining paper, 290, 343
moiré silk, 290
nurseries, 223
preparing for, 343-4
preparing to paint over, 339-40
ready pasted papers, 345
relief papers, 345
vinyl, 290, 345
washable, 345
woven textile, 290
walls, 288-97
alternative coverings, 291, 343
bathrooms, 192
brick finish, 158; *12*
children's rooms, 222, 224
city traditional houses, 28
colour, 67, 288
condition of, 289
damp, 280, 289

dining rooms, 137, 138
garden, 268, 270
high tech, 23, 24; *25*
insulation, 328
load-bearing, 88, 92-3
mirror-framed, 38, 291; *29*
nurseries, 223
one room living, 237
painting, 288, 291-7, 341
plaster, 289
plasterboard, 289
preparing for painting, 339
removing, 82, 86, 87, 88, 92-3
rooms near gardens, 123
rural living rooms, 120-1
sliding, 93
stencilling, 28, 192, 296, 297
studios, 241
textured, *16*
tiled, 291, 346-7
wood panelling, 289
workshops, 184
see also painting; *trompe l'oeil*; wallpapers
wardrobes, 195, 224, 314
children's rooms, 277
high tech, 19-20
location, 96
warehouses, converting, 56, 84, 238-9; *85, 91*
warmth: colours, 66
high tech and, 20
relaxation and, 130
wash stands, 204, 247
washing machines, 173, 209, 318, 328; *187*
Wassily chair, 70, *71, 117*
waste disposal units, 162
water beds, 196
water tanks, attic rooms, 251
watermills, converting, 85
Weallens, Jon, *47*
weather-boarding, *79, 83*
whirlpool baths, 216
Wilton carpets, 285
windmills, converting, 85
window boxes, 275
windows, 298-303
aluminium, 80, 298
attic rooms, 251, 254-5
bathrooms, 221
bedrooms, 194
blinds, 302
children's rooms, 225
development, 80
diamond panes, 80; *83*
dining rooms, 138
dormer, 252, 255; *250, 253*
double glazing, 298, 300, 328
draughts, 326
early houses, 76
extensions, 262-3
frames, 300

from the inside, 300-1
from the outside, 298
gable ends, 254
garden view, 265
inverted dormers, 252
legal requirements, 88
living areas, 108
locks, 324-5
painting, 341
picture, 255
in roofs, 251, 255
sash, 80, 300-1
security gates, 325
shutters, 136, 302
skylights, 156, 254; *255*
stained glass, 159
steel, 80
studies, 181
studio, 241
in warehouses, 84
see also blinds; curtains
wink chair, *73*
woks, 176
Wolfe, Tom, 71
wooden floors, 283
laying, 349
see also floorboards
wood graining, *49*
wood panelling, 289, 291
woodchip paper, 290, 343
woollen carpets, 285
word processors, 183
work areas, 179-87
cleaning cupboards, 186
dark rooms, 185
offices, 182-3
laundry rooms, 186; *187*
sewing rooms, 186; *187*
studies, 180-1
utility rooms, 186; *187*
workshops, 184-5
see also kitchens
work surfaces: children's rooms, 231
kitchens, 155, 162, 168; *171*
lighting, 156
Wright, Gareth, *263*
wrought iron furniture, *12*

Z

Zanotta, *172, 128*

ACKNOWLEDGEMENTS

The publishers would like to thank the following individuals and organizations for their assistance in the preparation of this book.

Abbreviations
t — top
b — bottom
c — centre
l — left
r — right

148 Astrohome, Neal Street, London WC2: table mats, plates, cups and saucers.
Cocktail Shop, Neal Street, London WC2: black-stemmed glasses.
Harvey Nicols, Knightsbridge, SW3: grey-handled cutlery.
149 tl: F. Trauffler Ltd, 57a Farringdon Rd, London EC1: rabbit dish, Apilco salt and pepper pots and plates.
Wedgewood, 34 Wigmore Street, London W1: jug and glass.
Harrods, Knightsbridge, London SW3: cutlery.
bl: Selfridges, Oxford Street, London W1: gold-rimmed bowl and cutlery.
Dartington Glass Ltd, 4 Portland Road, London W11: decanter and glasses. Wedgewood, gold rimmed china.
br: Astrohome: blue and yellow cutlery.
John Lewis, Oxford Street, London W1: plastic plates and glasses.
174/5 Selfridges **176** David Mellor, 26 James Street, Covent Garden, London WC2 **177** Lewis & Horning, 168 Drury Lane, London WC2; David Mellor **178** David Mellor **198** Harrods **199** tl: Hilary's Quilts (Dept HSB), 11 Priory Avenue, London W4; Harrods **200/1** Harrods

PHOTOGRAPHS
All credits are listed in the following order: page number, position on page, name of photographer, name of agent (where applicable). In addition, the name of the designer or architect is credited in italics at the end of some entries.

Abbreviations EWA — Elizabeth Whiting Associates, MBI — Mitchell Beazley International, MB — Michael Boys, RB — Richard Bryant, MD — Martin Dohrn, KK — Ken Kirkwood, MN — Michael Nicholson, JS — Jessica Strang, TSP — Tim Street-Porter, JV — John Vaughan.

9 KK/*John Pawson* **10** Richard Bryant/Arcaid/*Tom Brent* **12** t: MB/*Nicholas Hills*; b: Michael Boys/*Nicholas Hills* **13** l: ©Interiors; tr: MB/*Nicholas Hills*; br: MB/*Pradalié* **14** ©Interiors **15** t: MB/*Nicholas Hills*; b: ©Interiors **16** t: MB/*Nicholas Hills*; b: Ann Kelley/EWA **17** l: MB; tr: Clive Helm/EWA; br: MB/*Tricia Guild* **18** tl: RB/Arcaid/*Alan Dodd*; tr: MB/*Tricia Guild* **19** JV **20** KK/*Michael Hopkins* **21** l: KK/*Michael Hopkins*; tr: JS/*Colin Forbes*; br: RB/Arcais/*Eva Jiricna* **22** RB/Arcaid/*Eva Jiricna* **23** tr: RB/Arcaid/*Eva Jiricna*; tl: JV; b: JV **24** t: KK/*Michael Hopkins*; b: JV **25** KK/*Jan Kaplicky* **26** MN/EWA **27** MN/EWA **28** l: MN/EWA; r: Spike Powell/EWA/*Odette Azzagury* **29** tl: Lucinda Lambton/Arcaid; tr: MN/EWA/*Ken Turner*; b: MB/*Antony Redmile* **30** Tessa Musgrave/MBI **31** l: Spike Powell/EWA/*Odette Azagury*; r: JV **32** tl: Spike Powell/EWA; tr: MN/EWA/*Chester Jones*; b: Spike Powell/EWA/*Noel Stevenson* **33** tl: ©Interiors; tr: RB/Arcaid/*Richard Bryant*; b: ©Interiors **34** l: Santi Caleca/*Memphis de Lucchi*; r: JV **35** t: TSP/Peter Shire/*Memphis*; bl: TSP/*Peter Shire/Memphis*; br: TSP/EWA **36** tl: JV; tr: KK/*John Wright*; b: JV **37** l: Occhiomagico; r: KK/*John Wright* **38** t: TSP/EWA/*Spear*; b: Peter Aaron/ESTO **39** t: Marco Caselli/*Nanda Vigo*; bl; br: Santi Caleca **40** MB/*Francois Catroux* **42** l: MB/*David Hicks*; r: MN/EWA/*Dorit Egli* **43** l: MB/*Francois Catroux*; tr: MB/*David Hicks* **44** l: MB/*Antony Redmile*; r: MB/*Francois Catroux* **45** r: MB/*Francois Catroux* **46** t: MB/*Francois Catroux*; bl: MN/EWA; br: MN/EWA/*John Wright* **47** RB/Arcaid/*Jon Weallans* **48** RB/Arcaid/*Tom Brent* **49** RB/Arcaid/*Tom Brent* **50** l: TSP/*Peter Shire*; r: Spike Powell/EWA **51** r: TSP/EWA **52** t: TSP/EWA/*Piers Gough*; bl: Chris Garnham/*Duggie Fields*; br: Chris Garnham **53** tl: KK/*John Pawson*; bl: Marco de Valdivia/*Eva Jiricna*; tc: Marco de Valdivia/*Luis Barragan*; bc: MD/MBI/*Nigel & Midori Crump*; r: MD/MBI/*van Heyningen & Haward* **54** all KK/*John Pawson* **55** all KK/*John Pawson* **56** all MD/MBI/*Nigel & Midori Crump* **57** all MD/MBI/*Nigel & Midori Crump* **58** all Marco de Valdivia/*Eva Jiricna* **59** all Marco de Valdivia/*Eva Jiricna* **60** all MD/MBI/*van Heyningen & Haward* **61** all MD/MBI/*van Heyningen & Haward* **62** all Marco de Valdivia/*Luis Barragan* **63** all Marco de Valdivia/*Luis Barragan* **70** tl: Gebrüder Thonet; tr: *Hans Coray*/Zanotta SpA; c: *Le Corbusier*/Cassina SpA; b: *Alvar Aalto*/Artek **71** tl: *Gerrit Rietveld*/Cassina SpA; cl: *Marcel Breuer*/K.I. (UK) Ltd.; b: *C.R. Mackintosh*/Cassina SpA; tr: *Marcel Breuer*/K.I. (UK) Ltd.; cr: *Le Corbusier*/Cassina SpA **72** t: *Massimo Morozzi*/Cassina SpA; cl: *Fred Scott*/Hille Int'l; cr: *Vico Magistretti*/Cassina SpA; bl: *Charles Eames*/Herman Miller Ltd.; br: *Charles Eames*/Herman Miller Ltd **73** t: *Vico Magistretti*/Cassina SpA; bl: Design Council/*Peter Shire/Memphis*; br: *Toshiyuki Kita*/Cassina SpA **74** MD/MBI **75** t: MN/EWA/*Michael Hopkins*; lc, rc: MD/MBI; br: RB/Arcaid/*Tom Brent* **76** MD/MBI **77** tl: Ann Kelley/EWA; tr: MD/MBI; bl: Peter Aaron/ESTO/*Michael Graves*; br: Ezra Stoller/ESTO/*Robert Meier* **78** MD/MBI **79** MD/MBI **80** MD/MBI **81** MD/MBI **82** tl: MD; lc, rc: MD/MBI; b: TSP/EWA **83** MD/MBI — all **84** MD/MBI — both **85** tl, bl, bc, br: MD/MBI/; tr: Jon Bouchier/EWA **86** Marco de Valdivia **87** RB/Arcaid/*David Falla* **90** tl, tr: George Cserna/*George Ranalli*; bl: RB/Arcaid/*Eva Jiricna*; br: Camera Press **91** cl: TSP/EWA/Joan Sacks; tr: Jillian Nieman/EWA/*David Hodge*; bl: Marco de Valdivia; br: Marco de Valdivia **92** both JV **93** l: ©Abitare; r: Camera Press **95** tl: Jerry Tubby/EWA/*Jennifer Granville-Dixon*; bl: JV; br: Spike Powell/EWA/*David & Babs King* **96** Aldo Ballo **97** tl: Michael Dunne/EWA; tr: JS/*Colin Forbes*; b: TSP/EWA/*Michael Hopkins* **99** Steve Tanner/MBI **100** JV **101** tl: MB; tr: MN/EWA; b: MB **102** l: MN/EWA; r: MB/*Jenny Hall* **103** l: JV; r: Clive Helm/EWA **104** t: MD; bl: MB/*Jenny Hall*; br: JV **105** t: Marco de Valdivia; bl: KK/*John Wright* **106** JV **107** JV **108** l: JV; r: Mark Ross/*Tom Foederer* **109** JV **110** t: TSP/EWA/*Spear*; b: TSP/*Peter Shire* **111** t: TSP/EWA; bl: MB/*Tricia Guild*; br: Mark Ross/*Walker Group* **112** l: MB; c: TSP/EWA/*Moone Ruble Yudell*; t: JS/*Trene Beard*; cr: TSP/EWA; br: TSP/EWA **113** tl: MB/*Francois Catroux*; bl: MB/Michael Haynes; tr: MB/*Francois Catroux*; cr: MB/*Francois Catroux*; br: MB/*Pradalié* **114** tl: JV; cl: Neil Lorimer/EWA/*Zandra Rhodes*; bl: TSP/EWA/*Frank Gehry*; tr: Mark Ross/*Kevin Walz*; br: Camera Press **115** tl: TSP/EWA; cl: JS/*Dawn Zain*; br: Paul Warchol/ESTO/*Peter Stamberg*; tc: KK/*John Wright*; br: TSP/EWA; tr: MB/*Bob McLaren* **116** t: Santi Caleca; bl: JV; bc: JV **117** t: Mark Ross/*Adam D. Tihany, Intl*; b: JV **118** Jerry Tubby/EWA/*Dasha Shenkman* **119** t: ©Interiors; bl: Lucinda Lambton/Arcaid; br: Spike Powell/EWA/*Pierre Cabbiati* **120** bl: Spike Powell/EWA; r: JS **121** t: b: MB/*Tricia Guild* **122** Richard Einzig/Arcaid/*Ian Ritchie* **123** tl: Jillian Nieman/EWA//*Peter Ball*; tr, b: Peter Aaron/ESTO/*Joseph d'Uros* **124** t: TSP/EWA; b: Mark Ross/*Kevin Walz* **125** t: TSP/EWA; b: JV **126** ESTO/*Erickson/Kripacz* **127** tl: Richard Einzig/Arcaid/*Piano & Rogers*; bl: Spike Powell/EWA/*Pierre Cabbiati*; tr: Zanotta SpA; br: KK/*John Wright* **128** bl: Zanotta SpA; t: Maison Française/Christian Gervais; bc: KK/*John Wright* **129** l: MB/*Bob McLaren*; c: JV **130** t: MB/*Pradalié*; b: MB/*Francois Catroux* **131** l: TSP/EWA; r: MB **132** tl: Michael Crockett/EWA; bl: JS/*Oliver Morgan*; r: Santi Caleca **133** tl: Michael Crockett/EWA; bl: MB/*Bob McLaren*; r: RB/Arcaid/*Eva Jiricna* **134** *Brian Taggart* **135** l: RB/Arcaid/*Tom Brent*; r: Annet Held **136** bl: ©*Laura Ashley*; br: TSP/EWA **137** t: RB/Arcaid/*Jon Weallans*; bl: MB/*Jenny Hall*; bc: JV; br: Lucinda Lambton/Arcaid/*G. Boyd Harte* **139** tl: MN/EWA; bl: JV; br: Daniel Rozenczstroch/Gilles de Chabaneix **140** MD **141** MN/EWA **142** Mark Ross/*Kevin Walz* **143** l: Richard Einzig/Arcaid/*Richard Rogers*; tr: KK/*Alan Brown*; br: Richard Davies/EWA/*Rick Mather* **144** bl: *Le Corbusier*/Cassina SpA; tr: *Massimo Morozzi*/Cassina SpA; cr, br: *Piero de Martina Cassina SpA* **145** tl: *Oval 31*; bl: *Alvar Aalto*/Artek **146** bl: Gebrüder Thonet; tr: *Leila Corbett*; bl: David Cripps/EWA; br: Morley von Sternberg **148** Steve Tanner/MBI **149** Steve Tanner/MBI **150** tl: JV; tr: RB/Arcaid/*Eva Jiricna*; bl: Jerry Tubby/EWA; br: Fritz von der Schulenberg **151** tr: Marco de Valdivia; bl: Annet Held; br: MB/*Pradalié* **152** RB/Arcaid/*Eva Jiricna* **153** RB/Arcaid/*Eva Jiricna* **154** l: Santi Caleca; r: MN/EWA/*Campbell, Zogolovitch* **155** Aldo Ballo **156** RB/Arcaid/*Jon Weallans* **157** l: Neil Lorimer/EWA; r: Lucinda Lambton/Arcaid **158** l: MB; r: MD **159** t: Peter Aaron/ESTO; b: JV **160** TSP/EWA/*Piers Gough* **161** t: JV; b: Fritz von der Schulenberg; br: JV **162** Peter Aaron/ESTO/*Joseph d'Urso* **163** t: Michael Crockett/EWA; b: Richard Einzig/Arcaid/*Richard Rogers*; br: MN/EWA/*Johnny Grey* **164** MN/EWA/*Derek Walker* **165** t: TSP/EWA/*Piers Gough*; bl: MB/*Jenny Hall*; br: TSP/EWA **166** Neil Lorimer/EWA **167** l: TSP/EWA/*Peter Cook*; r: KK/*Jan Kaplicky* **168** t: TSP/*Peter Shire*; b: Jerry Tubby/EWA/*Isobel Czarska Designs* **169** l: KK/*John Wright*; r: Camera Press **170** tl: RB/Arcaid/*Eva Jiricna*; bl: David Cripps/EWA; tr: Ron Sutherland/EWA; br: JV **171** tl: Camera Press; tr: KK/*Pierre Botschi*; bl: Spike Powell/EWA; br: JS/*Sally Grover* **174** Steve Tanner/MBI **175** Steve Tanner/MBI **176** Steve Tanner/MBI **177** Steve Tanner/MBI **178** Steve Tanner/MBI **179** MN/EWA/*Chester Jones* **180** Clive Helm/EWA/*Alan Parker* **181** l: KK/*John Wright*; tr: MN/EWA/*Dorit Egli* **182** Santi Caleca **183** bl: Spike Powell/EWA; br: Clive Helm/EWA **184** l: JS/*Lou Klein*; r: JS/*Tarquin Cole* **185** l: TSP/EWA; r: TSP/*Peix Crawford* **186** Camera Press **187** l: MD/MBI; tr: MD/MBI/*van Heyningen & Haward*; br: KK/*John Pawson* **188** Richard Davies/EWA/*Rick Mather* **189** MB/*Tricia Guild* **190** t: ©Interiors; b: Daniel Rozenczstroch/Gilles de Chabaneix **191** tl: Daniel Rozenczstroch/Gilles de Chabaneix; b: TSP/EWA/*Piers Gough*; tr: Michael Nicholson/EWA **192** Spike Powell/EWA **193** Marco de Valdivia; b: Clive Helm/EWA **194** t: Richard Davies/EWA/*Michael Baumgarten*; bl: Spike Powell/EWA/*David & Babs King*; br: MB/*Tricia Guild* **195** tl: Michael Nicholson/EWA/*Michael Hopkins*; tr: ©Abitare **196** JV **197** l: MB/*David Hicks*; r: RB/Arcaid/*Eva Jiricna* **198** Steve Tanner/MBI **199** Steve Tanner/MBI **200** Steve Tanner/MBI **210** Steve Tanner/MBI **202** JV **203** l: KK/*John Wright*; r: Daniel Rozenczstroch/Gilles de Chabaneix **205** tl: Richard Davies/EWA/*Rick Mather*; tr: TSP/EWA; bl: ©Abitare **206** l: MB **207** Peter Aaron/ESTO/*Joseph d'Urso* **209** bl: RB/Arcaid/*Eva Jiricna*; tr: MN/EWA/*Edward Jones*; br: MN/EWA **210** l: Richard Einzig/Arcaid/JS/*John Hoskins*; bc: KK/*Richard Horden*; r: MN/EWA **211** KK/*Pierre Bötschi* **212** KK/*John Wright* **213** tl: JV; bl: Fritz von der Schulenberg; r: TSP/EWA **214** Mark Ross/*Kevin Walz* **215** l: MN/EWA/*Virginia Bates*; tr: MB/*Antony Redmile*; br: JV **216** t: RB/Arcaid/*Eva Jiricna*; bl: TSP/EWA; br: MB **217** MN/EWA **218** t: JV; b: MB/*David Hicks* **219** tl: RB/Arcaid/*Tom Brent*; tr: RB/Arcaid/*Eva Jiricna*; b: Spike Powell/EWA **220** tl: JV; tr Camera Press; b: Neil Lorimer/EWA **221** l: Richard Einzig/Arcaid/*Piano & Rogers*; tl: Spike Powell/EWA tr: Jerry Tubby/EWA/*Jan Pienkówski*; b: Neil Lorimer/EWA **222** ©Abitare **223** MD/MBI **224** RB/Arcaid/*Eva Jiricna* **225** tl: RB/Arcaid/*Eva Jiricna*; bl: MN/EWA/*Tricia Guild*; br: JS/*Chris Francis* **226** tl: MN/EWA; bl: Peter Aaron/ESTO **227** tl: MN/EWA; bl: MN/EWA/*Chester Jones* **228** bl: Jillian Nieman/EWA/*Peter Bell & Assoc.*; tr: TSP/EWA; br: Jillian Nieman/EWA/*Peter Bell & Assoc.* **229** tl: Jerry Tubby/EWA; bl: MN/EWA; r: Camera Press **230** l: JS/*Tarquin Cole*; r: Steve Colby/EWA **231** l: JS/*Jessica Strang*; r: Graham Henderson/EWA **234** JV **235** l: JV; r: JV **236** Annet Held **237** ©Interiors **238** l: MB/*Pradalié*; r: TSP/*Peix-Crawford* **239** t: Richard Davies/EWA/*Michael Baumgarten*; b: Morley von Sternberg **240** MD **241** l: JS/*Julia Aldridge*; r: Camera Press **242** t: TSP/EWA; bl: Clive Helm/EWA; br JS/*Sonny Howson* **243** t: JS/*Kati Dürer*; bl: Richard Davies/EWA; br: TSP/EWA **245** TSP/EWA **246** l: MN/EWA/*Andrew Chadwick*; r: MN/EWA/*Leila Corbett* **247** l: JS/*Jessica Strang*; r: KK/*Keith Garbett* **250** l: Gary Chowitz/EWA; tr: Annet Held; cr: Aldo Ballo; br: TSP/EWA **251** t: Santi Caleca; b: Clive Helm/EWA **252** t: MB; b: Ann Kelley/EWA **253** tl: Richard Davies/EWA/*Rick Mather*; b: JV; tr: MB/*Bob McLaren*; cr: Jerry Tubby/EWA/*Isobel Czarska Designs* **254** l: Mark Ross *Mojo/Stumer*; tr: JV; br: Marco de Valdivia **255** t: Mark Ross/*Udstad, Dandridge Assoc.*; bl: Annet Held; br: Clive Helm/EWA **256** JS/*Irene Beard* **257** tl, bl, Morley von Sternberg/*Benson/Forsythe*; tr: Clive Helm/EWA/*Philip Mercer*; br: Clive Helm/EWA **258** Ron Sutherland/EWA **259** t: Spike Powell/EWA/*David & Babs King*; b: *Clive Helm/EWA/Philip Mercer* **260** tl: TSP/EWA/*Robert Stern*; tr: Neil Lorimer/EWA/*Leila Corbett*; bl: Camera Press; br: Ianthe Ruthven/*Tony Crowther* ARIBA **261** Annet Held **262** MD/MBI **263** MD/MBI — all **264** t: TSP/EWA; b: MB **265** r: Ann Kelley/EWA; l: Daniel Rozenczstroch/Gilles de Chabaneix **266** l: MN/EWA/*Jeremy Linden*; r: JS **267** tl: Spike Powell/EWA; bl: Graham Henderson/EWA; tr: Daniel Rozenczstroch/Gilles de Chabaneix; br: MB **270** tl: Clive Helm/EWA; c: Jillian Nieman/EWA/*Mary Watson*; r: MB; bl: RB/Arcaid/*Peter Aldington* **271** t: JS/*Michelle Osborne*; b: Ann Kelley/EWA **272** t: JS; c: MN/EWA; bl: MN/EWA/*Ken Turner*; bc: Jillian Nieman/EWA/*Mary Watson*; br: JS **273** tl: Daniel Rozenczstroch/Gilles de Chabaneix; bl: EWA/*Stephen Teale*; tr: TSP/EWA; br: Spike Powell/EWA **274** Daniel Rozenczstroch/Gilles de Chabaneix — all **275** t, bl: Daniel Rozenczstroch/Gilles de Chabaneix; br: MN/EWA/*Ken Turner* **276** l: Michael Crockett/EWA; r: MN/EWA **277** t: Clive Helm/EWA; b: Annet Held **279** Tessa Musgrave/MBI **280** MD/MBI **281** tl: Jon Bouchier/EWA/*Isobel Czarska Designs*; bl: Neil Lorimer/EWA/*Smith*; r: David Cripps/EWA/*Lyn le Grice* **282** t: TSP/EWA/*Moore, Ruble, Yudell*; l: Michael Dunne/EWA/*Larry Durham*; r: TSP/EWA; b: Morley von Sternberg/*Paul Eddington* **283** t: Neil Lorimer/EWA; l: TSP/EWA/*Piers Gough*; r: JV **284** ©Bang & Olufsen **285** t: Peter Aaron/ESTO/*Robert A.M. Stern*; c, tr, br: Steve Tanner/MBI **286** TSP/EWA/*Andrew Batey* **287** tl, tr, c, bl, br: MD/MBI; cr: Camera Press **288** l: MB/*Pradalié*; c: RB/Arcaid/*Sue Ridge*; tr: JV; br: MD **289** l: Morley von Sternberg; r: JV **292** MD **293** JV **295** tl: MD/MBI; tr: JV; b: TSP/EWA/*Piers Gough* **296** tl: Tessa Musgrave/MBI; tr: David Cripps/EWA/*Lyn le Grice*; bl: RB/Arcaid/*Alan Dodd*; br: RB/Arcaid/*Bill Bennette* **297** Neil Lorimer/EWA **298** t: Annet Held; cl: MD/MBI; bl: Judith Parrish/EWA; r: Annet Held **299** tl: Daniel Rozenczstroch/Gilles de Chabaneix; tr: Annet Held; bl: Clive Helm/EWA; cr: MD/MBI; br: Judith Parrish/EWA **300** tl: Annet Held; tr: JV; bl: Mike St. Maur Sheil/EWA; br: JS/*Colin Forbes* **310** tl: Marco de Valdivia; tr: TSP/EWA; bl: Spike Powell/EWA; bc: Annet Held; br: Neil Lorimer/EWA **302** tl: JV; tr: Jon Bouchier/EWA/*Michael Tilley*; cl: MB/*Michael Haynes*; cr: KK/*Jan Kaplicky*; br: JV **303** bl: Marco Caselli; r: JV **304** tl: Annet Held; tc: Clive Helm/EWA; tr: MN/EWA; bl: Spike Powell/EWA; bc: EWA; br: Ann Kelley/EWA **305** l: Rodolfo Facchini/Stilnovo SpA/*Alberto Fraser*; r: MB/*Tricia Guild* **306** t: ESTO/*Gwathmey Siegel*; l: TSP/EWA; r: Camera Press **307** tl: MB/*David Hicks*; tr: MB; bl: MB/*Nicholas Hills*; br: MB/*David Hicks* **308** ©Abitare **309** ©Abitare **310** ©Abitare **311** tl: RB/Arcaid/*Jon Weallans*; bl: KK/*John Wright*; bc: Camera Press **312** l: JV; r: ©Abitare **313** l: ©Abitare; tr: MD/MBI; br: TSP/EWA **314** t: MD/MBI; b: Jillian Nieman/EWA **315** tl: Jon Bouchier/EWA/*Michael Tilley*; tc: MN/EWA; tr: MN/EWA/*Chester Jones*; b: Aldo Ballo **316** tl, tr: Camera Press; bl: RB/Arcaid/*Eva Jiricna*; br: Michael Dunne/EWA/*Michael Haynes* **317** t: Spike Powell/EWA; b: Richard Einzig/Arcaid/*Piano & Rogers* **318** t: Camera Press; b: Richard Davies/EWA/*Michael Baumgarten* **319** tl: MD/MBI; tr: RB/Arcaid; bl: JS/*Colin Forbes*; br: Richard Einzig/Arcaid/*Lattimore & Sugarman* **320** tl: KK/*Pierre Bötschi*; tr: Graham Henderson/EWA; bl: JS/*Oliver Morgan*; br: TSP/EWA.

ARTISTS
Paul Humphries 64-69; 244. Trevor Lawrence 138-155; 172/3; 204-208; 248/9; 268; 327. Hillary Gibson 269.